Third Edition

Central Library
Y Llyfrgell Ganolog
☎ 02920 382116

UNDERSTANDING TERRORISM

GROUPS, STRATEGIES, AND RESPONSES

James M. Poland
Professor Emeritus
California State University, Sacramento

Prentice Hall

Boston Columbus Indianapolis New York San Francisco Upper Saddle River
Amsterdam Cape Town Dub̶   ̶ich Paris Montreal Toronto
Delhi Mexico City Sao P̶   Singapore Taipei Tokyo

ACC. No: 02740411

363.325
POL

Editor in Chief: Vern Anthony
Acquisitions Editor: Tim Peyton
Editorial Assistant: Lynda Cramer
Director of Marketing: David Gesell
Marketing Manager: Adam Kloza
Marketing Assistant: Les Roberts
Production Editor: Rex Davidson
Project Manager: Susan Hannahs

Art Director: Jayne Conte
Cover Designer: Bruce Kenselaar
Cover Art: SuperStock
Full-Service Project Management: Sadagoban Balaji
Composition: Integra Software Services, Pvt. Ltd.
Printer/Bindery/Cover Printer: Bind-Rite Graphics
Text Font: 10/12 Times

Credits and acknowledgments borrowed from other sources and reproduced, with permission, in this textbook appear on appropriate page within text.

Copyright © 2011, 2005 Pearson Education, Inc., publishing as Prentice Hall, One Lake Street, Upper Saddle River, NJ 07458. All rights reserved. Manufactured in the United States of America. This publication is protected by Copyright, and permission should be obtained from the publisher prior to any prohibited reproduction, storage in a retrieval system, or transmission in any form or by any means, electronic, mechanical, photocopying, recording, or likewise. To obtain permission(s) to use material from this work, please submit a written request to Pearson Education, Inc., Permissions Department, Prentice Hall, One Lake Street, Upper Saddle River, NJ 07458.

Many of the designations by manufacturers and seller to distinguish their products are claimed as trademarks. Where those designations appear in this book, and the publisher was aware of a trademark claim, the designations have been printed in initial caps or all caps.

Library of Congress Cataloging-in-Publication Data

Poland, James M.
  Understanding terrorism : groups, strategies, and responses/James M. Poland.—3rd ed.
    p. cm.
  Includes bibliographical references and index.
  ISBN-13: 978-0-13-245776-7
  ISBN-10: 0-13-245776-8
  1. Terrorism. 2. Terrorism—Prevention. I. Title.
HV6431.P6 2010
363.325—dc22

                                                  2009028995

10 9 8 7 6 5 4 3 2 1

Prentice Hall
is an imprint of

www.pearsonhighered.com

ISBN-13: 978-0-13-245776-7
ISBN-10:   0-13-245776-8

To Barbara, Michael, and Amanda

CONTENTS

Preface   xi
Acknowledgments   xiii

Chapter 1   **Concepts of Terror and Terrorism   1**
Chapter Objectives   1
Introduction   1
Definitional Problems and Terrorism   2
Morality of Terrorism   4
Definitions of Terrorism   8
Terrorist Typologies   10
Terrorist Atrocities   14
Purpose of Terrorism   15
   Conclusions   16   •   Key Terms   17   •   Discussion Questions   17
   Web Sites   18   •   Endnotes   18

Chapter 2   **Historical Antecedents of Terrorism
and Violence   21**
Chapter Objectives   21
Introduction   21
Sicarii and Zealots: Religious Roots of Terrorism   22
The Assassins and Other Secret Societies   23
Narodnaya Volya   27
The Anarchist Tradition   29
Terrorism in the United States   31
Puerto Rican Independence   31
The Jewish Defense League   34
The Ideological Left   35
The Ideological Right   38
Single-Issue Terrorist   41
   Conclusions   43   •   Key Terms   43   •   Discussion Questions   44
   Web Sites   44   •   Endnotes   44

Chapter 3   **Violence and Terrorism: The Role of the Mass Media   48**
Chapter Objectives   48
Introduction   48
Contagion Theory, or the Copycat Syndrome   49

Propaganda Value and the "Deed"   53

United States   59

Internet and Terrorism   63

Censorship and Terrorism   65

Conclusions   68   •   Key Terms   69   •   Discussion Questions   69
Web Sites   70   •   Endnotes   70

Chapter 4   The Palestine Question and Al Qaeda   73

Chapter Objectives   73

Introduction   73

Palestine Resistance Movement   74

Historical Antecedents   74

Palestine Liberation Organization   77

Palestinian Extremism and the 1973 Yom Kippur War   78

Rejectionist Front: Historical Preview   80

Invasion of Lebanon   81

Hizballah   81

Palestinian Authority   88

Hamas and Islamic Jihad   88

Al Aqsa Martyrs Brigades   93

Al Qaeda   94

Conclusions   103   •   Key Terms   103   •   Discussion Questions   104
Web Sites   104   •   Endnotes   104

**Chapter 5   Designated Foreign Terrorist Organizations:
The "A List"   108**

Chapter Objectives   108

Introduction   108

Palestinian Groups   113

The Philippines and Southeast Asia   116

Algerian Groups   119

Religious Cults   120

European Groups   122

Colombia   126

Peru   128

Central Asia   129

Iran   132

Conclusions   133   •   Key Terms   134   •   Writing Assignment   134
Web Sites   135   •   Endnotes   135

Chapter 6   **The Dynamics of Hostage Taking and Negotiation**   **141**

Chapter Objectives   141

Introduction   141

Early History of Hostage Taking   142

Typologies of Hostage Takers   143

Time, Trust, and the Stockholm Syndrome   145

London Syndrome   148

Guidelines for Hostage Events   149

U.S. Experience: Hostage Rescue   153

The Good Guys Hostage Incident   156

Other Rescue Attempts   160

Surviving a Hostage Situation   164

    Conclusions 166 • Key Terms 167 • Discussion Questions 167
    Web Sites 167 • Endnotes 168

Chapter 7   **Contemporary Terrorism and Bombing**   **171**

Chapter Objectives   171

Introduction   171

Historical Perspective   172

Effects of an Explosion   176

Velocity and Explosives   179

Vehicle Bombs   181

Letter Bombs   185

Bombings Aboard Aircraft   188

    Conclusions 191 • Key Terms 191 • Discussion Questions 192
    Web Sites 192 • Endnotes 192

Chapter 8   **Suicide Bombers: A Global Problem**   **195**

Chapter Objectives   195

Introduction   195

Defining the Problem   199

Suicide Bombers in the Middle East   200

The Iraqi Insurgency   203

The Liberation Tigers of Tamil Eelam (LTTE)   205

Sikh Terrorism   206

Kashmiri Suicide Bombers   206

Kurdish Suicide Bombers: The PKK/Kadek, Kongra-Gel   207

Al Qaeda   208

Chechen Suicide Bombers   209

Other Suicidal Terrorist Groups   209

Summary   210

Security and Suicide Bombing   212

*Conclusions   214   •   Key Terms   214   •   Discussion Questions   214
Web Sites   215   •   Endnotes   215*

Chapter 9   Counterterrorist Measures: The Response   219

Chapter Objectives   219

Introduction   219

Security Measures   220

Intelligence Function   224

Counterterrorist Operations: Retaliation and Preemption   228

Covert Military Operations: Proactive Measures   231

Counterterrorist Operations: Reactive Measures   232

Special Operations   234

United Kingdom and Israel   235

National Guard   236

HRT and NEST   238

Chemical and Biological Terrorism   238

Legal Framework: Apprehension, Prosecution,
    and Punishment   239

Emergency Powers   241

Post-9/11 Legal Measures   243

*Conclusions   247   •   Key Terms   248   •   Discussion Questions   248
Web Sites   248   •   Endnotes   249*

Chapter 10   Future of Terrorism   252

Chapter Objectives   252

Introduction   252

Israel versus Palestinian Resistance Movement   253

Islamic Extremism   256

Low-Intensity Warfare   260

Superterrorism   262

Influence of Terrorism on Democracy   272

*Conclusions   274   •   Key Terms   274   •   Discussion Questions   275
Web Sites   275   •   Endnotes   275*

Glossary   280

Appendix: Maps   285

Index   291

PREFACE

Understanding Terrorism: Groups, Strategies, and Responses presents the essential lessons contained in the books, articles, and terrorist literature that have had the greatest impact upon the analysis of the terrorist strategy. The text is a synthesis in the respect that it brings together the divergent theories and methods that make up this dynamic field of scholarly inquiry. The book offers the various analytical approaches to the study of terrorism that identify terrorist groups, review terrorist tactics, and examine police and governmental responses to reduce or eliminate the incidence of terrorism.

The text is written for all those who will have to deal with future terrorist events and who today are struggling to understand the motivation of contemporary terrorist groups. This list includes criminal justice students, professionals in the criminal justice system, and any student wishing to gain more information on the phenomenon of "terrorism." To be well informed about terrorism, students and professionals in the field must be familiar with the concepts, techniques, and theories drawn from political science, social psychology, and sociology, as well as from the traditional criminal justice literature. The scholars who have assembled the knowledge on terrorism are obliged to relate their concepts of terrorism to the solution of the terrorist problem. The students and professionals in the field who must eventually confront the problem of terrorism are expected to keep up with new developments in terrorist theory and strategies and to possess special training, knowledge, and skills. Future trends indicate the necessity of increasing personal and scholarly awareness of the threat of terrorism to global peace. Thus, it is hoped that this book provides the information and knowledge to better understand the concept of terrorism.

However, terrorism must be placed in the proper perspective. The terrorist threat is in reality a multiplicity of real and imagined threats, each originating from a different source and each presenting a separate set of tactical and political problems. For example, the military retaliatory bombing raid against Afghanistan for assisting in terrorist attacks against American targets is viewed as deterrent retaliation. At the same time, few policy makers would suggest that the U.S. military send F-111 bombers to attack the headquarters of the KKK, Hamas, or Hizballah base camps in southern Lebanon. In addition, most terrorists are not career criminals, insane fanatics, or government surrogates, but ordinary individuals driven to violence by radical fundamentalism, nationalism, or extremist religious beliefs.

Clearly, the most confounding problem in the study of terrorism is arriving at a definition acceptable to all. Few people want to be called terrorists; terrorism is essentially what the other side has done. This is why there is no satisfactory political definition and no common academic consensus as to the essence of terrorism. For example, were the bombers of the marine compound in Beirut "terrorist criminals" or heroic "freedom fighters"? Which terms best describe the PIRA or the Tamil Tigers? Where there is political consensus, problems of definition are moot. Where there is no political consensus, definitions have a tendency to polarize differences. Ours are freedom fighters and commandos; yours are terrorist fanatics. So numerous are the definitions of terrorism proposed by scholars and policy makers that recently the focus has shifted to the aspect of the intimidation of "soft" civilian targets as an "unbiased" technique for defining terrorism. This textbook presents and compares several of the more popular definitions in the belief that each contributes to the growth of understanding terrorism.

WHAT'S NEW IN THIS EDITION?

1. The entire text has been updated to include references from 2007 to 2009.
2. The major thrust of the text follows the terrorism of al Qaeda after the 9/11 attacks.
3. There is a new section on the Internet and terrorism in Chapter 3.
4. In Chapter 4, the terrorism of al Qaeda in Iraq is analyzed.
5. The Iraqi insurgency and the use of suicide bombers are summarized.
6. The use of emergency powers by democratic governments around the world is examined. Post-9/11 legal measures enacted by the United States are also included, along with a review of the Patriot Act.

The fundamental concepts and theories of terrorism are summarized in Chapter 1. Chapter 2 briefly outlines the historical antecedents of terrorism. In Chapter 3 the role of the media in contributing to the increase in terrorism is examined. Terrorist groups active in the United States are reviewed. In Chapter 4, the Palestine–Israel conflict is reviewed and the structure and function of al Qaeda is analyzed. Chapter 5 outlines the "A list" of designated foreign terrorist organizations that pose a threat to the United States or its allies. Chapter 6 provides an overview of hostage taking and negotiation. In Chapter 7 the reader is introduced to the techniques involving explosive materials. The terrorist tactic of suicide bombings is explored in Chapter 8. Chapter 9 explains the analytic, political, legal, scientific, and behavioral responses that government policy makers have used to combat and solve the problem of terrorism. Finally, Chapter 10 attempts to look into the future and delineate potential areas of terrorism, such as nuclear terrorism and Islamic extremism. At the end of each chapter, a series of review/discussion questions are provided. The questions are designed to get students to critically think about the concepts, strategies, and responses to terrorism. The influence of terrorism on democratic states is also analyzed in terms of changes that might be anticipated as a result of a prolonged campaign of terrorism in a democracy.

As with most controversial subjects, the author must wrestle with his own bias and prejudice. I have done my utmost to present an unbiased, balanced view of contemporary terrorism in the modern world. This project was undertaken at the request of criminal justice students who continually complained that the literature on terrorism was overwhelming and confusing. I only hope that I have not added to that confusion.

Jim Poland

ACKNOWLEDGMENTS

I wish to express my gratitude to my wife, Barbara, who typed and edited the revisions from a tangle of handwritten pages, always encouraging and supporting my efforts in this endeavor. My special thanks to my children, Michael and Amanda, and my nephew, Trent Thompson, for reviewing and offering a critique of the manuscript.

I thank the following reviewers: Lee Ayers-Schlosser, Southern Oregon University; David Emmons, Richard Stockton State College; Daniel Juda, John Jay College of Criminal Justice; and Leon R. Kutzke, Chandler Gilbert Community College.

I continue to be indebted to the students of "Violence and Terrorism," Criminal Justice Division, California State University, Sacramento, for their continued interest in this topic. A special thanks to Lynda Cramer at Pearson Prentice Hall for her patience and guidance and Sadagoban Balaji for his editorial assistance.

CHAPTER 1

Concepts of Terror and Terrorism

CHAPTER OBJECTIVES
The study of this chapter will enable you to:

- Explore several definitions of terrorism
- Review several typologies of terrorism
- Discuss the purposes of terrorism
- Construct a basic typology of terrorism
- Appreciate the difficulty of law enforcement in dealing with terrorism
- Reflect on the moral justification of terrorism

INTRODUCTION

In recent years, small groups labeled as *insurgents*, *rebels*, *social revolutionaries*, *armies of national liberation*, *guerrillas*, *commandos*, *jihadists*, *freedom fighters*, and even *martyrs* have repeatedly demonstrated that certain tactics of random violence in democratic societies can trigger actions that often produce overwhelming fear. Such violent tactics attract the media, which ensures immediate worldwide publicity and can often cause democratic governments to overreact by tightening security. Before 9/11, the result of this tactical violence had been the gradual erosion of human rights and civil liberties in many parts of the world. For example, according to Sterling, the Tupamaros deliberately killed democracy by engaging in acts of indiscriminate terrorism that swept through Uruguay in the late 1960s and early 1970s.[1] As a result of this terrorism, the military seized power and established their own reign of state terror in 1973. Uruguay is a remarkable example of a democratic government being replaced by totalitarian rule. Political parties were banned, all citizens were required to register with the military regime, the press was tightly controlled, and thousands of people became political prisoners. This reign of terror lasted for twelve years. By April 1985, Uruguay finally returned to democracy.

Other examples of civil and human rights violations can be found in Northern Ireland. The continued escalation of terrorism in the region forced the British parliament to abolish the government of Northern Ireland and to impose direct rule and implement emergency powers.[2] Along with direct rule and emergency powers came warrantless searches, seizures, and arrests, the abolishment of jury trials, and internment.[3] In Canada, terrorism caused the government to invoke the War Measures Act of 1970, which temporarily abolished many civil liberties, including warrantless searches and arrests.[4] The Canadian government took these extreme measures in response to a double political kidnapping and a campaign of indiscriminate bombing by the Front for the Liberation of Quebec (FLQ).

Since 9/11, Western democratic governments around the world have again acted in a predictable manner to prevent indiscriminate acts of terrorism. For example, the United States has passed the **USA Patriot Act**, which gives law enforcement far-reaching police powers to detain immigrants, expand wire tapping, to use the military to patrol U.S. borders, and to conduct warrantless searches. In response to 9/11 and the Global War On Terrorism (GWOT), many countries have enacted repressive legislation in the name of protecting national security. When a country is at war, it claims the right to suspend normal democratic legal proceedings. In Australia, the United Kingdom, Russia, and Israel, antiterrorism laws give the police broad powers to search, detain, and prosecute suspected terrorists.

Terrorism is becoming the defining issue of the twenty-first century. The cycle of terrorist violence, governmental and military repressions, and vengeance is now quite commonplace. These facts alone create a need for a vigorous academic analysis of the use of terrorism and terror to achieve a political objective. The challenge for democratic governments is to balance civil and human rights with security and public safety. The function of the criminal justice system is to maintain the balance between liberty and law enforcement.

DEFINITIONAL PROBLEMS AND TERRORISM

The first analytical task facing scholars on **terrorism** is to define the term. At first glance, the definition of terrorism appears straightforward. Being held hostage for some vague political reason, the assassination of military and diplomatic personnel, and the suicidal car bombing of an embassy are considered acts of terrorism. Yet, as soon as one goes beyond these obvious examples, problems arise.

The term *terrorism* can produce extreme emotions, partly as a reaction to the indiscriminate nature of the violence and fear associated with it and partly because of its philosophical substance. The search for a definition that is both concise enough to provide an intelligent analytical premise and yet general enough to obtain agreement by all parties in the debate is laden with complexity. As a result, many observers and analysts get around the definitional problem by referring to one of several peremptory phrases, such as "one person's terrorist is another person's freedom fighter," "terrorism to some is heroism to others," "today's terrorist is tomorrow's Nobel Prize winner," and so on. These phrases, aphoristic though they may seem, outline the problem facing scholars who have attempted to define the limits of terrorism either for the purpose of developing some type of international agreement or to conduct scholarly research.

FIGURE 1.1   Former Israeli Prime Minister Menachem Begin (1913–1992) was the leader of the Zionist terrorist organization Irgun Zvai Leumi al Israel (IZL, National Military Organization of Israel) from 1943 to 1948. In 1978, along with Anwar Sadat of Egypt, Begin was awarded the Nobel Peace Prize for negotiating a peace treaty with Egypt.   (Getty Images Inc.—Hulton Archive Photos)

The problem of definition is further exacerbated by observers who frequently engage in the familiar rhetorical tactic of answering a question or a charge by leveling a countercharge. The key to this tactic is the speed and facility with which the "but what about" phrase can be used; that is, "but what about . . ." followed by some act of terrorism or violence allegedly committed by the opposition. Some examples are:

- **Al Qaeda** is supporting international terrorism, mass murder, and mayhem.
- BUT WHAT ABOUT the U.S. bombing of Serbia, Afghanistan, and the preempted invasion of Iraq?
- The suicide bombings of Hamas, al Aqsa, and Islamic Jihad are senseless acts of indiscriminate terrorism and mass murder.
- BUT WHAT ABOUT Zionist terrorism in Gaza and the targeted assassination of Palestinian leaders?
- The car bombing of the U.S. marine barracks in Beirut was a senseless, wanton act of terrorism and brutality.
- BUT WHAT ABOUT the U.S. naval shelling of innocent Lebanese villages in retaliation for the bombing of the marine barracks?

The purpose of such a tactic, according to Wilson, is to avoid the discussion of a specific issue by changing the subject in such a manner that implies the moral inferiority of your opponent. Moreover, the "but what about" response infers that the countercharge is precisely analogous to the original statement and, therefore, no distinctions among statements can be made. Thus, no distinction can be made between al Qaeda and the U.S. government, suicide bombers and the Israeli government, and suicidal car bombings and naval bombardment of enemy positions. The result is that the "but what about" strategy renders discussion virtually impossible, since analytical arguments are based on a willingness to make useful distinctions.[5]

The "but what about" tactic is also a clever and very old propaganda technique called **guilt transfer**. Tugwell describes guilt transfer as the switching of public attention away from the originator of the act toward the act of the adversary. For example, in 1987 when North Korea deliberately shot down a South Korean commercial jetliner carrying over one hundred people after it inadvertently wandered into North Korean airspace, the North Korean government responded by claiming the plane was on a spy mission for the United States. This claim was designed to erode both confidence in and the legitimacy of the United States acting through its surrogate South Korea. It was used to justify the shooting down of an unarmed civilian plane, diverting attention away from the original act while simultaneously stripping the United States and South Korea of any moral righteousness.[6] North Korea has long been on the U.S. State Department's list of state sponsors of international terrorism.

The tactic of guilt transfer has been widely criticized as one method for spreading disinformation. Obviously, many governments practice disinformation campaigns. Disinformation, however, is the anglicization of the Soviet term *desinformatsiya*. **Disinformation** is the deliberate spread of false, misleading, or incomplete information that is fed, passed, or confirmed to be from a targeted country, group, or individual.

It is in this way that the Palestinians justify random suicide bombings and hostage taking by claiming the perfidy of the Zionist state. The PIRA justifies the ambush murder of British soldiers by affirming that the British Army is an army of occupation on foreign soil and therefore takes its chances in Northern Ireland. The Armenian Secret Army for the Liberation of Armenia (ASALA) justifies the murder of the Turkish diplomatic corps by claiming the Turkish genocide of Armenians in 1915. Al Qaeda justifies the massacre of American citizens by claiming that the U.S. military presence in Arabia desecrates the land of Prophet Muhammad. The list goes on. Contemporary society appears to be particularly vulnerable to such tactics since a strong moral reference point for terror and violence is often lacking.

Furthermore, such terms as *international terrorism, transnational terrorism*, and *national terrorism* complicate the search for a working definition of terrorism. International terrorism most often refers to terrorist acts committed by offenders who represent the interests of a sovereign nation, for example, Hamas represents Gaza Palestinians. Transnational terrorists, such as Hizballah, operate across national borders, where the act of terrorism may affect more than one ethnic group. National terrorists—such as Basque separatists—seek to achieve political power within a single nation.

Reference to such statements and rhetoric should not convince the student that the search for a working definition of terrorism is fruitless. Wardlaw maintains that without a basic definition, it is impossible to say whether the phenomenon we call terrorism is a real threat to the stability of democratic nations or whether it is just another crime problem that eventually must be dealt with by the criminal justice system.[7] The fundamental problem in arriving at a definition acceptable to all is the moral issue associated with terrorism. As the reading of the literature should show, there are indeed many ambiguities about the morality of terrorism and about the meaning of related terms such as *terror, coercion, force*, and *violence*.

MORALITY OF TERRORISM

The scholarly analysis of the **morality** of terrorism has produced a wide range of observations. For example, Walter describes terror as an emotional state caused by specific acts or threats of violence, and terrorism as a compound of three elements: the act or threat of violence, the emotional reaction, and the social effects.[8] In 1934, Hardman referred to terrorism as activities involving a systematic use of violence but somehow sought to distinguish between mass violence and the terrorist method.[9] Moore described violence and terrorism as "negative compulsions" and stated there is an analogous relationship between violence and terrorism.[10] Rapoport, on the other hand, views terrorists and terrorism as involving individuals unconstrained by "moral limits" and acts of violence designed to cause extreme injury.[11] Rapoport argues that a moral distinction can be made between acts of political violence and indiscriminate random terrorism. Laqueur admits that terrorism has a wider meaning than violence and entitles his recent text *The New Terrorism.* According to Laqueur, the study of terrorism is about movements that use systematic terrorism to achieve political goals.[12] In fact, in 1977, Laqueur correctly predicted that the search for a comprehensive definition of terrorism would continue for a long time.[13]

Another scholarly analysis of terrorism is presented by Bell. Bell calls attention to the great diversity of the motivation of terrorists, distinguishing between psychotic, criminal, and self-dramatizing terrorists. Bell further claims that state terror has always been with us and that "attention has usually focused on the lone assassin or the tiny band of conspirators." Bell's primary concern is with transnational terrorism, which he defines as terrorists who operate across national borders and whose actions and political aspirations may affect individuals of more than one nationality.[14]

Other writers have been concerned with the responses to rebel or insurgent terrorism and the protection of individual rights. Gerstein observes that the terrorist is not a criminal but more of an outlaw. He argues that the purpose of terrorism is to cause feelings of fear, dread, and insecurity in

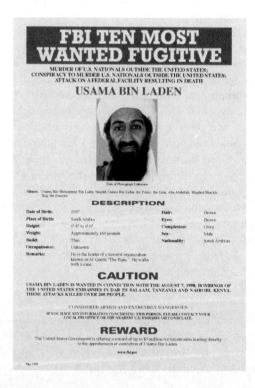

FIGURE 1.2 Most Wanted terrorist poster for Osama bin Laden, founder of the al Qaeda ("The Base") terrorist organization.   (AP/Wide World Photos)

the community. Gerstein maintains that individuals involved in terrorist violence forfeit their right to have rights.[15] Rapoport counters by arguing that some basic civil and legal rights may be forfeited but that there still remains a vital core of human and civil rights that should be protected no matter what the terrorist has done.[16] Rapoport believes that democratic governments often engage in torture, internment, and trials that do not accord full or normal due process when dealing with serious terrorist problems. For example, Amnesty International and investigative journalists have accused the United States, Northern Ireland, and Israel of establishing a planned program of torture, internment, and violations of due process in their efforts to prevent outrageous acts of indiscriminate terrorism.

While Gerstein and Rapoport dispute the relationship of moral principles and legal dogma, the noted political scientist Wilkinson is concerned with whether the domestic or international legal system should have jurisdiction over the apprehension and prosecution of suspected terrorists.[17] This is a very important question, as most captured terrorists claim that since they are freedom fighters or rebels and have a moral justification for using terrorist tactics, they should be treated in accordance with the rules of war. The claim has troubled many thoughtful writers who, for the most part, attempt to provide a careful distinction between the political, criminal, and common lawbreaker.[18] According to Dugard, international agreements are difficult to achieve because some governments protect escaping terrorists and actively support terrorist activity.[19] For example, the U.S. State Department has identified Iran, Cuba, North Korea, Syria, and Sudan as governments of state-supported terrorism. Former director of the CIA William J. Casey called governmental-sponsored terrorism "a weapons' system that obliterates the distinction between peace and war."[20] In addition, the U.S. State Department has identified forty-four foreign terrorist organizations (FTOs) that pose a threat to the United States (see Chapter 5). For example, terrorist training bases supported by al Qaeda have been located in Afghanistan, Iran, Syria, Libya, Yemen, and the Philippines.

Beginning in approximately 1988 and climaxing with the publication of Gunaratna's text *Inside Al Qaeda*,[21] there has been mounting evidence that al Qaeda has provided a substantial amount of weapons and training facilities to a variety of terrorist organizations. Al Qaeda's support may range from simply supplying suspected terrorists with weapons to directing and planning skyjackings, assassinations, and bombings. Gunaratna asserts, however, that al Qaeda is not the mastermind behind the world phenomenon called terrorism, but that al Qaeda does provide weapons, training, sanctuaries, and the right introductions to a widely fragmented and interconnected set of terrorist groups.[22] In other words, there is no global organization of terrorist groups, but there certainly are international ties that are exploited by al Qaeda. It must be made clear, however, that we do not know the extent of al Qaeda's involvement in global terrorism although al Qaeda seems to have a great deal of influence over several extremist Islamic terrorist groups listed by the State Department as foreign terrorist organizations. The financial backing for many terrorist groups probably comes not from the al Qaeda but from wealthy Arab nations and from criminal activities. Gunaratna's timely text suggests that we should take the claims of al Qaeda participation in international terrorism more seriously. To this end, a U.S. Senate subcommittee has been conducting hearings on both domestic and international terrorism since 1974.[23]

Herman has challenged the morality of defining terrorism by non-state terrorist groups. He maintains that many writers disregard the historical context of terrorism. He rejects their central thesis that acts of terrorism come from small groups because this view carefully ignores state- or government-sponsored terror. Herman declares that we should not forget the charges of American sponsorship of right-wing terrorism in U.S. client states in Latin America, which he refers to as the National Security States. Herman makes a careful distinction between retail terrorism, which is employed by isolated individuals or small groups, and wholesale terror, which is used by governments. Thus, retail terror is usually on a much smaller scale than pervasive wholesale terror.

Herman not only describes the techniques and extent of wholesale terror by regimes supported by the United States but also explores the financial interest of U.S. corporations in the Third World. He argues that U.S.-supported repression and terror results in the perpetuation of poverty and growing inequality, especially in Latin America. In quantitative terms, Herman affirms that U.S.-sponsored state or wholesale terrorism has victimized nearly a million people.[24]

Sageman provides a more contemporary example of wholesale terrorism. He argues that the war in Iraq has contributed to the increase of jihadist terrorism and the support for al Qaeda in the Muslim community. The invasion of Iraq has sparked a sense of moral outrage in Muslims throughout the world and has cast the United States as the real terrorist in the Middle East. The consensus in the U.S. intelligence community is that there was no operational presence of al Qaeda in Iraq before the invasion. Hence, the invasion of Iraq has bred a wave of global Islamist terrorism.[25]

However, Herman and Sageman do not clearly differentiate the strategies of the two types of terror. In Herman's view, the semantics of the morality of terrorism has a dualistic meaning. The term *morality* is used when applying moral values to our enemies, while *moralistic* refers to the morality of friends or ourselves.

More than a half-century ago, the principal ideologue of fascism, Sergio Panunzio, attempted to make a moral distinction between terror, terrorism, force, and violence. In Panunzio's analysis, terror represents the use of force to maintain the present social and political system, while terrorism is the application of violence to bring about the downfall of the existing social and political system.[26] Although force and violence seek to alter individual and collective behavior through coercion, intimidation, and fear, the distinction between terror/force and terrorism/violence apparently lies in the selection of victims. In Panunzio's eyes, the distinction can be clearly discerned:

> . . . between the torture of an editor of an opposition newspaper (terror) and the death of the housewife in the commission of a terrorist bombing (terrorism). For the terrorist anyone who is a member of society and not a member of his "revolutionary committee" is guilty of "complicity" with the "establishment" and hence exposed to violence.[27]

In other words, official state terror is used to attack and intimidate specific individuals or groups who threaten the existence of the state, while unpredictable, indiscriminate terrorism is directed at all members of society. Terrorism, then, is a strategy that exposes innocents to unpredictable attacks. The trait of this extraordinary violence is the indiscriminate, random nature of the violent act. There is every difference between the planned assassination of a leader of an oppressive regime and the shooting of innocent hostages who just happen to be available to the political terrorist. In sum, then, terror is the manufacture and spread of fear by legitimate authority or its official agent using the police or military, while terrorism is the manufacture and spread of fear by rebels, revolutionaries, insurgents, and freedom fighters, or other agents labeled "terrorists." The attempts to incorporate all the many manifestations of terrorism can be found in the difficulty in defining terrorism.

DEFINITIONS OF TERRORISM

Let us examine some of the more popular definitions of terrorism. Then we will attempt to clear away the rhetoric and formulate a more precise definition of terrorism. The lack of a precise definition causes three problems for criminal justice agencies:

1. Ambiguity over the distinction between common crime and political crime.
2. Lack of a comprehensive statistical base that may make it impossible to use statistical surveys, even though the State Department publication *Country Reports on Terrorism and the Rand Cooperation* does attempt to provide a statistical analysis of terrorism.
3. Difficulty in planning for tackling terrorist activity since philosophical definitions of terrorism differ.

However, no one definition of terrorism has gained universal acceptance. Despite decades of academic literature on the subject of terrorism, no commonly accepted definition has been found. Some popular definitions of terrorism are as follows:

1. All criminal acts directed against a state and intended or calculated to create a state of terror in the minds of particular persons or a group of persons or the general public (as defined by the 1937 League of Nations Convention, which was the first to attempt to define terrorism).[28]
2. Terror: violence committed by groups in order to intimidate a population or government into granting their demands.[29]
3. Terror is symbolic action designed to influence political behavior by extranormal means entailing the use or threat of violence.[30]
4. Terrorism may be defined as violent, criminal behavior designed primarily to generate fear in the community, or a substantial segment of it, for political purposes.[31]
5. Terrorism is the culturally unacceptable use or threat of violence directed toward symbolic targets to influence political behavior either directly through fear, intimidation, or coercion, or indirectly by affecting attitudes, emotions, or opinions.[32]
6. Terrorism is nongovernmental public violence or a threat performed by an individual or small group and aimed at achieving social or political goals that may be subnational, national, or international.[33]
7. Terrorism is the use of force, violence, or threats thereof to attain political goals through fear, intimidation, or coercion.[34]
8. In general, the word *terrorism* is used today to define almost all illegal acts of violence committed for political purposes by clandestine groups.[35]
9. The unlawful use of force or violence against persons or property to intimidate or coerce a government, the civilian population, or any segment thereof, in furtherance of political or social objectives.[36]
10. The term *terrorism* means premeditated, politically motivated violence, perpetrated against noncombatant targets by subnational groups or clandestine agents usually intended to influence an audience.[37]

Two common features are characteristic of nearly all definitions of terror and terrorism. First, terrorism is a technique for inducing **fear**. Terrorists attempt, by the nature of indiscriminate acts of violence, to use fear to achieve a variety of tactical and political objectives. Wilkinson addresses this point and notes that the key issue in defining terrorism lies in the ambiguous nature of fear.[38] We all have different thresholds of fear based on our personal and cultural backgrounds. Certain images and experiences are more terrifying than others, and it appears that those engaged in the business of terrorism know the right fear buttons to push. Therefore, terrorism has a more powerful impact on us than natural disasters such as floods, fires, or earthquakes. The 9/11 attacks confirmed our worst fears, demonstrating that terrorists have the ability and resolve to carry out suicide attacks in the United States. Wardlaw maintains that owing to the complex relationship between the subjective force of fear and the frequently irrational, individual response to fear, it becomes difficult to define terrorism accurately and to study it scientifically.[39] For this reason behavioral scientists have tended to disagree on a definition of terrorism that accurately reflects the subjective nature of fear and the methods used to arouse both individual and collective fear.

The second common denominator found in most incomplete definitions of terrorism is the reference to the achievement of a political objective. The political content of the act of terrorism distinguishes it from such ordinary criminal activities as murder, robbery, kidnapping, extortion, and hijacking, all of which are committed with far greater frequency by "nonterrorists" for motives of simple profit or passion. However, it is obvious that terror and terrorism need not be politically motivated. For example, criminals frequently resort to terrorist-type tactics for personal gain. Fleeing felons, upon encountering the police, will often take hostages and attempt to negotiate their escape. In fact, over 60 percent of all hostage-taking incidents in the United States involve criminal hostage takers, not political terrorists. Mentally disturbed persons may also terrorize others because of their condition. For example, it is very common in the United States for a mentally deranged person to hold his or her family members hostage. Likewise, political assassinations in the United States have been motivated not by political conspiracy, but by the mentally distraught offenders acting most often as an "agent of God." Some individuals may terrorize others because they are bored, sadistic, or angry, which causes them to engage in some type of violent act of protest against society. The distinctions between various forms of terrorism then are unclear, since criminals or psychopaths may use terror tactics and seek legitimacy by adopting political slogans and claiming to be political activists. In addition, terrorist organizations often recruit and collaborate with criminals and psychopaths.

However, what sets terrorism apart from other acts of violence is that terrorism is carried out in a very dramatic way to attract attention and create an atmosphere of fear that goes far beyond the actual victims of the violence. The distinction between actual victims and a target audience is the trademark of terrorism and separates it from criminal activity and other modes of armed conflict. Today, terrorism is a global theater.

These confusions, together with the pejorative usage of the word *terrorism*, make the problem of definition nearly insolvable. The problem is further complicated by writers who refuse to recognize that terrorism is not only a tactic of insurgents or political extremists but also a strategy of the state. All the same, in order to discuss the subject of terrorism in a meaningful way, it is necessary to accept some basic definition. For our purposes then, "Terrorism is the premeditated, deliberate, systematic murder, mayhem, and threatening of the innocent to create fear and intimidate in order to gain a political or tactical advantage, usually to influence an audience." Obviously this definition has limitations, but it attempts to distinguish between random murder and guerrilla warfare directed at the state. Moreover, this definition can be applied to terrorism from the left or right as well as terror practiced by a government or single-issue terrorist groups. Simply put, the purpose of terrorism is to terrorize. The contemporary terrorist uses terrorism as a preferred strategy rather than as a last resort. The terrorist prefers violence to other forms of political dissent. The routine nature of terrorist violence makes it difficult to distinguish completely between the political fanatic and the bloodthirsty killer. As pointed out earlier, the escalation of terrorism contributes to the spread of the totalitarian state. The next section explores several popular typologies of terrorism.

TERRORIST TYPOLOGIES

For years, political scientists have attempted to construct a consistent **typology** of terrorism, and many ingenious classifications have emerged (see Table 1.1). Probably the clearest framework for analyzing terrorism is provided by Wilkinson. Wilkinson categorizes four types of terrorism: (1) criminal, (2) psychic, (3) war, and (4) political. Criminal terrorism is defined as the planned use of terror for financial and material gain. Psychic terrorism is related to magical beliefs, myths, and superstitions induced by fanatical religious beliefs. War terrorism is the annihilation of the enemy through whatever means possible. Political terrorism is defined as the systematic use of violence and fear to achieve a **political objective**. Wilkinson lists seven specific characteristics of political terrorism:

1. The systematic use of murder, injury, or threats to realize a political objective such as revolution or repression.
2. An atmosphere of fear, coercion, and intimidation.
3. Indiscriminate attacks are made on noncombatants (soft targets)—no one in particular is the target; no one is safe.
4. Its unpredictability: the individual is unable to avoid injury or death.
5. Its abidance by no rules or conventions of war.
6. The savage methods of destruction used, such as car bombs, nail bombs, double bombs, and mass murder.
7. The moral justification for acts of terrorism, found in the group's political philosophy.[40]

Wilkinson further divides political terrorism into three types: revolutionary, subrevolutionary, and repressive. Revolutionary terrorism represents the "systematic tactics of terroristic violence with the objective of bringing about political revolution."[41] Four major points characterize this type of terrorism:

1. It is always a group activity rather than an individual act of violence.
2. The moral justification for the use of terror is always found in the revolutionary ideology.

TABLE 1.1   Characteristics of Terrorism

Characteristics	Political Terrorism	Domestic Violence
Objective	Political/religious	Profit, revenge, pain, passion, pleasure
Focus	Fear, panic, and intimidation	Fear of crime: carjacking, home invasion robbery, drive-by shootings
Selection of victims	Random, unpredictable, and indiscriminate	Prior association between victim and offender
Method	Nail bombs, car bombs, no warning bombs, trap bombs	Use of handguns in 60% of all homicides
Organization	Well planned	Spontaneous
Location	Public	Private residence
Sources of support	Financial, ideological, spiritual	Usually no support
Audience	Need media attention and recognition	Usually no media present

3. Terroristic leadership is an important element in recruiting people for terrorism.

4. The revolutionary movement must develop its own policy-making board, infrastructure, and code of conduct.[42]

The second category in Wilkinson's classification of political terrorism is subrevolutionary terrorism. This is defined as terror used for "political motives other than revolution or governmental repression." Subrevolutionary terrorism is directed at forcing the state to change its policy on a controversial political issue, warning state officials, or retaliating against the state for some act seen as reprehensible by the terrorist group.[43] For example, a clandestine antiabortion group, calling itself the "Army of God," has planted bombs in several abortion clinics in the United States to protest what it sees as unjust abortion laws.

Wilkinson's third category, repressive terrorism, is defined as "the systematic use of terror-istic acts of violence for the purposes of suppressing, putting down, quelling, or restraining cer-tain groups, individuals, or forms of behavior deemed to be undesirable by the oppressor."[44] Repressive terrorism relies heavily on the apparatus of the state security police, who are usually set apart from the rest of society. In fact, various aspects of contemporary terrorism were introduced to international affairs by a state rather than an independent terrorist organization. Hitler's SS and Gestapo used a variety of terrorist methods against the Jews. The final solution, or mass extermination, of the Jews of Europe represents the last phase of Hitler's terror campaign against them. This type of terrorism is also exemplified by the Black Hand operating in the Balkans prior to World War I, by the Red Hand in Algeria during and after political emancipation from France in the 1950s, by the White Hand terrorizing El Salvadorans in the 1960s, by the Ulster Defense Association in Northern Ireland, and by the Syrian Saiqa.[45] Wilkinson writes that initially this type of terror/terrorism is directed against specific opposition groups, but is frequently shifted to a much broader audience, for example, ethnic or religious minorities. Consequently, repressive terrorism by the state may be the most potentially dangerous form of present-day terrorism.

Hacker attempted to classify terrorists according to motives: crazies, criminals, and crusaders. According to Hacker, the emotionally disturbed (crazies) are driven by reasons of their own that often do not make sense to anybody else. He further delineates his classification into crazy terrorists from above (governmental terror) and crazy terrorists from below (psychotic terrorism). The latter category is very similar to the "motiveless" murder, where there is no moral justification for the act of terroristic violence other than individual recognition.

The motive of criminal terrorists is to simply achieve personal gain through illegitimate criminal behavior. Hacker outlines the difference between criminal terrorists from below, such as D. B. Cooper and members of crime syndicates, and criminal terrorists from above, such as individuals who consolidate governmental power through criminal activity and eventually adopt a strategy of terror to hold that power.

To Hacker, the real terrorists are the crusaders out to save the world, or at least part of it. Crusading terrorists are idealistically inspired, seeking no personal gain but prestige and power for a collective political goal, while acting for the interests of the "common good." Similar to crazies and criminal terrorists, crusading terrorists can be from above or below. However, he perceives the crusading terrorists from below as posing the greatest threat to global security and individual freedom. A common objective is to cause democratic governments to overreact and become repressive. Hacker's portrayal of terrorists is interesting, but most authors prefer a classification based on behavioral, political, historical, or sociological characteristics such as those listed by Wilkinson.[46]

Thornton identifies two broad classifications of the use of terrorism. The first is enforcement terror, which is used by governments to extinguish threats to their power and authority. The second is agitational terror, which specifies the terrorist activities of an organized group attempting to disrupt the existing political establishment and take political control. In a sense, Thornton discusses terrorism from above and terrorism from below.

A similar argument is acknowledged by May, who categorizes terrorism as regime of terror and siege of terror.[47] Regime of terror refers to the use of terrorism by the established political system, while siege of terror pertains to terrorism used by revolutionary movements. According to May, the regime of terror is the most insidious type of terrorism, but public attention is focused on the siege of terror due to the sensationalism of media reporting.

Gregor recognizes that terroristic violence has as its purpose not coercive sanction but some proximate end. He classifies terror into four distinctive groups:

- Instrumental terror is employed to impair the functioning of some system or institution.
- Demonstrative terror is used to bend entire populations to the purpose of others.
- Prophylactic terror is employed in anticipation of resistance or rebellion.
- Incidental terror involves those criminal acts—assaults, armed robbery, and kidnapping—that impact upon innocent victims and are in the service of the perpetrator's pathology, profit, or advantage.[48]

In a sense, terrorist acts are like natural catastrophes: everyone is a potential victim. Gregor observes that the most salient trait of terrorism is its indiscriminate nature. To him, the distinction is based on the selection of victims.

Schmid and de Graaf have presented an interesting classification of political terrorism distinguished by three principal types: (1) insurgent terrorism directed against the state, (2) state or repressive terrorism directed against less powerful segments of society, and (3) vigilante terrorism directed neither at the state nor on behalf of the state. Insurgent terrorism is further subdivided into three categories: (1) social revolutionary terrorism, which aims at causing worldwide revolution, (2) separatist, nationalist, or ethnic terrorism, which is concerned with radical changes in one part of society and not the entire political structure, and (3) single-issue terrorism, which is concerned with the granting of some privilege to a specific group.[49]

Schmid and de Graaf recognize that this typology concerns itself only with domestic and national terrorism while omitting international and transnational terrorism:

> . . . there is also so-called international terrorism. Its targets are sometimes foreign states and at other times foreign non-states. Its perpetrators are often non-state actors, but states also sometimes engage in it. Quite often, however, there is a mix of state and non-state actors who ally with each other. This allows for a multitude of combinations. If only states are involved as actors and targets, we might speak of interstate terrorism. In all other cases one might speak of transnational terrorism. Yet in fact there are so many variations possible.[50]

More recently, White argues for a tactical typology of terrorism that helps police officers to conceptualize their counterterrorist mission.[51]

Complicated as this picture may appear, it is less complex than the actual cases of reported international terrorism. For example, it has been reported that Palestinian terrorist groups have been associated with at least fourteen state and non-state terrorist actors. In truth, most acts of political terrorism are less international or transnational than it would seem at first analysis. Even the Palestinians have a major target of political terrorism in their frequent attempts to disrupt and destroy the Israeli state. Further study of the international aspects of terroristic violence seems likely to be fruitful.

From these general statements that have been made on the types of terrorism, we now seek to provide a reasonably comprehensive typology of terrorism. The focus of this typology is on the indiscriminate nature of terrorist violence and the selection of victims. Again, the problem of definition is recognized, but we must not overlook the fact that the victim is someone to be manipulated for purposes of creating intense fear.

Figure 1.3 outlines five distinct categories of terrorism: political, criminal, pathological, labor, and war.

The political nature of the purpose and origin of terrorism is the most important characteristic shared by such disparate groups as repressive state regimes or insurgent revolutionaries (e.g., Sendero Luminoso, **al Aqsa Martyrs Brigade**, al Fatah, al Qaeda, and a variety of neofascist groups).

Criminal "terrorists" are motivated by simple profit. Prison gangs, juvenile street gangs, and organized criminal cartels use fear to protect their turf and control criminal activity, especially drug trafficking.

The pathological terrorist may be motivated by greed, passion, pleasure, pain, or some undefined psychological aberration. The serial killer or mass murderer can certainly create an atmosphere of fear that easily paralyzes a large community.

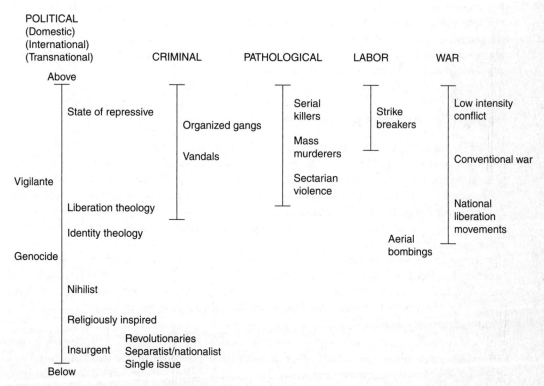

FIGURE 1.3 A typology of terrorism and violence.

The history of labor violence is one of constant confrontations between striking workers and company-supported strikebreakers. The industrialists of the nineteenth and twentieth centuries and their enforcers indiscriminately attacked striking workers, creating a situation of fear and intimidation. Workers often retaliated against company bosses with assassination and mayhem.

Finally, the best example of terrorism during a declared war is the indiscriminate aerial bombing of civilian targets. The purpose of aerial bombing is to spread panic and fear in civilian populations. The first concentrated aerial bombardment of a civilian target in modern warfare occurred at Guernica, Spain, on April 26, 1937, when Nazi German planes dropped 10,000 tons of explosives in support of Franco's rebel nationalist forces. Guernica was obliterated and thousands of civilians were killed.

Even though revolutionaries, criminals, or psychotics engage in terrorism, the gravest danger facing the world today comes from religiously inspired terrorist groups such as al Qaeda. These religiously inspired terrorist groups are especially difficult to counteract since they often use the newest terrorist strategy of the suicide bomber (see Chapter 8). Juergensmeyer writes that the recent attacks on the World Trade Center and the Pentagon are unique since they have no obvious military objective.[52] What makes religious terrorism so difficult to combat is that terrorist groups such as al Qaeda will not negotiate, compromise, or surrender. In addition, as Dershowitz points out, religiously inspired terrorist groups have no "return address," that is, a known location where they can be attacked without causing indiscriminate civilian casualties.[53]

In conclusion, the collected evidence for a consistent classification of terrorism is scarce and unreliable. The several studies explored here confirm the fact that diagnosis remains a matter for the individual ability of the researcher. This negative summation does not exclude the importance of a careful and comprehensive assessment of the adverse factors associated with the term *terrorism*. The choice of typologies remains a problem to be solved in relation to the purpose of the definition. In general, however, classification of terrorism could be improved by better research designs and by gaining an awareness of political, religious, social, and psychological determinants of terrorist and violent behavior.

TERRORIST ATROCITIES

Following the initial typology of Wilkinson, Shultz and Ivanesky discuss the varying degrees of extranormal violence used by terrorist guerrillas or revolutionaries.[54] In recent years, considerable attention has been paid to those terrorist instances where surface-to-air missiles or the indiscriminate bombing and shooting of large numbers of innocent civilians were used to terrorize the general population. This extranormal dimension can also be illustrated in other acts of violence such as shooting innocent travelers, shooting a teacher in the presence of the teacher's students, cutting off an ear or finger to dramatize the extortionist/kidnapper's demands, and "kneecapping" or shooting the legs of the victims to cause a permanent disability. Law enforcement authorities are concerned that terrorists will go nuclear or use chemical or biological weapons. The mystery and threat surrounding weapons of mass destruction make them an effective source of terrorist fear and manipulation. Neale offers a possible explanation for the cruel nature of terrorist **atrocity**.

> Terroristic violence must be totally ruthless, for moral scruples and terror do not mix and one or the other must be rejected. There can be no such thing as a weak dose of terror. The hand that controls the whip must be firm and implacable.[55]

TABLE 1.2   Summary of Typologies of Terrorism

Author	Types
Wilkinson	Criminal, psychic, war, political
Hacker	Crusaders, criminals, crazies
Thornton	Enforcement, agitational
May	Regime, siege
Gregor	Instrumental, demonstrative, prophylactic, incidental
Schmid and de Graaf	Insurgent, state, vigilante, social revolutionary, separatist
White	Political, criminal, foreign support, various gangs

Thus, terrorist atrocities serve several essential objectives for the terrorist. First and fore-most, they can produce pure terror or paralyzing fear. They are most effective when directed against specific critical groups. For example, in the popular revolutionary film *Battle of Algiers*,[56] the systematic assassination of police officers is portrayed in order to dramatize how to effectively paralyze the law enforcement community. More recently, the indiscriminate killing of police officers from ambush has been tried by the Provisional Irish Republican Army (PIRA) in Northern Ireland and the Black Liberation Army (BLA) in the United States.

The second major purpose of terrorist atrocities is to attract attention and gain sympathy through publicity. Thus, the more spectacular the act of terroristic violence, the more interest it arouses in the general population. Rapoport observes that reaction to the violence varies depend-ing on the audience. Viewing the atrocity may lead one audience to supply recruits, another to supply material aid, and yet another to offer encouragement.[57] Additionally, the terrorist atrocity may increase the prestige of the terrorist group and strengthen its acceptability and influence among other terrorist groups, for example, al Qaeda. The boldness of the act of terrorism may also strengthen the terrorist groups' claim that they are the only legitimate representatives of the "people." In sum, the terrorist atrocity of today is similar to the type of terror known as the "propaganda by the deed," so effectively used by nineteenth-century Russian anarchists

The third purpose of terrorist atrocities is to provoke the existing political establishment to commit counteratrocities. If the government is seen as employing the same tactics as the terrorist group, then potential sympathizers become allies and the strength of the terrorist group grows. The aim of the terrorist group is to *enrage* the establishment. Frequently, as Merari pointed out in his classification of terrorist groups, the target selected for the terrorist atrocity may enrage not only political bureaucrats but also rival ethnic and religious groups.[58] For example, the targets and victims of the Provisional wing of the Irish Republican Army (IRA) are both foreigners (British soldiers) and fellow country people (Ulster Protestants). There is no doubt that terrorist atrocities will continue since they produce outrage, publicity, and fear, which are the purpose of terrorism.

PURPOSE OF TERRORISM

The primary purpose, direction, and focus of terrorism is fear. However, contrary to popular belief, terrorism is not senseless, wanton destruction of life and property, and there are many reasons for acts of terrorism besides fear. Crenshaw believes that terrorism serves several func-tions: (1) to seize political power, (2) to affect public opinion and seize the media, (3) to maintain discipline within the terrorist organization and enforce obedience and conformity, (4) to discredit and disrupt the everyday operations of government, (5) to win new recruits, and (6) to project an image of strength that far exceeds their numbers.[59]

Likewise, Jenkins of the Rand Corporation expands on the following purposes of terrorism:

1. To provoke government overreaction, especially indiscriminate reaction.
2. To overthrow oppressive regimes.
3. To cause isolation and demoralization of individuals, creating an atmosphere of anxiety and insecurity.
4. To release prisoners and publish manifestos.
5. To immobilize security forces.
6. To obtain financial resources in order to purchase weapons and explosives.[60]

On the other hand, Herman argues that terrorism is a tactic to maintain power and to destroy and eradicate internal threats to that political power.[61] Schreiber believes that terrorism is an all-powerful and all-purpose method of action, the ultimate weapon.[62]

Therefore, while the principal effect of terrorism is fear and insecurity, terrorism may be used to achieve a variety of objectives: widespread publicity for the terrorists' cause, specific concessions, the provocation of repression, the dissolution of social norms, the enforcement of internal obedience, and the holding of hostages. A single terrorist incident may be aimed at accomplishing several of these objectives simultaneously.

Conclusions

Mencken said it best: "There's always an easy solution to every human problem—neat, plausible, and wrong."[63] So, too, with terrorism. In this chapter, we have surveyed many definitions of terrorism. Some are scholarly, such as Wilkinson's observations. Others are chic, such as Hacker's crusaders, criminals, and crazies. Still others argue that the real terror network is the state. The only common denominator seems to be that victims of terrorist acts are killed, injured, and threatened, and the acts are for the most part illegal.

Some recurring patterns were noted in the types of terrorist behavior and other violent offenses. However, no one terrorist group has an exclusive franchise on terrorism, and the causes of terrorism are as varied as the human condition itself. One of the objectives of this chapter was to introduce the student to the complexity of terrorism and to beware of easy, neat, and plausible explanations of terrorism.

Another major objective of this chapter was to set forth a conceptual framework for the study

of terrorism and the later evaluation of terrorist organizations. It is hoped that this chapter reflects the complexity of the phenomenon and encompasses the wide variety of terrorist types who engage in various forms of violent behavior. This chapter is probably best suited for exploring the theoretical rationale of terrorism rather than predicting what will occur in the future. If terrorism is a growth industry, then we can anticipate a steady escalation in the amount of terrorism in the years to come. As such, criminal justice students must be cognizant of the insidious nature of terrorism, from the state, from insurgent rebels, and religiously inspired terrorist groups. This problem is reflected in a major deficiency in the study of terrorism, which is, of course, the difficulty of operationally defining the term.

However, it must be emphasized that terrorism is neither wanton nor irrational. Terrorism is not mindless violence. It is a deliberate strategy with proximate ends. Terrorism has objectives, although they are often obscured by the fact that terrorist acts appear random and indiscriminate. The killing and terrorizing of seemingly innocent people who can be of no value to the terrorist cause may be very perplexing to criminal justice students. Terrorism, then, may be characterized as discriminate indiscriminate violence. Terrorism is discriminate since it has a definite purpose, but indiscriminate in that the terrorist has neither sympathy nor hate for the randomly selected victim. In order to understand this difficult paradox, we examine the historical antecedents of modern terrorism to outline historical trends and future prospects.

One of the intriguing aspects of the study of terrorism is the volume of historical literature associated with terrorism from below (rebels, insurgents, revolutionaries) as opposed to official state terror. There are several explanations. First, acts of terrorism by insurgents are dramatic, news-making events. The impact of the media cannot be overstated, as will be discussed in Chapter 3. Government by terror simply does not generate the news coverage that a suicide truck bombing does. Second, many people may see state terrorists as rational, political beings trying to hold on to their power, whereas insurgent terrorism is viewed as a last desperate act by the lunatic fringe. Third, even though state terrorism may be unjust and brutal, most citizens know what behavior or activities not to engage in to arouse the action of state security services. By contrast, rebellious terrorism seems random and thus presents a greater danger to the individual. The impression, therefore, is one of a society plagued by dangerous antisocial extremists threatening to destroy our way of life, while disregarding the more outrageous abuses of official government. Also, it is safer for the media to focus on small groups or individuals rather than governmental terror. Nevertheless, the immediate threat to the criminal justice system and the law enforcement community in the United States is not governmental terror but terrorism carried out by small groups dedicated to some vague political or religious objective. This text, therefore, concerns itself with terrorism from below, or insurgent terrorism. In the last decade, the amount of recorded terrorism has decreased, while the lethality of terrorism has increased. Over 3,000 innocent people were killed in the suicide attacks on the World Trade Center and the Pentagon.

Key Terms

al Aqsa Martyrs Brigade	fear	terrorism
al Qaeda	guilt transfer	typology
atrocity	morality	USA Patriot Act
disinformation	political objective	

Discussion Questions

1. Why is terrorism so difficult to define?
2. Compare and contrast the observations of Herman and Wilkinson.
3. Identify at least six purposes of terrorism.
4. Should police organizations be overly concerned with a precise definition of terrorism? Explain.
5. Discuss three current examples of guilt transfer. Review current media references of disinformation campaigns.
6. Outline Wilkinson's typology of terrorism. Construct your own typology.
7. Is terrorism ever morally justified? Explain fully.
8. Describe the difference between terror and terrorism. Do you agree or disagree with this distinction?
9. What distinguishes terrorism from other forms of violence?
10. How does criminal terror differ from political terror? Cite examples.

11. Give a contemporary example of:
    a. separatist/nationalist terrorism
    b. social revolutionary terrorism
    c. state or governmental terrorism
    d. pathological terrorism
    e. criminal terrorism
    f. religiously inspired terrorism
12. Why are democratic nations vulnerable to terrorism?

13. List three reasons for terrorist atrocities. Can you think of additional reasons?
14. Identify the following groups:
    a. FLQ   f. al Aqsa
    b. PIRA   g. al Qaeda
    c. ASALA   h. HAMAS
    d. PFLP   i. Hizballah
    e. Zionist

Web Sites

Center for the Study of Terrorism and Political Violence (CSTPV), St. Andrews, Scotland
http://www.st-andrews.ac.uk/academic/intel/research/cstpv

International Policy Institute for counter Terrorism (ICT), Herzlia, Israel
http://www.ict.org.il

U.S. Department of State, *Country Reports on Terrorism*, Washington, D.C.
http://www.state.gov/s/ct/rls/crt/

FBI home page: updated news and information on terrorism
http://www.fbi.gov

The Terrorism Research Center
http://www.terrorism.com

Endnotes

1. Claire Sterling, *The Terror Network: The Secret War of International Terrorism* (New York: Holt, Rinehart, and Winston, 1980), pp. 18–23.
2. Alfred L. McClung, *Terrorism in Northern Ireland* (New York: General Hall, 1983), pp. 224–27.
3. David Bonner, *Executive Measures, Terrorism and National Security* (United Kingdom: Ashgate Publishing Group, 2007), pp. 69–102.
4. Jan Schreiber, *The Ultimate Weapon: Terrorists and World Order* (New York: William Morrow and Company, Inc., 1978), p. 19. William Tetley, *October Crisis, 1970: An Insider's View* (Montreal, Canada: McGill-Queen's University Press, 2007), pp. 80–102.
5. James Q. Wilson, "Thinking about Terrorism," *Commentary*, 72 (July 1981), pp. 34–39.
6. Maurice A. J. Tugwell, "Guilt Transfer," in *The Morality of Terrorism: Religious and Secular Justifications,* eds. David C. Rapoport and Yonah Alexander (New York: Pergamon Press, 1983), pp. 275–90.
7. Grant Wardlaw, *Political Terrorism: Theory, Tactics and Countermeasures* (New York: Cambridge University Press, 1982), pp. 4–10.
8. Eugene V. Walter, *Terror and Resistance: A Study of Political Violence* (New York: Oxford University Press, 1969), p. 5.
9. Jacob Benjamin S. Hardman, "Terrorism," in *Encyclopedia of the Social Sciences,* eds. Edwin Robert Anderson Seligman and Alvin S. Johnson (New York: Macmillan Company, 1934), pp. 14, 575–76.
10. Barrington Moore Jr., *Terror and Progress— U.S.S.R.: Some Sources of Change and Stability in the Soviet Dictatorship* (Cambridge, MA: Harvard University Press, 1954), p. 11.
11. David C. Rapoport, "The Politics of Atrocity," in *Terrorism: Interdisciplinary Perspectives,* eds. Yonah Alexander and Seymore M. Finger (New York: John Jay Press, 1977), p. 47.
12. Walter Laqueur, *The New Terrorism: Fanaticism and the Arms of Mass Destruction* (New York: Oxford University Press, 1999), pp. 3–7.

13. ———, *Terrorism* (Boston, MA: Little, Brown and Company, 1977), p. 7.

14. Bowyer Bell, *Transnational Terror* (Washington, DC: American Enterprise Institute, 1975), pp. 3–10.

15. Robert S. Gerstein, "Do Terrorists Have Rights," in *The Morality of Terrorism: Religious and Secular Justifications,* eds. David C. Rapoport and Yonah Alexander (New York: Pergamon Press, 1983), p. 6.

16. David C. Rapoport, "The Politics of Atrocity," p. 47.

17. Paul Wilkinson, *Political Terrorism* (London: MacMillan, 1976), pp. 136–42.

18. For example, see Stephen Schafer, *The Political Criminal* (New York: Free Press, 1974); Tom Bowden, *The Breakdown of Public Security* (Beverly Hills, CA: Sage, 1977); Barton L. Ingraham, *Political Crime in Europe* (Berkeley, CA: University of California Press, 1979); Austin T. Turk, *Political Criminality* (Beverly Hills, CA: Sage, 1982).

19. John Dugard, "International Terrorism and the Just War," *Stanford Journal of International Studies,* 12 (1977), p. 21.

20. Central Intelligence Agency, *International and Transnational Terrorism: Diagnosis and Prognosis* (Washington, DC: U.S. Government Printing Office, 1976).

21. Rohan Gunaratna, *Inside Al Qaeda: Global Network of Terror* (New York: Columbia University Press, 2002); see also Rohan Gunaratna, *The Changing Face of Terrorism* (St. David's, PA: Eastern University Press, 2004).

22. Ibid., *Inside Al Qaeda*, pp. 70–76.

23. United States Congress, House, Committee on Internal Security, *Terrorism,* 93rd Congress (Washington, DC: Government Printing Office, 1974), Part 3 & Part 4.

24. Edward S. Herman, *The Real Terror Network: Terrorism in Fact and Propaganda* (Boston, MA: South End Press, 1983), pp. 4–16.

25. Marc Sageman, *Leaderless Jihad: Terror Networks in the Twenty-First Century* (Philadelphia, PA: University of Pennsylvania Press, 2008), pp. 91–93.

26. William Ebenstein, *Today's isms: Communism, Fascism, Capitalism, Socialism* (Englewood Cliffs, NJ: Prentice Hall, 1985), pp. 11–41; A. James Gregor, *The Ideology of Fascism: The Rationale of Totalitarianism* (New York: Free Press, 1969), pp. 170–75.

27. A. James Gregor, "Fascism's Philosophy of Violence and the Concept of Terror," in *The Morality of Terrorism,* eds. David C. Rapoport and Yonah Alexander (New York: Pergamon Press, 1982), p. 164.

28. Frederick Pollock, *The League of Nations* (London: Stevens and Son, 2003), p. 16.

29. "Terror," *Webster's Ninth New Collegiate Dictionary* (Springfield, MA: Merriam and Webster, Inc., 1983), p. 1218.

30. Thomas P. Thornton, "Terror as a Weapon of Political Agitation," in *Internal War: Problems and Approaches,* ed. Harry Eckstein (New York: Free Press of Glencoe, 1964), pp. 71–99.

31. National Advisory Committee on Criminal Justice Standards and Goals, Law Enforcement Assistance Agency, *Disorders and Terrorism* (Washington, DC: U.S. Government Printing Office, 1976), p. 3.

32. *U.S. Air Force Special Operations School* (Hurlburt Field, FL, July 1985).

33. David M. Krieger, "What Happens If? Terrorists, Revolutionaries, and Nuclear Weapons," *Annals of the American Academy of Political and Social Sciences,* 430 (March 1977), pp. 44–57.

34. Robert A. Friedlander, *Terrorism and The Law: What Price Safety?* (Gaithersburg, MD: International Association of Chiefs of Police, 1981), p. 3.

35. Lester A. Sobel, ed., *Political Terrorism* (New York: Facts on File, Inc., 1975), pp. 3–12.

36. Federal Bureau of Investigation Home Page, http://www.fbi.gov.

37. United States State Department, *Country Reports on Terrorism* (Washington, DC: Government Printing Office, 2009), p. V.

38. Wilkinson, *Political Terrorism,* p. 10; Paul Wilkinson, *Terrorism Versus Democracy: The Liberal State Response,* 2nd ed. (New York: Routledge, 2006), pp. 20–39.

39. Wardlaw, *Political Terrorism,* pp. 10–14.

40. Paul Wilkinson, *Terrorism and the Liberal State* (New York: Wiley, 1977), pp. 47–64. See also Paul Wilkinson, *Terrorism versus Democracy: The Liberal State Response* (New York: Frank Cass, 2000).

41. Wilkinson, *Political Terrorism,* p. 56.

42. Ibid., pp. 32–45.

43. Ibid., p. 38.

44. Ibid., p. 40.
45. Caroline Holland, "The Black, the Red and the Orange: System Terrorism versus Regime Terror" (unpublished manuscript, 1982), pp. 3–10.
46. Frederick J. Hacker, *Crusaders, Criminals, Crazies. Terror and Terrorism in Our Time* (New York: Bantam Books, 1978), pp. 3–38.
47. William F. May, "Terrorism as Strategy and Ecstasy," *Social Research,* 41 (Spring 1974), p. 277.
48. Gregor, "Fascism's Philosophy of Violence and the Concept of Terror," p. 159.
49. Alex P. Schmid and Janny de Graaf, *Violence as Communication: Insurgent Terrorism and the Western News Media* (Beverly Hills, CA: Sage, 1982), pp. 59–60. See also Alex Schmid and Albert J. Jongman, *Monitoring Human Rights Violations: State Violence, State Terrorism, and Human Rights* (Boulder, CO: Westview Press, 2003).
50. Schmid and de Graaf, *Violence as Communication,* p. 60.
51. Jonathan R. White, *Terrorism: An Introduction* (Belmont, CA: Wadsworth/Thomson Learning, 2002), pp. 14–15.
52. Mark Juergensmeyer, *Terror in the Mind of God: The Global Rise of Religious Violence* (Berkeley, CA: University of California Press, 2000).
53. Alan M. Dershowitz, *Why Terrorism Works: Understanding the Threat, Responding to the Challenge* (New Haven, CT: Yale University Press, 2002), p. 2.
54. Richard Shultz, "Conceptualizing Political Terrorism: A Typology," *Journal of International Affairs,* 32 (1978), p. 7; Ze'ev Ivianski, "Individual Terror: Concept and Typology," *Journal of Contemporary History,* 12 (1977), p. 43.
55. William D. Neale, "Terror: Oldest Weapon in the Arsenal," *Army,* 23 (August 1973), pp. 10–17.
56. Gillo Pontecorro, *Battle of Algiers,* film written by Franco Solivar (New York: Scribner, 1973).
57. David C. Rapoport, "Terror and the Messiah: An Ancient Experience and Some Modern Parallels," in *The Morality of Terrorism,* eds. David C. Rapoport and Yonah Alexander (New York: Pergamon Press, 1982), william d neale pp. 15–17; see also David C. Rapoport, ed., *Inside Terrorist Organizations* (London: Frank Cass, 2001).
58. Ariel Merari, "Classification of Terrorist Groups," *Terrorism,* 1 (1978), p. 331.
59. Martha Crenshaw, "The Causes of Terrorism," *Comparative Politics,* 13 (1981), p. 374; see also Martha Crenshaw and John Pimlott, eds., *Encyclopedia of World Terrorism* (Armonk, NY: Sharpe Reference, 1997).
60. Brian Jenkins, *International Terrorism: A New Mode of Conflict* (Los Angeles, CA: Crescent, 1975), pp. 4–7; see also Brian Jenkins, Paul K. Davis, and Stephen M. King, *Deterrence and Influence in Counterterrorism: A Component in the War on Al Qaeda* (Santa Monica, CA: Rand Corporation, 2002); Brian Jenkins, *Building an Army of Believers: Jihadist Radicalization and Recruitment* (Santa Monica, CA: Rand Corporation, 2007).
61. Herman, *Real Terror Network,* pp. 83–87.
62. Schreiber, *Ultimate Weapon,* p. 1.
63. Laurence J. Peter, *Peter's Quotations: Ideas for Our Time* (New York: Morrow, 1977), p. 410.

CHAPTER 2

Historical Antecedents of Terrorism and Violence

CHAPTER OBJECTIVES
The study of this chapter will enable you to:

- Identify historical trends in violence and terrorism
- Trace the relationship between ancient and modern terrorist groups
- Explore the difference between anarchism and terrorism
- Survey the historical evidence of violence and terrorism in the United States
- Develop an insight into the relationship between American value orientation and pervasive violence

INTRODUCTION

Although this is not a history of terrorism and our analysis does not emphasize terrorist groups of antiquity, some appreciation of their violent past is essential. The history of terrorism constitutes a major undertaking in its own right. That is not our intention here. However, it is important that we not ignore certain historical antecedents of terrorism and violence in order to appreciate the relationship between ancient and contemporary terrorist movements. War and revolution in general and the terrorist strategy in particular have a rich heritage.

The terms *terrorism* and *terrorist* have their roots in the French Revolution. Since that time, terrorism has been widely used to describe almost every form of violent behavior. Even though the term is relatively recent, the terrorist strategy is not. Criminal justice practitioners and students of the terrorist method sometimes ignore this important history or feel that terrorism is a contemporary phenomenon and thus new and unprecedented. The purpose of this chapter is to review some of the important attributes in the practice of terrorism as a political strategy. Particular attention is given to histrionic terrorism, or the fear-inducing aspect of terrorism and violent behavior.

SICARII AND ZEALOTS: RELIGIOUS ROOTS OF TERRORISM

The Jewish Sicarii (daggermen) and Zealot movements of ancient Palestine were the first groups to introduce terrorism as a strategy to produce panic or paralyzing fear for the purpose of accomplishing premeditated political objectives. The Sicarii and the Zealots, through acts of histrionic terror, successfully influenced a massive revolt against their colonial Roman rulers. However, the revolt ended after the Romans had encircled the Sicarii at Masada. Fearing retaliation by the Romans in the form of torture and death, the Sicarii refused to surrender and ended the siege of Masada by engaging in a dramatic mass suicide. Nearly a thousand Sicarii, including women and children, committed suicide rather than become Roman prisoners.[1]

The **Sicarii** were Jewish religious zealots who fomented a popular uprising in Palestine between A.D. 66 and 70. Like many popular uprisings, both historical and contemporary, the tactic of passive resistance was used as a first strategy to influence the apathetic. The Romans had abolished the Jewish monarchy and imposed direct rule over the Jewish community of Palestine. This action, along with the desecration of Jewish religious symbols and the arrest of important religious leaders, led to an escalation of the conflict. Roman soldiers began to use excessive force to break up demonstrations. This led to unorganized Jewish retaliation. At first a more moderate faction attempted to induce the Jewish community to reject the use of retaliatory violence. Roman soldiers committed several atrocities that resulted in the more radical Sicarii emerging as the dominant influence in the Jewish community. The Sicarii quickly went into action against the oppressive rule of the Romans, adopting a strategy of "pure terror." Rapoport notes that the Sicarii struck in broad daylight when the victim, either a Jewish moderate or a Roman soldier or a government official, was usually surrounded by witnesses and supporters.[2]

The intention of such high-risk assaults was to demonstrate that no circumstance could provide immunity from attack, and if the soldiers could not protect themselves, how could they provide security for citizens or government officials? This tactic, therefore, caused a situation of total uncertainty for the potential victim and certainly caused a sense of profound fear. No religious terrorist movement has ever been so successful. The Sicarii used a wide range of tactics designed to influence the Jewish community and to provoke, escalate, and inspire hatred between Jews and Romans. All efforts to find an acceptable political solution were frustrated by the terror tactics of the Sicarii. The primary purpose of Sicarii terrorist strategy, like that of so many terrorist groups today, seems to be the provocation of indiscriminate countermeasures by the established political system and to deliberately provoke repression, reprisals, and counterterrorism. To this end, the Sicarii were successful. Not only did a mass suicide occur at Masada, but also the Jewish community in Judea was decimated by Roman soldiers; and with a vengeance the Second Temple was destroyed in Jerusalem and the Jews were scattered to the four corners of the earth. The Diaspora had begun and would continue for 2,000 years, ending with the creation of Israel and the fulfillment of an ancient biblical prophecy.[3]

Parallels between the Sicarii and contemporary terrorism can be found in Northern Ireland and Palestine. For example, the tactic of passive resistance has a tendency to draw large numbers of participants into the conflict and dramatically raises the consciousness level of potential participants. In Northern Ireland, for instance, the current troubles began when the Northern Ireland Civil Rights Association protested peacefully against the Protestant majority and the British government. However, the peaceful marches soon escalated when police and British Security Forces overreacted. In one confrontation between Catholics and Protestants, British forces fired into the crowd, killing eight Catholics. Then on January 30, 1972, the Northern Ireland Civil Rights Association (NICRA) held an illegal protest march in reaction to the new British policy of internment. The march came to an abrupt end when British Security Forces fired into the marchers, killing thirteen and wounding at least twelve. The significant conclusion reached by a government investigation stated that "those who organized the illegal march created a highly dangerous situation in which a clash between demonstrators and security forces was inevitable."[4] The result was the deliberate provocation and the forthcoming retaliation and escalation by the newly formed Provisional Wing of the Irish Republican Army (IRA).

In Palestine, the contemporary counterpart of the Sicarii/Zealot movement was the Irgun Zvai Leumi-al-Israel (National Military Organization of Israel) and their leader, Menachem Begin. The Irgun directed its terrorist attacks against the British military government of Palestine between 1942 and 1948. They carried out numerous bombings and assassinations that eventually forced the British to abandon Palestine and turn the problem over to the newly formed United Nations. The frequent manifestos of the Irgun reiterated their slogan, "No Masada." In fact, Begin describes in his book *The Revolt* the determination of the Irgun to avoid a second Masada.[5] In the eyes of the British, however, the Irgun was considered the most violent and unrestrained terrorist organization of the modern era. For the British, there seemed to be no way out of the cycle of terror and counterterror. Begin and the Irgun were driven by history and despair to take on the mighty British Empire, mirroring the terror campaign of the Sicarii and the Roman Empire. Recently, the History channel, in a four-part series on terrorism, reported that Begin and the Irgun studied the terrorist strategies of the Sicarii and the IRA.[6]

A more overt reference to Sicarii can be found in Columbia. The Sicarios are a group of organized criminals who carry out assassinations and kidnappings for Columbian drug cartels. Mark Bowden describes the key role the Sicarios played in consolidating the power of the Medilin drug cartel in Columbia. The Sicarios assassinated police officers, members of rival drug cartels, and Columbian political officials for Pablo Escobar, the founder of the Medelin drug cartel. In Mexico, the word *Sicario* is used to identify contract killers who work for Mexican drug gangs.[7]

THE ASSASSINS AND OTHER SECRET SOCIETIES

A similar mixture of religious zeal and political extremism was the feature of a better-known religious sect called the **Assassins**.[8] The Assassins were a division of the Shi'ite Ismaili Muslim sect that appeared in the eleventh century and were finally extinguished in the thirteenth century by conquering Mongols. A religious despot, referred to as the "Old Man of the Mountains," was the acknowledged leader and founder of the Assassins. The Assassins gained widespread notoriety when the crusaders returned to Europe with stories of the murderers who killed their victims with golden daggers while under the influence of hashish. The hashish was to induce visions of paradise before the terrorists set out on their missions of assassination and terror. The name Assassin is derived from the Arabic *hashashin*, or "hashish-eaters." The Assassins planned the secret murder of their enemies from bases in Persia, Iraq, and Syria, where hundreds of devoted followers directed the activities of dedicated terrorists. The Assassins realized that the success of their organization depended on secrecy and a small number of dedicated followers to prevent detection from rival religious and political groups. So, they planned a long-term campaign of terror, often striking their victims at night while they slept. This program of terror by a small religious sect to maintain its religious autonomy succeeded in terrorizing the Middle East for two centuries. The legends about the Old Man of the Mountains and the Assassins have no doubt deeply inspired subsequent generations and apparently have motivated a campaign of suicidal bombings beginning in the 1980s by Hizballah, HAMAS, al Aqsa Martyrs Brigades, al Qaeda, and the Islamic jihad that continues to this day.

The newest group of Islamic assassins has promised to drive the U.S. military and all foreigners out of the Arabian Peninsula, and has carried out several high-visibility suicide bombing attacks. Al Qaeda is believed to be a coalition of Islamic Muslim religious fanatics influenced by the teachings of Osama bin Laden. They have taken credit for several spectacular terrorist suicide bombings, including the U.S. embassies in Africa, the U.S.S. Cole, the Pentagon, and the World Trade Center.

Other secret societies have existed for centuries in India and the Far East. The Thugs were a well-organized society of professional assassins who terrorized India for over 300 years. Unlike the Sicarii and the Assassins who killed their victims with daggers, the Thugs strangled their victims with a silk handkerchief. The choice of victims was random and indiscriminate; as a result they were feared throughout India, especially in the provinces of Punjab and Hindustan. They traced their origin to the religious dogma and practices of Kali, the Hindu goddess of destruction. The Thugs had complete contempt for death. Their political goals were not easily understandable and seldom did they terrorize members of the British Raj or Indian Rajah. Sporadic efforts were made to suppress the Thugs, but it was not until about 1837, through the cooperative efforts of the British military and various princely states, that the Thugs were driven underground. By 1852, the Thug religious cult had become extinct.[9]

The Thug phenomenon is yet another historical footnote to religious and secular terrorism. The same applies to the more fearsome secret societies in China that terrorized the countryside and urban areas for centuries.[10] Thug political objectives were for the most part vague or nonexistent. Many secret societies engage in the criminal activities of gambling, smuggling, extortion, and murder, hiring themselves out to the highest bidder. However, most secret Chinese societies despised foreigners. For that reason the Boxer Rebellion was encouraged by the union of several secret societies to rid China of all foreign influence. Even so, their political ambitions were limited to the control of criminal activities. In this respect they were more like the Mafia rather than a well-organized political terrorist movement.

The interest of the Fenian Brotherhood in revolutionary politics was probably more obvious, but it was still not a serious threat to the security of the United States or Ireland. The Fenians were an Irish American nationalist revolutionary secret society active during the 1860s. They derived their name from a legendary band of warriors in Ireland led by Finn MacCumhaill. Fenianism had as its major political objective the starting of a popular uprising in Ireland against colonial British rule. Irish communities in the United States as well as Australia, Canada, and South America supported the Fenians and revolution in Ireland. Their greatest opportunity came at the close of the U.S. Civil War when the Irish who fought for both the Union and the Confederacy were influenced by the Fenians to return to Ireland and prepare for the uprising that would finally defeat the British. The Fenians began a campaign of terror and assassination against the ruling British administration and Irish collaborators who supported the British. The British reacted quickly and suspended many civil liberties, including the enactment of the Habeas Corpus Act. A considerable number of rebels and potential rebels were arrested, thus destroying the planned uprising. The movement came to an abrupt end in both the United States and Ireland with the death of its founder, John O'Mahony, in 1877.[11]

According to Irish historian O'Farrell, the Fenian movement was a primitive attempt at revolution since it had no political program other than violent revolution based more on emotions and random terrorism than revolutionary discipline.[12] However, the emotional nature of Fenian rhetoric did awaken the latent revolutionary spirit of the Irish. The nationalist fervor of the Fenians eventually led to the formation of the Irish Republican Brotherhood, which has evolved into the oldest guerrilla army or terrorist group in the world today and probably the best known, the IRA.

The **Ku Klux Klan (KKK)** may not have been organized like an army, but its rhetoric has incited many Americans to join the most nefarious secret society in the United States. Its origin is somewhat sketchy, but historians seem to agree that the original Klan was organized by Southern Civil War veterans in Pulaski, Tennessee, in 1865. The name apparently is derived from the Greek word *kyklos*, from which comes the English *circle*. Klan was added for the sake of versification, and the Ku Klux Klan emerged. Laqueur reminds us that there are three Klans.[13] The first, a product of the Reconstruction period (1865–1876), was a secret, violent society organized to intimidate and spread fear among blacks and carpetbaggers. It was set up as the "Invisible Empire of the South" with a definable organizational structure. It was divided into state Realms, county Provinces, and individual Dens. The empire was presided over by a Grand Wizard with a descending hierarchy of Grand Dragons, Grand Titans, and Grand Cyclopses. There were also some minor functionaries known as giants, genii, hydras, furies, goblins, and nighthawks. They adopted intimidating symbols: wearing white hoods and robes and burning crosses. Symbolic threats gave substance to the power of terrorism and elevated the level of fear created by indiscriminate acts of violence. The more violent members escalated their level of fear through harassing, beating, and terrorizing blacks and white sympathizers, who were called scalawags.[14]

The second Klan (1915–1944), like the first, also stood for white supremacy; but in addition it campaigned for many other causes, such as American patriotism and attacks on bootleggers and

FIGURE 2.1 KKK members in white hoods and robes, waving Confederate flags, parade at a rally in Houston. (Bob Daemmrich/Stock Boston)

other law violators. This new KKK was organized at Stone Mountain, Georgia, in 1915 and proclaimed the protection and supremacy of white Protestants. The new Klan added Catholics, Jews, foreigners, and organized labor to its hate list. By the mid-1920s, membership had increased to between 4 and 5 million. The Klan controlled local politicians, judges, governors, and at least two U.S. senators. In 1928, the Democrats nominated Al Smith, a Roman Catholic, for president. This action produced a hate campaign against all Catholics, using the slogan "Keep the Pope out of the White House." The Klan was no longer a small secret society; instead it was a formidable political threat to freedom and democracy. This threat further manifested itself in the late 1930s when it was discovered that the Klan had a close association with members of the Nazi Party. Finally, the U.S. government began to arrest Klan members for a variety of civil rights violations and for unpaid back taxes. The Klan fell into disrepute and for the next twenty years was quiescent, but in the mid-1960s the civil rights movement renewed interest in the Klan and once again Klan membership began to grow.[15]

The emergence of the third Klan (1960–1975) began with accounts of beatings, shootings, and bombings in Southern communities carried out by Klansmen attempting to terrorize blacks and civil rights workers. Birmingham, Alabama, became known as "Bombingham, Alabama," after more than 100 bombs were detonated by apparent Klan members to intimidate blacks and civil rights workers. In fact, fifty bombings that occurred in the 1960s in Birmingham are to this day unsolved. Recently, one bombing that occurred in Birmingham in 1963 involving the deaths of four young girls was solved when Thomas Blanton, a grand dragon in the KKK, was arrested, tried, and convicted on May 8, 2002, and sentenced to life in prison.

Crosses were burned at Klan meetings and nightriders roamed the countryside. By 1966, the random, indiscriminate violence of the Klan had escalated and overwhelmed local law enforcement. The federal government stepped in and prepared an agenda to arrest and prosecute the top leadership of the Klan for the slaying of civil rights workers.[16] President Johnson even appealed to all Klan members to withdraw from the organization "before it is too late." Nevertheless, the Klan energetically participated in the hate campaign directed toward the civil rights movement. In the end, Klan members received little profit for their efforts.

In 2006, the Klan once again had a resurgence and an increase in membership. Hot-button issues such as illegal immigration, gay marriage, and urban crime have helped fuel an increase in Klan activity, with new Klan groups appearing in parts of the United States that have not seen such activity. For example, the Empire Knights of Ku Klux Klan formed in Florida in 2005 and quickly expanded across the South into the mid-Atlantic states and Oregon. In 2008, the Empire Knights proclaimed chapters in eighteen states. The Anti-Defamation League (ADL) has identified forty-four active Klan groups in the United States, claiming over 5,000 hard-core members with approximately 15,000 core supporters.[17]

The basic ideology of the Klan in the twenty-first century still supports white supremacy. Klan groups share the same emphasis on the so-called fourteen-word slogan—"We must secure the existence of our people and a future for white children." The fourteen-word slogan has become a rallying point for the white supremacist movement in the United States. Klan groups also still reflect their traditional beliefs of racial hatred and anti-Semitic bigotry. Justice Clarence Thomas in a 2003 decision characterized the Klan as a "terrorist organization, which in its endeavor to intimidate, or even eliminate those it dislikes, uses the most brutal of terrorist methods."[18]

Klan groups across the United States have aligned themselves with other white supremacy groups such as the neo-Nazi National Socialist Movement and the racist skinhead movement.

NARODNAYA VOLYA

Compared with the Sicarii, Assassins, Thugs, Fenians, Chinese secret societies, and Ku Klux Klan, the **Narodnaya Volya** was historically the most successful terrorist organization, even though its struggle with tsarist Russia lasted only from January 1878 to March 1881. The Narodnaya Volya (People's Will), organized as a socialist movement in Russia in the 1870s, was based on the concept that an overt campaign of political propaganda would excite the peasantry and workers and influence reforms in the regime. The movement first arose, like so many revolutionary movements, among intellectual and professional people. The writings of Herbert Spenser, August Comte, and John Stuart Mill encouraged the intellectuals; the teachings of Karl Marx dominated much of their ideology. The Narodnaya Volya was also enhanced by the failure of the ruling elite to recognize the legitimate grievances of the workers. The failure of tsarist Russia to respond to these grievances led to a split in Narodnaya Volya on how to react to the tsarist regime.[19]

The moderates believed that a concentrated propaganda campaign would incite the workers and undermine the authority of the tsar's regime. Another faction, led by the anarchist Bakunin, was convinced that the use of force and violence through a popular uprising would effect political changes.[20] Opposed to both approaches, Tkachev preached a doctrine of the forcible overthrow of the regime by dedicated revolutionaries, followed by a general education of the populace in communist teachings.[21] At first the extremists were rejected in favor of a strategy of peaceful reforms, but the tsar's regime overreacted and began to arrest and imprison many moderate members of Narodnaya Volya. The most famous political trial was the "trial of the 193" in 1878.[22] Several defendants were sentenced to death, others to prison, and still others were exiled. This action by the regime did not destroy Narodnaya Volya but widened the difference between moderates and extremists on the use of terrorism to overthrow the tsar. The radicals won the "debate" and immediately began a campaign of violent retaliation against the tsar's regime. The switch had been made from peaceful propaganda to the terrorist method. Narodnaya Volya set out to change the regime by acts of random terrorism directed toward the tsar's family and government officials.

This terrorism frequently involved the tactic of planned, selective assassinations. The key targets represented minor government officials, as well as the most visible symbols of the tsar's power: police and military personnel. However, their favorite target was, of course, the tsar. There were at least six recorded attempts on the life of Tsar Alexander II by Narodnaya Volya before an exploding bomb finally killed him. The tactic of selective assassination was also used to intimidate and coerce government bureaucrats who abused the power of their position. For example, several prominent police officials were assassinated for their brutal treatment of political prisoners.

Moreover, many members of Narodnaya Volya were realistic and recognized that a strategy of selective assassination could not topple the tsar's regime. Narodnaya Volya reasoned that a campaign of selective assassination would cause government officials to become overly security conscious, thus weakening their ability to cope with rising political dissatisfaction in the general society. One of the more articulate members of Narodnaya Volya explains:

> In a struggle against an invisible, impalpable, omnipresent enemy, the strong is vanquished not by arms of his own kind, but by the continuous exhaustion of his own strength, which ultimately exhausts him, more than he would be exhausted by defeat. . . . The terrorists cannot overthrow the government, cannot drive it from St. Petersburg and Russia, but having compelled it, for many years running, to neglect everything and do nothing but struggle with them, they will render its position untenable.[23]

At this stage in the struggle, the acts of terrorism were sporadic and often unsuccessful. But terrorist technology was in its early, evolutionary phase: the pistol, dagger, and crude explosive devices were being replaced by a new discovery, dynamite. Narodnaya Volya was the first terrorist organization to use dynamite on a wide scale. Crude bombs were fashioned that were both highly effective and very dangerous. The successful assassination of Alexander II was accomplished by the assassin approaching the tsar's carriage with a quantity of dynamite and blowing himself up along with the tsar. This act of terrorism caused the government to finally round up the leaders of Narodnaya Volya. Once the leadership was gone, the popularity of Narodnaya Volya began to decline. The attack that killed the tsar also doomed the Narodnaya Volya.

It is the terrorist ideology that distinguishes the "People's Will" from today's terrorist organizations. The Russian terrorists maintained that they had been forced to use murder since the tsarist government was corrupt and closed all possibilities of peaceful reform. They even promised to discontinue their terrorist activity once the government demonstrated its commitment to reforming the "system." Ivianski argues that Narodnaya Volya was desperately concerned about the concept of morality and terrorism.[24] Unlike terrorists today, the Narodnaya Volya would meticulously plan their assassinations to avoid the killing of innocent people. A favorite quote of the Russian terrorists is that they will not shed "one drop of unnecessary blood." The victim was always a person seen guilty of specific acts of brutality or corruption against the "people." The political goal was the thirst for basic freedoms embodied in the U.S. Bill of Rights. They had complete contempt for the anarchist element or pathological person who committed indiscriminate assassinations to overthrow a democracy. Where people were free to express their ideas through elected officials, Narodnaya Volya condemned the use of assassination and terrorism as a means of changing the system.

Though Narodnaya Volya did not completely understand the moral dilemma of the terrorist strategy, adherents did pay the moral price: one that established their reputations as noble, tragic, historical figures found in the novels of Dostoyevski and Turgenev. They had to accept death and even seek it in order to justify and recognize the aura of evil that surrounds an act of premeditated murder. Laqueur writes that the moral and intellectual distance between Narodnaya Volya and contemporary terrorists "is to be measured in light years."[25]

Even so, it must be pointed out that Russian terrorists of the period, including Narodnaya Volya, admired the rhetoric of Nechayev, encompassed in his *Revolutionary Catechism*. The portrait of the ideal terrorist and the terrorist method are dramatized in this document. This ideal type was distinguished by inhumanity and a lack of moral sensitivity. The terrorist was to denounce present-day social morality, be suspicious of friends, and have only one mission in life—the merciless destruction of the system. The *Revolutionary Catechism* is generally acknowledged to be the most cold-blooded manual of instruction in terrorist literature. It proposes a plan that has become familiar to all political terrorists. The function of the terrorist, who represents the vanguard of the revolution, must be to provoke governmental repression that would set the stage for a popular uprising. The *Catechism* glorified assassination as the tactic of political change. Nechayev advised that moderate political leaders should be the first targets of assassination since those remaining would represent the hardliners and would, therefore, be more useful in stimulating a popular revolution. Nechayev eventually became entangled in an internal struggle that resulted in the ritual murder of an innocent comrade. After the details of the murder became known to the Narodnaya Volya, Nechayev was discredited, and his influence in the Russian revolutionary movement declined. He was imprisoned for the murder of his comrade, and he later died of tuberculosis.[26]

However, the writings of Nechayev, particularly the *Revolutionary Catechism*, have inspired contemporary revolutionary theorists such as Debray[27] and "Che" Guevara.[28] Both writers outline the means of revolution by engaging in a campaign of indiscriminate terroristic violence designed to produce a situation of intense fear. For example, Guevara was unable to influence the peasants of Bolivia to support his revolution so he attempted to neutralize them by terrorizing village leaders and elders in a planned program of assassination and mutilation. Probably the best-known manual of terrorist strategy is presented in the *Mini-Manual of Urban Guerrilla Warfare*.[29] Its author, Carlos Marighella, was a dedicated Brazilian revolutionary who advocated terrorist action to destroy the existing democratic political system. The more radical and destructive, the better for the revolution. Marighella approved of the poisoning of food and water supplies, the sabotage of transport systems and oil pipelines, and a general strategy of the scorched-earth policy used by the military. He assumed that the populace would blame the government for resulting disasters. Typically for Marighella, the terrorist tactic of assassination was preferred over other violent acts. There is nothing intellectual in Marighella's dissertation, and the moral ambiguity in the use of the terrorist method is of no major concern. The *Mini-Manual* is nothing more than a rehash of some of the original ideas of Nechayev.

The *Document on Terror*[30] is yet another frightening review of the terrorist method. It offers a two-stage approach: (1) *general* terrorism, which is directed at the entire population, and (2) *enlightened* terrorism, which is motivated by selective attacks on specific groups. The author of this *Document* is unknown, although it is believed the manuscript was initially found on a dead KGB agent in the former Soviet Union. Eventually the *Document* made its way into Western Europe, appearing for the first time in 1948. It is not unreasonable to assume that the author was greatly influenced by Nechayev since much of the *Document* is a replication of the *Revolutionary Catechism*. It is also entirely possible that the sudden emergence of the *Document* was a propaganda ploy by anticommunists. In any event the suggested tactics of terrorism and the specific practices of terrorism are familiar elsewhere. (Later we discuss the al Qaeda manual, which is the most recent document on the terrorist strategy.)

In sum, Narodnaya Volya has passed into the pages of history. Other terrorists and revolutionaries sprang up in Russia. The 1905 uprisings and the well-documented Russian revolution of 1917 proved to be the final deathblow to tsarist Russia. The moral issue of the use of terrorist tactics so hotly debated by Narodnaya Volya posed no problem to the newly emerged Soviet communist state. State terror replaced insurgent terrorism with a savage brutality that the Narodnaya Volya would not have recognized.

THE ANARCHIST TRADITION

Another political ideology closely linked to terrorism is the anarchist tradition of assassination. Anarchism has frequently been associated with terrorism. The equation *anarchism = terrorism* is well documented and persistent in the literature.[31] This relationship is based on the political assassination of kings, heads of state, and other symbols of government in the nineteenth century. King Humbert of Italy; William McKinley, president of the United States; George I, king of Greece; Sadi Carnot, president of France; and Elizabeth, empress of Austria, were all assassinated by anarchists, thus supporting the popular opinion of anarchy.[32] However, most anarchists have not supported the terrorist method, so this association with terrorism may be unjustly deserved. In order to fully understand the doctrine of **anarchism,** Schmid suggests it is necessary to distinguish between three distinctive types: anarchism as a political ideology, anarchism as a movement, and the ambitions of individual anarchists.[33]

Three distinct principles form the basic analytical framework of anarchist dogma. First, anarchism is opposed to all forms of government that apply political, economic, and social coercion. In place of organized governmental systems, anarchists foresee voluntary arrangements of mature and independent human beings. Anarchists are uniformly anti-institution; thus, the repudiation of state, political party, associations, unions, churches, and all forms of institutionalized law. Second, anarchists believe that all political and religious ideologies are manifestations of the domination of institutional life and the ultimate submission of man to a formalized system of rules and laws. Anarchism is not only international in its approach but also anational. Thus, territorial boundaries cease to exist, and man belongs to one human community. Third, the objective of anarchism is a domination-free society, or total anarchy. Anarchy would replace institutional law with the self-organization of individual personalities who were committed to the "good" of society. Each individual would be left absolutely free. However, two exceptions applied. If any person attempted to injure another, all well-meaning persons would have the right to protect the aggrieved person; and law-abiding citizens could suppress the criminal element, but only through voluntary cooperation, not institutionalized legal rules.

The substance of philosophic anarchism is based on the creation of a "good" society that would exclude authority, repudiate violent methods of control, and strive toward anarchic organization. In order to achieve this blissful existence, dedicated and enlightened anarchists would set an example of their goodness by practicing the anarchist method in their isolated utopias. These islands of "freedom" would then be imitated by others seeking a more libertarian existence and the creation of a new organization of human relationships.[34]

Anarchism as a political movement gained prominence in the nineteenth century when it became associated with socialist doctrine and the influence of Bakunin.[35] But this relationship was short-lived. Led by the radical Russian revolutionary Bakunin, the anarchists were expelled from the first Socialist International because of a dispute over their reliance on organized violence and the use of the terrorist fear tactic of "propaganda by the deed." As a movement, anarchism survived until World War I in Russia and until the beginning of World War II in Spain. But in the United States the anarchists attained their greatest success by relying on labor unions as the main instrument of revolutionary struggle. For the most part labor unions did not engage in acts of terrorism in the United States.

Recently there has been a resurgence of anarchist ideals in the United States. American anarchist groups have become increasingly noticeable while demonstrating against globalization. Anarchists today are antiglobalization and anticapitalist. They are easily recognizable at demonstrations since they use a tactic known as the black bloc that was first introduced at the World Trade Organization Conference in 1999 in Seattle. Black clothing and masks are worn to avoid being identified by the police and to appear as one large group of people who support anarchist ideals. Black blocs have appeared at political rallies across the United States. Black blocing involves vandalism, rioting, street fighting, and attempts to provoke police officers to overreact. One of the most vocal anarchist groups in the United States is called Love and Rage. Love and Rage has a very strong activist orientation and its members have demonstrated against a variety of social issues including U.S. immigration policies, the war in Iraq and Afghanistan, global warming, and the support of capitalism. Supporters of Love and Rage call for the creation of an "anarchist-style" government and the destruction of American-style democracy. Through control of the states, they can move rapidly to transform society by implementing anarchist ideologies.[36]

However, the overwhelming majority of anarchists advocate the peaceful transformation of society by face-to-face interaction with the general population. The major spokesperson for anarchism today is Howard Zinn.[37] Professor Zinn states that anarchism is not about bombs, disorder, or chaos, but that anarchists today oppose racism, sexism, nationalism, capitalism, and globalization through peaceful confrontations with the ruling elite. The message of Professor Zinn and other supporters can be found on AnarchismToday.org.[38]

TERRORISM IN THE UNITED STATES

Before 9/11, to most Americans terrorism was a bomb that kills people in a far-off land or an assassin's bullet aimed at a foreign head of state. However, today terrorism has become a matter of grave concern in the United States. Witness the unprecedented use of barricades and metal detectors throughout the nation, the growth and refinement of special U.S. counterterrorist teams, the enactment of a wide range of antiterrorism legislation, including the Patriot Act, and the U.S. government's retaliatory air strikes against suspected terrorist bases in Afghanistan and Pakistan.

Fears that major terrorist campaigns could be launched in the United States are well founded. Terrorism in the United States tends to come from a variety of terrorist groups. Historically most terrorist groups that have been active in the United States are either transnational or strongly identified with separatist or leftist movements. The Federal Bureau of Investigation (FBI) has identified six categories of terrorist groups responsible for domestic terrorism in the United States. These include (1) Puerto Rican separatists, (2) Jewish extremists, (3) ideological left, (4) ideological right, (5) special interest groups, and (6) Islamic radicals.

Until the attacks on the World Trade Center and the Pentagon by al Qaeda, the use of political violence and terrorism in the United States has not been sufficiently serious to warrant much attention from academic analysts, law enforcement authorities, or governmental policy makers. However, since 9/11 the United States has launched a multifront war on terrorism utilizing all the military, legal, economic, and legislative tools available. Before we examine more closely the war on terrorism, we review the nature of terrorism in the United States.

Historically, the most serious terrorist attacks committed in the United States have been linked to nondomestic issues. The most active and firmly implanted terrorist group in the United States for over thirty years is motivated by a desire for Puerto Rican independence.

PUERTO RICAN INDEPENDENCE

The most active terrorist groups in the United States have been groups seeking Puerto Rican independence. After the Spanish–American War, Puerto Rico was ceded to the United States by the Treaty of Paris, December 19, 1898. By 1900, the U.S. Congress had established a civil government on Puerto Rico, and American citizenship was granted to its residents. In 1948, the first native governor was elected and steps were taken by the United States to proclaim the Commonwealth of Puerto Rico. But Puerto Rican nationalists wanted total independence from the United States, not the proposed commonwealth status.[39]

In October 1950, the Puerto Rican nationalists conducted an uprising that was quickly suppressed by loyal government troops. As part of the uprising, two Puerto Rican extremists dramatized their desire for independence by attempting to assassinate President Truman.[40] On November 1, 1950, while Truman was in residence at the Blair House, located across the street from the White House, the Puerto Rican nationalists fired several shots, killing a District of Columbia police officer who engaged the Puerto Rican assassins in a brief gun battle. Truman escaped unharmed, but the nationalists were successful in attracting widespread publicity and media attention in the United States to their cause of independence. They attracted international attention on March 1, 1954, when several Puerto Rican nationalists invaded the House of Representatives in the U.S. Capitol while Congress was in session and shot and wounded five Congressmen.[41] Puerto Rico is currently a self-governing political entity associated voluntarily with the United States and is no longer considered a U.S. colonial territory. But several Puerto Rican nationalist/separatist groups have challenged this concept of "independence."

Formed in 1974, the most active Puerto Rican terrorist group is **Fuerzas Armadas de Liberation Nacional (FALN),** the Armed Forces for National Liberation.[42] The FALN is apparently the merger of two nationalist movements, the Armed Commandos of Liberation and the Armed Independence Revolutionary Movement of the 1960s. The introduction of the FALN occurred on October 16, 1974, with the bombing of five banks in New York City.[43] Since its formation, the FALN has claimed responsibility for over 200 bombings on the United States mainland and in Puerto Rico. Their most deadly attack occurred on January 20, 1975, when a powerful pipe bomb destroyed the Fraunes Tavern in New York, killing four persons and injuring sixty-three others.[44] Even though the ideological underpinning of the FALN is the belief in Puerto Rican independence, many of its communiqués concern themselves with the rhetoric of the far left. The bombings of the New York banks and Fraunes Tavern were carried out to denounce American imperialism, the exploitation of the working class by bankers and stockbrokers, and the U.S. military presence in Puerto Rico.

The FALN is not the only Puerto Rican terrorist group. Too often Puerto Rican terrorist groups are seen as a single entity, but in reality they consist of several competing factions that often cooperate with each other.

All the Puerto Rican separatist groups have been active since 1974, concentrating primarily on the destruction of property, especially American corporations with interests in Puerto Rico, the U.S. military based in Puerto Rico, and the federal government. However, the FALN and Macheteros (machete wielders) have no apparent feelings of remorse for the indiscriminate taking of lives. On the contrary, it is often their intent to inflict maximum injury and death. One of their most spectacular operations was the ambush on December 3, 1979, of a navy bus carrying unarmed U.S. sailors to their daily assignments.[45] Two sailors were killed and ten others were seriously wounded. This ambush involved the classic terrorist tactic of the stalled vehicle blocking the road, then the emergence of the terrorists firing automatic weapons indiscriminately into the crowded bus. The Italian Red Brigades, PFLP, IRA, Red Army Faction (RAF), and Basque separatists have used this ambush maneuver satisfactorily. After the bus attack, three ROTC officers were ambushed as they left the campus of the University of Puerto Rico. One was seriously wounded, the other two escaped unharmed. Like the victims on the bus, the ROTC officers were unarmed.

One incident stands out as a clear indication of the indiscriminate nature of attacks on U.S. military personnel in Puerto Rico by the FALN. Four U.S. sailors on shore leave in San Juan were just leaving a popular nightclub when a car drove alongside and cut them down with automatic weapons. One sailor died and three were seriously wounded. Additional attacks on U.S. military personnel were recorded in Illinois and New York. Possibly the most dramatic and theatrical attack on the U.S. military occurred on January 12, 1981, when the FALN and the Macheteros entered the Puerto Rican National Guard headquarters at Muniz Air Base and destroyed approximately $60 million in jet aircraft.[46] Later investigation revealed that the terrorists entered the base by penetrating a security fence, evaded armed guards by wearing military uniforms, and planted twenty-one bombs in the intake manifolds and wheel wells of eleven jet fighters. The attack on the air base was carried out by eleven FALN and Macheteros terrorists to dramatize their solidarity with eleven members of the FALN who were then on trial in Evanston, Illinois.

The symbolic nature of the attack on Muniz Air Base may be a subtle cue to the "expressive symbolism" of Puerto Rican culture. Jarger and Selznick pursue this hypothesis and stress the degree of attachment or intensity of meaning in the expressive symbolism of a culture.[47] They argue that culture consists of sharing symbolic experiences and that shared experiences eventually become part of normative behavior. If this hypothesis is valid, then agents of the criminal justice system may have missed some important cues sent by Puerto Rican terrorist groups. By analyzing past terrorist actions of Puerto Rican nationalists and terrorist groups, it may be possible to predict with some degree of accuracy the date, time, and target of subsequent attacks.

Another example of the expressive symbolism theory took place at midnight March 1, 1982, when four explosions tore through the financial district of New York City.[48] The explosions were timed to commemorate the March 1, 1954, assault on the U.S. Congress. The FALN claimed credit for the bombings, stating that it was a strike against U.S. imperialist forces that are suppressing the Puerto Rican people. The FALN, like other terrorist groups, often celebrate commemorative dates by violence and terrorism.

In addition to bombings, the FALN has also taken over buildings and held hostages as a selective propaganda tactic. On March 15, 1980, armed terrorists of the FALN seized the Bush and Carter-Mondale election headquarters in Chicago and New York.[49] The terrorists threatened and terrorized campaign workers and ransacked the offices, seizing the records of campaign contributors. Law enforcement officials speculated that the lists of contributors contained the names of possible victims of assassination or kidnapping. Shortly after this assault, on April 4, 1980, eleven members of FALN were arrested in Evanston, Illinois, during the planning of an apparent robbery and kidnapping.[50] Subsequently, the eleven FALN members, including the acknowledged leader, Carlos Alberto Torres, were tried and convicted for a variety of offenses and sentenced to long prison terms. The FBI proclaimed, "We have decapitated their leadership." But FALN terrorists never stopped the bombing campaign initiated in 1974; they were merely slowed until new recruits could be found. By December 30, 1981, the sentencing procedure had been completed for the eleven FALN members arrested earlier. On New Year's Eve, 1982, to protest the long prison terms for dedicated "freedom fighters," the FALN placed four bombs at federal and local government buildings in New York City.[51] The four bombs were timed to explode at approximately thirty-minute intervals. An FALN communiqué stated: "This is the FALN, we are responsible for the bombings in New York City today. Free Puerto Rico. Free all political prisoners and prisoners of war."

The bombing campaign continued through the 1980s with continued attacks on federal facilities and U.S. corporations doing business in Puerto Rico. During the 1970s and 1980s, the FALN took credit for 146 bombings in the United States, mostly in New York and Chicago. By the late 1980s, sixteen additional members of the FALN were apprehended and sentenced to long prison terms. In sum, it was effective police work that ended the FALN terrorist organization. The FBI intelligence service and local police investigators developed a picture of the FALN's structure, tactics, and bomb-making ability that eventually led to the arrest of key members of the group. Policing is an effective strategy to penetrate terrorist groups and ultimately eradicate the group.

However, in November 1999, President Clinton granted clemency to the sixteen FALN terrorists, who were freed from prison. The U.S. attorney general and the FBI vehemently objected to the freeing of FALN terrorists. In fact, the FBI picketed the White House for several days in protest. The freed FALN terrorist gang members returned to Puerto Rico. The terrorism of the Puerto Rican independence movement has stalled with few terrorist incidents recorded over the last two decades.

THE JEWISH DEFENSE LEAGUE

The **Jewish Defense League (JDL)** was founded in 1968 by Rabbi **Meir Kahane** in New York City to protest the Soviet treatment of Jews, to support the Jewish state of Israel, and to protect elderly Jewish citizens.[52] Members of the JDL, whom Kahane called the Jewish Panthers, are trained in the use of weapons and karate to defend themselves against the threat of anti-Semitism. The motto of the JDL is "Never Again," a reminder of the Jewish Holocaust. Despite the fact that terrorist activity by the JDL appears to be declining, acts of anti-Semitism by white supremacy groups have sparked renewed interest in the JDL. During the early 1980s and 1990s, the terrorist activities and hate crimes of white supremacy groups were primarily directed at Jewish targets. Several incidents occurred in California: arson attacks on Jewish businesses, the desecration of Jewish cemeteries, an assault on the Center for Jewish Studies, and an attack on a day care center in Los Angeles.

Initially the JDL made headlines by marching with baseball bats through black neighborhoods of New York City, where attacks on elderly Jews had occurred, and by planting bombs in the former Soviet United Nations' offices to protest the treatment of Russian Jews.[53] But in 1971, Kahane emigrated to Israel, where he became equally infamous as the leader of an even more militant Zionist organization, Kach (Hebrew for "thus"). Kahane is supported by a small group of Zionist extremists who advocate the total expulsion of Arabs from Israel. Kahane was arrested more than 100 times while in Israel for inciting violence. He is the only Jew ever to be held in Israel under administrative detention or imprisoned without trial for alleged security offenses.[54] In New York he was sentenced to five years' probation for conspiracy to manufacture explosives. Kahane frequently returned to the United States on fund-raising expeditions.

FIGURE 2.2 Rabbi Meir Kahane (1932–1990) founded the Jewish Defense League (JDL) in 1968 in New York to combat the rise of anti-Semitism. Kahane emigrated to Israel in 1971 and founded the Kach ("Thus") political party. (Images, Peter L. Gould/Getty Images Inc.—Hulton Archive Photos)

On November 5, 1990, while on a fund-raising tour in New York City, Kahane was assassinated by an Egyptian immigrant named El Saiyyed Nosir. In a curious twist of fate, police investigators discovered that Nosir was part of an Islamic terrorist cell. Eventually other members of the terrorist cell were arrested and convicted for the bombing of the World Trade Center in 1993. The assassination of Kahane also inspired Baruch Goldstein, a disciple of Kahane, to attack Muslim worshipers in the shrine of the Tomb of the Patriarchs in Hebron in 1995, where he killed forty Muslims while they knelt in prayer.

The extremist rhetoric of Kahane and Kach has apparently affected the target selection of the JDL in the United States. According to media reports, a faction within the JDL attacked targets it believes are conspiring against the Jewish race and the state of Israel. This faction has bombed the French, Lebanese, and Egyptian diplomatic delegations in New York City. It also bombed the West German airline offices of Lufthansa in New York City. The extremist element of the JDL apparently views Middle East peace initiatives with the Palestinian Arabs as threatening to the principles of Zionism.

On December 8, 2001, Irv Rubin, the leader of an extreme faction of the JDL, was arrested for planning to bomb a Muslim mosque and the offices of U.S. Congressman Darrell Issa in Los Angeles. Congressman Issa is of Arab descent and supports the establishment of a Palestinian state in Israel. Before Rubin could be brought to trial, he allegedly committed suicide at the Metropolitan Detention Center in Los Angeles. In sum, Kahane and the JDL represent the most vengeful, extreme, and confrontational views of the Jewish people. Even so, the official Web site of the JDL (www.jdl.org) unconditionally condemns terrorism of all forms. More traditional Jewish and Zionist organizations, such as the ADL, condemn the terrorist activities of the JDL.

THE IDEOLOGICAL LEFT

Left-wing ideology and terrorism were all-pervasive in the United States between the late 1960s and the mid-1980s. Left-wing ideologies include a variety of Marxist-Leninist, anarchical and antiglobalization groups. The rhetoric of the left is reflected in their propaganda. For example, the left believes that the political and social structure of the United States is totally corrupt. Their anticapitalist slogans call for the working class to throw off the chains of corporate corruption and take over the means of production. The left claims to be the champion of the exploited and downtrodden in society. They believe that only violence and terrorism will bring about change in society. Subsequently, groups on the left have carried out several bank and armored car robberies, planted bombs at military facilities and businesses, and assassinated several "capitalists." One such left-wing group emerged in the 1970s.

The **Revolutionary Armed Task Force (RATF)** first emerged after an unsuccessful attempt to ambush a Brinks's armored bank truck in New York on October 20, 1981.[55] After the abortive holdup attempt, law enforcement officials arrested eleven people. Later investigation revealed that the individuals were members of an unknown "guerrilla" group calling itself the Revolutionary Armed Task Force.[56] As investigators began to reconstruct the holdup attempt, they discovered and arrested several fugitives from violence-prone revolutionary groups of the late 1960s and early 1970s, including the Weather Underground, the Black Liberation Army, the Republic of New Africa, and the May 19 Communist Organization. This new relationship between fugitives from the 1960s and 1970s was unique. Law enforcement officials believe it is the first time that black dissident groups joined with predominately white middle-class groups to use crime and terrorism in their dream of overthrowing the established power in the United States.

In effect, the formation of the RATF suggests that political differences that kept black and white radical groups from cooperating in the 1970s may have been overcome. During the late 1960s, radical white university students who eventually formed the **Weather Underground Organization (WUO)** tried in vain to form an alliance with violent members of the growing black power movement.[57] The advocates of black power, however, tended to abhor the affluent white middle-class status and backgrounds of the Weatherman, often expressing contempt for the lack of total commitment to revolutionary ideals by white militants. Eventually internecine disputes about who should lead the revolution developed within both the black power movement and the white revolutionary groups. That subsequently led to radical organizational splits in both groups. The failure to encourage support among racial minorities, for example, resulted in the East Coast branch of the WUO breaking away and forming the May 19 Communist Organization (CO).[58] The May 19 CO derived its name from the birthdays of Malcolm X and Ho Chi Minh. The group devoted itself entirely to strengthening and developing links with elements of the radical black, Hispanic, and women's movements. Communication channels were established with members of the **Black Liberation Army (BLA)**, many of whom were in prison. In turn, the members of the BLA would recruit hardened black criminals by convincing them that American society was racist and unjust. The bible for left-wing groups, Marighella's *Mini-Manual of Urban Guerrilla Warfare*, stated that revolution could only be successful in the United States when it combines elements of black prison inmates and radical white college students. The May 19 CO also made contact with the Republic of New Africa (RNA), another black extremist group.[59]

The RNA was formed in March 1968 as part of the Black Government Conference sponsored by the Malcolm X Society. The purpose of the conference was to establish a national black movement to be known as the RNA. The stated goal of the RNA was to establish a separate black nation by annexing the states of Georgia, Louisiana, Alabama, Mississippi, and South Carolina. The FBI reports that over 400 members were recruited between 1968 and 1972. The recruits were organized into a group known as the Black Legion (BL), which was to support and defend the principles of the newly formed "African republic." Between 1969 and 1972, the RNA became involved in several shootouts with police and FBI agents. Following the shootouts, RNA activity began to decline. By 1976, the RNA was considered to be a loosely knit organization that generated little financial or popular support. In fact, the FBI discontinued investigation of RNA activities on July 9, 1976. However, the RNA continues to seek self-government and land, offering online courses in radical black liberation theology. The RNA membership has close ties to the BLA.[60]

The BLA appeared in February 1971, when the Black Panther Party split into the Newton faction and the Cleaver faction.[61] Eldridge Cleaver called for the overthrow of the U.S. government by creating a climate of paralyzing fear. The BLA campaign of fear was to begin with the indiscriminate ambush killing of uniformed police officers. Members of the BLA murdered uniformed police officers in New York, New Jersey, and San Francisco. In January 2007, eight former members of the BLA were arrested and charged with the murder of a San Francisco police officer. The eight, labeled the "San Francisco 8" by the media, await trial. They were also involved in numerous bank robberies, bombings, and prison escapes. Today most members of the BLA have either been killed in shootouts with the police or incarcerated in U.S. prisons. Cleaver, once branded the "nation's greatest threat" by J. Edgar Hoover, eventually became disillusioned with the BLA and became a preacher. He spent his later years preaching nonviolence. He died in 1998, at age 62, from natural causes.

The oldest and most active of the revolutionary groups affiliated with the RATF is the Weatherman Underground Organization, a revolutionary group dedicated to the violent overthrow of the U.S. government. The WUO began as a paramilitary support group of Students for a Democratic Society (SDS). The SDS, founded in 1960, called for an alliance of blacks, students, peace groups, and liberal organizations and publications to influence the "liberal" policies of the Democratic Party. By 1965, the SDS had organized the first "anti-Vietnam War" march in Washington, DC. The "March on Washington" stimulated interest in the SDS, and the number of local chapters grew to 100 in six months. As the SDS gained in popularity among students, draft resistance became its top priority. After the escalation of the Vietnam War, the SDS split into several competing factions, each advocating violence and indiscriminate terrorism. The most vocal and prominent was the WUO.[62]

At the Chicago national convention of the SDS in June 1969, the Weatherman faction surfaced with a position paper titled "You Don't Need a Weatherman to Know Which Way the Wind Blows." (The phrase is contained in the Bob Dylan song "Subterranean Homesick Blues.") The paper attempts to define a political ideology based on aggressive and prolonged guerrilla tactics that would overthrow the U.S. economic system and its "military-industrial complex" and replace it with a classless society: world communism. The Weatherman style evolved over the summer of 1969. Members began to seriously study revolutionary doctrine, especially the writings of Mao. By 1970, the WUO changed its tactics and came into the open, claiming responsibility for several bombings, including the bombing of the U.S. Capitol on March 1, 1971.[63] With the end of the Vietnam War, interest in the WUO declined, and internal battles split the original organizational structure.

In 1976, internal dissension split the WUO. The heavily feminist faction, the "Revolutionary Committee" (RC), broke away from what it called the "Central Committee" (CC).[64] After 1977, nothing was heard from the WUO, either under its own name or under the RC or CC names. However, no evidence suggested that the WUO ceased to exist. Then, during 1978 and 1979, several WUO members surfaced and came "above ground" but would not reveal the status of the group. Ultimately the FBI closed its domestic security case against WUO since it could not be substantiated that the group was involved in criminal or "revolutionary terrorist" activities. The WUO has not claimed credit for any criminal or terrorist activities since late 1977.

Nonetheless, the FBI believed that the RATF was composed of a group of "survivors" from the WUO, BLA, RNA, and May 19 CO, who had been responsible for a series of bombings directed at U.S. government and corporate facilities. Revolutionary cells of the RATF using a variety of names had carried out the bombings. The most active names were the United Freedom Front (UFF) and the Armed Resistance Unit (ARU). The UFF and ARU were believed to be directly linked to the RATF through the WUO and May 19 CO. The practice of claiming terrorist attacks under different group names may be a clever attempt used by RATF to bypass federal laws that at the time provided for the prosecution of members of an organization involved in illegal activity. Therefore, members linked to any RATF revolutionary cells could not be indicted for a bombing committed by the UFF unless they could be directly tied to that group.[65]

The FBI maintains that the UFF and ARU are one and the same. They arrived at this conclusion by citing the similar language used in communiqués issued after each bombing, the consistency in target selection, and the materials used in bomb construction. It is important to recognize that terrorist groups use a variety of aliases to frustrate counterterrorist efforts and to persuade the police and mass media that a variety of formidable "radicals" are active and prepared to attack the "system" of "American imperialism."

By the mid-1980s, the recent history of left-wing groups ended, and all supporters of the left were in either hiding or prison. After the fall of the Soviet Union, leftists were deprived of a coherent ideology, and after 1990, left-wing terrorism in the United States virtually disappeared.

Left-wing terrorism was short-lived in the United States. As Cronin maintains, "the left-wing groups of the 1970's were notorious for their inability to articulate a clear vision of their goals that could be handed down to successors after the first generation of radical leaders departed or were eliminated."[66]

THE IDEOLOGICAL RIGHT

Right-wing extremism has waged a continuous assault against the values supported by the U.S. Constitution since the KKK emerged after the Civil War. The terrorist activities of the KKK succeeded in "liberating" the old Confederacy from white Republicans, expelling Union soldiers from the South and dominating the lives of Southern blacks for many years. The early Klan terrorism was based primarily on the principles of patriotism and nationalism. The success of Klan extremism can be traced to four important conditions needed for the terrorists' strategy to be effective: (1) postwar disruption and economic chaos; (2) solidarity based on nationalist pride; (3) terrorist objectives limited to destabilization of the "system"; and (4) the established governmental system lacking the resources to conduct an effective counterterrorist campaign. These conditions certainly existed after the Civil War, World War I, and the Vietnam War: historical periods when Klan violence reached its greatest peak.

The Klan has evolved into a variety of "right-wing" extremist groups that vary greatly in the use of the terrorist strategy. For example, the Sheriff's Posse Comitatus (SPC) has murdered police officers from ambush, and the group calling itself the Order is responsible for a series of bank and armored car robberies. The Covenant, the Sword, and the Arm of the Lord (CSA) consists largely of young idealists who embrace religious revival, spiritual regeneration, patriotism, and nationalism. The CSA, although founded on Christian fundamentalist religious principles, believed that "society" was going to collapse. So they began to arm and train their members for the coming racial and religious "war."

The legacy of right-wing extremism introduced by the KKK has taken on a new dimension. Not only is the old patriotism and nationalism heard to suppress the threat of social revolution, but also fundamentalist religious ideas supported by a growing number of Christian Identity churches has provided a rallying point for right-wing extremism. (Christian Identity churches support a religious belief based on racism and anti-Semiticism, proclaiming white supremacy.)

The growth of right-wing extremism, which was relatively quiet in the 1970s, is a continuing source of major concern for the criminal justice system. Groups such as the Order, Posse Comitatus, American Nazi Party, the Aryan Nations, and the CSA, a variety of white supremacy groups, survivalists, skinheads, and militias still pose a serious threat to the values of constitutional liberty in the United States.

One of the most dangerous right-wing hate groups in the United States is probably the neo-Nazi **National Alliance** founded by **William Pierce.** The National Alliance came to prominence when it was discovered that a fictionalized story entitled the *Turner Diaries* was the inspiration behind several criminal high-visibility terrorist acts. Convicted bomber Timothy McVeigh was reported to be a devoted reader of the *Turner Diaries*, which details a bombing scenario that is very similar to the Oklahoma City bombing. The book also provided a blueprint for the Order, a violent right-wing group that robbed banks, armored cars, and murdered several people in the 1980s. The *Turner Diaries* was also required reading for the Aryan Republican Army, which committed twenty-two bank robberies and bombings in the Midwest between 1992 and 1996, before they were apprehended by the FBI, convicted, and sentenced to long prison terms.[67]

THE TURNER DIARIES

Andrew Macdonald

FIGURE 2.3 *The Turner Diaries* has become the "bible" for some white extremist hate groups. It was written by William Pierce under the pseudonym Andrew MacDonald.

The sequel to the *Turner Diaries*, called *Hunter*, also by William Pierce, relates a story dedicated to Joseph Paul Franklin, who confessed to murdering eighteen people between 1977 and 1980 in an attempt to start a race war in the United States. Franklin's victims included interracial couples, African Americans, and Jews. Franklin, a serial killer who was convicted for murder and sentenced to multiple life sentences, is praised in the *Hunter* as a white patriot. William Pierce died of natural causes in 2002. After Pierce's death, the National Alliance was severely weakened and split up into competing factions.

The **World Church of the Creator (WCOTC)**, founded in 1973 by Ben Klassen, hailed Adolf Hitler as the greatest white leader the world has ever known. The church, whose battle cry is RaHoWa, an acronym for Racial Holy War, supports the survival, expansion, and advancement of the white race through the use of violence. In the 1990s, the WCOTC was identified by the FBI as the most violent right-wing group in the United States. In 1993, Ben Klassen committed suicide and the leadership of the church was taken over by Matthew Hale, an attorney from East Peoria, Illinois.[68] Hale revitalized the WCOTC, eventually changing the name to the "Creativity movement." On January 9, 2003, Hale was arrested in Chicago for planning to have a federal judge murdered. On April 6, 2005, Hale was sentenced to forty years in prison for soliciting an undercover informant to kill a federal judge. Since Hale's incarceration, the WCOTC has split into several groups supporting white supremacy and anti-Semitism.

The **Phineas Priesthood** is yet another violent right-wing group that has gained some popularity among white supremacists. Richard Hoskins, an anti-Semitic and racist, is the author of *Vigilantes of Christendom: The Story of the Phineas Priesthood*, a book that inspired the justification of anti-Semitic and racist acts of violence. Unlike other white hate groups, the

Phineas Priesthood does not require membership. There are no meetings, rallies, or newsletters. An individual becomes a member when he/she commits a Phineas act, that is, any violent activity against nonwhites or Jews. Bryon de la Beckwith, who was convicted for killing civil rights leader Medgar Evers, wrote that he finally attained the status of being accepted into the Phineas Priesthood.[69] Paul Hill, the antiabortion terrorist, was convicted of murdering an abortion doctor and his escort in 1994. Hill had written an essay advocating the commission of "Phineas actions" against abortion doctors.

In sum, there are, of course, certain similarities in practice between terrorist groups that support the ideological right and the ideological left. For example, their targets in many cases are identical; they prefer violent action rather than a nonviolent approach; and on occasion they have trained together. The similarity is further strengthened when ideologically opposed terrorist groups take credit for the same terrorist event. Viewed from the center, then, all extremist groups, whether right or left, appear identical; however, we would be making a serious error if we took this literally for there are significant differences between the ideological right and left (see Table 2.1).

First of all, they occupy specifically different positions in relation to the governmental power structure. Even though both right and left may plan to overthrow the existing political structure, right-wing extremists often have allies and supporters in the police, armed services, and among wealthy, conservative corporate executives and business people. Ordinarily, groups on the left do not have such sponsors. The overlap between the Klan and local police agencies throughout the South is well documented, although admittedly this relationship is often exaggerated. Consider, for example, the campaign undertaken by the FBI and local law enforcement agencies against members of the Aryan Nations and the Order.

A confrontation between right and left extremist groups occurred in Greensboro, North Carolina, in November 1979. During an anti-Klan rally, five members of the Communist Workers Party (CWP) were slain by the KKK and the American Nazi Party. In the subsequent trial, the Klansmen and Nazis were found not guilty of both murder and conspiracy. However, in

TABLE 2.1   Comparison of Left-Wing and Right-Wing Terrorist Groups in the United States

Characteristics	Left Wing	Right Wing
Ideology	Marxism[a]	CIM[b]/Neo-Nazi
Economic views	Procommunist socialist	Anticommunist work ethic
Base of operations	Urban areas	Rural areas
Tactical approach	Cellular/use of safe houses	National Alliance camps/compounds
Targets/funding	Armored trucks/bank robbery	Armored trucks/bank robbery
Terrorism	Capitalist targets	Federal law enforcement agencies

[a]Marxism: a political ideology that supports the historical idea of class conflict advocated by Karl Marx.

[b]CIM (Christian Identity Movement): a racial supremacist religious group that supports the belief that white Aryans are the chosen people of God and nonwhites and Jews are biologically inferior to white people. Most recently, there has been a resurgence of neo-Nazi activity by racist skinhead groups. Skinhead groups are affiliated with other more established white supremacist groups, such as the Klan, National Socialist Movement, American Front, Creativity Movement, Nazi low riders, Hammerskin Nation, Volksfront, White Revolution, and PEN1 (Public Enemy #1). The ADL (Anti-Defamation League) has identified over 100 racist skinhead groups throughout the United States that have been involved in hate crimes, drug trafficking, and street terrorism.

a later civil suit brought against Klansmen, Nazis, and three police officers, the court found them liable for the wrongful death of one of the CWP victims and ordered them to pay $355,100 in damages. The Greensboro police were accused of complicity and support for Klan actions against the CWP victims.

Right-wing extremists generally attack "alien" targets. Targets are carefully chosen on the basis of race, religion, ethnic origin, or ideology. In the case of the Greensboro incident, ideology and race provoked the Klan assault. The targets are quite frequently "out groups" competing for scarce economic resources. Right-wing terrorists would prefer to arouse the support of the masses as an ethnic (Aryan race) or religious (Christian Identity church) nation to attack communists, aliens, and nonbelievers. Today, religious fundamentalism provides the medium by which right-wing groups express their political views. Right-wing groups inspiring nationalist pride can be highly effective when an entire community or nation defines itself on the basis of race, nationality, or religion. Terrorism can be an effective strategy for exciting communal violence. In short, right-wing terrorist groups are inspired by the political principles of fascism.

SINGLE-ISSUE TERRORIST

The most recognizable single-issue terrorists are those seeking a change in government policy on one specific issue. Under this heading, three issues have gained importance: abortion rights, animal rights, and environmental issues or "ecoterrorism." Smith explores the idea that over the past two decades some of the more popular social issues have attracted radical elements that now form an extremist militant core prepared to use threats, intimidation, and violence to achieve their objectives.[70] During the 1980s, the United States recorded over forty bombings of abortion clinics. In the 1990s, the attacks on abortion clinics began to escalate with assaults on individual clinic workers, an increase in arson and bombings, and the murder of abortion doctors.

Antiabortionists are guided by an underground manual *Army of God*, which provides detailed instructions on various forms of violence and terrorism directed specifically at abortion clinics and workers. The initials AG were found on several abortion buildings that were bombed in the 1980s. Mike Bray, a convicted abortion clinic bomber, was accused by Ted Koppel, host of ABC's *Nightline*, of being the author of *Army of God*,[71] although Bray would not confirm or deny authorship. However, Bray did author *A Time to Kill*, the definitive text on what he considers the ethical justification for antiabortion violence, where he defends the use of terrorism and the murders of abortion clinic doctors.[72] There is every reason to believe that attacks on abortion clinics will continue in the future. Antiabortion extremists have vowed to continue the use of "terrorist" tactics until the federal government overturns *Roe* v. *Wade*.[73] For those who see abortion as simply baby killing, the federal government and the support of abortion clinics will remain the enemy.

Like the antiabortionists, animal rights and environmental extremists discovered that they shared some common objectives. They distrust the mass media, despise the government, and maintain that large corporations exploit the resources of the world. Although animal and environmental rights extremists are considered domestic terrorists, they are international in scope. Today the popular term *ecoterrorism* is widely used to describe violent activity of animal and environmental extremists. Obviously, most people are in favor of protecting animals and saving the environment. However, most people do not send letter bombs to corporations, set up booby traps intent on injuring loggers, or firebomb department stores that sell furs.

The Animal Liberation Front (ALF) and the violent ecology movement began in England in the 1970s and 1980s.[74] Both concepts eventually spread to the United States. The movements had their strongest support in the American West. Like the antiabortion groups, a novel served to inspire the ecoterrorists. *The Monkey Wrench Gang*[75] told the story of a group of ecologists who travel through several Western states destroying bulldozers, damaging private property, and burning billboards, and other structures that harm the environment. "Monkey wrenching" has become the symbol of ecoterrorism.

Crimes of ecoterrorists include bombs attached to cars of animal researchers, raids against fur farms, a string of firebombs in London department stores, use of noxious chemicals, destruction of animal research labs, threats to individuals, and widespread arson of new construction sites throughout the United States. Dyson states that when the total economic impact of ecoterrorism is calculated, it illustrates that the United States and England have been victimized by a long-term terrorist campaign.[76] The FBI estimates that between 1976 and 2005 the ALF and Earth Liberation Front (ELF) have committed more than 1,100 criminal acts in the United States, resulting in damages estimated at $110 million.

In the past decade, ecoterrorism has spawned numerous groups supporting a variety of animal and ecological causes. The ALF, Band of Mercy, Animal Rights Militia, and Paint Panthers endorse animal rights. The ELF and Earth First! want to save the planet. Many ecoterrorist groups have Web sites where they publicize their criminal terrorist activities. For example, one writer provides explicit details for raiding animal farms, while another describes the use of arson to force land developers, ski lodges, research labs, and farms out of business to save the environment. A review of the rhetoric of ecoterrorists is very clear. They are illogical extremists who referred to animal farms as concentration camps. They want to destroy all new building construction and force everyone to be vegetarians. The FBI concludes that ecoterrorists "have become the most active criminal extremist elements in the United States." On November 27, 2006, President Bush signed the Animal Enterprise Terrorism Act into law. Under this Act, any effort to interfere with animal research that makes researchers or their families fear for their safety is now punishable by up to five years in prison.

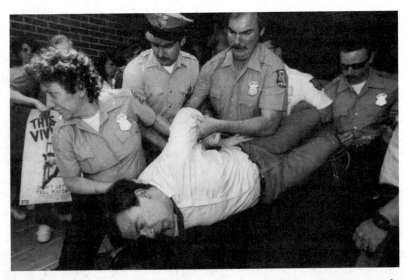

FIGURE 2.4 Police arrest animal rights advocates while demonstrating against the use of animals for experimentation in Bethesda, Maryland. (Marcy Nighswander/AP/Wide World Photos)

There is every reason to believe that attacks by antiabortion groups and ecoterrorists will continue in the future. The Task Force on Violence against Abortion Providers still investigates more than 100 violations a year of the Freedom of Access to Clinic Entrances (FACE) Act. Ecoterrorist cells remain difficult to infiltrate and identify. Therefore, it is likely that ALF and ELF will continue their terrorist and criminal activities.

Conclusions

There is sufficient cause to suspect that terrorism will intensify in the United States. The numerous groups that this chapter has identified illustrate that extremists could find justification in their perceived grievances against the United States or governments sympathetic to the United States. Additionally, controversial issues such as abortion and nuclear disarmament or even the liberation of animals could escalate and include acts of indiscriminate terror. International issues could also excite campaigns of domestic terrorism. For example, U.S. military intervention in Afghanistan, Iraq, and elsewhere could provoke the type of antiwar violence prevalent during the Vietnam War.

Finally, irrational acts by individuals who seek recognition, revenge, and retaliation by hijacking airplanes, seizing hostages, assassinating government representatives, or bombing federal and state facilities must be anticipated. The U.S. homeland will face a persistent terrorist threat from evolving Islamic extremist groups, especially al Qaeda. Al Qaeda will remain the most serious terrorist threat to the U.S. homeland, the war on terrorism's newest front. Table 2.2 summarizes the future of terrorism in the United States. Chapter 4 discusses Middle East terrorism and the rise of homegrown al Qaeda and Islamic radical terrorism that threatens the U.S. homeland.

Key Terms

anarchism
assassins
Fuerzas Armadas de Liberation
    Nacional (FALN)
Jewish Defense League (JDL)
Ku Klux Klan (KKK)
Meir Kahane

Narodnaya Volya
National Alliance
Phineas Priesthood
Revolutionary Armed Task
    Force (RATF)
Sicarii
Turner Diaries

World Church of the Creator
    (WCOTC)
William Pierce
Weather Underground
    Organization/Black
    Liberation Army
    (WUO/BLA)

TABLE 2.2   Future of Terrorism in the United States

Type	Future	Major Causal Issue
International	Increases	al Qaeda/Osama bin Laden/supporting Islamic terrorism
Domestic		
Left wing	Significant decreases	Fall of communism/FBI convictions
Right wing	Increases (worldwide)	Distrust federal government/rise of Christian Identity churches
Single issue	Increases	Environmental issues/antiabortion/animal rights
Puerto Rican	Decreases	Decline after vote to maintain Commonwealth status/ President Clinton granted clemency

Discussion Questions

1. Describe the terrorist tactics used by the Sicarii.
2. What major attribute distinguishes Narodnaya Volya from contemporary terrorist groups?
3. Discuss and identify the following "terrorist" publications. Why are they important?
   a. *Revolutionary Catechism*
   b. *Mini-Manual of Urban Guerrilla Warfare*
   c. *Document on Terror*
   d. *Turner Diaries/Hunter*
   e. *Army of God*
   f. *Time to Kill*
   g. *Vigilantes of Christendom: The Story of the Phineas Priesthood*
   h. *Monkey Wrench Gang*

4. What is histrionic terrorism?
5. Who were the Assassins? Compare and contrast the terrorist acts of the Assassins with those of HAMAS, the al Aqsa Martyrs Brigade, and Hizballah.
6. Identify and define three distinct types of anarchism.
7. How do left-wing and right-wing terrorist groups differ?
8. Outline the major differences between the first, second, and third Klans.
9. What are the core beliefs of the Phineas Priesthood?
10. Do you think right-wing hate and terrorist groups are a dangerous threat to the United States? Explain fully.

Web Sites

Anti-Defamation League (ADL)
http://www.adl.org/adl.asp

Rand Corporation (Criminal Justice and terrorism topics)
http://www.rand.org

Southern Poverty Law Center (Klan watch)
http://www.splcenter.org

The Terrorism Research Center
http://www.terrorism.com

Terrorist Group Profiles
http://www.milnet.com

Center for the Study of Terrorism and Political Violence
http://www.st-andrews.ac.uk

Endnotes

1. E. Mary Smallwood, *The Jews under Roman Rule: From Pompeii to Diocletian: A Study in Political Relations* (Leiden, Netherlands: Brill, 1981), pp. 133–38.
2. David C. Rapoport and Yonah Alexander, eds., *The Morality of Terrorism: Religious and Secular Justifications* (New York: Pergamon, 1983), pp. 16–23.
3. For example, see Samuel G. Brandon, *Jesus and the Zealots. A Study of the Political Factor in Primitive Christianity* (New York: Scribner, 1967); David Roberts and Fabio Bourbon, *The Holy Land: Yesterday and Today* (Cairo: American University Press, 1996); Gerard Chaliand and Arnaud Blin, *History of Terrorism: From Antiquity to al Qaeda* (Berkeley, CA: University of California Press, 2007).

4. Lord Widgery, *Report of the Tribunal Appointed to Enquire into the Events on Sunday, 30th January, 1972 in Londonderry* (London: HMSO, 1972), p. 6.
5. Menachem Begin, *The Revolt: Story of the Irgun*, rev. ed. (New York: Nash, 1977), p. 47.
6. History Channel, *100 Years of Terror* (New York: A & E Television Networks, 2000).
7. Mark Bowden, *Killing Pablo: The Hunt for the World's Greatest Outlaw* (New York: Penguin Press, 2002), pp. 58–59, 167–69.
8. For example, see Marshall G. S. Hodgson, *The Order of Assassins* (The Hague: Morton, 1955); Bernard Lewis, *The Assassins: A Radical Sect in Islam* (New York: Basic Books, 1968), Chapter 2; Enno Franzius, *History of the Order of Assassins* (New York: Funk and Wagnalls, 1969); Bruce

Hoffman, *Inside Terrorism* (New York: Columbia University Press, 1998).

9. For example, see George Bruse, *The Stranglers— The Cult of Thuggee and Its Overthrow in British India* (New York: Harcourt, Brace and World, 1969).

10. For example, see Jean Chesneaux, ed., *Popular Movements and Secret Societies in China, 1840–1950* (Stanford, CA: Stanford University Press, 1972).

11. For example, see Wilfred Neidhardt, *Fenianism in North America* (University Park, IL: Pennsylvania State University, 1975); William D'Arcy, *The Fenian Movement in the U.S.: 1858–1886* (Washington, DC: Catholic University Press, 1947); R. V. Comerford, *The Fenians in Context: Irish Politics and Society, 1884–1882* (Dublin: Wolfhound Press, 1985).

12. Patrick J. O'Farrell, *Ireland's English Question: Anglo-Irish Relations 1534–1970* (New York: Schocken Books, 1972), pp. 138–43.

13. Walter Laqueur, *Terrorism* (Boston, MA: Little, Brown and Company, 1977), p. 10; Laqueur, *The New Terrorism: Fanaticism and the Arms of Mass Destruction* (New York: Oxford University Press, 1999), pp. 107–9.

14. For example, see David M. Chalmers, *Hooded Americanism: The First Century of the Ku Klux Klan 1865–1965* (Garden City, NY: Doubleday, 1965); Jonathan R. White, *Terrorism: An Introduction* (Belmont, CA: Wadsworth/Thompson Learning, 2002), p. 222; Joseph T. McCann, *Terrorism on American Soil: A Concise History of Plots and Perpetrators from the Famous to the Forgotten* (Boulder, CO: Sentient Publishing, 2006).

15. William P. Randel, *The Ku Klux Klan: A Century of Infamy* (Philadelphia, PA: Chilton, 1965); David M. Chalmers, *Hooded Americanism: The History of the Ku Klux Klan* (New York: Franklin Watts, 1981), pp. 190–325.

16. White, *Terrorism*, pp. 220–32.

17. For example, see Anti-Defamation League, *Ku Klux Klan Rebounds* (New York: ADL, 2007), http://www.adl.org.

18. *Virginia* v. *Black*, et al., 538 U.S. 343(2003). A First Amendment case–the act of cross burning.

19. For example, see Astrid Von Borcke, "Violence and Terror in Russian Revolutionary Populism, The Narodnaya Volya, 1879–1883," in *Social Protest, Violence, and Terrorism in 19th and 20th Century Europe*, eds. Wolfgang J. Mommsen and Gerhard Hirschfeld (London: MacMillan, 1982), pp. 48–62; Ronald Seth, *The Russian Terrorists: The Story of Narodniki* (London: Barrie and Rockliff, 1967).

20. James Joll, "Anarchism: A Living Tradition," in *Anarchism Today*, eds. David E. Apter and James Joll (New York: Anchor, 1972), pp. 245–61.

21. Franco Venturi, *Roots of Revolution: A History of the Populist and Socialist Movements in 19th Century Russia* (New York: Knopf, 1960), pp. 389–428.

22. William E. Mosse, *Alexander II and the Modernization of Russia* (New York: MacMillan, 1958), p. 159.

23. Sergius Stepniak, *Underground Russia: Revolutionary Profiles and Sketches from Life* (New York: Scribner, 1892), p. 32.

24. Ze'ev Ivianski, "The Moral Issue: Some Aspects of Individual Terror," in *The Morality of Terrorism: Religious and Secular Justifications*, eds. David C. Rapoport and Yonah Alexander (New York: Pergamon, 1983), pp. 229–57.

25. Laqueur, *Terrorism*, p. 4.

26. For example, see Sergei Nechaev, "Catechism of the Revolutionist," in *Daughter of a Revolutionary*, ed. Michael Confino (London: Alcove, 1982); Robert Payne, *The Life and Death of Lenin* (New York: Simon and Schuster, 1964), pp. 24–29.

27. Regis Debray, *Revolution in the Revolution: Armed Struggle and Political Struggle in Latin America* (New York: Grove Press, 1967).

28. Ernesto (Che) Guevara, *Episodes of the Revolutionary War* (New York: International Publishers, 1968).

29. For example, see Carlos Marighella, "The Mini-Manual of Urban Guerrilla Warfare," in *Urban Guerrilla Warfare*, ed. Robert Moss (London: Institute for Strategic Studies, 1971); Carlos Marighella, *The Terrorist Classic: Manual of the Urban Guerrilla*, trans. Gene Hanrahan (Chapel Hill, NC: Documentary Publishers, 1985).

30. "Document on Terror," in *The Morality of Terrorism: Religious and Secular Justifications*, eds. David C. Rapoport and Yonah Alexander (New York: Pergamon, 1983), pp. 186–216.

31. For example, see George Woodcock, *Anarchism (Broadview Encore Editions)* (New York: Broadview Press, 2004); David L. Miller, *Anarchism* (London: J. M. Dent and Sons, 1984).

32. James Joll, *The Anarchists* (Cambridge, MA: Harvard University Press, 1980); Laqueur, *Terrorism*, pp. 14–15.

33. Alex P. Schmid, *Political Terrorism: A Research Guide to Concept Theories, Databases, and Literature* (New Brunswick, NJ: Transaction Books, 1983), p. 52.

34. For example, see Robert Nozick, *Anarchy, State and Utopia* (New York: Basic Books, 1977); Robert D. Kaplan, *The Coming Anarchy: Shattering the Dreams of the Post Cold War* (New York: Random House, 2000).

35. For example, see Richard B. Saltman, *The Social and Political Thought of Michael Bakunin* (Westport, CT: Greenwood, 1983); Paul McLaughlin, *Mikhail Bakunin: Philosophical Basis of His Anarchism* (New York: Algora Publishers, 2002).

36. For example, see "Nine Years of the Love and Rage Revolutionary Anarchist Federation," (2007), http://www.libcom.org.

37. For example, see Howard Zinn, et al., *A People's History of American Empire* (New York: Metropolitan Books, 2008).

38. For example, see AnarchismToday.org. In their view, democracy creates injustice because it leads to the enslavement and the exploitation of the world. The notion of democracy undermines the creation of a fair and just social system.

39. For example, see Robert W. Anderson, *Party Politics in Puerto Rico* (Stanford, CA: Stanford University Press, 1965).

40. National Commission on Causes and Prevention of Violence, *Assassination and Political Violence* (Washington, DC: U.S. Government Printing Office, 1968), pp. 58–59.

41. Ibid., p. 29.

42. Patricia Atthowe, "Terrorism: The FALN's Undeclared War," *Defense and Foreign Affairs Digest* (1978), p. 48.

43. U.S. Congress, Senate, Committee on the Judiciary, *Hearing on FALN Clemency* (Washington, DC: U.S. Government Printing Office, September 15, 1999).

44. Ibid., January 25, 1975, pp. 1, A10.

45. Ibid., December 4, 1979, pp. 1, A10.

46. Ibid., January 13, 1981, pp. 1, A12.

47. Gertrude Jaeger and Phillip Selznick, "A Normative Theory of Culture," *American Sociological Review*, 29 (1964), pp. 653–69.

48. *New York Times*, March 1, 1982, pp. 1, DI 1.

49. Ibid., March 16, 1980, pp. 1, 45.

50. Ibid., April 5, 1980. pp. 1, A7.

51. Ibid., January 1, 1983, pp. 1, A23.

52. "Meir Kahane: A Candid Conversation with the Military Leader of the Jewish Defense League," *Playboy* (October 1972), p. 69.

53. "Anti-Soviet Zionist Terrorism in the U.S.," *Current Digest of the Soviet Press*, 23 (1971), pp. 6–8.

54. *Time*, August 13, 1984, p. 26.

55. *New York Times*, October 20, 1981, p. A1.

56. Ibid.

57. Stuart Daniels, "The Weathermen," *Government and Opposition*, 9 (autumn 1974), pp. 430–59.

58. For example, see *The Split of the Weather Underground Organization* (Seattle, WA: John Brown Book Club, 1977).

59. Brent L. Smith, *Terrorism in America: Pipe Bombs and Pipe Dreams* (Albany, NY: State University of New York, 1994), p. 99.

60. U.S. Congress, Senate, Committee on the Judiciary, Subcommittee on *Security and Terrorism*, Committee on the Judiciary, U.S. Senate, 97th Congress, February 4, 1982 (Washington, DC: U.S. Government Printing Office, 1982), pp. 41–43.

61. Ibid., p. 44.

62. For example, see G. Louis Heath, *Students for a Democratic Society* (Metuchen, NJ: Scarecrow, 1976).

63. *New York Times*, March 1, 1971, p. 1.

64. *The Split of the Weather Underground Organization*, pp. 4–7.

65. U.S. Congress, Subcommittee on *Security and Terrorism*, pp. 52–81.

66. Audrey K. Cronin, "How al Qaida Ends: The Decline and Demise of Terrorist Groups," *International Security*, 31 (Summer 2006), p. 23.

67. Anti-Defamation League (ADL) Web site: http://www.adl.org/adl.asp.

68. World Church of the Creator (WCOTC) Web site: http://www.creator.org.

69. Mark Juergensmeyer, *Terror in the Mind of God: The Global Rise of Religious Violence* (Berkeley, CA: University of California Press, 2000), p. 154.

70. G. Davidson Smith, "Single Issue Terrorism: Canadian Security Intelligence Service," *Commentary*, 74 (1998), p. 46.

71. Ted Koppel, *Nightline*, March 9, 1998.

72. Michael Bray, *A Time to Kill: A Study Concerning the Use of Force and Abortion* (Portland, OR: Advocates for Life Publications, 1994), pp. 4–26.

73. Ibid., p. 158.

74. Bryan Denson and James Long, "Ecoterrorism Sweeps the American West," *Portland Oregonian* (September 26, 1999), p. 1; Joanie Marie Dybach, "Domestic Environmental Terrorists: Philosophies and Practices as Predictors of Future Threat," thesis, California State University, Sacramento, Spring 2002.

75. For example, see Edward Abby, *The Monkey Wrench Gang* (Salt Lake City, UT: Roaming the West, 1975); Also, Bob Torres, *Making a Killing: The Political Economy of Animal Rights* (Oakland, CA: AK Press, 2007).

76. William E. Dyson, *Terrorism: An Investigator's Handbook* (Cincinnati, OH: Anderson Publishing, 2001), p. 24.

██ ██ ██ █ ██ ▬▬▬▬▬▬▬▬▬▬▬▬▬▬▬▬▬▬▬▬▬▬▬▬▬▬▬

CHAPTER 3

Violence and Terrorism: The Role of the Mass Media

CHAPTER OBJECTIVES

The study of this chapter will enable you to:

- Explore the relationship between television and the escalation of violence in American society
- Analyze the nature of contagion theory
- Outline historical trends of skyjacking
- Detail the uses of propaganda by terrorist groups
- Interpret the use of a hunger strike as a media attention strategy
- Recognize the insidious nature of censorship
- Evaluate law enforcement and media relations

INTRODUCTION

Modern terrorist groups make extensive use of the mass media, particularly the electronic media. One of the major purposes of a terrorist act is to inform the world. We are reminded by Crenshaw that "the most basic reason for terrorism is to gain recognition or attention."[1] Advertising the aims of the terrorist groups and the specific act of terrorism is extremely important to the success of the terrorist incident. In fact, publicity and attention are the only objectives in many cases.

For example, on September 10, 1976, five members of the Croatian National Resistance, or Fighters for Free Croatia (CFF), hijacked a Boeing 727 with sixty-three passengers and the flight crew aboard. The odyssey began in New York and ended some thirty hours later in Paris. The hijackers made stops in Montreal, Newfoundland, London, and Paris. The demands of the Croatians included the publication of their manifesto in its entirety in the *New York Times*, *Chicago Tribune*, *Los Angeles Times*, and the *International Herald Tribune.* This manifesto outlined Croatian grievances against the Yugoslav government and the Tito regime. Furthermore, the Croatians demanded that pamphlets be scattered over New York, Chicago, Montreal, London, and Paris. These pamphlets proclaimed that the world would not have peace until Croatia had the same freedoms that other nations enjoy. On board the hijacked plane, the Croatians had planted a fake bomb and threatened to injure the passengers. The plane was forced to land in Newfoundland, where thirty-five passengers were unexpectedly released. The hijackers then continued on to Paris, where they finally surrendered to the police and were returned to the United States. After dismantling his fake bomb and being taken into custody by the FBI, one of the hijackers announced, "Well, that's showbiz!" So for the price of five one-way tickets to Chicago, the printing of some pamphlets, the ingredients for at least two bombs, worth a total of approximately $400, the Croatians received media attention worth millions of dollars of advertising, and they captured the attention of millions of people for some thirty hours. Certainly the purpose of this act of terrorism was to gain publicity for a political cause. To this end, the Croatians were successful. However, they were not the first terrorist group to use this attention-getting strategy.[2]

CONTAGION THEORY, OR THE COPYCAT SYNDROME

In the last fifty years, our days and nights have been illuminated by the electronic media. Television and the Internet have transformed our time at a rate unmatched by any past technology or social idea, including the printing press. In fact, television viewing and the Internet are preferred to reading books, journals, magazines, and newspapers. Many of our earliest memories represent images transmitted by television. Our heroes (the police-action dramas), symbols (the prevalent use of firearms and drugs), shared values (the use of force, coercion, and intimidation), and behavior (the effect of product advertising) are influenced by prolonged television viewing and surfing the Internet. The images projected on the television screen flood into our homes seven days a week, and many of these images reinforce the violence theme. This daily barrage of television violence is perceived as "entertainment" by the television networks. During the years since the introduction of television into our lives, real-life violence has risen to epidemic proportions, and acts of political violence and terrorism have become pandemic. Has television brought on this explosion of domestic violence and international terrorism, or does it merely reflect a dangerous social trend? Jenkins of the Rand Institute thinks television has stimulated the growth of terrorism and violence from insurgent terrorist groups, or terrorism from "below."

Jenkins argues that terrorism is theater; therefore, terrorists want a lot of people watching and listening.[3] The world has hardly noticed the struggle of developing countries in Africa, Latin America, and the Middle East, where the tactics of terrorism and guerrilla warfare are widespread. But a handful of Palestinian "freedom fighters" have demonstrated the importance of media attention. In September 1970, the theatrical introduction of the *new* terrorism, holding completely innocent hostages and making outrageous political demands, began with the carefully staged **skyjacking** of three airliners. A total of 276 persons were held hostage and brought to an abandoned World War II airfield in Jordan. Another much larger jumbo jet that had been too big to land in Jordan was wired with explosives and blown up in Cairo. What followed was a six-day hostage-taking media event.

The **Popular Front for the Liberation of Palestine (PFLP)** proudly claimed credit for the incident. The initial demands of the PFLP involved a complicated exchange of hostages and Palestinians imprisoned in Israel, West Germany, France, and England, but these demands most certainly were secondary. The primary purpose of the terrorist action was later explained at a news conference by one of the skyjackers, Bassani Abu Sherif: "It was a direct assault on the consciousness of international opinion. What mattered most to us was that one pays attention to us."[4] Television crews and news reporters from around the world converged on the scene, and regular press conferences were held with hostages and the spokesman of the PFLP. These scenes were broadcast to millions of viewers. The Palestinian issue had finally erupted onto the world scene. Eventually the hostages were bussed to Amman, and the planes, worth $30 million, were wired with explosives and blown up. Negotiations began to break down, Jordanian troops attacked the PFLP, and civil war broke out in Jordan. The Palestinians referred to that month as **Black September**. After several days of intense fighting, the hostages were freed by the Jordanian army, and the PFLP was driven out of Jordan.

Film of the entire incident—the exploding planes, the hostage negotiation, the civil war, and finally the release of the hostages—was immediately prepared to inform the entire world. The reporter who put together the film, David Phillips, was honored at the Cannes Television Festival for his exclusive coverage of the affair. He had unwittingly provided the Palestinian Resistance Movement and the PFLP with the publicity the Palestinians so desperately wanted. The full meaning of this terrorist tactic was realized when other Palestinian groups and "freedom fighters" around the world emulated the new terrorist strategy of taking hostages and making political demands.

There is no doubt that the copycat, or **contagion effect**, is motivated by the media. The basis for contagion theory is that any time someone does something new and novel and is successful, others will attempt to imitate that success. This is particularly evident in the case of skyjacking. The chronicles of air piracy, or skyjacking, reveal five distinct trends. First, a series of skyjackings occurred in the early 1950s when individuals as well as small groups attempted to escape the tyranny of Eastern Bloc countries. Most of the aircraft were diverted to airfields in West Germany and France. The passengers of these skyjacked aircraft were merely innocent captives, not pawns used in a deadly game of blackmail. The second trend also involved the attempted escape of some rather desperate skyjackers from Cuba to the United States in the late 1950s and the early 1960s. Several skyjackings originated in the United States where aircraft were forced to land in Cuba. For the most part, the skyjackers just wanted to return home or flee Cuba. Third, a new trend began in 1968 that was to encompass the entire world. This new form of skyjacking was introduced by the PFLP when an Israeli El Al airliner was seized.[5] The status of innocent passengers quickly changed to that of political hostages; a new category of victims had been created. The phenomenon began to spread when other political terrorist groups as well as criminals hijacked aircraft for the purposes of making political demands or extortion. The role of the media seems to have significantly influenced this type of skyjacking.

The eminent psychiatrist Hubbard, who has interviewed hundreds of skyjackers, writes that skyjackers often kept scrapbooks and detailed notes of skyjacking incidents in order to understand how to carry out a skyjacking.[6] Although not terrorism, the parachute hijackings provide an excellent example of media influence. On November 12, 1971, a young Scotsman living in Canada hijacked a DC-8. He carried his own parachute and threatened to blow up the aircraft if he was not given $50,000. The hijacker was eventually overpowered by the crew and turned over to the police. However, the incident received considerable publicity in U.S. news reports.[7] On November 24, 1971, a successful parachute skyjacking was accomplished by a hijacker using the name of **D.B. Cooper**.[8] Cooper's extortion demands included $200,000 and four parachutes. D.B. Cooper parachuted out of the aircraft somewhere between Portland, Oregon, and Reno, Nevada, never to be seen again. This skyjacking received enormous media attention, and D.B. Cooper became a folk hero of sorts, with the pop media contributing songs, poems, and short stories glorifying this success. If D.B. Cooper imitated the young Scotsman, then media report-ing provided the impetus for a whole series of parachute hijackings following D.B. Cooper's "success." Subsequently, twenty-seven such hijackings were attempted in the United States, Europe, Japan, Latin America, and Australia. Undoubtedly, media reporting of skyjackings tantalizes would-be emulators with the promise of recognition and reward.

The media played a decisive role in fostering the parachute hijackings that followed the Cooper episode. For example, precise details were reported on the type and proper use of the parachute. Therefore, it is reasonable to conclude that if these details had not been printed and described by the media, imitations would have been rare. In fact, in two cases the hijacker demanded $200,000 and four parachutes, identical to the D.B. Cooper ultimatum. Yet another indication of media-fostered contagion is that twenty of the twenty-seven hijackings occurred in the United States and Canada, and seven cases were separated from each other by eight days or less.[9] Of the twenty-seven parachute skyjackers, only D.B. Cooper is still a fugitive. Other hijackers were killed by the police, committed suicide, or were arrested after making the para-chute jump. The case histories for media-induced contagion seem incontestable when applied to parachute hijackings.

The fourth skyjacking trend involves two specific groups of people. After the Mariel boat lifts from Cuba in 1981, thousands of Cubans made their way to the United States. Many eventu-ally became disillusioned with life in the United States and longed for their native Cuba. So, the quickest and most inexpensive way to return to Cuba was to hijack an airliner. In 1982, there were ten such hijackings that originated in the United States. Airline policy required that all passengers and carry-on luggage be screened through metal detectors. The Cuban skyjackers used carry-on explosive devices that went undetected by metal security devices. Gasoline bombs, dynamite, and improvised explosive devices were used in order to intimidate crews and passen-gers. Security, however, was further tightened, especially in Florida, and the skyjackings were discontinued by early 1983. In the summer of 1984, Iranian dissidents protesting the cruelty of the Khomeni regime hijacked airliners in Iraq, Egypt, Cyprus, and Italy. Like the Cuban hijack-ers, the Iranians possessed "liquid explosives" and threatened to blow up the airliners. The moti-vation for the Iranian skyjackings was twofold: to seek political asylum in the democratic West and to gain publicity for their counterrevolution in Iran. On September 9, 2008, three Britons of Pakistani descent were convicted of conspiracy to commit murder in an **al Qaeda** plot to blow up commercial aircraft. The suspects planned to explode hydrogen peroxide-based bombs on seven transatlantic flights in midair, an alleged attempt to match the massacre of 9/11.

A fifth type of skyjacking is the use of the hijacked aircraft as a flying bomb by Islamic terrorists. There are several examples of this category of skyjackers that will be discussed in the next chapter. In sum, the media spread the idea of the "gasoline bomb" hijackings as well as the know-how and techniques on how to do it. It is surprising that a "how to" text on air hijackings has not been mass marketed. All the same, other poignant examples of contagion theory and imitation are evident in the media.

The wave of cases involving product tampering spread terror and fear throughout the United States in the early 1980s. The discovery of cyanide-laced Tylenol in several pharmacies in the Midwest created a serious epidemic of product-tampering incidents. The media widely reported tactics used in the Tylenol incident. Soon other products, including patent medicines, beverages, and food products, were found to have been tampered with by imitators of the Tylenol strategy. This type of extortionist tactic eventually made its way to Japan. In October 1984, an extortionist gang threatened to place 100 packets of cyanide-laced candy onto grocery shelves. The Japanese extortionists demanded $410,000 in ransom from the candy manufacturer, who refused to pay. The candy caper has been emulated throughout Japan by other extortionist gangs who threaten to place poisoned candy in stores that are frequented by large numbers of children. This product tampering emerged again in March 1986 in the United States. Again, Tylenol was the unfortunate victim. The Tylenol incident was followed by the tampering of three additional products: Teldrin, Contac, and Diatec.

Films that are seen in theaters and in reruns on television are also an influential medium through which acts of violence and terrorism are encouraged and emulated. In 1979, the gang warfare films *Boulevard Nights* and *The Warriors* so aroused teenage audiences around the country that during several showings they started shooting in the theaters. Eight people were killed at these films and five were wounded. The Academy Award–winning film *The Deerhunter* provides yet another example of emulation by people repeating the Russian roulette scene. Several suicides and accidental deaths due to imitation of the film scene were reported to the police. Nevertheless, television network executives and film producers maintain that media presentations affect all kinds of human behavior, from helping, sharing, and altruism to decisions about what products to buy, and, of course, aggression. On the other hand, social science investigations reveal that exposure to media violence and terrorism leads to the creation of fear, anxiety, insensitivity, and emulation. If the social scientists are correct, then perhaps media distributors should concentrate more on the themes of sharing, altruism, and helping rather than the brutality, violence, and terrorism that presently dominate television and film airtime.

In the **Good Guys** hostage-taking incident in Sacramento in 1991, the media reported that the hostage takers were influenced by the highly stylized Hong Kong gangster films. *A Better Tomorrow* and *Bullet in the Head* were popular among the Good Guys hostage takers. Investigators believed that such films inspired the four young Vietnamese to take hostages at the Good Guys electronics store.[10] (More specifics on the Good Guys incident can be found in Chapter 6.)

Clearly, certain acts of terrorist violence often make abnormal behavior seem justified. Several examples are evident. First, seldom are the perpetrators of terrorist acts ever punished. This fact is not lost on potential terrorists. Second, the terrorist act is often portrayed as justified. The Irish Republican Army (IRA), al Qaeda, and Palestinian extremists all feel justified in using terrorist violence to gain media attention. Third, terrorist violence is often characterized by avoiding injury or death to innocent victims. In other words, the terrorist group is forced to use extranormal violence because of alienation, frustration, and a lack of political power. Fourth, the extraordinary coverage of terrorist incidents encourages identification with the group by other irresponsible "rebels." Fifth, the terrorist group is often portrayed as having great strength, power, and support. In reality terrorist groups are impotent without the media, which impulsively concentrate on the violence or potential for violence. Sixth, the act of violence is overdramatized in an entertainment way, where a disproportionate amount of time is spent photographing victims, scenes of violence, and interviewing terrorists. The causes, issues, and viewpoints that produced the act of violence are overlooked for the dramatic value of the violence. Thus, an unrealistic and exaggerated image that both invokes and stimulates acts of terrorism by others is presented.[11]

Finally, the frivolousness in the news coverage of terrorist violence involving suicide bombings, car bombs, assassinations, and hostage taking where groups and individuals are often referred to as rebels, freedom fighters, commandos, guerrillas, protesters, dissidents, rioters, extremists, or jihadists may cause confusion among people. For example, Peter Jennings referred to the Palestinian hostage takers of Israeli athletes during the 1972 Munich Olympics as guerrillas and commandos. Moreover, suicide bombers are often called freedom fighters or martyrs. This confusion may be interpreted by organized terrorist groups as a justification for acts of violence. The distinction between freedom fighter and commando is significant. The connotation implies that if one is fighting for his freedom, then conventional rules of warfare need not apply. The present media trend apparently favors the legitimization and the reporting of all methods of violence or terrorism as pursuit of "freedom." This may set a dangerous precedent since "freedom fighter" and "terrorist" are concepts that defy precise definition. Hence, groups that specialize in acts of terrorism against the "oppressor" now become freedom fighters. The revival of the concept of freedom fighter presents serious implications for the protection of human rights. If the most brutal acts of terrorism directed at innocent civilian targets are justified in the name of freedom, human rights will suffer a severe setback. Today, hundreds of freedom fighters exist in the world—evidence that contagion and imitation are perpetrated by news media interpretation of acts of political violence. In the same view, the growth of terrorism must not be defined simply in terms of contagion and imitation but also in terms of propaganda.

PROPAGANDA VALUE AND THE "DEED"

Propaganda is the dissemination of facts, arguments, half-truths, or lies in order to influence public opinion. The making of propaganda involves a systematic effort to persuade a mass audience by deliberately presenting one-sided statements. One-sided presentations often spread and convey unrealistic images by concentrating only on the good points of one position and the bad points of another. In a colloquial sense, then, propaganda is used to refer to someone else's efforts as persuasion while one's own are described as informational or educational. The communication is clearly propaganda when it appeals to the emotions and sentiments of the target audience. In analyzing any specific political-terrorist propaganda campaign in either a historical or contemporary sense, several questions arise:

1. Who are the groups that initiate the propaganda campaign?
2. What objectives are they trying to accomplish?
3. By what strategies are objectives sought?
4. What political resources and assets does the group begin with?
5. What outcomes are desired by the group?
6. How extensive is media coverage of specific incidents?

In modern totalitarian states, government officials monopolize the means of communication. At the other extreme are democratic pluralistic states where freedom of the press is considered an important, fundamental civil right. In a free society, the media compete for audiences, and circulation is often stimulated by the reporting of violent events. In some respects, the media has replaced government as an authority figure. In political-terrorist incidents, it has become evident to the leaders of terrorist/revolutionary movements that they can greatly enhance the chances of success by using propaganda to win popular support and to recruit new members. The eagerness of the media to respond to terroristic violence is a perverse incentive to organized terrorist groups, as well as the criminally unstable and fanatical individual. Terrorist propaganda depends on accessible networks of communication. The violence and terrorism by al Qaeda and in Northern Ireland provide an example of competing political ideologies, all desperately trying to influence public opinion.

Osama bin Laden has been interviewed by several journalists from CNN, ABC, CBS, *Time* magazine, Pakistani TV stations, and the Arab-speaking news network al Jazeera. For instance, Peter Bergen, a CNN reporter, actually visited and interviewed Osama bin Laden at his mountain hideout in Afghanistan in 1998. Bergen was the first journalist to provide Osama bin Laden a forum to discuss his hatred for America and the West. Since 9/11, Osama bin Laden has produced several videotapes that glorify the attacks on the World Trade Center and the Pentagon, which have been eagerly broadcast around the world.[12]

In Northern Ireland, there are several competing political philosophies. These include the British military, a British-supported government, Protestant paramilitary groups such as the Ulster Volunteer Force (UVF); Ulster Defense Association (UDA); Ulster Freedom Fighters (UFF); Red Hand Commandos (RHC), Loyalist Volunteer Force, the Catholic left (Free Ireland Saor Eire); and the IRA. But the most prominent and "newsworthy" group is the **Provisional wing of the IRA** (**PIRA**, or Provos). The objective of PIRA is to influence the British to withdraw support from the dominant Northern Ireland Protestant community, which controls the economy, and to provoke the British military into open warfare that eventually would bring about the withdrawal of Britain's 20,000 combat troops.

In this propaganda war, PIRA held clandestine press conferences with exclusive television interviews on the British Broadcasting Corporation (BBC), Independent Television (ITV), and the American Broadcasting Company (ABC). In one of these interviews, David O'Connell, PIRA chief of staff, proclaimed that the Provos would conduct a bombing campaign in Great Britain. One week later several bombs were detonated in Birmingham with the loss of twenty-one innocent lives. In another interview conducted by ABC, O'Connell described the tactics and moral justification for PIRA's indiscriminate attacks against the British military and the Royal Ulster Constabulary (RUC). This interview was part of a documentary titled *To Die for Ireland*, which was widely distributed in the United States.[13] In yet another interview, PIRA invited an American-TV film crew to accompany a terrorist squad on an actual terrorist mission. The TV crew filmed the Provos loading a car with explosives and then driving it to a city street where it was blown up, injuring several people and causing extensive property damage.[14] Certainly, the impact of such deeds is heightened by the willingness of the media to participate in the propaganda aims. In one respect, PIRA has bombed their way into the hearts and minds of the "people."

The bombing strategy of PIRA is also used to influence the coverage of other events in Northern Ireland and Great Britain. According to PIRA chief of staff O'Connell, the first car bombs were placed in London to *bomb* the election in Northern Ireland from the front pages.[15] The strategy was successful and taught the Provos a very valuable lesson. As one PIRA source stated, "Last year taught us that in publicity terms one bomb in Oxford Street is worth ten in Belfast. It is not a lesson we are likely to forget."[16]

They did not forget, for on October 11, 1984, PIRA tried unsuccessfully to wipe out the entire British government in a savage hotel bombing. About nine hours after the blast, the PIRA claimed responsibility, asserting that it had set off a 100-pound gelignite bomb in an attempt to kill the "British Cabinet and Tory warmongers." The British prime minister, Margaret Thatcher, thirteen of her twenty-member cabinet, and many of her senior advisors were staying at the Grand Hotel in Brighton when at about 3:00 A.M. a thundering explosion ripped out a 500-square-foot section of the hotel's facade. The prime minister escaped injury, but others were not so fortunate. Four government officials were killed and forty were seriously injured. It was one of the boldest and most outrageous terrorist attacks against British government officials in Great Britain or Northern Ireland. A spokesman for the Provos promised more terrorist strikes in the future:

> Thatcher will now realize that Britain cannot occupy our country, torture our prisoners and shoot our people in their own streets and get away with it. Today we were unlucky. But remember, we have only to be lucky once. You will have to be lucky always."[17]

The attack triggered a wave of anger and a strong condemnation of the PIRA by prominent world political leaders. In fact the attack seemed to provide a rallying point for the British prime minister and the British public. Nevertheless, the Provos accomplished their propaganda aims of putting the British government on the defensive and dominating media coverage. For two consecutive weeks the media published details of the bombing, the status of victims, the political position of the PIRA, and the tightening of security measures to protect British government officials.

The PIRA strategy of concentrating on spectacular acts of terrorist bombing is not the only tactic to attract the media. Perhaps the most effective propaganda tactics have been the well-publicized **hunger strikes** by the PIRA and the INLA (Irish National Liberation Army) in 1980–1981. On October 27, 1980, seven Provos began a hunger strike in Maze Prison, Belfast. The strike lasted for fifty-three days with no deaths. At the same time, three women members of the PIRA and twenty-three men who supported the Irish nationalist cause joined in the strike. The hunger strikers wanted segregation from "common criminals" and to be granted "political prisoner status." They also wanted an independent investigation of prison brutality and torture. The hunger strike was eventually ended through clergy intervention, family pressure, and when prison officials agreed to review the strikers' request. But by the beginning of 1981, the Provos concluded that British prison officials had no intention of granting political prisoner status to members of PIRA or INLA.[18]

Plans to renew the hunger strike were developing, and Bobby Sands, a PIRA terrorist, began a new strike on March 1, 1981, from his prison cell. All terrorist activity of PIRA and INLA was discontinued so that world attention might be focused on the hunger strike of Bobby Sands. At about the same time, an opportunity for Sands to run for political office arose when the representative from his district suddenly died. Sands won the election on April 9 and then died on May 5. Nonetheless, the deaths of Sands and other PIRA hunger strikers demonstrated to the British government that the hunger strikes' target audience had been reached. Until the deaths of the hunger strikers, there appeared to be little support for PIRA's political program. Now world media attention was attracted to Northern Ireland and the hunger strike.[19]

FIGURE 3.1   Funeral procession for PIRA member Bobby Sands who died after a sixty-four-day hunger strike at Maze Prison, Belfast, Northern Ireland. (S.P. Hennesay/Getty Images, Inc.—Hulton Archive Photos)

The propaganda impact of Sands's protest, election, and death equaled or exceeded that of any other terrorist incident carried out by the PIRA. There were massive parades in Belfast, Londonderry, Dublin, and several British cities. The British Parliament spent countless hours debating the issue of political prisoner status and how to react to international pressures to free the prisoners. Riots, shootings, and bombings escalated in Northern Ireland against the British military and the police. The media coverage of Sands's funeral involved no less than 164 TV crews. The event received international recognition and no doubt greatly enhanced the political image and prestige of the Provos. Needless to say, the British were distressed by the PIRA's propaganda victory, especially in Europe and America, and at least a few members of the British Parliament recommended that the government take steps to stop the procession of dying hunger strikers. By October 3, 1981, ten PIRA and INLA hunger strikers had died. But it was not British capitulation to the hunger strikers' demands that stopped this retinue of death.

Like previous hunger strikes, clergy and family members urged PIRA and INLA to discontinue the protest. The Provos rejected this appeal and announced the hunger strike would continue until the British granted political prisoner status to all Irish nationalists in British and Irish jails. In spite of the Provos's adamant position, as Irish prisoners lapsed into unconsciousness toward the end of their hunger strikes, family members were permitted to take control; and most consented to the forced feedings of the strikers. Thus, the eight-month hunger strike was called off, and a very effective propaganda campaign came to an end. The entire world was now aware of the "troubles" in Northern Ireland.

Three days after the hunger strike ended, one of the demands was conceded to by prison officials. The Irish nationalists (PIRA and INLA) now had the right to wear their own clothes, but they would not be granted the status of political prisoners.

The hunger strike proved to be a dramatic event and touched the lives of everyone in Northern Ireland, the Republic of Ireland, and the United Kingdom. Television news coverage of the event vividly described the pain and agony associated with death due to starvation. The history of propaganda makes it clear that in order for propaganda to be effective it must be in devoted hands. The most important factor is certainly the emotional involvement of the participants. In terms of propaganda value, the Irish nationalist hunger strike, like religiously motivated suicide bombers, represents the ultimate act of propaganda: the willingness to sacrifice one's life for political or religious beliefs. The violent past of PIRA appears finally to be over. In 2008 after four decades of terrorism, the PIRA agreed to decommission, destroy their weapons cache, and disband. The British military pulled its troops out of Northern Ireland on July 28, 2008. However, the Irish hunger strikers claimed they had been murdered by the British and that their protest was not an act of suicide.

Unlike the Irish hunger strikers, German terrorists of the notorious Baader-Meinhoff gang did use their bodies as an ultimate propaganda weapon. On October 18, 1977, four members of the Baader-Meinhoff gang committed suicide while incarcerated in Stammheim prison, a maximum-security institution. It was later determined that handguns were smuggled into the prison by attorneys for the gang. The plan was to commit suicide by shooting themselves in the back of the head, execution style. The method was intended to suggest that they had been murdered or executed by the West German "fascist" state. Many people believed this account, and the media were full of speculation that prison guards had murdered the members of the gang. An independent commission of forensic pathologists reconstructed the scene of the mass suicide and concluded that the victims had indeed committed suicide. The evidence was conclusive, but by then the propaganda value generated by the suicides indicated that few people believed the findings of the commission. This form of terrorism and propaganda making, therefore, selects its victims from its own ranks with the intention of having the guilt attributed to the enemy.[20] By the late 1990s, the Baader-Meinhoff gang had faded into the history of terrorism.

In yet another act of terrorism designed for its propaganda value, five members of the little-known Armenian Revolutionary Army shot their way into the Turkish ambassador's residence in Lisbon, Portugal, on July 24, 1983, and vowed to blow it up. Shortly after the Armenian terrorists seized the ambassador's residence, negotiations appeared fruitless, and the police planned to assault the building and free several Turkish hostages. However, the residence had been wired with explosives by the terrorists; as the police approached, the explosives were detonated, killing all inside the building, including the five Armenian terrorists. A typewritten message signed by the Armenian Revolutionary Army was later found in the residence; it stated, "We have decided to blow up this building and remain under the collapse. This is not suicide nor an expression of insanity, but rather our sacrifice to the altar of freedom." Ostensibly, Armenian terrorist groups want the world to believe that this "self-sacrifice" is necessary because the Turkish government refuses to acknowledge the realities of the Armenian genocide that allegedly and systematically killed thousands of Armenians between 1894 and 1915.[21]

The tactical objective of the Armenians, as well as the PIRA and the Baader-Meinhoff gang, was to propagandize politics as a drama in which the forces of good and evil stand opposed to one another. The strategy of self-sacrifice by the Armenian Revolutionary Army was no doubt intended to induce a sense of guilt among Turkish government officials and dramatize the self-righteousness of the Armenian cause to the entire world; that is, the acknowledgment of the Armenian genocide. The marked success of this tactic was designed to capture media attention and influence the Armenian community. On September 10, 1984, the U.S. Congress agreed to set aside a day of remembrance for the 1.5 million Armenians killed in this century's first recorded act of genocide. Thus, April 24 has been designated to remember the Armenian genocide of 1915. The U.S. Congress was careful to state that this action was not an endorsement of Armenian terrorism or an acknowledgment of Turkish complicity in the Armenian genocide. In Chapter 8 we take a much closer look at suicide terrorism.

An alternative to this self-destructive type of terrorism is another popular propaganda strategy that does not create a news event but instead intrudes on other newsworthy events to maximize propaganda. The most successful of such events was the decision to take Israeli athletes hostage during the 1972 Munich Olympic Games. The popularity of the Olympic games ensured Palestinian extremists that millions of people would be watching the Olympics on television. On September 5, 1972, eight Palestinian terrorists of the Black September Organization took eleven Israeli athletes hostage and captured the attention of 800 million to 1 billion spectators. The terrorists demanded the release of 200 Arab prisoners being held in Israel. However, as the tense drama unfolded, it became apparent that the release of prisoners was secondary to the propagandistic nature of the event. A Palestinian explained it like this:

> We recognize that sport is the modern religion of the Western world. We knew that the people of England and America would switch their television sets from any program about the plight of the Palestinians if there was a sporting event on another channel. So we decided to use their Olympics, the most sacred ceremony of this religion, to make the world pay attention to us. We offered up human sacrifices to your gods of sport and television. And they answered our prayers.[22]

After Munich, nobody could ignore the Palestinians or their cause. The media did not hesitate to cooperate and broadcast the bloody spectacle via satellite to all continents. In the Arab world, the Black September were widely applauded, and thousands of Palestinians joined various Palestinian extremist groups in the wake of this public-relations success.[23] However, the operation, which began with military precision, ended in failure. Five Palestinian terrorists were killed, all eleven Israeli athletes were killed, and one police officer was killed in a firefight that took place at the Furstenfeldbruck airport. But the military failure of the terrorist incident did not detract from the propaganda triumph. On the contrary, the spectacular nature of the attack reinforced its emotional appeal. The Palestinian cause once more exploded onto the international political scene. Part of the world condemned the attack as a savage, barbaric act of murder; others defended the Palestinian terrorists as dedicated nationalists willing to sacrifice their lives for Palestinian nationalism. The Palestinians were not advocating world revolution; instead they wanted the creation of a Palestinian state and recognition of the Palestinian people. Certainly other patriots in the world saw this as a plausible goal, and a compromise with Israel was not altogether impossible.[24]

The breakthrough came two years later, in November 17, 1974, when the chairman of the Palestine Liberation Organization (PLO), Yasir Arafat, addressed the United Nations General Assembly. The event was widely televised and Arafat received a standing ovation. The idea that a compromise was feasible on the Palestinian–Israeli issue had become a shared opinion in international politics. The PLO was later granted observer status at the United Nations. Apparently the consciousness of the world and the media had been aroused by several sensational Palestinian terrorist acts. The taking of hostages, skyjacking, and the detonation of bombs can be very effective communication strategies. Nevertheless, the propaganda war between the Palestinians and Israelis continues. We discuss this conflict further in Chapter 4.

The skill of propaganda making and communication manipulation was most clearly evident in the kidnapping of Aldo Moro by the Italian **Red Brigades** in 1978. Aldo Moro, one of Italy's leading political figures, was held captive for fifty-five days. During this period, the Red Brigades were able to manipulate the media by spreading false information, lies, and rumors concerning the condition of Aldo Moro. For example, the Red Brigades claimed that Moro had been "executed by suicide," that he had been tried by a people's court and confessed to crimes against society, and that he divulged state secrets about corruption, graft, and bribery in Italian politics. The whole nation was held in a state of tension waiting for the next communiqué by the Red Brigades. In fact, rival newspapers, magazines, and television newscasts competed for the communiqué, and circulation more than doubled for the printed media. The government tried unsuccessfully to stop the communiqués from being published, and Italy began to look like a nation under siege. Ordinary civil and human rights were suspended while the Italian police and military searched the country trying to locate Moro and the Red Brigades.[25]

Since the Red Brigades indirectly controlled the Italian media, they were able to create a situation of terror, fear, and anxiety as well as to provoke the Italian government to overreact by suspending normal legal procedures.[26] The Italian media overwhelmingly condemned the kidnapping and the eventual murder of Aldo Moro. But by merely reporting only what the Red Brigades wanted, the media were easily manipulated and the incident that normally would have become a matter of police investigation and one family's tragedy instead became another chapter in international terrorism and the political instability of Italian politics. The media defended their publication of Red Brigades' communiqués by rationalizing that it was the public's right to know. However, the various Italian communities became polarized over the affair and identified with a variety of positions. Most, of course, identified with the victim, sharing his sense of desperation and impotence. Others identified and supported the Red Brigades, sharing their sense of revenge against a corrupt political system.

Still others identified with the police, sharing their moral dilemma of balancing liberty, freedom, and individual rights. The Red Brigades very skillfully used the media to translate an isolated act of physical violence into one of "psychic terror" that affected millions of Italians. Of all terrorist propaganda strategies, media concentration on one isolated terrorist incident is probably the most insidious. The media give modern terrorism much of its power, for without media cooperation it is doubtful that the Red Brigades would have eluded the police for so many years. Beginning in the late 1980s, the terrorist activities of the Red Brigades began to decline. Internal dissension, operation failures, and the arrest of the group's leaders hastened its decline. Many Red Brigade members became informers after the Italian government established an amnesty program. By the early 1990s over 4,000 members of the Red Brigades had been arrested. The group has been largely inactive since that time.[27] Although the Red Brigades were dismantled, several smaller groups have continued to carry out terrorist operations in Italy. On September 12, 2008, Italian police arrested twenty-one members of the Fighting Communist Party for a series of bombings and assassinations.

UNITED STATES

The United States has also experienced the manipulation of the mass media by political extremists. Probably the most daring act of media exploitation was carried out by the then little-known Black Panther Party (BPP). The Black Panthers appeared on the scene in the late 1960s in Oakland, California. The **Black Panthers** had been trying to mobilize the mass of lower-class blacks for several years without much success. The group owed its popularity almost entirely to clever manipulation of the mass media. They first gained national attention in 1969 by their massed entry into the California Legislature, wearing paramilitary uniforms and carrying "unloaded" rifles. The Legislature, in session, was debating a proposed bill to make it unlawful to carry loaded guns in California. The Black Panthers invited the media to witness this scene of armed extremists on the floor of the California State Legislature. The incident made the headlines and newscasts across the United States. The Panthers were suddenly catapulted onto the national scene. They were invited to participate in speaking engagements and were eagerly sought by the national media, both print and electronic, to tell their story. The *Black Panther* newspaper was established and became an immediate success with circulation rising to 200,000 copies by 1971. In this paper, the Black Panthers advocated armed resistance, urban guerrilla warfare methods, and the indiscriminate terrorist tactic of murdering uniformed police officers. Even though the Black Panthers were capable of issuing their own propaganda statements, they still relied heavily on the national media to spread their exaggerated rhetoric about violence and revolution. The strategy of the Black Panthers was to use the media to introduce a technique of "liberation" through propaganda by deed that would "awaken all oppressed people of the world."[28]

By the mid-1990s, the BPP was recast as the New Black Panther Party of Self-Defense (NBPP) and had been "hijacked" by the Nation of Islam (NOI). As of 2009, the leader of the NBPP is Malik Zulu Shabazz. Shabazz has a long record of racism and anti-Semitism that includes promoting conspiracy theories about Jewish foreknowledge of the 9/11 terrorist attacks. Shabazz also claims that Jews developed and controlled the transatlantic slave trade to the Americas. Shabazz and the NBPP continue to attract media attention by attending racially charged events around the United States. The Anti-Defamation League (ADL) considers the NBPP the most anti-Semetic and racist black extremist group in the United States. On January 9, 2009, the U.S. Justice Department filed suit against the NBPP of Philadelphia for alleged voter intimidation at a North Philadelphia polling station on November 4, 2008.

FIGURE 3.2 During an anti-Vietnam War demonstration, protesters wave "Free Bobby Seal" banners. Seal, along with Huey Newton, founded the Black Panther Party for Self-Defense. The Panthers urged all blacks to arm themselves for the "liberation" struggle. By 1971, Seal abandoned the use of violence and endorsed a nonviolent strategy that focused on providing community services to African Americans. (Alon Reininger/Getty Images Inc.—Hulton Archive Photos)

Perhaps the most adroit manipulation of the media by terrorists in the United States was the terrorism of the **Symbionese Liberation Army (SLA)**. This California army, consisting of less than a dozen soldiers, managed to influence media attention for two years by kidnapping Patricia Hearst on February 4, 1974. The SLA held not only Patty Hearst hostage but also her father, Randolph Hearst, ruler of the media empire that included the *San Francisco Examiner.* After the abduction of Patty Hearst, the SLA demanded that the entire text of all their demands be published in Hearst-owned newspapers. Randolph Hearst was warned that a failure to do so would endanger the safety of his daughter. The SLA–Patty Hearst saga became one of the most publicized stories in media history. For example, between 1974 and 1976, Patty Hearst, who was taken hostage and who allegedly turned terrorist, made the cover of *Newsweek* seven times.[29]

The public was treated to a variety of taped and printed communiqués from the SLA and their hostage. In one message on February 12, 1974, the SLA announced their demands for the release of Patty Hearst. The SLA demanded a food distribution program be planned by Randolph Hearst. The program was to distribute $70 worth of "quality food" to each and every person in need in California. It was estimated that 5 million people in California were living below the poverty level. Such a program would have cost Randolph Hearst approximately $400 million. Unable to accommodate such an outrageous demand, Randolph Hearst set up a $2 million food distribution program. Thousands of people in Oakland and San Francisco showed up at four announced locations to receive the free food. The plan to distribute the food was ill conceived, and soon fighting broke out for the free food. The scenes of unruly mobs fighting for food were broadcast by the three major television networks to over 80 million viewers. The Robin Hood image projected by the program of taking from the rich and giving to the poor turned into chaos.

Thus, a second food giveaway program was demanded by the SLA with the stipulation that media coverage of the giveaway be suspended. This second free food program was successful in the sense that the orderly distribution of the food was achieved. The Robin Hood image of the SLA

FIGURE 3.3   Patty Hearst, a.k.a. "Tanya," with a machine pistol. In the background is the symbol of the SLA, the seven-headed cobra. (CORBIS BETTMANN)

began to grow. In fact, one reporter noted that the "tone of the press in the Bay area is subdued and even sympathetic toward the SLA."[30] Even so, the only apparent convert to the preposterous rhetoric of the SLA was Patty Hearst, who became Tanya (named after a female companion of Che Guevara). Tanya allegedly became an ardent supporter of the political aims of the SLA. The initial skill the SLA had demonstrated in manipulating the media ultimately was overshadowed by the entertainment value of the exploits of the SLA. To date, three movies and twelve books have capitalized on the story, not to mention hundreds of dramatic embellishments by journalists who covered the story and produced countless articles. The FBI finally cornered the SLA in Los Angles in May 1975. In a shoot-out with the FBI and the Los Angles police department, seven members of the SLA were killed. By November 2005, the remaining SLA members were finally apprehended, convicted, and sentenced to prison for a 1975 bank robbery and murder in Sacramento, California.[31]

Another expressive case of media manipulation and propaganda making involved an obscure **Hanafi** Muslim religious sect. Led by Hamaas Abdul Khaalis and twelve followers, the sect seized 134 hostages in three buildings in Washington, DC, on March 9, 1977. During the takeover, one hostage was shot and sixteen were subsequently injured. Unlike most hostage takers, Khaalis was seeking revenge. He demanded the release from prison of three members of a rival Black Muslim sect who had been convicted for the murders of his family, including three children. Khaalis wanted to administer his personal interpretation of Islamic justice. A secondary demand was that a movie released that day, *Mohammed, Messenger of God*, be banned from American theaters because Khaalis regarded it as heretical.[32] The first demand was out of the question and could not be negotiated, but the second was met when producers of the film agreed to remove it from distribution. This represented a clear victory for the terrorists, for they temporarily had the power to censor the film media. Even so, the movie was later shown in various U.S. cities.

The incident lasted for some thirty-nine hours, and involved the media in other ways as well. Khaalis called local reporters to discuss his demands. Even more often, news reporters called Khaalis. This greatly complicated the process of negotiation since the negotiators began to lose control of the situation. One reporter disclosed to Khaalis that several people were hiding on the top floor of one of the buildings where hostages were being held. Yet another reporter insulted and infuriated Khaalis by referring to him as a Black Muslim. Khaalis's family had been slain by Black Muslims, and he demanded an immediate apology from the newscaster or a hostage would be killed in retaliation for the remark. On the advice of police negotiators, the reporter publicly apologized for the blunder. Nevertheless, the episode did nothing to ingratiate the media to the hostages. As one of the hostages later responded:

> As hostages, many of us felt that the Hanafi takeover was a happening, a guerrilla theater, a high-impact propaganda exercise programmed for the TV screen, and second-arily for the front pages of newspapers around the world. . . . The resentment and anger of my fellow hostages toward the press *is* . . . that the news media and terrorism feed on each other, that the news media, particularly TV, create a thirst for fame and recognition. Reporters do not simply report the news. They help create it. They are not objective observers, but subjective participants—actors, scriptwriters, and idea men.[33]

The Hanafi incident finally ended when Khaalis agreed to negotiate with Islamic interme-diaries. There is no doubt that media interference prolonged this incident and endangered the lives of the hostages.[34]

In sum, the preceding section has attempted to describe some historical propagandist uses of the news media by terrorist groups. This is, of course, only a limited survey of examples. However, it is possible to summarize the main points. Table 3.1 represents a list of propagandist uses of the media by terrorist groups.

TABLE 3.1 Propagandist Uses of Mass Media by Modern Terrorist Groups

 1. Instill fear in a mass audience
 2. Polarize public opinion
 3. Gain publicity by agreeing to clandestine interviews
 4. Demand publication of a manifesto
 5. Provoke government overreaction
 6. Spread false and misleading information
 7. Bring about the release of prisoners
 8. Attract converts and support to a cause
 9. Coerce the media by assaulting journalists
10. Profit from "free advertising"
11. Discredit public officials monitoring the hostage crisis
12. Divert public attention by bombing their way onto front page
13. Use the media to send messages to comrades in another country
14. Excite the public against the legitimate government
15. Bolster the terrorist group's morale
16. Gain the Robin Hood image by fighting "injustice"
17. Obtain information on counterterrorist strategies
18. Identify future victims
19. Acquire information about popular support for the terrorist group
20. Exploit the exaggerated media image of a powerful, omnipotent group

Source: Adapted from Alex P. Schmid and Janny de Graff, *Violence as Communication* (London and Beverly Hills, CA: Sage, 1982), pp. 53–54.

This propagandist use of the media by terrorist groups has resulted in yet another conflict involving the law enforcement community. The different roles of law enforcement and the media are certain to result in conflict since each sees the other as interfering with its functions and community responsibilities. However, it appears that one of the greatest dangers that faces the United States and the criminal justice system is from the Internet.

INTERNET AND TERRORISM

Clearly, terrorist groups are using the Internet to spread fear, panic, and terrorism. By 2004, nearly all the terrorist groups identified by the U.S. State Department as "Foreign Terrorist Organizations (FTOs)" had established sites on the Internet. There is little doubt that terrorist groups are exploiting the unique opportunities offered by the Internet. We need to pay more attention to the dangers posed by terrorists' use of the Internet. Terrorist groups with very different political agendas make use of the Internet. They are united in their readiness to use terrorist tactics to distribute propaganda, to communicate with supporters, and to execute operational plans. The Internet is an ideal arena for promoting the goals of terrorist groups. According to Weimann, the Internet offers terrorist groups:

1. Fast flow of information;
2. Easy access to the Web;
3. Anonymity of communication;
4. Little or no censorship, government control, or regulation;
5. Availability of huge audiences spread throughout the world;
6. A multimedia environment that offers videos, graphics, books, songs, films, posters, and games;
7. An inexpensive way to advertise history, grievances, goals, and objectives;
8. The ability to spread propaganda by using several different languages; and
9. Overcoming geographic distances.[35]

Islamic terrorists, anarchists, racists, hate groups, nationalists, separatists, and left-wing revolutionaries all find the Internet an excellent method for getting their message out to the public.

There are seven significant ways in which contemporary terrorist groups tap into the Internet. First, political terrorism has been characterized as a form of psychological warfare. For example, terrorist groups use the Internet to spread disinformation, to communicate threats to create fear and panic, and to provide frightening images of violence and death. The beheadings of American journalist Daniel Pearl and civilian contract workers in Iraq are one example. A videotape of the beheadings was replayed on several terrorist Web sites. Terrorist groups can also manipulate the psychological fears of people by promoting "cyberterrorism." For example, cyberterrorists can create fear and intimidation by claiming they can bring down commercial aircraft in midair, disable air traffic control systems, or disrupt worldwide financial computer systems, causing the collapse of the stock market. The cyberterrorist threat is often so exaggerated by the media that the public believes that a cyber attack is imminent.

Today, Osama bin Laden and al Qaeda concentrate their psychological warfare on the Internet. Despite the fact that al Qaeda has been crippled by arrests, the killing of several of its leaders, and the destruction of its training bases in Afghanistan, they still can conduct a terrorist fear campaign. Since the massacre of September 11, 2001, al Qaeda has announced impending mass casualty attacks against the United States on its Web sites. These warnings receive considerable media attention, which in turn generates widespread feelings of insecurity throughout the

United States. In other words, where will al Qaeda strike next? In 2008, an al Qaeda editorial posted on the Web announced that "America is in retreat and now is the time for Jihadi martyrs to strike the great Satan."

Second, the Internet has expanded opportunities for terrorist groups to attract attention and gain publicity. In the past, terrorist groups depended on the print media and television for publicity. Now, the use of the Internet offers terrorist groups the chance to frame their own message and shape how they are perceived by a wider audience. In this way, terrorist groups can fashion their own image and the image of their adversaries. For instance, many terrorist Web sites skillfully use the "but what about" tactic to illustrate the moral inferiority of their adversary. In other words, the terrorist group attempts to shift the blame for their violent actions onto the "enemy."

Third, the Internet is a vast digital library. It provides the user with nearly limitless pages of information, much of it free. Terrorist groups can obtain from the Net a wide variety of information concerning potential targets. A great deal of data is easily retrievable concerning public buildings, nuclear facilities, military bases, airports, and police counterterrorism strategies. Verton maintains that al Qaeda has large Internet databases containing details of potential targets in the United States and Europe.[36] Al Qaeda sifts through the Internet, collecting intelligence information on hard as well as soft targets. The Internet provides al Qaeda the opportunity to study not only the susceptibility of security systems but also the structural weaknesses of potential targets. In fact, an al Qaeda training manual, recovered in Manchester, England, after a raid on an al Qaeda safe house in 2002, encouraged the "mujaheddin" to use Internet sources when collecting information on potential targets.[37]

On a Web site operated by al Qaeda called Sawat al Jihad or "Voice of Jihad," Jihadists are encouraged to spread viruses and sabotage U.S. and Israeli Web sites. Sawat al Jihad discusses specific targets, including hard targets such as the U.S. historical landmarks and soft targets such as shopping malls, nightclubs, and train stations. Jihadists have come to rely on al Qaeda Internet sites as a virtual substitute for terrorist training camps. In addition, al Qaeda Web sites have become a source of inspiration for the perpetrators of terrorist attacks. For example, in March 2004, the Madrid train station bombers killed 191 people. Their computers revealed fifty downloaded books and manuals written by extremist Islamic ideologues that provided not only inspiration but also instructions on bomb making.[38]

Fourth, terrorist groups use the Internet to solicit funds. Al Qaeda depends on donations filtered through charities and affiliated terrorist groups that use Web sites, chat rooms, and political forums. Hizballah uses Internet sites across the Middle East encouraging supporters to donate to the cause of jihad. The key message of Hizballah is that donations will be used to purchase weapons for the destruction of Israel. Hizballah's extensive network of Web sites, published in several languages, is an important tactic for collecting donations. Using online ads, Web surfers worldwide can be certain donations will reach Hizballah offices in Lebanon.[39] Al Qaeda, Hizballah, and other FTOs have come to realize that soliciting funds through the Internet is just as important to their cause as suicide bombing, hostage taking, and assassination. In the battle for hearts and minds, it's "money" that provides the lubricant for terrorist groups.

Fifth, the recruitment and mobilization of supporters are also significant to the success of terrorist groups. Al Qaeda seeks converts by using Web site technologies, such as audio and digital videos of suicide bombings and beheadings to capture the interest of Web browsers. Al Qaeda, like any multinational corporation, goes looking for recruits. For example, the SITE Intelligence Group provides details of an al Qaeda Internet recruitment campaign to recruit fighters to travel to Iraq and attack U.S. military forces and civilian contractors.[40] Recruiters also roam online chat rooms, YouTube, Myspace, cybercafés, and electronic bulletin boards reaching out to potential new recruits. The ability of the Internet to mobilize the terrorist groups' members is best illustrated by the Israeli incursion into Lebanon in July 2006. When Israeli military forces stormed into Southern Lebanon, thousands of Hizballah fighters responded to an Internet message to mobilize and confront the Israelis. A U.S. Senate report on terrorism and the Internet states that Hizballah's Internet infrastructure consists of fifteen to twenty Web sites in five languages.[41]

Sixth, the Internet is the repository of dozens of sites providing information on how to construct chemical, radiological, and conventional explosive devices. Terrorist groups, through the Internet, share any new information on how to construct a wide range of bombs. Al Qaeda's manual, referred to as the *Encyclopedia of Jihad*, offers detailed instructions on how to organize a terrorist cell and execute bombing attacks.[42] Hamas shares operative know-how for assembling a Qassam rocket. Specifications for **Qassam rockets** are published on Hamas Web sites and have transformed the strategic equation of the Israeli–Palestinian conflict.[43] Hamas now has the capability to strike deep into Israel, raising the level of fear and panic in Israeli communities. In addition, *The Terrorist's Handbook* and *The Anarchist Cookbook* are two well-known manuals that offer detailed instructions on how to construct a wide variety of explosive devices and can be easily downloaded.

Finally, terrorist groups also use the Internet to plan and coordinate specific attacks. The 9/11 hijackers relied heavily on the Internet in planning and coordinating the attacks on the World Trade Center and the Pentagon. Federal agents discovered thousands of coded messages related to the planning and coordination of the 9/11 attacks on the computer of Abu Zubaydah, who masterminded the 9/11 massacre. To conceal their identity, the 9/11 mass murderers used the Internet in public places, such as the public libraries and Internet cafes, to avoid detection by federal intelligence agents. Three weeks before the 9/11 attacks, Mohammed Atta received a coded message that read: "The semester begins in three more weeks. We've obtained 19 confirmations for studies in the faculty of law, the faculty of urban planning, the faculty of fine arts and the faculty of engineering."[44] The faculties referred to the World Trade Center, Pentagon, and U.S. Capitol.

The ethos of suicide bombing is firmly embedded in the planning strategy of al Qaeda. Martyrdom is an important characteristic of al Qaeda. Suicide terrorism is well suited to achieving the objectives of al Qaeda at a minimum cost to the organization. In fact, the second in command of al Qaeda, Ayman **al Zawahiri**, sets forth his planning strategy for suicide operations in "Knights Under the Prophet's Banner."[45] Al Zawahiri states that the careful planning of suicide bombings can be used not only to create panic but also to mobilize supporters and attract new recruits. According to al Zawahiri, jihad is an ideological struggle with the United States—a war without any truce. The "Knights of the Prophet's Banner" is easily downloaded and widely read by Islamic jihadists.

Since 9/11, terrorist groups supporting a variety of ideological beliefs, such as racist, Marxist, separatist, and nationalist, have all learned the great virtues of the Internet. Lack of censorship, ease of access, potential audiences, and anonymity have been recognized as key strategies in achieving terrorist goals. Terrorist groups now understand the value of the Internet and exploit it to support their objectives.

CENSORSHIP AND TERRORISM

The concept of a free press is not held in very high esteem by many governments of the world. It has been recorded by the United Nations that few countries have a free press.[46] In fact, in some Third World countries governmental leaders sarcastically state that a free press is irrelevant in a country when the general population represents an illiteracy rate of over 90 percent. Nevertheless, countries exist where an escalation of terrorist activity has led to media **censorship**. For example, in 1967 the government of Uruguay closed a local newspaper for publishing a communiqué of the **Tupamaros**.[47] By 1973, the military government of Uruguay had passed legislation that prohibited "the publication of oral, written, or televised information, commentaries, or impressions that directly or indirectly mention or refer to those persons who conspire against the nation or against antisubversive operations, excluding official communication."[48] Furthermore, the news media was prohibited from any criticism of government measures to combat and repress the terrorism of the Tupamaros. The Tupamaros were considered the vanguard of a successful terrorist movement that inspired terrorist groups around the world. Many terrorist groups, such as the SLA, PFLP, al Qaeda, the Red groups of the 1970s in Europe, and Latin American terrorist groups of the 1990s, followed the organizational principles of the Tupamaros.

Likewise, in Argentina the government suspended media publication of the names of two popular terrorist groups: the Montoneros and the Ejercito Revolucionario del Pueblo (ERP). In April 1976 a governmental proclamation prohibited the Argentinian media from reporting, commenting, or mentioning politically related acts of violence. In addition, the political viewpoints of groups considered in opposition to the ruling elite could not be printed without first being reviewed by a government censor. Hundreds of journalists were arrested, kidnapped, and interned in prison without regard to individual rights because they violated the restrictions of Argentinian government censorship.[49]

To some degree what has occurred in Uruguay and Argentina has been true for other countries experiencing escalating terrorism. For example, in Sri Lanka the government has prohibited any reporting of terrorist activities by the news media.[50] In Lebanon, reports of political violence are closely censored by the ruling government.[51] In Rhodesia-Zimbabwe, media censorship was imposed to prevent the spread of political violence and terrorism throughout the country. An examination of the South African media illustrates a self-imposed censorship since only governmental responses toward combating terrorism are reported, not the acts of terrorism. The Republic of Ireland censors all interviews with representatives of the IRA, the Sinn Fein, and the UDA.[52] The Israeli government requires that all news material relating to incidents of in-progress terrorist acts be routed through a military censor who then decides if the information is aiding the terrorists or hampering the operations of the police or Defense Forces.

In Denmark, the publication of Mohammed cartoons sparked rioting throughout the Muslim world. Muslims viewed the cartoons as offensive to Mohammed and the Islamic religion. Eleven people were reported killed in the rioting. The European Union (EU) has banned certain words from being searched on the Internet. Key words to be filtered are "terrorism," "bomb," "kill," and "genocide." The EU censorship has been met with widespread criticism. The Attorney General of Australia has proposed banning all books, DVDs, and games that incite racist and religious violence. Of particular interest to Australians is the banning of all material on how to become a suicide bomber. Reportage is not the only part of freedom of the press that has experienced governmental censorship. The well-known "bible" of leftist guerrilla and terrorist groups, the *Mini-Manual of Urban Guerrilla Warfare*, is outlawed in Latin America and several Western European countries.[53]

In sum, censorship may reduce the value of the terrorist strategy by hampering the spread of fear, but it cannot prevent terrorists from engaging in other forms of political violence. The grievances and political aspirations of terrorist groups will remain whether censored or not. In some countries, such as Uruguay and Argentina, terrorist incidents increased after the imposition of censorship. It could well be that pro-government forces will feel freer to engage in terrorist acts against those who oppose the government knowing they will not be exposed or criticized by the media. For example, the mass terrorism and executions carried out by Hitler and Stalin were possible only because the victims were not aware of what was going on, since Hitler and Stalin each had complete control of the media. Therefore, if censorship is considered, one should first ask, "Whose best interests does the introduction of censorship serve?" There are, of course, arguments both pro and con for censorship. In Table 3.2, a review of the literature on the arguments for and against censorship is presented by Schmid and de Graaf.[54]

TABLE 3.2   Censorship and Terrorism

Arguments for Censorship	Arguments against Censorship
1. Insurgent terrorists use the media as a platform for political propaganda that also helps them to recruit new members to their movement.	1. If the media would keep quiet on terrorist atrocities, the violent perpetrators might be judged less negatively by sections of the public.
2. Since publicity is a major and in some cases the unique reward sought by terrorists, censorship would make terrorism a less desirable strategy.	2. With psychotic terrorists, publicity can be a substitute for violence. Without media attention, their threats might be translated into acts.
3. Detailed coverage of incidents by the media provides potential terrorists with a model that increases their chances of success in their own acts.	3. Political terrorists boycotted by the media might step up their level of violence until the media have to cover their deeds.
4. Information broadcast during incidents can be useful to terrorists.	4. If the media did not report on terrorism, rumors would spread, which might be worse than the worst media reporting.
5. Media presence during acts of hostage taking can endanger hostages.	5. During siege situations, media presence can prevent the police from engaging in indefensible tactics, causing unnecessary loss of lives among hostages and terrorists.
6. Reporting on acts of terrorism can produce imitative acts.	6. If terrorism would be treated with silence, governments could label quasi- or non-terroristic activities by political dissenters as terrorism; uncontrolled government actions might be the result.
7. In cases of hostage taking and kidnapping, media reports can cause panic with the kidnapper so that he kills the victim.	7. If the media would censor terrorism, the public would suspect that other things are censored as well; credibility in the media will decline.
8. People who have so little respect for other people's lives as terrorists do should not be enabled to command public attention only because they use violence.	8. Suppression of news on terrorism might leave the public with a false sense of security. People would be unprepared to deal with terrorism when directly faced with it.
9. Sadism in the public might be activated by reporting terrorist acts.	9. The lack of public awareness of certain terroristic activities would keep the public from fully understanding the political situation.

(continued)

TABLE 3.2 Continued

Arguments for Censorship	Arguments against Censorship
10. Media reports on terrorist outrages might lead to vigilantism and uncontrolled revenge acts against the group the terrorists claim to speak for.	10. The feeling of being deprived of vital information might create a public distrust in the political authorities.
11. Negative news demoralizes the public while "good news makes us feel good."	11. The assertion of insurgent terrorists that democratic states are not really free would gain added credibility if freedom of the press were suspended.

Source: Adapted from Alex P. Schmid and Janny de Graaf, *Violence as Communication* (London and Beverly Hills, CA: Sage, 1982), p. 172.

In conclusion, some forms of guidelines on media coverage of terrorism are desirable and defensible. The question is who should promulgate such guidelines. Kehler et al. argue that some form of media regulation is absolutely essential since media coverage of terrorist episodes often endangers innocent lives. They cite incidents where the press negotiated with hostage takers, where journalists entered security zones, and where hostage rescue efforts were hampered by live broadcasts of the rescue team moving into position. Kehler et al. conclude that it is the broadcast industries' responsibility to create and enforce media guidelines for terrorist situations.[55] If the media formulate the guidelines, then they may be seen as self-serving. Acts of violence, particularly spectacular acts of terrorist hostage taking or high-visibility suicide bombings, serve to heighten viewer interest and increase circulation. The challenge for the media is to maintain interest while at the same time not allowing the media to be manipulated by terrorists. If the government formulates the guidelines, those guidelines will support and protect the government's position first. In the long run, that could be detrimental to public relations. What is recommended, then, is a joint governmental/police/media commission that would best serve the interests of the two competing parties: law enforcement and media. If the United States is going to find a solution that will decrease the probability of media intrusion into ongoing terrorist events and make the media more aware of the consequences of some of their dramatic and romantic portrayals of terrorist acts, then that solution is going to have to come through an informed dialogue by both parties. The greatest ally law enforcement has in its struggle with terrorism is the media. Differences between law enforcement and the media are bound to exist, but these differences should not obscure their mutual interest in saving the lives of hostages and in the preservation of an orderly society.

Conclusions

Laqueur notes that the terrorist's act by itself is nothing, "publicity is all."[56] Since terrorists need to advertise their acts of violence on the world stage, one would anticipate that they would be masters of the communication process. Certainly terrorist groups have failed to fully manipulate the means of communication. The present-day terrorist scenario is to let the media communicate the terrorist act to the viewing public. Given the increased sophistication of terrorists and the need of the electronic media to provide "good" pictures, it can only be a matter of time before the level of violence is escalated to produce nightly news. Thus, instead of channels of communication reporting news-making events, terrorist groups actually create the news by amplifying the level of violence. This is certainly the case today with al Qaeda. Seldom does an evening newscast pass without several references to al Qaeda.

Terrorist groups that simply distribute manifestos and other printed material to the media detailing grievances or political demands quickly learn that there is little chance their views will be published by the national or international media. Therefore, terrorists rely on spectacular acts of violence. Experience has demonstrated that the media will report all the details of a terrorist attack, including specific details of the group responsible for the attack. The more blood that is shed, the greater the news coverage (if it bleeds, it leads). Terrorist groups want to communicate their message to the world. What better tactic than through the use of outrageous acts of indiscriminate violence.

Guerrilla wars have been waged for fifty years by ethnic and religious minorities in Angola, Morocco, Northern Ireland, Spain, Eastern Europe, and Uganda with little effect or recognition by a large viewing audience. However, when a small number of Palestinians moved their armed struggle from Israel to Western Europe, their grievances quickly became news-making events around the world. The Palestinians understood that access to the media magnified their voice and eventually put pressure on Western governments to seek a resolution to the Palestinian question.

Terrorism is a dynamic process, and the media represent an important asset to the success of terroristic events. Thus, the media should regularly evaluate the changing strategies used by terrorists, the increasing threats posed to society by incompetent reporting of terrorist attacks, and the responsibility of accurately reporting on terrorist attacks. Unfortunately, there is no foolproof way for the media to avoid being used by terrorist groups in the future. Former prime minister of the United Kingdom Margaret Thatcher said it best, "It is up to the media to deprive terrorists of the 'oxygen of publicity' on which they thrive."[57]

The next chapter explores terrorism in the Middle East with a special emphasis on al Qaeda and the Palestine Question.

Key Terms

Black Panthers	hunger strike	Symbionese Liberation Army
Black September	Popular Front for the Liberation	(SLA)
censorship	of Palestine (PFLP)	Tupamaros
contagion effect	Provisional wing of the IRA	al Qaeda
D.B. Cooper	(PIRA)	Qassam rockets
Good Guys	Red Brigades	al Zawahiri
Hanafi	skyjacking	

Discussion Questions

1. Describe the origins of Black September.
2. What is contagion theory, or the copycat syndrome?
3. What precautions can commercial airlines take to protect passengers from the threat of skyjacking?
4. Identify the historical trends in skyjacking. Speculate as to what is next.
5. Develop a set of guidelines for supporting censorship.
6. Present an argument for the introduction of government censorship in ongoing terrorist events.
7. How did the Black Panther Party generate media attention?
8. Why is the 1972 Munich Olympics considered a turning point for international terrorist groups?
9. Describe the hunger strike by INLA and PIRA in 1981.
10. Defend the role of the media in terrorist incidents.
11. Evaluate the role of the Internet in spreading fear and intimidation.

Web sites

The Irish Hunger Strikes—A Commemorative Project
http://larkspirit.com/hungerstrikes

Media, Peace and Conflict Programme
http://www.mediapeace.org

Brookings Institution, Washington, DC—Role of the
Press in the Anti-Terrorism Campaign
http://www.brookings.edu

MSN Encarta and Research
http://encarta.msn.com

The Middle East Research Institute
http://www.memri.org

The Center of Public Integrity: Investigative Journalism
in the Public Interest
http://www.publicintegrity.org/main.html

Aljazeera, Arab News Network—The most popular in
the Middle East
http://english.aljazeera.net

Endnotes

1. Martha Crenshaw, "The Causes of Terrorism," *Comparative Politics*, 13 (1981), p. 396.
2. J. Bowyer Bell, *A Time of Terror. How Democratic Societies Respond to Revolutionary Violence* (New York: Basic Books, 1978), pp. 11–23.
3. Brian Jenkins, *International Terrorism: A New Mode of Conflict* (Los Angeles, CA: Crescent, 1975), p. 4.
4. Peter Jennings, *Hostage: An Endless Terror* (ABC Documentary Film, 1978).
5. David Phillips, *Skyjack* (London: Hairap, 1973), p. 72; Bruce Hoffman, *Inside Terrorism* (New York: Columbia University Press, 1998), p. 67.
6. David Hubbard, *The Skyjacker. His Flights of Fancy* (New York: Macmillan, 1973), pp. 16–30.
7. James Avery, *The Sky Pirates* (London: Ian Allan, 1973), p. 75; Robert T. Holden, "The Contagiousness of Aircraft Hijacking," *American Journal of Sociology*, 91 (1986), p. 902.
8. Marcia M. Trick, "Chronology of Incidents of Terroristic, Quasi-Terroristic and Political Violence in the U.S.: January 1965 to March 1976," in *Disorders and Terrorism*, National Advisory Committee on Criminal Justice Standards and Goals (Washington, DC: U.S. Government Printing Office, 1977), p. 563; Gabriel Weimann and Conrad Winn, *The Theater of Terror: Mass Media and International Terrorism* (New York: Longman Publishing Group, 1994), p. 215.
9. Ibid., pp. 563–83.
10. James M. Poland and Michael J. McCrystle, *Practical, Tactical and Legal Perspectives on Terrorism and Hostage Taking* (Lewiston, NY: Edwin Mellon Press, 2000), pp. 108–15; Michael Smith and Bernadette Tarallo, "Who Are the Good Guys?: The Social Construction of the Vietnamese Other," in *The Bubbling Cauldron: Race, Ethnicity, and the Urban Crises*, eds. Michael Smith and Joe R. Flagin (Minneapolis, MN: University of Minnesota Press, 1995), pp. 50–76.
11. For example, see William A. Hachten and James F. Scotton, *The World News Prism: Global Media in an Era of Terrorism* (Ames, IA: University of Iowa Press, 2002).
12. Peter L. Bergen, *Holy War, Inc.: Inside the Secret World of Osama bin Laden* (New York: Free Press, 2001), pp. 1–22.
13. *To Die for Ireland* (ABC Documentary Film, 1980).
14. U.S. Congress, Senate, Committee on the Judiciary, Subcommittee to Investigate the Administration of the Internal Security Act and Other Internal Security Laws, *Part 5. Hostage Defense Measures*, Hearings, 94th Congress, July 25, 1975 (Washington, DC: U.S. Government Printing Office, 1975), pp. 275–76.
15. J. Bowyer Bell, *IPI (International Press Institute) Report* 25 (June 1976), p. 4.
16. Michael Moodie, "The Patriot Game: The Politics of Violence in Northern Ireland," in *International Terrorism in the Contemporary World*, ed. Marius H. Livingston (Westport, CT: Greenwood Press, 1978), p. 98.
17. *Time*, October 22, 1984, p. 50; Bruce Hoffman, *Inside Terrorism* (New York: Columbia University Press, 1998), p. 182.

18. For example, see David Beresford and Peter Maas, *Ten Men Dead: The Story of the 1981 Irish Hunger Strike* (New York: Atlantic Monthly, 1997); Kevin Toolis, *Rebel Hearts: Journeys within the IRA's Soul* (New York: St. Martin's Press, 1997).
19. Ibid.
20. Alex P. Schmid and Janny de Graaf, *Violence as Communication* (London and Beverly Hills, CA: Sage, 1982), p. 5; See also Joanne Wright, *Terrorist Propaganda: The Red Army Faction and the Provisional IRA, 1968–1986* (New York: St. Martin's Press, 1991).
21. Michael M. Gunter, "The Armenian Terrorist Campaign against Turkey," *Orbis*, 27 (summer 1983), pp. 447–77; See also Henry Morgenthau, *The Murder of a Nation* (New York: Armenian General Benevolent Union of America, 1974).
22. Christopher Dobson and Ronald Paine, *The Carlos Complex: A Pattern of Violence* (London: Hodder and Stroughton, 1977), p. 15.
23. Frederick Hacker, *Crusaders, Criminals, Crazies: Terror and Terrorism in Our Time* (New York: Bantam, 1978), p. 223.
24. For example, see Simon Reeve, *One Day in September* (New York: Arcade Publishing, 2000).
25. *Time*, March 28, 1977, p. 13; *Newsweek*, May 22, 1978, p. 35; See also Richard Drake, *The Aldo Moro Murder Case* (Boston, MA: Harvard University Press, 1996).
26. Ernesto Fiorillo, "Terrorism in Italy: Analysis of a Problem," *Terrorism*, 2 (1979), pp. 261–70.
27. For example, see Robert C. Gardner, *Red Brigades: The Story of Italian Terrorism* (New York: Palgrave MacMillan, 1990); Raimondo Catanzaro, *The Red Brigades and Left-Wing Terrorism in Italy* (New York: Palgrave MacMillan, 1991); Robert C. Meade, *Red Brigades: The Story of Italian Terrorism* (New York: St. Martin's Press, 1990).
28. Charles E. Silberman, *Criminal Violence Criminal Justice* (New York: Random House, 1978), pp. 157–59; See also Jennifer B. Smith, *An International History of the Black Panther Party* (New York: Garland Publishing, 1999).
29. For example, see Vin McLellan and Paul Avery, *The Voices of Guns* (New York: Putnam, 1977), p. 22; Leslie Payne, *The Life and Death of the SLA* (New York: Ballantine Books, 1976); Patricia Hearst, *Every Secret Thing* (New York: Doubleday, 1981).
30. Desmond Smith, *The Nation*, March 30, 1974, pp. 392–94.
31. For example, see James Monaco, *Celebrity: The Media as Image Maker* (New York: Delta, 1978), pp. 65–78; Robert B. Pearsall, *The Symbionese Liberation Army* (New York: Rudopi BV Editions, 1974); Sharon D. Hendry, *Soliah: The Sara Jane Olson Story* (New York: Cable Publishing Inc., 2002).
32. Michael J. McMains and Wayman C. Mullins, *Crisis Negotiations: Managing Critical Incidents and Hostage Situations in Law Enforcement and Corrections* (Cincinnati, OH: Anderson Publishing, 1996), pp. 13–15.
33. Charles Fenyvesi, *The Media and Terrorism* (Chicago, IL: Field Enterprises, 1977), p. 28.
34. Poland and McCrystle, *Practical, Tactical, and Legal Perspectives of Terrorism and Hostage Taking*, p. 45.
35. For example, see Gabriel Weimann, *Terror on the Internet: The New Arena, the New Challenges* (Washington, DC: USIP Press, 2006).
36. Dan Verton, *Black Ice: The Invisible Threat of Cyberterrorism* (New York: McGraw Hill, 2003), pp. 3–24
37. Kathy Gannon, "Manual of Jihad Details Terrorist Tactics," *War on Terrorism* (October 2, 2001), *http://seattlep-i.newsource.com*.
38. Paul Hamilos and Mark Tran, "21 Guilty, 7 cleared over Madrid Train Bombings" (October 31, 2007), *http://guardian.co.uk*.
39. "Hizballah—the Party of God," *http://alamshrig.hiof.no/lebanon*. There are 25 websites on the Internet that host and support Hizballah.
40. "al Qaeda Trolls Net," (September 14, 2003), *http://siteintelgroup.org*.
41. For example, see Clay Wilson, *Botnets, Cybercrime, and Cyberterrorism: Vulnerabilities and Policy Issues for Congress* (Washington, DC: Congressional Research Service, 2008).
42. Gannon, "Manual of Jihad Details Terrorist Tactics," Lesson 9.
43. "Senate Report on Terrorism and the Internet," (July 14, 2008), p. 7, *http://militantislammonitor.org*.
44. Timothy L. Thomas, "al Qaeda and the Internet: The Danger of Cyberplanning," *Parameters*, (Spring, 2003), pp. 112–23.
45. Ayman al-Zawahiri, "Knights Under the Prophet's Banner: The al Qaeda Manifest," *Military Review*, 85, 1(January 2005), pp. 83–92.

46. Peter M. Sandman, David M. Rubin, and David B. Sachsman, *Media: An Introductory Analysis of American Mass Communication* (Englewood Cliffs, NJ: Prentice Hall, 1976), p. 165.

47. James Kohl and John Litt, eds., *Urban Guerrilla Warfare in Latin America* (Cambridge: MIT Press, 1974), p. 186.

48. Jordon J. Paust, "International Law and Control of the Media: Terror, Repression and the Alternatives," *Indiana Law Journal, 53* (1978), pp. 644–45.

49. United States Congress, House Committee on Internal Security, *Terrorism*, Hearing, 93rd Congress, 2nd Session (Washington, DC: U.S. Government Printing Office, 1974).

50. Paust, *Indiana Law Journal*, p. 661.

51. Ibid.

52. Alfred McClung Lee, *Terrorism in Northern Ireland* (New York: General Hall, 1983), p. 48.

53. Francis M. Watson, *Political Terrorism* (Washington, DC: R. B. Luce, 1976), p. 93.

54. Schmid and de Graaf, *Violence as Communication*, p. 172.

55. Christopher P. Kehler, Greg Harvey, and Richard Hall, "Perspectives on Media Control in Terrorist-Related Incidents," *Canadian Police College Journal*, 6 (1982), pp. 226–58.

56. Walter Laqueur, "The Futility of Terrorism," *Harpers* (March 1976), p. 104.

57. Rushworth M. Kidder, "Manipulation of the Media," in *Annual Editions: Violence and Terrorism 91–92* (Guilford, CT: McGraw-Hill Dushkin, 1991), p. 118.

CHAPTER 4

The Palestine Question and Al Qaeda

CHAPTER OBJECTIVES
The study of this chapter will enable you to:

- Trace the historical antecedents of the Arab–Israeli conflict
- Identify extremist groups affiliated with the PLO
- Compare and contrast the Palestine Question and al Qaeda
- Discuss the Zionist Movement
- Explore the escalation of terrorism in democracies
- Speculate as to the nature of terrorism in the twenty-first century

INTRODUCTION

In this chapter, the focus is on the Palestine Question and Osama bin Laden and al Qaeda. The organizational structure, motives, and methods of the Palestine Liberation Organization (PLO) will be explored. The second section examines the motives and terrorist activities of al Qaeda. The evolutionary development of the al Qaeda network is also examined.

After the attacks carried out by al Qaeda bombers on September 11, 2001, many puzzled Americans asked, "Why do they hate us so much?" The answer to this simple question is very complex. A few explanations for this hatred for Americans can be found in the so-called clash of civilizations, the poverty amid oil wealth, the oppression and corruption of Arab governments, a crisis within the Islamic faith, and the presence of U.S. military forces on the Arabian Peninsula. However, at the top of the list of any explanation is American support for the Jewish state of Israel. For many Arabs, the survival of the State of Israel symbolizes everything that is wrong in the Middle East. Anti-American emotions run high across the Arab and Muslim world fueled by the Palestinian/Israeli conflict.

PALESTINE RESISTANCE MOVEMENT

The most inventive, successful, and sometimes ruthless non-state terrorists have been the various Palestinian extremist factions. The success of Palestinian terrorists has no doubt inspired other freedom fighters and rebels around the world. In fact, much of the increase in world terrorism can be directly traced to the success of Palestinian extremist groups.

For more than twenty years, the world had ignored the fate of the displaced Palestinians. Then in 1968 the Palestinians carried their struggle from the borders of Israel to the rest of the world by capturing media attention for their cause. Spectacular hostage-taking episodes, outrageous bombings, and barbaric assassinations catapulted obscure Palestinian extremist groups onto the world scene. Today the conflict between Israel and the Palestinians and the Arab world in general has become a central issue in international politics. At the forefront of this conflict is the PLO, which claims to represent the interests of all Palestinians.[1] The stated objective of the PLO is the "liberation of Palestine, the elimination of Israel as a political entity."[2] What follows is a brief history of the evolution of the Palestinian–Israeli conflict.

HISTORICAL ANTECEDENTS

Beginning in the late-nineteenth century, two powerful political forces emerged in Palestine: political **Zionism** and Arab nationalism.[3] Political Zionism represented the yearning for Jewish political and religious self-determination in the Promised Land. The ultimate objective of the Zionists was the creation of a Jewish state in Palestine. Arab nationalists, of course, had other ideas, and as the Ottoman Empire began to disintegrate after World War I, both Zionist and Arab nationalists saw an opportunity to realize a passionate dream of self-determination in Palestine (see Figure 4.1, Map 1). However, as World War I ended, Palestine was placed under the administration of a British mandatory government that was officially committed to the creation of a Zionist/Jewish state in Palestine (see Figure 4.1, Map 2).[4]

British Foreign Secretary Lord Arthur Balfour stated in a written document that "Palestine shall be reconstituted as a national Home of the Jewish people."[5] This document was subsequently referred to as the **Balfour Declaration**. Although the Balfour Declaration was not a legally binding document, it did strengthen the cause of the world Zionist movement and stimulate Jewish immigration to the Promised Land. The British also verbally promised to give the Arabs of Palestine the opportunity to once again become a nation in the world. For the next thirty years, the British pursued an inconsistent policy in Palestine that permitted both the growth of a Zionist/Jewish economic and social infrastructure and the existence of a separate Arab national movement.

In short, the British mandate seriously underestimated both the rise of Arab nationalism and the determination of the Zionists to create a Jewish state in Palestine. It seems evident that Britain's conflicting promises and policies would ultimately lead to strife between Arabs and Jews and to endless problems for Britain in Palestine. Thus, the indecision of the British, the impatience of the Zionists, and the political immaturity of the Arabs helped to launch a chain of events that produced the "Question of Palestine."

Before the United Nations Partition Plan for Palestine (see Figure 4.1, Map 3) was put into effect, a series of terrorist acts were carried out by Zionist gangs. The two most active Zionist gangs in Palestine in the 1940s were the **Irgun Zvai Leumi al Israel** (IZL: the National Military Organization of Israel) and Lohemey Heruth Israel (LEHI: Fighters for the Freedom of Israel), also known as the **Stern Gang**. The Irgun and Stern Gang evolved in the eyes of the British into the most violent terrorist organizations of the modern era.[6] The Irgun and Stern Gang launched a

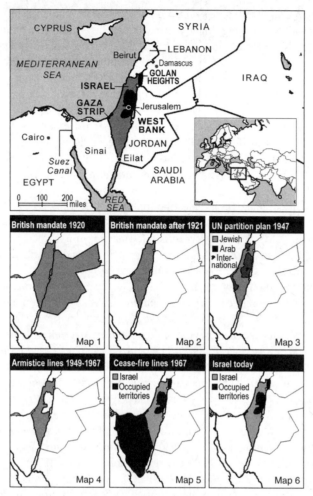

FIGURE 4.1   Israel's changing boundaries: 1920–2003. Maps courtesy of www.theodora.com/maps, used with permission.

series of terrorist attacks against British soldiers, British Mandate government officials, and Arab Palestinians. According to Begin in his book *The Revolt*,[7] the purpose of the terrorist attacks was to undermine British rule in Palestine, create a climate of fear and panic in Palestine, and to attract international media attention to Palestine. The Irgun and Stern Gang strategy was to publicize Zionist grievances against the British and to claim the right to establish a Jewish state. Between 1944 and 1948, terrorism by the Irgun and Stern Gang was at its worst.

The Irgun's most spectacular terrorist attack was the bombing in July 1946 of the King David Hotel in Jerusalem. Explosives were placed on two floors that housed the nerve center of British rule in Palestine. Ninety-one people were killed and forty-five were injured, including British, Arabs, and Jews. Hoffman maintains that the bombing of the King David Hotel remains one of the world's most lethal terrorist acts of the twentieth century.[8]

Then on April 9, 1948, the Irgun and Stern Gang set out to attack the Palestinian village of Deir Yassin, located on the outskirts of Jerusalem. The objective was to take over Deir Yassin, which controlled the high ground above the City of Jerusalem. Before dawn, about 120 members of the Irgun and Stern Gang converged on Deir Yassin. The Palestinian Arabs offered little resistance and the Irgun and Stern Gang quickly overwhelmed the villagers. According to the Arab version and some Jewish witnesses and British journalists, the Zionist fighters or terrorists conducted an indiscriminate massacre of the villagers, including women, children, and the elderly. In all more than 250 people were randomly slaughtered. The attack on Deir Yassin was a turning point in the 1948 war. Historian Benny Morris recalls that the massacre of Palestinians at Deir Yassin was the one single event of the 1948 war that precipitated the flight of Arab villagers from Palestine.[9] Eventually, Deir Yassin became a symbol of Zionist cruelty and everything that has happened to Palestinians. The 1948 war ended with the establishment of the State of Israel (see Figure 4.1, Map 4) on May 15, 1948, and the destruction of the Palestinian community. The atrocity at Deir Yassin set in motion a cycle of assault and retaliation between Palestinians and Israelis that continues to this day.

By 1947, the British mandate in Palestine found Arab and Jewish demands irreconcilable and turned the problem over to the newly formed United Nations. A United Nations Commission reviewed the Palestine Question and recommended partitioning the country (see Figure 4.1, Map 3). The United Nations was now committed in principle to a divided Palestine. The Partition Plan was eagerly accepted by the Zionists and unequivocally rejected by the Palestinian Arabs. The British mandate ended on May 14, 1948; the new Jewish state of Israel was proclaimed the following day. The invading armies of five surrounding Arab countries immediately challenged the Jewish assertion of statehood, but in this first of eight major Arab–Israeli wars, Israel was able to consolidate its independence and extend its authority over all of Palestine except for the West Bank and the Gaza Strip (see Figure 4.1, Map 4). Palestine ceased to exist after the 1948 war, and more than 700,000 Palestinian Arabs fled or were forced out of Palestine or off their land by the new Israeli state.[10] The Palestinians were now stateless and relegated to refugee status. The Diaspora, or dispersal, had passed from one people, the Jews, to another, the Palestinians.

The end of the 1948 war did not bring peace; rather, it left a legacy of hate. The Arabs, defeated and humiliated, were determined to reverse the decision in future wars. Since the 1948 war, Israel has fought seven major wars: 1956 Suez War, 1967 June War, 1968–1970 War of Attrition, 1973 Yom Kippur War, 1982 PLO war in Lebanon, 2006 war against Hizballah in Lebanon, (known as the July War), and the 2008–2009 war against Hamas in the Gaza Strip.[11] Israel is the strongest military power in the Middle East. Its conventional forces are far superior to those of its surrounding neighbors, and it is the only state in the region with nuclear weapons. According to Flapan, the Israelis believe that they have become a mini-superpower in the world and can continue indefinitely to rule over the Palestinians and to annex Arab and Palestinian land.[12] If this is so, then Israel ignores the historical context of the Jewish people, which contends that people suffering from dispersion, homelessness, and refugee conditions yearn for freedom and independence and that the oppression of another people can only lead to violence and terrorism.

For example, the Zionist movement gained strength out of the suffering of the Jewish people in Eastern Europe. By the late 1880s, a series of communal riots spread throughout Eastern Europe and Russia. The Russian word for these communal riots is *pogrom*, or devastation. The pogroms set in motion a vast movement of Eastern European Jews seeking to escape poverty, discrimination, and the indiscriminate destruction of Jewish communities. The Zionist Jews believed they could only be safe by having their own country. A small number of Jews began to emigrate to the Promised Land of Palestine, but it was the Holocaust that provided the final push of Jewish migration into Palestine. At the end of World War II, the survivors of Nazi death camps arrived in Palestine. The recommendation for the creation of a Jewish state by the United Nations was motivated largely by empathy for the devastation inflicted on European Jews by the Nazi state. In turn, the 1948 War of Independence of the Jewish state led to the uprooting of more than 700,000 Palestinian Arabs from their homes. La Guardia argues that if the Jews were victims of the Nazis, the Palestinians are in many ways "victims of the victims."[13] In Israel, the Holocaust is known as the **Shoah**, the Catastrophe. The exodus of Palestinians after the 1948 war is known as Al Nakba, also the Catastrophe. The Palestinians relegated to refugee status yearn for a return to Palestine.

Thus, Palestinian refugee camps administered by the United Nations after 1948 have become breeding grounds for terrorism. The generation of Palestinians who were born and raised in the refugee camps has erupted on the world stage of international terrorism. Condemned to refugee status after the 1948 war, Palestinian social structure and political institutions were shattered and ceased to be a major factor in the Arab–Israeli conflict, at least until the formation of the PLO in 1964.

PALESTINE LIBERATION ORGANIZATION

In January 1964, the first Arab summit was held in Cairo, and steps were taken to create the Palestine Liberation Organization (PLO). The PLO was organized to provide greater unity to the fragmented Palestinian community and to adopt a new tougher strategy on the "liberation of Palestine." Ahmed Shuqairy, an articulate, resolute Palestinian diplomat, was assigned the task of developing the structure of the PLO. Wide disagreement about the formation, structure, and goals of the PLO made this a difficult task. Particularly vocal in its criticism of the planned organization of the PLO was a group of "freedom fighters" known as **al Fatah**, led by Yasir Arafat. Nisan argues that Arafat and the leadership of Fatah wanted to begin an armed struggle with Israel in the form of guerrilla/terrorist attacks against "soft" Israel targets.[14] Fatah, which is an acronym formed by reversing the initial letters of Harakat Tahrir Filastin (the Palestine

FIGURE 4.2 Holocaust survivors from Buchenwald concentration camp. From July 1937 to March 1945, over 200,000 prisoners passed through Buchenwald, over 40,000 were killed and 21,000 were liberated. Buchenwald is located 5 miles from Weimar, Germany. (CORBIS BETTMANN)

Liberation Movement), proclaimed through its official publication, *Filastinuna* (our Palestine), that the strategic use of terrorism should be to disrupt the Jewish state and that "Palestine is the only road to Arab unity."[15]

Even though Fatah would later develop a complex strategy of guerrilla warfare and suffer numerous internal conflicts, its political ideology was simple. The liberation of Palestine could only be accomplished by armed Palestinians, and the struggle with the Zionist Israelis could not be controlled by unstable Arab regimes. Fatah was greatly influenced by the success and simplistic terrorist strategy of the Algerian terrorist organization, the Front for National Liberation (FLN). Miller argues that one of the reasons for the continued survival of Fatah has been the decision to avoid the "confusing ideological traps" that would be the downfall of other Palestinian resistance groups.[16]

While Fatah emphasized the liberation of Palestine by Palestinians, the Arab Nationalist Movement (ANM) stressed that only through total Arab unity and power could Palestine be recovered from Israel. However, the ANM eventually split over a disagreement in ideology, and some members adopted a more radical position. For example, the two most ideological of the ANM resistance groups, the **Popular Front for the Liberation of Palestine (PFLP)** formed by Dr. George Habash, and the Popular Democratic Front for the Liberation of Palestine (PDFLP) adopted a Marxist political orientation. Both the PFLP and PDFLP were later to distinguish themselves by introducing a "new" strain of terrorism onto the international scene. During the course of this bitter internecine warfare between the moderate leadership of the PLO, the ANM, and Fatah, Fatah began to escalate its terrorist/guerrilla actions against Israel. By the end of 1965, Fatah had logged a total of thirty-nine successful raids against "soft" Israeli targets.[17] Fatah had proved itself capable of sustaining a continued level of guerrilla/terrorist activity against Israel. While these guerrilla operations by Fatah did not destroy the Jewish state, they were a constant irritant and provided a source of pride for Fatah in the Palestinian Diaspora.

The terrorist/guerrilla actions by Fatah eventually forced the Israelis to retaliate against Fatah bases in Syria, Egypt, and Jordan. These Israeli retaliation raids in turn prompted increased public clamor, particularly in Jordan, to finally destroy Israel. Once again hostilities seemed imminent, and the outbreak of the third Arab–Israeli war seemed inevitable. When it came, the 1967 June War was a devastating defeat of the armies of Syria, Egypt, and Jordan. The Arab defeat further aggravated the Palestinian people, forcing some 400,000 Palestinian Arabs to join the 700,000 refugees of 1948.[18] Israel now occupied the West Bank, Gaza, Golan Heights, and the Sinai Peninsula (see Figure 4.1, Map 5). But the humiliating Arab defeat catapulted Fatah and Arafat into the leadership of the PLO. The moderate leadership of the PLO was discredited after the 1967 war, and by July 1968, terrorist/guerrilla groups took over the PLO and Arafat was elected chairman. The Question of Palestine now exploded onto the international scene in a series of well-planned terrorist incidents designed to attract media attention for the Palestinian cause that continues to this day.

PALESTINIAN EXTREMISM AND THE 1973 YOM KIPPUR WAR

In order to attract maximum world attention, the PLO-affiliated PFLP introduced the hijacking of aircraft. It was the first terrorist group to do so. The PFLP planned and directed a series of spectacular air hijackings of international flights between July 1968 and September 1970. Fifty innocent people were killed and scores were injured. Despite the success of the well-staged hijackings, hijackers were apprehended and convicted in European countries; they were quickly released after other planes had been hijacked and hostages were exchanged for convicted hijackers.[19]

Again there was an escalation of Palestinian terrorism. Israeli retaliation and the continued Israeli occupation of Arab lands acquired during the 1967 war led to renewed military confrontation between Israel and its Arab neighbors. On October 6, 1973, Syria and Egypt invaded the "**occupied territories** of Palestine." Sachar considers the **Yom Kippur War** in October 1973 to be the most brutal of the eight Arab–Israeli wars and the most traumatic experience for Israelis.[20]

For the first time the Arabs achieved significant military successes. Unlike the Israeli victories in 1948, 1956, and 1967, the 1973 war produced a credible military performance by the Arab forces and proved to the Arabs that the Israeli military machine was not invincible. The 1973 war restored Arab self-respect and produced a new pragmatism among Arab leaders on the basis of military superiority of Israel and the lack of unity in the Arab world. This new pragmatism also forced the PLO to review its strategy for the liberation of Palestine in order to meet the post-October 1973 war situation.

Under the leadership of Yasir Arafat, the PLO National Council in 1974 agreed to pursue a diplomatic or political solution with Israel by opening up negotiations for a Palestinian homeland on the West Bank and Gaza. However, several members of Arafat's Fatah rejected any negotiations with Israel while the smaller, more extremist groups such as the Popular Front for the Liberation of Palestine, the Palestine Liberation Front, and the Arab Liberation Front withdrew from the PLO executive committee in protest. Arafat, in a desperate effort to prevent the disintegration of the PLO, reluctantly concluded that "half a loaf was better than none," while keeping alive the vision that someday pre-1948 Palestine would be returned to the Palestinians by peaceful means.

FIGURE 4.3 Yasir Arafat addresses the United Nations General Assembly in 1974 and the PLO is granted observer status. Arafat was born in 1929 in Cairo to a Palestinian father and Egyptian mother. In 1994, Arafat received the Nobel Peace Prize along with Shimon Perez and Yitzhak Rabin for their efforts to create peace in the Middle East. (UPI/CORBIS BETTMANN)

Even more important, by renouncing their more extreme terrorist tactics, the moderate PLO factions were able to win public support throughout the world since many countries were prepared to support a Palestinian national home. Thus, in 1974, the PLO received recognition from more than 100 countries throughout the world, obtained overwhelming backing for favorable UN General Assembly resolutions, and also gained wide popular support, especially in the Third World. Then on November 17, 1974, Arafat addressed the UN General Assembly to a standing ovation, and the PLO obtained observer status at the UN. The PLO could now attempt to influence and initiate UN resolutions on the Palestine Question. A more favorable media image of the PLO began to appear. As a result, moderate Palestinian leaders encouraged their followers to pursue a path of diplomacy and negotiation in the hope that it would eventually pay off. Nonetheless, this path did not diminish Israel's opposition to the PLO and the creation of a Palestinian state, and did not win meaningful support from the United States for a Palestinian entity in Israel. Since the PLO's stated tactic of moderation and peace with Israel, increasing numbers of moderate Palestinians joined the "rejectionists," leading to several splits in Fatah and the PLO.[21] By the late 1980s, another split occurred with the formation of Hamas and Islamic Jihad.

REJECTIONIST FRONT: HISTORICAL PREVIEW

Since 1974, the rejectionist PLO factions have been composed of two important groups. First, for ideological reasons, one faction has completely rejected the "half a loaf" idea, even if it were offered to them. Second, the other faction liked the "half a loaf" notion but was convinced that Israel would never voluntarily and peacefully surrender the "occupied" territories and that the United States would never pressure Israel into negotiations for a Palestinian state. Believing that no diplomatic solution was feasible for the recovery of Palestine, which nearly the entire world considered legitimate, the rejectionists concluded that the only alternative open to them was armed struggle, that is, terrorism and guerrilla warfare. Thus, the rejectionists had nothing to lose by going for the "whole loaf." Arafat's position was widely criticized by extremist Palestinian elements, and he was accused of wasting precious time by pursuing the unattainable through peaceful diplomacy and negotiation.

Over the years, many of Arafat's most ardent followers deserted him to pursue the escalation of violence and terrorism without negotiations with Israel. For example, on December 27, 1985, Palestinian terrorists attacked the El Al ticket counter at the Rome and Vienna airports, randomly killing 17 innocent victims and seriously wounding 116 more. Responsibility for the unprovoked, indiscriminate shooting spree was claimed by the Abu Nidal faction, and the media quickly christened Abu Nidal the master of international terrorism.[22] Although little known in the West, Abu Nidal was well known within the PLO and by the Israeli Mossad. The Abu Nidal faction had claimed credit for hundreds of terrorist incidents and assassinations, including the attempted assassination of Arafat. Abu Nidal was eventually sentenced to death in absentia for his attempt to kill the PLO chairman, although other assassination attempts have been more successful.[23] An estimated ninety moderate PLO leaders and supporters have been murdered by the Abu Nidal faction. Equally ruthless have been random indiscriminate attacks against non-Palestinian targets. For example, the Abu Nidal faction killed several people in random grenade attacks on synagogues in Rome and Vienna in 1982.[24] By the late 1980s, the **Abu Nidal Organization (ANO)** began to decline and Abu Nidal (a.k.a. Sabri al Bana) was later found dead in a Baghdad hotel from an apparent suicide in October 2002. But the most serious challenge to the existence of the PLO and the leadership of Arafat came with the Israeli invasion of Lebanon on June 6, 1982.

INVASION OF LEBANON

The war in Lebanon, the sixth major Arab–Israeli war, was a large ground force operation launched by Israel into Lebanon to finally destroy the PLO and root out its infrastructure, which supported terrorist attacks on the settlements and civilian inhabitants of northern Israel. Israeli ground units struck with lightning speed and precision, destroying PLO training camps and capturing hundreds of international terrorists caught by the surprise Israeli blitzkrieg. After five days of fighting, the PLO was bottled up in West Beirut. The siege of Beirut lasted for several weeks and finally ended when UN negotiators planned the safe withdrawal of PLO fighters to several Arab host countries.[25]

The war in Lebanon became a turning point for both Israel and the PLO and generated an international crisis of unprecedented dimensions. Spontaneous protests erupted in Israel, Europe, and the United States in reaction to the blockade of Beirut and the savage massacre in the Sabra and Shatila Palestinian refugee camps. The Israeli-supported Lebanese right-wing Christian **Phalangist** militia killed 700 to 2,000 unarmed Palestinian refugees. The Israel military was later charged with complicity in the atrocities at Sabra and Shatila, and Israeli citizens demanded a change in government.[26] But the Lebanon war dragged on for three years. All of the Israeli objectives of the war, including the destruction of the PLO, were shattered. The initial promise by Israeli Prime Minister Begin of a two-day limited military action against PLO military bases resulted in Israel's longest war, with heavy Israeli, Palestinian, and Lebanese casualties. Finally, on June 7, 1985, the Israelis pulled most of their ground troops out of Lebanon, leaving reserve forces in southern Lebanon to prevent a return of the PLO. In May 2000, the Israeli military finally pulled all its forces out of Lebanon. However, the distressing reality is that the destruction of PLO terrorist camps and the ejection of PLO fighters from Beirut have not diminished the PLO's leading role in the Palestinian struggle for independent nationhood. In fact, not only was the PLO still basically intact, but the Israeli invasion of Lebanon created an even more implacable enemy: Hizballah.

HIZBALLAH

The name **Hizballah** literally means "the Party of God." Hizballah was established after the Israeli invasion of Lebanon in 1982 and is an umbrella organization of various Lebanese Shi'ite groups that adhere to the ideals of the Iranian revolution of 1979. In late 1982, Iran sent fighters from its elite Iranian Revolutionary Guards to Lebanon to establish an Islamic movement that would wage holy war, or jihad, against Israel. The principal goal of Hizballah is to create an Islamic republic in Lebanon, headed by religious clerics. Friedman maintains that after the Israeli invasion of Lebanon, Palestinian and Lebanese extremists found common ground for their hatred of the Israeli Zionists.[27] By the mid-1980s, Hizballah had consolidated its hold over parts of Lebanon and moved its headquarters to the Bekaa Valley. Hizballah then established depots for weapons, began to recruit fighters, and distributed aid to South Lebanon Shi'ites in the form of money, food, and medical supplies. Hizballah hoped to gain the support of the local population through social service activities.[28]

In 1983, Hizballah introduced a new tactic into the lexicon of terrorism: suicide bombing. In a series of well-planned truck suicide bombings in Beirut in 1983, Hizballah was able to finally cause the multinational force, which was sent to Beirut to oversee the evacuation of PLO fighters, to "quit" Lebanon. The U.S. embassy, the U.S. marine barracks, the French Paratroop Brigade, and the U.S. embassy annex were all destroyed by suicide truck bombings, with a total of over 360 lives lost. Hizballah extended its reach in Lebanon by kidnapping dozens of Western hostages from a variety of countries for economic and political gain. Eighteen Americans were held hostage in Lebanon during the period from 1983 until the release of Terry Anderson in 1991. Three American hostages were killed.[29]

Hizballah has also demonstrated the ability to plan and execute acts of terrorism far from Lebanon. After a thorough investigation into the suicide bombing of the Israeli embassy in Buenos Aires in 1992, the Argentine Supreme Court issued a warrant for the arrest of Hizballah leader **Imad Mughniyah**. Imad was also on the FBI's most wanted terrorist list for the hijacking of a U.S. commercial jet and the murder of one of its passengers. Mughniyah and Hizballah were also responsible for the truck bombing of the Argentine-Jewish Mutual Association in July 1994 that left nearly 100 fatalities. Mughniyah is believed to be responsible for more American deaths than any other terrorist before the 9/11 attacks. His life as a wanted terrorist came to an abrupt end on February 12, 2008, when he was killed by a car bomb in Damascus, Syria.[30]

But the real battle between Israel and Hizballah has been on the Lebanese–Israeli border. Southern Lebanon has been the battleground between Israeli Defense Forces (IDF) and Hizballah fighters. Israel's presence in Lebanon is the primary justification for Hizballah's terrorist operations. Hizballah has indiscriminately launched thousands of Katyuska rockets from Lebanon at Israeli communities in the northern part of Israel. Hizballah, operating from its home territory, enjoys the support of the local populace as a movement fighting to liberate Lebanon. Hizballah has always maintained that they are not terrorists but a "national liberation movement" trying to drive Westerners and Israelis out of Lebanon. Between 1990 and 2000, Hizballah attacked Israeli positions in Southern Lebanon with snipers, mortars, and placed remote-controlled bombs to ambush Israeli convoys and patrols. On average, Hizballah inflicted between twenty and twenty-five casualties a year on the Israelis. On February 28, 1999, Hizballah claimed its biggest prize when it killed Israeli Brigadier General Erez Gerstein along with two aides with a roadside bomb.[31] Due to the high number of casualties, Israel wanted to withdraw its troops from Southern Lebanon. Therefore, in accordance with UN Security Resolution 425, Israeli forces redeployed from Southern Lebanon to Northern Israel at the end of May 2000. However, the redeployment did not end the terrorism of Hizballah against Northern Israel.

Hizballah continues to conduct military provocations by firing into Israeli territory and conducting cross-border raids. Since the pullout, Israel has recorded 100 terrorist attacks along the northern border of Israel. Hizballah continues to arm itself with the continued backing of Iran. On January 3, 2002, the Israelis seized a ship carrying fifty tons of advanced weapons supplied by Iran. The destination of the weapons was both the Palestinian Authority and Hizballah. The kidnapping of three Israeli soldiers patrolling inside Israeli territory by Hizballah further escalated the tension between Israel and Hizballah. As of the end of 2008, the whereabouts of the three soldiers is unknown, and they are presumed dead. Hizballah, in violation of UN Resolution 425, has refused to disarm and justifies its continued military action against Israel by demanding that Israel "liberate" land in Northern Israel known as Shaba Farms, which allegedly belongs to Lebanon. Hizballah also demands the release of Lebanese prisoners held in Israeli jails. Israel has refused to release terrorists and murderers. Hizballah contends that the return of Lebanese territory and prisoners justifies continued terrorist/military operations against Northern Israel.[32]

Israel has initiated a number of major military strikes against Lebanon over the past forty-five years, but previously had fought only one genuine war on Lebanese territory—the 1982 war to destroy the PLO guerrilla groups. In the summer of 2006, Israel once again invaded Southern Lebanon and fought a thirty-four-day war against Hizballah and their Lebanese supporters. On

July 12, 2006, Hizballah made a cross-border raid into Israel that killed and captured several Israeli soldiers. In response, the IDF launched a major air campaign in Lebanon.

Israel's main objective in the 2006 war was to destroy Hizballah's effectiveness as a fighting force. In particular, the Israelis were determined to eliminate the thousands of missiles and rockets that could strike Northern Israeli civilian communities. The Israelis were confident they could use air strikes to take out Hizballah missile sites. However, Ophir states that this strategy was destined to fail since Hizballah had from 10,000 to 16,000 rockets and missiles widely dispersed and located in mosques, homes, caves, and other hiding places in Southern Lebanon.[33] Moreover, Rubin maintains that even if the air strikes did destroy a large portion of Hizballah's inventory of missiles, Iran and Syria were prepared to send replacements.[34] It became apparent to the Israelis that air strikes were not having an effect on Hizballah, as missiles and rockets continued to rain down on Northern Israeli communities during the entire thirty-four-day war. In late July 2006, the Israelis sent in thousands of ground troops, believing that "boots on the ground" would be more successful than air strikes to defeat Hizballah once and for all. However, the Israeli ground offensive stalled and failed to produce a clear victory over Hizballah. Israel had no choice but to accept a UN-negotiated ceasefire on August 14, 2006.

When the war finally ended on August 14, both sides declared victory. Most independent observers believe that Hizballah clearly defeated the IDF.[35] Hizballah retained thousands of missiles and rockets that still today threaten Israel. In addition, Hizballah's political position in Lebanon was greatly improved by the war. Hizballah's popularity and support were widespread not only in Lebanon but across the Arab and Islamic world. Israel, on the other hand, failed to achieve its original objective of eliminating the Hizballah threat. The Israeli government appointed the *Winograd Commission* to investigate Israel's military performance and answer the question: How did the terrorist organization Hizballah defeat the superior IDF? Its findings included a very critical assessment of Israel's planning of the war. In particular, the Winograd Commission stated that Israel's political and military leaders failed to recognize Hizballah's guerrilla strategy and pursued goals that were unclear and could not be achieved. Overall, the Winograd Commission viewed the Second Lebanon war as a missed opportunity for Israel to destroy the terrorist Hizballah organization.[36]

Meanwhile, the second Lebanon war has complicated the U.S. government's global war on terrorism (the GWOT) in two ways. First, the war reinforced the anti-American hysteria in the Arab and Muslim world. The media widely reported that, during the fighting, Israel was being supplied with American weapons, including cluster bombs and missiles. According to Amnesty International, the Israeli bombing campaign killed over 1,100 Lebanese civilians.[37] Israeli bombs also did extensive damage to the infrastructure of Lebanon, destroying airport runways, roads, bridges, water pumping stations, and commercial business areas. Undoubtedly, the perception of U.S. involvement in the Second Lebanon war will help al Qaeda and other terrorist organizations find new recruits and supporters who want to not only attack Israel but also the United States.

Second, the conflict increased the prestige of Hizballah in Lebanon. The Arab and Muslim world saw Hizballah's impressive performance against a far superior Israeli military force as a great victory. By late fall of 2006, Hizballah, encouraged by its success against the Israelis, began to threaten the pro-American democratic government of Lebanon. There is the real possibility that Hizballah's actions could restart the Lebanese civil war.

Hizballah is now the major political party in Lebanon that represents the Shi'ite Muslims. Hizballah holds 14 of 128 seats in the Lebanese Parliament. In addition, Hizballah now controls eleven of thirty seats in the Lebanese cabinet. Unlike other militias in Lebanon, Hizballah has refused to disarm; thus, Hizballah is as well armed as the Lebanese army. Although Hizballah does not directly threaten the United States, it does threaten Israel. It is clearly attempting to take over the Lebanese government and establish an Islamic state in Lebanon. There is no doubt that the 2006 war in Lebanon has been a disaster for the Lebanese people as well as a major setback for both Israel and the United States' GWOT.[38]

In sum, it is doubtful that Israel can defeat Hizballah. Hizballah is well organized, well trained, and has the financial and logistical support of Iran and Syria. In the Arab world, Hizballah's popularity is widespread. Hizballah is the only guerrilla/terrorist group or Arab state to force Israel back from territory it has conquered. Hizballah's eighteen-year campaign of terrorism and guerrilla war against Israeli control of a self-declared security zone in Southern Lebanon has also inspired the second intifada against Israel. Hamas and Islamic Jihad cite Hizballah as providing the inspiration and the terrorist technology to destroy Israel. In fact, Hizballah believes that it is Allah's plan to bring all the Jews to Israel and then kill all the Jews. Note the words from a hadith, or saying, of Prophet Muhammad:

> The last hour will not come until the Muslims fight against the Jews, and the Muslims kill them, and until the Jews hide themselves behind a stone or a tree, and a stone or a tree says: "Muslim or Servant of Allah there is a Jew behind me; come and kill him."[39]

In conclusion, eight major Arab–Israeli wars have been fought, and on occasion the fighting threatens to erupt into a superpower confrontation between the United States and the Arab world. This superpower confrontation remains an ominous undertone in any Arab–Israeli crisis—one of the few regional conflicts that could actually provoke a nuclear war. Despite U.S. involvement and Arab intervention, the heart of the Israeli–Palestinian conflict is the dispute over what each considers its rightful homeland. Both sides, Palestinian and Israeli, are utterly convinced that the land is theirs. There is little agreement between Israelis and Palestinians, with no resolution in sight. The alternative to peaceful negotiation is protracted regional wars and a continued escalation of international terrorism by desperate, revengeful Palestinians led by the PLO and Hizballah.

In summary, the PLO is an umbrella group consisting of eight major extremist groups and several minor factions. In addition, the PLO provides a general organizational framework for all Palestinian community life. The five major extremist groups are al Fatah, al Saiqa, PFLP, PDFLP, and the PFLP-GC. The PLO attempts to project a unified organization of Palestinian nationalists working for the liberation of Palestine and the destruction of Israel. Moreover, members of the PLO attempt to portray themselves as guerrilla fighters in the image of guerrilla movements in Latin America or Asia. However, this may not be the case.

The PLO is splintered. In fact, the PLO does not appear to be unified on anything, including social outlook, economic interests, or relationship with Israel. Each group pursues its own self-interest, and group leaders view each other with deep suspicion, taking precautions against being assassinated by rival factions. Internal clashes by competing groups occur as frequently as clashes with Israelis. According to Gabriel, some PLO-affiliated groups often clash over the control of illegal drug traffic, prostitution, and smuggling, especially in Lebanon.[40] The Palestinian groups are also divided along ideological lines. They range from the nationalism of al Fatah to the Marxist PFLP, from the extremist terrorism of the PFLP-GC to the rejectionist front led by Abu Nidal. Table 4.1 outlines the extremist PLO-affiliated organizations.

TABLE 4.1 PLO-Affiliated Extremist Terrorist Groups

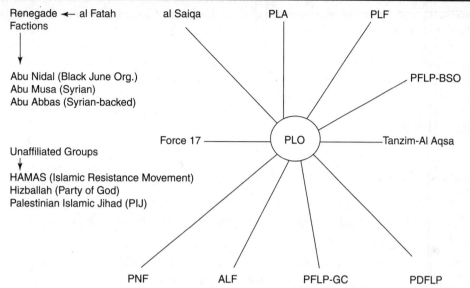

Renegade ← al Fatah
Factions

↓

Abu Nidal (Black June Org.)
Abu Musa (Syrian)
Abu Abbas (Syrian-backed)

al Saiqa   PLA   PLF

PFLP-BSO

Force 17 —— PLO —— Tanzim-Al Aqsa

Unaffiliated Groups

↓

HAMAS (Islamic Resistance Movement)
Hizballah (Party of God)
Palestinian Islamic Jihad (PIJ)

PNF   ALF   PFLP-GC   PDFLP

1. al Fatah is the oldest and largest of the PLO organizations cofounded by Yasir Arafat. Fatah has dominated the coalition of the PLO ever since Arafat was chairperson.
2. al Saiqa (Thunderbolt) is the second largest PLO-affiliated group formed after the 1967 June War. Although Saiqa is independent, most of its support comes from Syria. Saiqa has often been referred to as the terrorist arm of the Syrian Army.
3. The PFLP, founded by George Habash, supports a Marxist ideology. The PFLP is highly ideological and radical; acts of spectacular terrorism are almost its exclusive activity.
4. The PFLP-GC, led by Ahmed Jibril, has been responsible for numerous terrorist attacks against Israeli soft targets. PFLP-GC claims its major support comes from Libya.
5. The PDFLP, formed by Nayef Hawatmeh, is a splinter group of the PFL. The PDFLP is said to have close ties Iran and Syria.
6. The Palestine Liberation Army (PLA) is a regular standing military force of some 15,000 Palestinians financed primarily by the PLO and Syria.
7. The Arab Liberation Front (ALF), like Saiqa, conducts its operations almost exclusively against Israeli targets.
8. The Palestine National Front (PNF) was formed after the 1973 October War. The PNF con-ducts its operations primarily in the West Bank.
9. The Palestine Liberation Front (PLF) is a splinter group of the PFLP-GC. The PLF sought to escape Syrian influence in favor of alliance with al Qaeda.
10. Renegade al Fatah factions consist of three primary groups: (1) Abu Nidal faction, (2) Abu Musa faction, and (3) Abu Mohammed Abbas faction. The Abu Abbas faction was responsible for the seajacking of the Achille Lauro in 1985.
11. The Black September Organization (BSO) was formed in 1970 after the Jordanian Army drove the PLO and affiliated groups out of Jordan. The BSO's most spectacular terrorist operation was the taking of Israeli athlete hostages at the Munich Olympic Games in 1972.

Note: For a more comprehensive coverage of the genealogy of the PLO, see Yonah Alexander, *Palestinian Secular Terrorism, Profiles of Fatah, Popular Front for the Liberation of Palestine, Popular Front for the Liberation of Palestine-General Command, and Democratic Front for the Liberation of Palestine* (Leiden, The Netherlands: Hotei Publishing, 2003).

The role of the PLO has changed in reaction to the post-Lebanon period. The reality of the situation is that both Israel and the Palestinians have a time bomb on their hands. Extremist elements on both fronts are becoming more vocal, and acts of terrorism are bound to increase within the "occupied territories" and on the international scene. On April 14, 1987, in an unprecedented meeting between Arafat and rival guerrilla groups, a bid was made to unite the once-powerful PLO. However, that effort to unify the PLO failed. Rejectionist groups, such as the PFLP's George Habash, after four years of internal strife, have once again joined with Arafat in the armed struggle against Israel. Table 4.2 outlines the chronology of historical events in the continuing conflict between Israel, the Palestinians, and surrounding Arab nations. However, much has changed since 1987 and the first intifada.

TABLE 4.2   Chronology of Significant Events

A.D. 70	Destruction of the second Temple: Jewish Diaspora
Sixth century	After death of Prophet Muhammad, Arabs conquer Palestine
1897	First Zionist Congress held in Switzerland
1917	Palestine becomes a British mandate: Balfour Declaration
1929	Jewish agency established: Haganah formed
1937	British Peel Commission proposes partition of Palestine
1947	UN recommends partition of Palestine
1948	State of Israel is created; first Palestine war
1950–1955	Peace fails: border violence, blockade, boycott, and isolation of Israel
1956	Second Palestine War: Suez War
1957	Arafat forms al Fatah and the Palestine Liberation Movement
1964	PLO established
1967	Third Arab–Israeli war: June War; War of the Setback; Israel expands territory; UN Security Council Resolution 242
1968–1970	Escalation of terrorism by PFLP and Fatah; first terrorist skyjacking; Black September formed; War of Attrition, Fourth Arab-Israeli conflict
1972	Munich Olympic massacre by Black September; Israeli retaliation
1973	Fifth Arab–Israeli war: Yom Kippur War; War of Ramadan
1974	Arafat addresses UN General Assembly and PLO given observer status at UN
1975	Civil war breaks out in Lebanon: Damour destroyed by Saiqa
1976	Entebbe hijacking/Israeli counterterrorist strike
1978	Bus incident: thirty killed by PDFLP; Israel retaliates and invades Lebanon
1980	Camp David peace talks; Israel and Egypt
1981	Annexation of Golan; Reagan Peace Plan; Fez Peace Plan
1982	Israeli occupation ends in Sinai; Sixth war –invasion of Lebanon and the dispersion of PLO; massacre at Sabra and Shatila
1983–1984	Atrocities continue in Lebanon; PLO internal struggle; terror bombings of multinational force

TABLE 4.2   Continued

1985	Terror attacks at Rome and Vienna Airports by Abu Nidal faction; seajacking of *Achille Lauro* by Abu Abbas faction; Israeli bombing of PLO headquarters in Tunisia
1986	U.S. bombing of PLO-supported terrorist training centers in Libya
1987	PLO reconciliation
1988	Arafat renounces terrorism and declares Palestinian statehood
1990	Iraq invades Kuwait; Iraq will withdraw from Kuwait if Israel withdraws from occupied territories
1991	Gulf War ends; Palestinians (400,000) flee Kuwait; Madrid Peace Conference
1992	Hamas and Islamic Jihad deported to Lebanon; Rabin elected prime minister of Israel
1993	Oslo Accords signed in Washington, DC, between Israel and PLO
1994	Baruch Goldstein massacres twenty-nine Palestinian Muslims praying in Hebron Mosque; Hamas begins suicide-bombing campaign
1995	Rabin assassinated by right-wing Israeli Jew
1996	Arafat elected "president" of the PA; Ayyash killed by Israelis; triggers new wave of suicide bombings; Hizballah and Israel exchange fire on Lebanese border; Israel opens tunnel under Temple Mount; sparks first gun battles between Israelis and Palestinians
1997	Netanyahu (prime minister) continues building new Israeli settlements on West Bank
1999	Barak elected prime minister of Israel and continues peace talks with Arafat
2000	IDF withdraws from Southern Lebanon; Sharon visits Al Aqsa mosque, igniting the second intifada
2001	Sharon elected prime minister; Bush supports Palestinian statehood; IDF attacks PA compound and Ramallah
2002	IDF captures arms shipment from Iran bound for PA; Bush accuses Arafat of supporting terrorism; 200 Israeli reservists refuse to serve in occupied territories
2003	Suicide bombings continue; stalled peace talks revived when United States introduces "Road Map" to peace; Hamas and Palestinian Islamic Jihad reject any peace proposals
2004	International Court of Justice (ICJ) rules Israeli security fence must be torn down; Yassar Arafat dies; Yassin Rantessi (Hamas) and Khalil assassinated by Israelis
2005	Mahmoud Abbas elected PA President, Sharm El Sheikh Conference; Israel pulls out of Gaza and four West Bank cities
2006	Hamas upsets Fatah/PLO in Palestinian elections; Olmert elected PM of Israel; Israel versus Hizballah—seventh war
2007	Palestinian Unity Agreement—Hamas and Fatah agree to share power; later, Hamas ousts Fatah from Gaza in bloody coup; joint Israeli-Palestinian Declaration; Israel destroys Syrian nuclear structure
2008–2009	President Bush visits Middle East; Mughniyah killed by car bomb; IDF vs. Hamas—Gaza war (eighth war); Hamas rockets continue to strike Israeli cities

PALESTINIAN AUTHORITY

On January 1, 1996, in a democratic election, the Palestinian communities on the West Bank and the Gaza Strip chose their first popularly selected government known as the Palestinian Authority. The **Palestinian Authority** is an autonomous government established after the **Oslo Peace Process**. The Oslo Peace Accords granted Palestinians control of Gaza and a limited area of the West Bank. The Accords, signed in Washington, D.C., in September 1993, were another attempt to partition Palestine into an Arab and Jewish sate. The Palestinian voters elected an eighty-eight-member Palestinian Council (PC) and the chairman of the executive authority. The Palestinian Authority also has a cabinet of thirty ministers appointed by the president. After recognition by Israel of the PLO as the legitimate representatives of the Palestinian people, the PLO evolved into the Palestinian Authority. Yasir Arafat, the chairman of the PLO, was elected "president" of the Palestinian Authority with overwhelming public support.

The Fatah faction of the PLO continues to dominate the affairs of the Palestinian Authority. Most senior Palestinian government officials are in fact members of Arafat's Fatah organization. The PLO is still the main umbrella organization of the Palestinian national movement. Like the PLO, Arafat continued to dominate the affairs of the Palestinian Authority until his death (from natural causes) in 2004. La Guardia maintains that Arafat ruled the Palestinian Authority like a fiefdom, controlling all the finances, travel requests, and patronage.[41] After the start of the al Aqsa intifada, Arafat was granted even more power.

On September 28, 2000, the eve of the Jewish New Year (Rosh Hashanah), the leader of the Israeli opposition party (Likud), Ariel Sharon, visited the Temple Mount in Jerusalem. Flanked by an entourage of security officers, Sharon claimed he had a right to visit Temple Mount. Temple Mount contains the remains of the Second Jewish Temple, the holiest structure in Judaism. Unfortunately, the al Aqsa mosque, the third holiest site in Islam, is built on top of the remains of the Second Temple. The al Aqsa mosque is the site where Prophet Muhammad reportedly ascended into heaven. The visit by Sharon sparked a spontaneous Palestinian riot that quickly spread through the West Bank, Gaza, and among Israeli Arabs. Since then, the Palestinians have called their revolt the al Aqsa intifada, or uprising. The al Aqsa intifada quickly became a sequel to the first intifada that lasted from 1988 to 1992.

The al Aqsa intifada caused Arafat to declare a state of emergency to make arrests, prohibit demonstrations, and take action against organizations engaged in terrorism. Arafat had arrested hundreds of Hamas and Islamic Jihad extremists. Initially, Palestinian Authority security police routinely patrolled together with IDF and worked with Israeli intelligence officers to disrupt the terrorist activities of Hamas and Islamic Jihad. However, the Palestinian Authority has made little progress in preventing terrorism or unifying Gaza and West Bank cities under Palestinian Authority control. In recent years, the Palestinian Authority has been accused by Hamas of corruption, lack of accountability, waste of public funds, and a lack of public trust. The main challenge to the Palestinian Authority comes from Hamas and Islamic Jihad.

HAMAS AND ISLAMIC JIHAD

Hamas is a uniquely Palestinian Islamic fundamentalist movement inspired by the tactics and rhetoric of Hizballah. Hamas was formed during the early stages of the first intifada in 1987. The basic goals of Hamas are to destroy Israel, the PLO, and the peace process with Israel. Hamas' favorite attack strategy is the suicide bombing of Israeli "soft" civilian targets. Hamas

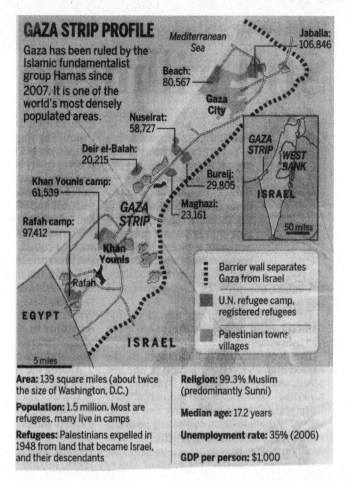

GAZA STRIP PROFILE

Gaza has been ruled by the Islamic fundamentalist group Hamas since 2007. It is one of the world's most densely populated areas.

Mediterranean Sea

Jabalia: 106,846

Beach: 80,567

Gaza City

Nuseirat: 58,727

Deir el-Balah: 20,215

Khan Younis camp: 61,539

Rafah camp: 97,412

GAZA STRIP

Bureij: 29,805

Maghazi: 23,161

Khan Younis

Rafah

EGYPT

GAZA STRIP   WEST BANK

ISRAEL

50 miles

ISRAEL

5 miles

▮▮▮ Barrier wall separates Gaza from Israel

▮ U.N. refugee camp, registered refugees

▮ Palestinian towns villages

Area: 139 square miles (about twice the size of Washington, D.C.)

Population: 1.5 million. Most are refugees, many live in camps

Refugees: Palestinians expelled in 1948 from land that became Israel, and their descendants

Religion: 99.3% Muslim (predominantly Sunni)

Median age: 17.2 years

Unemployment rate: 35% (2006)

GDP per person: $1,000

FIGURE 4.4   Gaza Strip Profile—Eighth War, December 2008 to January 2009; Israeli Defense Forces versus Hamas. (CIA World Factbook) http://www.cia.gov/library/publications/the-world-factbook/geos/gz.html.

and Islamic Jihad began to bomb Israeli civilian targets after the Hebron massacre by Baruch Goldstein. Since 1994, Hamas and Islamic Jihad have carried out over one hundred suicide bombings. The suicide bombers have targeted buses in major Israeli cities as well as cafés, shopping malls, and other "soft" civilian targets. The honor of dying for Palestine and the certainty of going to Paradise convinced young Palestinian men and some women to volunteer to become martyrs. The Israel assassination of Yihya Ayyash, known as "the Engineer" for his bomb-making skills, also precipitated a series of deadly suicide bombings, killing more than sixty Israelis and injuring hundreds. Ayyash was the first hero of the military wing of Hamas. Tactically, the assassination of Ayyash was a brilliant operation for Israel, but in many ways it was a strategic blunder.[42]

Hamas is an acronym for *Harakat al-Muqawama al-Islamiyya*, or the Islamic Resistance Movement. Hamas is also the Arabic word for "zeal or enthusiasm." Hamas believes the only way of liberating Palestine from the Israeli Zionists is by jihad or holy war. The central tenet of Hamas

FIGURE 4.5 Suicide bus bombing in Jerusalem that killed nineteen people and injured seventy-four others on June 18, 2002. The bus carried many students on their way to school. Hamas claimed responsibility for the suicide attack. (AP/Wide World Photos)

is to establish an Islamic state in *all* of pre-1948 Palestine. Hamas insists that international conferences and peace initiatives are a waste of time. According to Hamas, the only way to recover Palestine from the Jewish Zionists is by armed struggle, terrorism, and jihad. Hamas receives funding from Iran, wealthy Gulf Arab states, and Palestinian expatriates, and it conducts fundraising and propaganda activities in the United States, Canada, and Western Europe. Contributions go to charitable activities for destitute Palestinian families served by Hamas' network of social service agencies. Hamas draws much of its support from its network of schools, nurseries, clinics, and mosques. The United States or Americans have not been directly targeted by Hamas, although some Americans have been victims of suicide bombers in Israel. Hamas presents itself as the group that inspired the first intifada in 1987 and as the direct heir of Sheikh Izz al-Din al-Qassam, the founder of the first armed Palestinian resistance in the 1930s.[43]

The Izz al-Din al-Qassam is the military wing of Hamas. In its first stages of operation, the Izz al-Din al-Qassam carried out kidnappings and executions of Palestinians suspected of collaborating with Israel. Izz al-Din al-Qassam is responsible for most of the serious attacks, including suicide bombings, assaults on Israeli settlements, the launching of Qassam rockets, and "guerrilla" warfare, against Israel since early 1992. Hamas' charter declares that Israel must be destroyed, and there is no compromise with Israel for a single inch of Palestinian territory.[44]

For over forty years, the Palestinians were encouraged by the United States, the European Union (EU), and Israel to hold free and democratic elections. In January 2006, they finally held free elections and the result was totally unexpected. Instead of the moderate PLO/Fatah faction winning, it was the Islamist terrorist group Hamas that was proclaimed the winner. In short, a terrorist group had won the right to rule the Palestinian Authority while still refusing to recognize the right of Israel to exist.[45]

The shock of the Hamas victory to the PLO/Fatah was considerable. It was well known in the Palestinian community that the PLO/Fatah had been defeated in the election because corrupt and incompetent officials dominated the PLO. The Palestinians apparently wanted new leadership and thus supported Hamas candidates. The shock to the United States, Israel, and the EU was probably even greater. The United States and the EU regarded Hamas as a terrorist organization. As a result, it was out of the question for the United States or the EU to have diplomatic relations with a Hamas-led Palestinian government. In fact, Hamas proclaimed that there will be no peace with Israel—"We are adhering to the liberation of Palestine and Jerusalem."[46]

To complicate the situation even further, a power struggle between Hamas and Fatah erupted into internecine warfare in Gaza. On June 14, 2007, after ten days of heavy fighting between Hamas and Fatah, Hamas overran the last stronghold of Fatah in Gaza and declared victory. The Palestinians were once again fighting among themselves, while Israel watched from the sidelines. Hamas has been in firm control of Gaza since Israel pulled its military forces out of Gaza in 2005 and Fatah retreated to the West Bank in 2007. Gaza is currently ruled by Hamas and the West Bank by Fatah. Palestinians are now divided into two distinct entities ruled by two different political ideologies; the Islamist extremist Hamas and the nationalist Fatah.

The future for the establishment of a Palestinian state in Gaza and the West Bank and the reopening of peace talks with Israel does not look promising. However, from the Israeli perspective, the current political and territorial division of Hamas and Fatah may make it easier for Israel to control the two competing "terrorist" factions. In fact, Israel, the United States, and the EU have planned a strategy to isolate and boycott Hamas with the objective of forcing Hamas to the negotiating table and renounce the use of terrorism.[47] This international isolation of Hamas, however, has pushed it closer into the orbit of Iran and Syria. According to Schanzer, Iran provides the political, spiritual, and economic backing for Hamas, along with training Hamas fighters to attack both Fatah and Israelis.[48] Hamas continues to send suicide bombers and launch Qassam rockets into Israel. In sum, it has accomplished two of its original objectives: the peace process has been destroyed and the PLO/Fatah organization has been left ineffective. The third objective of Hamas calls for the destruction of Israel and the extermination of the Jewish people. How, then, can Israel, the United States, and the EU engage in negotiations with a terrorist group that supports genocide? In the end, the conflict between Hamas and Israel will continue to fester, doing further damage to the Middle East peace process.

The conflict between Israel and Hamas erupted into a full-scale war on December 27, 2008, with a devastating series of Israeli air strikes. Flying at 28,000 feet, the Israelis destroyed over one hundred Hamas targets, including a Hamas police graduation ceremony that killed dozens of police recruits. In the opening days of the air attacks, Israel reported that over two hundred Hamas commanders and fighters were killed. Dozens of Hamas government buildings and missile launch sites were also destroyed. The Israelis called the Gaza war "**Operation Cast Lead**," which hoped to achieve three goals. The Israelis wanted to destroy Hamas' ammunition depots, rocket-launching sites, and a tunnel system between Egypt and Gaza used for smuggling weapons and explosives.[49]

Beginning in 2005, when Israel pulled its military and settlements out of the Gaza Strip, Hamas began firing a barrage of rockets and missiles into Israel, killing and wounding dozens of Israeli citizens. The rocket fire and mortar shelling by Hamas and other Palestinian terrorist groups became the major terrorist threat to Israeli communities. Gradually, the Hamas rockets became more sophisticated and deadly, putting nearly 1 million Israeli civilians within range of the rockets. Hamas had stopped their terrorist suicide-bombing campaign in favor of heightening fear in Israeli communities by the indiscriminate nature of missile attacks.

Israel tried several options to put pressure on Hamas to stop the rocket and missile attacks, including economic sanctions, border controls, a security barrier that separates Gaza from Israel (see Figure 4.4), targeted attacks against Hamas leaders, and ground incursions. Each of these generally acceptable strategies did not stop or even show a decline in the escalating missile attacks on Israeli civilian populations. Hamas is committed to the utter destruction of Israel and the Jewish people. What choice did Israel have to stop the rocket and missile attacks? No democracy in the world would tolerate the daily barrage of missiles being fired at its cities without taking action.[50]

On January 3, 2009, after eight days of bombing, the Israeli government sent ground troops into Gaza on a search and destroy mission: search for missile-launching sites and destroy Hamas. Hamas had a military force of approximately 20,000 well-trained men who were supported financially by Iran, Hizballah, and Syria. The Israeli tanks and ground forces quickly drove through Gaza, destroying missile-launching sites and overwhelming Hamas fighters. Many Hamas fighters sought refuge among the civilian population of Gaza. A deliberate strategy of Hamas was the use of Gaza citizens as human shields. Approximately 1,300 Palestinians, many of them children, were killed. The Israelis estimate that over 600 Hamas fighters and political leaders were killed. However, the Israelis did not destroy Hamas or all the missile-launching sites. In fact, while the fighting was going on in Gaza, Hamas continued to launch rockets and missiles toward Israeli cities. After twenty-two days of fighting, Israel declared a cease-fire that was followed by Hamas calling for a cease-fire. The results of the Gaza war were 1,300 Palestinians killed, approximately 1,400 rocket and missile sites destroyed, and $2 billion in property damage. On the Israeli side, thirteen Israelis were killed: ten soldiers and three civilians.[51]

There is little doubt that Hamas, like Hizballah, may emerge stronger from this one-sided war. In whatever manner Israel responds to Hamas terrorism, Hamas wins. If Israel does nothing, Hamas taunts the Israeli government as being weak. If Israel responds to the threat of Hamas terrorism, as they did in the Gaza war, Israel is accused of a "disproportionate" response. Most Israelis are under no illusion that Hamas has been eliminated. Israelis know that future wars with the terrorist Hamas are inevitable. However, they do realize that on the horizon looms the ultimate terrorist threat—a nuclear Iran.[52]

Likewise, the Palestinian Islamic Jihad (PIJ) views the "Zionist Jewish entity" as the main enemy of Islam and vows to destroy Israel by force. Unlike Hamas or Fatah, the PIJ does not participate in the political process. The PIJ rejects any two-state solution to the Palestine problem in which Israel and Palestine coexist. Palestinian students founded the PIJ after a split with the Palestinian Muslim Brotherhood in Gaza in 1979. The founders of the PIJ were inspired by the successful Islamic revolution in Iran in 1979. The ideology of the PIJ fosters the liberation of Palestine as a precondition for the unification of the Arab and Muslim world. In other words, the jihad for the liberation of Palestine by various Islamic movements around the world is the first step toward the greater jihad and the establishment of one united Islamic community. Not only did the PIJ consider the Iranian revolution as a model for worldwide jihad, they also accepted the principle of religious Islamic clergy leading their movement.

The PIJ and the EIJ (Egyptian Islamic Jihad) have carried out joint terrorist attacks against Egyptian targets and Israeli targets in the Gaza. One such attack was the assassination of Egyptian President Anwar Sadat in October 1981. In the eyes of the PIJ, the concept of jihad, or struggle, is to be taken literally. The true follower of Islam must use any means available to achieve a just Islamic society. Trickery, deceit, violence, and terrorism are acceptable options available to the jihad soldier. The PIJ has carried out dozens of suicide bombing attacks in Israel. Between 1995 and 2008, PIJ suicide-bombing attacks have claimed the lives of over 160 Israelis.[53] Israeli intelligence reports that Hamas and PIJ have also coordinated simultaneous suicide-bombing attacks. For example, in a combined attack on March 4, 1996, a suicide bomber detonated a 20-kilogram nail bomb in Jerusalem, killing thirteen Israeli civilians. In another joint attack, two consecutive bombs exploded near Netanya, Israel, killing twenty Israeli soldiers while they were awaiting transportation to their military base.[54] Like Hamas, the PIJ has never struck directly at the United States. The combined terrorist activities of Hamas and the PIJ form a very dangerous and determined fundamentalist Islamic terrorist association striving to destroy the State of Israel. Another group that has vowed to destroy Israel is the al Aqsa Martyrs Brigades.

AL AQSA MARTYRS BRIGADES

The **al Aqsa Martyrs Brigades** was created from Arafat's Fatah movement and has been one of the driving forces behind the second intifada. The al Aqsa Martyrs Brigades derives its name from the al Aqsa mosque located atop the contested holy site in Jerusalem known to the Arabs as the Noble Sanctuary and to the Jews as Temple Mount. Muslims believe that Prophet Muhammad ascended into heaven on a white horse from the al Aqsa Mosque. The Brigades appeared on the scene shortly after the outbreak of the al Aqsa intifada in late September 2000. Israeli intelligence services claim that the Brigades is a branch of the **Tanzim**[55] ("organization" in Arabic). The Tanzim is also associated with Arafat's Fatah Movement. The Brigades ideology is firmly rooted in Palestinian nationalism, not Islamic fundamentalism, and they carry out the same type of suicide bombings as Hamas and Islamic Jihad. The Brigades were the first to use female suicide bombers. The first documented case of a female suicide bomber occurred on February 18, 2002, when a young Palestinian woman approached an Israeli checkpoint and detonated explosives strapped to her body.[56]

Like Hamas and the PIJ, the Brigades were inspired by the violence and terrorism of Hizballah. The leadership of the Brigades incorrectly assumed they could emulate the strategy of Hizballah in forcing Israel to withdraw from South Lebanon by inflicting many casualties on Israel. Hamas, PIJ, and the Brigades answered Fatah's call for "rivers of blood in the streets of Tel Aviv." Hizballah succeeded because it had a clear objective, its fighters were well disciplined, and it concentrated mainly on Israeli military targets rather than random suicide bombings. In contrast, the al Aqsa Brigades, as well as Hamas and PIJ, have failed to draw a distinction between military and civilian targets, or between occupied territories and the state of Israel. They choose "soft" targets such as civilians in Israel and Israeli settlers on the West Bank. Al Aqsa stages the majority of their suicide bombings in Israel. Suicide bombings in Israel only strengthen the resolve of the Israelis to keep fighting the Palestinians, since backing down would only make it easier for suicide bombers to attack Israel. The Brigades have outscored the PIJ and Hamas, both in the number and deadliness of its suicide attacks.[57]

To date, the al Aqsa Martyrs Brigades has taken credit for over 300 terrorist attacks in which Israeli citizens have been killed and injured. In addition to suicide bombings, the Brigades have carried out sniper attacks, car bombings, hostage takings, stabbings, and assaults on Jewish settlements. Some examples follow: shooting spree at a kibbutz in Northern Israel that killed seven Israelis, including three children; suicide bombing in a Jerusalem café that killed twenty-one and wounded more than fifty people; sniper attack on an Israeli army checkpoint that killed ten Israeli soldiers. Al Aqsa attacks became even more deadly after it is believed the Israelis assassinated Raed Karmi, the West Bank leader of the Brigades, on January 14, 2002. Al Aqsa announced it would heighten its suicide-bombing campaign to avenge the death of Karmi.[58] In January 2008, the Brigades joined with Hamas and the PIJ in launching Qassam rockets into Israel from Gaza. Hamas, the PIJ, and al Aqsa have launched over three thousand rockets and mortar shells into Israel between February 2006 and December 2008.

Israel has responded to the al Aqsa intifada by establishing a policy of preventive action. The policy has become known as "targeted assassinations." Israel has used helicopter gunships, car bombs, tanks, and snipers to kill dozens of Palestinian guerrillas/terrorists. The Israelis maintain that the most efficient way of fighting "terrorism" is to decapitate the leadership and destroy the command structure of terrorist organizations by targeting specific terrorist leaders who are actively involved in planning or coordinating terrorist attacks and who are beyond the reach of the law. Critics of the targeted assassination policy state that the assassinations often led to Palestinian revenge attacks and aggravate the cycle of violence. In sum, the tactics of al Aqsa and the second intifada have evolved into a second war of attrition between Israelis and Palestinians. The al Aqsa Martyrs Brigades, Hamas, and the PIJ are all on the U.S. State Department's list of designated Foreign Terrorist Organizations. At the top of that list is the most dangerous international terrorist group, al Qaeda. This next section examines the role of al Qaeda in motivating terrorism and extremist religious beliefs.

AL QAEDA

Gunaratna states that **al Qaeda** is the first multinational terrorist organization of the twenty-first century, and it presents the world with a new type of terrorist threat. Since the introduction of contemporary terrorism by Palestine nationalists, no groups have emerged resembling al Qaeda—a worldwide terrorist movement that threatens global stability. Al Qaeda's most spectacular terrorist attack was the suicide assault on the World Trade Center and the Pentagon. The method of attack represented a combination of the familiar tactic of skyjacking and the newest terrorist attack method of suicide bombing. By perpetrating one of history's greatest massacres on September 11, 2001, al Qaeda demonstrated the magnitude of the escalating threat and the sophistication of its planning.[59]

On September 11, 2001, four separate teams of terrorists, nineteen men in all, hijacked four airplanes. At 7:58 A.M., United Airlines Flight 175 left Boston's Logan Airport bound for Los Angeles. The hijackers clearly knew that the flight would take them within 50 miles of Manhattan, close enough to use the Twin Towers of the World Trade Center as a visual landmark. Flight 175 struck the South Tower of the World Trade Center about 9:05 A.M. American Airlines Flight 11 took off from Logan Airport just after UAL 175 at 7:59 A.M., also en route to Los Angeles International Airport. About 50 miles into New York State, Flight 11 abruptly turned south and followed the Hudson River Valley down to New York City. Flight 11 impacted the North Tower of the World Trade Center at 8:45 A.M. United Airlines Flight 93 left Newark International Airport at 8:01 A.M. en route to San Francisco. Just before reaching the outskirts of Cleveland, Ohio, Flight 93 suddenly made a 180-degree turn and headed back southeast toward Pittsburgh. Flight 93 crashed nose-first in an empty field about 80 miles from Pittsburgh at 10:10 A.M. The passengers of Flight 93 were attempting to regain control of the plane from the hijackers when it crashed, killing all aboard. The destination of Flight 93 apparently was either the White House or the U.S. Capitol building. At 8:10 A.M., American Airlines Flight 77 took off from Dulles International Airport for Los Angeles. Flight 77 crashed into the ground next to the west side of the Pentagon at 9:40 A.M. Witnesses stated that Flight 77 was in a dive when it hit the Pentagon, causing the deaths of 189 people.[60]

We probably will never know exactly how the hijackers seized control of the aircraft. What we do know is that the hijackers were armed with pepper spray, box cutters, and small knives, and claimed they had smuggled bombs on board the planes. At that time, passengers were allowed to carry small knives on commercial aircraft. Apparently, some passengers and crew had

FIGURE 4.6 World Trade Center South Tower burst into flames after being struck by hijacked United Airlines Flight 15 as the North Tower burns following an earlier attack by a hijacked airliner in New York City on 9/11. (Corbis/Reuters)

their throats slit to intimidate the other passengers/hostages. Some of the hijackers had trained in the use of martial arts, while others trained as pilots and flew the planes. All received their training at U.S. flight schools and workout facilities. Each hijacked aircraft had five suicidal hijackers, with the exception of Flight 93, which had four. Apparently one of the hijackers missed the flight. The alleged twentieth hijacker, **Zakarias Moussaoui**, was arrested for visa violations before the September 11 attacks.

In August 2001, the owner of a flight school in Minnesota was perplexed by a strange request by a man who wanted to enroll in his flight school. The request was from Zackarias Moussaoui, who wanted to learn to steer a commercial jet, but not how to take off and land. He was prepared to pay in cash the $8,000 fee for attending the flight school. Between August 13 and August 15, 2001, Moussaoui attended the Pan Am Intenational Flight Academy in Minneapolis for simulator training on the Boeing 747. Moussaoui also made inquiries about starting a crop dusting company. The owner of the flight school thought Moussaoui's requests were quite unusual, and notified the FBI. The police later discovered that Moussaoui was in contact with Islamic extremist groups in Pakistan and al Qaeda in Afghanistan. On December 11, 2001, Moussaoui was indicted by the grand jury for committing a range of terrorist offenses. Moussaoui told the FBI that he was simply interested in learning to fly. Moussaoui was the only person to be specifically charged with the September 11 attacks.[61] After further investigation, in February 2008, the U.S. government charged six Guantanamo detainees with a variety of criminal offenses related to the 9/11 attacks.

In sum, all the hijacked flights took off within a twelve-minute time span. All were fully fueled for a transcontinental flight with a low number of passengers. There is no doubt that the hijackers carefully surveyed the hijacked flights. The fact that the hijackers worked as a team probably intimidated the surprised passengers.

The al Qaeda terrorist achieved full tactical and operational surprise. The 9/11 al Qaeda terrorists were able to develop their tactical plans, infiltrate the United States, distribute money, and, once inside the United States, coordinate their forces, all without detection by the U.S. intelligence community. Fundamentally, the 9/11 attack was a low-tech terrorist assault. The 9/11 attackers displayed more ingenuity than technological know-how. Al Qaeda demonstrated that mass casualty terrorist attacks can be carried out without resorting to biological, chemical, or improvised nuclear weapons. To better understand the motives behind the 9/11 attacks, we must answer the question, "What is al Qaeda?"

Al Qaeda ("the base" or "the base of Allah's support") was founded by Osama bin Laden and other extremist Muslim fundamentalists in the early 1980s to support the war effort in Afghanistan against the former Soviet Union, which invaded Afghanistan in December 1979. By 1989, the Afghanistan mujahedin (an alliance of Muslim fighters) had defeated the Soviet Union. The victory of the mujahedin in Afghanistan eventually led to the jihad movement organized by Osama bin Laden. The now-trained mujahedin fighters left Afghanistan, returning to their own countries with a desire to continue the jihad.

From 1989 to 1991 al Qaeda was headquartered in Afghanistan and Pakistan. In late 1991, the leadership of al Qaeda, including Osama bin Laden, relocated to the Sudan. While in the Sudan, Osama bin Laden continued to develop the financial and organizational structure of al Qaeda. Then, in 1996, al Qaeda left Sudan and once again relocated to Afghanistan, where they now had the support of the **Taliban** (religious students), the ruling party in Afghanistan. The goal of the Taliban was to create the perfect Islamic state. The goal of al Qaeda and Osama bin Laden was to create a worldwide Islamic revolution. The two groups consolidated their forces, developing training facilities and logistics, and sharing financial resources, and began to export their brand of Islamic extremism. All members of al Qaeda pledged an oath of allegiance or *bayat* to Osama bin Laden and al Qaeda. Emboldened by the defeat of the Soviet Union, al Qaeda began to focus its attentions toward the United States, whom Osama bin Laden referred to as the "King of Satan."[62]

Al Qaeda and bin Laden violently opposed the United States for several reasons. First, the United States was regarded as an *infidel* because it was governed by principles that supported the evil and decadence of society. Second, the United States was seen as supporting other *infidel* governments and institutions, particularly Saudi Arabia, Egypt, and Israel. Third, al Qaeda opposed the United States and the United Nations for the preemptive invasion of Iraq by the United States and the coalition forces. Fourth, the principle objective of al Qaeda was to expel U.S. military forces from Saudi Arabia and the Arabian Peninsula. Bin Laden viewed the buildup of U.S. forces in the Middle East as a prelude to an American occupation of Islamic countries. Fifth, al Qaeda supported the Palestinian resistance movement and the *intifada* to recover Islamic holy sites in Palestine and to destroy the state of Israel.

While bin Laden and al Qaeda are genuinely angered by what they regard as the decadent West, the theft of Arab oil, the U.S. support of corrupt Arab governments, and the U.S. military presence on Arab lands, they are also hostile to the United States for supporting Israel and the harsh treatment of the Palestinians by the Israelis. Bin Laden has been a proponent of the Palestinian cause since he was a young man. According to Scheuer, a CIA intelligence officer, al Qaeda and bin Laden have long supported the Palestinians and have hostile attitudes toward the United States for its unconditional support of Israel.[63]

Moreover, the 9/11 Commission confirmed that bin Laden and key al Qaeda members were motivated both by their hatred for Israel and by U.S. support for Israel. For example, the Commission noted that bin Laden tried to reschedule the 9/11 attacks to the fall of 2000 after Israeli political leader Ariel Sharon provoked a riot between Israeli police and Palestinians at the Temple Mount. The Commission maintains that bin Laden wanted to punish the United States for supporting Sharon and Israel. The Commission also states that the Palestine Question primarily inspired Khalid Sheikh Mohammed, whom it describes as "the principal architect of the 9/11 attacks." By his own account, Khalid Sheikh Mohammed's hatred toward the United States stemmed from his violent disagreement over U.S. foreign policy favoring Israel.[64]

By 1992, al Qaeda began to issue *fatwahs* that U.S. military forces stationed on the Arabian Peninsula must be attacked and driven from Arabia. In fact, bin Laden's very first fatwah, released in December 1994, directly addressed the Palestinian issue. Bin Laden refers explicitly to Muslim blood being spilled in Palestine and Iraq and blames it all on an American–Israeli conspiracy. A *fatwah* is a religious ruling that sanctions the use of violence and jihad against *infidels*; namely, the United States and Israel. The role of clerical authority in sanctioning terrorists' operations has always been critical to al Qaeda.[65]

Beginning around 1992, bin Laden, working together with members of the *fatwah* committee of al Qaeda, disseminated fatwahs to members and associates of al Qaeda that the U.S. military forces stationed on the Arabian Peninsula and in Somalia should be attacked. Similarly, al Qaeda clerics and Osama bin Laden have supported and given their blessing to the use of suicide attacks, which are forbidden by Islamic law. On August 23, 1996, al Qaeda issued a declaration of jihad against the Americans occupying the land of the two holy mosques to expel the heretics from the Arabia Peninsula. Then, on February 23, 1998, bin Laden endorsed a fatwah under the heading of the "International Islamic Front for Jihad on the Jews and Crusaders." The fatwah stated that Muslims should kill Americans, including civilians, anywhere in the world where they can be found. Bin Laden, on or about May 29,

1998, endorsed the development of weapons of mass destruction to terrorize the enemies of God; that is, the United States and Israel. In June 1999, bin Laden issued further threats, stating in an interview on Arabic-language television that all American males should be killed. After the 9/11 attacks, bin Laden praised the suicide bombers and vowed that the United States would not enjoy security until infidel armies leave the Arabian Peninsula and the United States stops supporting Israel. Then, on October 10, 2001, al Qaeda issued another fatwah that all Muslims had a sacred duty to attack U.S. targets around the world. Bin Laden and al Qaeda have proclaimed dozens of fatwahs since 1994, calling for deaths of Americans and Israelis.

Since the "fatwah programs," lethal attacks officially attributed to al Qaeda are included in Table 4.3, which identifies only a small number of al Qaeda attacks. For a complete list of al Qaeda attacks, see http://www.historycommons.org/timelines.

TABLE 4.3   Terrorist Attacks Linked to Osama bin Laden and al Qaeda

Attributed to al Qaeda	
1992	Bombed hotel in Yemen housing U.S. troops
1993	Bombed World Trade Center
1993	Somalia fire fight; eighteen U.S. soldiers killed by al Qaeda–trained extremists
1995	Bombed National Guard building in Riyadh, Saudi Arabia; five U.S. soldiers killed
1996	Bombed U.S. military housing known as Khobar Towers in Dharan, Saudi Arabia; nineteen Americans killed
1998	Suicide bombings of U.S. embassies in Nairobi and Dar es Salaam, East Africa; 230+ killed, over 5,000 injured
1999	Planned Millennium Bombing attacks in Jordan and Los Angeles airport; prevented by arrests
2000	Suicide bombing of the destroyer, U.S.S. Cole, in Aden, Yemen; seventeen sailors killed, thirty-nine injured
2001	Suicide bombing of World Trade Center and Pentagon; 3,000 killed
2003	Multiple suicide bombings in Morocco; thirty-two killed at five locations
2003	Multiple suicide bombings in Saudi Arabia; forty killed
2004	Shooting rampage in Saudi Arabia; twenty-two people killed; coordinated car bomb attacks in Egypt; 40 killed and 182 wounded U.S. consulate in Jedda attacked with bombs and gunfire; nine killed, fifteen wounded
2005	Coordinated bombings in London; 52 killed, 700 injured Coordinated bombings Sham el Sheikh; 88 killed, 400 wounded Coordinated suicide bombing attack in Amman; 63 killed, 100 wounded Suicide bombers attack Saudi Arabia oil facility; four killed, seven injured
2006	Islamic Maghreb in coordinated bombing attacks kill 20, wound 100 in Algeria
2007	Algeria sustains dozens of suicide and car bombings that kill 50 and wound over 200
	Attempted assassination of Benazir Bhutto and suicide bomb that kills twenty-four and wounds fifty

TABLE 4.3   Continued

	Assassination of Benazir Bhutto in Pakistan; al Qaeda's al Zawahiri claims credit; ensuing riots kill twenty-six and wound hundreds
2008	Suicide attacks in Algeria killed fifty-five and wounded hundreds
	Car bomb and rocket attack on U.S. embassy in Yemen, killing sixteen; twenty-five suspects (al Qaeda) arrested

Suspected by al Qaeda—Pre-9/11

1995 & 1998	Attempted assassinations of President Mubarak of Egypt
1995	Yousef and Abu Sayyaf plan to blow up twelve U.S. passenger jets, assassinate Pope John Paul II, and bomb CIA headquarters in Virginia; plot uncovered by police
1995	Conspiracy to bomb tunnels and public buildings in New York City; plot uncovered by police
1995	Suicide bombing of Egyptian embassy in Pakistan; eighteen killed, eighty injured
1997	Suicide shooting spree in Luxor, Egypt, by Egyptian Islamic Jihad; sixty-two killed
1999	Skyjacking India Airlines by HUM, a Kashmiri group

Suspected by al Qaeda—Post-9/11

April 2002	Suicide attack on an ancient synagogue in Tunisia; twelve German tourists killed—Islamic Army claimed credit for attack
May 2002	Suicide bombing of bus in Karachi killing eleven French engineers—suspect al Qaeda-affiliated group Jaish-e-Mohammad (JEM)
June 2002	Arrest of Jose Padilla for plotting a "dirty bomb" attack in United States
June 2002	Suicide bombing of U.S. Consulate in Karachi; 10+ killed—suspect al Qaeda-affiliated group HUM
September 2002	Al Qaeda car bomb kills 22+ in Kabul in attempt to assassinate Afghani President Karzai
September 2002	Six members of al Qaeda cell arrested in Buffalo, New York
October 2002	Assassination of U.S. Diplomat Lawrence Foley in Jordan; two members of al Qaeda confessed
October 2002	Suicide bombing of French oil tanker in Yemen; same M.O. as attack on U.S.S. Cole
October 2002	Suicide bombing in Bali, Indonesia by Jemaah Islamiya; 200+ killed
November 2002	Suicide bombing of Israeli-owned Paradise Hotel in Kenya; ten killed, simultaneous missile attack on Israeli airliner

As the 1990s progressed, it became quite clear that al Qaeda attacks concentrated on "symbolic targets" representing the U.S. military and economic institutions. Al Qaeda operations suggest several traits worthy of concern to the criminal justice system. First, long-range planning is the hallmark of al Qaeda success. The planning for the attacks on the U.S. embassies in 1998 took five years from its inception. The planning for the attacks on the U.S.S. Cole, World Trade Center, and Pentagon took several years to prepare. Al Qaeda does not act spontaneously. Second, al Qaeda has the ability to conduct simultaneous operations. Gunaratua observes that simultaneous terrorist attacks are rare since few terrorist groups have enough skilled operators, logisticians, planners, and dedicated followers.[66] Third, al Qaeda places a great deal of emphasis on operational security. Several al Qaeda manuals, captured by U.S. troops in Afghanistan, stress the need for tight security and the compartmentalized planning of operations.[67] Al Qaeda terrorist attacks often occur with little or no warning. Fourth, al Qaeda has a flexible command structure and a very diverse member-ship that cuts across ethnic, class, and national boundaries. It is neither a single group nor a coalition of groups. Al Qaeda has terrorist cells worldwide, and supports independent terrorist movements that participate in planned al Qaeda attacks. Al Qaeda's high command is run by a vertical leadership structure that provides strategic direction and tactical support.[68] Falk sums up the leadership of al Qaeda as a "network that could operate anywhere and everywhere, and yet was definitively situated nowhere."[69] Al Qaeda does not have a home address. Fifth, al Qaeda strictly follows a cell structure whose members seldom know one another.

Al Qaeda terrorist attacks generally involve three distinct phases. First, intelligence collects information and conducts surveillance on the intended target. The attack team then rehearses the operation in an al Qaeda training camp. Next, an al Qaeda support team arrives in the target area, organizes safe houses and vehicles, provides forged documents if necessary, and, when appropriate, selects the type of weapons and explosives that will be used. Finally, the strike team arrives in the target area and completes the assigned terrorist mission. Due to the success of recent suicide attacks, it is likely to remain the preferred tactic of al Qaeda and affiliated groups for the near future.[70]

Al Qaeda's global network, which has been confirmed to exist in at least fifty-five countries, has survived by strictly following the principles of operational security outlined by Osama bin Laden.[71] The success of al Qaeda is due in large part to an inspirational leader with exceptional organizational and business talents. As of this writing, the elusive Osama bin Laden has eluded capture or has not been confirmed dead. Who is Osama bin Laden?

In Arabic, Osama means "young lion." Born in Riyadh, Saudi Arabia, in 1957, one of fifty-two siblings, Osama is the seventeenth son of the eleventh wife of Mohammed bin Laden, a Middle East tycoon who made billions of dollars in the construction business on the Arabian Peninsula. After the death of his father, Osama allegedly inherited over $300 million. He wan-dered about the Middle East for several years, eventually settling in Saudi Arabia to study engineering at the Saudi University. While at the university, Osama was greatly inspired by the writings and teachings of Abdullah Azzam, a Palestinian who promoted jihad against Israel, and Abdul Zindani, the godfather of the Egyptian Islamic Jihad. Azzam was hostile to the United States because he viewed the United States as a corrupt and licentious society that uncondition-ally supported Israel. So inspired, Osama eventually made his way to Afghanistan. He began to recruit mujahedin and set up training bases to support the Afghan war against the Soviets. Ultimately, about 25,000 Arabs and Muslims arrived in Afghanistan to join the jihad against the Soviets. The pullout of the Soviets from Afghanistan in 1989 left behind a transnational force of Islamic fighters who, under the leadership of Osama, began to export terrorism and guerilla war around the world.[72]

Eventually, the United States became the major protagonist of al Qaeda and Osama bin Laden. After the 9/11 attack, the United States declared war on terrorism—a war that will contin-ue for some time to come. In one respect, al Qaeda is the latest manifestation of anti-American and anti-Western feelings in the Islamic world. A new generation of Islamic radicals appears to have a lot in common with Nazi Germany and Japanese extremists of World War II, which is embodied in the love of heroism and death. In other words, current Islamic extremists of al Qaeda are comparable to Japanese kamikazi pilots and the German cult of heroes, for whom "happiness lies only in sacrificial death." Nowhere is the sacrificial death more evident than in Iraq.

Since the U.S. invasion in 2003, suicide bombings in Iraq have killed thousands of Iraqi civilians, coalition forces, and U.S. troops. Suicide bombings have been a tactic used by other terrorist groups, such as Hamas and Hizballah, but the frequency and lethality of the suicide bombings in Iraq are unprecedented.[73] The groups that are responsible for the majority of suicide bombings are **al Qaeda in Iraq (AQI)** and its allies Ansar al-Sunna and the Islamic State of Iraq (ISI). AQI refers to the group created by **Abu Musab al Zarqawi**. In January 2006, AQI, the dominant insurgent group in Iraq, created the Mujahedin Shura Council that claimed to be a collection of insurgent groups. AQI then created the ISI in 2006.

Before the invasion of Iraq by the United States, al Qaeda was unknown in Iraq. After the invasion of Iraq, al Qaeda became a major player in the ongoing insurgency in Iraq. The Bush administration identified al Qaeda as the central threat to the stability of Iraq. In fact, in April 2008, the top commander of U.S. forces in Iraq, General David H. Petraeus, referred to AQI as public enemy No. 1 for the U.S. forces in Iraq.[74]

AQI is a Sunni Muslim terrorist group that seeks to disrupt the civil peace in Iraq by using conventional terrorist bombing tactics as well as suicide bombings. Eventually, AQI wants to establish the ISI as part of a caliphate or as part of a single transnational Islamic state.[75] AQI was established by Abu Musab al-Zarqawi, an Osama bin Laden "wannabe," who arrived in Iraq shortly before the U.S. invasion in March 2003. Zarqawi and AQI favored high-profile attacks on civilian, military, and religious targets. Some of the more notable attacks attributed to AQI follow:

- In August 2003, the suicide bombings of the Jordanian embassy, the sacred Shi'ite mosque in Najaf, and the U.N. headquarters in Baghdad (which forced the UN to withdraw from Baghdad).

TABLE 4.4   Evolution of al Qaeda in Iraq

1999–2001	Tawhid wal Jihad (Group of Monotheism and Holy War)
	• organized by Abu Musab al-Zarqawi to recruit and train radical jihadists
2001–2004	Ansar al-Islam (Partisans of Islam)
	• radical movement in the Kurdish area of Iraq; Zarqawi makes contact with Ansar
2003–2004	Tawhid wal Jihad in Iraq
	• Zarqawi begins suicide bombings and beheadings
October 2004	al Qaeda in Iraq
	• bin Laden gives Zarqawi support
January 2006	Mujahedin Shura Council (MSC)
	• al Qaeda in Iraq merges with several smaller Iraqi groups
October 2006	Islamic State of Iraq
	• after the death of Zarqawi the MSC disbands

- The February 2006 bombing of Shi'ite Islam's holiest shrine, the al Askari Mosque in Samara. The bombing severely damaged the golden dome of the Mosque, setting off a wave of sectarian violence that resulted in over 10,000 deaths.
- A series of suicide bombings in Baghdad that killed hundreds in November 2006, igniting a firestorm of sectarian violence between Sunni and Shi'ite Muslims.
- In June 2006, the kidnapping, torture, and execution of two American soldiers in Baghdad. The bodies of the two soldiers were dragged through the streets of Baghdad. U.S. forces located their badly mutilated bodies three days later.
- Between 2004 and 2007, the beheadings of foreign hostages, Iraqi police officers, and infidel Shi'ites. Many of the beheading videos were placed on al Qaeda Web sites. The beheading of U.S. citizen Nick Berg was widely distributed on the Internet, with Zarqawi personally carrying out the beheading.

Zarqawi's reign of terror in Iraq ended on June 7, 2006, when he was killed by a U.S. air strike outside of Baghdad. In August 2007, the National Intelligence Estimate concluded that AQI still had the ability to carry out high-profile attacks.[76] Yet, the Pentagon reported that the Multinational Force had captured over thirty-six senior AQI leaders as well as several members of AQI's media wing, which produced and disseminated videos of suicide bombings and beheadings.[77] On October 28, 2008, a U.S.-led raid on an al Qaeda stronghold in eastern Syria killed an AQI high-ranking commander who smuggled foreign fighters into Iraq. These foreign fighters, mostly Sunni Muslims, are believed to be responsible for thousands of Iraqi and American civilian and military deaths. Even though much of AQI's network and leadership has been decimated, it has shown in the past the capacity to regenerate. Rear Admiral Gregory Smith warns us that AQI has been slowed but not defeated.[78]

Despite the initial success in capturing and killing al Qaeda leaders, the United States failed to significantly weaken the organizational structure of al Qaeda or capture bin Laden and al Zawahiri. In fact, al Qaeda has been involved in more terrorist attacks in a wider geographical area since the attacks of 9/11. These attacks have spanned the globe; Europe, Asia, Africa, and the Middle East have experienced outrageous terrorist attacks by al Qaeda–affiliated groups. Al Qaeda's modus operandi now includes a repertoire of more sophisticated explosive devices and an alarming rise of suicide bombings. The organizational structure of al Qaeda has evolved such that it has become a more viable terrorist group and a more dangerous enemy. For instance, Sageman warns that al Qaeda encourages independent thought and action from lower-level jihadi terrorists, or leaderless resistance.[79] Attacks in London, Madrid, Bali, and Beirut illustrate the effectiveness of low-level operatives carrying out mindless terrorist actions against a civilian population.

Furthermore, the 2008 *Annual Threat Assessment of the Director of National Intelligence* reports that "using the sanctuary in the border area of Pakistan, al Qaeda has been able to maintain a cadre of skilled lieutenants capable of directing the organization's operations around the world." The report also observed that "al Qaeda is improving the last key aspect of its ability to attack the United States: the identification, training, and positioning of operatives for an attack in the Homeland."[80] Bruce Riedel, a former CIA agent of 29 years, acknowledges that "al Qaeda is a more dangerous enemy today than it has ever been before."[81] Jones and Libicki charge that part of the reason for al Qaeda's regeneration was a perception by the Bush administration that there is a battlefield solution to the "war" on terror.[82] Research indicates that terrorist groups seldom are destroyed by the use of military force. In Chapter 10, we will analyze a more promising strategy for eliminating terrorist groups like al Qaeda.

The next chapter explores the relationship of al Qaeda with other terrorist groups and reviews the designated foreign terrorist organizations (FTOs).

Conclusions

For more than forty years, the international community has been combating Palestinian terrorism; it is probable that at least in the near future Palestinian terrorism will continue. The tenacity of Palestinian terrorist activity has gained worldwide sympathy for the Palestinian cause, Hamas, and the PLO/PA. More than 200 countries have officially recognized the PLO/PA, which has a permanent representative at the United Nations. The PLO/PA and Hamas seek to achieve their objectives through a strategy of "protracted struggle." This strategy is partly based on unprovoked attacks on civilian targets, especially suicide bombings. There have been a limited number of attacks by Palestinian terrorist groups on military targets.

In implementing their strategy of protracted struggle, Hamas and the PLO/PA enjoy several important advantages that could continue indefinitely. First, the PLO/PA has a large recruiting pool located in the many refugee camps throughout the Arab world and within the Palestinian Diaspora. Second, the various Palestinian terrorist groups have been provided with sanctuaries in several Arab countries, including Libya, Syria, Sudan, and Lebanon. Third, Palestinian terrorist groups enjoy financial, political, and military aid from the Arab world. Hamas, for example, receives funding from Iran.

In the forseeable future, all these advantages seem unlikely to change. Although the Israeli military blitz of 2008–09 disrupted the infrastructure of Hamas and the PLO/PA, it is only a matter of time before the PLO/PA and Hamas regroup.

Hamas and the PLO/PA have stated peace will only come by complete Israeli withdrawal from the West Bank and Gaza Strip; the evacuation of Israeli settlements, East Jerusalem, and the Old City as the capital of the new state of Palestine; and the right of return for Palestinian refugees to Israel. Palestine is still the issue. Likewise, the global war on terrorism is likely to continue for some time to come. At this point in the war, it appears that the strategy of attacking Afghanistan has been a tactical success. The U.S. bombing campaign and ground troops have destroyed, disabled, and dispersed al Qaeda leadership and forces. The nerve center of al Qaeda has been dispersed, and the annihilation of the Taliban disrupted the primary base of al Qaeda operations that had been providing training and organizational direction. However, AQI is a still active and dangerous force that the United States may be fighting for many years.

Al Qaeda continues to threaten a megaterrorist attack in the United States. For example, on January 10, 2007, al Qaeda supporters stated they possess dirty bombs and virus bombs and will use them against the Americans. Al Qaeda will not negotiate and will not surrender. The terrorist may be difficult to defeat in the future.

Key Terms

Abu Musab al Zarqawi
Abu Nidal Organization (ANO)
al Aqsa Martyrs Brigades
al Qaeda
al Qaeda in Iraq (AQI)
Balfour Declaration
Fatah
fatwah
Hamas

Hizballah
Imad Mughniyah
Irgun/Stern Gang
Occupied Territories
Operation Cast Lead
Oslo Peace Process
Palestinian Authority
Phalangist

Popular Front for the Liberation
of Palestine (PFLP)
Shoah
Taliban
Tanzim
Yom Kippur War
Zakarias Moussaoui
Zionism

Discussion Questions

1. Identify and define the following terms:
   a. Zionism
   b. Arab nationalism
   c. Diaspora
   d. Balfour Declaration
   e. British mandate colony
2. Describe the United Nations Partition Plan for Palestine in 1947.
3. Define the difference between a soft target and a hard target. Why do you think Hamas and al Qaeda concentrate on attacking soft targets?
4. List Palestinian terrorist groups affiliated with the PLO.
5. Why were the 1982 and 2006 wars in Lebanon a failure for Israel?
6. What is al Qaeda?

7. Identify and discuss the terror tactics of the following groups:
   a. Hamas
   b. Hizballah
   c. al Aqsa Martyrs Brigade
   d. Islamic Jihad
8. Describe the strategy of al Qaeda attacks.
9. Why did the United States invade Iraq?
10. Explain the 9/11 massacre; that is, the how and why of the attack.
11. Why is Osama bin Laden opposed to the United States?
12. Argue for or against the Israeli strategy of attacking terrorist groups by using "targeted assassinations."

Web Sites

Official Web site of the Multinational Force—Iraq
http://www.mnf-iraq.com

The Palestinian Human Rights Monitoring Group
http://www.phrmg.org

Frontline, "Shattered Dreams of Peace"
http://www.pbs.org

Middle East Intelligence Bulletin
http://www.meib.org

Terror Attack Database
http://www.ict.org.il

Endnotes

1. Edward W. Said, *The Question of Palestine* (New York: Times Books, 1979), p. 25.
2. John N. Moore, ed., *The Arab-Israeli Conflict*, Volume III (Princeton, NJ: Princeton University Press, 1974), pp. 706–11; See also, David W. Lesch, *The Arab-Israeli Conflict: A History* (London: Oxford University Press, 2007).
3. Fred J. Khouri, *The Arab Israeli Dilemma* (Syracuse, NY: Syracuse University Press, 1985). pp. 1–3.
4. Mark A. Heller, *A Palestinian State: The Implications for Israel* (Cambridge, MA: Harvard University Press, 1983), p. 1.
5. Walter Laqueur, ed., *The Israeli-Arab Reader* (New York: Bantam, 1969), p. 18.
6. J. Bower Bell, *Terror Out of Zion: The Shock Troops of Israeli Independence* (New York: Avon Books, 1977), pp. 237–39.

7. Menachem Begin, *The Revolt: Story of the Irgun* (Jerusalem: Steimatzky, 1988).
8. Bruce Hoffman, *Inside Terrorism* (New York: Columbia University Press, 1999), p. 51.
9. Benny Morris, *The Birth of the Palestinian Refugee Problem 1947–1949* (New York: Cambridge University Press, 1988), pp. 82–86; See also Benny Morris, *Righteous Victims: A History of the Zionist-Arab Conflict, 1881–1999* (New York: Knopf, 1999).
10. Said, *The Question of Palestine*, p. 45; Joseph Massad, "Palestinians and Jewish History: Recognition or Submission," *Journal of Palestine Studies*, 30 (Autumn 2000), pp. 52–58.
11. For example, see Howard M. Sachar, *Egypt and Israel* (New York: Richard Marek, 1982); Simon Dunstan, *The Yom Kippur War: The Arab-Israeli War of 1973* (London: Osprey Publishing, 2007).

12. Simha Flapan, "Israelis and Palestinians: Can They Make Peace," *Journal of Palestine Studies*, 15 (Autumn 1985), p. 21; See also, Guy Ben Porat, *Failure of the Middle East Peace Process: A Comparative Analysis of Peace Implementation in Israel/Palestine, Northern Ireland, and South Africa* (New York: Palgrave MacMillan, 2008).

13. Anton La Guardia, *War without End: Israelis, Palestinians, and the Struggle for a Promised Land* (New York: St. Martin's Press, 2003), pp. 154–57.

14. Mordechai Nisan, "The PLO and the Palestinian Issue," *Middle East Review*, 28 (Winter 1985), p. 55; See also Mordechai Nisan, *Israel and the Territories: A Study in Control, 1967–1977* (Ramat Gan, Israel: Turtledove Publishers, 1978).

15. James W. Amos III, *Palestine Resistance: Organization of a Nationalist Movement* (New York: Pergamon Press, 1980), p. 56; See also, Yezid Sayigh, *Armed Struggle and the Search for State: The Palestinian National Movement, 1949–1993* (Oxford, England: Oxford University Press, 2006).

16. Aaron D. Miller, *The PLO and the Politics of Survival* (New York: Praeger Publisher, 1983), p. 19; See also, Anat N. Kurz, *Fatah and the Politics of Violence: The Institutionalization of a Popular Struggle* (East Sussex, England: Sussex Academic Press, 2006).

17. Helen Cobban, *The Palestinian Liberation Organization: People, Power, and Politics* (Cambridge: Cambridge University Press, 1983), p. 33.

18. Said, *The Question of Palestine*, p. 118; Edward W. Said, "What Israel Has Done: Seeking to Eliminate the Palestinians as a People, It Is Destroying Their Civil Life," *Nation*, 274 (May 6, 2002), p. 20.

19. Julian Becker, *The PLO: The Rise and Fall of the Palestine Liberation Organization* (New York: St. Martin's Press, 1984), p. 74; See also, Walter Laqueur, ed., *The Israel-Arab Reader: A Documentary History of the Middle East*, 7th Rev. ed. (New York: Penguin, 2008).

20. Sachar, *Egypt and Israel*, pp. 222–23.

21. Alain Gresh, *The PLO. The Struggle Within: Towards an Independent Palestinian State* (London: Zed Books, Ltd., 1985), pp. 146–49.

22. Thomas L. Friedman, *New York Times*, January 1, 1986, sec. 1, p. 4; See also, Thomas L. Friedman, *From Beirut to Jerusalem* (New York: Anchor Books, Doubleday, 1989).

23. Yossi Melman, *The Master Terrorist: The True Story behind Abu Nidal* (New York: Adams Books, 1986), pp. 69–82.

24. *Time*, 127 (January 13, 1986), pp. 31–32.

25. Richard A. Gabriel, *Operation Peace for Galilee: The Israeli-PLO War in Lebanon* (New York: Hill and Wang, 1985), pp. 53–57; Itamar Rabinovich, *The War for Lebanon, 1970–1985* (Ithaca, NY: Cornell University Press, 1985), pp. 138–50.

26. Kahan Commission Report, *The Beirut Massacre* (Princeton, NJ: Karz-Cohl, 1983), pp. 50–99; Avi Shlaim, *The Iron Wall: Israel and the Arab World* (New York: W.W. Norton and Co., 2002), pp. 416–19.

27. Friedman, *From Beirut to Jerusalem*, p. 43.

28. For example, see Magnus Ranstorp, *Hizb'allah in Lebanon: The Politics of the Western Hostage Crisis* (New York: Palgrave MacMillan, 1997); Hala Jaber, *Hezbollah* (New York: Columbia University Press, 1997); Augustus Richard Norton, *Hezbollah: A Short History* (New Jersey: Princeton University Press, 2007).

29. Terry Anderson, *Den of Lions: Memoirs of Seven Years* (New York: Crown Pub., Inc., 1993), pp. 335–46; Judith Palmer Harik, *Hezbollah: The Changing Face of Terrorism* (London: I.B. Tauris, 2005), pp. 12–45.

30. "FBI Ties Iran to Argentine Bombing in '94," *Washington Post* (August 8, 1998), p. 3; Nicholas Blanford, "Mughniyah Murder Could Trigger Retaliation," (February 16, 2008), *http://arabamericannews.com.*

31. Israeli Defense Forces, "Major Incidents in Lebanon in 1999," *http://www.idf.il.*

32. For example, see Amal Saad-Ghorayeb, *Hizbullah: Politics and Religion* (London: Pluto Press, 2002); Ann Byers, *Lebanon's Hizbollah: Inside the World's Most Infamous Terrorist Organization* (New York: Rosen Publishing Co., 2002).

33. For example, see Noam Ophir, "Look Not to the Skies: The IDF vs. Surface-to-Surface Rocket Launchers," *Strategic Assessment* (Jaffee Center for Strategic Studies, Tel Aviv University) 9, 3 (November, 2006).

34. Uzi Rubin, "Hizbollah's Rocket Campaign Against Northern Israel: A Preliminary report," *Jerusalem Issue Brief* (Jerusalem Center for Public Affairs) 6, 10 (August 31, 2006).

35. For example, see Alastair Crooke and Mark Perry, "Winning the Ground War," *Asia Times Online* (October 13, 2006); Anthony H. Cordesman, "Preliminary Lessons of the Israeli-Hizballah War," *Center for Strategic and International Studies* (Washington, DC, August 17, 2006).

36. "Winograd Commission Final Report," *Council on Foreign Relations* (January 30, 2008), *http://www.cfr.org/publication*; Gregory Levey, "Israel's Surge of Despair," Salon.com (February 15, 2007).

37. Amnesty International, "Israel/Lebanon: Deliberate Destruction or 'Collateral Damage': Israeli Attacks on Civilian Infrastructure," Report MDE18/007/2006 (August 23, 2006), *http://www.amnesty.org*.

38. "Hezbollah (a.k.a. Hizbollah, Hizbu'llah)," *Council on Foreign Relations* (August 13, 2006), *http://www.cft.org/publication/9155*; See also Adam Shatz, "In Search of Hezbollah," *New York Review of Books* (April 29, 2004); Rafael D. Frankel, "Israel Troubled That the War in Lebanon Drove Its Enemies Closer," *Christian Science Monitor* (September 22, 2006).

39. Robert Spencer, *Islam Unveiled: Disturbing Questions about the World's Fastest Growing Faith* (San Francisco, CA: Encounter Books, 2002), pp. 45–47.

40. Gabriel, *Operation Peace for Galilee*, p. 37.

41. La Guardia, *War without End*, p. 304; "A Window on the Workings of the PA: An Inside View," *Journal of Palestine Studies*, 30 (Autumn 2000), p. 88.

42. For example, see Samuel M. Katz, *The Hunt for the Engineer: How Israeli Agents Tracked the Hamas Master Bomber* (Guilford, CT: Lyons Press, 2002); Elaine Landau, *Suicide Bombers* (Breckenridge, CO: Twenty-First Century Books, 2006); Rosemarie Skaine, *Female Suicide Bombers* (Jefferson, NC: McFarland and Co., 2006).

43. For example, see Yonah Alexander, *Palestinian Religious Terrorism: Hamas and Islamic Jihad* (New York: Transnational Publishers, 2002); Shaul Mishal and Avraham Sela, *The Palestinian Hamas* (New York: Colombia University Press, 2000); Jeroen Gunning, *Hamas in Politics: Democracy, Religion, Violence* (New York: Columbia University Press, 2008).

44. For example, see Khalid Harub, *Hamas: Political Thought and Practice* (Washington, DC: Institute for Palestine Studies, 2000); Zaki Chehab, *Inside Hamas: The Untold Story of the Militant Islamic Movement* (New York: Nation Books, 2008).

45. For example, see Michael Irving Jensen, *The Political Ideology of Hamas: A Grassroots Perspective* (London: I.B. Tauris, 2009).

46. Aaron D. Pina, "Fatah and Hamas: The New Palestinian Factional Reality," *Congressional Research Service Reports and Issues Brief* (Michigan: Thomson Gale, March 13, 2007).

47. For example, see Isaac Kfir and Adam E. Stahl, "Hamas: A Gun in One Hand, A Qu'ran in the Other," *International Institute for Counterterrorism* (Herzliya, Israel, 2007), *http://www.ict.org*.

48. Jonathan Schanzer, *Hamas vs. Fatah: The Struggle for Palestine* (New York: Palgrave Macmillan, 2008), pp. 14–46

49. Ethan Bronner, "Israelis United on Gaza War as Censure Rises Abroad," *New York Time* (January 12, 2009), *http://www.nytimes.com*.

50. Anthony H. Cordesman, "The 'Gaza War': A Strategic Analysis," *Center for Strategic and International Studies* (February 2, 2009), *http://www.csis.org/media/csis/pubs/090202_gaza_war.pdf*.

51. Ethan Bronner and Sabrina Tavernise, "The Gaza War in Microcosm," *International Herald Tribune* (February 3, 2009), *http://www.iht.com/*.

52. Max Boot, "No Room for Israel Under America's Umbrella," *Financial Times* (January 27, 2009), *http://www.ft.com/home/us*.

53. Israeli Ministry of Foreign Affairs, "Palestinian Violence and Terrorism," (October 9, 2008), *http://www.mfa.gov*.

54. Israeli Defense Forces homepage, *http://www.idf.il*.

55. Council on Foreign Relations; Al Aqsa Martyrs Brigades, *http://www.terrorismanswers.com*.

56. Jerrold Kessel, "Female Suicide Bombers New Weapons," (February 28, 2002), *http://www.cnn.com*; Skaine, *Female Suicide Bombers*, p. 22.

57. La Guardia, *War without End*, pp. 347–48; Ronen Sebag, "Lebanon: The Intifada's False Premise," *Middle East Quarterly*, 9 (Spring 2002), pp. 13–22.

58. Guardian Unlimited, "Militants Avenge Israeli Killing," *http://www.guardian.co.uk*.

59. Rohan Gunaratna, *Inside al Qaeda: Global Network of Terror* (New York: Columbia University Press, 2002), p. 1; David C. Rapoport, "The Fourth Wave: September 11 in the History of Terrorism," *Current History*, 100 (December 2001), pp. 419–25.

60. Brian M. Jenkins, "The Organizations Men: Anatomy of a Terrorist Attack," in *How Did This Happen? Terrorism and the New War*, eds. James F. Hoge Jr. and Gideon Rose (New York: Public Affairs, 2001), pp. 1–4.

61. *United States of America* v. *Zacarias Moussaoui*, U.S. District Court for the Eastern District of Virginia, *http://www.usdoj.gov/ag/moussaouiindictment.htm.*

62. Peter L. Bergen, *Holy War, Inc.: Inside the Secret World of Osama bin Laden* (New York: Free Press, 2001), pp. 143–59.

63. For example, see Michael Scheuer, *Through Our Enemies' Eyes: Osama bin Laden, Radical Islam and the Future of America* (Washington, DC: Potomac Books, Inc., 2007).

64. *The 9/11 Commission Report: Final Report of the National Commission on Terrorist Attacks Upon the U.S.* (New York: Norton, 2004), pp. 144–47.

65. Gunaratna, *Inside al Qaeda*, pp. 22–28; See also Jane Corbin, *Al Qaeda: In Search of the Terror Network That Threatens the World* (New York: Thunders Mouth Press, 2002).

66. Gunaratna, *Inside al Qaeda*, pp. 55–67.

67. Kathy Gannon, *Manual of Jihad Details Terrorist Tactics: The al Qaeda Manual* (October 2, 2001), *http://www.seattlepi.com*; See also *Manual of Afghan Jihad*, Terror Manual is an A-B-C Primer for Attackers, 9/21/01, *http://www.foxnews.com.*

68. Gunaratna, *Inside al Qaeda*, p. 54; See also, Bruce Riedel, *The Search for al Qaeda: Its Leadership, Ideology, and Future* (Washington, DC: Brookings Institution Press, 2008).

69. Richard Falk, *The Great Terror War* (New York: Olive Branch Press, 2003), p. 6.

70. For example, see William E. Dyron, *Terrorism: An Investigator's Handbook* (Cincinatti, OH: Anderson Publishing, 2001); Lawrence Wright, *The Looming Tower: al Qaeda and the Road to 9/11* (New York: Alfred A. Knopf, 2006).

71. Yonah Alexander and Michael S. Swetnam, *Usama bin Laden's al Qaida: Profile of a Terrorist Network* (New York: Transnational Publishers, 2001), p. 31.

72. For example, see Anthony J. Dennis, *Osama bin Laden: A Psychological and Political Portrait* (New York: Wyndham Hall Press, 2002); Marc Sageman, *Leaderless Jihad: Terror Networks in the Twenty-First Century* (Philadelphia: University of Pennsylvania Press, 2008).

73. Determining the exact number of suicide bombings in Iraq is nearly impossible. Bombing attacks are so frequent that the media often does not bother to investigate each reported suicide bombing. Nevertheless, several sources have attempted to compile a list of suicide bombings in Iraq; for example, The Rand Corporation has compiled the following list:
2003—25
2004—140
2005—478
2006—300
2007—189
2008—115+

74. General David H. Petraeus, "Report to Congress on the Situation in Iraq," (April 8–9, 2008).

75. Seth G. Jones and Martin C. Libicki, *How Terrorist Groups End: Lessons for Countering al Qa'ida* (Santa Monica, CA: Rand Corporation, 2008), pp. 83–90.

76. National Intelligence Estimate, "Prospects for Iraq's Stability: Some Security Progress But Political Reconciliation Elusive," (National Intelligence Estimate, August, 2007), *http://www.dni.gov/nic/NIC_home.html.*

77. Rear Admiral Greg Smith, "Multinational Force—Iraq Operational Update," (November 7, 2007), *http://www.mnf-iraq.com.*

78. Ibid.

79. Sageman, *Leaderless Jihad*, pp. 77–87.

80. J. Michael McConnell, *Annual Threat Assessment of the Director of National Intelligence for Senate Select Committee on Intelligence* (Washington, DC, February 5, 2008), p. 6.

81. Bruce Riedel, "al Qaeda Strikes Back," *Foreign Affairs*, 86, 3 (May–June, 2007), p. 24.

82. James and Libicki, *How Terrorist Groups End*, pp. 115–20.

CHAPTER 5

Designated Foreign Terrorist Organizations: The "A List"

CHAPTER OBJECTIVES

The study of this chapter will enable you to:

- Identify foreign terrorist organizations (FTOs) that pose a threat to the United States and its allies
- Understand the objectives of Islamic terrorist groups
- Review the political ideologies of designated FTOs
- Describe the influence of al Qaeda on the objectives of the designated FTOs
- Discuss the criteria for selection as an FTO
- Compare and contrast national/separatist FTOs and Islamic fundamentalist FTOs

INTRODUCTION

In this chapter, we examine those groups identified by the U.S. State Department as foreign terrorist organizations (FTOs). The Antiterrorism and Effective Death Penalty Act of 1996 established the current statutory requirements of U.S. policy toward foreign terrorist groups. The **Antiterrorism Act** sets forth a formal list of FTOs. The legal criteria for designation as an FTO stipulates that the terrorist organization must meet three specific principles: (1) The group must be a foreign organization; (2) must engage in terrorist activity as defined by U.S. law; and (3) the terrorist activity must threaten the security of the United States, which is broadly defined as national defense, foreign relations, and economic interests.

In October 1997 thirty FTOs were initially designated by then Secretary of State Madeleine Albright. FTO designations expire in two years, unless explicitly removed by the Secretary of State. However, groups can be added or removed from the list at any time. The first biennial review of designations occurred in 1999 when al Qaeda was added to the list, and the Democratic Front for the Liberation of Palestine (DFLP), the Khmer Rouge, and the Manuel Rodriquez Patriotic Front of Chile were dropped from the list. In September 2000, the first out-of-cycle change to the list was the addition of the Islamic Movement of **Uzbekistan** (IMU). In 2001 and 2002, Secretary of State Colin

Powell had designated the following groups to the list: the Real IRA, United Self-Defense Forces of Colombia, al Aqsa Martyrs Brigade, Asbat al-Ansar, Jaish-e-Mohammed, Lashkar-e Tayyiba, **Salafist** Group for Call and Combat (GSPC; in September 2006, the GSPC merged with al Qaeda and changed its name to al Qaeda in the Islamic Maghreb (AQIM)), Jemaah Islamiya, and Kahane Chai (Kach). As of April 30, 2008, there are a total of forty-three groups designated as FTOs. (See Table 5.1 for complete list.)

TABLE 5.1   U.S. State Department's Designated Foreign Terrorist Organization List, March 2008

Name/Orientation	Primary Area(s) of Operation	Primary Goal(s)
Abu Nidal Organization (ANO) *Palestinian nationalist*	Middle East, Asia, Europe	Anti-Israel, opposes moderate Arab regimes, seeks independent Palestinian state, rejects Middle East Peace Process
Abu Sayyaf Group (ASG) *Islamic extremist*	Philippines	Seeks Iranian-style Islamic state on one of the Philippines's southern islands
al-Aqsa Martyrs Brigade *Palestinian nationalist*	Middle East	Seeks establishment of independent Palestinian state; rejects Middle East Peace Process
al Shabaab (the Youth) *Formed in 2004 Islamic (Sunni) extremist*	Somalia	Establish the rule of Sharia in Somalia; jihadists who wage war against enemies of Islam; affiliated with al Qaeda
Ansar al Sunnah (Soldiers of Islam) *Islamic (Sunni) extremist*	Iraq (Kurdistan)	Drive U.S. out of Iraq and establish Islamic state in Iraq
al Qaeda* *Islamic extremist*	Worldwide	Opposes "non-Islamic" regimes, strongly anti-Western, seeks to "reestablish the Muslim State" throughout the Persian Gulf; responsible for U.S. embassy bombings in East Africa (1998), bombing of the U.S.S. Cole (2000), and attacks on the World Trade Center and Pentagon (2001)
al Qaeda in Iraq *Islamic (Sunni) extremist*	Iraq, Pakistan, Afghanistan	Drive U.S. and coalition forces out of Iraq
Armed Islamic Group (GIA) *Islamic extremist*	Algeria, France	Antiforeign, anti-Algerian government, seeks to establish Islamic state; frequently massacres civilians
Asbat al-Ansar *Palestinian nationalist*	Middle East	Seeks establishment of independent Palestinian state; rejects Middle East Peace Process
Aum Shinrikyo (Aum Supreme Truth) *Religious Cult*	Japan, Russia	Seeks to bring about Apocalypse; responsible for 1995 sarin gas attack on Tokyo subway, resulting in 12 dead and over 5,000 injured
Euzkadi Ta Askatasuna (ETA) (Basque Fatherland & Liberty) *Separatist (Marxist-Leninist)*	Spain, France	Anti-Spanish government, anti-French government, seeks independent Basque state in northern Spain and southern France

(continued)

TABLE 5.1   Continued

Name/Orientation	Primary Area(s) of Operation	Primary Goal(s)
al-Gama'a al-Islamiyya (IG)* (Islamic Group) *Islamic extremist*	Egypt	Anti-Egyptian government; seeks to establish Islamic state; responsible for attack on tourists at Luxor, Egypt (1997)
Communist Party of the Philippines/New People's Army (CPP/NPA) *Marxist*	Philippines	Seeks to overthrow the government of the Philippines and replace it with a leftist, Marxist-oriented regime
Continuity Irish Republican Army	Northern Ireland and Irish Republic	Unification of Ireland and refuse to decommission
Hamas *Islamic extremist*	Israel, Gaza Strip	Anti-Israel, seeks to establish Palestinian Islamic state; tactics include large-scale suicide bombings; missile attacks on Israel; rejects Middle East Peace Process
Harakat ul-Mujahedin (HUM) *Islamic extremist*	Pakistan, Kashmir (northern India), Afghanistan	Anti-Indian; seeks Islamic rule in Kashmir and throughout the world
Hizballah* *Islamic (Shia) extremist, closely linked to Iranian government*	Lebanon	Seeks to establish Islamic theocracy in Lebanon and to reduce non-Islamic influences in the Middle East; responsible for suicide truck bombings of U.S. embassy and marine barracks (1983) and U.S. embassy Annex in Beirut (1984), among other terrorist acts
Islamic Jihad Group *Islamic (Sunni) extremist*	Uzbekistan	Split from the IMU; seek to create Islamic rule in Uzbekistan
Islamic Movement of Uzbekistan (IMU) *Coalition of Islamic militants*	South Asia, Tajikistan, Afghanistan, Iran, Kyrgyzstan, Pakistan	Seeks to overthrow Uzbekistan's secular government and replace it with an Islamic theocracy
Jaish-e-Mohammed (JEM) (Army of Mohammed) *Islamic extremist*	Pakistan and Kashmir	Anti-Indian; seeks to unite Kashmir with Pakistan
Jemaah Islamiya (JI) *Islamic extremist*	Southeast Asia	Seeks to overthrow secular governments in Southeast Asia and create an Islamic state, or "Darul Islam Nusantara," linking Malaysia, Indonesia, and the Muslim-dominated southern Philippines
Egyptian al-Jihad (EIJ) *Islamic extremist*	Egypt	Anti-Egyptian government, seeks to establish Islamic state; original *al-Jihad* responsible for assassination of Egyptian President Anwar Sadat (1981)

(continued)

TABLE 5.1   Continued

Name/Orientation	Primary Area(s) of Operation	Primary Goal(s)
Kahane Chai* *Jewish extremist*	Israel, West Bank	Seeks to continue Kach founder's rejectionist agenda, considered more militant than Kach party from which it sprang
Kongra-Gel (formerly Kurdistan Workers' Party [PKK]) *Separatist (Marxist-Leninist)*	Turkey, Europe, Middle East, Asia	Anti-Turkish, seeks to establish independent Kurdish state in southeastern Turkey
Lashkar-e Tayyiba (LT) (Army of the Righteous) *Islamic (Sunni) extremist*	Pakistan, Kashmir, India	Seeks to drive India from the disputed Kashmir region; strongly anti-United States; Mumbai attack
Lashkar I Jhanyvi *(Army of Jhang) Islamic (Sunni) extremist*	Pakistan, India	Focus on anti-Shia attacks and allied with Taliban and al Qaeda
Liberation Tigers of Tamil Eelam (LTTE) *Separatist insurgent*	Sri Lanka	Anti-Sri Lanka government; seeks to establish independent Tamil state in Sri Lanka
Libyan Islamic Fighting Group	Libya	Overthrow Kadhafi; today aligned with al Qaeda
Moroccan Islamic Combatant Group *Islamic (Sunni) extremist*	Western Europe, Moroccan diaspora communities	Responsible for Madrid train bombing; allied with al Qaeda in Iraq
Mujahedin-e-Khalq Organization* (MEK or MKO) *Marxist–Islamic, Iranian dissident*	Iraq, Iran; worldwide operation	Seeks to overthrow Iranian government, has expressed anti-Western sentiment in the past
National Liberation Army (ELN) *Marxist-Leninist*	Colombia	Seeks removal of United States and other foreign businesses (especially petroleum industry) from Colombia and revolution to establish Marxist-Leninist government
Palestine Islamic Jihad—Shiqaqi Faction (PIJ) *Islamic extremist*	Middle East	Anti-Israel, rejects Middle East Peace Process, seeks to establish Islamic Palestinian state
Palestine Liberation Front—Abu Abbas Faction *Palestinian nationalist*	Israel, Gaza, West Bank, Egypt	Anti-Israel; rejects Middle East Peace Process; seeks to establish independent Palestinian state; responsible for seizure of *Achille Lauro* cruise ship (1985), during which an American was murdered
Popular Front for the Liberation of Palestine (PFLP) *Marxist–Palestinian nationalist*	Israel, West Bank, Syria, Lebanon	Anti-Israel, rejects Middle East Peace Process, seeks to establish independent Palestinian state
Popular Front for the Liberation of Palestine—General Command (PFLP-GC) *Marxist–Palestinian nationalist*	Israel, West Bank, Lebanon, Egypt	Anti-Israel, rejects Middle East Peace Process, seeks to establish independent Palestinian state; broke from PFLP in 1968 because PFPL-GC founder believed PFLP too focused on diplomacy, not engaging in enough violence

(continued)

TABLE 5.1 Continued

Name/Orientation	Primary Area(s) of Operation	Primary Goal(s)
Real Irish Republican Army (RIRA) *Dissident Republican splinter group*	Northern Ireland, Irish Republic, Great Britain	Seeks the removal of British forces from Northern Ireland and the unification of Ireland; includes many former members of the PIRA
Revolutionary Armed Forces of Colombia (FARC) *Marxist-Leninist*	Colombia	Seeks overthrow of current government and ruling class of Colombia
Revolutionary Organization 17 November *Marxist/Communist*	Greece	Seeks to replace Greek establishment with communist system, rid Greece of United States, EU, and NATO presence, end Turkish military presence on Cyprus; responsible for numerous assassinations, including several U.S. government officials
Revolutionary People's Liberation Party/Front (DHKP/Q) *Marxist*	Turkey	Seeks to remove United States and NATO presence from Turkey and foment a revolution to overthrow Turkish government
Revolutionary Nuclei (Formerly Revolutionary People's Struggle [ELA]) *Extreme leftist, Marxist*	Greece	Anti-Greek government, seeks removal of U.S. military forces from Greece
United Self-Defense Forces of Colombia (AUC) *Narcoterrorist, paramilitary*	Columbia	Generally restricts actions to attacks against insurgent groups
al Qaeda in the Islamic Maghreb (AQIM) (formerly Salafist Group for Call and Combat [Groupe Salafiste Pour la Predication et le Combat]) *Islamic extremist*	Algeria, France	Antiforeign, anti-Algerian government, seeks to establish Islamic state in Algeria
Shining Path (Sendero Luminoso) *Neo-Maoist*	Peru	Anti-Peruvian government, antiforeign, seeks peasant revolutionary regime; particularly brutal and indiscriminate
East Turkistan Islamic Movement (ETIM) *Islamic extremist*	China	Seeks to establish an independent Islamic republic in Xinjiang province
Special Purpose Islamic Regiment (SPIR), Islamic International Brigade (IIB), Riyadus- Salikin Reconnaissance, and Sabotage Battalion of Chechen Martyrs (RS) *Islamic Separatist Extremist*	Russia, Chechnya, Caucasus Region	Establish an independent Chechen Republic based on Wahhabi sect of Islam

*Groups that have a presence in the United States.

Source: U.S. State Department, Office of Coordination for Counterterrorism, Country Reports on Terrorism, Chapter 6, Terrorist Organizations, U.S. Government Printing Office (April 30, 2008).

The greatest advantage of creating such an FTO list is symbolic. The list calls attention to terrorist groups, making it clear that the United States is closely monitoring their activities and cooperating with other governments to disrupt their terrorist activities. Henceforth, this chapter examines the background, structure, ideology, and terrorist activities of the designated FTOs. Much can be learned from an historical analysis of each of the FTOs designated by the secretary of state. What follows is a brief description of the designated FTOs. Several of the designated FTOs are covered in other chapters; for example, Hizballah, Hamas, al Aqsa Martyrs Brigade, Liberation Tigers of Tamil Eelam, and al Qaeda can be located in Chapters 4 and 8.

PALESTINIAN GROUPS

Abu Nidal Organization,[1] also known as Arab Revolutionary Brigades, Black June, the Revolutionary Council

The Abu Nidal Organization (ANO) was founded by Sabri al-Banna, the son of a wealthy Palestinian landowner. After the 1948 war in Palestine, the newly formed Israeli government confiscated all the property owned by the al-Bannas. The al-Bannas, now destitute, were forced to live in a series of Palestinian refugee camps on the West Bank. By 1968, Sabri had joined Arafat's **Fatah** movement and changed his name to Abu Nidal (The Father of the Struggle). The ANO began its terrorist operations in 1973 and by late 1974 declared its opposition to Arafat's PLO. The stated goals of the ANO are (1) the destruction of Israel and the creation of an independent Palestinian state, (2) demoralization of any Israeli–Palestinian peace talks, and (3) armed struggles as the first priority of the Palestine resistance movement. The ANO represents a model of secular Palestinian fundamentalism whose sacred goal is the liberation of Palestine from the "Zionist entity."

Since 1974, the ANO is believed to have committed over 90 attacks, killed over 300 people, and wounded over 650 in 20 countries. The ANO is a highly secretive and vengeful Palestinian group, selecting recruits from Palestinian refugee camps in Lebanon, Gaza, and the West Bank. New recruits receive military-type training in Libya and Iraq. Some recruits specialize in assassination tactics, while others train in the techniques of bomb making. Estimates of ANO membership range from 400 to 1,000. The ANO has a central committee structure that serves as a decision-making body with several functional committees such as military, finance, and operations that plan terrorist attacks.

The ANO has indiscriminately bombed dozens of airports in Europe, North Africa, and the Middle East. They have assassinated at least sixty moderate members of the PLO and attempted to assassinate Yassir Arafat three times. In June 1982, Marwan al Banna was convicted of the assassination of the Israeli ambassador to England. The ambassador's assassination was the pretext Israel used to invade Lebanon in 1982. They have hijacked planes in Egypt, Lebanon, and France. They have kidnapped numerous victims for ransom, and have carried out at least three suicide bombings. By the late 1990s, the ANO was no longer considered an active threat. Media reports indicated that the ANO had broken apart after a series of internal feuds, internecine warfare, defections, and a lack of funding. In August 2002, it was reported that Abu Nidal (Sabri al-Banna), suffering from leukemia, died at his Baghdad home of several gunshot wounds. It is unclear whether his death was a suicide or an assassination. The notorious Abu Nidal (Sabri al-Banna), the man whom the U.S. government called the "most dangerous terrorist in the world," has passed into the back pages of the history of terrorism.

Asbat al-Ansar[2]

Asbat al-Ansar (Band of Partisans), founded in 1985, is a radical Islamic Palestinian organization. The Asbat al-Ansar is based in the Palestinian refugee camp of Ayn al-Hilwah, outside the ancient city of Sidon in southern Lebanon. Like the AQIM [formerly the Algerian Group for Call and Combat (GSPC)], the Asbat al-Ansar advocates the Islamic practice of Salafism. Salafism's message is utopian, and its adherents seek to completely transform the Muslim community (*umma*) to ensure that Islamic belief systems should eventually dominate the world. The Asbat al-Ansar has two primary objectives: (1) to replace the power-sharing government of Lebanon with an Islamic state, and (2) to oppose any peace plan with Israel. Asbat al-Ansar has maintained close ties to al Qaeda in Iraq, supplying weapons, training, and recruits to AQI.

Beginning in the early 1990s, Asbat al-Ansar carried out a series of terrorist attacks on domestic non-Islamic targets in Lebanon, such as nightclubs, Christian churches, and rival Palestinian and Lebanese Islamic groups in Southern Lebanon. Then in 2000, after reportedly receiving financial support from Osama bin Laden and al Qaeda, Asbat al-Ansar upped the scale of their attacks by assaulting the Russian embassy in Beirut with rocket-propelled grenades. Shortly after 9/11, Asbat al-Ansar gained some notoriety when Lebanese police discovered a plot to bomb the Beirut embassies of the United States, United Kingdom, and Jordan.

Since the Israeli Defense Forces redeployed from Southern Lebanon in May 2000, the Lebanese government has attempted to gain control of the many Palestinian refugee camps without much success. The Palestinian refugee camps, like Ayn al-Hilwah, have become autonomous enclaves controlled by extremist Islamic groups. Thus, Asbat al-Ansar has become the principle power broker over a largely radicalized group of disenfranchised Palestinians accountable to no one. Comprising about 400 extremists, Asbat al-Ansar has little difficulty recruiting new members from Palestinian refugee camps in Lebanon.

Palestine Liberation Front (PLF)[3]

Ahmad Jibril founded the secular PLF in 1959. By 1967, the PLF had merged with several other Palestinian groups to form the Popular Front for the Liberation of Palestine (PFLP), while Jibril formed a new organization called the Popular Front for the Liberation of Palestine-General Command (PFLP-GC) in 1968. In 1977, the PLF was reestablished after an internal struggle within the PFLP-GC and **Abu Abbas** emerged as the new leader of the PLF. Despite the many changes in leadership and organizational structure, the PLF did not lose sight of its objectives— the destruction of the Israeli/Zionist state, the recovery of Palestine, and the establishment of a secular Palestinian state.

Although the PLF has not carried out a major terrorist attack since May 1992, the Abu Abbas faction of the PLF still remains on the U.S. State Department's list of designated FTOs. The most notorious terrorist act committed by the PLF was the seajacking of the Italian cruise ship, the *Achille Lauro*, on October 7, 1985, off the coast of Egypt. In the events that followed, an elderly, wheelchair-bound Jewish-American citizen was killed and thrown overboard. The seajackers were apprehended, tried, and convicted in Italy and sentenced to long prison terms. Abu Abbas escaped and was sentenced by Italy to life imprisonment in absentia. The United States also wants to try Abu Abbas for the *Achille Lauro* seajacking. Following the *Achille Lauro* affair, Abu Abbas moved the PLF to Iraq. On April 16, 2003, Abu Abbas was apprehended in Baghdad by U.S. military forces and later died from heart failure while he was in custody.

During the 1980s and early 1990s, the PLF committed a series of destructive terrorist attacks against Israeli "soft" targets. After dropping out of sight for a decade, the PLF reappeared in November 2001, when Israeli police arrested fifteen members of a PLF terrorist cell. The Israelis believe the cell was planning a series of terrorist car bombings against civilian targets. The main support, both military and financial, for the PLF came from Saddam Hussein and Iraq. In support of Palestinian suicide bombers, Saddam offered a stipend of $25,000 to the families of those who participate in such attacks. Israeli government officials maintain that PLF members are active distributors of the "suicide" funds. The PLF took part in the 2006 Palestinian elections and did not win a seat in the Palestine National Council.

Popular Front for the Liberation of Palestine (PFLP)[4]

The PFLP traces its roots to the 1948 war in Palestine and the establishment of the Israeli state. By the late 1960s, under the leadership of **George Habash**, the PFLP began to take a more active role in the recovery of Palestine. The PFLP considers itself at the vanguard of Palestinian guerrilla organizations dedicated to liberating all of Palestinian territory and creating a democratic socialist Palestinian state. The PFLP bases its political ideology on a combination of Marxist doctrine and Palestinian nationalism. The PFLP views the destruction of Israel as the key element in bringing about a worldwide communist revolution. It was the first Palestinian organization to attract worldwide media attention by introducing the terrorist tactic of skyjacking. After several high-visibility skyjackings by the PFLP, the "Palestine Question" exploded onto the international scene.

In May 2000, an aging George Habash resigned as the leader of the PFLP and was replaced by Abu Ali Mustafa. Once the second intifada broke out in September 2000, the PFLP carried out dozens of car bombings, shootings, and suicide bombings in the West Bank. In September 2001, Mustafa was assassinated by Israel, and his successor was Ahmed Sadat. Under Sadat, the PFLP retaliated for the assassination of Mustafa by killing Israeli Tourism Minister Rehavam

FIGURE 5.1 Dr. George Habash, founder of the PFLP, is a Greek Orthodox who was driven out of his house in Lydda by the Israeli Army after the 1948 Middle East war. Habash graduated from medical school at American University in Beirut in 1951. Here he is seen with a female member of the PFLP, Maha Abu Kahli. (Getty Images Inc.—Hulton Archive Photos)

Zeevi, which has led to a series of revenge and retaliation killings in 2002 and 2003. Between 2004 and 2008, the PFLP carried out several suicide bombings in Israel.

After Arafat's Fatah organization, the PFLP is the most important of the PLO-affiliated organizations. The PFLP has nearly ceased international terrorist operations, concentrating today on "guerrilla" attacks against Israel although PFLP terrorist activities have been seriously disrupted by Israeli arrests and assassinations since the start of the second intifada. Currently, the PFLP is about 800 strong with headquarters in Damascus, Syria. In response to U.S. pressure, on May 5, 2003, Syria closed the office of the PFLP and deported several of its members to the West Bank. The PFLP is very active in Palestinian politics and has Web sites in both Arabic and English.

Popular Front for the Liberation of Palestine-General Command (PFLP-GC)[5]

The PFLP-GC is a secular, Marxist-Leninist communist group known for its unequivocal rejection of any political settlement or peace process with Israel. Since its beginning the PFLP-GC has relied on state sponsors of terrorism such as Syria, Libya, and Iran. In 1968, after an internal dispute within the PFLP between George Habash and Ahmed Jibril, the PFLP-GC was formed under the leadership of Jibril.

The PFLP-GC continues to oppose any peace initiatives by the Palestinian Authority to negotiate and make concessions to Israel. In the 1970s and 1980s, the signature terrorist attack method of the PFLP-GC was the in-flight bombing of commercial aircraft. On February 21, 1970, the PFLP-GC's first in-flight bombing occurred aboard a Swiss Air flight from Zurich to Tel Aviv that killed forty-seven passengers and crew. Between 1970 and 1980 the PFLP-GC was credited with nine bombings and attempted bombings of in-flight aircraft and airport concourses. Even though two Libyan intelligence agents were charged with the bombing of **Pan Am 103** over Lockerbie, Scotland, police investigators believe substantial evidence exists that implicates the PFLP-GC. To date no member of the PFLP-GC has been charged with the bombing of Pan Am 103.

Clearly the most active period for the PFLP-GC was during the 1970s and early 1980s. Throughout the 1990s PFLP-GC terrorist activity declined. Similar to the PFLP and PLF, the PFLP-GC saw an opportunity to once again enter the terrorist arena with the introduction of the second intifada. In 2001 and 2002, the PFLP-GC carried out several attacks against Israeli settlements in the Golan Heights and the Northern Galilee. The probability that the PFLP-GC will once again resume large-scale terrorist attacks depends on the extent provided by state sponsors such as Iran and Syria. The PFLP-GC is well known in the Palestinian and Arab communities for its conventional military expertise. Reports indicate that the PFLP-GC possesses Soviet SA-7 antiaircraft missiles. Now that the conflict between Israelis and Palestinians has escalated since the election of Hamas, the PFLP-GC is expected to become more involved in terrorist attacks. By 2007, terrorist operations by the PFLP-GC had killed an estimated 165 people. On May 21, 2002, a powerful car bomb killed Jihad Jibril, a leading figure in the PFLP-GC's organizational hierarchy. Ahmed Jibril, his father, believes the Israelis assassinated his son, and he has sought revenge ever since.

THE PHILIPPINES[6] AND SOUTHEAST ASIA

Abu Sayyaf Group (ASG)

The Abu Sayyaf Group (Bearer of the Sword) was formed in 1991 after it split from the Moro National Liberation Front (NLF). The stated objective of Abu Sayyaf is to create an Iranian-style zjority. The Abu Sayyaf is the most violent Islamic group in the Philippines, waging a separatist war against the Philippine government and the so-called Christian "settlers" from the Northern Philippine islands. It has claimed credit for numerous bombings, assassinations, kidnappings for ransom, and extortion payments from corporations and businesses on the island of Mindanao.

Philippine police linked Abu Sayyaf to Ramzi Yousef's "**bojinka plot**" or big bang. The bojinka plot involved a plan to blow up eleven commercial jets while in flight, assassinate Pope John Paul and President Clinton, and blow up the CIA headquarters in Langley, Virginia. The plan was to use a suicide bomber dressed as a priest to kill the pope and another suicide bomber to fly a small plane, in a kamikaze-style attack loaded with explosives, into the CIA headquarters. The police discovered the plan after a fire broke out in a Manila apartment rented by Ramzi Yousef. The apartment contained bomb-making materials, information on commercial jet flights, the itinerary of Pope John Paul's visit to Manila, diagrams of CIA headquarters at Langley, and literature proclaiming the merits of membership in Abu Sayyaf. However, Ramzi Yousef and his Abu Sayyaf co-conspirators escaped before the arrival of the police.

Police intelligence sources believe that Abu Sayyaf has strong ties to Middle Eastern terrorist groups. Abu Sayyaf members fought with the mujahedin against the Soviets in Afghanistan in the 1980s. Mohammad Khalifa, a wealthy Saudi businessman, is accused of being the main financier of Abu Sayyaf. Khalifa has a notorious reputation for funding Islamic extremist movements. Also, Osama bin Laden and al Qaeda provide training, funding, and material support for Abu Sayyaf. On February 14, 2008, Abu Sayyaf attempted to assassinate the president of Philippines, Gloria Arroyo.

The arrival of Afghan veterans and the training and leadership of al Qaeda have transformed Abu Sayyaf into a dangerous terrorist threat. Today the Abu Sayyaf is better trained, better armed, and better organized than other Philippine Islamic terrorist groups. The conflict on Mindanao has killed over 50,000 people since it began in 1972.

Communist Party of the Philippines/New People's Army (CPP/NPA)

Unlike Abu Sayyaf, the CPP/**NPA** terrorist acts have been confined to the Philippines. The NPA is active in the Northern Philippines, especially in Metropolitan Manila. The CPP/NPA was founded by Jose Maria Sison in 1969 and supports a Maoist-communist political doctrine. The goal of CPP/NPA is to overthrow the Philippine government by conducting a prolonged guerrilla war and to establish a Maoist communist government. The NPA is the guerrilla force of the CPP and has a membership of over 15,000 fighters. The CPP/NPA opposes the presence of any U.S. involvement in the Philippines. The NPA has murdered and kidnapped several U.S. military personnel stationed in the Philippines. For example, in April 1974, three U.S. naval personnel were killed near Subic Bay. In April 1989 U.S. Army Special Forces Colonel James Rowe was killed from ambush in Manila; in May 1995 two U.S. airmen were killed as they returned to Clark Air Base. The NPA has kidnapped dozens of U.S. corporate executives abroad, demanding ransom which was then used to financed their activities. Michael Barnes, general manager of Geothermal, Inc., was kidnapped while driving on his way to work. The NPA kidnappers demanded a $10 million ransom payment for Barnes's release. A Philippine counterterrorist team eventually rescued Barnes.

The Philippine government has not been able to suppress the communist insurgency of the CPP/NPA. The NPA is too well established to be completely overwhelmed or even neutralized by the Philippine government. To this end the Philippine government has engaged in a series of peace talks aimed at stabilizing the country. In 2001, the CPP met with Philippine government officials in Oslo for a series of peace talks. However, the peace talks were discontinued after three Philippine legislators were assassinated and eighteen Philippine soldiers were killed from ambush by the NPA. Despite the on-and-off peace talks, the NPA continues to engage in terrorist activities, killing and wounding hundreds of innocent people between 2004 and 2008. In 2006 media reports indicated that over forty people have been killed by NPA attacks. The terrorist attacks by the NPA will likely continue for some time to come. Although designated as an FTO, the NPA will have a difficult time gaining support from other organizations sympathetic to their cause. In the face of such challenges as Abu Sayyaf and the CPP/NPA, the Philippine government may slow the violence and terrorism down, but the insurgency probably can only be ended through a negotiated settlement.

Jemaah Islamiya (JI)[7]

The Jemaah Islamiya was first identified as a dangerous terrorist group in the late 1990s, with their headquarters in Indonesia. The name Jemaah Islamiya translates into Islamic communities. The goal of JI is to create an Islamic state consisting of Singapore, Malaysia, parts of Indonesia, and the Southern Philippines. Indonesia is the world's most populous Islamic state. The JI does not recognize the arbitrary borders established by European colonial powers over the last 300 years. In particular, JI is closely associated with the Abu Sayyaf in the Southern Philippines. The overall plan of the JI is to establish a pan-Islamic state throughout Southeast Asia (Figure 5.2).

FIGURE 5.2 Bali bombing suspect Imam Samudra shouts "Allah Okbar" (God is Great) after being sentenced to death on September 10, 2003. Member of Jemaah Islamiya executed on November 9, 2008, by firing squad. (AP/Wide World Photos)

The U.S. State Department believes it has clear evidence that JI has close ties to Osama bin Laden's global terrorist network. For example, FBI Chief Robert Mueller singled out JI as al Qaeda's leading collaborator in Southeast Asia. JI receives military training, financial assistance, and sophisticated bomb-making skills from al Qaeda. JI's most devastating terrorist attack was the indiscriminate suicide bombing of two nightclubs in Bali, Indonesia. The **Bali bombing** was Southeast Asia's first recorded suicide bombing.

On October 12, 2002, two powerful bombs exploded simultaneously in the resort of Kuta, blowing up two nightclubs, killing over 190 people, and injuring hundreds more. More than half of those dead and injured were Australians. The suicide bombing resulted in the largest loss of Australian lives in one operation since World War II. However, the JI claimed that their primary target was Americans. Few Americans were killed or injured. Police authorities maintain that the targets of the Bali bombing were foreign tourists. Targeting foreign tourists has been a favorite tactic of terrorist groups operating in Southeast Asia. Several suspects were arrested and convicted. Three suspects were sentenced to death. The sentences were carried out on November 8, 2008.

In sum, JI began as a model religious group for resisting the "evil" ways of secular Western societies. By the late 1990s, the JI evolved into a revolutionary/terrorist force determined to eliminate Western influence in Southeast Asia. JI is intent upon waging war against the West and restoring Islam as the dominant global ideology.

ALGERIAN GROUPS[8]

Armed Islamic Group (GIA) and al Qaeda in the Islamic Maghreb (Formerly GSPC)

The Armed Islamic Group, known by the French *Groupe Islamique Arm* or GIA, is a violent splinter group of Algeria's largest Islamic group, the Islamic Salvation Front. After winning independence from France in 1962, Algeria was governed by the FLN, a violent socialist terrorist organization. In 1991 the FLN, for the first time since 1962, permitted all-party elections. When the Islamic Salvation Front, a party of radical Islamists, won the election, the FLN nullified the victory, installed a military government, and banned all Islamic political organizations. The GIA emerged to fight against the FLN-supported, military-dominated government.

The goal of the GIA is to overthrow the current Algerian government and replace it with a fundamentalist Islamic state. The GIA is antisecular and antiintellectual. The GIA has destroyed over 1,000 schools and murdered more than 200 teachers in Algeria since the early 1990s. The GIA has massacred thousands of civilians, killed more than 100 European expatriates in Algeria, carried out a series of deadly bombings in Paris that killed dozens of innocent victims, kidnapped foreign nationals for ransom, hijacked several aircraft, and killed over sixty journalists.

Police intelligence believes that GIA has some connection to al Qaeda, but it is unclear what that connection might be. Osama bin Laden recruited many Algerians to fight in Afghanistan during the 1979–1989 Soviet war. However, the objectives of the GIA are more local than the ambitious objectives of Osama bin Laden for a global jihad or holy war. The GIA has not targeted U.S. citizens in Algeria though Ahmed Ressam, a member of the GIA, was arrested and convicted for planning a millennium-eve attack on the Los Angeles International Airport. At the time of his arrest, Ressam was driving a car loaded with explosives.

The GIA supports its terrorist activity by robbing banks, imposing "revolutionary taxes" on rural Algerian villagers, and donations from supporters outside of Algeria, such as Iran and Sudan. However, in January 2006, the Algerian government announced the capture of the leader of the GIA, Nourredine Boudiafi, and the dismantling of several GIA terrorist cells. The GIA's role in the current violence in Algeria appears to have decreased. Even so, the U.S. State Department believes GSPC is the most dangerous terrorist group today in Algeria. The GSPC eventually evolved into AQIM.

In 1996, the GSPC broke away from the GIA and subsequently changed its name to al Qaeda in the Islamic Maghreb. The split occurred for two primary reasons. First, AQIM adhered to the rigid and utopian principles of the Salafist branch of Islam. The Salafis believe Islam should be returned to its purest roots, supposedly practiced in the time of Prophet Muhammad. The Salafis set the best example for how Islam is to be practiced and cite their cause as the ideological justification for jihad or holy war. Second, the AQIM vowed to end the indiscriminate attacks, carried out by the GIA, against innocent civilian and noncombatant targets. The goals of the AQIM are to overthrow the secular Algerian government, replace it with a strict interpretation of Muslim Salafist beliefs, organize high-profile terrorist attacks throughout Europe, and spread Salafism throughout the Muslim world. Unlike the GIA, the AQIM concentrates its terrorist attacks on Algerian government officials, public bureaucrats, and Algerian soldiers and police rather than the massacre of innocent Algerian civilians.

The signature attack strategy of the AQIM is to set up false roadblocks that often result in the capture of Algerian government workers. AQIM has also proclaimed the use of suicide attacks as a primary method to advance the goals of the jihad. They acquire many of their weapons by raiding military and police barracks in the mountainous regions of Algeria. The AQIM also has strong ties with al Qaeda since many AQIM members fought against the Soviets in Afghanistan and later trained in al Qaeda terrorist camps. Since 2006, AQIM has claimed credit for attacks under its new name. In July 2008, AQIM issued several warnings that expanded its targets beyond Algeria and France, to include the United States. The AQIM accuses the United States of leading a "crusade" against Muslims and has sent hundreds of fighters to Iraq. The U.S. State Department estimates that 9–20 percent of foreign fighters in Iraq came from North Africa. According to the Combating Terrorism Center at the West Point military academy, Algerian terrorist groups conducted 106 significant terrorist acts in 2008.

RELIGIOUS CULTS

Aum Shinrikyo (Aum Supreme Truth)[9]

The Aum Shinrikyo is a Japanese apocalyptic religious cult that drew widespread attention after it perpetrated a **sarin gas** attack on the Tokyo subway system in March 1995. The Aum Shinrikyo was the first non-state terrorist group to carry out a large-scale chemical weapon attack against innocent civilians. By being the first terrorist group to use chemical weapons in an indiscriminate attack on noncombatants, the Aum Shinrikyo raised the level of fear on the psychological shock value of using weapons of mass destruction.

The Aum Shinrikyo cult supports a belief system that incorporates religious aspects of Hinduism, Christianity, New Age Believers, and Tibetan Buddhism. The founder and leader of Aum Shinrikyo is a half-blind yoga instructor named **Shoko Asahara** who wanted to first take over Japan and then the rest of the world. According to the revelations of Asahara, sometime around the year 2000 the United States would attack Japan using weapons of mass destruction. In the ensuing chaos, Asahara and Aum Shinrikyo would emerge and take control of Japan. But Asahara could not wait for a U.S. attack. Instead, he wanted to accelerate the process by planning the sarin gas attack in the hope that the United States would get the blame.

FIGURE 5.3 Shoko Asahara, the Aum Shinrikyo doomsday cult founder, is currently in prison awaiting execution for the 1995 sarin gas attack in Tokyo. (AP/Wide World Photos)

During the investigation that followed the sarin gas attack, police confirmed that Aum Shinrikyo carried out nine additional chemical weapons attacks in Japan and attempted seven attacks using biological weapons. For example, in June 1993, the Aum attempted to release anthrax spores from a Tokyo office building. In February 1994, the Aum traveled to Africa to analyze the use of Ebola as a weapon of mass destruction. On March 15, 1995, the Aum planned to release botulinum toxin in the Tokyo subway system but abandoned that plan in favor of the sarin gas attack. The Aum was capable of producing enough sarin gas to kill over 4 million people. Police also discovered an arsenal of chemical agents including VX, phosgene gas, and hydrogen cyanide that could easily be weaponized.

Before the sarin gas attack, Aum Shinrikyo had over 65,000 followers worldwide. After the sarin gas attack, Aum claims a following of 2,000 members worldwide. Asahara was tried, convicted, and sentenced to death for the sarin gas attack. On September 15, 2006, Asahara lost his final appeal against the death penalty. Several of Aum's adherents were also arrested, convicted, and sentenced to death for the sarin attack in Tokyo. Today the Aum Shinrikyo has a new leader, Fumihiro Joyu, and a new name, *Aleph*. Aleph is the first letter in the Hebrew alphabet and means new beginning, age of benevolence, or liberation of the soul.

The apocalyptic ethos of Aum Shinrikyo does not fit easily into the political objectives espoused by other terrorist groups. Aum Shinrikyo was obsessed with manufacturing and using weapons of mass destruction to "jump start" the biblical cataclysm—Armageddon.

Kahane Chai (Kach)[10]

Kahane Chai (Kahane Lives) and Kach (Thus! or Take) are two of the best-known violent Jewish extremist groups active in Israel today. Kahane Chai and Kach are the outgrowth of the anti-Arab and messianic teachers of Rabbi Meir Kahane. The forerunner of the Kach movement was the terrorist group called the Jewish Defense League (JDL), which was founded by Kahane in New York in 1968 to fight anti-Semitism. Unlike the JDL, the political objectives of Kahane Chai and

Kach are the expulsion of all Palestinian Arabs from the Jewish state of Israel and the restoration of the biblical lands of Israel.

Kahane wanted to transform the image of Jews as a weak and vulnerable people into a proud Jewish nation. In 1970, Kahane moved to Israel and formed the extremist Kach movement, preaching "terror against terror." Kahane and the Kach movement gained widespread support in Israel. In 1984, Kahane was elected to the Israeli Knesset as a representative of the Kach Party. Then on November 5, 1990, Kahane was assassinated in New York by an Egyptian Islamic fundamentalist while speaking to a group of his constituents. After his death, Kahane's son Binyamin formed the splinter group Kahane Chai, while Baruch Marzel took over the leadership of the Kach movement.

In 1994, the Israeli government banned both Kahane Chai and Kach and declared them to be terrorist organizations. However, the Kahane Chai and Kach continued to draw supporters from Israel and sympathetic Jewish communities in the United States. In September 1999, an Israeli court convicted several members of Kahane Chai, including Binyamin Kahane, of sedition. Then in January 2001, Palestinian gunmen killed Binyamin Kahane and his wife as they drove through the West Bank city of Hebron. Another Kach member was arrested in April 2002 for the attempted bombing of a Palestinian school and hospital in Jerusalem. Both Kahane Chai and Kach organize protests against the Israeli government and harass and threaten Palestinians. Both groups have claimed responsibility for a series of shootings and car bombings on the West Bank against "soft" Palestinian targets. Kahane Chai supports the belief that the West Bank is the biblical homeland of the ancient Hebrews.

The U.S. State Department estimates that Kach and Kahane Chai have fewer than 100 members and since 2002 have been suspected of "low-level" attacks in the West Bank. However, unconfirmed reports state that the Kahane Chai and Kach disbanded in 2008.

EUROPEAN GROUPS

The ETA (Euskadi Ta Askatasuna) Basque Fatherland and Liberty[11]

Basque nationalists seeking to establish an independent Basque nation in the regions of northern Spain and southwestern France formed the ETA in 1959. ETA maintains that Basques should have full independence from Spain. The political ideology supported by the ETA is nationalistic in nature with a "loose" commitment to Marxist philosophy. ETA has claimed responsibility for hundreds of car bombings, shootings, and kidnappings. The primary target of ETA terrorists is Spanish and French security forces and high-profile Spanish government officials. For example, Admiral Luis Carrero Blanco, the next in line to succeed Franco as "dictator" of Spain, was assassinated in 1973 by a powerful car bomb. ETA often follows shootings and assassination attempts with high explosions that are designed to divert attention away from ETA operatives and destroy any evidence left at the crime scene. ETA terrorist activities have claimed the lives of over 800 victims, half of whom have been Spanish security forces.

ETA's membership is believed to be about twenty to twenty-five hard-core members with several hundred ardent supporters. ETA members operate in small self-sufficient cells that make if difficult for the police to penetrate and develop informants. At various times, ETA has received "terrorist" training in Libya, Lebanon, Cuba, the Colombian FARC, and Nicaragua and also has close ties with the Provisional Irish Republican Army (PIRA) in Northern Ireland. Funding for ETA activities comes from bank robberies, kidnappings for ransom, drug trafficking, and extortion of "Basque revolutionary taxes" from wealthy Basque businessmen. ETA has not directly targeted U.S. interests.

Even though ETA is a domestic terrorist group, the United States and the European Union recognize ETA as a global terrorist organization. In 2002, the U.S. State Department redesignated ETA as Specially Designated Global Terrorists (SDGTs), requiring businesses, governments, and financial institutions to take specific legal measures to prevent ETA terrorism. In March 2006, ETA stunned the Spanish government by declaring a "permanent ceasefire." However, the cease-fire did not stop a more radical faction within ETA from continuing bombing of civilian targets and the assassination of Spanish police officers.

The struggle between ETA and the Spanish government has persisted for over forty-five years. Spain's antiterror campaign has resulted in the arrest of more than 100 suspected ETA members, the dismantling of several ETA cells, and the recovery of over 400 pounds of high explosives. On July 22, 2008, Spanish police believed they had finally dismantled the most dangerous ETA cell by arresting several ETA top-ranking commanders. Nevertheless, the struggle for an independent Basque state is far from over. ETA has survived fascist dictators, paramilitary counterterrorist groups, and internecine warfare. The future of ETA terrorism no doubt will continue for some time to come. ETA maintains that its support for independence is similar to that in the cases of Kosovo, Palestine, and Northern Ireland.

The Real Irish Republican Army (RIRA)[12]

The RIRA, or Oglaigh na h-Eireann, is a hard-line splinter group of between 50 to 100 members that broke away from the PIRA in late 1997. The founding members of the RIRA objected to the ceasefire called by the PIRA and to the involvement of the Republican movement in the peace process known as the Good Friday Agreement. The ultimate objective of the RIRA is the disruption of the peace talks between British Protestants and PIRA negotiators, as well as the unification of Northern Ireland and the Republic of Ireland.

The hard-liners of the RIRA wanted to continue with a campaign of violence and terrorism against the presence of British security forces in Northern Ireland. After heated debate over the proposed peace process, one of the leaders of the PIRA council, Michael McKevitt, resigned his position as quartermaster general. McKevitt's resignation was significant since he was in charge of procuring and storing weapons for the PIRA. As quartermaster general, McKevitt transformed RIRA into the best-armed terrorist organization in Western Europe, possessing a sizable amount of explosives, ammunition, and weapons. Led by McKevitt, the newly formed RIRA announced the ceasefire was over and the peace talks were irrelevant.

The goals of the RIRA support the terrorist strategy of (1) the indiscriminate bombing of town centers in Northern Ireland, (2) the attacking of police and British security forces with car bombs and homemade mortars, (3) the robbing of banks to secure funds for its terrorist activities, and (4) the spreading of fear, panic, and intimidation on the British mainland by the use of car bombs and incendiary devices.

The tactic of blowing up town centers eventually led to the massacre at **Omagh**, a market town in Northern Ireland. The Omagh bombing was the deadliest bombing in the thirty-year history of the "Irish troubles." On August 15, 1998, the town center of Omagh was destroyed by a powerful car bomb that killed thirty people and injured over 200. The public outrage over the Omagh bombing, which killed and injured Protestants and Roman Catholics, forced the RIRA to declare a suspension of bombing activities.

However, the suspension did not last long and the RIRA took its "armed struggle" to the British mainland. In 2000 and 2001, the RIRA targeted British police and military barracks, the BBC television center, MI-6 intelligence center, and the London postal depot. However, by late 2001, British and Irish authorities had arrested over forty RIRA members, including the leader and founder of the RIRA, Michael McKevitt. In February 2003, five members of the RIRA were arrested in London for conspiracy to bomb several targets in England. On February 7, 2008, the RIRA announced it intends to "go back to war" by opening up a new offensive against "legitimate targets," and apologized for the Omagh bombing.

The future of the RIRA remains uncertain. The Omagh atrocity turned the Irish Catholic community against the tactics of the RIRA. Despite the arrests and lack of support from Roman Catholics, some RIRA members will most likely continue to carry on the armed struggle and attempt to derail the Good Friday peace process.

Revolutionary Organization 17 November[13]

The Revolutionary Organization **17 November** was formed in 1973 in Athens, Greece, in honor of thirty-four university students who were killed by police during a peaceful student demonstration. The objectives of 17 November include the expulsion of U.S. military bases from Greece, the removal of Turkish forces from Cyprus, the severing of Greece's association with NATO, and the withdrawal of Greece from the EU. The political ideology supported by 17 November is Marxist-Leninist in nature centered around the anti-Greek establishment and anticapitalist and anti-imperialist beliefs.

The organization launched its terrorist campaign in 1975 with the assassination of Richard Welch, the CIA's station chief in Athens. Over the next twenty-seven years, 17 November continued sporadic terrorist attacks in metropolitan Athens. These terrorist attacks included rocket attacks, car bombings, PIRA-style improvised mortar assaults against military bases and government buildings, and assassinations of Greek and American diplomats. It was the most elusive terrorist group in Europe, completely eluding police for over twenty-seven years. Police investigators believe that the tight organizational structure, largely self-taught and rarely consulting with other terrorist groups, accounted for the elusiveness of 17 November. In total, 17 November is credited with over 100 attacks and twenty-three fatalities between 1975 and 2002.

However, the terrorist activities of 17 November may be over or at least slowed down. On June 29, 2002, Savas Xiros, a member of 17 November, was on his way to carry out a bombing when the bomb prematurely detonated, injuring Xiros and resulting in his capture. Police interrogation and the discovery of a revolver on Xiros linked him to several bombings and assassinations. Shortly thereafter, Xiros confessed, and fourteen members of 17 November were arrested, including the former university professor Alexandros Giotopoulos. Giotopoulos, the chief ideologue of 17 November, was identified as the shooter in the Welch murder. Greek police maintain that the active membership of 17 November is less than twenty terrorists. By March 2003, fourteen members of 17 November were found guilty and sentenced to long prison terms.

Despite the capture of 17 November, Greek authorities suspect that it had close ties with another Greek terrorist organization known as the Revolutionary Nuclei or ELA. The ELA may be an umbrella group for several smaller Greek terrorist groups.

Revolutionary Nuclei (formerly ELA)[14]

Like 17 November, the Revolutionary Nuclei (RN), also known as the Revolutionary People's Struggle or ELA, is active in Greece. The ELA began in 1971 in opposition to the military government that ruled Greece. Similar to 17 November, the ELA was anticapitalist, anti-imperialist, and supported the political ideals of Marxism. The ELA became known as the blue jean bombers. Explosives wrapped in blue jeans or jeans material were the signature bomb of the ELA. The ELA dropped out of sight and has not claimed credit for a terrorist attack since 1995.

In 1996, a new group known as the RN began claiming credit for a series of bombings directed at the economic institutions of Greece. In fact the RN attacked the same targets as the ELA. It appears that the RN was a splinter group of the former ELA. The RN has taken credit for bombing dozens of "soft" symbolic targets of Greek "capitalism" and U.S. "imperialism." Unlike 17 November and the ELA, the RN precedes their bombings by warning the intended victims. To date there has been only one bombing incident that caused injury or death. The bombing of a meeting of the European Commission in Athens in April 1999 killed an innocent bystander. The RN has not claimed credit for a terrorist bombing attack since late 2000. As long as the RN avoids the type of bombings that cause personal injury, there is probably no reason that it will not remain a dangerous annoyance to Greece.

Revolutionary Peoples Liberation Party/Front (RPLP/F)[15]

The RPLP/F is an anti-Western Marxist-socialist group. The primary goal of the RPLP/F is to "liberate" Turkey from American influence and establish an independent socialist state in Turkey. The group also opposes the U.S.-led war in Afghanistan and Iraq, the search for al Qaeda leaders, and the presence of NATO in Turkey. The RPLP/F was originally established in 1978 as Devrimci Sol or **Dev Sol** (Revolutionary Way). The RPLP/F formed as a dissident faction of Dev Sol, attacking Turkish national security interest and military targets.

The RPLP/F began to intensify its terrorist campaign in the late 1980s, continuing to attack soft Turkish government targets. However, in 1990 RPLP/F changed its target selection and began attacking foreign business interests and military installations in Turkey. For example, RPLP/F assassins murdered British businessmen and American defense contractors, launched rockets at the U.S. consulate in Istanbul, and detonated bombs at several U.S. Air Force facilities in Turkey. By 1998, a faction of RPLP/F claimed to have committed a total of 1,000 terrorist operations such as massacres, disappearances, bombings, and murders throughout the country of Turkey. However, since 2004 no terrorist incidents have been claimed by RPLP/F.

Despite the internal feuding between the RPLP/F and Dev Sol, the RPLP/F still poses an ongoing terrorist threat to Western national security interests in Turkey. The preemptive U.S. strike against Iraq in March 2003 presents a continued danger to U.S. interests in Turkey from the RPLP/F. The group has been intensely outspoken against U.S. military operations in Iraq and Afghanistan. Even though the RPLP/F is of major concern to the Turkish government and the United States, the threat from the Kurdish Workers Party (PKK) is the cause of more concern for Turkish authorities.

The Kurdish Workers Party (PKK), now known as KADEK or Kongra Gel[16]

Inspired by Marxist political doctrine, the Kurdish Workers Party, or PKK, was formed in 1974. The goal of the PKK was to establish a Marxist-communist state in predominantly Kurdish southeast Turkey. Like all new groups, the PKK lacked funding, weapons, and recruits. In order to finance its activities, the PKK carried out a series of daring bank robberies and became involved in narcotics trafficking. A large portion of narcotics supplied to Western Europe passed through PKK dealers. The PKK was then able to purchase a sizable quantity of weapons and attract mostly idealistic Kurdish students to their cause. By 1980, the PKK moved their operation to the Beka'a Valley in Lebanon where they received "terrorist" training from various Palestinian factions. However, support for the Marxist agenda of the PKK was only minimal among the

Kurdish communities of Turkey. Thus, by 1984 the PKK changed its direction and focus, concentrating more on the nationalistic goals of the Kurdish people and less on the political ideology of Marxism. The PKK's new objective was the "liberation of Kurds" and the creation of an independent United Democratic Kurdistan in Turkey, Syria, Iran, and Iraq. The PKK has since toned down its rhetoric and pursues the cultural and political rights for the ethnic Kurdish population in Turkey.

To this end the PKK began its terrorist campaign by assassinating Turkish diplomats, bombing Turkish commercial interests in Europe, attacking Turkish resorts, kidnapping foreign tourists for ransom, suicide bombings of Turkish government facilities, and indiscriminate bombing attacks against soft Turkish civilian targets. Thousands of Turks were killed and injured in the terrorism blitz by the PKK in the 1990s. Then on February 16, 1999, Turkish authorities captured Abdullah **Ocalan**, the founder and leader of the PKK, in Nairobi, Kenya. The capture of Ocalan drastically reduced the terrorist activity of the PKK. In April 2002, the PKK changed its name to Kurdish Freedom and Democracy Congress (KADEK). Nevertheless, the name change did not affect the overall goal of Kurdish nationalism and the creation of an independent Kurdish state. In fact, to complicate the war in Iraq, Turkish troops entered Northern Iraq in an effort to destroy the PKK or KADEK. However, Turkish troops were unsuccessful. By April 2009, Northern Iraq had become a staging ground for PKK attacks against Turkey.

COLOMBIA

The People's Revolutionary Army: Fuerzas Armadas Revolucionarias de Colombia (FARC)[17]

FARC was formerly established in 1964 as the military wing of the Colombian Communist Party. Motivated by Marxist ideology, FARC is determined to overthrow the Colombian government. FARC actually controls about 40 percent of Colombia, has a large guerrilla force of 18,000 armed fighters, and is heavily involved in narcotics traffic. It is involved in all the processes of drug trafficking from "taxing" the growers of coca and poppy plants to controlling the manufacturing laboratories and distribution centers to foreign illegal drug markets. Drug trafficking provides a huge source of income for FARC. Drugs are often traded for weapons and explosives, to attract new recruits, and to fund FARC terrorist operations. The profits derived from narcotics traffic have made FARC the richest terrorist group in the world.

Kidnapping and extortion provide other sources of income for FARC. Since the early formation of FARC, kidnapping and extortion have been their signature terrorist tactic. The FARC, together with the National Liberation Army (ELN), account for the majority of kidnappings in Colombia. Since 1980 FARC and the ELN have kidnapped over 100 Americans, thirteen of whom were murdered. On April 11, 2002, FARC kidnapped thirteen Colombian lawmakers from a government building in Cali. On June 28, 2007, the FARC reported the death of eleven of the Colombian lawmakers. Ingrid Betancourt, a well-known figure in Colombian politics, was taken hostage in February 2002. Colombian security forces finally rescued her on July 2, 2008. FARC has also committed numerous bombings of oil pipelines, Colombian Army posts, police barracks, banks, bridges, and soft noncombatant targets.

While the conflict between FARC and the Colombian government appears to be a domestic issue, many international players are now involved. Drug profits have demonstrated the global reach of FARC by attracting Cubans, Iranians, Germans, al Qaeda, and other Latin American "insurgent" groups. The latest evidence of interaction between FARC and another terrorist group was the arrest of three suspected PIRA members in August 2001. Apparently the PIRA introduced FARC to the use of sophisticated car bombs and long-range mortar attacks in exchange for narcotics.

The FARC has been involved in on-and-off peace talks with the Colombian government since 1980. According to some observers, FARC enters the peace process because it legitimizes their cause for social justice. The future does not look bright for Colombia. FARC has huge cash reserves from drug trafficking and ransom payments. The cycle of civil war and political corruption, together with the U.S. appetite for drugs, ensures the continued existence of FARC.

The National Liberation Army: Ejercito de Liberacion Nacional (ELN)[18]

The ELN is yet another Marxist guerrilla organization involved in Colombia's thirty-five-year-old civil war. In 1997, after several attacks on American interests in Colombia, the ELN was added to the U.S. State Department's list of FTOs. Like FARC, the ELN has murdered dozens of Colombian political leaders and business owners who oppose their Marxist agenda. ELN's present strength is estimated at about 4,000.

Unlike FARC, Roman Catholic clergymen led the ELN until the emergence of Nicolas Rodriguez, its present leader. The ELN derives its funding from kidnapping and extortion. In 2001, for example, the ELN held over 800 hostages for ransom and received over $200 million for their release. The victims of ELN kidnappings are mostly foreign oil companies' employees. By 2005, the ELN became involved in drug trafficking. The terrorist activities of the ELN closely resemble those of FARC—bombings, assassinations, and kidnappings for ransom. Nonetheless, the terrorist activities of the ELN and FARC have not gone on unchallenged. The United Self-Defense Forces of Colombia (AUC) appeared in 1997 with the goal of eliminating the ELN and FARC and are, in fact, responsible for the majority of civilian casualties in Colombia's civil war.

United Self-Defense Forces of Colombia: Autodefensas Unidas de Colombia (AUC)[19]

The AUC emerged from an earlier Colombian group known as MAS or "death to kidnappers." The notorious drug czar Pablo Escobar formed MAS after his sister was kidnapped in 1981. MAS eventually grew into one of the most feared paramilitary groups in Colombia. As the drug trade expanded, the paramilitaries gained strength and prestige among the Colombian military and drug traffickers. By the late 1980s, there were several such paramilitary groups, including MAS that protected wealthy landowners and drug dealers in Northern Colombia from the "guerrilla" activities of FARC and the ELN. In 1997, the AUC was formed as an umbrella group to unite several paramilitary organizations in Colombia.

The objectives of the AUC were to destroy the Marxist guerrilla groups, FARC and ELN, put an end to kidnappings and extortion, and gain recognition by the Colombian government as a legitimate political entity. The AUC had a paramilitary force of about 8,000 members. It actively recruited members from families that are terrorized by the "guerrilla" activities of the ELN and FARC.

However, the AUC has expanded its target selection beyond the Marxist guerrillas and citizens who support them to include the murder of trade union members and human rights activists. The AUC also wants its share of the Colombian drug trade. In 2002, Attorney General Ashcroft indicted several members of the AUC on charges of smuggling approximately 17 tons of cocaine into the United States since 1997. On May 13, 2008, thirteen AUC commanders were extradited to the United States to answer charges of murder, kidnapping, and drug trafficking against U.S. citizens in Colombia. Furthermore, the Colombian government has "outlawed" all paramilitary groups in Colombia, although some experts believe that strong ties exist between the Colombian military and the AUC. The AUC is responsible for the largest number of killings and massacres in Colombia. It committed over 100 massacres in 2001, a typical terror tactic used to intimidate the peasant population of Colombia. A ceasefire was declared and the Colombian government began to negotiate peace terms with the AUC. By February 2006, over 17,000 members of the AUC turned in their weapons, and the AUC began to demobilize. The AUC is no longer a major threat to Colombia, although some AUC cadres are still involved in narcotics and drug trafficking. Another Marxist terrorist group is also active in Peru.

PERU

Sendero Luminoso (SL or Shining Path)[20]

The Sendero Luminoso formed as a splinter group of the Communist Party of Peru. The SL bases its political ideology on the Maoist ethos of its founder **Abimael Guzman**. A philosophy professor at the University of Huamanga in Peru, Guzman adopted the Maoist model of insurgency for the SL. The university connection of Guzman provided the SL with a convenient source of recruitment, which targeted impressionable university students. Guzman, who had visited China during the Cultural Revolution, advocated the complete overthrow of Hispanic social structures and their replacement by a Maoist centralized socialist system run by indigenous peoples of Peru.

Beginning in 1980, the SL launched their first attacks on agriculture areas of central Peru in an attempt to isolate rural communities from urban areas. In the process, the SL murdered local Peruvian government officials and terrorized the local peasant populations into submission. Despite the intimidation of local peasants, the SL profited from the protection of cocoa farmers. It also derived financing for its political agenda by robbing banks, extorting a "revolutionary tax" from corporations, and kidnapping for ransom.

The SL has a wide range of targets to select from. These include government officials, foreign diplomats, corporations, and rival "revolutionary" groups. The attack methods used by SL consist mostly of car bombings, assassinations, attacks on the infrastructure of Peru, and the torture of suspected collaborators. The U.S. State Department estimates that the SL is responsible for over 30,000 deaths since 1980. In one such attack, the SL conducted a campaign of genocide against the Ashaninkas Indians. The Ashaninkas are the largest ethnic group in Peru's forest region. The SL was seeking revenge against the Ashaninkas who signed an agreement with the Peruvian government to organize counterterrorism squads. The single most destructive act by the SL was the double bombing in a busy shopping district of Lima. Two car bombs containing about 1,000 kilograms of explosives were detonated by the SL, killing twenty-four people and injuring over 200 others. By 1990, Alberto Fujimori was elected president of Peru after promising to rid Peru of terrorism by the SL.

Fujimori suspended the Peruvian constitution in 1992, giving the police more power to go after the SL. By early 1993, the Peruvian police had captured Guzman and 300 members of the SL. The capture of Guzman marked the decline of the SL, which then split into two factions, creating a crisis of leadership for the group. One faction advocated a continuation of the armed struggle, while another faction wanted to negotiate a peace deal with the Peruvian government.

In spite of these setbacks, the SL has recently expanded its interest in drug trafficking. The booming Peruvian cocaine industry as well as a lucrative market for opium poppies has contributed to the renewed efforts of the SL to recruit new members. In September and October of 2008, the Peruvian government stepped up its assault on SL training camps, killing several SL recruits. The recent escalation in narcotrafficking and kidnapping for ransom indicates the SL may be in the process of building up its "war chest." The future outlook for Peru appears to suggest a continued struggle between security forces, drug trafficking, and the terrorism of the Sendero Luminoso.

CENTRAL ASIA

Jammu/Kashmir[21]

The U.S. State Department lists four Islamic groups active in Kashmir and Pakistan. The groups are:

> Harakut ul-Mujahedin (HUM) or Islamic Freedom Fighters formed in 1985
>
> Lashkar e-Tayyiba (LT) or Army of the Pure created in 1990
>
> Jaish e-Muhammad (JEM) or Army of Muhammad established in 2000
>
> Lashkar e-Jhangvi (LIJ) or the Army of Jhangvi founded in 1996

The goal of HUM, LT, JEM, and LIT (hereafter known as the Groups) strives to create a pan-Islamic Empire in Central Asia, unifying **Jammu/Kashmir** and Pakistan. Although some of the Groups' leaders have also called for a worldwide jihad, the Groups follow a predominately anti-Western and anti-India terrorist agenda. The Groups can trace their origins to the Afghan–Soviet War where they fought alongside the Taliban against the Soviet Union. After the Afghan war, many **mujahedins** joined the struggle to "free" Kashmir. The Groups have a combined strength of several thousand fighters.

The Groups have carried out hundreds of terrorist attacks against Indian military troops and civilians in Kashmir. Traditionally, the attack methods used by the Groups are car bombs, rocket-propelled grenades, and, most recently, suicide attacks. The Groups also carry out massacres of Hindu, Sikh, and Shia communities in Kashmir and Pakistan. Kashmir is one of the world's most violent places. According to the U.S. State Department, since the terrorism began in the early 1990s, approximately 60,000 people have been killed.

Some recent terrorist incidents include the following. A leading JEM member was arrested for the murder of American journalist Daniel Pearl, a correspondent for the *Wall Street Journal*. On December 24, 1999, HUM hijacked an Indian Airlines flight from Nepal to Afghanistan. The hijacking ended after the Indian government capitulated and released several members of HUM from Indian jails. On December 13, 2001, in a combined suicide assault the LT and JEM attacked the Indian parliament, killing twelve people and wounding several others. The LIJ, besides attacking anti-Western targets, is involved in a bitter sectarian rivalry with the Shia community of Pakistan. After the assassination of the LIJ leader by a Shia "terrorist," the LIJ began attacking Shia clergy, mosques, and communities in retaliation. On February 22, 2003, the LIJ attacked a Shia mosque in Pakistan where nineteen people were killed while engaged in a Muslim prayer service.

Both Pakistan and India claim Kashmir as part of their sovereign territory. The decades-long conflict over Jammu/Kashmir has brought Pakistan and India close to nuclear war. Additionally, the Groups in Central Asia appear to be funded, trained, and supplied by Osama bin Laden and al Qaeda. The Pakistani groups all support the rhetoric of al Qaeda and the religious tenets of the Taliban, calling for the destruction of America and death to "Western crusaders." The Pakistan—India conflict over Kashmir is probably the most dangerous conflict in the world today since both countries have a nuclear military option.

Islamic Movement of Uzbekistan[22]

Uzbekistan is another country that has been transformed by religious fanaticism and al Qaeda's money and weapons. The IMU was created in 1998 calling for the overthrow of the Uzbek government and replacing it with an Islamic state. In 2001, the IMU expanded its original goal of an Islamic state in Uzbekistan to establishing an Islamic state in all of Central Asia. The membership of the IMU is made up of mostly Uzbeks, but also includes other Central Asian nationalities and ethnic groups. The IMU has declared a jihad in Central Asia in order to create an Islamic religious system based on a literal interpretation of the Sharia and Islamic law.

The IMU operates largely in the Ferghana Valley on the Uzbek-Kyrgyz border where it receives support and protection from local villagers. The total membership of the IMU is unknown; however, the U.S. State Department estimates that the IMU has several thousand active fighters. The IMU has close links to al Qaeda, the former Taliban of Afghanistan, and the HUM in Pakistan. It derives its main funding source from the lucrative drug trade of Afghanistan. The network of IMU operatives aid drug traffickers in the smuggling of heroin and opium into Russia and Europe. Apart from smuggling drugs, the IMU also sells drugs throughout Central Asia. Besides the involvement in drug trafficking, it also has taken hostages for ransom, including four Americans who eventually escaped.

The IMU is responsible for a series of indiscriminate car bombings in the Uzbek capital of Tashkent, where numerous people were killed. The IMU were among the most dedicated foreign mercenaries who fought against U.S. forces in Afghanistan in October 2001. IMU fighters were also among the Taliban prisoners who were incarcerated at Guantanamo Bay, Cuba. According to Ahmed Rashid, the IMU recently made contact with Uighur Muslims from **Xinjiang** province of China, fulfilling their promise to unite all of Central Asia under one Islamic state. The noted professor John Esposito maintains that the IMU poses the greatest security threat to the peace of Central Asia. The media report that in mid-2008, over a dozen IMU terrorists were arrested in Germany while preparing to raid a U.S. military installation in search of weapons and explosives.

East Turkestan Islamic Movement (ETIM)[23]

The East Turkestan Islamic Movement is a Muslim separatist movement based in China's western Xinjiang province. Xinjiang province is a sparsely populated region that borders several countries, including Afghanistan and Pakistan. The Uighur people formed the ETIM. The **Uighurs** are the largest Turkish-speaking ethnic minority in Xinjiang. The Uighurs support a moderate form of Sufi Islam. The goal of the ETIM is the creation of an independent state called East Turkestan. China has long viewed the separatist activities of the ETIM as a threat to its territorial integrity. The Chinese government maintains that since 1990 the ETIM has been responsible for over 200 terrorist attacks, killing 162 people and injuring hundreds.

According to Chinese officials, the ETIM has indiscriminately bombed buses, marketplaces, and government buildings and assassinated local government authorities, Muslim clerics who do not support them, and innocent civilians; they have also attacked Chinese military bases. Even though the ETIM has focused on Chinese targets, it planned to attack the U.S. embassy in the Kyrgyz capital of Bishkek, in May 2002. China claims that the ETIM has cells operating throughout Central Asia. Although the U.S. State Department asserts that the ETIM has a close relationship with al Qaeda, which supports them with money and weapons, Hahsan Mahsum, the leader of the ETIM, has denied any relationship between the ETIM and al Qaeda. However, ETIM insurgents fought in the ranks of al Qaeda and the Taliban during Operation Enduring Freedom.

U.S. intelligence officials report that twenty-two Uighurs were captured in Afghanistan and detained at Guantanamo Bay, where they confessed to the ETIM's link to al Qaeda.

Although the ETIM has carried out numerous terrorist acts against Chinese targets over the last decade, critics view the U.S. decision to recognize ETIM as a terrorist group a political move to secure China's support during the UN Security Council debate over a resolution to go to war with Iraq. In fact, human rights groups have accused China of repressing the Uighur people. Likewise, the United States has accused China of using the war on terrorism as a pretext to control political dissent in Xinjiang province.

Xinjiang, China's largest province, is estimated to have about 40 million people, including 8 million Uighurs. The province has large deposits of natural gas, oil, and uranium. The native Uighurs resisted China's occupation of Xinjiang, but failed to gain support from neighboring Muslim states. Since the mid-1980s, China has consolidated its power over the Xinjiang province and sees the increase of Uighur "terrorism" as a potential threat to Chinese hegemony in the region. In the period leading up to the Olympics in Beijing, it was widely reported that ETIM would try to disrupt the Olympic Games. No terrorist attacks occurred during the 2008 Olympic Games in Beijing.

Chechen Terrorist Groups[24]

On February 14, 2003, Secretary of State Colin Powell designated four Chechen organizations as terrorist groups. These include:

1. The Special Purpose Islamic Regiment (SPIR)
2. The Islamic International Brigade (IIB)
3. Riyadus-Salikin Reconnaissance
4. Sabotage Battalion of Chechen Martyrs

The Chechen terrorists are engaged in a bloody ethno-nationalist struggle for the independence of the Republic of **Chechnya** from 150 years of Russian domination. In general, the Chechens are a largely Muslim ethnic group that has resided for centuries in the mountainous Caucasus region and has continually resisted Russian subjugation. The conflict between Chechens and Russians was heightened during World War II. The Soviet dictator Josef Stalin accused the Chechens of collaborating with the Nazis and forcibly deported the entire Chechen population to the Central Asian Republic of Kazakhstan. Thousands of Chechens perished, and the survivors were only permitted to return to Chechnya after the death of Stalin in 1953.

The Chechen terrorist groups adhere to the passionate fundamentalism of the Wahhabi sect of Islam. In addition to Chechen independence, Chechen terrorist groups seek to create a fundamentalist-style Islamic state throughout the entire Caucasus region. As followers of the Wahhabi sect of Islam, Chechen terrorists have transformed the Chechen civil war for national liberation into a religiously inspired jihad. The U.S. State Department believes that Chechen terrorist groups have direct links to al Qaeda. Chechen extremists reportedly fought alongside al Qaeda and Taliban forces against the U.S.-supported Northern Alliance in late 2001. The Taliban regime was the only "government" to recognize Chechen independence. Popular support for Chechen independence is widespread among Muslims throughout the world.

Chechen terrorists are responsible for committing numerous acts of terrorism, including hostage takings, assassinations, and indiscriminate bombings. According to the U.S. State Department, all four groups were directly involved in the taking of over 800 hostages at Moscow's Dubrovka Theater in October 2002, an incident that resulted in the deaths of 129 hostages, including two Americans. In December 2002, in a dual suicide bombing attack on the headquarters of Chechnya's Russian-supported government, eighty-three people were killed. In May 2002, a bomb blast during a military parade in Grozny killed forty-one people, including seventeen children. The most brutal and notorious attack occurred in September 2004 when Chechen terrorists attacked a school in Beslan in an effort to take children as hostages. After a three-day siege, Russian counterterrorism forces overran the hostage takers. More than 300 people were killed, most of them children. All but one of the thirty-two Chechen terrorists were killed.

The future of Chechen terrorism remains uncertain. The deaths of two popular terrorist group leaders, Arbi Barayev and Amir al-Khattab, have left a vacuum in the leadership of Chechen terrorist groups. However, there is a possibility that large-scale terrorist attacks against targets in Moscow will continue. The ties between Chechen groups and al Qaeda can be traced back to the Soviet occupation of Afghanistan, where Chechens joined Osama bin Laden. Later, the Chechens joined the Taliban in the Afghanistan civil war of 2001. Vladimir Putin has continually stressed that Chechen terrorists are part of the global jihad of al Qaeda. If the March 23, 2003, referendum, where the majority of Chechens accepted political autonomy under continued Russian rule, does not hold, then an escalation of terrorism by determined Islamic fundamentalists may begin.

IRAN

Mujaheddin-e Khalq (MEK)[25] or Peoples Mojahedin Organization of Iran (PMOI)

The **MEK** can trace its origins back to the early 1960s and the formation of the National Liberation Movement of Iran. The MEK first sought to overthrow the shah of Iran, Reza Pahlavi. In the late 1970s, the MEK fought in guerrilla operations during the Iranian revolution that eventually forced the capitulation of the shah's government. However, due to its radical Marxist ideology the MEK was left out of the power structure formed by the Ayatollah Khomeini after the Iranian revolution. Since the late 1970s, the MEK has turned against the government of Iran and continues to wage an armed struggle. Iraq previously provided the MEK with financial, logistical, and military support. The MEK remains the most powerful opposition group to the Islamic Republic of Iran. The MEK attacked targets in Iran and assassinated Iranian government officials from bases in Iraq. Prior to the U.S. invasion of Iraq, several thousand MEK fighters were located in twenty bases scattered throughout Iraq. After the invasion of Iraq in 2003, U. S. forces bombed MEK bases because of their alliance with Saddam Hussein. By early 2004, MEK and U.S. forces entered into a cease-fire agreement. The United States reportedly captured over 6,000 MEK fighters and 2,000 pieces of military hardware. As of April 2009, MEK fighters are kept under U.S. military guard in a camp outside Baghdad.

The MEK's worldwide campaign of terrorism against the Iranian government has continued since the 1970s. The MEK participated in the taking of American hostages in Tehran in 1979. In 1981, the MEK planted bombs in the office of the Islamic Republican Party in Tehran, killing several high-ranking Iranian officials. In April 1992, the MEK carried out bombings and assaults on Iranian embassies located in thirteen different countries. In 2001 and 2002, the MEK carried out regular attacks and cross-border raids from Iraq on Iranian military targets. In Tehran, the MEK conducts frequent attacks against Iranian political leaders.

The MEK had its own conventional military force protected by Iraq. In the past, the MEK assisted Iraq in the repression of the Kurds and other ethnic minorities in northern Iraq. The MEK has an extensive support system throughout the Iranian diaspora. In sum, the MEK has conducted numerous bombings, assassinations, and hostage takings against the Iranian government. Undoubtedly the MEK will continue the armed struggle to overthrow the Islamic Republic of Iran and replace it with a Marxist/socialist governmental system. However, after the defeat of Saddam Hussein and Iraq, the MEK lost its most ardent support. The future of the MEK is uncertain. In January 2009, the EU removed MEK from its list of terrorist organizations, thereby unfreezing millions of dollars owned by the MEK. The United States is expected to follow the EU and remove MEK from its list of FTOs.

Conclusions

Foreign terrorist organizations differ not only in terrorist objectives but also in size, strength, terrorist tactics, ideological goals, outside support, anti-U.S. orientation, the use of suicide bombers, and popular community support. Despite the diversity of designated FTOs, they do share a basic structure. The root causes of terrorism, such as poverty, political corruption, religious conflict, and ethnic turmoil, create opportunities for terrorist groups to exploit. The belief that the use of terrorism as a legitimate strategy to effect political change is a fundamental problem enabling terrorist groups to develop and mature.

FTOs must have a physical base from which to operate. Many states around the world offer safe havens, both physical and virtual, to terrorist groups. Supporting states provide safe houses, training grounds, financial networks, and reliable communication systems. Once operating in a safe environment, the terrorist organization can begin to develop and expand. With help of state sponsors, the terrorist threat today can now disperse training, logistics, and leadership not just regionally but globally.

Furthermore, many FTOs have become self-sufficient by exploiting the global criminal environment to support their terrorist operations. For example, FARC, ELN, and SL are heavily involved in cocaine trafficking in Colombia and Peru. Pakistani and Kashmiri groups profit from the poppy fields of Afghanistan, and Abu Sayyaf is involved in kidnapping for ransom in the Philippines. FTOs are increasingly using criminal activities to support and fund terrorist objectives. Thus, FTOs often operate in states that have weak and ineffectual central governments.

Moreover, the terrorist threat is flexible and transnational in nature. FTOs often work together sharing intelligence, training, planning, and carrying out terrorist attacks. In 2001, three members of the PIRA were apprehended in Colombia, suspected of training FARC in how to make sophisticated car bombs in exchange for cocaine. The connections between al Qaeda and FTOs throughout Central and Southeast Asia further highlight the dynamic network of interconnected terrorist groups.

Figure 5.4 illustrates how FTOs operate on three distinctive levels. At the first level are those FTOs that function primarily in a single country. State-level FTOs have a limited global reach but may expand if allowed to develop their organizational structure unchecked by governmental authorities. The second level is FTOs that have a regional influence and may cross contiguous borders to carry out terrorist operations. The third category represents FTOs with global influence. FTOs with a global reach span several regions, and their objectives are transnational and even global, such as al Qaeda.

The three types of FTOs (state, regional, global) are linked together in two basic ways. First, FTOs can cooperate by sharing intelligence, resources, safe havens, personnel, and expertise. Second, FTOs can support each other by fostering the same ideological agenda, such as a pan-Islamic state in Southeast Asia. The inner-connected nature of many of the designated FTOs necessitates that legitimate governments pursue a rigorous policy of law enforcement and at times military action.

However, the designated FTOs do not completely capture the "B list" of ad hoc groups, fringe

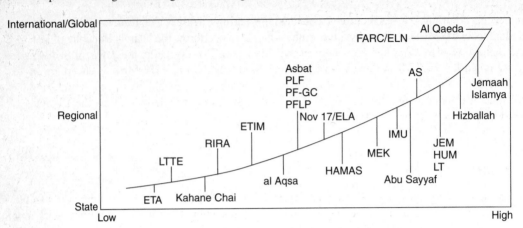

FIGURE 5.4   Threat severity of designated foreign terrorist organizations to United States.

groups, and less established terrorist groups, who are just as dangerous as the designated "A list." In other words, the war on terrorism is not a campaign with an identifiable beginning and an ending.

Terrorism perpetrated by the FTOs probably cannot be defeated but only reduced, prevented, and maybe controlled. Jenkins said it best—"Terrorism is a growth industry."

Key Terms

Abimael Guzman	Fatah	Pan Am 103
Abu Abbas	George Habash	Salafist
Antiterrorism Act	Jammu/Kashmir	Sarin gas
Bali bombing	MEK	Shoko Asahara
Basque	mujahedin	17 November
Bojinka Plot	NPA	Uighurs
Chechnya	Ocalan	Uzbekistan
Dev Sol	Omagh	Xinjiang
FARC		

Writing Assignment

Select one of the designated FTOs outlined in this chapter and prepare a *threat* analysis. You are to follow the threat analysis guidelines.

GUIDELINES FOR THREAT ANALYSIS PAPER

You are to conduct a threat analysis of a FTO outlined in this chapter that has been identified as posing a threat to the United States or its interests.

    A. Motivation: Stated goals
      1. Political philosophies
      2. Ideological support

      a. International support and cooperation
      b. Umbrella or cover group
    3. Spiritual or religious "support"
    4. Historical background/significant dates
    5. Role of the United States
  B. Tactics and Strategies
    1. Selection of victims and target discrimination
    2. Media manipulation
      a. Propaganda methods
      b. Use of disinformation
    3. Type of weapons, explosives, or equipment

4. Methods of attack: bombing, hostage taking, and assassination
5. Criminal activities: narcotics and drugs, bank robberies, kidnapping for ransom
6. Community support
   a. Geographic region
   b. State sponsors
7. Profile of group membership
   a. Strength
   b. Recruitment
   c. Training
8. Past terrorist activities
   a. Patterns
   b. Trends
   c. Successes and failures
   d. Benchmark incidents
9. Financial support

C. Terrorism Counteraction
   1. Response of the criminal justice system
   2. Government response
      a. Treaties
      b. Conventions
      c. Intelligence gathering
      d. Military action
   3. Effectiveness of legal measures
D. Future Threat
   1. Vulnerabilities and potential targets
   2. Security measures
E. Your opinion and final analysis

Your threat analysis should be five to eight pages in length, typed and double spaced, with at least ten references. No more than four references may be from Internet sources.

Web Sites

U.S. Department of State: *Foreign Terrorist Organizations*
http://www.state.gov

Center for Defense Information (CDI): *Terrorism Project*
http://www.cdi.org

Foreign Policy: *Magazine of Global Politics, Economics, and Ideas*
http://www.foreignpolicy.com

Council of Foreign Relations: *Terrorism Questions and Answers*
http://www.terrorismanswers.com

Jane's: *Jane's World Insurgency and Terrorism*
http://www.janes.com

START: National Consortium for the Study of Terrorism and Responses to Terrorism
http://www.start.umd.edu

Institute for the Study of Violent Groups
http://www.isvg.org

Endnotes

1. For example, see Carl A. Wege, "The Abu Nidal Organization," *Terrorism*, 14 (January–March 1991), pp. 59–66; Yossi Melman, *The Master Terrorist: The True Story behind Abu Nidal* (New York: Adams, 1986); "TVI Profile Report: Fatah Revolutionary Council (FRC)," *TVI Profile*, 8 (1989), pp. 5–8; Patrick Seale, *Abu Nidal* (London: Arrow Books Limited, 1992); Clifford Simonsen and Jeremy R. Spindlove, *Terrorism Today: The Past, the Players, the Future* (Upper Saddle River, NJ: Prentice Hall Inc., 2000), pp. 141–44.

2. For example, see Jeffery A. Builta, *Extremist Groups: An International Compilation of Terrorist Organizations, Violent Political Groups, and Issue Oriented Militant Movements* (Chicago, IL: Office of International Criminal Justice, University of Illinois at Chicago, 1996), pp. 573–95; Sara M. Ellenbogen, *Revolutionaries and Reformers: Contemporary Islamist Movements in the Middle East* (Albany, NY: State University of New York Press, 2003); CDI: Center for Defense Information, *http://www.cdi.org.*

3. For example, see "U.S. Says Palestinian Guerrilla Chief Abu Abbas Must Be Tried," *Agence France-Presse* (January 13, 2003), *http://www.clari.net/*; Neil C. Livingstone and David Halevy, *Inside the PLO: Covert Units, Secret Funds, and*

the War against Israel and the United States (New York: Morrow Publishing, 1990); "Hijack Backwash," *Nation*, 241 (October 26, 1985), pp. 395–96; Stephen Segaller, *Invisible Armies: Terrorism into the 1990's* (New York: Harcourt-Brace-Jovanovich, 1987); Brian Marshall, "Palestine Liberation Front (PLF)," *Jane's Information Group* (May 21, 1999); Antonio Cassere, *Terrorism, Politics, and Law: The Achille Lauro Affair* (Williston, VT: Blackwell Publishers, 1989).

4. For example, see Bruce Hoffman, *Inside Terrorism* (New York: Columbia University Press, 1998), pp. 66–69; Harold M. Cubert, *The PFLP's Changing Role in the Middle East* (New York: Frank Cass Publishers, 1997); Samuel M. Katz, *Israel versus Jihad: The Twenty Year War against a Master Terrorist* (New York: Paragon House Publishers, 1993); Popular Front for the Liberation of Palestine, *A Radical Voice from Palestine: Recent Documents from the Popular Front for the Liberation of Palestine* (Montreal, Canada: Abraham Guillen Press, 2002); Livingstone and Halvey, *Inside the PLO*, pp. 75–88; Laleh Khalili, *Heroes and Martyrs of Palestine: The Politics of National Commemoration* (New York: Cambridge University Press, 2007); Popular Front for the Liberation of Palestine official Web site, *Political Strategy*, http://www.pflp-pal.org/strategy.html.

5. For example, see David Tal, "The International Dimension of PFLP-GC Activity" (January 1, 1990), http://www.ict.org.il/; Sofia Adape, *In the Spotlight: The Popular Front for the Liberation of Palestine: General Command* (PFLP-GC) (November 13, 2002); Center for Defense Intelligence, http://www.cdi.org/; Peter Janke, *Guerilla and Terrorist Organizations: A World Directory and Bibliography* (New York: MacMillan Publishing, 1983), p. 253; Terrorism Questions and Answers, *Palestinian Leftists*, Council on Foreign Relations, http://www.terrorism-answers.com/; Richard J. Chasdi, *Serenade of Suffering: A Portrait of Middle East Terrorism* (New York: Rowman and Littlefield Publishers, 2001); James L. Gelvin, *The Israeli-Palestine Conflict: One Hundred Years of War* (New York: Cambridge University Press, 2007).

6. For example, see Dirk J. Barreveld, *Terrorism in the Phillipines: The Bloody Trail of Abu Sayyaf, Bin Laden's East Asian Connection* (Carlsbad, CA: Writer's Club Press, 2001); Thomas M.

McKenna and Barbara D. Metcalf, *Muslim Rulers and Rebels: Everyday Politics and Armed Separatism in the Southern Phillipines* (Berkeley, CA: University of California Press, 1998); Greg Williams, *13 Days of Terror: Held Hostage by Al Qaeda Linked Extremists—A True Story* (New York: New Horizon Press, 2003); Thayil J. S. George, *Revolt in Mindanao: The Rise of Islam in Phillipine Politics* (Kuala Lumpur: Oxford University Press, 1980); Larry Niksch, *Abu Sayyaf: Target of Philippine-U.S. Antiterrorism Cooperation* (Washington, DC: CRS Report for Congress, January 24, 2008), pp. 1–14; CRS Report for Congress, *Abu Sayyaf: Target of Phillipine-U.S. Anti-Terrorism Cooperation* (January 25, 2002), http://www.fas.org/irp/crs/RL31262.pdf; David Kilcullen, *The Accidental Guerrilla: Fighting Small Wars in the Midst of a Big One* (New York: Oxford University Press, 2009), pp. 186–261.

7. For example, see Simon Elegant, "The Jihadi's Tale: The Confessions of Two Bali Bombers Tell of Their Hatred for the West—And Their Ties to Osama bin Laden," *Time International*, 161 (January 27, 2003), p. 16; Keith Suter, "Terror in Paradise: The Bali Bombing," *Contemporary Review*, 282 (January 2003), pp. 1–7; Greg Barton, *Jemaah Islamiyah: Radical Islam in Indonesia* (Singapore: Singapore University Press, 2005); "Bali Bombing Suspect's Extraordinary Admission," *Sydney Morning Herald* (February 11, 2003), http://www.smh.com.au/.

8. For example, see Terrorism Questions and Answers, *Armed Islamic Groups: Algerian Islamists*; Builta, *Extremist Groups*, pp. 573–95; Ellen Bogan, *Revolutionaries and Reformers*, pp. 76–84; Walter Laqueur, *The New Terrorism: Fanaticism and the Arms of Mass Destruction* (New York: Oxford University Press, 1999), pp. 130–34; Martin Stone, *The Agony of Algeria* (New York: Columbia University Press, 1997); Andrew J. Pierre and William B. Quandt, *The Algerian Crisis: Policy Options for the West* (Washington, DC: Carnegie Endowment for International Peace, 1996); Hamou Anurouche, "Algeria's Islamic Revolution: The People versus Democracy?" *Middle East Policy*, 5 (January 1998), pp. 82–103; Peter O. St. John, "Algeria: A Case Study of Insurgency in the New World Order," *Small Wars and Insurgencies*, 7 (Autumn 1996), pp. 196–219; Lauren Vriens,

"Armed Islamic Group," *Council of Foreign Relations* (June 27, 2008), *http://www.cfr.org.*

9. For example, see Robert Jay Lifton, *Destroying the World to Save It: Aum Shinrikyo, Apocalyptic Violence, and the New Global Terrorism* (New York: Henry Holt, 1999); Jessica Stern, *The Ultimate Terrorists* (Cambridge, MA: Harvard University Press, 1999); David E. Kaplan and Andrew Marshall, *The Cult at the End of the World: The Terrifying Story of the Aum Doomsday Cult, from the Subways of Tokyo to the Nuclear Arsenals of Russia* (New York: Crown, 1996); Kyle B. Olson, "Aum Shinrikyo: Once and Future Threat," *Emerging Infectious Diseases*, 5 (July/August 1999), pp. 16–18; Angus M. Meier, "Terrorism and Weapons of Mass Destruction: The Case of Aum Shinrikyo," *Studies in Conflict and Terrorism*, 22 (January/March 1999), pp. 79–91; D. W. Brackett, *Holy Terror: Armageddon in Tokyo* (Trumbull, CT: Weatherhill, 1996); Manabu Watanabe, "Religion and Violence in Japan Today: A Chronological and Doctrinal Analysis of Aum Shinrikyo," *Terrorism and Political Violence*, 10 (Winter 1998), pp. 80–100; Joseph Felter and Brian Fishman, "al Qaida's Foreign Fighters in Iraq," *Combating Terrorism Center at West Point* (2008), *http://www.ctc.usma.edu;* Seth Jones and Martin C. Libicki, *How Terrorist Groups End: Lessons for Countering al Qa'ida* (Santa Monica, CA: Rand Corporation, 2008), pp. 45–63; See Religion News Blog, *http://www.religionnewsblog.com.*

10. For example, see Jewish Defense League, *http://www.jdl.org/index.shtml;* Mark Juergensmeyer, *Terror in the Mind of God: The Global Rise of Religious Violence* (Berkeley, CA: University of California Press, 2000), pp. 52–59; Robert Friedman, *The False Prophet: Rabbi Meir Kahane—From FBI Informant to Knesset Member* (London: Faber and Faber, 1990); Ehud Sprinzak, *Brother against Brother: Violence and Extremism in Israeli Politics from Altalena to the Rabin Assassination* (New York: Free Press, 1999); Meir Kahane, *The Story of the Jewish Defense League* (Radnor, PA: Chilton Book, 1975); Reuven Paz, "The Threat of Jewish Terrorism in Israel," *Terrorist Organization Profiles* (August 30, 1998), *http://www.ict.org/;* Jessica Stern, *Terror in the Name of God: Why Religious Militants Kill* (London: Harper Perennial, 2004).

11. For example, see Wayne Anderson, *ETA: Spain's Basque Terrorists* (New York: Rosen Publishing Group, 2003); Paddy Woodworth, *Dirty War, Clean Hands: ETA, the GAL and Spanish Democracy* (New Haven, CT: Yale University Press, 2003); The Terrorism Research Center, *ETA: Euzkadi Ta Askatasuna* (March 2002), *http://www.terrorism.com/terrorism/ETA.shtml;* Stanley Payne, *Basque Nationalism* (Reno, NV: University of Nevada Press, 1975); William A. Douglass and Joseba Zulaika, "On the Interpretation of Terrorist Violence: ETA and the Basque Political Process," *Comparative Studies in Society and History*, 32 (April 1990), pp. 238–58; Gorka Espiau Idoiaga, "The Basque Conflict: New Ideas and Prospects for Peace," *U.S. Institute of Peace* (April 2006), *http://www.usip.org/index.html;* Judith Miller, "The Other Terrorism," *City Journal*, 18, 2 (Spring 2008), *http://city-journal.org/.*

12. For example, see Ed Moloney, *A Secret History of the IRA* (New York: W. W. Norton, 2002); David J. Whittaker, ed., *Terrorism Reader* (New York: Routeledge, 2003), pp. 89–107; Paul Rogers, "Political Violence and Economic Targeting: Aspects of Provisional IRA Strategy, 1992–97," *Civil Wars*, 3 (2000), pp. 1–30; J. Bowyer Bell, *The IRA, 1968–2000: Analysis of a Secret Army* (London: Frank Cass, 2000); "Ulster: Arrest in Omagh Bombing," *New York Times* (February 20, 2003), p. A6; James Dingley, "The Bombing of Omagh, 15 August 1998: The Bombers, Their Tactics, Strategy and Purpose behind the Incident," *Studies in Conflict and Terrorism*, 24 (November–December 2001), pp. 451–66; Eighteen Report of the Independent Monitoring Commission (May 1, 2008), *http://www.independentmonitoringcommission.org/;* Sue G. Mahan and Pamala L. Griset, *Terrorism in Perspective* (New York: Sage Publications, Inc., 2007), pp. 27–30.

13. For example, see Leonard Doyle, "The Cold Killers of 17 November Who Always Go Free," *London Observer* (September 28, 1997), p. 1; George Kassimeris, *Europe's Last Red Terrorists: The Revolutionary Organization 17 November* (New York: New York University Press, 2003); "Greece Confronts Its Past," *New York Times* (March 7, 2003), p. A26; "Major Arrests in Greece," *Macleans* (July 29, 2002), p. 11; C. Buhayer, "Europe-Greece Finally Takes on

17N," *Jane's Terrorism and Security Monitor* (July 1, 2002), *http://www.jtsm.janes.com/*; "Greece to Begin Trial Involving Long Elusive Terrorist Group: 27 Years Went by without Any Arrests," *New York Times* (March 3, 2003), p. A3.

14. For example, see U.S. Department of State, *Country Reports* (2008); John Murry and Richard Ward, *Extremist Groups* (Chicago, IL: University of Illinois, 1996), pp. 384–89; Janke, *Guerrilla and Terrorist Organizations*, p. 41; Dora Antoniou, "Fighting Revolutionary Struggle, Revolutionary Nuclei," *Kathemerini* (August 29, 2002), *http://www.ekathimerini.com/* (Greece's International English Language Newspaper); Spiros Ch. Kaminaris, *Greece in Middle Eastern Terrorism* (June 28, 1999), *http://www.ict.org/*.

15. For example, see Ely Kanion, "Islamic Terrorist Activities in Turkey in the 1990s," *Terrorism and Political Violence*, 15 (Winter 1998), pp. 101–21; Dennis A. Pluchinsky, "Academic Research on European Terrorist Developments: Pleas from a Government Terrorist Analyst," *Studies in Conflict and Terrorism*, 15 (January/March 1992), pp. 13–24; Russell D. Howard and Reid L. Sawyer, eds., *Terrorism and Counterterrorism: Understanding the New Security Environment* (Guilford, CT: McGraw-Hill/Dushkin, 2002), p. 576; Noriyuki Katagari, "In the Spotlight: Revolutionary People's Liberation Party/Front (RPLP/F)," *Center for Defense Intelligence* (November 5, 2002), *http://www.cdi.org/*.

16. For example, see Abbas Vali, ed., *Essays on the Origins of Kurdish Nationalism* (Costa Mesa, CA: Mazda Publications, 2003); Henri J. Barkey and Graham E. Fuller, *Turkey's Kurdish Question* (New York: Rowman and Littlefield Publishers, 1998); Michael M. Gunter, *The Kurds and the Future of Turkey* (New York: St. Martin's Press, 1997); Svante E. Cornell, "The Kurdish Question," *Orbis*, 45 (Winter 2001), pp. 31–46; Michael Radu, "The Rise and Fall of PKK," *Orbis*, 45 (Winter 2001), pp. 47–63; Nur Bilge Criss, "The Nature of Terrorism in Turkey," *Studies in Conflict and Terrorism*, 18 (January/March 1995), pp. 17–37; Edgar O'Ballance, *The Kurdish Struggle, 1920–94* (London: MacMillan Press, 1996); Asa Lundgren, *The Unwelcome Neighbour: Turkey's Kurdish Policy* (London: I.B. Tauris, 2007), pp. 80–89.

17. For example, see Abua Guillermorpieto, "Waiting for War; Elections Are a Few Weeks Away, and the Country Is Bracing for an Explosion," *New Yorker*, 78 (May 13, 2002), pp. 49–57; "Colombia: Trial of IRA Suspects Starts," *New York Times* (December 3, 2002), p. A10; Kirk Semple, "The Kidnapping Economy," *New York Times Magazine* (December 3, 2002), p. 46; Roman D. Ortiz, "Insurgent Strategies in the Post-Cold War: Revolutionary Armed Forces of Colombia," *Studies in Conflict and Terrorism*, 25 (March–April 2002), pp. 127–44; James Petras, "The FARC Faces the Empire," *Latin American Perspectives*, 27 (September 2000), pp. 134–43; David J. Whittaker, *Terrorism: Understanding the Global Threat* (London: Longman, 2002); Robin Kirk, *More Terrible Than Death: Massacres, Drugs, and America's War in Colombia* (New York: Public Affairs, 2003); Michael Shifter, "Colombia on the Brink: There Goes the Neighborhood," *Foreign Affairs*, 78 (July–August 1999), pp. 14–20; Ingrid Betancourt, *Until Death Do Us Park: My Struggle to Reclaim Colombia* (New York: Harper Perennial, 2008); Thomas A. Marks, "A Model Counterinsurgency: Uribe's Colombia (2002–2006) v. FARC," *Military Review*, 87, 2 (March 2007), pp. 41–57; Voces de Colombia, ELN homepage (March 9, 2009), *http://www.eln-voces.com/*.

18. For example, see Bert Ruiz, *The Colombian Civil War* (Jefferson, NC: McFarland, 2001); Gary M. Leech, *Killing Peace: Colombia's Conflict and the Failure of U.S. Intervention* (Minneapolis, MN: Information Network of the Americas, 2002); Gabriel Garcia Marquez, *News of a Kidnapping* (New York: Knopf, 1997); Ana Carrigan, *The Palace of Justice: A Colombian Tragedy* (New York: Four Walls Eight Windows, 1993); Daniel Garcia-Pena, "The National Liberation Army (ELN) Creates a Different Peace Process," *NACLA Report on the Americas*, 34 (September 2000), p. 34; "Pastrana: Rightist Paramilitaries a Greater Threat Than Leftist Guerrillas," *United Press International* (February 8, 2001), p. 1.

19. For example, see Max G. Manwaring, *Nonstate Actors in Colombia: Threat and Response* (Carlisle, PA: Strategic Studies Institute, U.S. Army War College, 2002); Richard L. Maullin, *Soldiers, Guerrillas, and Politics in Colombia* (Lexington, MA: Lexington Books, 1973);

Angel Rabasa and Peter Chalk, *Colombian Labyrinth: The Synergy of Drugs and Insurgency, and Its Implications for Regional Stability* (Santa Monica, CA: Rand Corp., 2001); David Spencer, *Colombia's Paramilitaries: Criminals or Political Force* (Carlisle, PA: Strategic Studies Institute, U.S. Army War College, 2001); Javier Giraldo, *Colombia: The Genocidal Democracy* (Monroe, ME: Common Courage Press, 1996); Robin Kirk "Colombian Human Rights Defenders Killed, Kidnapped," *NACLA Report on the Americas*, 32 (March–April 1999), pp. 1–4; Sergio Ferragut, *A Silent Nightmare: The Bottom Line and the Challenge of Illicit Drugs* (2007), *http://www.Lulu.com.*

20. For example, see James Ron, "Ideology in Context: Explaining Sendero Luminoso's Tactical Escalation," *Journal of Peace Research*, 38 (September 2001), pp. 569–93; William Rosenau, "Is the Shining Path the 'New Khmer Rouge,'" *Studies in Conflict in Terrorism*, 17 (October–December 1994), pp. 305–13; "Sendero Luminoso: Peruvian Terrorist Group," *Department of State Bulletin: Fact Sheet*, 89 (December 1989), pp. 49–53; Simon Strong, *Shining Path: A Case Study in Ideological Terrorism* (London: Research Institute for the Study of Conflict, 1993); David Scott Palmer, ed., *The Shining Path of Peru* (New York: St. Martin's Press, 1994); Yael Shahar, "Sendero Luminoso: Insurgency Resurgent," *International Institute for Counterterrorism* (October 29, 2008) http://www.ict.org.il/; Michael Reid, *Forgotten Continent: The Battle for Latin America's Soul* (New Haven, CT: Yale University Press, 2008).

21. For example, see Dilip Haro, *War without End: The Rise of Islamic Terrorism and Global Response* (London: Routledge, 2002); David D. Taylor, *Kashmir* (Oxford, England: Clio Press, 2000); United States Congress: Subcommittee on the Middle East and South Asia, *The Current Crisis in South Asia, June 6, 2002* (Washington, DC: U.S. Government Printing Office, 2002); John F. Burns, "Kashmir's Islamic Guerrillas See Little to Fear from U.S.," *New York Times* (December 24, 2001), p. B5; Husain Haqqani, "The Gospel of Jihad," *Foreign Policy* (September–October 2002), pp. 72–75; Robin Wright, "The Changing Face of Islam; the Chilling Goal of Islam's New Warriors," *Los Angeles Times* (December 28, 2000), p. A1; Hazel Courteney, Sudhir Sreedhar, and Manish Saxena, *Jihadis in Jammu and Kashmir: A Portrait Gallery* (Santa Monica, CA: Sage Publications, 2003); Robert G. Wirsing, *India, Pakistan and the Kashmir Dispute: On Regional Conflict and Its Resolution* (New York: St. Martin's Press, 1998); Vijay Karan, *War by Stealth: Terrorism in India* (New Delhi, India: Viking Press, 1997); Kanchan Lakshman, "The Expanding Jihad," *South Asia Intelligence Review*, 6, 32 (February 18, 2008).

22. For example, see Andrei Kamakin, "Central Asia," *Current Digest of the Post-Soviet Press*, 52 (September 13, 2000), pp. 19–21; Ahmed Rashid, "They're Only Sleeping: Why Militant Islamicists in Central Asia Aren't Going Away," *New Yorker*, 77 (January 14, 2002), pp. 34–42; Ahmed Rashid, *Jihad: The Rise of Militant Islam and Central Asia* (New Haven, CT: Yale University Press, 2002); John L. Esposito, *Unholy War: Terror in the Name of Islam* (New York: Oxford University Press, 2002); Mohammed E. Ahrari, *Jihadi Groups, Nuclear Pakistan, and the New Great Game* (Carlisle, PA: Strategic Studies Institute, U.S. Army War College, 2001); Sean D. Hill and Richard H. Ward, eds., *Extremist Groups: An International Compilation of Terrorist Organizations, Violent Political Groups and Issue-Oriented Militant Movements* (Huntsville, TX: Institute for the Study of Violent Groups, Sam Houston State University, 2002); Adeeb Khalid, *Islam After Communism: Religion and Politics in Central Asia* (Berkeley, CA: University of California Press, 2007), pp. 168–90.

23. For example, see Matthew Forney, "China's New Terrorists," *Time International*, 160 (September 23, 2002), p. 14; Nader Hasan, "China's Forgotten Dissenters: The Long Fuse of Xinjiang," *Harvard International Review*, 22 (Fall 2000), pp. 38–42; Joshua Kurlantzick, "Among the Uighurs: Muslim Minority of West China," *World and I*, 18 (March 2003), pp. 156–57; Azat Akimbek, "The Making of a Nationalist," *Index on Censorship*, 27 (March/April 1998), pp. 173–76; Michael Dillon, "We Have Terrorists Too," *World Today*, 58 (January 2002), pp. 25–28; Charles Horner, "The Other Orientalism: China's Islamic Problem,"

National Interest, 67 (September 2002), pp. 37–46; Anthony Davis, "Xinjiang Learns to Live with Resurgent Islam," *Jane's Intelligence Review*, 8 (September 1996), pp. 417–21; Roger Milton and Ben Bohane, "The New Crusade," *Asiaweek*, 27 (March 2, 2001), pp. 24–26; James A. Millward, *Violent Separatism in Xinjiang: A Critical Assessment* (Washington, DC: East-West Center Washington, 2004).

24. For example, see Brian Glyn Williams, "Commemorating 'the Depotation' in Post Soviet Chechnya," *History and Memory: Studies in Representation of the Past*, 12 (Spring–Summer 2000), pp. 101–10; Francois Jean, "Chechnya: Moscow's Revenge," *Harvard International Review*, 22 (Fall 2000), pp. 16–25; Miriam Landkoy, "Daghestan and Chechnya: TheWahhabi Challenge to the State," *SAIS Review*, 22 (Summer–Fall 2002), pp. 167–92; Olga Oliker, *Russia's Chechen Wars 1994–2000: Lessons from Urban Conflict* (Santa Monica, CA: Rand Corporation, 2001); Christopher Panico, *Conflict in the Caucasus: Russia's War in Chechnya* (London: Research Institute for the Study of Conflict and Terrorism, 1995); Paul J. Bolt, et al. (eds.), *The United States, Russia and China: Confronting Global Terrorism and Security Challenges in the 21st Century* (Westport, CT: Praeger Security International, 2008), pp. 93–97; Timothy Phillips, *Beslan: The Tragedy of School No. 1* (London: Granta U.K., 2008); John B. Dunlop, *The 2002 Dubrovka and 2004 Beslan Hostage Crises: A Critique of Russian Counterterrorism* (Stuttgart, Germany: Ibidem-Verlag, 2006).

25. For example, see James A. Phillips, "U.S. Policy and the Future of Iran," *Heritage Foundation*, *http://www.heritage.org/Research/MiddleEast/bg. 194.cfm*; Rokhsareh S. Shoaee, "The Mujahid Woman of Iran: Reconciling Culture and Gender," *Middle East Journal*, 41 (Autumn 1987), pp. 519–38; Ervand Abrahimian, *The Iranian Mojahedin* (New Haven, CT: Yale University Press, 1988); Dilip Hiro, *Iran: The Revolution Within* (London: Center for Security and Conflict Studies, 1988); Amir Taheri, *The Spirit of Allah: Khomeini and the Islamic Revolution* (Bethesda, MD: Adler and Adler, 1986); Peoples Mojahedin Organization of Iran, homepage (March 2009), *http://www.english. mojahedin.org/pagesEn/index.aspx*; Foreign Affairs Committee of the National Council of Resistance of Iran, *http://www.ncr-iran.org*; Alireza Jafarzadeh, *The Iran Threat: President Ahmadinejad and the Coming Nuclear Crisis* (New York: Palgrave Macmillan, 2008).

CHAPTER 6

The Dynamics of Hostage Taking and Negotiation

CHAPTER OBJECTIVES
The study of this chapter will enable you to:

▪ Sketch the historical precedents of hostage taking

▪ Describe at least three categories of hostage takers

▪ Explain the Stockholm Syndrome

▪ Recognize the need for hostage guidelines

▪ Review hostage survival strategies

▪ Trace the historical experience of U.S. hostage-taking rescue attempts

▪ Describe the Good Guys hostage-taking incident.

INTRODUCTION

The last decade has witnessed a dramatic increase in hostage taking as a preferred tactic of political terrorists. The theatrical nature surrounding terrorist hostage situations has also provided the stimulus for the increase of criminal and psychotic hostage-taking episodes. The high visibility of instant media coverage of the hostage incident has also forced democratic governments and police administrators to develop extensive hostage antiterrorist training programs.

U.S. government statistics reveal that nearly 5,000 people throughout the world have been taken hostage in 2007; unofficially, several times that number may have been taken hostage.[1] The onslaught of political, criminal, and psychotic hostage-taking incidents has challenged the criminal justice system to develop new countermeasures to control such crime. Recently hostage takers have demanded everything from the freeing of inmates during a prison riot, to the payment of a $100 million ransom for the release of a wealthy businessperson, to political asylum of Cuban skyjackers in the United States, and to demands that Russia end the war in Chechnya. No community or country is immune to the growing phenomenon of hostage taking.

Hostage-taking incidents can occur anytime, anywhere. A simple domestic dispute can quickly escalate into a hostage-taking situation, or a spectacular sporting event, like the Olympic Games, can become the object of a hostage taking. The location of a hostage taking can be a government office, a library, or state prison. For the police, hostage taking has become commonplace. In fact, some criminal justice institutions can be described as "hostage prone"—particularly courthouses, jails, and prisons. Police officials responsible for the administration of such facilities must be prepared for the possibility of a hostage taking.

In this chapter, therefore, some of the basic factors related to government and police response to hostage takings are examined. Additionally, a **typology** of hostage takers will be presented; furthermore, the psychological manifestations of the **Stockholm Syndrome**, identification with the aggressor, response of the hostage victim, and techniques for surviving a hostage taking are explored. The purpose here is to alert the reader to the complex problems associated with a variety of hostage-taking scenarios. But first, a brief historical review of hostage taking is in order.

EARLY HISTORY OF HOSTAGE TAKING

Hostage taking has a long relationship with rebellion and warfare. For example, the Roman Empire suppressed revolts in Italy, Spain, and Gaul by requiring the vanquished tribes to give hostages as a guarantee of their future good behavior.[2] Earl of Tyrone used similar tactics in Ireland during the sixteenth century, and they were again used during the French Revolution. More recently, during World War II, Nazi Germany would take hostages in retaliation for acts of sabotage and assassination. In one such incident, during the Nazi occupation of Czechoslovakia in 1942, 10,000 Czech hostages were taken by the Nazis and randomly executed in reprisal for the attempted assassination of Reinhard Heydrich.[3] Likewise, today nuclear strategy based on the alleged balance of power is, as Schelling states, "simply a massive and modern version of an ancient institution: the exchange of hostages."[4]

However, a qualitative distinction in the selection of hostage victims appeared in the twelfth century. In Europe, the hostage holding of a member of the nobility was considered to be an effective future bargaining tool. The best-known example was the abduction of Richard the Lionhearted by rival noblemen in Austria in 1193. In order to secure the release of Richard, a large ransom was paid to the Austrians. Similarly, Fredrich Barbarossa seized hundreds of noblemen and high-ranking military leaders in order to secure a favorable peace treaty with Milan in 1158. This pattern of holding powerful government officials or wealthy business tycoons as hostages has continued to the present, although today non-state hostage takers have become more widespread. The taking of hostages to achieve political objectives by non-state hostage takers has occurred with regularity in the United States, Northern Ireland, Spain, France, Italy, Germany, and Latin America.[5]

For example, the Zapatistas in Mexico in the spring of 1994 abducted several wealthy Mexican business tycoons and released them only after the payment of large ransoms. Equally, in Colombia, literally thousands of people were taken hostage and held for ransom between 1997 and 2008. The U.S. State Department has labeled Colombia the kidnapping capital of the world. Colombian terrorist groups such as FARC (Revolutionary Armed Forces of Colombia) and the ELN (National Liberation Army) are responsible for most of the kidnappings and hostage takings.[6]

Thus, in the case of political terrorists, the strategy of taking high-ranking corporate officials hostage accomplishes four objectives for the terrorist organization:

1. The organization acquires large sums of ransom money needed to finance further terrorist activities.
2. The publicity generated by media attention brings the group national and international recognition.
3. The victim is often viewed as exploiting the poor people, which translates into much needed grassroots community support.
4. The free enterprise system is weakened by the intimidation of foreign investments.

TYPOLOGIES OF HOSTAGE TAKERS

There are a number of possible ways to categorize hostage takers, each of which may be used for decision-making purposes, developing negotiating styles, or for academic analysis. The first step in an academic analysis of hostage taking is the creation of a hostage-taking typology. Stratton has identified three broad categories and delineates them as follows: (1) the mentally ill hostage taker, (2) the criminal hostage taker, and (3) the social, political, religious, or ethnic crusader hostage taker.[7] The mentally ill hostage taker most often seeks recognition from the intense media exposure that follows the hostage episode. The mentally ill hostage taker also has the ability to exercise considerable power over the police. This is especially true in the barricade/hostage situation where the hostage taker threatens suicide. This hostage-taking event can easily develop into a spectacle, emulating a Cecil B. deMille Hollywood production. For example, on April 3, 1986, a barricaded hostage taker in a crowded South Chicago tenement killed two hostages and was holding one captive and threatening suicide.[8] The building was surrounded by 150 police officers. The hostage taker demanded a pizza be delivered and vowed not to surrender until he had watched a movie on TV. He was permitted to watch his movie and eat his pizza uninterrupted by the police. In a related incident, a barricaded suspect holding two teenage hostages in a Newport, Kentucky, house held off police SWAT teams for over thirty hours, demanding heroin and $20,000 in ransom for the release of the hostages before being killed by a police sharpshooter.[9]

Virtually every police agency in the United States has its own version of the mentally disturbed hostage-taking scenario. The number of incidents is endless. Cooper suggests that the mentally disturbed hostage taker is a person with limited individual power who feels persecuted by the world or a segment of it and strikes back by attempting to physically control someone.[10] Mentally disturbed hostage takers are the most difficult to negotiate with since their actions are irrational and unpredictable.

Criminal hostage takers, on the other hand, are generally the most rational and predictable to negotiate with because they do not want to be arrested. Approximately 60 percent of all hostage-taking incidents in the United States are a result of criminal hostage takers. Criminals who are fleeing the scene of a felony, such as an armed robbery, often take hostages as a last resort when faced with the unexpected arrival of the police. The fleeing felon can most likely be negotiated out of a potentially dangerous situation by delineating the seriousness of the crime of kidnapping (hostage taking) or false imprisonment, as well as the charge of armed robbery. However, some criminals may try to convince the police they are political terrorists rather than criminals, thus complicating the negotiating process. This was the case when a man claiming to be a Palestinian guerrilla burst into a French courtroom and attempted to free two of France's most notorious criminals.[11] The two French criminals who were on trial for a series of armed robberies were provided with guns, and 35 hostages were taken, including the judge and jury. During the course of the courtroom siege, hostages were released sporadically; after two days, French police negotiators were able to convince the hostage takers that their escape was futile. The political cause proclaimed by the hostage takers was obscure, and few people understood their rhetoric. But what seemed to be yet another hostage tragedy ended with no injuries or deaths.

The social, political, religious, or ethnic crusader hostage taker is most often a member of a group falling within our definition of terrorism. The terrorist hostage taker generally has a strong commitment to a cause or a political ideology. Organizations that seek social change (e.g., Hizballah), political change (the Real IRA and the Palestinian Islamic Jihad of Israel), or independence for ethnic minorities (the ETA Basque separatist movement in Spain or the Tamils in Sri Lanka) are well known to the world because of their extranormal acts of terrorism and the publicity these acts generate through intense media involvement. Such groups are the most difficult to negotiate with because of their total commitment to a cause. The crusader terrorist is rational and often enters a hostage-taking situation with preconceived demands and identified limits as to how far the negotiator can be pushed in meeting the stated demands. Therefore, through extensive planning, individual determination, and the ability to manipulate the media, the negotiation process is quite complicated.

Other criminal justice writers have also analyzed the three-way classification of hostage takers. Middendorff has identified three types of hostage takers: (1) politically motivated offenders, (2) those seeking to escape from something to somewhere, and (3) those seeking personal gain. Middendorff argues that the classification of hostage takers can only be based on motives.[12]

Like Middendorff and Stratton, the New York City hostage-negotiation training program identifies three categories of hostage takers: (1) professional criminals, (2) psychotics, and (3) terrorists. Trainers from that program claim that each type of hostage taker requires a different approach to handling the situation in the process of negotiation. In other words, different motives would require different response strategies by police **negotiators**. For example, a ransom demand can have quite a different meaning for the professional criminal and the political terrorist. The professional criminal may use the ransom for personal gratification, while the terrorist may use the ransom to purchase guns and explosives to further his terrorist activity.[13]

Richard Kobetz lists five types of hostage-taking situations: (1) prison takeovers and escape situations in which hostages are seized; (2) aircraft hijackings; (3) seizures of business executives, diplomats, athletes, and cultural personalities; (4) armed robberies in which innocent bystanders are seized to effect an escape; and (5) seizures of hostages by mentally disturbed individuals seeking personal recognition. Clearly, his typology involves a synthesis of hostage taker, hostage, and motive. Each category has its own unique features that demand an individual response by police negotiators.[14]

Cooper maintains that hostages are seized by those who perceive the hostage-taking event as a way of setting up a bargaining position that cannot be achieved by other means. He argues for a typology of seven hostage takers: (1) political extremists, (2) fleeing felons, (3) institutionalized persons, (4) estranged persons, (5) wronged persons, (6) religious fanatics, and (7) mentally disturbed persons. Cooper recognizes that his classification is subject to wide criticism since many categories may overlap. But from a police operational point of view, this classification can be used as a guide for action in organizing police/hostage training programs.[15]

Goldaber describes nine categories of hostage takers: (1) suicidal personality, (2) vengeance seeker, (3) disturbed individual, (4) cornered perpetrator, (5) aggrieved inmate, (6) felonious extortionist, (7) social protestor, (8) ideological zealot, and (9) terrorist extremist. The value of

Goldaber's typology is that it reveals the complexity of responsive action by the police. For example, negotiating with a suicidal bank robber as opposed to a nonsuicidal bank robber, or a vengeance-seeking terrorist as opposed to a social protestor, requires an extraordinarily complex police response.[16]

The Los Angeles Sheriff's Office states that an understanding of the type of person holding hostages aids the negotiator in identifying the motivation of hostage takers. The Los Angeles Sheriff's Office, then, classifies hostage takers into four broad categories: (1) mentally disturbed persons, (2) common criminals, (3) prisoners, and (4) terrorists. The FBI first introduced the four categories in the mid-1970s. Since then the four-category hostage-taker typology has become the standard for state and local law enforcement agencies in the United States.[17]

The creation of a hostage typology is a useful first step in coordinating police responses. This is the case even though no natural categories of hostage takers exist. The creation of any typology is bound to be arbitrary, reflecting the training and discipline of those who construct them. The most realistic arrangements are those that are able to reduce the subjectivity of the categories. Certainly, this is no easy task. Nonetheless, a typology clearly indicates that different responses (to different hostage types) require a wide variety of police strategies, negotiating skills, and tactical responses. Based on the previous review, we now seek to provide a reasonable typology of hostage takers. The typology is based on the hostage taker's motivation, with the creation of three broad categories and several subcategories. Conceivably, an individual hostage taker could be a psychotic, criminally inclined, or a political terrorist. (See Table 6.1.)

We will now review some of the general negotiating guidelines that apply most often to all hostage-taking situations.

TIME, TRUST, AND THE STOCKHOLM SYNDROME

The most important factor in any hostage negotiation situation is time. The first few minutes appear to be the most dangerous since the emotional level of both hostage takers and hostages is extremely unpredictable. The confusion, fear, and anxiety at the initial stage of the hostage-taking event predominate and can produce injury and death. However, as time passes and the agitated emotions of the hostage takers and the hostages subside, a period of calm begins. Generally, the longer the hostage-taking incident continues, the greater the probability the hostages will be released unharmed. This phenomenon can be explained in several ways. The passage of time allows the Stockholm Syndrome an opportunity to manifest itself. The term "Stockholm

TABLE 6.1 Typology of Hostage Takers

Criminal	Political Terrorist	Psychotic
Fleeing felon	Seeking media recognition for a cause	Mentally deranged
Prison inmate riots	Social protestor	Suicidal
Extortionist kidnapper	Religious zealot	Angry
Barricaded suspect	Seeking vengeance	Seeking personal recognition
	Air hijacking	Estranged from family
	State as hostage taker	Barricaded suspect

Syndrome" is commonly used by the mass media to describe the positive relationship that develops between the hostage victim and the hostage taker. The Stockholm Syndrome was first observed on August 23, 1973, when a single gunman intent on robbery entered a bank in Stockholm, Sweden. The police interrupted the robbery attempt, whereupon the gunman took four bank employees hostage and retreated into an 11-foot by 42-foot carpeted bank vault. The hostage taking was to continue for 131 hours, affecting the lives of the hostages and giving rise to the psychological phenomenon eventually referred to as the Stockholm Syndrome.

The Stockholm Syndrome appears to be an unconscious emotional response to the traumatic experience of victimization. In the Stockholm bank robbery case, the armed bank robber was able to negotiate the release from prison of his former cellmate. This cellmate then joined the bank robber in the vault, further complicating negotiating procedures. Now there were four hostages and two hostage takers. During the course of the negotiations, it was discovered that the hostages feared the police more than they feared their captors. In a phone conversation with the prime minister of Sweden, one of the hostages expressed the feelings of the entire group when she stated, "This is our world now . . . sleeping in this vault to survive. Whoever threatens this world is our enemy. The robbers are protecting us from the police." Eventually, after 131 hours, the bank siege ended, but for weeks after, the hostages complained to psychiatrists that they had chronic nightmares over the possibility that the hostage takers might escape and abduct them again. Yet strangely enough, the hostages felt no hatred toward their abductors. In fact, they felt emotionally indebted to the hostage takers for allowing them to remain alive and saving them from the police.[18]

The Stockholm Syndrome has been observed around the world in a variety of hostage situations. Since the Stockholm hostage incident, a variety of kidnap/hostage victims have exhibited behavior similar to the hostages of the 1973 Stockholm event. Patty Hearst was abducted by the Symbionese Liberation Army (SLA); and for the first fifty-seven days of her captivity, she was kept blindfolded, locked in a walk-in closet, and subjected to physical and sexual abuse by her captors. During this time, Patty Hearst was forced to confess past misdeeds and was manipulated so that she became very hostile toward her family, especially the Hearst media empire. Eventually she became part of the SLA, even changing her name to "Tania," and participated in SLA criminal activities. She remained loyal to the SLA up to the time of her capture by the police. At her trial, Patty claimed she had been brainwashed, coerced, and intimidated by the SLA to participate in several bank robberies. She was convicted and sentenced to seven years in prison. However, President Carter freed her after she served twenty-two months. In 2001 President Clinton granted Patty Hearst a full pardon.[19]

In 2003, Brian Mitchell and Wanda Barzee abducted fourteen-year-old Elizabeth Smart. Mitchell believed he was a Mormon prophet and kidnapped Smart to be his "wife." Smart was held captive for nine months, when she was physically and psychologically abused. She was threatened repeatedly with a knife, tied to a tree, kept isolated in a hole in the ground, and reportedly was raped. She was taken into public places with Mitchell and Barzee and forced to wear a long robe, a heavy veil, and prohibited from talking to anyone. Despite her treatment, Smart had a number of opportunities to escape but did not. Upon her safe return, there was wide community criticism that she had gone unrecognized while in public and not sought help or tried to escape. After the capture of Mitchell and Barzee, Smart repeatedly asked what would happen to her captors, showing ongoing concern for their welfare. Mitchell and Barzee were declared mentally incompetent to stand trial.[20]

In yet another kidnap episode from Vienna, Austria, widely reported by the media, Wolfgang Priklopil abducted ten-year-old Natascha Kampusch while on her way to school. She was held captive for eight years, confined in a custom-built basement under Priklopil's house, where she was beaten, sexually abused, and photographed. She had several opportunities to escape—even went on a ski trip with her abductor—but did not. Kampusch claims that her captor threatened to kill her if she tried to escape. Finally, Kampusch, by then eighteen-years-old, escaped. Priklopil, while fleeing the police, jumped in front of a moving train and committed suicide. Kampusch expressed remorse and grief over Priklopil's death. She actually reported that her captivity was a good thing since she was not exposed to the negative influences of life.[21]

Participants in the hostage drama are cast together in a life-threatening environment where each must adapt in order to stay alive. The positive bond that develops between hostages and hostage takers serves to unite them against the outside influence of the police. Many similarities exist between the Stockholm case, Patty Hearst, Elizabeth Smart, and Natascha Kampusch. Persons previously unknown to the victims had abducted them. They were held in close confines, isolated from the rest of the community, and under the control of the abductor. All experienced some sexual, physical, or psychological abuse during their captivity. They all experienced a continuing threat to their survival. All the victims had opportunities to escape, with the exception of the Stockholm incident, which they did not attempt. After their rescue, all the victims showed sympathy toward their abductors, and all were relatively young (between 10 and 20 years of age) at the time they were abducted.[22]

Actually the Stockholm Syndrome has been known for quite some time to the psychiatric community, where it often is referred to as "identification with the aggressor." The Stockholm Syndrome had been recognized many years ago in psychological studies of other hostage, prisoner, or abusive situations such as abused children, battered spouses, prisoners of war, cult members, and concentration camp survivors. By any name, the syndrome works in favor of the police negotiator. The Stockholm Syndrome may manifest itself in three ways: (1) the positive feelings of the hostages toward the hostage takers; (2) the reciprocal, positive feelings of the hostage takers toward the hostages; and (3) the negative feelings of both the hostages and hostage takers toward the police and the government.[23] Strentz defends the position that hostages regress to an earlier period of development when they are in a state of extreme dependence and fear.[24] This situation is not unlike a parent/child relationship in which the child is emotionally attached to its parents. The positive feelings act as a defense mechanism to ensure the survival of the hostage. Simon and Blum maintain that hostages are in a cognitive bind. On the one hand, they are dependent on the hostage taker for their survival. On the other hand, they are dependent on the police for their rescue. Thus, the hostage is placed in a double jeopardy situation.[25]

Despite the involuntary manifestation of the Stockholm Syndrome, it is not a magical relationship that affects all hostage-taking incidents. It is interesting to contrast the Stockholm, Hearst, Smart, and Kampusch incidents with the experiences of older captive hostages. In the 1980s, dozens of people were taken hostage in Beirut, Lebanon. For example, Brian Keenan, thirty-five years old, was held for over 4 years; Terry Waite, forty-eight years old, was held for 5 years, and Terry Anderson, thirty-eight-years-old, was held for 8 years. They did not develop a bond of sympathy with their captors. On the contrary, they were hostile, angry, and wanted to repay their hostage takers in kind. In Iran, during the U.S. hostage crisis that lasted 444 days, few of the freed hostages had any favorable commentary about their captors. In order to prevent the positive feelings the hostage takers might feel toward the hostages, Iranian hostage takers would frequently change guards, and keep some hostages isolated and others blindfolded for long periods of time. In fact, one of the returning hostages stated "students told him of being trained in the summer of 1979 at Palestine Liberation Organization camps on how to handle hostages."[26]

Aronson maintains that most people cannot harm another person unless the victim has been dehumanized.[27] Favaro et al., in their study, described the Stockholm Syndrome as an indicator of the trauma caused by the isolation and dehumanization that is experienced by hostages.[28] When hostage takers and hostages are isolated together in a building, airplane, or a bank vault, a process of humanization apparently occurs. A hostage can then build empathy with the hostage taker while still maintaining his or her dignity and individuality, thus lessening the possibility of being physically abused or executed. The exception is the antisocial hostage taker, demonstrated by four Iranians in December 1984.[29] The four seized a Kuwaiti airliner and took refuge in Tehran. Two American hostages were summarily executed, and several other hostages reported being beaten, burned with cigarettes, and having their hair set on fire. Fortunately, this type of hostage incident is rare, and in most situations the Stockholm Syndrome will be present. As time passes and positive experiences begin to develop between hostage takers and hostages, the hostage's chance of survival becomes much greater.

Certainly the relevance of the Stockholm Syndrome to the police negotiation process is clear. The syndrome's presence may save the life of hostages as well as hostage takers. Understanding the ultimate effects of the syndrome may also prevent the police from resorting too quickly to the use of deadly force. The experience of positive contact often prevents the hostage taker from injuring a hostage he or she has come to know and in some cases to love. Solomon reminds us that the level of the Stockholm Syndrome increases with better treatment of the hostage(s) by the hostage taker(s).[30] The police negotiator can foster the Stockholm Syndrome by (1) asking to check on the health of a hostage, (2) discussing the family responsibilities of the hostage with the hostage taker, and (3) requesting information on the treatment of the hostage. The police negotiator should not understate the importance of the human qualities of the victim or hostage. Hostage-taking episodes are complex and no two hostage events are the same. However, the Stockholm Syndrome does appear as an identifiable pattern of behavior present among victims of hostage-taking incidents that can be exploited by police negotiators.

Time is also important because it allows a "friendly" relationship between the hostage takers and the negotiator to develop. By stalling for time, the negotiator can use several strategies to build rapport and trust with the hostage takers. The improvement of trust between hostage takers and negotiator reduces the likelihood that victims or hostages will be harmed and increases the likelihood that the hostage takers will seriously consider the negotiator's suggestions. Miron and Goldstein outline several techniques for developing trust and rapport between negotiator and hostage takers, which include (1) self-disclosure, (2) empathy, (3) being a good listener, (4) being understanding and showing personal interest in the hostage taker's problems, (5) reflecting on the hostage taker's feelings, and (6) not rejecting outright all demands.[31] The primary role of the negotiator is to establish a favorable and supportive climate with the hostage takers. Even though **time and trust** are generally considered to be the most important factors in the hostage-taking episode, other management and psychological considerations are also very important.

LONDON SYNDROME

The London Syndrome is yet another complex concept that occasionally occurs during a hostage-taking crisis. In 1980, hostage takers seized the Iranian embassy in London and took twenty-six people hostage. After six days of unproductive negotiations with the hostage takers, the British Special Air Services (SAS) planned to assault and rescue the hostages. While the SAS planned their assault and rescue, one of the hostages was shot and killed by the hostage takers, and his body was unceremoniously thrown out onto the street. The death of the hostage was the signal for the SAS to assault and attempt to rescue the remaining hostages. Thus began Operation Nimrod, one of the few major counterterrorist rescue operations to occur in front of television cameras. The rescue mission lasted eleven minutes. During the ensuing firefight, four of the five hostage takers were killed and one was captured. In the after-action report, the SAS noted that the hostage killed earlier after negotiations broke down was the only hostage killed or injured by the hostage takers. In fact, the hostages who survived the ordeal reported no physical abuse by the Iranian hostage takers.

Further investigation revealed that the hostage who was killed continually argued with the hostage takers and would at times physically challenge them. After several hours of haranguing the hostage takers, the argumentative hostage was shot and killed and his body removed from the hostage location. Hence, the term **London Syndrome** refers to a situation in which a hostage continuously argues or otherwise threatens the hostage takers and the hostage is killed by the hostage takers.[32] Several incidents since the London embassy rescue appear to verify the syndrome. The admonition is as follows: "Don't argue with hostage takers because they will eventually eliminate the argumentative hostage." Obviously, the hostage takers have the power.

The best-known incident involving the London Syndrome was the murder of Leon Klinghoffer.[33] Leon Klinghoffer was a passenger aboard the Italian cruise ship the *Achille Lauro*, which was seajacked by four Palestinian hostage takers on October 7, 1985. Once in control of the ship, the hostage takers demanded the release of fifty Palestinians being held in Israeli jails. When the negotiations began to falter, the hostage takers brutally murdered the sixty-nine-year-old, wheelchair-bound Leon Klinghoffer, dumping his body and wheelchair into the sea. Reportedly, Klinghoffer confronted the hostage takers and became extremely argumentative, even spitting on the hostage takers. Apparently agitated by the behavior of Klinghoffer, the hostage takers killed him, but killed no other hostages. Even so, there are specific recommended guidelines to resolve hostage-taking incidents.

GUIDELINES FOR HOSTAGE EVENTS

After the drama of the Munich Olympics in 1972, democratic nations recognized a need to deal with political hostage-taking incidents on more than an ad hoc basis. Eleven Israeli hostages, five Palestinian hostage takers, and one police officer were killed when negotiations collapsed and Munich police attempted to rescue the hostages.[34] The Palestinian hostage takers, who represented a group calling themselves the Black September Organization, demanded the release of thirty-four "fedayeen" incarcerated mainly in Israeli jails along with Ulrike Meinhof and Andres Baader, the founders of the infamous Red Army Faction of West Germany. The West Germans refused, but after a complicated negotiation process, they promised the Palestinian hostage takers safe passage to Egypt with their hostages. When Israeli hostages and their Palestinian captors arrived at the Furstenfeldbruck airport, German police sharpshooters were waiting for them. In the ensuing gun battle, the terrorists threw hand grenades into the helicopters holding the Israeli hostages, killing all on board. Police captured three terrorists after the gun battle. The West German police were widely criticized for their use of deadly force. The massacre at Munich caused police administrators worldwide to carefully review and analyze police response to political hostage-taking situations. Police and democratic governments suddenly became conscious of their lack of understanding of terrorist hostage takers and the vulnerability of society's institutions. The Munich Olympics was a turning point. A series of well-trained, elite military units were organized, and the improvement of hostage negotiation skills was undertaken in response to the newest form of criminality: hostage taking.[35]

The circumstances surrounding every hostage-taking situation are somewhat different; however, there are recommended guidelines appropriate for most hostage situations. The selection and training of negotiators is crucial since they provide the link between police authorities and hostage takers. Negotiators should be trained in hostage management strategy, terrorist ideologies, and the psychology of hostage takers. In the case of the **Munich Olympics**, no specifically trained negotiator was available. Several police and government officials representing West German, Israel, U.S., and Arab delegations attempted to negotiate the release of the Israeli hostages without success. One reason for this failure is that high-ranking officials acted as negotiators. Negotiators should be lower- or middle-ranking police officers that report to a decision maker. This buys time since the negotiator must always consult with his or her superiors before a decision is made. Other advantages are that unfavorable decisions will be accepted as coming from "higher-ups" and not the negotiator and, therefore, will not influence the trust that has developed, it is hoped, between negotiator and hostage taker. The negotiator can also direct his or her attention to the immediate task of building rapport with the hostage takers and not be obstructed by management responsibilities.

Cooperation of the media is also essential not to reveal the tactical plans and resources of the police or military. In the Munich incident, no limit was placed on media reporting of West Germany's tactical response.

A chain of command must be established to ensure that communication among responding personnel is free of interference. Communications, firepower, assistance to negotiators, and related resources should be the responsibility of one ranking official. In Munich, there was no chain of command. Eventually, the police chief of Munich took over the management of the hostage situation.

All police and nonpolice personnel must be readily identifiable and distinguishable from hostages and hostage takers. In the event of an unexpected firefight, police personnel obviously

FIGURE 6.1 A masked hostage taker of the Black September Organization appears on the balcony in front of the location where Israeli athletes are being held hostage at the 1972 Olympic Games in Munich, Germany. (AP/Wide World Photos)

must not be mistaken for hostage takers. In the Munich Olympics incident, a police officer was killed when he was mistaken for one of the Palestinian hostage takers.

The exact number and identity of hostage takers must be ascertained as quickly as possible. In the event of an assault, the police/fire team must be able to distinguish the difference between hostages and hostage takers beyond mere clothing because hostage takers can easily switch clothing or other similar items to confuse or test the trustworthiness of the police. For example, in Munich the police misjudged the number of Palestinian hostage takers, assuming that there were only five holding the Israelis at the Olympic Village. Instead, there were eight. Five sharpshooters were stationed at strategic locations and instructed to "take out" the terrorists after they arrived at the Furstenfeldbruck airport with the hostages. Even under the best of conditions, it would have been difficult for the sharpshooters to kill all of the hostage takers before they retaliated against the hostage Israeli athletes. The problem was compounded when one of the police sharpshooters prematurely opened fire. Three hostage takers were disabled, but the others turned on the bound and helpless Israeli hostages with grenades, killing all. If possible, the negotiating team should make every effort actually to see all the hostages and hostage takers.[36]

The negotiator should avoid any shifts in location of hostages by the hostage takers. Most likely this demand is for an airplane, bus, or car for the purpose of escape. Once the hostage-taking location is moved, the negotiator loses the control of the situation that might possibly have been established at the original location. The movement of hostages creates a setting of unpredictability and compounds the task of the negotiator. This loss of control by the negotiator may prompt the mistimed use of deadly force to rescue the hostages, since new resources and new people for the hostage takers are now available. In the Munich incident, hostages were moved from the Olympic Village to a waiting bus, then to helicopters that flew them to a nearby airport where hostages and hostage takers were to escape to Egypt aboard a waiting 737 commercial jet.

If hostage takers request others, such as relatives or friends, to be present at the scene, the negotiator should avoid this and stall the hostage taker. Like shifts in location, the presence of hostage takers' relatives or friends (religious or governmental) adds that element of unpredictability to the scenario. Friends or relatives may aid the hostage taker, become hostages, or act as an audience for the hostage taker who has suicidal tendencies. The way of handling such a request, rather than outright refusal, is to stall for time. However, there are exceptions, as with all guidelines. The Hanafi Muslim siege of Washington, DC, in 1977, for example, was resolved only after three outside negotiators representing the Islamic faith were requested; they successfully negotiated the release of the hostages,[37] although some experts believe that everything is negotiable.[38]

Certain items are universally accepted as non-negotiable. Obviously, you would not want to negotiate for new weapons, explosives, or more ammunition, which would increase the level of power or violence potential of the hostage takers. Crelinsten and Szabo cite two additional nonnegotiable policies that are commonly adhered to by police negotiators throughout the world: (1) no exchange of hostages and (2) no concessions without something in return.[39] Other non-negotiable items are drugs, narcotics, and alcohol. A hostage situation becomes unpredictable and unduly dangerous when intoxicating substances are introduced. As with requests for others and shifts in location, the negotiator should stall for time.

The use of tricks and deceit by the negotiator during a hostage situation is yet another difficult management consideration. On the one hand, critics of the use of deception maintain that the negotiator must consider the long-term effects of dishonest negotiation because of widespread media reporting of the hostage incident. Then, hostage takers involved in the next incident may not trust any negotiators, thereby reducing the probability of a peaceful resolution of the incident. On the other hand, tricks and deceit are viewed as viable strategies if they work and hostage lives are saved. Evidence indicates, however, that tricks and deceit are likely to be more successful with psychotic and criminal hostage takers than with fanatical and devoted political terrorists. The dilemma is a realistic one and ultimately the use of deception should be based on the circumstances of each individual hostage situation. Generally, the negotiator should avoid promising to meet demands he cannot deliver, especially if the hostage incident generates intense media coverage that is observed by future hostage takers seeking to demonstrate the perfidy of a rival government or the treachery and brutality of the police. The reporting of a hostage-taking event in the United States might reach an audience of 40 million people. What's the chance that some borderline psychotic may be stimulated to take part in some future hostage-taking episode?

Finally, a style of negotiation or overall hostage strategy based on mutual concession is recommended. After reviewing hundreds of hostage-taking incidents, three styles of negotiation have been observed: (1) win/lose, or agitation, (2) harmony, and (3) mutual concession. The agitation style forces the hostage taker into a position where he has no other recourse but to harm the hostages. The negotiator who is more interested in harmony gives in easily, granting the demands of the hostage taker. The preferred style is, of course, one based on compromise, problem solving, and mutual concession.

In sum, the few guidelines highlighted in this section point out the complexity of hostage negotiations. A hostage incident is more than a few "crazy people" seeking recognition. In effect, hostage incidents are contests of power between police and governments on the one hand and a variety of hostage takers on the other hand, the latter representing criminals, political terrorists, and psychotics. The understanding of this power relationship should be an important element in formulating hostage-taking strategies by the police in order to cope with future hostage incidents. What has been the U.S. experience in responding to hostage-taking crises?

FIGURE 6.2 American hostages in blindfolds are paraded by their Iranian captors at the U.S. embassy in Tehran, Iran, on November 4, 1979. (CORBIS BETTMAN)

U.S. EXPERIENCE: HOSTAGE RESCUE

The most difficult decision during a hostage-taking episode concerns the appropriate time to use force and conduct a rescue attempt. The police and military record in using hostage rescue teams to free hostages is a mixed one. For every spectacular, successful hostage rescue operation, there are many more spectacular failures. A historical review of hostage-taking incidents illustrates the difficulty involved in hostage rescue attempts. The hostage rescue attempt must be perfectly timed and coordinated to catch the hostage takers by surprise and save as many hostage lives as possible. All of this raises the risk of a failed rescue attempt. No two hostage situations are exactly the same. In hostage-taking incidents the type of location may be similar (such as a house, public building, airplane), but the circumstances can vary greatly. What type of hostage takers are involved? What type of weapons do the hostage takers have? What impact will a successful or failed rescue attempt have on the community? What outside support do the hostage takers have? The United States has a long history of hostage rescue attempts, which include a few successes but a far greater number of failures. The following is a representative sample of U.S. government experiences in reacting to political hostage-taking episodes.

The earliest recorded hostage rescue attempt occurred in 1805 when President Thomas Jefferson attempted to rescue 307 Americans being held by Barbary pirates. The Barbary states of Tripoli, Tunis, Algiers, and Morocco had continually harassed American shipping in the Mediterranean Sea, where they seajacked passing American vessels, sold their cargoes, and held their crews for ransom. By 1805, President Jefferson had dispatched the U.S.S. *Philadelphia* to Tripoli to neutralize the Tripolitan Barbary pirates. While the U.S.S. *Philadelphia* was in pursuit of a Tripolitan pirate ship, it ran aground, and 307 U.S. sailors were taken hostage and held for a large ransom. President Jefferson refused to pay the ransom, stating that a ransom payment would only encourage the other Barbary states to take Americans hostage. After failed negotiations with the Tripolitan Barbary pirates, President Jefferson was convinced that the best course of action was to organize an expeditionary force to rescue the hostages. The U.S. expeditionary force or "hostage rescue team" landed on the shores of Tripoli, threatening to march on the capital city and destroy it if the hostages were not freed. The Barbary pirates countered with a threat of their own to kill the U.S. hostages if the expeditionary force did not pull back from the capital city of Tripoli. The stalemate lasted for several days. Finally, President Jefferson agreed to pay $60,000 in ransom for the U.S. hostages. Many people considered the rescue attempt a failure since President Jefferson eventually gave in to most of the demands of the Barbary pirates.[40]

Another 100 years passed before the United States was once again faced with a major hostage crisis overseas. In May 1904, Ion Perdecaris and his stepson were taken hostage in Morocco by a Berber chieftain. What eventually became known as the "Perdecaris incident" prompted President Theodore Roosevelt to immediately dispatch a unit of the U.S. Navy to rescue his close friend Perdecaris and his stepson. Turner reports that President Roosevelt's dramatic moves on behalf of two Americans electrified the country and ensured his reelection.[41] However, the U.S. Navy could do little in its efforts to secure the release of the two hostages. The hostage takers threatened to kill the hostages rather than surrender. Once again, a president of the United States was forced to make a deal with hostage takers. The hostage takers received almost everything they demanded, including a large ransom, and Perdecaris and his stepson were released unharmed.[42]

One of the most unusual and lesser-known hostage-taking incidents involving negotiations occurred in January 1945. In Santo Tomas University, located in Manila, over 5,000 American and British civilians were being held as prisoners of war by the Japanese. The returning General Douglas MacArthur wanted the prisoners released as soon as possible in order to boost the morale of invading American troops. MacArthur ordered General William Chase to go to Manila and free the prisoners. As Chase and his column of tanks and infantry arrived at Santo Tomas University, the Japanese barricaded themselves in the courtyard and threatened to kill the American prisoners. Chase negotiated with the Japanese for three days. On the first day of negotiation, Chase was allowed to send in food and medical supplies for the American and British prisoners. By the second day, the Japanese agreed to release all the children and the most seriously ill and wounded prisoners. Finally, Chase and the Japanese reached a mutual agreement. All the American prisoners were freed, and the Japanese soldiers were permitted to leave Santo Tomas University without their weapons and join elements of the Japanese army still fighting on the outskirts of Manila.[43]

Chase used many of the negotiating tactics considered standard procedure in hostage negotiations today. For example, Chase wisely used the element of time and dragged negotiations out for three days to calm the terrified Japanese hostage takers. He first negotiated for the release of sick and injured prisoners. He did not set deadlines for ending the crisis. He never gave up anything without getting something in return. He had a keen understanding of the personality of the Japanese commander. He would not negotiate for weapons and ammunition. He avoided dismissing any Japanese demand as trivial. He skillfully used the threat of force and violence. At one point in the negotiations, he warned the Japanese if one American was harmed, the entire American brigade would attack the University (hostage stronghold). In sum, General Chase used his common sense and performed as a well-trained hostage negotiator.

The hostage incident that stirred the American public to demand immediate rescue was the seizing of the U.S.S. *Pueblo* by North Korea in early 1968. The *Pueblo* was a noncombatant, lightly armed, intelligence-gathering ship with eighty-three sailors on board. A North Korean torpedo boat fired on *Pueblo*, killing a sailor. The *Pueblo* was boarded, the crew was blindfolded, hands tied, and several were beaten. The North Koreans took the *Pueblo* to Wonsan, Korea, where the eighty-three sailors became hostages of the North Korean military. The North Koreans laid out their demands, which President Johnson refused to acknowledge. Instead, he called up 14,787 Air Force and Navy reservists, along with 372 aircraft, and positioned several aircraft carriers off the coast of North Korea, threatening to rescue the American seamen by force. North Korea stood firm, insisting that President Johnson acknowledge their demands. In the end, President Johnson agreed to the demands of the hostage-taking North Koreans, who insisted that the United States was spying on North Korea. Again, the threatened rescue mission failed, the hostage takers obtained almost everything they demanded, and the hostages were freed unharmed.[44]

On May 12, 1975, a Cambodian gunboat seized the **S.S. Mayaguez**, an unarmed container ship off the coast of Cambodia. Thirty-nine American seamen were taken hostage. President Ford, seeking to avoid a *Pueblo*-type incident, immediately prepared to launch a military rescue of the thirty-nine hostages. He and his advisors prematurely concluded that it was futile to negotiate for the release of the hostages with "international pirates." Accordingly, that left only a military-style rescue option. U.S. aircraft and Marines were ordered to rescue the hostages with a land and sea assault, a costly rescue operation. Eighteen Marines were killed when they engaged the Cambodians, and twenty-three Marines lost their lives in a helicopter accident while preparing for the rescue operation. More U.S. troops were killed than the number of hostages taken by the Cambodians. At about the same time the tactical assault began, the Cambodian hostage takers released the thirty-nine American hostages unharmed. The rescue attempt lacked accurate and timely intelligence data. President Ford's decision to rescue the thirty-nine hostages was widely supported by the U.S. Congress, as well as presidential candidate Jimmy Carter. The Mayaguez incident marked the last official battle of U.S. involvement in the Vietnam War.[45]

The most spectacular attempt to rescue U.S. hostages occurred during President Carter's term in office. On November 4, 1979, Iranian terrorists seized the American embassy in Tehran, and fifty-three Americans were taken hostage. Simon reports that preparation for an eventual military rescue operation was begun shortly after the embassy was overrun.[46] However, the implementation of a hostage rescue would be delayed until a coherent plan could be designed and rehearsed. By early April 1980, negotiations with the Iranian hostage takers were at a stand-still, and President Carter announced that the United States was breaking off diplomatic relations with Iran. The stage was set for a rescue attempt. Unlike the previous rescue attempts, the newly formed counterterrorist team, **Delta Force**, was specially trained and prepared to rescue the American hostages in Iran. On April 11, 1980, President Carter ordered a military rescue mission for the American hostages, implemented by Delta Force on April 25, 1980.

Operation Eagle Claw, the code name for the hostage rescue operation in Iran, caught many people by surprise. Few people really expected the United States to attempt such a high-risk military rescue. Nonetheless, the rescue mission was plagued by unforeseen circumstances that doomed it from the start. In brief, the rescue plan was for eight helicopters to rendezvous with six C-130 tactical air transports about 150 miles southeast of Tehran. (The code name for the rendezvous point was **Desert One**.) The helicopters were to refuel and then, under the cover of darkness, fly to the outskirts of Tehran, rest until the following evening, and then, in buses and cars provided by Iranian intelligence agents, drive to the U.S. embassy and rescue the American hostages.[47]

However, en route to the Desert One location, two of the helicopters experienced engine problems and were forced to land in the Iranian desert, where the crew abandoned them. The remaining six helicopters became disoriented in a fierce, unpredicted desert sandstorm and lost their way. Thus, the six helicopters arrived at the rendezvous point almost one hour late. The six C-130s encountered no difficulties en route and arrived safely at Desert One. Unfortunately, a third helicopter was judged unsafe to continue the rescue mission, leaving five remaining helicopters, one below the minimum outlined in the original rescue plan. Not wanting to attempt the rescue mission with fewer than six helicopters, President Carter gave the order to abort the hostage rescue mission. As one of the remaining helicopters moved into position for refueling, it collided with a C-130. Both aircraft burst into flames, sending exploding shell casings in all directions and endangering the other aircraft.[48]

Eight members of the 140-man rescue team died in the collision, and their remains were left behind. Sick argues that the decision to leave the bodies of the rescue team behind was prompted by the urgency to flee the area before the Iranian military discovered the flames.[49] The remaining rescue team safely fled the Iranian desert. There is little doubt that the Iranian hostage rescue attempt was an utter disaster for the United States.

In fact, Paul Ryan, a high-ranking military official, maintains that the planning for such a rescue mission was inconceivable and was doomed to failure from the very start.[50] Even several American hostages believed the rescue mission had little chance of success.[51] Eventually, the Iranian military recovered the eight bodies of the rescue team and put them on display in front of the American embassy for the whole world to see. The failed rescue attempt was a great propaganda victory for Iran and a humiliating defeat for the U.S. Delta Force.

The Iranian hostage rescue mission is still widely debated, and it raised several questions regarding the problems associated with the hostage rescue operations. For example, the chances for failure were high since the hostage takers could easily kill all the hostages once the rescue

FIGURE 6.3   Iran releases American hostages who were held captive in Tehran for 444 days. The freed hostages arrive at Rhein-Main Air Base in the then West Germany on January 21, 1981. (UPI/CORBIS BETTMAN)

effort began, even though the United States believed it caught the Iranians by surprise. It is conceivable that the Iranians could have learned of the rescue mission and could have been waiting to ambush the U.S. Delta Force once it entered the U.S. embassy. There is no doubt that the risks for a successful hostage rescue attempt in Iran were great. However, those who planned the Iranian rescue mission were confident that the highly trained rescue team, Delta Force, would succeed. The commandos of Delta Force were ready to distinguish themselves in the annals of hostage rescue operations, but unforeseen circumstances would postpone that effort. Probably the most bizarre hostage-taking incident and rescue attempt occurred at the Good Guys electronics store in Sacramento, California.

THE GOOD GUYS HOSTAGE INCIDENT[52]

On April 4, 1991, shortly after 1:00 P.M., four armed Asian males entered the **Good Guys** electronics store in Sacramento, California, in an apparent attempted robbery, and held forty-one men, women, and children hostage in a siege that was to last more than eight hours. Before the hostage-taking incident ended, three hostages were killed, and the hostage takers wounded eleven others. During the tactical assault by members of the Sacramento Sheriff's Selective Enforcement Detail (SED), three hostage takers were killed, and another suspect was seriously wounded. The hostage takers were described as part of a loosely knit Asian gang. According to the police, the four hostage takers belonged to an Asian gang called the Oriental Boys, although the police maintained that the hostage-taking incident was not in any way gang related.

The Good Guys incident reflects a type of hostage-crisis negotiation seldom encountered; that is, negotiating with unfamiliar culture. Hammer observes that hostage-taking episodes involving significant cultural differences in beliefs, values, and communication style offer a difficult and uncertain negotiation situation.[53] The rules and principles commonly practiced by skilled negotiators may not be sufficient when cultural dynamics are present. The Good Guys hostage incident is a rare case of intercultural crisis negotiation.

The Good Guys hostage takers were four South Vietnamese males who arrived in Sacramento in 1980 with their parents. Three of the Good Guys hostage takers were brothers. The Nguyen brothers—Long Khoc, 17; Loi Khoc, 21; Pham Khoc, 19—lived with their parents and three other siblings in a cramped, two-bedroom apartment complex in South Sacramento. The father of the three Nguyen brothers was a former soldier in the South Vietnamese army who first fled North Vietnam and then fled to Malaysia by fishing boat after the communist takeover of South Vietnam in 1975. Loi Nguyen was a high school dropout, while his brothers Long and Pham attended continuation high school for students with academic problems. Long Nguyen had previously been arrested for burglary and school vandalism. The three Nguyen brothers were fascinated with firearms and often talked of war and being in combat. The fourth member of the "gang" was Cuong Van Tran, 17, who came from an affluent family. Cuong Tran attended high school with Pham and Long Nguyen and, like Long, had a juvenile record of burglary and vandalism. On the day of the Good Guys hostage-taking episode, the Nguyen brothers asked their parents' permission to go fishing on the Sacramento River. However, they took a detour that eventually resulted in one of the most bizarre hostage-taking incidents ever recorded in California.

The Nguyen brothers and Cuong Tran attacked the Good Guys electronics store. According to surviving hostages, they moved quickly through the electronics store with trained, brutal precision and began rounding up hostages. One hostage stated that they moved through the store like trained commandos. They eventually secured forty-one hostages within a defensive perimeter in the front of the store. The four hostage takers were armed with three 9-mm Parabellum 15-shot magazine pistols and a pump action 12-gauge shotgun. Loi Nguyen purchased their weapons at a West Sacramento gun store after waiting the required fifteen days for purchases of pistols. The fifteen-day waiting period is designed to give police authorities time to make a background check on gun buyers. The four hostage takers also had a quantity of .45 caliber ammunition in their possession.

The first police response came after dispatchers received a 911 call for a "robbery in progress, shots fired." At first police assumed they were dealing with ordinary holdup men, possibly attempting to escape from a botched stickup. When the first officers on the scene surrounded the building, it became apparent that this incident was no ordinary robbery-in-progress call. A tense standoff began between the police and the hostage takers who threatened to kill the hostages. Fearing for the safety of the hostages, the first officer on the scene attempted to negotiate with the hostage takers, who demanded his bulletproof vest in exchange for a hostage. The police officer gave up his bulletproof vest, and the hostage takers released a woman and two children. The bulletproof vest was retrieved by a hostage and taken into the store, where the hostage takers tested it by firing a single shot into it. The surviving hostage taker was wearing the bulletproof vest. Thereafter, the hostage takers gave the police more demands. By this time the SED had arrived, and several trained police snipers surrounded the electronics store.

By mid-afternoon, the nature of the hostage-taking incident began to unfold. In a passionate diatribe, the hostage takers outlined their demands. First, they wanted forty 1,000-year-old ginseng plants or roots, and they wanted the police to cook ten of the ginseng plants to make tea and serve it to them. They also wanted four bulletproof vests, the kind of vests that cover a person from the toes to the neck. They also wanted $4 million in cash and transportation to Thailand, where they intended to shoot Viet Cong. They demanded a helicopter with a capacity for forty people to transport them to Sacramento Metropolitan Airport. They also demanded a .45 caliber pistol.

If these demands were not met, the hostage takers stated that they would start shooting the hostages at 6:00 P.M. They renewed their demands for bulletproof vests and transportation out of the country. They did not renew their demand for money or ginseng plants. In the meantime, the SED team had gained access to a rear storage room in the Good Guys store by entering through the ceiling in an adjoining store. Additionally, the SED team installed a camera lens in the wall of the Good Guys store, enabling them a partial view of the hostages gathered near the main entrance of the store. The hostage situation then entered the negotiation phase.

One of the hostage takers, known as Thailand, began to negotiate with the Sacramento sheriff's negotiator. The media described the performance of the sheriff's negotiating team as professional and efficient during the siege. Thailand wanted to know when the mayor would arrive at the scene and told the police negotiator he knew they would not be able to get out of the store, but still the hostage takers refused to surrender. Thailand renewed his demand for the release of one hostage for one bulletproof vest. Thailand eventually became agitated with the stalling tactics of the police negotiators and turned the negotiation over to another hostage taker, known only as Number 1. Number 1 then replaced Thailand and also threatened to kill the hostages if the bulletproof vests were not placed in front of the store immediately. Number 1 stated, "We call the shots here," not the police. In fact, Number 1 did not believe the police negotiator had the power to meet any of the hostage takers' demands. At one point, a hostage was put on the phone and reiterated the hostage takers' demands for the release of three hostages for three bulletproof vests, stating that the situation was critical and he was in danger of being killed.

By 7:30 P.M. tension began to mount, and the hostage takers tied the hands of several hostages behind their backs and tethered the hostages together. Hostages would later report a frightening ordeal of taunting, constant threats of death, and brutal beatings. The hostage takers flipped coins to see whom they were going to shoot first. The hostage takers told several hostages they would shoot them in the leg first, then the chest, and finally shoot them in the head. Even so, one hostage was sent out by the hostage takers to notify the police that the hostage takers were very serious, and if their demands were not met, hostages would die. When this hostage did not return to the hostage scene with the police response, the hostage takers became very angry. A negotiated settlement rapidly deteriorated.

A second hostage was shot in the leg and sent out to renew the hostage takers' threat that they were serious. The hostage takers demanded three bulletproof vests immediately or another hostage would be shot. The police negotiator stalled; another hostage was shot in the leg, and a third hostage was shot in the back after he collapsed to the floor. The police negotiator then decided to give the hostage takers one bulletproof vest. The bulletproof vest was placed in front of the main entrance to the store. The hostage takers sent a female hostage, who was tethered to a long length of rope with her hands tied to retrieve the bulletproof vest. The police, fearing more hostages would be shot, decided that the time had come to launch an attempted rescue mission. The rescue plan was to begin when the bulletproof vest was retrieved from the front of the store. The plan seemed simple enough (See Figure 6.4.).

As the female hostage opened the door to pick up the bulletproof vest, an SED sharpshooter, his rifle mounted on a tripod, was given the go ahead to shoot a hostage taker standing near the front entrance as the door was opened. The action by the sharpshooter was the signal to other SED team members hidden in a rear storage room to "take out" the remaining hostage takers and rescue

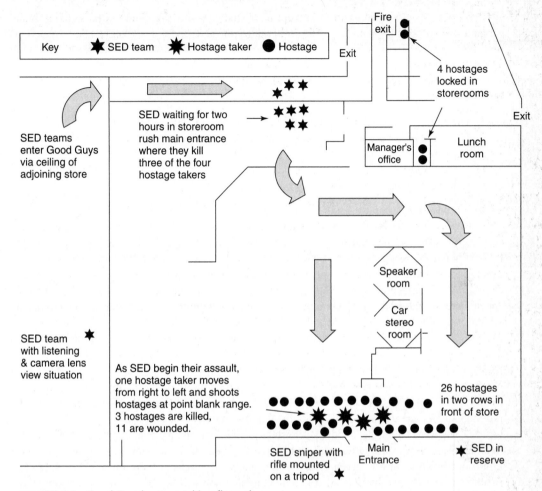

FIGURE 6.4   Good Guys hostage-taking floor plan.

the hostages. However, as the door swung open, the police sniper's bullet shattered the glass door but missed the hostage taker. The hostage takers then turned on the hostages who were lying facedown on the floor in the front of the store and began to shoot several hostages in the back and head. At about the same time, the SED team emerged from the storage room and engaged the hostage takers in a brief but deadly gun battle. Three hostage takers were killed, and one was seriously wounded. The surviving hostage taker, Loi Khoc Nguyen, was convicted on February 9, 1996, of fifty-one counts of murder and assault and was sentenced to life in prison without the possibility of parole.

The Good Guys hostage incident, and the manner in which it was resolved, has much to teach us. The Good Guys incident highlights the special problems of cooperation, personnel, and negotiations that occur when the hostage event involves multiple offenders and many hostages. It is a good example of the careful and coordinated use of highly skilled police personnel. The Good Guys incident underscores how crucial to the outcome are the negotiator's efforts to understand the hostage takers' motivations. Certainly the motivation behind the Good Guys incident was notoriety. The Nguyens and Tran were poor students who could not hold a steady job and blamed their problems on society. The irrationality of the Good Guys hostage takers' demands and the childlike display of anger illustrate the need to develop new strategies for dealing with this type of terrorist psychotic criminal hostage taker.

The Good Guys hostage-taking incident identifies several important topics relevant to hostage negotiations:

1. The need for patience and deliberation, balanced with appropriate levels of force.
2. The expressive versus instrumental motivations of the hostage takers.
3. The timing of rescue missions.
4. Language differences between the negotiator and hostage takers (in the Good Guys incident the hostage takers spoke very poor English).
5. Hostage taking as a desperate cry for attention and affiliation.

Reportedly, the Nguyen brothers and Cuong Tran were Hong Kong movie fanatics. All four youths watched the highly stylized films whose gun-toting detectives and gangsters fought it out amid Hong Kong streets and back alleys. The real motivation in the Good Guys hostage-taking incident may be these Hong Kong videos. Gangster films such as *A Better Tomorrow* and *Bullet in the Head* were popular among Vietnamese youth in the late 1980s. Police investigators speculate that such films' gang shooting scenes, in which gunmen coolly flipped coins to decide which of the hostages would be shot first, influenced the Good Guys hostage-taking incident.

In *Bullet in the Head*, three best friends, blood brothers from Hong Kong looking to make a name for themselves, travel to Vietnam during the war to smuggle drugs and instead begin to fight the Viet Cong. While in Vietnam, the blood brothers are searching for their souls. They cannot decide whether they are good guys or bad guys. Along the way the brothers are captured by the Viet Cong and tortured. Eventually, the brothers escape from the Viet Cong. Hence the rationale—the bad guys take hostages at the Good Guys electronic stores.

A few weeks after the Good Guys hostage-taking incident, the Sacramento Sheriff's department received a threatening letter signed by the Brothers of the Dragon: "On 4-4-91 you have killed our brothers in Sacramento for no reason. For this reason there must be revenge. The Brothers of the Dragon have decided in a meeting a lesson will be made." On the margins of the letter were the Vietnamese words that embody the gangster theme, words that many Vietnamese gang members have tattooed on their skin: Tinh, Tien, Tu, Toi, Thu—Love, Money, Prison, Sin, Revenge. However, the Brothers of the Dragon never carried out the threat.

Obviously, future negotiators will need to add an increased understanding of cultural awareness to their archives on negotiator behavior. Even so, groups motivated by political and religious beliefs have proven to be the most difficult, dangerous, and threatening for law enforcement to negotiate with. Negotiators must understand the group they confront.

OTHER RESCUE ATTEMPTS

Entebbe and Beyond

The raid on **Entebbe Airport** in Uganda by Israeli commandos has been considered the model for successful military hostage rescue attempts. Whenever the United States or other countries are confronted with a high-visibility hostage situation, the question often raised is whether they can duplicate the success of the Israelis. In a daring hostage rescue mission in 1976 that has yet to be duplicated, the Israelis flew more than 2,500 miles to Entebbe Airport in Uganda and freed over 100 Israeli hostages. During the raid three hostages were killed, along with seven hostage takers, forty Ugandan soldiers, and the Israeli operational leader of the rescue mission. Simon points out that the raid on Entebbe was unique and aided by several factors that are unlikely to be present in other hostage-taking episodes.[54]

First, the Israelis helped train the Ugandan military forces in the tactics of counterterrorism and hostage rescue. Thus, they were familiar with the Ugandan military defenses that surrounded Entebbe Airport. The Israelis also knew the physical layout of Entebbe Airport since an Israeli construction firm built much of it. Additionally, the rescue operation caught nearly everyone by surprise. The raid on Entebbe was the first long-range hostage rescue operation, and terrorist hostage takers were not yet familiar with counterterrorist military-style operations. The Israeli success at Entebbe stimulated the United States and other countries to develop their own counterterrorist and hostage rescue capabilities, with the result that several other countries have conducted successful hostage rescue missions. A few notable examples follow.

On Christmas Eve, 1994, four members of the **Armed Islamic Group (GIA)** of Algeria, posing as baggage handlers, boarded an Air France jetliner in Algiers and took 227 passengers and twelve crew members hostage. The hijackers were armed with AK-47s and at least two handguns. They demanded the release of their spiritual leader, who was being held in an Algerian jail, or hostages would be killed. Five hours after the hostage taking began, the hostage takers unexpectedly released nineteen women and children, although two hostages were brutally killed and their bodies thrown from the aircraft. On the second day of the hostage standoff, the hostage takers released more women and children and killed a third hostage. The hostage takers then issued a new demand. They wanted to leave Algiers and fly to Paris, the original destination of the hijacked plane. The Algerian government reluctantly allowed the plane to leave for Paris with a stop in Marseille for refueling. The elite French GIGN (Gendarmerie Nationale) counterterrorist hostage-rescue team was waiting.

As the hijacked plane sat on the runway in Marseille, negotiations were stalled, and the hostage takers would not surrender. The hijackers gave a new deadline for their demands and threatened to begin killing more hostages if their demands were not met. Not wanting to see another innocent hostage killed, GIGN assaulted the plane. The hostage rescue team yanked open the doors of the plane and threw "flash bangs" to confuse the hostage takers. Flash bangs produce a loud noise and a brief intense light designed to disorient hostage takers. Next the rescue team exchanged rapid bursts of gunfire with the hostage takers. In the end, the hostage-taking ordeal lasted for fifty-four hours; twenty-five people were injured, including thirteen hostages, nine members of the rescue team, the pilot, and two crew members. The four hostage takers were killed during the assault and rescue. The entire rescue operation took only seven minutes.[55]

The hijackers actually wanted to fly the plane into the Eiffel Tower and explode it over Paris. Freed hostages reported that the hostage takers had planted dynamite under the seats of the plane. The hijackers also demanded the plane's fuel tanks be filled with three times the amount of fuel to reach Paris. Because negotiators believed that the hijackers were creating a bomb, they decided to attempt a hostage-rescue effort. The rescue of the hostages was one of the most successful since the raid on Entebbe. It now seems clear that the terrorist GIA learned an important lesson. The plan was defeated partly because the hijackers could not fly the plane. The terrorist activities of the GIA have greatly decreased. Intelligence authorities believe that many GIA members have merged with al Qaeda in the Islamic Maghreb.[56]

On December 17, 1996, Peru faced a hostage-taking crisis that would last for 126 days.[57] During a reception being held at the Japanese ambassador's residence in Lima, twenty terrorist hostage takers from MRTA, or the **Tupac Amaru**, suddenly appeared and took several hundred guests hostage. The Tupac Amaru is a symbol of rebellion in Peru. In 1572, the name belonged to an Incan chief who attempted to overthrow Spanish colonial rule in Peru. Thus, the name became a rallying cry for Peruvian peasants through the centuries. By the early 1980s the Tupac Amaru would become one of the most dangerous terrorist groups in Peru. In terrorist attacks across Peru, the group killed thousands of innocent civilians. However, after the election of a new Peruvian president, who vowed to eliminate terrorism in Peru, hundreds of members of Tupac Amaru were either killed or apprehended by Peruvian police. By late 1996, Peru's president boasted that he had "knocked out" terrorism in Peru. It seemed that way until the evening of December 17, 1996.[58]

During a reception, twenty terrorist hostage takers of the Tupac Amaru overran the Japanese ambassador's residence and took 600 of Peru's political, religious, and social elite hostage. Within minutes police arrived on the scene and engaged the hostage takers in a forty-minute gun battle, capturing six of the hostage takers. After about an hour, the hostage takers had secured the Japanese ambassador's residence and began to negotiate for the release of the hostages. In a goodwill gesture, the hostage takers released all the women and elderly hostages. By the fifth day the hostage takers released 225 additional hostages. After the ninth day, the Tupac Amaru held 103 hostages. The Tupac Amaru demanded the release of 400 prisoners from Peruvian jails, including the wife of the leader of the hostage takers. In addition, an improvement in Peruvian prison conditions was demanded for all prisoners. The Peruvian government took a hard-line stance and refused to negotiate and make concessions for the release of the hostages. Instead, the Peruvian government formulated a complicated rescue plan.

The rescue plan was to build five tunnels under the hostage-taking location (Japanese ambassador's residence) that would allow a counterterrorist team to storm the site. Also, the Peruvians began to collect intelligence information on the daily routine of the hostage takers. The Peruvian president made his last negotiated offer that if hostages were freed the hostage takers would be granted political asylum in Cuba. The hostage takers refused. Tension and stress were building among negotiators, hostage takers, and hostages. A negotiated settlement seemed remote. Then on April 20, 1997, the 140 members of the Peruvian Counterterrorist Team gathered in the tunnels awaiting the signal for the attempted rescue. After two days the rescue team was in place, and on April 22, 1997, the rescue operation commenced. Explosives were placed at several locations that allowed the tactical team to breach the residence and engage the Tupac Amaru in a twenty-three-minute gun battle. All fourteen hostage takers were killed. The hostage takers were completely taken by surprise. Two members of the counterterrorist team were killed, and one hostage died of a heart attack during the rescue. The daring rescue mission was an extraordinary success attributed to "state of the art" surveillance, superior intelligence information gathering, and careful, meticulous planning.[59]

On October 23, 2002, Russia was faced with an unusual hostage-taking event involving multiple hostages and multiple hostage takers. Fifty heavily armed Chechen hostage takers, including twenty women, seized over 800 hostages at a theater in central Moscow. The hostage takers identified themselves as members of the 29th Division of the Chechen Army. The Chechen hostage takers, dressed in camouflage clothing, wore suicide explosive belts around their bodies. They took up positions around the theater and planted mines and explosive charges at the entrances and exits of the theater. The women hostage takers moved into the crowded theater and sat among the terrified audience, threatening to detonate the suicide explosive belts wrapped around their bodies. During the next several hours, the hostage takers allowed water to be delivered to the hostages and released about eighty hostages, mostly women and children. Two hostages were killed when they attempted to escape.

The Chechen hostage takers demanded an end to the war in Chechnya between the Russian military and Chechen rebels. In addition the hostage takers wanted Russia to pull all its troops out of Chechnya within a week. If the Russians did not meet the demands of the Chechen hostage takers, hostages would be killed, and the theater would be blown up. The hostage takers said they were ready to die along with the hostages if their demands were not met. Negotiations dragged on for three days. The hostage takers would not give up, and the Russian government would not give in.

Meanwhile, Russian counterterrorism troops and police surrounded the theater while the Russian special operations hostage-rescue team (Alpha) prepared to conduct a rescue of the hostages. On Saturday, October 26, the hostage takers presented a new demand that if Russian troops did not begin to pull out of Chechnya by 6:00 A.M., they would begin to execute the hostages. Fearing for the lives of the hostages, the Russians decided to attempt a risky rescue mission.

Under the cover of darkness, using night vision goggles, the hostage-rescue team moved into place around the theater. Once the rescue team was in place, the Russians released a deadly narcotic gas into the theater's ventilation system. The gas quickly immobilized the hostages and the hostage takers who were knocked unconscious. The rescue team blew a hole in the wall of the theater, entered, and killed forty-seven of the unconscious Chechen hostage takers and disarmed the explosive devices. Three hostage takers escaped but were apprehended two hours later. At first the rescue effort appeared to be successful. The gas was only to render the hostages and hostage takers unconscious for a short period of time. However, this was not the case.

The gas the Russians used was **Fentanyl**, an opiate-based narcotic a hundred times more powerful than morphine. Fentanyl not only causes extreme drowsiness but can also cause breathing to stop. Unfortunately Fentanyl killed 129 innocent hostages. Russian negotiators maintained that the use of the deadly gas was necessary in order to neutralize the hostage takers who were strapped with explosives and threatening to kill everyone. The Russians insisted that Fentanyl by itself could not have resulted in the deaths of so many hostages. Rather the deaths of the hostages resulted from their weakened condition: lack of movement, hunger, dehydration, severe stress, and a lack of oxygen after three days of being held captive. President Putin defended the rescue operation by stating we "managed to do the impossible" and saved most of the 800 hostages.[60]

Throughout the last few years, there have been several terrorist hostage-taking incidents carried out by Chechen rebels. For example, Chechen rebels have taken mostly Russian hostages at schools, hospitals, and hijacked airplanes, ships, and busses all in an effort to force Russia to grant independence to Chechnya. In sum, in the breakaway Russian republic of Chechnya, Russia says it is fighting terrorism, while Chechen rebels say they are fighting for independence. The outcome seems to be an ongoing war that will continue for many years to come.

In summary, the rescue operations illustrate the importance of training, planning, and the use of high-tech equipment. In addition, the effective use of diversions or distractions is apparent. The use of flash bangs and disabling gas illustrate the need for creative planning to gain a few seconds' advantage over the hostage takers. Split-second timing and close-quarters combat are skills often necessary for the safe release of the hostages. However, it must be restated that every hostage situation is different, and the tactical rescue attempt is never the same. A decisive turning point in the formation of highly trained hostage rescue units was the Munich Olympic hostage-taking episode. Thousands of people worldwide have been held hostage since the late 1960s. Many former hostages believe that once "you are a hostage, you will be a hostage the rest of your life." The following section offers some suggestions on how to survive the trauma of a hostage-taking event.

SURVIVING A HOSTAGE SITUATION

Past experience has shown that people who are prepared suffer the least physical abuse and emotional trauma when taken hostage. Even though every hostage situation is somewhat different and every individual reacts differently, the following proposed guidelines may prove useful in surviving the growing threat of the sudden, unpredictable captivity of being held hostage. So, how does one prepare to be a hostage?

The most critical points of any type of hostage situation come at the moment of capture and release. The important thing is to remain calm and not panic. During the capture phase of the incident, the hostage should avoid unnecessary or unexpected movements, crying out for help, or making loud noises. Obviously, the initial reactions of hostages are fear, disbelief, and shock. This fear must quickly be overcome so that the hostage can regain composure and recognize the reality of captivity. At the initial phase of captivity, should the hostage resist or surrender? Generally, this is a personal decision based on the circumstances and the amount of danger involved in trying to escape. Because of the uncertainty involved at the moment of capture, it is recommended that the hostage reassure the hostage taker of his or her intention to cooperate. The potential hostage must also be psychologically prepared to cope with blindfolds, gags, being bound, and drugs. Blindfolds and hoods are used to disorient and confuse the hostage. Gags prevent talking or shouting out and being bound hand and foot prevents escape. Being blindfolded, gagged, and bound, the hostage then becomes a mere object, less than a human being, making it easier for the hostage taker to assault the hostage.[61]

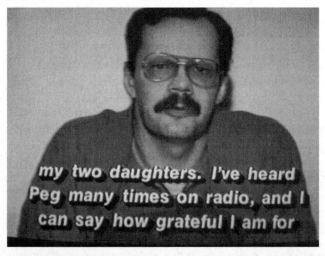

FIGURE 6.5   American journalist Terry Anderson was held hostage in Beirut, Lebanon, from March 1985 to December 1991. Anderson describes how he survived seven years as a hostage of Islamic extremists in his book *Den of Lions*. (AP/Wide World Photos)

After the initial phase of captivity, the hostage must adjust. There are several recommendations: (1) exercise when possible and keep fit, (2) keep a sense of humor by remembering that others have survived similar or worse situations, (3) try to establish a routine; this gives the hostage the feeling of control over the environment, (4) try to keep a sense of time orientation by inwardly recording time, place, and routine of the hostage takers, (5) if singled out, try to relate to the hostage taker as a human being—for example, mention personal events, emphasizing children and family, (6) do not let hostage takers dehumanize you, (7) when physically beaten, do not be a hero; show pain; if you have any medical problems, notify the hostage takers immediately, (8) if interrogated by the hostage takers, tell the truth; avoid embellishments that will cause damage later in the situation, and (9) do not try to escape unless the probability of success is high.[62]

During the capture phase, the captors may also heighten fear by loading and unloading weapons in the presence of hostages, by staging mock executions, by dramatic displays of temper, by physical abuse, and by continually threatening to kill the hostages. But time is in the favor of the hostages. The longer the hostage situation continues, the greater the chance hostages will be released unharmed. Passage of time without rescue or release is quite depressing. To overcome this depression, the hostage can establish rapport with the hostage taker but should not fake interest in support for the hostage taker's cause. Terrorist hostage takers will use that support for propaganda purposes.

The most dangerous phase of any hostage-taking situation is during a negotiated release or a tactical rescue attempt. Seventy-five percent of all casualties occur during release and rescue operations. If a negotiated release is agreed upon, hostage takers may be nervous and fearful of a double cross, anxious to escape capture and punishment. Therefore, hostages must not act in any manner that would endanger their lives, such as an angry outburst toward the hostage takers. In the case of a tactical rescue attempt, hostages must avoid panic and remain as calm as possible. The tactical rescue is based largely on surprise and shock. During the rescue phase, hostages and hostage takers will experience momentary panic and fear. Confusion may also result from gunfire, explosions, and tactical team members shouting instructions to both hostages and hostage takers. The hostage must avoid the impulse to flee during the rescue operation. Rescue team members can easily mistake hostages for hostage takers. The safest response for hostages is to immediately drop to the ground and lie as flat as possible.[63]

The experience of being a hostage does not end with the resolution of the situation either by negotiated release or tactical rescue. Generally, the victimization hostages live through can be either uncomplicated or pathological. Following the hostage crisis, many hostages develop a variety of psychological problems, including nightmares, phobias, depression, and startle reactions. For example, five years after the Iranian hostage episode, at least one-half of the American hostages reported still having nightmares about their captivity in Iran.[64] A hostage may not suffer depression until after the situation has ended. The intense media coverage of hostage incidents makes celebrities of some hostages. This certainly was the case during the seventeen-day captivity of TWA 847 in June 1985. However, as the celebrity status begins to recede, depression may occur. Ochberg identifies additional psychological manifestations of post-release hostages, including paranoid reactions, obsessions, idiosyncratic difficulties, and the Stockholm Syndrome.[65]

For some people (high-risk corporate executives, diplomats, correctional personnel, and ranking military personnel) preparing for captivity is just as important as preparing tighter security measures to avoid being captured. Therefore, potential targets should realize what their own

TABLE 6.2   Hostage Event

Normal Response	Pathological Response
Outcry: fear, sadness, anger, rage	**Overwhelmed:** emotional reaction of panic and fear
Denial: "This cannot be happening to me"	**Extreme avoidance:** using drugs/alcohol to avoid pain
Intrusion: voluntary thoughts of the event	**Flooded states:** disturbing nightmares and thoughts of the event
Working through: facing reality of situation	**Psychosomatic responses:** developing new ailments
Completion: going on with life	**Character distortions:** long-term distortions of ability

instinctive reactions will be during captivity, what hostage takers might expect hostages to do, and what hostages can do to overcome the psychological and physical pressures of being held captive.

In sum, the psychological literature identifies five states of **hostage reaction** to captivity. The five states can be categorized into a normal response and a pathological response. The emotional impact of being held hostage has a devastating effect on some hostages—they may never outlive the experience of having been held hostage. (See Table 6.2.)

Conclusions

Hostage taking will continue to escalate because of the proven benefits of intense publicity and as a cost-effective method of extorting a ransom. Hostage taking does work. It works for criminals except in those countries where the police are efficient and trusted by the populace. In the 1970s, for example, Italy has reported the hostage taking of 334 people by criminal gangs and ransoms of $185 million paid for the release of the victims.[66] It works for terrorists except where states are repressive. Terrorist groups have taken thousands of people hostage and millions of dollars have been paid in ransom by businesses and private citizens. But above all, the taking of hostages brings terrorists, psychotics, and criminals publicity and recognition. For example, little was known of Palestinians, Chechens, Peruvian rebels, Croatians, jihadists, or Kashmiris until their criminal acts of hostage taking filled the media. One factor that could disrupt the trend of hostage taking is to establish stringent security measures. More effective security measures should deter and reduce attacks on corporations, embassies, airlines, and individuals by raising the potential risks, and the costs to hostage takers

in terms of death or imprisonment. Another factor that could impinge on the escalation of hostage taking is the universal application of a no-ransom policy. If a policy of no ransom or no concessions were uniformly applied without major exceptions, then the probability of reducing hostage episodes might rise dramatically.

The possibility also exists that terrorists or psychotics could take mass hostages involving not just individual victims or corporations but the governments they represent. Nuclear threats by terrorists against major cities are not an unlikely scenario confined to paperback novels. Another reasonable conclusion is that as hostage taking increases, governments will be forced to devote sizable resources and money to the protection of key communication networks, nuclear plants, and energy systems. Recall that 9/11 began as a hostage-taking incident. Finally, the need to improve negotiation skills and tactical responses is imperative if we expect to effectively manage the hostage crisis. The next chapter examines the most common act of terrorism in the world today—indiscriminate bombing.

Key Terms

Armed Islamic Group (GIA)
Delta Force
Desert One
Entebbe Airport
fentanyl

Good Guys
hostage reaction
London Syndrome
Munich Olympics
negotiator

S.S. Mayaguez
Stockholm Syndrome
time and trust
typology
Tupac Amaru

Discussion Questions

1. Why was the Munich Olympics a turning point in hostage negotiation strategies and tactical response?
2. Describe the Stockholm Syndrome.
3. Why will hostage taking continue to be a major problem for police agencies?
4. How realistic is a repeat of the Good Guys hostage incident?
5. You are negotiating with a psychotic terrorist hostage taker who is prepared to surrender. As he approaches the door, he recognizes a police sniper stationed on a nearby rooftop. He runs back inside and begins to threaten the hostages, claiming you set him up to be killed. What would you say or do to get negotiations "back on track"?
6. Shortly after 9:00 P.M., Sacramento State University is invaded. Six terrorists led by I.M. Violent burst into the Social Science building carrying automatic weapons, a shotgun, and a sword. They seize forty-five students and take control of the building. When N.O. Wayout attempts to escape, he is shot in the arm by one of the terrorists. I.M. Violent shouts at the startled students, "They killed my comrades, destroyed my country, and tortured our women. Now, they will listen to us or hostages will die."

Your assignment is to resolve the incident. You are part of the negotiating team. Consider the following:

   a. Phases of hostage-taking events
   b. Management requirements
   c. Negotiating strategies
   d. Media relations
   e. A rescue plan
   f. Building rapport with the hostage takers
   g. You know one of the hostages is an off-duty police officer
7. How have the tactics of hostage takers changed over the last decade?
8. How do you determine when the Stockholm Syndrome is not developing?
9. Develop your own typology of hostage takers.
10. What differentiates criminal and political terrorist hostage-taking episodes?
11. List and describe at least six hostage-taking guidelines that are present in every hostage-taking incident.

Web Sites

Terrorism Research Center
http://www.terrorism.com

United Nations Website on Terrorism
http://www.un.org/terrorism

Human Rights Databank
http://www.hri.ca

Amnesty International
http://www.amnesty.org

United Nations Human Rights Web site
http://www.ohchr.org/English

Victims Information
http://www.ncjrs.gov

Endnotes

1. "National Counterterrorism Center: 2007 Report on Terrorism," (April 30, 2008), p. 29, *http://www.nctc.gov.*

2. Robert B. Asprey, *War in the Shadows. The Guerrilla in History* (London: MacDonald and Jane's, 1975), p. 20; Joel Allen, *Hostages and Hostage Taking in the Roman Empire* (Cambridge, MA: Cambridge University Press, 2006), pp. 44–48.

3. J. Bowyer Bell, *Assassin: The Theory and Practice of Political Violence* (New York: St. Martin's Press, 1979), p. 102; Callum Macdonald, *The Killing of Reinhard Heydrich: The SS "Butcher of Prague"* (New York: Da Capo Press, 1998), pp. 184–87.

4. Thomas C. Schelling, *The Strategy of Conflict* (London: Oxford University Press, 1973), p. 239; Brian Michael Jenkins, *Will Terrorists Go Nuclear* (Amherst, New York: Prometheus Books, 2008), pp. 241–76.

5. Clive C. Aston, "Political Hostage Taking in Western Europe: A Statistical Analysis," in *Perspectives on Terrorism*, eds. Lawrence Z. Freedman and Yonah Alexander (Wilmington, DE: Scholarly Resources, 1983), p. 100; John C. Griffiths, *Hostage: The History, Facts, and Reasoning Behind Political Hostage Taking* (London: Andre Deutsch, 2003), pp. 72–87.

6. For example, see Ann Hagedorn Auerbach, *Ransom: The Untold Story of International Kidnapping* (New York: Henry Holt, 1998); Kirk Semple, "The Kidnapping Economy," *The New York Times Magazine* (June 3, 2001), p. 46; Ana Carrigan, "Pawns of War: The Colombian Hostage Crisis," (November 15, 2007), *http://www.opendemocracy.net/about.*

7. John G. Stratton, "The Terrorist Act of Hostage Taking: Considerations for Law Enforcement," *Journal of Police Science and Administration*, 6 (1978), pp. 123–24.

8. *Sacramento Bee* (April 4, 1986), sec. A, p. 10.

9. Ibid. (December 31, 1985), sec. A, p. 8.

10. H. H. A. Cooper, *The Hostage Takers* (Boulder, CO: Paladin Press, 1981), pp. 53–61.

11. *Time Magazine* (December 23, 1985), p. 35.

12. Wolf Middendorff, *New Developments in the Taking of Hostages and Kidnapping: A Summary* (Washington, DC: National Criminal Justice Reference Service, 1975), pp. 1–9.

13. Frank Bolz Jr., "The Hostage Situation: Law Enforcement Options," in *Terrorism: Interdisciplinary Perspectives*, eds. Burr Eichelman, David A. Soskis, and William H. Reid (Washington, DC: American Psychiatric Association, 1983), pp. 99–116.

14. Richard Kobetz, *Hostage Incidents: The New Police Priority* (Gaithersburg, MD: International Association of Chiefs of Police, undated mimeo).

15. Cooper, *The Hostage Takers*, pp. 1–3.

16. Irving Goldaber, "A Typology of Hostage Takers," *Police Chief* (June 1979), pp. 21–22.

17. Los Angeles Sheriff's Office, *Special Enforcement Bureau (SEB): Hostage Guidelines* (July 1998).

18. David A. Soskis and Clinton Van Zandt, "Hostage Negotiation: Law Enforcement's Most Effective Non-lethal Weapon," *FBI Management Quarterly*, 6 (1986), pp. 1–8; Nils Bejerot, "The Six-Day War in Stockholm," *New Scientist*, 61 (1974), pp. 486–87.

19. Katherine Ramsland, "The Claiming of Patty Hearst," *http://www.crimelibrary.com.*

20. For example, see Maggie Haberman and Jeane MacIntosh, *Held Captive: The Kidnapping and Rescue of Elizabeth Smart* (New York: Avon Books, 2003); Tom Smart and Lee Benson, *In Plain Sight: The Startling Truth Behind the Elizabeth Smart Investigation* (Chicago, IL: Chicago Review Press, 2005).

21. Katy Duke, "Respect My Privacy says Kidnap Victim," (August 27, 2006), *http://www.guardian.co.uk;* Allan Hall and Michael Leidig, *Girl in the Cellar: The Natascha Kampusch Story* (New York: Harper Collins, 2007); Martin Fido, *True Crime* (London: Carlton Books Ltd., 2007), pp. 352–56.

22. M. Namnyak et al., Stockholm Syndrome: Psychiatric Diagnosis or Urban Myth," *Acta Psychiatrica Scandinavica*, 117, 1 (January 2008), pp. 4–11.

23. Murray S. Miron and Arnold P. Goldstein, *Hostage* (New York: Pergamon, 1979), p. 9.

24. Thomas Strentz, "Law Enforcement Policy and Ego Defenses of the Hostage," *F.B.I. Law*

Enforcement Bulletin (April 1979), p. 4; Thomas Strentz, *Psychological Aspects of Crisis Negotiation* (London: CRC Press, 2005), pp. 243–56.

25. Robert I. Simon and Robert A. Blum, "After the Terrorist Incident: Psychotherapeutic Treatment of Former Hostages," *American Journal of Psychotherapy*, 41 (April 1987), pp. 194–200.

26. Robert D. McFadden, Joe B. Treaster, and Maurice Carroll, *No Hiding Place* (New York: Times Books, 1981), p. 120.

27. Elliot Aronson, *Social Animal* (San Francisco, CA: W. H. Freeman, 1972), p. 168.

28. Angela Favaro et al., "The Effects of Trauma Among Kidnap Victims in Sardinia, Italy," *Psychological Medicine*, 30 (2000), pp. 975–80.

29. *Sacramento Bee* (December 11, 1984), sec. A, p. 1.

30. V. M. Solomon, "Hostage Psychology and the 'Stockholm Syndrome:' Captor, Captive and Captivity," *Dissertation Abstracts International*, 43 (1982), p. 1269.

31. Miron and Goldstein, *Hostage*, pp. 101–02.

32. Thomas Strentz, *FBI Hostage Negotiation Training Program* (San Diego, CA, March 17, 1986); Strentz, *Psychological Aspects of Crisis Negotiation,* p. 233.

33. For example, see Antonio Corsese, *Terrorism, Politics and Law: The Achille Lauro Affair* (Malden, MA: Blackwell Publishers, 1989); Adam Dolnik and Keith M. Fitzgerald, *Negotiating Hostage Crises with the New Terrorists* (New York: Praeger Security International, 2007), pp. 149–50.

34. Manfred Schreiber, *After Action Report of Terrorist Activities 20th Olympic Games Munich, West Germany FRG* (September 1972), p. 14.

35. Simon Reeve, *One Day in September: The Full Story of the 1972 Munich Olympics Massacre and the Israeli Revenge Operation "Wrath of God"* (New York: Arcade Publishing, 2006), pp. 20–48.

36. Ibid., pp. 105–15.

37. Miron and Goldstein, *Hostage*, pp. 53–62.

38. For example, see Frank Bolz, Kenneth J. Dudonis, and David P. Schulz, *Counterterrorism Handbook: Tactics, Procedures, and Techniques* (New York: Elsevier, 1990); George Jonas, *Vengeance: The True Story of an Israeli Counter-Terrorist Team* (New York: Simon and Schuster, 2005).

39. Ron A. Crelinsten and Denis Szabo, *Hostage Taking* (Lexington, MA: Lexington Books, 1979), p. 53.

40. Jeffery D. Simon, *The Terrorist Trap: America's Experience with Terrorism* (Bloomington: Indiana University Press, 1994), pp. 29–33; Joseph Wheelan, *Jefferson's War: America's First War on Terror 1801–1805* (Jackson, TN: Public Affairs, 2005), pp. 159–80.

41. Stansfield Turner, *Terrorism and Democracy* (Boston, MA: Houghton Mifflin, 1991), pp. 8–9.

42. For example, see Godfrey Fisher, *Barbary Legend: War, Trade and Piracy in North Africa* (Westport, CT: Greenwood, 1974).

43. For example, see Frederic H. Stevens, *Santo Tomas Internment Camp* (New York: Stratford House, 1946); Emily Van Sickle, *The Iron Gates of Santo Tomas* (Chicago, IL: Academy Chicago, 1992); Robert B. Holland, *The Rescue of Santo Tomas: Manila WWII* (Paducah, KY: Turner Publishing Co., 2003).

44. For example, see Ed Brandt, *The Last Voyage of the USS Pueblo* (New York: Norton Press, 1969); Lloyd M. Bucher, *Bucher: My Story* (New York: Doubleday, 1970); Mitchell B. Lerner, *The Pueblo Incident: A Spy Ship and the Failure of American Policy* (Lawrence, KS: University Press of Kansas, 2003).

45. For example, see Richard G. Head, *Crisis Resolution: Presidential Decision Making in the Mayaguez and Korean Confrontations* (Boulder, CO: Westview Press, 1978); Christopher Jon Lamb, *Belief Systems and Decision Making in the Mayaguez Crisis* (Gainesville, FL: University of Florida Press, 1989); Ralph Wetterhahn, *The Last Battle: The Mayaguez Incident and the End of the Vietnam War* (New York: Da Capo Press, 2001).

46. Simon, *The Terrorist Trap*, pp. 125–35.

47. For example, see Charlie A. Beckwith and Donald Knox, *Delta Force* (New York: Dell Books, 1983); James H. Kyle, *The Guts to Try: The Untold Story of the Iranian Hostage Rescue Mission by the On-the-Scene Desert Commander* (New York: Orion Books, 1990).

48. For example, see Gary Sick, *All Fall Down: America's Tragic Encounter with Iran* (New York: Random House, 1984); David P. Houghton, *U.S. Foreign Policy and the Iran Hostage Crisis* (New York: Cambridge University Press, 2001); Massoumeh Ebthkar, *Takeover in Iran: The Inside Story of the 1979 U.S. Embassy Capture* (London: Talonbooks, Limited, 2001); Mark Bowden, *Guests of the Ayatollah: The First Battle*

in America's War with Militant Islam (New York: Atlantic Monthly Press, 2006).

49. Sick, *All Fall Down*, pp. 35–55.

50. Paul B. Ryan, *The Iranian Rescue Mission: Why It Failed* (Annapolis, MD: Naval Institute, 1985), pp. 31–39.

51. McFadden, Treaster, and Carroll, *No Hiding Place*, pp. 115–25.

52. Glen Craig, Sheriff, Sacramento County Sheriff's Office, *Training Video on Good Guys Incident* (Sacramento: Sacramento County Sheriff's Office, April 1991); Lisa Joseph, *Heads or Tails: A True Hostage Story of Terror, Torture, and Ultimate Survival* (Orange, CA, 2003).

53. Mitchell R. Hammer, "Negotiating Across the Cultural Divide: Intercultural Dynamics in Crisis Incidents," in *Dynamic Processes of Crisis Negotiation: Theory, Research, and Practice*, eds. Randall G. Rogan, Mitchell R. Hammer, and Clinton R. Van Zandt (Westport, CT: Praeger, 1997), pp. 105–15.

54. Simon, *The Terrorist Trap*, pp. 3391–93; See also Iddo Netanyahu, *The Jonathan Netanyahu Story: The First Battle in the War on Terrorism* (Green Forest, AR: New Leaf Press, 2003).

55. *San Francisco Chronicle* (December 27, 1994), p. 1.

56. Chris Hansen, "The Lesson of Air France Flight 8969," (February 6, 2003), *http://www. msnbc.com.*

57. *Sacramento Bee* (December 18, 1996), p. Al.

58. For example, see Suzie Baer, *Peru's MRTA: Tupac Amaru Revolutionary Movement* (New York: Rosen Publishing Group, 2003); Gordon McCormick, *Sharp Dressed Men: Peru's Tupac Amaru Revolutionary Movement* (New York: National Book Network, 1993).

59. The Rescue, *Pride Is First for the President* (April 24, 1997), *http://www.geocities.com/ CapitolHill/6502/pride.htm*; Suzie Baer, *Peru's MRTA*, pp. 18–42.

60. Christian Caryl and Eve Conant, "Show of Nerve," *Newsweek* (November 4, 2002), pp. 44–46; Paul Murphy, *The Wolves of Islam: Russia and the Faces of Chechen Terror* (Dulles, VA: Potomac Books, Inc., 2004), pp. 188–92.

61. For example, see Frank Bolz, *How to Be a Hostage and Live* (New York: Carol Publishing Group, 1987); Terry Anderson, *Den of Lions: Memoirs of Seven Years* (New York: Crown, 1993); Nathan Andrews, *Hostage Taking Can Seriously Damage Your Health and other Stories* (Lulu.com, 2008), pp. 7–92.

62. For example, see Robert K. Spear and Michael Moak, *Surviving Hostage Situations* (Leavenworth, KS: Universal Force Dynamics, 1989); Ben Weir and Carol Weir, *Hostage Bound, Hostage Free* (Philadelphia, PA: Westminster Press, 1987).

63. For example, see Frank Bolz, Kenneth J. Dudonis, and David P. Schulz, *Counterterrorism Handbook: Tactics, Procedures and Techniques* (Boca Raton, FL: CRC Press, 2002).

64. *Sacramento Bee* (January 19, 1986), sec. A, p. 1.

65. Frank Ochberg, "Hostage Victims," in *Terrorism: Interdisciplinary Perspectives*, eds. Burt Eichelman, David Soskis, and William Reid (Washington, DC: American Psychiatric Association, 1983), p. 86.

66. Richard Clutterbuck, *Kidnap and Ransom: The Response* (London: Farber and Farber, 1978), pp. 158–64.

CHAPTER 7

Contemporary Terrorism and Bombing

CHAPTER OBJECTIVES
The study of this chapter will enable you to:

- Identify the effects of an explosion
- Explore the historical antecedents of explosive materials
- Distinguish between low- and high-velocity explosives
- Describe the phases of blast/pressure
- Examine several vehicle bomb attack methods
- Outline a law enforcement strategy to cope with vehicle bombs
- Explore incidence of aircraft bombings
- Develop a security program to prevent injuries due to mail bombs

INTRODUCTION

In spite of the spectacular nature of hostage-taking incidents, nothing personifies contemporary terrorism more than indiscriminate bombing. Certainly everyone is familiar with the popular caricature of the nineteenth-century anarchist/terrorist, dressed in a long, black coat and broad-brimmed hat with eyes bulging, about to throw a round, black bomb with a fuse extending from the top into a crowd of unsuspecting victims. Unfortunately, the terrorist using the bomb is still the most important strategic attack method of modern terrorism. Slightly more than one-half of all recorded fatalities in 2007 were from bombings.[1] The U.S. State Department reports that between 2000 and 2008 over 60 percent of all recorded terrorist incidents were bombings.[2] According to the National Counterterrorism Center (NCTC), 4,543 terrorist bombings occurred in 2007, recording 11,194 deaths and 30,098 injuries.[3] However, the majority of bombings in 2007 occurred in Iraq and Afghanistan. Regardless of whose statistics we use, little doubt remains that bombing is the terrorist weapon of choice. Several factors have contributed to the escalation of bombing as a preferred tactic by today's terrorist groups.

First, bombings are the most effective method of launching a terrorist attack. **Carlos Marighella** writes, "Terrorism is accomplished by placing a bomb . . . so that its destructive power causes an irreparable loss of life to the *enemy*; committed with extreme cold-bloodedness, while acting with bold decisiveness" (my emphasis).[4] Indeed, terrorist bombings are lethal, indiscriminate, and cold-blooded. Several examples illustrate the point. In September 1986, fourteen terrorist bombs indiscriminately exploded in several French cities, killing fifteen people; the U.S. embassies in Kenya and Tanzania were bombed in August 1998, killing over 200 people and injuring 5,000 others. In October 2002, a powerful car bomb killed 192 people in Bali, Indonesia, and a midair terrorist explosion aboard Pan Am 103 killed 258 Americans. In June 2006, Iraqi terrorists in Baghdad randomly bombed trains, busses, and busy market plazas, killing more than 200 innocent victims. The most devastating bombings between 2005 and 2009 have occurred in Iraq with the introduction of the deadly suicide bomber. Suicide bombers have killed hundreds of Iraqi civilians. Nothing so symbolizes the Iraqi resistance to the U.S. occupation of Iraq as the ubiquitous suicide bomber. (Suicide bombings are discussed in Chapter 8.)

Second, explosives and bomb technology are easily accessible to terrorist groups at a relatively low financial cost. In fact, several "mayhem" manuals are available, which graphically illustrate the simplicity of bomb making.[5] Third, although the making of clandestine explosive devices requires some degree of technical expertise, one person can easily handle the entire process. Fourth, bombings involve far less risk to the terrorist bomber since improved timing devices allow sufficient opportunity for the terrorist to escape detection or injury. Fifth, Internet sources provide detailed instructions on bomb making. Finally, the larger the terrorist explosion, the more vigorous the media coverage. Media interest is in "good" pictures—"if it bleeds it leads." Indeed, bombings provide graphic scenes of mayhem, mutilation, and death, as witnessed in the media coverage on 9/11, the Madrid train bombings, or the London subway attacks.

The focus of this chapter is on types of explosives, effects of explosions, and terrorist bomb attack methodologies. Its purpose is to provide criminal justice students with a general understanding of the nature of explosions and explosives. But first, a brief review of the historical development of explosive devices is relevant.

HISTORICAL PERSPECTIVE

The oldest known explosive and propellant is **black powder**. As with most discoveries that are centuries old, the name of the inventor and even the country of its origin remain in dispute. The principal claimants for the discovery of black powder are the Chinese, the Romans, the Hindus, the Greeks, the Arabs, the English, and the Germans. For example, the Chinese and the Romans of the fourth century were familiar with black powder pyrotechnic displays, while the ancient Greeks manufactured an incendiary composition, similar to that of black powder, referred to as "Greek Fire."

In England, Roger Bacon is generally credited with the invention of black powder in the thirteenth century. However, Bacon apparently was not aware of the projecting qualities of black powder although he was aware that black powder was unstable, made a thunderous noise when exploded, and terrified people. By the fourteenth century, Berthold Schwarz, a German friar, used black powder as a propelling agent; he is generally acknowledged as the inventor of firearms.

Eventually, in Europe, black powder became known as Schwarzpulver. Until the seventeenth century, black powder was used as a propellant charge. Cannonballs, for example, were made of solid pieces of stone or iron. But the development of hollow cast iron balls introduced the use of black powder as explosive filler, thus introducing crude bombs that could be thrown or used as mines. These bombs could easily be ignited by a time fuse.

Laqueur records several incidents where black powder bombs were used with great effect, especially in the terrorist Fenian bombing of Clerkenwell Prison in 1867 in which twelve persons were killed and 120 injured.[6] The unpredictable nature of black powder, however, made it extremely dangerous to handle, and many people blew themselves up while making bombs. Terrorist bombing was made much easier but probably more dangerous with the invention of nitroglycerine and **dynamite**.

Nitroglycerine, the basis of high explosives, was discovered in 1847 by an Italian chemistry professor at the University of Turin.[7] But the discovery of nitroglycerine remained more or less a scientific curiosity until 1867, when the eminent scientist Alfred Nobel mixed nitroglycerine with an absorbent material, thus making it safer to handle. Nobel also invented the blasting cap to provide a safe and dependable way to detonate dynamite. Nobel's epoch-making discovery of dynamite ushered in a new era of high explosives.[8] Dynamite was widely believed to be the ultimate weapon, and anarchist/revolutionary groups of the period based their whole strategy on its use. However, terrorists, anarchists, and revolutionaries quickly discovered that they could not bomb their way into the hearts and minds of the people. The exaggerated hope of dynamite as the ultimate weapon was not fulfilled. Clearly, the dynamite bomb was not the all-destroying weapon of the future, but it had become a symbol of fear and intimidation. Dynamite continues to be one of the most popular high explosives used by modern terrorist groups.[9]

With the introduction of military explosives shortly before the outbreak of World War I, the technological development of high explosives accelerated. Military explosives differ from commercial explosives such as black powder and dynamite in several respects. Military explosives have a much greater shattering effect, have high rates of detonation, and are relatively insensitive to impact, heat, shock, and friction. Military explosives also must be usable underwater and be of convenient size, shape, and weight for combat use. The most widely used military explosive is TNT (trinitrotoluene). TNT is widely used as a main charge in aerial bombs, artillery shells, and mortar rounds. TNT cannot be detonated by heat, shock, or friction, as black powder or dynamite can.[10]

Another popular military explosive, discovered during World War II and in wide use today, is the mysterious Composition 4 (C-4). **C-4** is the notorious "plastic" explosive, a yellow, putty-like substance that closely resembles children's modeling clay. C-4 is easy and safe to handle and can be molded into a variety of shapes. It has no odor, has a greater shattering effect than TNT, and detonates at a much higher rate.[11] Yet another well-known military explosive is pentaerythritol-tetranitrate, commonly known as PETN.[12] **PETN** is a high explosive in linear form that has a variety of military as well as some commercial uses. It closely resembles ordinary clothesline and is also referred to as datachord, primex, or primacord. Like C-4, PETN is resistant to heat, shock, and friction.

After the first bombing of the World Trade Center in 1993, yet another high explosive came into prominent use. Ammonium nitrate **fertilizer** bombs have been used by a variety of terrorist groups, including the **PIRA**, Tamil Tigers in Sri Lanka, and Middle East groups. Most recently the **Jemaah Islamiya** (JI) used a fertilizer bomb in Bali, Indonesia, on October 20, 2002, which killed over 192 people. Ammonium nitrate is a strong oxidizer and mixed with other materials can cause a massive explosion.

FIGURE 7.1   Timothy McVeigh confers with his attorneys at the federal prison in El Reno, Oklahoma. McVeigh was convicted for the terrorist bombing of the Murrah Building and executed on June 11, 2001. (AP/Wide World Photos)

In the bombing of the Murrah Building in Oklahoma City, **Timothy McVeigh** described how he mixed three fifty-five-gallon drums of liquid nitromethane with 108 fifty-pound bags of ammonium nitrate fertilizer. McVeigh then placed a high explosive known as Tovex sausage around the AN-FO to act as a booster. In the end he had mixed 7,000 pounds of explosives. The explosion would release more energy than the **blast** from a ton of dynamite. McVeigh would use datachord or PETN to set off a nonelectric blasting cap that would instantaneously transfer a spark to the Tovex, setting off the explosive mixture of ammonium nitrate and nitromethane. The result was the death of 168 people and the worst terrorist bombing in U.S. history until the 2001 attack on the World Trade Center.[13] (See Figure 7.2.)

The ample range of explosive materials now available to contemporary terrorist groups has produced a shock wave of worldwide bombings. The commercial explosives, black powder and dynamite, can be easily purchased or stolen from construction or mining sites while military explosives are provided to terrorist groups by such "terrorist" nations as Iraq, Sudan, Iran, Libya, or Syria.[14] New types of delayed fuses are also available to terrorist groups. These include electrically fired devices and bombs fired by pressure, by chemical methods, and by X-ray-sensitive fuses. Even the most powerful bombs can be easily concealed in letters, parcels, shopping bags, suitcases, or vehicles. The technological advances in the manufacture of explosives have produced limitless opportunities for today's terrorist bombers. But the greatest threat of terrorist bombing comes from the very real possibility of nuclear terrorism. Jenkins warns the international community that nuclear blackmail by terrorists is the future threat to democratic nations.[15]

Several future nuclear terrorist scenarios have been identified. First, terrorists now have the technology to construct a fission-type nuclear device. Second, terrorists could contaminate a city with nuclear waste material by detonating a **dirty bomb** in midair and allowing the wind to let the radiation drift over the target.

A dirty bomb is a conventional explosive salted with radioactive isotopes in order to spread nuclear material over a wide area. It is much easier to construct a "dirty nuke" than to build a

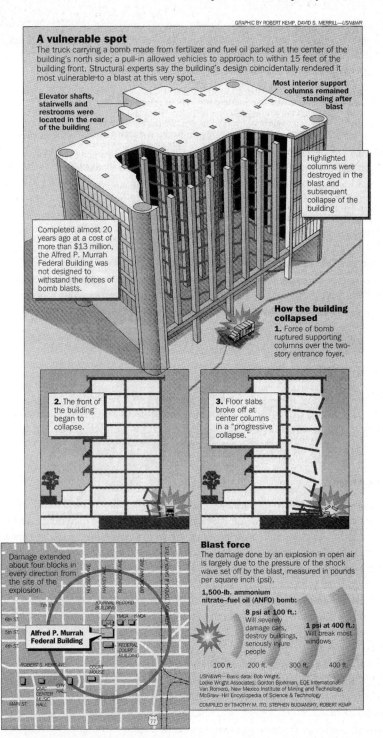

FIGURE 7.2 Bombing of Murrah building—Oklahoma City, 1995. (Copyright 1995 U.S. News & World Report, L.P. Reprinted with permission.)

conventional nuclear bomb. In addition to killing a large number of people, the panic created by a "dirty nuke" would be devastating. A "dirty nuke" is a pure terror weapon. On May 2, 2002, Jose Padilla was arrested in Chicago after allegedly planning a "dirty bomb" attack in the United States. Padilla is believed to be a follower of Osama bin Laden and trained in terrorist camps in Afghanistan. On January 22, 2008, Padilla, who changed his name to Abdullah al-Muhajir, was sentenced to seventeen years in prison for supporting terrorism and conspiring to kill people in an overseas jihad.

Third, a terrorist group could seize a nuclear facility and cause a meltdown. Finally, long-range missiles or mortars, causing widespread nuclear fallout, could attack a nuclear facility. Theoretically possible, these nuclear scenarios pose a serious threat to the entire world.[16]

As the technology of bombing has become more complicated, terrorist groups have greatly increased their technical expertise and the competency required to handle sophisticated explosive material. When manufactured explosives are not available, the ingredients necessary to produce an improvised explosive device are easily obtained. The ingredients required to construct home-made bombs are virtually unlimited and can easily be obtained in hardware or drug stores without arousing much suspicion. Such seemingly innocuous items as starch, flour, sugar, and ammonia-nitrate fertilizers can be treated to become effective explosives. But still, the most widely used main charge explosive is black powder. For example, the black powder pipe bomb is the most popular type of clandestine explosive device used in the United States. The next section reviews the three primary effects of an explosion.

EFFECTS OF AN EXPLOSION

When an explosive is detonated, the black powder, stick of dynamite, block of TNT, or chunk of C-4 is instantaneously converted from a solid into a rapidly expanding mass of gases. The detonation will produce several secondary effects, but three primary effects produce the greatest amount of damage: **fragmentation**, blast pressure, and secondary fires, as illustrated in Figure 7.3.

Fragmentation

A simple fragmentation bomb is a quantity of explosive filler placed inside a length of pipe capped at each end with a piece of time fuse used for detonation. Once detonated, the explosion will produce a number of shattered fragments from the pipe. These fragments are propelled outward from the point of detonation at extremely high velocity. These small, high-velocity fragments reach a speed of approximately 2,700 feet per second.[17] The bomb fragments travel in a straight line until they lose velocity and fall to the earth or become embedded in an object. In order to increase the number of small, high-velocity fragments flying through the air, the inside of the pipe is often filled with glass, nails, bullets, razor blades, or staples, thereby increasing the number of people killed and injured. Another fiendish explosive device used by terrorist groups to increase the amount of fragmentation, or *shrapnel*, is one in which a couple of sticks of dynamite has a two-inch layer of nails or staples taped on the outside. This type of device is referred to as an IRA nail bomb. Figure 7.4 illustrates the typical pipe bomb and IRA nail bomb.

However, the most destructive fragmentation terrorist explosive device is the vehicle bomb. The configuration of a vehicle bomb is limited only by the imagination of the bomber. Whether a car, van, or truck is used, the consequences are overwhelming. Not only does the explosion create fragments from the vehicle, but in many cases the vehicle is loaded with bullets, scrap metal, or a large quantity of nails to increase the amount of fragmentation. Typically, vehicle bombs contain

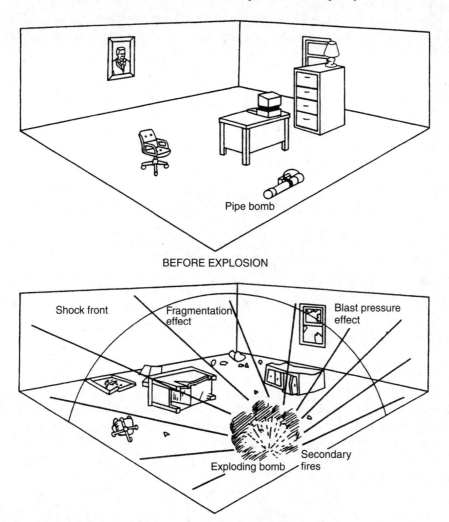

BEFORE EXPLOSION

FIGURE 7.3 Fragmentation, blast pressure, and secondary forces produced by an explosion.

high explosives such as dynamite, TNT, or "plastic." For example, the FBI estimates that the truck driven into the **Marine compound** in Beirut in October 1983 contained approximately 12,000 pounds of TNT.[18] The explosion collapsed a four-story building, left a crater approximately 30 feet deep by 40 feet wide, and killed 241 Marines as they lay sleeping in their bunks.[19] In addition to injuries created by the fragmentation effect, the blast pressure effect can also contribute to increased casualties.

Blast Pressure

The detonation of an explosive charge produces very hot expanding gases. These gases exert pressures of approximately 700 tons per square inch and rush away from the point of detonation at velocities up to 7,000 miles per hour. This mass of expanding gases travels outward in a concentric pattern from the point of origin of the explosion like an immense wave, destroying any object in its

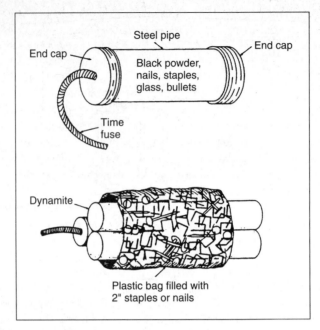

FIGURE 7.4 Black powder pipe bomb and dynamite nail bomb.

path. Similar to a giant ocean wave rushing to meet the beach, the further the pressure wave travels from the point of origin of the explosion, the less power it has until it disappears completely. This wave of pressure is called the blast pressure effect of an explosion. There are two distinct phases to the blast pressure effect: (1) positive pressure phase and (2) negative pressure phase.[20]

FIGURE 7.5 Bombing of the U.S. Marine Compound in Beirut on October 23, 1983. Rescue workers search the debris for survivors. Two hundred and forty-one marines were killed in the bombing. Hizballah/Islamic Jihad claimed credit for the bombing. (Zouki/AP/Wide World Photos)

The positive pressure wave is formed at the moment of detonation when the surrounding atmosphere is compressed into a rapidly expanding circle. The leading edge of the positive pressure wave is called the shock front. As the shock front begins to move outward from the point of detonation, closely followed by the positive pressure wave, it introduces a sudden, crushing one-two punch to any object in its path. Therefore, when the positive pressure wave struck, for example, the walls of the Marine compound, the shock front delivered a massive blow to the building followed instantly by the positive pressure phase. The shock front shattered the walls of the compound, while the positive pressure waves violently pushed the walls outward in a radiating pattern away from the point of detonation. The entire process of shock front and positive pressure waves lasts only a fraction of a second. The positive pressure waves will continue to dissipate until all the wave's power is expended.[21]

The negative pressure phase occurs as the outward compression of air by the positive pressure phase causes a partial vacuum at the point of detonation. The partial vacuum causes the displaced air to reverse its movement and rush inward to fill the void left by the positive pressure phase. The displaced air has mass and power as it returns toward the point of origin of the explosion. Even though the negative pressure phase is not as powerful as the positive pressure phase, it still has great velocity. In comparative terms, the positive pressure wave is comparable to a hurricane, while the negative pressure phase can be compared to a high wind.

As the displaced air rushes toward the point of origin or detonation, it will strike and move objects in its path of destruction. For example, when negative pressure waves struck the already damaged Marine compound, it caused additional portions of the battered building to topple. However, in the negative pressure phase, objects are pulled toward the center of detonation. The negative pressure phase lasts about three times longer than the positive pressure phase and is less powerful in its destruction.

Secondary Fires

The final effect produced by an explosion is the secondary fires, or thermal effect. The secondary fires created by the detonation of low- or high-velocity explosives vary greatly. At the instant of detonation, there is a bright flash, or fireball, that often causes a fire. Only when highly combustible materials are near the point of detonation will secondary fires erupt. For example, if a pipe bomb containing 5 pounds of black powder is detonated inside a building, the fires generally result from ruptured fuel lines or shorted electrical circuits. Generally, secondary fires cause the least amount of damage of the three primary detonation effects. The next section briefly clarifies the distinction between low- and high-velocity explosives.

VELOCITY AND EXPLOSIVES

The most widely acclaimed system for the classification of explosives is according to the rate of velocity or detonation of explosion. Two major groups of explosives have been identified: (1) low-velocity explosives and (2) high-velocity explosives.

Low-velocity explosives have rates of detonation below 3,000 feet per second. For example, the most popular low-velocity explosive in use today is black powder, which has a velocity rating of approximately 1,312 feet per second.[22] By comparison, straight dynamite, which is at the low end of high-velocity explosives, has a velocity rating of between 7,000 and 18,000 feet per second. The primary use of low-velocity explosives is as a propellant. The expanding gases of a low-velocity explosive such as black powder have a pushing effect rather than the shattering effect of high-velocity explosives. Low-velocity explosives, that is, black powder, gunpowder, or smokeless powder, are used in a variety of legitimate ways such as the manufacture of fireworks, flares, sporting propellants, blasting and mining operations, and the construction of safety fuses.

Black powder is a mechanical mixture of three common ingredients: (1) potassium nitrate or saltpeter, (2) charcoal or carbon, and (3) sulfur. The explosive characteristics of black powder occur only when the three ingredients are thoroughly mixed together. There are several recipes for the making of black powder; however, the most widely accepted formula is 75 percent salt-peter, 15 percent charcoal, and 10 percent sulfur. The composition of black powder has changed little since it was introduced in the thirteenth century in Europe. It can also be found in a range of colors, from black to gray to brown. In addition, the form of black powder may differ: the grains range from very fine to very coarse. The size of the grains controls the burning speed of black powder; large grains burn more slowly than smaller grains, fine grains burn more rapidly and explode more quickly. Thus, terrorists prefer the fine grain black powders for making homemade pipe bombs.

Black powder is also one of the most hazardous low-velocity explosives. It is easily ignited and can explode, when not confined, for no apparent reason. It is susceptible to friction, heat, and static electricity. Static electrical sparks can easily initiate black powder fires and explosions. Therefore, police officers and other criminal justice personnel working with black powder should wear self-grounding shoes and static-free clothing and work with wooden tools. Additionally, unlike other explosives, black powder does not deteriorate with age.

The black powder pipe bomb is the most widely used clandestine explosive device in the United States, and a number of people have blown themselves up while attempting to make the device. For instance, in one representative year, 1982, 35 percent of all recorded injuries in the United States due to bombings involved the persons who made the bombs. In 2006, the Bureau of Alcohol, Tobacco, and Firearms (BATF) reported that there were 3,445 explosive incidents in the United States, resulting in 14 fatalities and 135 injuries.[23] Bombs show no allegiance to their makers. In sum, black powder is an extremely unpredictable low-velocity explosive that should be handled with extreme care.

The most widely used high-velocity explosive is dynamite, which is a combination of liquid nitroglycerine, oxidizers, and an absorbent material. Dynamite is relatively easy to obtain in the United States either by theft or through legal purchase. Consequently, terrorists and criminal bombers prefer dynamite. Commercial dynamites differ widely in their strength and sensitivity. Straight dynamite, for example, is a mixture of liquid nitroglycerine; sodium nitrate, which supplies the oxygen for complete combustion; and wood pulp or ground meal to absorb the shock of the nitroglycerine. The strength of commercial straight dynamite is determined by the percentage of nitroglycerine by weight in the dynamite formula. For example, 60 percent dynamite means the dynamite contains 60 percent nitroglycerine and is quite powerful. When detonated, dynamite gives off a gray-white smoke. Dynamite is usually found in stick form, wrapped in colored wax paper, but is available in a variety of sizes, shapes, strengths, and packages. In addition to straight dynamites, ammonia dynamites, gelatin dynamites, and ammonia-gelatin dynamites are in wide use today in commercial operations.[24]

Other high-velocity explosives are manufactured for military use. These include TNT, C-4, and PETN. The TNT recovered by law enforcement personnel generally comes in the form of 1/4, 1/2, or 1-pound blocks. After TNT is exposed to sunlight, its light-yellow to light-brown color gradually turns to dark brown. TNT gives off a dirty gray smoke when detonated.

C-4 is an improved version of C-3. C-3 was developed for the Korean War but had a tendency to be brittle and break up. C-3 was difficult to handle in hot or cold environments.

TABLE 7.1 Types of Explosives

Low Velocity		High Velocity
Black powders		Dynamite
Smokeless powders	Military	TNT
Gun powders: detonate at 40 feet per second	Explosives	C-4
		PETN: detonates at 21,000 feet per second
		Ammonium nitrate
		Fertilizer bombs

Subsequently, C-4 was developed for the Vietnam War. C-4 contains 90 percent of the explosive compound RDX, has no odor, and is white to light tan in color. Table 7.1 summarizes the types of explosives most commonly used by modern terrorist groups and criminal bombers.

Now that we have identified the effects of an explosion and the types of explosive materials, our attention turns to the diverse and innovative attack methodologies of modern terrorist groups and criminal bombers.

VEHICLE BOMBS

The use of a vehicle as a bomb delivery system is not new, but it has become the tactic most preferred by such terrorist groups as the PIRA and various Middle East factions, especially in Iraq. Typically, the types of vehicles used to "deliver" explosive materials have been cars and vans. However, with the escalation of terrorism, explosive devices have also been planted on railway cars, busses, large trucks, and airplanes to create increased casualties and to attract greater media attention.

The attack methodologies used to date by terrorists and criminal bombers include the following: (1) placing explosive materials on or in a car to kill the occupants; (2) the use of a vehicle as a launching system for rocket-propelled munitions; (3) the use of a vehicle as a booby trap or antipersonnel device to ambush law enforcement personnel, members of the military, or bomb disposal experts; (4) the use of a hostage for the transportation and delivery of explosives; (5) the use of a vehicle as a fragmentation device when a large amount of explosives is used; (6) the use of multiple vehicle bombs in a coordinated terrorist strike; and (7) the use of a vehicle in a suicide, or "kamikaze," attack. Terrorist groups use all these methods today, but the trend seems to be toward the indiscriminate car bomb, loaded with explosives, parked on a busy commercial street with the purpose of creating fear and panic by killing a large number of innocent bystanders. A review of car bomb attack methods follows.

Historically, **car bombs** have been used for the purpose of killing the occupants. The car served merely as another location for the act of murder. The motives for such killings were no different than other types of murders that were committed with guns, knives, or poisons. These motives included retaliation, revenge, anger, suicide, financial gain, or hate–love triangles. The procedure for many of these car bombings was to place 2–5 pounds of dynamite under the hood on the left side of the engine, under the front seat, on the gas tank, under the dashboards, or any place on the car that would have the greatest killing effect on the intended target.[25]

Organized crime figures of the 1920s, 1930s, and even the 1980s and 1990s are notorious for using car bombs to intimidate rival gangs and to eliminate competition. The practice is still used today. In one incident in 1985, a car bomb was used to murder a government witness who agreed to testify against organized crime figures in a Chicago gambling case.

Likewise, hundreds of accounts exist in which car bombs were used in domestic arguments. In one case, known as the "baby food bombing," the bomber placed two explosive devices contained in baby food jars under the front seat of his spouse's car. The jars were wired to the car's ignition system. Brodie maintains that the most effective place to hide a bomb is under the driver's seat, which is also the most common area for bombs to be placed in domestic quarrels.[26]

Car bombs have also been used in the selective assassination of political figures throughout the world. For example, a remote-controlled bomb killed Orlando Letelier, the former Chilean ambassador to the United States, as he drove through a quiet residential street in Washington, DC. The bomb, a 1.5-pound mixture of TNT and plastic explosive, was fastened to the undercarriage of Letelier's car. The explosion killed Letelier and two passengers as they unsuspectingly drove to work.[27]

Another fairly common terrorist bomb attack method is to place an explosive charge inside a vehicle and park the vehicle along the route of the intended victim. On April 14, 1993, while in Kuwait, there was an attempt to assassinate former President George Bush by using a car bomb. Bush was the target of an assassination plot directed by Iraqi intelligence. Kuwaiti police discovered a 175-pound car bomb, including the remote control detonators, the plastic explosives, and the electronic circuitry. The car bomb had been parked near the motorcade route taken by former President Bush. The bomb was to be set off using a remote control device that would have been lethal for nearly a quarter of a mile. The bomb was disarmed after an Iraqi informant told Kuwaiti police where it was located. Using a remote control switch, the terrorist bomber needs only await the arrival of the intended victim. When the victim is within range, a signal is transmitted to the explosive charge, causing detonation. The remote-controlled car bomb is a popular PIRA tactic.

On August 27, 1979, a cleverly planned double car bombing on the border between Northern Ireland and the Republic of Ireland killed eighteen British paratroopers. A vehicle containing 1,100 pounds of explosives was parked inconspicuously on a country road. As a British troop convoy passed the vehicle, the PIRA bombers detonated the bomb by remote control. Ten British soldiers were killed, and the force of the blast hurled their vehicle 50 feet into the air. British reinforcements quickly arrived at the scene, and a second 800-pound bomb was detonated remotely, killing another eight British paratroopers. The use of two explosive devices or the double bomb is a frequently used PIRA tactic. This PIRA attack inflicted the heaviest loss of life on British soldiers since 1921 when an ambush by Irish Republican rebels killed thirty-five British troopers.[28]

A second variation of the vehicle bomb attack method is to use the vehicle as a munitions-launching system. This terrorist strategy is used to fire rockets and mortars at the intended target—again, a favorite strategy of the Provos.

A stolen flatbed truck that concealed a makeshift mortar-launching system welded to the truck's frame was used by the PIRA to attack a heavily fortified police barracks in Newry, Northern Ireland.[29] Nine shells were launched from a distance of 250 yards away, scoring a direct hit on the Royal Ulster Constabulary police barracks, killing nine police officers and seriously wounding thirty-seven others. Police in Northern Ireland suspected the mortars were fired by remote control. The stolen flatbed truck had been parked on a hill overlooking the rear entrance of the police barracks, making an easy target for the PIRA bombers. Mortar attacks by the PIRA are quite frequent in Northern Ireland but in the past have been notoriously inaccurate. For example, the PIRA fired eighteen mortar rounds from a flatbed truck at a police station and training center in Belfast.[30] The mortar rounds fell harmlessly, and no one was seriously injured. On February 7, 1991, in a daring, well-planned attack, the PIRA attempted to assassinate British Prime Minister John Major at 10 Downing Street with a salvo of mortar rounds fired from a van. A section of the van's roof had been cut away to allow the firing of the homemade "rockets." Three mortar rounds fell within 40 feet of 10 Downing Street, the residence of the British prime minister. The "rockets" shattered the upper windows of the building, where Prime Minister Major was in a meeting with British cabinet members. No one was killed or injured. Such attacks, whether successful or not, receive significant media attention, again publicizing the cause of the Republican movement and the "courageousness" of the Irish Republican Army. Similar attacks involving the firing of rockets from moving vehicles have been used by Hizballah and Hamas.

The third variation of the vehicle bomb attack method involves the use of the bomb-laden vehicle to ambush law enforcement and military personnel. The ambush attack method usually involves a stolen car or rental vehicle expertly wired with a remote-control firing device. The vehicle bomb is then parked near a police station house or along routes frequented by police or military personnel. As security vehicles approach, the vehicle bomb is detonated without warning, usually killing the unsuspecting security officers.

In July 2007, AQI detonated a booby-trapped truck in Baghdad, Iraq, while four Iraqi security officers were inspecting it, killing two and seriously wounding the others. Hundreds of Iraqi and American soldiers and police officers have been killed by such devices. The tactic has also been used in Spain, Greece, Australia, and the United States. For example, Basque separatists or terrorists in Spain killed two police officers with a remote-control vehicle bomb, as they were about to investigate a complaint of a suspicious vehicle. In Athens, Greece, a car bomb was detonated by remote control as a police bus was passing, killing two and wounding fourteen. In Melbourne, Australia, two rental cars packed with explosives were parked at the front entrance to police headquarters. The first car bomb was detonated, causing little damage and few injuries; however, the second car bomb was detonated fifteen minutes later, after a large crowd had gathered at the scene of the first bomb. This second car bomb, or double bomb, caused many casualties, including the serious wounding of fifteen police officers. In the United States, the booby-trapped car bomb was the signature bomb of the FALN. In one such incident, a number of police officers and firefighters were injured by an exploding van while responding to a fire alarm. Eyewitness accounts indicate that the van was parked and then set on fire. As firefighters attempted to put out the flames, a remote-controlled firing device detonated the van. The FALN later claimed credit for the blast in a telephone call to the *New York Times*.[31]

The fourth type of vehicle attack bomb uses the vehicle to deliver or gain access to the intended target. The PIRA was the first terrorist group to popularize this method, which uses the following strategy. In order to penetrate security checkpoints and gain a closer position to the intended target, the PIRA would kidnap a close family member of a legitimate employee (such as a government employee or prison guard) of the bombing target. The legitimate employee would then be instructed to deliver the bomb vehicle to his place of employment. If the employee refused, then the family member being held hostage would be threatened with injury or death. With few choices, the employee would deliver the explosive device using his legitimate identification to penetrate security checkpoints. The tactic has also been used repeatedly in Iraq, resulting in the deaths of hundreds of innocent bystanders.

In the August 2003 bombing of the United Nations Headquarters Compound in Baghdad, explosives were surreptitiously planted in the vehicle of an embassy employee. Unaware that the vehicle contained a large quantity of explosives, the unsuspecting employee was allowed to pass a security checkpoint and park the vehicle on the embassy grounds where sometime later the explosives were detonated, killing twenty-two people including the United Nations envoy to Iraq.

In the fifth variation of the vehicle terrorist attack method, large quantities of explosives are used; and glass, bullets, or small pieces of metal are contained inside the bomb vehicle. Bomb vehicles containing explosive substances in excess of 100–500 pounds and randomly parked in a heavily residential area to maximize the killing of innocent civilians are not unusual.

During the Iraqi insurgency, AQI and affiliated groups carried out hundreds of such bomb attacks. Between June 2003 and June 2006, an estimated 538 car bombs were detonated in Iraq, killing thousands of Iraqis and American soldiers. These vehicle bombs were parked on busy commercial and residential streets, thereby increasing the number of civilian casualties.

On June 25, 1996, Muslim terrorists from the Saudi Hizballah detonated a petroleum tanker truck containing approximately 4,000 pounds of ammonium nitrate fertilizer and RDX explosives on the perimeter of the U.S. apartment complex known as **Khobar Towers** in Dhahran, Saudi Arabia. The apartment complex housed U.S. Air Force personnel and their families. The bomb-laden truck initially was denied entry into the Khobar facility but eventually was parked outside the concrete barriers surrounding the facility. The driver got out of the truck and sped away in a small white car driven by another man. The resulting explosion left an 85- by 35-foot crater that killed nineteen U.S. Air Force personnel and injured 500 others. Thirteen Saudis and a Lebanese were indicted on June 22, 2001, on charges of murder and conspiracy for the Khobar towers bombing. The 48-count indictment alleges that the fourteen men were members of the Islamic terrorist group Hizballah, which received financial and spiritual support from Iran. The indictment states that the conspiracy was driven by a desire to drive Americans from Saudi Arabia.[32]

The sixth vehicle attack method uses multiple bombs hidden on vehicles of public transportation. This terrorist attack method involves placing explosive devices, timed to explode during rush hours, on busses or trains, thereby creating mass casualties of innocent civilian bystanders. The method has been used by various Palestinian factions, the PIRA, and more recently by Tamil separatists in Sri Lanka, Kashmir militants in India, and AQI. The intent of such indiscriminate bombings is to gain media attention and create intense fear in the general community. There is no doubt that the selective terrorist bombing of public transportation will continue to escalate. The establishment of effective security controls for all public transportation is difficult to institute.

The seventh bomb attack method involves vehicle bombs containing large quantities of explosives driven by suicide bombers. The most sensational suicide bombings have occurred in the Middle East and have been directed against U.S. targets. On October 23, 1983, a truck loaded with the equivalent of 12,000 pounds of TNT was driven into the Marine compound in Beirut.[33] According to the FBI, this vehicle bomb created the largest conventional blast ever seen by explosive experts. In a simultaneous attack on the French multinational peacekeeping force, a suicide truck bomber killed fifty-eight French paratroopers. Then, on November 5, 1983, a suicide truck bomber penetrated the Israeli military compound in Tyre, Lebanon, killing sixty people.[34] In less than two weeks, suicide truck bombers had killed 359 members of the military forces of the United States, France, and Israel.

The suicide bomb attack method has fully emerged as a strategic weapon that enables nations with inferior military forces to gain a degree of strategic equality with more powerful military forces. Defenses against the suicide car or truck bomb are difficult to maintain. They consist of physical barriers, vehicle mazes, use of increased buffer distances, and well-armed security guards instructed to fire on suspicious vehicles. The fear of the vehicle bomb exists not only in the Middle East. Washington, DC, has been given the look of a government under siege with highway barriers and armed security guards protecting entrances to the White House, U.S. Capitol, and other important government structures. The psychological impact of the suicide bomber has created a situation of overwhelming fear in the United States as well as the Middle East. One must remember that the focus and direction of terrorism is to create fear. Certainly the suicide vehicle bomb accomplishes this major objective of terrorist violence.

In sum, the evolution of the vehicle bomb attack method has produced some definitive trends. The bigger the explosion, the greater the casualties, and the more intense the media coverage, the greater the publicity for the terrorist group. Since we concluded in earlier chapters that terrorist groups are imitative rather then innovative, they have certainly monitored the successes of vehicle bomb tactics. Most likely, we can anticipate the increased use of vehicle bombs by terrorist groups around the world.

As the use of vehicle bombs escalates, law enforcement personnel must devise alternative tactics to identify practical ways to stop the bombing—obviously an extremely difficult responsibility. In some cases, such as with the suicide bomber, it becomes a formidable task to prevent or deter infiltration into an area without seriously disrupting daily routines. However, security forces (law enforcement, military, or sentries) must be on the alert and have sufficient training to handle the vehicle bomb on an individual basis. From the terrorist perspective, the true genius of the vehicle attack method is that the objective and the means of attack are often beyond the imagination of those responsible for providing security and establishing bomb-training curriculums. Security personnel must understand that the vehicle bomb is a fully established mode of indiscriminate political violence. But the use of deadly parcel bombs is probably the most heinous bomb attack method.

LETTER BOMBS

According to Laqueur, Russian terrorists of the 1880s first introduced the terrorist tactic of preparing **letter bombs**. Russian terrorists made plans to conceal small quantities of explosives in little parcels, then mail the parcels to the tsar and other government officials. However, because of the insurmountable technical difficulties in handling explosives, this plan apparently was not carried out. Additionally, anarchist writers of the 1880s, such as Most, Bakunin, and Nechaev, recommended sending letters and small parcels containing incendiary explosives as a tactic to spread fear among government leaders and bureaucrats. Nonetheless, the first recorded use of a letter bomb or parcel bomb occurred in 1895 when a young German anarchist sent a 25-pound black powder bomb to a Berlin police officer. The bomb was intercepted at the Berlin post office and rendered harmless. By the beginning of World War I, some of the technical difficulties of making letter bombs were overcome, and several prominent European political leaders were killed or seriously injured by exploding parcels. Through the years various terrorist groups, including the Irgun, the Palestine resistance groups, and the IRA, have used letter bombs to spread fear and to introduce "new" terror tactics since the police and potential targets were alert to most of the old terror bomb attack methods.[35]

Theodore Kaczynski, better known as the **Unabomber**, is serving four consecutive life sentences in connection with sixteen parcel bombings and attempted bombings he committed in seven states between 1978 and 1995. Kaczynski's parcel bombs injured ten people and killed three. Two of the fatalities occurred in Sacramento. Kaczynski was motivated by his hatred for advancements in high technology. His bombings had targeted carefully selected individuals, victims he blamed for technological achievements in the United States. Kaczynski acted alone and was not part of any terrorist organization[36]

FIGURE 7.6   Theodore John Kaczynski, a.k.a. the Unabomber, is led into court in Sacramento, CA, where he pled guilty to a series of bombings that killed three people, two in Sacramento. Kaczynski was sentenced to life in prison without the possibility of parole. He is serving his time at a supermax prison in Florence, Colorado. (Michael Gallacher/Getty Images, Inc—Liaison)

Through trial and error the technological problems associated with the construction of letter bombs have been greatly reduced. Explosive devices now can easily be concealed within letters and small packages. The letter bomb creates a far greater security risk than the car bomb or planted bomb. Letter bombs are antipersonnel devices and serve two offensive terrorist functions. First, they may be designed to kill or maim a specific target. Since letter bombs contain only a small amount of explosive material, their intended effect is to injure and maim. Injury from an exploding letter bomb is caused by the explosive shock and the blast pressure, not from fragmentation. Second, letter bombs may be used to harass and intimidate the general public.

Even though the use of letter bombs is an ideal terrorist attack method, they are used infrequently compared with other bomb attack methods, such as the vehicle bomb. Letter bombs tend to be the preferred terrorist tactic during periods of a brief, intensive terrorist bombing campaign directed against specific targets. Palestinian terrorists waged a terrorist letter bomb campaign against Israeli and American targets in 1972. As with other bomb attack methods, the high-risk targets of letter bombs are embassies, corporations, defense-related industries, police, and government offices. Historically, letter bombs have been sent to a variety of targets.

For example, between 1977 and 1983, eighty-four recorded letter-bomb incidents occurred in twenty-three different countries. The United States was the favorite target, with nineteen incidents reported, while forty-seven letter bombs were mailed to Western European targets. By far the favored addresses for letter bombs have been diplomats, to whom forty of the eighty-four letter bombs were sent. Seven people were killed and fifty-one others injured in the eighty-four reported letter bomb attacks. Terrorist groups representing eighteen different ethnic identities claimed credit for forty-three (51.1 percent) of the eighty-four letter bombs, with the senders of the remaining forty-one undetermined. Various Irish extremist groups and individuals sent eleven of the deadly letter bombs to British targets, accounting for the largest number of letter bombs sent among known ethnic terrorists.[37]

In another letter-bomb campaign that occurred between December 1996 and January 1997, sixteen letter bombs disguised as holiday greeting cards were delivered through the mails to targets in the United States and United Kingdom. Thirteen of the letter bombs were mailed to the offices of the *Al Hayat* newspaper in New York City, Washington, DC, and London. One bomb detonated in the London office of *Al Hayat*, seriously injuring two people. *Al Hayat* is an independent Arabic-language daily newspaper published in London with worldwide distribution and circulation.

All sixteen letter bombs bore a December 21, 1996, Alexandria, Egypt, postmark without a return address. The bombs were in plain white envelopes, with computer-generated addresses. Three of the letter bombs were discovered at the federal penitentiary in Leavenworth, Kansas. This is still an open case and the FBI currently offers a $5 million reward for information about the perpetrators.[38]

Letter bombs or parcel bombs may be constructed to fit within almost any familiar container. This list includes all types of mail deliveries. Mail bombs are designed to detonate as the letter or package is opened. The explosive charge is activated by the release of a spring-loaded striker system or an electrical circuit. The most common type of mail devices encountered by postal security officers has been sent in large envelopes or small packages. The typical terrorist letter bomb weighs between 2 and 3 ounces and fits neatly into an envelope approximately 5 3/4 inches by 4 inches by 1/4 inches.[39]

In order to function, letter bombs must contain an explosive charge, a detonator, and a fuse to set off the detonator. The type of explosive preferred by letter bombers is C-4, but if C-4 is unavailable, other fast-burning explosives, including various black powder mixtures, can also be used. The most common type of fuse used in letter bomb construction is the percussion fuse. The percussion fuse operates on the same principle as a firing pin in a gun. The spring is released carrying a striker that impacts upon the detonator, igniting the explosive charge. The detonator most commonly discovered in letter bombs is the type used in commercial mining operations. This type of detonator is cylindrical in shape, has a very thin copper casing, and is about 3/16 inch (5 millimeters) in diameter. It is hoped that the identification and understanding of these principles of letter bomb construction will help security and police officers to detect and recognize suspected mail explosive devices.

Some specific things to look for in a suspected letter bomb are the following: (1) letter bombs cannot be constructed of extremely small size or placed in very thin, ordinary envelopes; (2) letter bombs are generally unbalanced, and are heavier on one side or the other; (3) an explosive mail device may have wires or spring holes in its outer wrapping; (4) certain categories of explosives may leave a greasy film on the envelope or paper wrapping, which may also indicate that the explosive is extremely unstable; (5) an unusual odor such as an almond smell may be present; (6) if the envelope is taped down on all sides, it may contain a spring-loaded booby trap; and (7) inspection of the stiffness of the contents of the envelope may reveal the presence of folded paper, cardboard, or an explosive device. The key indicator that an explosive device may be present in an envelope is *feel*. If the suspected letter bomb does not bend or flex and has a feeling of springiness at the top, bottom, or sides of the envelope, this is a clear sign that an explosive device is present. (See Figure 7.7.)

As in other bomb-attack methods, the target of the bombers should not assume that only one explosive device exists. Letter bombers have been known to send several explosive devices to the same address. Therefore, all mail deliveries for several weeks should be carefully examined. There are several excellent books, monographs, and pamphlets that outline the correct procedure for handling suspected letter bombs and parcel bombs.[40]

Letter bombs are a continued hazard to the high-risk population of diplomats, corporate executives, government officials, and police officers. Therefore, the risks of receiving letter

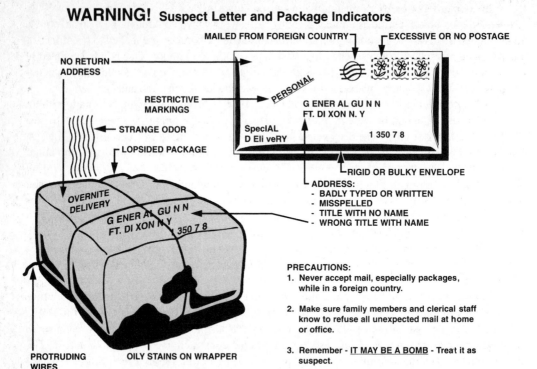

WARNING! Suspect Letter and Package Indicators

FIGURE 7.7 Package and letter bomb recognition.

bombs must be continually reevaluated and updated. Criminal justice management and rank-and-file employees alike must be trained in letter bomb recognition and the proper emergency procedures for handling explosive mail devices.

BOMBINGS ABOARD AIRCRAFT

The bombing of in-flight aircraft is yet another extranormal terrorist attack method. Modern high-performance civil aircraft are extremely vulnerable to in-flight bombing attacks. There are numerous ways of planting bombs on aircraft, even with the heightening of security measures. The motivations behind such terrorist attacks are many, but regardless of the motive, it is apparent that bombers of aircraft hope to destroy all tangible evidence by creating midair explosions. The design of the explosive device and methods of concealment are limited only by the ingenuity of the bomber. Therefore, security arrangements and technical methods of detecting hidden explosive devices on board aircraft must be superior to that of the skillful bomber. If, however, bombers of aircraft are able to penetrate security measures and the aircraft is destroyed, then every effort must be made to quickly recover victims and debris from the explosion. At times the problems of recovery may seem insurmountable, especially if the explosion occurred over deep ocean waters or the aircraft is widely scattered over desert or jungle landscapes. Such was the case after a midair bomb explosion occurred off the coast of Ireland on September 21, 1985.

An Air India Boeing 747 Flight 182 en route to London from Vancouver, British Columbia, Canada, disintegrated in midair about 110 miles off southwestern Ireland, killing all 329 people on board.[41] The midair explosion occurred less than an hour after another explosive device detonated at the Air India baggage check station in Tokyo, killing two baggage handlers and seriously wounding several workers. Sikh extremists seeking political autonomy from India claimed both bombings. After a lengthy investigation, Air India officials concluded that a plastic explosive device, concealed in the forward cargo hold, escaped metal detectors and was the cause of the midair explosion. Indian forensic scientists reconstructed the debris and examined the remains of victims recovered at the scene of the explosion and further determined that two bombs were used by the Sikh terrorists.

On February 11, 2003, Inderjit Singh Reyat pled guilty to manslaughter for his part in the bombing of Air India Flight 182. Reyat had earlier been sentenced to ten years for the Tokyo bombing. Reyat, as the bomb maker, was sentenced to five years for the bombing of Flight 182. Two other codefendants were found not guilty and released. The motivation for the two attacks was related to Sikh extremists' ambitions to create an independent Sikh nation in India called Khalistan. Air India was considered a legitimate target by Sikh terrorists since it is a highly visible symbol of the Indian government. However, 280 of the 329 passengers on board Flight 182 were Canadian citizens and 22 were Indian nationals.[42]

In yet another midair explosion, this one inside a TWA jetliner bound for Athens, four people were hurled to their deaths.[43] The explosion blew a 9- by 3-foot hole in the side of the aircraft; the four innocent victims were sucked out of the hole at approximately 15,000 feet and fell to their deaths. Palestinians claimed credit for the TWA bombing, saying it was in retaliation for a U.S. military strike against Libya. Fortunately, this type of terrorist bombing attack is rare compared with car bombs and letter bombs.

On December 21, 1988, a bomb hidden in the cargo hold of **Pan Am Flight 103**, a Boeing 747, destroyed the aircraft. The bombing occurred at 31,000 feet over the Scottish village of Lockerbie, killing all 259 passengers on board as well as eleven people on the ground. Investigators were able to identify the luggage that contained the bomb, which led them to two Libyan suspects. The investigation continued for three years when U.S. and British officials concluded that two Libyans, one a member of the Libya intelligence service, had organized the bombing. In March 1993, the United States was able to convince the United Nations to impose economic sanctions on Libya. Eventually Libyan leader Muammar Qaddafi turned over the two accused Libyans in hopes of having the economic sanctions lifted. The trial began in May 2000, conducted by a Scottish Court sitting in the Netherlands. On January 20, 2001, the Court returned a verdict of guilty for the Libyan intelligence officer Abdel Bassit Ali–al Megrahi and sentenced him to twenty years in prison. His alleged accomplice, Laman Khalifa Fhimah, was acquitted.[44]

Statistics on explosions aboard aircraft between 1949 and 2001 indicate that eighty aircraft were damaged or destroyed by the detonation of an explosive device while in flight. Of the eighty aircraft damaged or destroyed, seventeen aircraft were totally destroyed. In all, 1,148 passengers and crew lost their lives. The bombings occurred in various parts of the world covering thirty-eight countries and affecting forty-three airlines. During that same period, the United States recorded the damage or destruction of 15 aircraft with a total loss of 126 lives.[45]

To some extent the increase in fatalities can be attributed to the larger size of aircraft used by civil air carriers rather than the increased effectiveness of terrorist bombers. An analysis of the statistics also reveals that the three most popular areas to secrete explosive devices aboard aircraft are cargo baggage holds, the passenger cabin, and the lavatory.

In view of the little information available to students of criminal justice, a brief review of several in-flight aircraft bomb attacks is presented.[46]

1. **United Airlines DC–68 (November 1, 1955)**
   This aircraft was on a scheduled flight to Portland, Oregon. Approximately 11 minutes after takeoff from San Francisco an explosion disintegrated the aircraft. A dynamite bomb located in the number 4 *baggage compartment* detonated, killing thirty-nine passengers and five crew.

2. **Canadian Pacific Airlines DC–68 (July 8, 1965)**
   An explosive device planted in the *passenger cabin* area detonated, separating the tail section from the aircraft. All fifty-two aboard were killed. The explosion occurred over British Columbia.

3. **British Airways Comet 48 (October 12, 1967)**
   On a scheduled flight to Nicosia, Cyprus, at about 28,000 feet an explosion ripped through the tourist *passenger cabin.* All sixty-six aboard were killed. The recovery of victims and debris revealed evidence of an explosion.

4. **Cathway Pacific Airways CV 880 (June 15, 1972)**
   En route from Thailand to Hong Kong, a bomb in a suitcase under the *passenger seat* exploded killing eighty-one passengers and crew.

5. **Air Vietnam B-727 (September 15, 1974)**
   A skyjacker boarded the aircraft in Saigon and ordered the flight to go to Hanoi. The pilot convinced the skyjacker that the plane was low on fuel and therefore a forced landing was necessary. While in the landing pattern, the skyjacker for some reason detonated two hand grenades in the *cockpit.* The pilot lost control of the aircraft and seventy passengers and crew were killed.

6. **Gulf Air Bahrain B–737 (September 23, 1983)**
   About 30 miles from the airport in Kuwait, a bomb exploded in the *baggage compartment.* While attempting a forced landing in the desert, the aircraft crashed, killing 112 people.

7. **Air India B–747 (June 21, 1985)**
   Approaching the coast of Ireland at approximately 30,000 feet, the aircraft disintegrated, killing 329 people. Subsequent investigation revealed plastic explosives had been planted in the *baggage compartment* and the *lavatory.*

8. **Brazilian TAM Fokker 100 (July 9, 1997)**
   An unknown explosive device detonated in flight, killing one passenger and injuring seven others, including the bomber. The device blew a hole in the *fuselage* of the aircraft. The plane landed safely. A passenger, intent on suicide, brought the explosive device on board in his carry-on baggage.

9. **Russian Airways (May 30, 2000)**
   A homemade improvised explosive device was discovered on board. The device consisted of 400 grams of TNT, a clock mechanism, detonator, battery, and connecting wires. The device was hidden in a tea box in the rear *lavatory* of the plane. The device was discovered just before takeoff.

10. **American Airlines Boeing 767 (December 23, 2001)**
    Richard Reid, an alleged member of al Qaeda, attempted to ignite an explosive device concealed in his shoes. The device contained several ounces of C-4. Passengers and crew overpowered Reid before he could detonate the explosive device. The Miami flight, which

originated in Paris, contained 185 passengers and 12 crew members. The plane landed safely. Richard Reid pleaded guilty and admitted he was a member of al Qaeda. In January 2003, Reid was sentenced to life in prison for over thirty years.

11. **Volga-Avia Express TU-134 and Siberia Airlines TU-154 (August 24, 2004)**
Two almost simultaneous explosions were carried out by Chechen female suicide bombers while the aircraft were in flight, killing eighty-nine passengers and crew. Bombs were smuggled on board the aircraft with the help of airport security personnel.

In sum, the effectiveness of civil-aviation security measures will continue to test the determination of terrorist bombers. Acts of aircraft bombings and attempted bombings are on the increase. This increase in the number of explosions and the number of explosive devices detected by airport security indicates that perhaps aircraft bombings may become the primary threat to civil air carriers as opposed to hijackings. Despite the preventive measures taken of strengthening security systems, it is believed that civil aviation will remain a tempting and vulnerable target to the mentally disturbed, criminal, and terrorist bomber.

Conclusions

We have reviewed the effects of explosions, types of explosive devices, and bomb attack methodologies, including the use of car bombs, letter bombs, and the bombing of aircraft. This review suggests that terrorist bombers have demonstrated clearly and convincingly that they are willing to escalate the threshold of violence beyond what was previously believed attainable because of stricter police and military security measures. However, stricter security measures have not prevented car bombs or suicide terrorist bombers from turning Baghdad into a city of fear. During the month of December 2007, Iraqi insurgents, in an attempt to drive the United States out of Iraq, detonated dozens of bombs in Baghdad in a ten-day period. Two hundred people were killed and scores were injured. Although the Iraqi car bombs and suicide bombings were serious, they were not catastrophic. Nevertheless, the vehicle bombs and suicide terrorist bombings in Iraq may be a harbinger of a more lethal future for democratic countries. Dedicated terrorist groups could easily carry out intensive terrorist bombing campaigns.

Therefore, police officers and government security personnel need technical training in bomb recognition, identification of explosive materials, and bomb construction. Too often law enforcement agencies wait until an incident occurs before a decision is made to take precautionary measures for the future. There is no substitute for the well-informed and well-trained police officer.

The next chapter explores a special kind of terrorist bombing—the suicide bomber.

Key Terms

black powder	dynamite	Marine compound
blast	fertilizer	Pan Am Flight 103
C-4	fragmentation	PETN
car bombs	Jemaah Islamiya	PIRA
Carlos Marighella	Khobar Towers	Timothy McVeigh
dirty bomb	letter bombs	Unabomber

Discussion Questions

1. List at least five factors that have contributed to the escalation of terrorist bombing.
2. Describe the difference between commercial and military explosives.
3. Explain the effects of an explosion.
4. Distinguish between the positive and negative pressure phase of an explosion.
5. Discuss the difference between low- and high-velocity explosives.
6. Identify and explain at least five terrorist vehicle bomb attack methods. What strategies would you

suggest to prevent the recurring problem of vehicle bombs?
7. Compare and contrast the car bomb and letter bomb methodologies.
8. Describe several techniques for identifying suspected letter bombs.
9. Why are aircraft so vulnerable to terrorist attack?
10. Outline a bomb-training program for police and security personnel.
11. Compare and contrast the bombing campaign of Palestinian terrorists with that of Iraqi insurgents.

Web Sites

Sourcebook of Criminal Justice Statistics 2001
http://www.albany.edu/sourcebook/

Nobel e–Museum
http://www.nobelprize.org

Bureau of Alcohol, Tobacco, and Firearms
http://www.atf.gov

International Association of Bomb Technicians and Investigators

http://www.iabti.org

International Association of Arson Investigators
http://www.firearson.com

National Center for Forensic Science
http://www.ncfs.ucf.edu

Endnotes

1. U.S. Department of State, *Country Reports on Terrorism: 2007* (Washington, DC: U.S. Government Printing Office, 2008).
2. U.S. Department of State, *Terrorist Bombings* (Washington, DC: U.S. Government Printing Office, 2002), p. 1.
3. U.S Department of State, *National Counterterrorism Center: 2007 Report on Terrorism* (April 30, 2008), pp. 24–31.
4. Carlos Marighella, *The Terrorist Classic: Manual of the Urban Guerrilla*, trans. Gene Hanrahan (Chapel Hill, NC: Documentary Pub., 1985), p. 84.
5. For example, see William Powell, *Anarchist Cookbook* (New York: L. Stuart, 1971); Andrew MacDonald, *The Turner Diaries* (Arlington, VA: National Vanguard Books, 1985); Alberto Bayo, *150 Questions for a Guerrilla* (Boulder, CO: Paladin Press, 1975); Joseph P. Stoffel, *Explosives*

and Homemade Bombs (Springfield, IL: Charles C. Thomas, 1972).
6. Walter Laqueur, *Terrorism* (Boston, MA: Little, Brown, 1977), p. 92; Walter Laqueur, *Voices of Terror* (Naperville, IL: Sourcebooks, Inc. 2005), pp. 185–90.
7. Arthur P. Van Gelder and Hugo Schlatter, *History of the Explosives Industry in American* (New York: Arno Press, 1972), p. 315; Jack Kelly, *Gunpowder: Alchemy, Bombards and Pyrotechnics, The History of Explosives that Changed the World* (New York: New York: Basic Books, 2004), pp. 109–20.
8. For example, see Ragnar Sohlman, *The Legacy of Alfred Nobel* (London: Bodley Head, 1983); Herta E. Pauli, *Alfred Nobel: Dynamite King, Architect of Peace* (Whitefish, MT: Kessinger Publishing, LLC, 2008).

9. For example, see Chris Gray, *Dynamite: A Century of Class Violence in America 1830–1930* (New York: Rebel Press, 1990); William J. Borbidge, *Bombs: Defusing the Threat* (Jacksonville, FL: Institute of Police Management and Technology, 1999).

10. For example, see Department of the Army, *Field Manual 5-250 Explosives and Demolitions* (Washington, DC: U. S. Government Printing Office, 1992); Erasmus Morgan Weaver, *Notes on Military Explosives* (Whitefish, MT: Kessinger Publishing, LLC, 2007).

11. Robert R. Lenz, *Explosives and Bomb Disposal Guide* (Springfield, IL: Charles C. Thomas, 1971), p. 56; Rudolf Meyer, Josef Köhler, and Axel Homburg, *Explosives*, 6th ed. (Germany: Wiley-VCH, 2007), pp. 237, 255.

12. H. J. Yallop, *Explosion Investigation* (Edinburgh, Scotland: Scottish Academic Press, 1980), p. 90; Meyer, Köhler, and Homburg, *Explosives*, pp. 250–54.

13. Lou Michel and Dan Herbeck, *American Terrorist: Timothy McVeigh and the Oklahoma City Bombing* (New York: Regan Books, 2001), pp. 215–18; Stuart A. Wright, *Patriots, Politics, and the Oklahoma City bombing* (New York: Cambridge University Press, 2007), pp. 173–96 and 207–14.

14. U.S. Department of State, *Terrorist Bombings*, p. 4.

15. Brian Jenkins, "Terrorism and Nuclear Safeguards Issue," *Rand Paper Series P-5611* (Santa Monica, CA: Rand Corp., 1984), p. 1; Brian Jenkins, *Will Terrorists Go Nuclear* (Amherst, NY: Prometheus Books, 2008), pp. 183–243.

16. Neil C. Livingstone and Terrell E. Arnold, eds., *Fighting Back: Winning the War against Terrorism* (Lexington, MA: D. C. Heath, 1986), pp. 32–33; Jenkins, *Will Terrorists Go Nuclear*, pp. 323–68.

17. Yallop, *Explosion Investigation*, pp. 75–77; James T. Thurman, *Practical Bomb Scene Investigation* (Florida: CRC Press, 2006), pp. 159–62.

18. *New York Times* (October 23, 1983), sec. 1, p. 1; Eric Hammel, *The Root: The Marines in Beirut, August 1982–February 1984* (Osceola, WI: Zenith Press, 2005), pp. 285–326.

19. For example, see Eric Hammel, *The Root* (New York: Harcourt Brace Jovanovich Publishers, 1985); Jacqueline Akhavan, *The Chemistry of Explosives* (Cambridge, England: Royal Society of Chemistry Information Services, 1998).

20. Charles L. Roblee and Allen McKechnic, *The Investigation of Fires* (Englewood Cliffs, NJ: Prentice Hall, 1981), p. 98; Jonas A. Zukas and William Walters, *Explosive Effects and Applications* (New York: Springer, 2002), pp. 45–112.

21. For example, see Paul W. Cooper and Stanley R. Kurowski, *Introduction to the Technology of Explosives* (New York: Wiley-VCH, 1997); M. A. Cook, *The Science of High Explosives* (Malabar, FL: Robert E. Krieger Publishing, 1985); Jehuda Yinon, *Forensic and Environmental Detection of Explosives* (New York: John Wiley, 1999); Zukas and Walters, *Explosive Effects and Applications*, pp. 34–112.

22. Van Gelden and Schlatter, *History of Explosives Industry*, p. 281; Maurice Marshall and Jimmie C. Oxley, eds., *Aspects of Explosives Detection* (New York: Elsevier Science, 2008), pp. 12–23.

23. U.S. Bureau of Alcohol, Tobacco, and Firearms, *Explosives Incidents 1982* (Washington, DC: U.S. Government Printing Office, 1983), p. 6; BATC, *Fact Sheet: U.S. Bomb Data Center* (September, 2008), www.atf.gov.

24. Van Gelden and Schlatter, *History of Explosives Industry*, pp. 403–16; Zukas and Walters, *Explosive Effects and Applications*, pp. 45–94.

25. Thomas G. Brodie, *Bombs and Bombings* (Springfield, IL: Charles C. Thomas, 1972), p. 92; Richard Esposito and Ted Gerstein, *Bomb Squad: A Year Inside the Nation's Most Exclusive Police Unit* (New York: Hyperion, 2007), pp. 96–105; Mike Davis, *Buda's Wagon: A Brief History of the Car Bomb* (New York: Verso, 2008), pp. 24–62.

26. Brodie, *Bombs and Bombings*, p. 98.

27. John Dinges and Saul Landau, *Assassination on Embassy Row* (New York: Pantheon, 1980), pp. 2–15.

28. *London Times* (August 28, 1979), p. 1; Timothy Shanahan, *The Provisional Irish Republican Army and the Morality of Terrorism* (United Kingdom: Edinburg University Press, 2009), pp. 42–96

29. *San Francisco Chronicle* (March 2, 1985), sec. A, p. 8.

30. *Sacramento Bee* (September 5, 1985), sec. A, p. 12.

31. John W. Ellis, *Police Analysis and Planning for Vehicular Bombings: Prevention, Defense, and Response* (Springfield, IL: Charles C. Thomas, 1994), pp. 156–64.

32. Rewards for Justice, *Bombing of Khober Towers, http://www.rewardsforjustice.net.*

33. *Report of the DOD Commission on Beirut International Airport Terrorist Act* (Washington, DC: U.S. Government Printing Office, October 23, 1983), pp. 84–86.

34. *The New York Times* (November 5, 1983), sec. 1, p. 14.

35. Laqueur, *Terrorism*, pp. 94–95.

36. For example, see John E. Douglas and Mark Olshaker, *Unabomber: On the Trail of America's Most Wanted Serial Killer* (New York: Pocket Books, 1996); Robert Graysmith, *Unabomber: A Desire to Kill* (Washington, DC: Regency Publishing, 1997); Nancy Gibbs, Lance Morrow, and Jill Smolowe, *Mad Genius: The Odyssey, Pursuit, and Capture of the Unabomber Suspect* (New York: Warner Books, 1996).

37. U.S. Department of State, *Terrorist Bombings*, pp. 4–6.

38. FBI Homepage, *http://www.rewardsforjustice.net.*

39. Graham Knowles, *Bomb Security Guide* (Los Angeles, CA: Security World, 1976), p. 93.

40. For example, see Knowles, *Bomb Security Guide*, pp. 96–102; Frank Moyer, *Police Guide to Bomb Search Techniques* (Boulder, CO: Paladin Press, 1981), pp. 137–46; Richard Clutterbuck, *Living with Terrorism* (London: Faber & Faber, 1976), pp. 83–91; Esposito and Gerstein, Bomb Squad: *A Year Inside the Nation's Most Exclusive Unit*, pp. 262–65.

41. *New York Times* (September 21, 1985), sec. 1, p. 1.

42. For example, see Kim Bolan, *Loss of Faith: How the Air India Bombers Got Away with Murder* (Toronto, Canada: McClelland and Stewart, Limited, 2005).

43. *New York Times* (June 24, 1985), sec. 1, p. 1.

44. For example, see John Crawford, *The Lockerbie Incident: A Detective's Tale* (Oxford, UK: Trafford Publishing, 2006); Richard A. Marquise, *Scotbom: Evidence and the Lockerbie Investigation* (New York: Algora Publishing, 2006).

45. U.S. Department of Transportation, Federal Aviation Administration, Office of Civil Aviation Security, *Explosions Aboard Aircraft* (Washington, DC: U.S. Government Printing Office, 2005), pp. 1–13.

46. Ibid.

CHAPTER 8

Suicide Bombers: A Global Problem

CHAPTER OBJECTIVES
The study of this chapter will enable you to:

- Explore the nature of suicide bombing
- Describe the motivation of suicide bombers
- Identify terrorist groups involved in suicide bombing
- Understand the complexity of suicide
- Develop strategies to interdict suicide bombings
- Speculate as to the future of suicide bombing attacks

INTRODUCTION

In recent years, the terrorist strategy of suicidal bombings has created increasing fear and widespread media attention. Suicide bombings are an incredibly cost-effective method of terrorism. While some suicide bombings are directed toward military targets, most are directed toward civilians. Such events as the suicide bombing of the United States marine barracks in Beirut in 1983, the assassination of Rajiv Gandhi in 1991, the countless suicide bombings in Iraq, the numerous suicide bombings against innocent civilians in Israel since March 1996, the suicide bombing of the U.S.S. Cole in 2000, and the devastating suicide bombings of the World Trade Center and the Pentagon on September 11, 2001, have caused widespread alarm.

It is hardly surprising that the suicide bombers themselves have become one of the most feared terrorist weapons. Suicide is a particularly awful way to die. Suicidologists agree that the mental suffering leading up to suicide is usually prolonged, intense, and well thought through.[1]

The suicide bombers discussed in this chapter are those who carry explosive charges on their bodies or by various vehicles such as a car, truck, boat, bicycle, or an airplane. Unlike previously noted acts of suicidal terrorism, the suicide bomber's intent is to cause a maximum number of innocent casualties. However, the ultimate goal of suicide bombers goes well beyond causing a high number of casualties. Suicide bombers produce fear, intimidation, and anxiety in the larger population. A suicide bombing attack ensures full media coverage and ranks with other outrageous acts of terrorism, such as midair explosions or the threatened use of weapons of mass destruction such as nuclear bombs, anthrax, or smallpox. For our purposes, a suicide bombing is defined as "a politically motivated violent attack carried out by an individual who is fully aware and purposely causes his or her own death by blowing himself or herself up along with the intended target usually to influence an audience." The offender's death is a precondition for the success of the suicide bombing attack.

Suicide bombings, as well as the fear suicide bombers promote in the general population, is not a new phenomenon. In fact, the suicide bombings of the U.S.S. Cole, the World Trade Center, and the Pentagon are reminiscent of earlier suicidal attacks against the United States that may be a template for contemporary suicide bombing attacks. Indeed, if we examine the historical record, it will become clear that strong parallels exist between the Japanese **kamikaze** pilots of World War II and the perpetrators of the recent suicide bombings aimed especially at Israeli and American military and citizen targets.

The most infamous example of suicide bombers occurred during World War II when Japanese kamikaze[2] pilots slammed their bomb-laden planes onto the decks of U.S. naval vessels in the Pacific. In effect, the kamikaze, or Divine Wind, was a flying bomb. Indeed, the term *kamikaze* is now synonymous with suicide attack. The Japanese High Command believed the only way to stop the advancing U.S. naval forces was to organize suicide bombing attack units. The organized suicide attacks were seen by the Japanese military as an effective battle tactic against the overwhelming superiority of U.S. forces.

Popular images of psychopathic fanatical kamikaze pilots, however, appear to be exaggerated. Sasaki writes that kamikaze pilots were volunteers between 17 and 25 years of age, well educated, and well trained, with many attending various military pilot-training programs.[3] Even so, why would a Japanese pilot volunteer for certain death? There seem to be several reasons. Extreme patriotism was one certain factor. Complete reverence for the emperor—who was considered a god in Japanese society—was another factor. Some Japanese pilots believed that if one died for the emperor and was praised in the Yasukuni Shrine,[4] he would be in paradise forever. Thus, the kamikazes considered it an honorable mission to take revenge against the advancing U.S. military forces and felt it was a great honor to be selected from the group of volunteers for a suicide bombing attack. Inoguchi and Nakajima report that most of the volunteer kamikaze pilots were extremely depressed at the thought of a U.S. invasion of the Japanese home islands and the eventual loss of the war.[5] Robins, in his landmark study, reminds us that nowhere is the danger of suicide more acute than in the mood disorders of depression and manic depression.[6] Suicidologists have long agreed that depression is at the heart of all suicidal behaviors. In sum, Pineau reports that the depressed kamikaze pilots believed that everlasting happiness would follow the suicide attacks on U.S. military forces; thus, there was nothing to fear.[7]

In spite of the heroism and self-sacrifice of the kamikaze pilots, they were relatively ineffective and contributed little to the Japanese war effort. Craig describes

FIGURE 8.1   A Japanese kamikaze pilot ties on a ceremonial headband with the rising sun design before crashing his bomb-laden plane onto American naval vessels. (Getty Images, Inc.—Hulton Archive Photos)

the kamikaze suicide bombing attacks as the "tactics of despair."[8] Nearly a thousand Japanese kamikaze pilots were lost and over 100 U.S. naval vessels were damaged or destroyed. The dream of halting the advancing U.S. Navy by suicide bombing attacks remained unrealized.

Suicide bombers again attracted attention during the last two decades of the twentieth century. During that time, twenty-two different terrorist organizations and their sponsors in eighteen different countries have used suicide bombing attacks in an attempt to realize their political objectives. (See Table 8.1.)

In addition, the *threat* of a suicidal terrorist bombing attack increasingly has become a useful terrorist tactic in attempts to intimidate "unfriendly" governments. Since 9/11, government buildings in Washington, DC, and U.S. embassies around the world have been barricaded. The United States is on heightened security alert to prevent kamikaze-style suicide attacks involving vehicles or airplanes. The media have reinforced these threats by describing the recruitment and training of suicidal terrorists, especially in Islamic countries. Hundreds of so-called fanatical Palestinian suicide bombers offering to sacrifice their lives for the destruction of Israel have been portrayed on the evening news. However, the suicide bombing capital of the world is currently in Iraq. Since the U.S. invasion of Iraq in March 2003, nightly newscasts are filled with the daily suicide bombing attacks. In 2008, Iraq recorded nearly 150 suicide bombings. In fact, the 2008 figure is low compared with the 478 recorded suicide bombings in 2005. By sheer volume, Iraq is now the global center of suicide bombings.[9]

TABLE 8.1   Suicide-Bombing Events

Group	Country of Origin	Motive	Target
Kamikaze	Japan	Tactical	U.S. naval vessels in Pacific
Abu Sayyaf	Southern Philippines	Separatists/ independence	Philippine government/ Roman Catholics
al Aqsa	Israel/Palestine	Revenge/retaliation	Israeli civilians
al Qaeda	Afghanistan/Yemen	Islamic revolution/ revenge	United States/Israel
al Qaeda in Iraq	Iraq	Tactical	Iraqi security forces, U.S. military
al Qaeda in Islamic Maghreb	Algeria	Islamic fundamentalist	United States/the West Infidels
Chechens	Chechnya/Russia	Chechen independence	Russian military
Gama (Egypt)	Egypt	Retaliation	Foreign tourists in Egypt
Hamas	Palestine/Israel	Revenge	Israeli "soft" (nonmilitary) targets
Hizballah	Lebanon/Iran	Tactical/revenge/ image	Multinational Force Lebanon/Israel
Iraqi "nationalists"	Iraq	Expulsion of U.S. military	United States military and foreign diplomats
Iranians	Iran	Tactical	Iraqi military
Islamic Jihad	Egypt	Retaliation/revenge	Foreign tourists in Egypt
Islamic Jihad	Lebanon/Iran	Expulsion of foreigners/revenge	United States/Israel
Jemaah Islamiya	Indonesia	Expulsion of foreigners/revenge	Australian civilians
Kashmiris	India	Union with Pakistan	Indian government and military officials
Lashkar e-Tayyeba	Pakistan	Islamic state	India/Kashmir
LTTE	Sri Lanka	Tactical/inspire recruits	Sri Lankan and Indian government and military
MNLF	Southern Philippines	Separatists/ independence	Philippine government/ Roman Catholics
PFLP	Israel/Palestine	Revenge/retaliation	Israeli civilians
PKK	Turkey	Revolution/ separatists	Turkish military and soft targets
Sikhs	India	Independence/ separatists	Indian hard and soft targets

DEFINING THE PROBLEM

There are no simple theories for suicide bombings nor are there strategies with which to predict suicide bombing attacks. Nevertheless, Kushner and Pedazhur point out that much knowledge exists about who commits suicide bombings.[10] For example, the research on suicide bombers reveals vulnerable age groups, social backgrounds, gender, methods used, locations, times chosen, and types of bombing devices. However, researchers are less certain as to why people carry out suicide bombing attacks. The complexity and privacy of the suicidal mind is a difficult barrier to overcome. The motives of a suicidal person are quite complex. Inevitably, the research literature on **suicidology** reflects the complexities and inconsistencies in our understanding of suicide bombing attacks.

However, suicide to attain a collective political goal is not confined to just suicide bombing attacks. Suicide is quite prevalent among terrorist groups. Suicide by self-inflicted starvation or a **hunger strike** has a long history. In Ireland, for example, the hunger strike has been a characteristic form of political protest used by the Republican movement for many years. In March 1981, the nationalists groups Provisional Irish Republican Army (PIRA) and **Irish National Liberation Army (INLA)** began a hunger strike that continued until October 1981. When it finally ended, ten hunger strikers were dead. The hunger strikers believed that self-induced starvation was the only logical means of bringing public attention to their cause and was the price to be paid for winning national liberation from British domination of Northern Ireland. According to Beresford, PIRA and INLA planned to end the hunger strike only after the British government granted their political demands.[11] Potential hunger strikers were lined up and ready to take the place of a "striker" once he died. It was only pressure from family members on the leadership of PIRA and INLA that finally ended the hunger strike, which probably saved the lives of dozens of young PIRA and INLA nationalists.

The notorious Baader-Meinhoff[12] terrorist gang in the then West Germany carried out another form of suicide to support political objectives in the late 1960s. After a prolonged series of bombings, hostage takings, and attempted assassinations, the Baader-Meinhoff gang was finally apprehended, convicted, and sentenced to life in prison. While there, the gang planned an elaborate scheme to "discredit" the West German government and continue the "revolution." Handguns were smuggled into the maximum-security prison housing the Baader-Meinhoff gang by their attorneys. Three members of the gang then committed suicide by self-inflicted gunshots. The scheme of the suicide was intended to suggest that prison authorities had, in fact, murdered them. An independent investigation revealed that the three members of the Baader-Meinhoff gang had indeed committed suicide by self-inflicted gunshots, and one gang member had hanged herself.

Another example of suicide for a political cause is **self-immolation**. Suicide by fire or self-immolation is a rare form of suicide, and is almost always associated with political protests. Self-immolation is without exception the most fanatical form of political protest. In the late 1960s, an epidemic of suicides and attempted suicides by burning occurred in Southeast Asia after a Buddhist monk set fire to himself on a busy thoroughfare in Saigon to protest the war in Vietnam. Suicide by fire seems to be best understood as an extreme form of political protest designed to bring attention to a specific political problem. In one sense, the self-immolations of the late 1960s had a profound effect on the peace movement in the United States. After several public self-immolations, public opinion against the Vietnam War began to shift from the battlefield to the negotiating table. The tremendous media coverage of

FIGURE 8.2 Buddhist monk commits ritual suicide by self-immolation in Saigon, South Vietnam, to protest religious persecution by the South Vietnamese government in June 1963. (AP/Wide World Photos)

the self-burnings ensured that the political nature of the Vietnam War would not go away. Furthermore, Jamison states that suicide by burning is a rational act where the victims are well aware of what they are doing.[13] More recently Carlson reports that several members of the Falun Gong spiritual group committed suicide by self-immolation in Beijing, China.[14] According to Dallman and Yamamoto, the Falun Gong has been protesting against the oppressive Chinese government for interfering in their religious activities.[15]

In sum, suicide to protest political conditions has a contagious aspect, as well as an indisputable appeal as the solution of last resort. Lifton describes suicide—by self-starvation, self-inflicted gunshots, self-immolation, or suicide bombings—as "symbolic immortality."[16] In other words, Lifton claims that human beings require a sense of immortality in the face of inevitable death. Hazani takes Lifton's paradigm further and refers to a variety of suicidal acts of terrorism as "sacrificial immortality."[17] Accordingly, extreme political movements such as the PIRA, **Hamas**, al Aqsa, al Qaeda, and the Tamil Tigers require members to sacrifice their lives, by suicide if necessary, for the furtherance of political and nationalistic objectives. If this is the case, then:

1. What common background characteristics are related to suicide bombers?
2. What terrorist groups sponsor and support the tactic of suicide bombings?
3. How are suicide bombers selected or why do they volunteer?
4. Why have suicide bombings occurred at this historical period?
5. Is it possible to predict the next target of a potential suicide bombing attack?

SUICIDE BOMBERS IN THE MIDDLE EAST

The most well-known contemporary suicide bombers originated in the Middle East. Suicide bombing attacks began in Lebanon on April 18, 1983, when a suicide bomber driving a van carrying approximately 400 pounds of high explosives drove into the U.S. Embassy in **Beirut**, killing sixty-three and injuring hundreds more. Among the dead were sixteen Americans, including the CIA station chief in Lebanon. The newly formed Shi'ite terrorist group, **Hizballah**, claimed credit for the attack. Then on October 23, 1983, a suicide bomber, also from Hizballah, drove a three-quarter ton truck loaded with 12,000 pounds of TNT into the U.S. marine barracks in Beirut, killing 241 marines. A simultaneous suicide bombing attack was carried out against the French multinational force in Beirut, killing sixty French paratroopers and maiming dozens more.

Martin and Walcott report that between the spring of 1983 and the summer of 1985, there was an unprecedented number of suicidal bombings carried out by Hizballah, Islamic Jihad (Islamic Holy War), and other competing Lebanese Shi'ite factions in Lebanon. In the thirteen months prior to the suicidal bombing of the marine barracks, Hizballah and Islamic Jihad had participated in 118 car bomb attacks. During that time Hizballah suicide bombers attacked a variety of targets, including the U.S. military, rival Shi'ite groups, the Israeli military forces in southern Lebanon, and the Syrian military. Of the 118 car bombs, at least forty were, in fact, suicide car bombings.[18] Schweitzer estimates that Hizballah was responsible for fifty suicide bombing attacks between 1983 and 1999.[19]

There is no denying that the Beirut suicide bombings made a marked impression on world public opinion and launched the career of Hizballah as a dangerous terrorist group that continues to this day. Even though there is a strong Islamic prohibition against suicide, Hizballah clerics grant religious dispensation to suicide bombers on the eve of their suicidal mission. Hizballah clerics rationalize that death from a suicide bombing attack is no different from deaths of soldiers who enter battle knowing that some of them will be killed. On the basis of this perverted moral logic, Hizballah could then recruit, train, and deploy young Shi'ite men and women in suicidal bombing missions.

By late 1999, Hizballah discontinued its suicide bombing attacks in favor of other "tactical" considerations. Hizballah suicide bombing attacks have also inspired a number of terrorist groups in other countries as well as the Middle East. The most prolific suicide bombers struggling to recover Palestine from the Israelis have been the Palestinian Hamas, Palestinian Islamic Jihad (PIJ), the Palestinian al Aqsa Martyrs Brigade, and the PFLP.

Although the PFLP, al Aqsa, Islamic Jihad, and Hamas targets are not as spectacular as the U.S. marine headquarters in Beirut, the series of suicide bombing attacks in Jerusalem and elsewhere in Israel are just as vicious. For example, Hamas initially focused its suicide attacks against Israeli military targets but found that security surrounding military targets made suicide bombing an unacceptable tactic. As a result, Hamas shifted its suicide bombing attacks to innocent civilians in crowded Israeli cities. The Israeli home page (www.israel.org) lists more than 140 suicide bombing attacks since 1993. These attacks, carried out by Islamic Jihad, Hamas, PFLP, and al Aqsa, caused over 540 fatalities and the wounding of over 3,000 innocent victims.[20]

Beyer describes a typical suicide bombing attack that occurred on a crowded bus carrying Israeli students to classes in the city of Jerusalem in 1995.[21] A lone Arab passenger sitting in the back of the bus suddenly reached into the book bag he was carrying and detonated a high explosive bomb filled with nails. Police later estimated the improvised explosive device contained about ten pounds of plastic explosive. The blast instantly incinerated the suicide bomber and four Israelis seated nearby. In addition to the five killed, 107 others were injured, some very seriously. Ten years later, in similar attacks that occurred in February and March 2005, hundreds of Israeli civilians were killed and wounded. The bombs were packed with nails, razor blades, staples, ball bearings, and nuts and bolts to deliberately increase the number of Israeli casualties.

The fear generated by such suicidal attacks has a profound impact on the personal security of Israeli citizens. The horror is compounded by the fact that the bombers purposefully killed themselves. Who would carry out such atrocities and why? Obviously, to question suicide bombers directly involved in suicide attacks is not possible. However, Hamas, PIJ, al Aqsa, and PFLP suicide bombers often make videotapes the night before the suicide attacks. Oliver and Steinberg,[22] in their definitive research on Hamas suicide bombers, had access to several of the videotapes. The videotapes were used to memorialize the young suicide bombers and to illustrate to other potential suicide recruits the honor of a heroic "suicide" death for Palestine. The video-tapes show young Hamas recruits strapping high-velocity explosives to their waists and stating that the choice of martyrdom was an opportunity to meet God. At this point there is no turning back for the suicide bomber. The suicide bombers appear to be attracted by a straightforward message of religion and nationalism.

Israeli filmmaker Dan Setton produced a documentary film about Hamas suicide bombers. The film *Suicide Bombers: Secrets of the Shaheed* is a series of interviews of Hamas members who tried to carry out suicide attacks against Israeli targets but failed. The film portrays the recruitment of suicide bombers in Gaza mosques through the time when, strapped with explosives, they try to blow themselves up. These surviving suicide bombers are alive only because bombs failed to detonate or police intervened before bombs could be set off. From the surviving suicide bombers, Setton puts together a profile of a "typical" suicide bomber: unobtrusive, uneducated, raised within poor families who have no criminal record, and capable of blending easily into a crowd. Even their closest family members are unaware of plans to carry out a suicide bombing attack. Setton is bewildered by how calm the suicide bombers were before their planned attack.[23] But Jamison insists that suicidal people are calmer after deciding to kill themselves because they are relieved of the anxiety and pain related to life.[24]

Setton continues that some suicide bombers are lured by visions of beautiful virgins waiting for them in paradise. In order to prepare for death, suicide bombers perform a bizarre ritual by visiting cemeteries at night and sleeping among the graves of **martyrs**. In one film sequence, a jailed bomb maker casually diagrams how a suicide bomb works. Setton portrays the leaders of Hamas, who have no plans to sacrifice their own lives, as manipulative, cynical, and charismatic.

Even though Setton's film presents a so-called "inside look" at the motivation for suicide bombings, Merari has other ideas. Merari maintains that Hamas clerics use three strategies to convince young Muslims to die for Palestine. One technique is to force or trick people to carry out suicidal bombing missions against their will. Merari illustrates one such incident involving a 16-year-old who was apprehended by Israeli police before he could detonate the suicide bomb. The boy claimed he had been forced to go on a suicide-bombing mission after Hamas threatened to kill his family. A second tactic is to seek out mentally disturbed persons who may harbor suicidal tendencies or suffer from other aberrant psychological conditions. A third strategy is to brainwash or indoctrinate potential young recruits to believe that to die for God and Palestine is a great honor—as many kamikaze pilots believed that it was a great honor to die for the defense of Japan and the emperor. In sum, suicide bombing has become a vital part of the struggle to destroy Israel and establish an independent Palestine.[25]

Another explanation for the motivation of Palestinian suicide bombers is what Muir refers to as the paradox of dispossession or "the less one has, the less one has to lose."[26] Nasr reports that the majority of Palestinian suicide bombers had no money, no job, no opportunities, no property, little respectability, few skills, little education, and believed their lives were meaningless without taking revenge against the "Zionists."[27]

Beck et al., in an extensive study, stated that one of the most consistent warning signs of suicidal behavior is a sense of hopelessness, despair, and negative feelings about the future.[28] **Emile Durkheim** argued that the egotistical suicidal person becomes detached from society, family, and religion and becomes so deluded in his personal beliefs and feelings that suicide appears to confirm the righteousness of a suicidal attack.[29] Being surrounded by unprecedented violence every day, potential Palestinian suicide bombers were living very depressed and desperate lives. Thus, it became easy to make the transition from a "nobody" to instant recognition as a martyr for Palestine. Katz believes that the simplicity of the suicide bombing attack had great appeal to the leaders of Hamas, since the "hopelessness and helplessness" described the inner feelings of Palestinian people living under Israeli occupation for over thirty-five years.[30]

In theory, the Islamic suicide bomber is required to submit to the will of Allah, but it is his own personal decision to go on a suicide bombing attack. In practice, the candidates for suicide bombing attacks are thoroughly indoctrinated, chosen by Islamic leaders, and assured that after martyrdom they will be in heaven with the Prophets. Their families will be financially taken care of, and their afterlife will be filled with perfection. Laqueur refers to the Middle East suicide bomber as a sort of deluxe martyrdom.[31] The Islamic martyr will live on in paradise, eating exquisite food, living in golden palaces, and surrounded by beautiful young virgins, and their families will be provided with monthly stipends. In contrast, suicide martyrs outside of the Islamic faith carry out suicide bombings without the promise of an elaborate reward structure.

Kramer has argued that Islamic suicide bombing attacks are intended to be expressions of both religious faith and nationalistic fervor.[32] There is little doubt that religious fervor, nationalism, and perhaps mental illness is a dangerous mix. Undertaking a suicide bombing attack provides a way of adding meaning to a life that has little prospect of future success. As a young Palestinian stated to Nasra Hassan of the *New Yorker Magazine*, "the youth of the Islamic resistance who blow themselves up in order to cause casualties are considered the greatest of those who die, because they die as martyrs."[33] Clearly a qualitative difference exists between those *willing* to die and those *wanting* to die. There are dozens of articles on the Internet that justify the suicide bombing attacks by Palestinian youth for Palestinian nationalism and Islamic beliefs. In fact, Jerozolimiski writes that the selection of suicide bombing is an integral aspect of Palestinian terrorism taught to Palestinian children at a very early age.[34]

In conclusion, Hizballah, Hamas, PIJ, al Aqsa, and the PFLP suicide bombing attacks are the most well known due to the instant media coverage of such events. But the most effective and brutal campaign to utilize suicide bombing attacks to date has been the Iraqi insurgent groups.

THE IRAQI INSURGENCY

The insurgency in Iraq consists of a myriad of anti-Iraqi terrorists and their supporters who are engaged in a guerrilla war with United States and Iraqi security forces. In a preemptive strike, the United States and coalition forces invaded Iraq in March of 2003 to overthrow Saddam Hussein. The United States and several other countries believed that Saddam Hussein posed a grave threat to the world. Intelligence officials warned the United States that Saddam was in the process of developing nuclear weapons and speeding up efforts to produce biological and chemical weapons, especially weaponized anthrax and smallpox. In addition, several U.S. political leaders, including Vice President Dick Cheney, were obsessed with proving that Saddam was responsible for the 9/11 attacks.[35] Other writers argued that evidence suggested Iraq aided or perhaps planned the 9/11 attacks and that Iraq was the "center of world terror."[36] The war hawks within the Bush administration lost no time making the case that a preemptive strike against Iraq was essential to winning the war on terrorism.

Clearly, Saddam Hussein was a brutal tyrant in pursuit of weapons of mass destruction, who desired to be the next Saladin of the Middle East. However, according to Mearsheimer and Walt, Saddam's own incompetence put his dangerous objectives out of reach. His army was weakened by a decade of United Nations sanctions and the defeat of the 1991 Gulf War. Iraq's military power looked strong on paper but was easily rolled over in the 2003 U.S. invasion. Saddam had no weapons of mass destruction. United Nations' inspection teams eliminated Iraq's nuclear program and destroyed Saddam's biological and chemical stockpiles as well. There was no convincing evidence linking Saddam and Osama bin Laden, who were, in fact, hostile to each other. Saddam had nothing to do with the 9/11 attacks. At that time bin Laden and al Qaeda were in Afghanistan and Pakistan, not Iraq. As U.S. and coalition forces rolled through Iraq in March 2003, they encountered limited resistance from the Iraqi military. But as coalition forces reached the outskirts of Baghdad, they were met by an Iraqi police officer driving a car full of explosives. Thus, Iraq recorded its first suicide-bombing event. The ubiquitous suicide bomber has become the symbol of the Iraqi insurgency, while the war in Iraq has turned into a strategic disaster for the United States.[37]

Since suicide bombing was first introduced by Hizballah in 1981, the world has recorded a total of 1,800 suicide bombings in 27 countries, with over 900 suicide bombings in Iraq. Thus, over one half of all suicide bombings have occurred in Iraq between 2003 and 2009. Prior to March 2003 there were no suicide bombings in Iraq. Yet, today Iraq leads the world in suicide bombings. Increasingly, female suicide bombers are being used in Iraq. In 2008 over thirty-five female suicide bombers were used against targets in Iraq. However, a most interesting feature is that the majority of suicide bombers in Iraq are not female or even Iraqis. The majority of suicide bombers in Iraq come from neighboring countries like Syria, Egypt, Jordan, Saudi Arabia, and even North Africa and Europe.[38] According to Professor Hafez, there are nineteen nationalities represented in Iraq as suicide bombers.[39] In the past, the question revolved around what motivates a young man or woman to become a suicide bomber. Today the question is more complex—what motivates young Muslim men to travel to Iraq to become suicide bombers?

Little has been known about foreign suicide bombers in Iraq until the October 2007 U.S. raid on an **AQI** base in Sinjar, a small town in northwest Iraq near the Syrian border. During the raid on Sinjar, the U.S. military discovered documents and computer data that belonged to AQI. The documents and computer data offered a unique look at foreign fighters in Iraq. The more than 750 personnel records discovered during the raid indicated that Saudi Arabia was the country of origin of 41 percent of foreign fighters in Iraq. Many of the Sinjar records had a "work" field category that primarily distinguished between suicide bombers and fighters. Apparently, the category designation reflects the "assignment" that foreign recruits to AQI had upon arrival in Iraq. In fact, many foreign recruits were required to sign suicide contracts before entering Iraq to ensure they will commit a suicide attack. For example, the translated version of the Sinjar records converts the Arabic word *istishhadi* in a variety of ways such as "martyr," or "suicide bomber." The word itself means "martyrdom seeker." Therefore, *istishhadi* likely refers to AQI recruits intended for suicide attacks. The Sinjar documents reveal that an astonishing 75 percent of suicide bombers in Iraq between August 2006 and August 2007 were in fact foreign fighters seeking martyrdom.[40]

Unlike many of the indigenous suicide bombers in AQI, foreign fighters are not insurgents or criminals. Foreign suicide bombers are likely motivated by religious ideology or factors that a native Iraqi would find difficult to understand. Professor Hafez outlines several factors that may contribute to the making of a foreign suicide bomber in Iraq. The first factor is related to Muslim rage against the United States for the invasion of Iraq. Muslims throughout the Islamic world wondered "Why Iraq?" since there are tyrants all over the world. To many Muslims, the invasion of Iraq was a sign of U.S. arrogance and the abuse of U.S. power against a far weaker opponent. Second, Palestinian suicide bombers and the al Asqa intifada (against a superior Israeli military force) inspired the foreign jihadists. Third, foreign jihadists mobilized to support each other in foreign conflicts since the Afghan-Soviet war. Muslim fighters had developed a series of networks across the Muslim world, making it easier to travel from one Islamic country to another. Many Muslims saw the war in Iraq as the classical defense of jihad.[41]

Professor Hafez's fourth factor is that a Sunni insurgency provided an opening for foreign fighters to "get into Iraq," and join the insurgency against the United States. The foreign fighters and suicide bombers were Sunnis who were primarily attacking Shi'ite civilians, Iraqi police officers, and security personnel. Fifth, the culture of martyrdom is at the heart of the explanation of why the world has seen the upsurge of Muslim suicide bombers. The culture of martyrdom relates back to the Palestinian–Israeli conflict where Palestinian suicide bombers were viewed by the Muslim world as heroic figures. Muslims around the world believed the Palestinian suicide bombers were defending their land, honor, religion, and family. The tactic of suicide bombing by Palestinians receives near-universal support from the Arab media and Muslim clerics. Thus, suicide bombers were to be emulated and admired as courageous figures of the jihad. The culture of martyrdom appears to be the most significant factor in attracting "jihadists" to volunteer as suicide bombers in Iraq.[42]

There is little doubt that foreign suicide bombers have drawn Iraq into a disastrous civil war. In one sense, Iraq has become a "field of dreams" for foreign fighters seeking expertise in terrorist tactics and the opportunity to become a martyr. Professor Hafez's valuable study on the use of suicide bombers alerts the world to the difficult challenges of coping with the growing phenomena of "martyrdom suicide attacks." Prior to 2000 and the invasion of Iraq, the most active suicide bombers were the **Liberation Tigers of Tamil Eelam** (**LTTE**), a Tamil separatist group of Sri Lanka.

THE LIBERATION TIGERS OF TAMIL EELAM (LTTE)

Since the early 1970s, the Tamils, provoked by government discrimination in education, culture, language, and restricted opportunities in the professions, have demanded the creation of a separate Tamil state in the northern and eastern regions of Sri Lanka (to be called Eelam—homeland). By the late 1970s, an all-out archetypical separatist/terrorist war was being waged by the most violent and hard-line Tamil organization, the LTTE. Terrorism had reached epidemic proportions, and Sri Lanka was descending into an outright civil war. According to Grosscup, inspired by the suicide tactics of Hizballah, which had forced the multinational force out of Lebanon, the LTTE shifted its terrorist attacks from ambush and assassination of Indian troops to suicide bombing attacks.[43]

Gunaratna tells us that between July 1987 and December 2000, LTTE carried out over 170 suicide attacks in Sri Lanka and southern India and was responsible for 62 percent of suicide bombing attacks worldwide.[44] Thousands of innocent bystanders have been killed and maimed in LTTE suicide attacks. Joshi contends that LTTE actually has suicide units called the **Black Tigers**, comprising both men and women who are more than willing to participate in suicide-bombing attacks.[45] In fact, the LTTE has a unique feature not found in other international or national terrorist groups. Every member of the LTTE carries a cyanide capsule around his/her neck. Upon capture he/she may swallow the cyanide capsule to avoid disclosing the group's secrets during coercive interrogation. The media report many instances of LTTE terrorists who take the cyanide capsule rather than risk capture and interrogation that most likely would force them to betray their organization. Joshi reports that many young Black Tigers live under the delusional belief that they will not be harmed and will survive the suicide bombing attack.[46]

The primary focus of LTTE suicide bombing attacks has been the ruling political party in Sri Lanka. The LTTE is the only terrorist group to assassinate two heads of state by a suicide bombing attack. Rajiv Gandhi, former prime minister of India, was assassinated on May 21, 1991, when a female suicide bomber approached him with a bouquet of flowers as a welcoming gesture to his arrival in Sri Lanka. Concealed in the bouquet and around the body of the assassin was a high-explosive bomb packed with small ball bearings to increase the shrapnel effect. The powerful bomb killed Gandhi plus twenty-eight innocent bystanders and wounded hundreds more. In 1993, the president of Sri Lanka was assassinated when a male suicide bomber from LTTE detonated an explosive charge wrapped around his body. Juergensmeyer reminds us that hostilities in Sri Lanka are exacerbated by the religious struggles between the Hindu Tamil minority and the Buddhist Sinhalese majority.[47] Elsewhere in India, **Sikh** and **Kashmiri** extremists have occasionally resorted to suicide bombing as a terrorist tactic in their efforts to gain independence from India.

SIKH TERRORISM

The most serious violence and terrorism between Sikh separatists and the Indian government began after Indian troops invaded the Golden Temple on June 5, 1984, the most holy shrine to Sikh believers.[48] In a two-day military operation to drive Sikh militants from the Golden Temple, over 2,000 Sikhs were killed. What outraged the Sikh community most was the desecration of their most sacred shrine, the Golden Temple, by Indian troops. On October 31, 1984, Sikh extremists seeking revenge for the Golden Temple massacre assassinated Indira Gandhi, prime minister of India. On the following day, angry Hindu mobs slaughtered thousands of innocent Sikhs in Delhi and elsewhere in India. After the rioting, Sikh militants became even more fervent for their need to establish a separate Sikh nation. Marwah and Mahmood contend that the heavy-handed response and torture of Sikh militants by the Indian government helped to increase the ranks of the Sikh nationalist movement and create Sikh suicide martyrs.[49] Similar to the LTTE, Hamas, and Hizballah, young Sikh extremists from a variety of competing factions from 1981 to 1994 viewed martyrdom as an honorable and holy way to die, even in a suicide bombing attack.

Vinayak's investigation into the first Sikh suicide bombing attack provides some insight into the suicide bombing strategy. The young Sikh suicide bomber practiced for the suicide-bombing event for several weeks. As the suicide bomber prepared to leave on his mission, he gave a note to one of his companions stating that his act of suicide was to honor the memory of the martyrs of the Golden Temple. Apparently inspired by his dedication, other young Sikhs became suicide bombers, giving new life to the Sikh separatist movement. By the mid-1990s, Sikh terrorist groups were penetrated by the Indian police and ceased to be a major threat to the Indian government, although the Sikh community still demands the creation of an independent Sikh nation.[50]

KASHMIRI SUICIDE BOMBERS

In Kashmir, where Muslims are the majority, another separatist movement began in 1986. The decades-old dispute between India and Pakistan over the hegemony of Kashmir erupted when the Muslim United Front called for secession from India. By May 1989, the separatists began referring to themselves as "holy warriors" and calling for a jihad (holy war) against the Hindu government of India. The violence and terrorism between India and Kashmiri separatists continued to escalate, and thousands of people from both sides were killed and maimed by indiscriminate bombings. By the late 1990s, the bombing campaign by various competing Kashmiri Muslim factions gave way to the use of suicide bombers. Accordingly, ten suicide bombings occurred in the year 2001.[51] For instance, on December 13, 2001, in an unprecedented attack, five suicide bombers attacked the Indian parliament in Delhi, killing twelve, including the suicide attackers, and injuring twenty-two. The suicide attack on the Indian parliament once more brought India and Pakistan (which allegedly supports Kashmiri terrorism) to the brink of war.

Juergensmeyer reports that Islamic clerics have little interference in recruiting young Kashmiri Muslim men to fight in a holy war.[52] Similar to the al Qaeda suicide bombers of 9/11, Kashmiri suicide bombers are young, well-educated, middle-class recruits who appear to be *willing* to die for God and country. Khurshid states that groups such as the Kashmiri Liberation Front, the Lashkar e-Tayyiba (Army of the Pure), and the Muslim United Front have little trouble attracting young Kashmiri males to carry out suicide bombing attacks against the Indian military forces in Kashmir or soft civilian targets in India.[53]

On November 26, 2008, Mumbai, India, was the target of a ferocious "suicide" attack that lasted for 60 hours; 172 people were killed and 239 were injured. Unlike other attacks in India, which consisted of anonymously planted bombs or suicide bombers, the Mumbai attack consisted of ten members of Lashkar e-Tayyiba (LET) armed with AK 47s and hand grenades. The assailants attacked ten locations in Mumbai, including two luxury hotels, a railway station, and a Jewish cultural center. The terrorists entered the railway station and hotels and began spraying gunfire and throwing hand grenades at innocent bystanders. Police and army units engaged the terrorists from LET, which is closely aligned with al Qaeda, in a running gun battle that lasted over 60 hours. Nine of the terrorists were killed and one was taken alive. According to Indian police interrogators, the surviving terrorist "sang like a canary," revealing the detailed planning and preparation for the assault on Mumbai. Interrogators discovered that the terrorists had no escape plan and expected to die as martyrs. The motive for the Mumbai attack was to retaliate against India's occupation of Kashmir.[54]

KURDISH SUICIDE BOMBERS: THE PKK/KADEK, KONGRA-GEL

Another group that has resorted to suicide bombing attacks is the **PKK (Kurdistan Workers Party)**, also called **Kadek, Kongra-Gel, and KGK**. The PKK is composed of Turkish Kurds and represents the same ruthless brand of terrorism as do other notorious Middle East terrorist groups. They have murdered more than 10,000 people, mostly innocent Turks and Kurds. The PKK began as an orthodox revolutionary group in 1974, but has evolved into a nationalist/separatist religious group seeking to establish an independent Islamic Kurdistan in Turkey. Criss reports that the PKK received "terrorist" training sponsored by Hizballah in the Bekaa Valley in Lebanon.[55] While training there the PKK discovered the "terrorist strategy" of the suicide bombing attack and emerged as a deadly terrorist group ready to wage war against the Turks.

The PKK resorted to suicide bombing attacks beginning on June 30, 1996, when a female suicide bomber dressed as a pregnant woman in order to conceal the explosives she had hidden beneath her dress. She detonated the bomb, killing herself and ten innocent Turkish victims. Ergil contends that between 1994 and 1996 the PKK carried out twenty-one suicide or attempted suicide bombing attacks.[56] The PKK resorted to suicide bombing terrorism at a time when the Turkish military was gradually destroying the infrastructure of the PKK. In order to boost the morale of its membership and continue to struggle for a separatist Kurdish nation, suicide bombing attacks were chosen. The PKK, under Abdullah Ocalan's leadership, believed that the willingness to sacrifice one's life for Kurdish national goals would consolidate their membership, inspire young Kurds, and cause intense fear among the Turkish population. Apparently the tactic of suicide bombing did not work. After the capture of Abdullah Ocalan in June 1999, the Kurdish suicide bombing campaign was called off. The PKK has returned to the use of conventional terrorist/guerrilla war tactics against Turkey.

AL QAEDA

Osama bin Laden and his terrorist group al Qaeda (the Base or the Base of Allah's support) recently have successfully carried out suicide bombings against the United States. Al Qaeda is responsible for two of the most spectacular and lethal suicide bombing attacks in recent years. The coordinated suicide bombing attacks against the World Trade Center and the Pentagon, which killed over 3,000 innocent people, and the attack on the American embassies in Nairobi and Dar-es-Salaam in August 1998, which killed 300 and left at least 5,000 wounded, demonstrate the lethality of well-planned acts of suicide bombings. Osama bin Laden and al Qaeda demonstrated that with careful planning and dedicated followers, even the United States was vulnerable to a suicide bombing attack.

Gunaratna states that in a suicide attack reminiscent of the kamikaze, in October 2000 two al Qaeda suicide bombers approached the destroyer, the U.S.S. Cole, in the port of Aden, Yemen, in a small boat and detonated an enormous amount of explosives. The explosion ripped a 40- by 450-foot hole in the Cole, killed seventeen American sailors, and injured thirty-three others. The attack was intended to show the powerlessness of the United States in the face of Islam's embrace of martyrdom. The zeal of the two suicide bombers was meant to intimidate and demoralize the United States while simultaneously acting as an inspiration to Muslims around the world. A billion-dollar U.S. warship, armed with sophisticated twenty-first-century high-tech equipment, was all but destroyed by a small boat operated by "martyrs." This act conveys the message that world superpowers are easily vulnerable to suicide attack. Emboldened by the attack on the Cole, al Qaeda has demonstrated that a combination of religious zeal and technical know-how can produce horrific results. Gunaratna maintains that suicide attacks are likely to remain al Qaeda's preferred terrorist strategy for the foreseeable future. Al Qaeda will continue to plan spectacular suicide attacks against high profile or symbolic targets (embassies, naval vessels, government buildings, and famous landmarks) in the United States.[57]

Al Qaeda–affiliated groups also claimed responsibility for two recent suicide bombings. On May 8, 2002, a suicide car bomber of the Jaish-e-Mohammed (Army of Mohammed), a Pakistani terrorist group supported by al Qaeda, pulled up alongside a busload of French guest workers in Pakistan and detonated a powerful bomb, killing fourteen people. In Tunisia on April 11, 2002, the Islamic Army for the Liberation of the Holy Sites claimed credit for the suicide truck bombing of an historic synagogue in Tunis, killing nineteen people. The Islamic Army for the Liberation of the Holy Sites announced that the synagogue bombing was in retaliation for Israeli crimes against the Palestinians. Unlike the kamikaze, al Qaeda has adopted suicide bombing as a strategic "first" choice.

According to a study by the Afghanistan Conflict Monitor, eighty suicide bombings occurred between 2007 and 2008 in Afghanistan. The study concluded that over 60 percent of the suicide bombers are people with physical disabilities. The Taliban and al Qaeda recruited people who had been crippled by unexploded shells or land mines to carry out suicide bombings. Al Qaeda and the

Taliban claim that disabled Afghanis are easily recruited as suicide bombers. Afghan suicide bombers live in poverty, are unable to find work, and often agree to carry out suicide attacks in exchange for al Qaeda and the Taliban providing for their families. Al Qaeda has been able to spread its ideology, create an army of believers, radicalize its followers, recruit suicide bombers, and incite them to action. Al Qaeda's activities and goals are dedicated to a global jihad.[58]

CHECHEN SUICIDE BOMBERS

Chechen separatists carried out over fifteen suicide bombings between June 2000 and September 2004. A wave of suicide truck bombings was carried out against Russian military forces in Chechnya in 2000. After the Russian military declared that Chechen rebel resistance had been crushed, the suicide bombers struck. The vast majority of Chechen suicide bombings have targeted government compounds and military installations. For example, five nearly simultaneous suicide truck-bombing attacks occurred in four Chechen towns on July 4, 2000. In each of the bombings, large trucks were loaded with explosives. Suicide bombers drove them into buildings housing Russian military troops. Over eighty Russian soldiers and police officers were killed and hundreds were wounded. Commander Kattab, leader of the Chechen rebels, proudly claimed credit for the bombings stating that "the Kremlin military adventure had no prospects for success against the dedication of the Chechen martyrs." Once again the twin motivators of religion and nationalism have inspired the use of the terrorist strategy of suicide bombing attacks.[59]

The vast majority of Chechen suicide bombers are women. Such Chechen women, also known as **Black Widows**, are motivated by their grief and despair and independently volunteer for the role of suicide bombers. Chechen insurgent leaders discovered that the use of female suicide bombers was a very effective method for attacking high-profile targets in Chechnya. Therefore, Chechen suicide attacks imply a strategic rationale. Pape maintains that suicide terrorism is not motivated by irrational people or as an expression of fanatical hatred, but as a strategic effort to achieve a political objective.[60] In this case, it was the establishment of an independent Chechnya. In sum, the strategic goal of Chechen suicide attacks is to liberate the Chechnya homeland, attract supporters, obtain media recognition, and solicit funding. By 2005, Chechen suicide bombings virtually came to an end. Russia and Chechen insurgents signed a cease-fire and began peaceful negotiations to eventually set up a Chechen homeland. In the meantime, a pro-Russian administration rules Chechnya today.

On December 6, 2003, two female Chechen suicide bombers attempted to enter the Russian parliment, but the explosives detonated prematurely. Five people were killed and fourteen were injured.

OTHER SUICIDAL TERRORIST GROUPS

Several additional terrorist groups have claimed suicide bombing as part of their terrorist strategy. Egypt's two leading terrorist groups—Gama'a el-Islamiya and the Egyptian Islamic Jihad—have taken credit for at least two suicide bombing attacks. A Gama'a member had been held in the police barracks awaiting extradition to Egypt. In a retaliatory attack, a Gama'a suicide bomber drove a vehicle loaded with high explosives into a police barracks in Croatia in October 1995. Several police officers were injured by the attack. The Gama'a member they were attempting to rescue was killed in the ensuing attack.

In November 1995 the Egyptian Islamic Jihad sent two suicide bombers to attack the Egyptian Embassy in Pakistan in retaliation for Egyptian and Pakistani cooperation in extraditing fugitives of the Egyptian Jihad group to Egypt to stand trial for a variety of terrorist-related offenses. The attack resulted in fifteen fatalities and dozens of seriously injured victims. Like the suicide attacks on the United States by al Qaeda, the suicide bombings of the Egyptian Gama'a and Jihad illustrate that terrorist groups are not hesitant to export suicide attacks to other countries.

The Philippines has witnessed occasions of suicide bombing attempts in the southern Philippine islands of Mindanao. Three Islamic separatist groups, **Abu Sayyaf**, the Moro National Liberation Front, and the Rajah Soliaman Movement (RSM) have attacked Philippine military bases with suicide bombers. After police interrogation, several members of Abu Sayyaf claimed that Osama bin Laden is providing training for Abu Sayyaf and RSM in terrorist techniques and suicide bombing attacks.[61]

SUMMARY

There is little doubt that suicide bombings generate a great deal of fascination and panic among the general population. If, according to the creed of terrorist groups, bombing attacks are considered "propaganda by deed," then the suicide bombing attack is the ultimate propaganda. The impression created by martyrs willing to sacrifice themselves is that the cause is worthy and God is "on our side." In the case of Muslim suicide bombers, however, the Koran does not permit suicide in principle. At the same time, it is the religious duty of every Muslim to fight and die in defense of Allah and Islam—certainly a confusing religious doctrine.

Islamic fundamentalists may live without hope, be poverty stricken, deeply religious, and nationalistic, but only a fraction of them have considered going on suicide bombing attacks. Is there a fraction of suicide bombing candidates who are more idealistic, more easily manipulated by terrorist group leaders, and more willing to sacrifice their lives? Is there perhaps an inclination to overlook the so-called real motives for suicidal behavior? What is the justification for the current appeal of suicide bombing attacks?

For the moment, suicidologists know that some groups of individuals are much more likely to kill themselves: those who suffer from depression, manic depression, drug and alcohol addiction, schizophrenia, personality and mental health disorders, patients recently released from mental hospitals, and adolescents.[62] The World Health Organization estimates that worldwide over 1 million people commit suicide every year.[63] Jamison estimates that the figure may be twice as high.[64] Worldwide, suicide is the second leading cause of death for females between the ages of 15 and 40. Among males of the same age group, suicide is the fourth leading cause of death. By any standard, suicide in general is a crucial public health problem. Hence, it may be relatively easy for such groups as Hizballah, Hamas, Islamic Jihad, al Aqsa, or AQI to convince prospective suicide bombers to die as martyrs for Allah and the motherland.

Merari argues that religion is unimportant to a suicide bomber and that an individual who wishes to die for personal reasons makes the choice.[65] In fact, Merari contends the terrorist group simply provides the framework and legitimacy for committing the suicide bombing. He continues that there is no evidence to suggest that religious or political leaders could convince a nonsuicidal person to carry out a suicidal bombing attack. Alvarez tends to support the notion that no one mental illness or event causes suicide and no one knows the motivation behind the killing of self.[66]

In addition, the tendency for suicide bombing attacks to incite imitation is persistent, especially if the suicide is highly publicized and romanticized. In 1975, the sociologist David Phillips introduced the phrase "Werther Effect" to describe the phenomenon of suicide contagion.[67] Many researchers believe that highly publicized media accounts of suicide bombing events lead to an increase in suicidal behavior.[68] Motto agrees that suicide has the strongest impact on young people and that the images and context of the suicide are far more important than the act of suicide itself.[69]

Berkan and the American Association of Suicidology offer the following general media guidelines for reporting suicide incidents that may contribute to a reduction or lessening of suicide bombing attacks.[70]

1. Providing sensational coverage of suicide bombing attacks.

    By its nature, news coverage of a suicidal bombing heightens public awareness and fear. Researchers believe this practice is associated with contagion and suicide **clusters**.[71] Police and news reporters can reduce the sensationalism by limiting the morbid details and avoiding the use of dramatic photographs.

2. Presenting suicide bombing as a tactic for reaching political goals.

    Suicide bombing is usually a rare act of a disturbed person. If suicide bombing is presented as an effective means of destroying Israel or the United States, for example, suicide may be perceived by a potentially suicidal person as a viable "military" strategy. In almost thirty years of terrorist suicide bombings, terrorist campaigns have not been won in Iraq, Palestine, Sri Lanka, Chechnya, or any other nation.

3. Glorifying suicide bombers.

    Such actions may contribute to suicide contagion by suggesting to a susceptible young person or an emotionally disturbed person that a great deal of honor and glory is associated with the suicide bombing attack. The innocent victims of a suicide bombing are often only given cursory coverage, while extensive coverage is devoted to the suicide bomber, his/her motives, and his/her tactics.

4. Presenting simplistic explanations for suicide bombings.

    Any type of suicide is a very complex interacting of many factors. There is more to a suicide bomber's motives than "Allah Akbar." Research on suicidology supports the thesis that people who commit suicide have a history of personal, social, and mental health problems. An overwhelming number of suicides are linked to psychiatric illnesses. At the heart of many suicides are mood, anxiety, and personality disorders. Acknowledgment of these problems will surely demonstrate the complexities involved in suicide bombing attacks.[72]

5. Illustrating and reporting "how to" descriptions of suicide bombing techniques.

    Describing technical details about the method of bombing may be undesirable. Providing details of the mechanism and procedures used to complete the suicide bombing may inspire other suicidal persons. For example, in the documentary *The Shaheed*, a bomb maker casually sketched the simplicity of making a bomb carried by a suicide bomber. Suicide incites imitation and repetition. Livingstone has argued that emphasis on violent acts committed by terrorist bombers may stimulate like-minded terrorists to repeat the same behavior. In Livingstone's view, the evidence suggests that detailed media coverage of suicide bombing attacks is apt to lead to a rash of similar imitative suicide bombings.[73]

In sum, with the exception of Palestinian groups and AQI, most of the terrorist groups involved in suicide bombing attacks actually have either stopped using it or significantly reduced it. According to Jacqard, the difference between suicide attacks by al Qaeda and other terrorist groups is the capacity and the global reach of al Qaeda to inflict mass casualties through the use of chemical or biological weapons.[74] Today the greatest potential risk of suicide bombing attacks is the use of weapons of mass destruction. Stern warns us that the use of a chemical, biological, or nuclear weapon by a suicide bomber is now a reality.[75]

Despite all the information available on suicide and suicide bombers, law enforcement still has not been able to protect communities from the lethality of a suicide bombing attack. What can the criminal justice system do to prevent suicide bombings from occurring in the future?

SECURITY AND SUICIDE BOMBING

A practical problem that confronts the planning of suicide bombings is the extent of physical security surrounding potential targets. Some targets, such as government officials or embassies, may have elaborate and sophisticated security systems to prevent a suicide bombing attack. Other targets are largely unprotected, such as unguarded buildings and unarmed civilians. Therefore, terrorist suicide bombers will always have opportunities to carry out attacks, since it is impossible to provide protection for all possible targets. The result of such uneven security means that some targets will always be vulnerable to a suicide bombing attack. So what can be done to protect vulnerable citizens from a determined suicide bomber?

While the very size of a large urban area makes it difficult to protect all possible targets, following a few practical security recommendations can reduce the possibilities of carrying out a suicide-bombing attack.

- First, the deployment of a large number of uniformed soldiers and police may afford some security as they increase the likelihood that suicide bombers will be intercepted on the way to an attack.
- Second, the introduction of intense surveillance of potential targets will make it difficult for suicide bombers to move about undetected. For example, the installation of high-density TV cameras can provide coverage of a vulnerable area.
- Third, the use of covert observation posts on the roofs of houses combined with surveillance equipment can supply information on suspicious persons.
- Fourth, the use of helicopters hovering over areas that are most vulnerable will help, especially to supplement the observation posts.
- Fifth, the setting up of checkpoints will make it difficult for the suicide bomber to move about undetected and should act as a deterrent as the suicide bomber runs the risk of being identified before he or she can carry out one's mission.
- Sixth, the use of dogs can detect explosives concealed in vehicles and on individuals.

In sum, some protection may be possible against suicide bombing attacks, but it is impossible to protect everything and everyone all the time. A determined suicidal terrorist bomber may not be deterred by security measures. The limitations on the amount of physical protection create vulnerabilities that are exploited by terrorist groups planning suicide bombing attacks. As potential targets are hardened, suicide bombers seek out softer targets. In January 2000, an individual bent on committing suicide drove his eighteen-wheeler into the south porch of the State Capitol in Sacramento, California. Surveillance cameras showed the eighteen-wheeler barreling up the steps of the California Capitol building into the portico and bursting into flames. Fortunately, the driver of the semi-truck was not a suicide bomber. Instead, he was a suicidal person who had spent much of his life in prison and mental institutions and apparently suffered from a variety of mental health and mood disorders. There is little doubt, however, that potential suicide bombers studied how easy it was to attack a hard target such as the California Capitol building.

Security measures alone are not sufficient to prevent suicide bombings. The collection of intelligence information is the key to a successful **interdiction** of a suicide bombing attack. Potential suicide bombers need support in order to plan and execute a successful suicide attack. Dershowitz observes that the vast majority of suicide bombers do not act alone and are part of complex organizational structures.[76] Suicide bombers are recruited, trained, and promised rewards by the organization that sends them on suicide attacks. Therefore, by taking preventive measures it may be possible to interdict future suicide bombing attacks. The decision to send a suicide bomber is almost always made by others. A few proactive measures follow.

- First, family members may notice a change in the behavior of a son or daughter planning a suicide attack and notify authorities and perhaps prevent the suicide attack from occurring.
- Second, a successful counterstrategy requires comprehensive intelligence of the recruitment, selection, and training of the suicide bombers. The potential suicide bomber must be identified either when he or she joins the terrorist organization or during the period of "basic training."
- Third, the person who recruits the potential suicide bomber usually follows him or her throughout his "military" preparation and "spiritual" awakening before the planned suicide attack.
- Fourth, the operational groundwork for the suicide attack includes preparation of the explosive device at a clandestine bomb factory, location of a safe house for the suicide bomber, and finally the transport of the suicide bomber and the explosives to the target area without being detected by the police, military, or watchful citizens.
- Fifth, the leaders of terrorist organizations who support and create an atmosphere for the use of suicide attacks should be identified. There is little doubt that the tactic of suicide bombing is devised and approved by terrorist organizational leaders.

In short, the intelligence apparatus of nations under attack by suicide bombers should concentrate on interrupting the preparations and planning of a suicide attack in order to neutralize the suicide attack in its preparatory stage. When contending with the phenomenon of suicide bombings, nations under attack must keep in mind that suicide operations are not the act of a desperate irrational terrorist or a lone "madman." Rather, suicide attacks are well-planned, well-organized strategic operations that include extensive preparation and the involvement of a large support staff. Therefore, countering suicide bombings requires a combination of target hardening and intelligence gathering to interdict the terrorist organizations responsible for suicide attacks.

Another, perhaps surer, strategy for preventing suicide bombings, especially in Iraq and Israel, may be for the United States to end the occupation of Iraq and the Israeli government to end the occupation of Palestinian territory and to cease the construction of Israeli settlements in the "occupied territories." Bahour concludes that only Israel can stop the suicide bombing attacks by returning the "occupied territories" to the Palestinians.[77] For many of these groups, the Palestinians included, the political objective for suicide bombers is, most often, the achievement of an independent state. Thus, it may be posited that in most cases of suicide bombing, the best prevention strategy is a political settlement in which some kind of independence is granted. In the wake of September 11, how we respond to suicide bombings and terrorism is becoming the defining issue of our time.

Conclusions

There are no simple theories for suicide bombing, nor are there strategies to predict it. Some groups use disabled people, while other groups use women and foreign fighters. As yet, no one has found a way to stop it. Suicide bombing has a contagious aspect associated with it, and it has an indisputable appeal as the solution of last resort.

The leadership of terrorist organizations also has discovered a number of positive benefits of the suicide attack method. First, many casualties can be expected. Second, widespread media coverage is assured. Third, the suicide bomber can choose the time and place of the attack. Fourth, there is no need to plan an escape and risk being captured and interrogated. Fifth, the suicide attack method is least costly in terms of "battlefield losses." Finally, success is almost guaranteed.

Suicide bombing has become the new benchmark of religious devotion and nationalistic pride. In fact, the suicide bomber also believes he or she benefits from participating in a suicide attack. For example, fulfillment of a religious obligation and eternal life in paradise are certainly benefits. The suicide bomber improves his/her social status in the community and may receive economic rewards for his/her family as more benefits.

For these reasons, suicide bombing will continue to be part of the terrorist strategy of many terrorist organizations. Suicide bombing, which has quadrupled over the last twenty years, is without argument the most serious problem facing the war on terrorism. The world is now facing the very real threat of a suicide attack using weapons of mass destruction (WMD). The next chapter concentrates on counterterrorist measures—the best response to the growing threat of terrorism.

Key Terms

Abu Sayyaf
AQI
Beirut
Black Tigers
Black Widow
cluster
Emile Durkheim
Hamas

Hizballah
hunger strike
interdiction
Irish National Liberation Army
   (INLA)
Kamikaze
Kashmiri
Kurdistan Workers Party (PKK)

Liberation Tigers of Tamil
   Eelam (LTTE)
martyrs
self-immolation
Sikh
suicidology

Discussion Questions

1. Who were the kamikazes?
2. What is the Yasukuni Shrine?
3. Identify the country of origin of the following groups:
   a. PKK
   b. Hizballah
   c. Sikhs
   d. Abu Sayyaf
   e. Black Tigers
   f. MNLF
4. Explain the concept of "suicide clusters."
5. What motivates suicide bombers?

6. Why do you think suicide bombing is a "tactical" choice of terrorist groups?
7. Describe the analysis of suicidologists and the motivation for individual acts of suicide.
8. What terrorist group participates in the largest number of recorded suicide attacks? Why?
9. Develop a strategy to interdict and prevent suicide bombings.
10. Discuss the "benefits" of the suicide-bombing strategy for the terrorist organization and the terrorist bomber.

Web Sites

The International Policy Institute for Counter-Terrorism
http://www.ict.org.il/

Israeli Ministry of Foreign Affairs
http://www.mfa.gov.il/MFA

The Jerusalem Post
http://www.jpost.com

Washington Report on Middle East Affairs
http://www.wrmea.com/

American Association of Suicidology
http://www.suicidology.org/

Combating Terrorism Center at West Point
http://www.ctc.usma.edu

Endnotes

1. For example, see Bruce Hoffman, *Inside Terrorism* (New York: Columbia University Press, 1998); Kevin Crosby, Joong-oh Rhee, and Jimmie Holland, "Suicide by Fire: A Contemporary Method of Political Protest," *International Journal of Social Psychiatry*, 23 (1977), pp. 60–69; Martin Milton and Judy Crompton, "Recent Research on Suicide," *Counseling Psychology Review*, 16 (2001), pp. 28–33; James Rogers, "Theoretical Grounding: The 'Missing Link' in Suicide Research," *Journal of Counseling and Development*, 79 (Winter 2001), pp. 16–25; Edwin Shneidman, ed., *Comprehending Suicide: Landmarks in 20th Century Suicidology* (Washington, DC: American Psychological Association, 2001); John Westefeld, et al., "Suicide: An Overview," *Counseling Psychologist* 28 (July 2000), pp. 445–510; Talal Asad, *On Suicide Bombing* (New York: Columbia University Press, 2007).

2. Kamikaze or Divine Wind is a term originally applied by grateful Japanese to a typhoon that destroyed a Mongol invasion fleet in 1281. Revived in 1945, kamikaze applied to pilots who flew planes loaded with explosives into U.S. naval vessels.

3. Mako Sasaki, "Who Became Kamikaze Pilots and How Did They Feel toward Their Suicide Mission," *Concord Review* (2000), *http://www.tcr.org*.

4. Yasukuni (Peaceful Country) is a shrine dedicated to Japanese war dead. If a war hero is buried in the Yasukuni Shrine, he becomes godlike and deserves reverence from all visitors. The shrine is dedicated to the Shinto code of Bushido. It is the most important shrine in the Shinto hierarchy of shrines. In one respect the Yasukuni is equivalent to Arlington Cemetery. The shrine contains a special room for kamikaze pilots.

5. Rikihei Inoguchi and Tadashi Nakajima, *The Divine Wind* (Annapolis, MD: United States Naval Institute, 1958), pp. 36–52.

6. For example, see Eli Robins, *The Final Months: A Study of the Lives of 134 Persons Who Committed Suicide* (New York: Oxford University Press, 1981).

7. Roger Pineau, "Spirit of the Divine Wind," *U.S. Naval Institute Proceedings*, 84 (January 1958), pp. 23–29.

8. William Craig, *The Fall of Japan* (New York: Dell Books, 1967), pp. 1–14.

9. For example, see Mohammed Hafez, *Suicide Bombings in Iraq: The Strategy and Ideology of Martyrdom* (Washington, DC: U.S. Institute of Peace Press, 2007).

10. Harvey Kushner, "Suicide Bombers: Business as Usual," *Studies in Conflict and Terrorism*, 19 (October–December 1996), pp. 329–37; Ami Pedazhur, *Root Causes of Suicide Terrorism: The Globalization of Martyrdom* (New York: Routledge, 2006), pp. 54–80.

11. David Beresford, *Ten Men Dead The Story of the 1981 Irish Hunger Strike* (Jackson, TN: Atlantic Monthly Press, 1997), p. 97.

12. The Baader-Meinhoff gang, so named after its founders, was active in the Federal Republic of Germany in the 1970s. The original name of the Baader-Meinhoff Gang was the Red Army Faction (RAF). The gang strongly believes that an armed campaign of terrorist violence against the state was the highest form of class struggle.

13. Kate Jamison, *Night Falls Fast: Understanding Suicide* (New York: Vintage Books, 1999), pp. 142–45.

14. Peter Carlson, "For Whom the Gong Tolls," *Washington Post* (February 27, 2000), p. 1; See also, David Ownby, *Falun Gong and the Future of China* (United Kingdom: Oxford University Press, 2008), pp. 214–19.

15. Christine Dallman and Isamu Yamamoto, "China's Falun Gong, the World Is Watching . . . and Joining," *Christian Research Journal*, 22 (February 2000), pp. 22–45.

16. For example, see Robert Lifton, *Destroying the World to Save It: Aum Shinrikyo, Apocalyptic Violence and the New Global Terrorism* (New York: Metropolitan Books, 1999), pp. 292–95; Robert Lifton, *The Broken Connection: On Death and the Continuity of Life* (New York: Simon and Schuster, 1979).

17. Moshe Hazani, "Sacrificial Immortality: Toward a Theory of Suicide Terrorism and Related Phenomena," in *The Psychoanalytic Study of Society*, eds. C. Boyer, et al. (Hillsdale, NJ: Analytic Press, 1993), pp. 415–42.

18. David Martin and John Wolcott, *Best Laid Plans: The Inside Story of America's War Against Terrorism* (New York: Simon and Schuster, Inc., 1988), pp. 125–45; See also, Robert A. Pape, *Dying to Win: The Strategic Logic of Suicide Terrorism* (New York: Random House, 2005), pp. 129–39.

19. Yoram Schweitzer, *Suicide Terrorism: Development and Characteristics* (Herzlija, Israel: The International Policy Institute for Counterterrorism, 2000), *http://www.ict.org.il/*.

20. Israeli Ministry of Foreign Affairs (2008), *http://www.israel.org/mfa/home.asp;* See also, Michael V. Uschan, *Terrorism in Today's World: Suicide Bombings in Israel and Palestinian Terrorism* (Milwaukee, WI: World Almanac Library, 2006).

21. Lisa Beyer, "Jerusalem Bombing," *New York Times* (August 21, 1995), p. 1.

22. For example, see Anne Marie Oliver and Paul Steinberg, *The Road to Martyr's Square: A Journey into the World of the Suicide Bomber* (New York: Oxford University Press, 2001); Anne Marie Oliver and Paul Steinberg, "The Politics of Apocalypse in the Underground Media of the Islamic Resistance Movement (HAMAS)," *Center for Millennial Studies* (Boston, MA: Boston University Press, 1997).

23. *Suicide Bombers: Secrets of the Shaheed*, written and directed by Dan Setton (Set Productions, 1998). Presentation of CineMax: Reel Life.

24. Jamison, *Night Falls Fast*, pp. 125–27.

25. Ariel Merari, "The Readiness to Kill and Die: Suicide Terrorism in the Middle East," in *Origins of Terrorism: Psychologies, Ideologies, Theologies, States of Mind*, ed. Walter Reich (Washington, DC: Woodrow Wilson Center Press, 1998), pp. 192–207.

26. William K. Muir, *Police: Streetcorner Politicians* (Chicago, IL: University of Chicago Press, 1977), p. 61.

27. For example, see Kameel B. Nasr, *Arab and Israeli Terrorism: The Causes and Effects of Political Violence* (Jefferson, NC: McFarland, 1997); Raphael Israeli, *Islamikaze: Manifestations of Islamic Martyrology* (London: Frank Cass Publishers, 2003).

28. Aaron T. Beck, et al., "Relationship between Hopelessness and Ultimate Suicide: A Replication with Psychiatric Outpatients," *American Journal of Psychiatry*, 147 (1990), pp. 190–95.

29. For example, see Emile Durkheim, *Suicide: A Study in Sociology* (New York: Simon and Schuster, 1997); Durkheim et al., *On Suicide* (New York: Penguin Classics, 2007).

30. For example, see Samuel Katz, *The Hunt for the Engineer: How Israeli Agents Tracked the HAMAS Master Bomber* (New York: Fromme International Publishing, 1999).

31. Walter Laqueur, *The New Terrorism: Fanaticism and the Arms of Mass Destruction* (Oxford: Oxford University Press, 1999), pp. 140–47.

32. Martin Kramer, "The Moral Logic of Hizballah," in *Origins of Terrorism: Psychologies, Ideologies, Theologies, States of Mind*, ed. Walter Reich (Washington, DC: Woodrow Wilson Center Press, 1998), pp. 131–57; See also Barbara Victor, *Armies of Roses: Inside the World of Palestinian Women Suicide Bombers* (Emmaus, PA: Rodale Press, 2003).

33. Nasra Hassan, "Letter from Gaza: An Arsenal of Believers: Talking to the 'Human Bombs,' " *New Yorker* (November 11, 2001), pp. 36–42.

34. Adam Jerozolimiski, "Islamic Jihad Is Running Four Camps in the Gaza Strip at Which Eight to Twelve-Year-Olds Learn the Importance of Becoming a Suicide Bomber," *Jerusalem Post* (July 20, 2001), p. l.

35. David E Sanger and Robin Toner, "Bush and Cheney Talk Strongly of Qaeda Links with Hussein," *New York Times* (June 18, 2004), p. 1.

36. William Safire, "Saddam and Terror," *New York Times* (August 22, 2002), p.1.
37. John J. Mearsheimer and Stephen M. Walt, *The Israeli Lobby and U.S. Foreign Policy* (New York: Farrar, Straus and Geroux, 2007), pp. 227–29.
38. Peter Bergen, et al., "Bombers, Bank Accounts, and Bleedout: al Qa'ida's Road In and Out of Iraq," (New York: Combating Terrorism Center at West Point, July 2008), pp. 54–63, *http:// www.ctc.usma.edu.*
39. Hafez, *Suicide Bombings in Iraq*, pp. 251–54.
40. Bergen, et al., "Bombers, Bank Accounts, and Bleedout," pp. 57–59.
41. Hafez, *Suicide Bombings in Iraq*, pp. 14–24.
42. Ibid., pp. 224–26.
43. Beau Grosscup, *The Newest Explosion of Terrorism* (Far Hills, NJ: New Horizon Press, 1998), pp. 234–67; See also, Dennis McGilvray, *Crucible of Conflict: Tamil and Muslim Society on the East Coast of Sri Lanka* (North Carolina: Duke University Press, 2008).
44. For example, see Rohen Gunaratna, *International and Regional Security Implications of the Sri Lankan Tamil Insurgency* (St. Albans, United Kingdom: International Foundation of Sri Lankans, 2000); John Horgan, *Teach Yourself Understanding Terrorism* (New York: McGraw-Hill, 2009).
45. Charu Joshi, "Ultimate Sacrifice," *Far Eastern Economic Review* (June 1, 2000), pp. 64–67.
46. Ibid.
47. Mark Juergensmeyer, *Terror in the Mind of God: The Global Rise of Religious Violence* (Berkeley, CA: University of California Press, 2000), pp. 112–13.
48. The Golden Temple in Amristar in Punjab Province of India is the symbol of strength of Sikh people worldwide. The Golden Temple is the heart of Sikhism and is equivalent to St. Peters in Rome and Temple Mount in Jerusalem.
49. For example, see Cynthia Mahmood, *Fighting for Faith and Nation: Dialogues with Sikh Militants* (Philadelphia, PA: University of Pennsylvania Press, 1997); Ved Marwah, *Uncivil Wars: Pathology of Terrorism in India* (New Delhi, India: Harper-Collins India, 1995).
50. Ramsen Vinayak, "Striking Terror," *India Today* (September 30, 1995), p. 27.
51. *BBC News* (2001), *http://news.bbc.co.uk/.*
52. Juergensmeyer, *Terror in the Mind of God*, p. 210.
53. For example, see Salmon Khurshid, *Beyond Terrorism: New Hope for Kashmir* (New Delhi, India: UBS Publications, 1994).
54. Bill Roggio, "Analysis: Mumbai Attack Differs From Past Terror Strikes," *The Long War Journal* (November 28, 2008), *http://www.longwarjournal. org;* See also Jeremy Kahn and Salman Masood, "More Mumbai Links to Pakistan and Hostage Abuse," *The New York Times* (December 4, 2008), p. 1, *http://www.nytimes.com.*
55. Nur Criss, "The Nature of PKK Terrorism in Turkey," *Studies in Conflict and Terrorism*, 18 (January–February 1995), pp. 17–38.
56. Dogu Egil, "Suicide Terrorism in Turkey," *Civil Wars*, 3 (2000), pp. 37–54.
57. For example, see Rohen Gunaratna, *Inside al Qaeda: A Global Network of Terror* (New York: Columbia University Press, 2002); Roland Jacqard, *In the Name of Osama Bin Laden: Global Terror and the Bin Laden Brotherhood* (London and Durham, NC: Duke University Press, 2002).
58. "Over 60 Percent of Suicide Bombers are Physically Disabled," Human Security Report Project, *Afghanistan Conflict Monitor* (October 22, 2008), *http://www.afghanconflictmonitor.org.*
59. *The Russia Journal* (July 8, 2000), *http://www. russiajournal.com/.*
60. Pape, *Dying to Win*, pp. 116–25.
61. "The War Comes Home," *Asiaweek* (October 26, 2001), pp. 24–27; See also, Rommel C. Banlaoi, "The Rise of Rajah Soliaman Movement: Suicide Terrorism in the Philippines," *Institute of Defense and Strategic Studies* (IOSS Commentaries, October 9, 2008).
62. For example, see Edwin Shneidman, *Definition of Suicide* (New York: Aronson, Jason Publishers, 1995); Edwin Shneidman, *Voices of Death* (New York: Harper and Row, 1980).
63. For example, see World Health Organization, *Figures and Facts about Suicide: World Health Organization Mental and Behavioral Disorders Team* (Geneva: World Health Organization, 2001).
64. Jamison, *Night Falls Fast*, p. 48.
65. Ariel Merari, "The Readiness to Kill and Die: Suicide Terrorism in the Middle East," in *Origins of Terrorism: Psychologies, Ideologies, Theologies, States of Mind*, ed. Walter Reich, (Washington, DC: Woodrow Wilson Center Press, 1998), pp. 192–207.

66. For example, see Alfred Alvarez, *The Savage God: A Study of Suicide* (London: Weidenfeld and Nicolson, 1971); Thomas Joiner, *Why People Die by Suicide* (Cambridge, MA: Harvard University Press, 2007), pp. 16–46.

67. David Phillips, "The Influence of Suggestion on Suicide: Substantive and Theoretical Implications of the Werther Effect," *American Sociological Review*, 39 (June 1974), pp. 340–54; See also, J. W. Von Goethe (trans. R. D. Boylan), *The Sorrows of Young Werther* (Scotts Valley, CA: Create Space, 2008), *http://www.createspace.com.*

68. Drew Velting and Madelyn Gould, "Suicide Contagion," in *Review of Suicidology*, ed. W. Maris, et al. (New York: Guilford, 1997), pp. 3–22; Ira Wasserman, "Imitation and Suicide: A Reexamination of the Werther Effect," *American Sociological Review*, 49 (June 1984), pp. 427–36.

69. Jerome A. Motto, "Suicide and Suggestibility— The Role of the Press," *American Journal of Psychiatry*, 124 (August 1967), pp. 252–56.

70. For example, see William Berkan, *A Guide to Curriculum Planning in Suicide Prevention* (Madison: Wisconsin Department of Public Instruction, 1990).

71. For example, see Loren Coleman, *Suicide Clusters* (Boston, MA: Faber and Faber, 1986).

72. For example, see Shneidman, *Definition of Suicide*; Shneidman, *Voices of Death.*

73. For example, see Neil Livingstone and Terrell Arnold, *Fighting Back: Winning the War against Terrorism* (Lexington, MA: Lexington Books, 1986); Neil Livingstone, *The War against Terrorism* (Lexington, MA: Lexington Books, 1982).

74. Jacqard, *In the Name of Osama Bin Laden*, p. 48.

75. Jessica Stern, *The Ultimate Terrorists* (Cambridge, MA: Harvard University Press, 1999), pp. 84–85.

76. Alan Dershowitz, *Why Terrorism Works: Understanding the Threat, Responding to the Challenge* (New Haven, CT: Yale University Press, 2002), pp. 29–30.

77. Sam Bahour and Leila Bahour, Are Palestinians Human (2002), *http://www.awitness.org/.*

CHAPTER 9

Counterterrorist Measures: The Response

CHAPTER OBJECTIVES

The study of this chapter will enable you to:

- Understand the major trends in counterterrorist tactics that may have an impact on future policy decisions
- Differentiate between reactive and proactive counterterrorist strategies
- Identify steps in the intelligence-gathering process
- Describe the difficulties in the application of covert operations
- Explain the need for a legal framework that increases the opportunity of prosecution of terrorists
- Discuss the various strategies for defeating the spread of terrorism, such as the USA Patriot Act (2001)

INTRODUCTION

In the preceding chapters it was stated that contemporary terrorism produces a credible threat to the security and stability of democratic nations. The social impact of an indiscriminate terrorist campaign of bombing, suicide bombing, or hostage taking cannot be overstated. Democratic governments must respond to the nature of the potential threat of terrorism. However, since contemporary terrorism first erupted onto the world stage in the late 1960s, that response has been less than adequate. In 1970, the U.S. State Department recorded 302 terrorist incidents around the world.[1] Democratic governments reacted in near panic since they had neither a common response nor the resources or equipment to counter terrorism. This lack of a coordinated response became particularly evident during the attack on the World Trade Center and the Pentagon on September 11, 2001. The result has been a critical examination of counterterrorism strategies and governmental policy decisions regarding a viable response to the growing threat of indiscriminate terrorism.

President Bush stated that the U.S. government has a sacred duty to protect the homeland from terrorist attacks. On October 8, 2001, President Bush established the **Office of Homeland Security** with the responsibility of creating a national strategy to mobilize, organize, and secure the U.S. homeland from terrorist attacks. In July 2002 President Bush released the first *National Strategy for Homeland Security.* The terrorist attacks of September 11, 2001, reinforced the threat of large-scale attacks in the United States, and the anthrax attacks that followed marked the first fatal use of a biological weapon in the United States.[2]

In attempting to implement the strategy, police and government officials may take positive action at three different stages of possible involvement in combating terrorism. The first stage is to deter acts of terrorism before they occur. Several options can be identified: (1) tighten security measures at airports, nuclear plants, or any critical industry; (2) design a general public awareness program to reduce sympathy for the terrorist cause and provide an early warning system of the terrorist threat level; (3) develop effective intelligence gathering that leads to the apprehension of terrorists; and (4) find the causes of increased terrorist activity, particularly terrorist acts directed at democratic nations. If these steps fail, then police and government officials must "manage" the terrorist incident or respond with the maximum use of force.

The second stage involves such strategies as improving hostage negotiation skills and the use of various elite military units, either working within existing armed forces or as an auxiliary to counterterrorist police squads. The responsibility of these specialized military units is to provide a quick reaction force to respond to **skyjackings**, kidnappings, bombings, and assassinations. By the late 1970s, no self-respecting democratic nation or police agency was without its own highly trained, elite, counterterrorist SWAT team. By 2002, the use of a military counterterrorist strike force was expanded to include preemptive or retaliatory measures to prevent terrorist attacks or to punish terrorist organizations.

Finally, if the act of terrorism is successfully completed and the terrorist escapes from the scene, then law enforcement authorities must locate, apprehend, prosecute, and convict the terrorist. Therefore, the third stage involves the enactment of domestic antiterrorist legislation and the acknowledgment of international treaties. To this end, the USA Patriot Act enhances law enforcement's ability to fight terrorism. In sum, the focus of this chapter is to examine several policy options open to police and government officials in their efforts to combat terrorism. The intent is not to analyze specific policies in depth but rather to explore several possible considerations for controlling, combating, responding, and reducing terrorist acts.

SECURITY MEASURES

Typically, security measures include intrusion detection systems, barriers, panic alarms, uniformed guards, and a highly visible patrol force. The concept of deterring acts of terrorism is based on the old police formula for preventing crime, that is, *desire + opportunity = crime.* The police have little effect on controlling the desire to commit crime, but the opportunity to carry out a criminal event can be greatly reduced by a highly visible patrol force. Likewise, the opportunity to execute a terrorist act can be significantly reduced by tightening the security around potential targets. For example, once security measures were adopted seriously by commercial air carriers and airports, skyjackings were reduced by 65 percent.[3] In 1973, the introduction of metal detectors and uniformed security guards further reduced the number of skyjackings of domestic and international flights. Approximately ten skyjackings a year have been recorded worldwide between 1973 and 2002.[4] Undoubtedly the number of skyjackings can be reduced.

Securing aircraft from all potential terrorist threats is a monumental task. In general, passengers, crew, and cargo placed on the aircraft as baggage, or nonpassenger cargo such as mail or general cargo, can cause potential terrorist threats. There is no screening technology that is completely foolproof. Equally important is the fact that much of the nonpassenger cargo carried on commercial passenger aircraft is only casually screened for explosive material.[5] The task of screening nonpassenger cargo is hampered by physical and technical limitations such as the lack of screening equipment for bulky cargo and the space to set up screening equipment.

According to Burshtein, cargo aircraft pose a significant terrorist threat. In fact, in December 2003, the Department of Homeland Security issued a warning that al Qaeda may be planning to use cargo planes to carry out attacks on nuclear plants, bridges, or dams in the United States. The potential for cargo aircraft to cause even greater damage than passenger aircraft if flown into a building or other group target is amplified by the greater kinetic energy provided by the substantially greater weight of cargo aircraft.[6]

Airport security primarily depends on two security strategies. The first is the use of behavioral profiling. Although profiling is a very controversial technique, a well-trained security person can often detect suspicious passengers or potential terrorist hijackers. The second strategy relies on detection technology. After the 9/11 attacks, the Transportation and Security Administration introduced a variety of sophisticated detection systems to ensure safe air travel. For example, advanced X-ray technologies, biometrics identification, castscope, explosive detection systems, explosive trace detection, paperless boarding passes, threat image projection, trace portals, sensit, and whole body imaging are now in place at most U.S. airports.[7]

The goal of the U.S. Department of Homeland Security, through the Transportation Security Administration (TSA), is to protect the transportation systems of the United States. This protection goes well beyond the physical screening of airline passengers. It begins with intelligence information gathered by multiple law enforcement agencies, including the FBI, CIA, and NSA. Every passenger manifest is checked against terror watch lists. In addition, law enforcement personnel observe individual behaviors and activities in the airport milieu, often with the assistance of pilots, flight crews, and airport managers—all in an effort to prevent acts of terrorism and skyjacking.[8]

The 9/11 attacks shattered the illusion of national security. All Americans who traveled by air became potential terrorist targets. The 9/11 attacks made airline safety a national obsession. By 2009, the TSA had established twenty layers of security to ensure the safety of the traveling public. Each layer alone is capable of preventing a terrorist attack. In combination, the security value of the layer system creates a much stronger, formidable security system. A terrorist organization or a "lone wolf" who has to outwit multiple layers of security is likely to be deterred or apprehended during an attempted skyjacking.[9]

More than eight years after the 9/11 attacks, al Qaeda's top leaders are still at large, presiding over a reorganized global terrorist network, determined to continue their terrorist attacks against the United States. Supporters of al Qaeda have made several attempts to penetrate airline security in the United States and abroad. Richard Reid tried to detonate a bomb hidden in his shoe; an al Qaeda training manual recovered in Afghanistan encouraged al Qaeda operatives to hijack airplanes and fly them into the Statue of Liberty, football stadiums, and nuclear power plants; in 2004, British police uncovered a plot to fly a hijacked airliner into a passenger terminal at Heathrow Airport; in 2005, federal authorities prevented a plot to hijack a plane and crash it into the U.S. Bank Tower, the tallest building in Los Angeles; and in 2007, a scheme to blow up transatlantic airplanes with liquid explosives was uncovered by police in London. Al Qaeda or al Qaeda "wannabes" have not given up on finding a way to penetrate airline security. The layered approach to airline safety appears to be working.

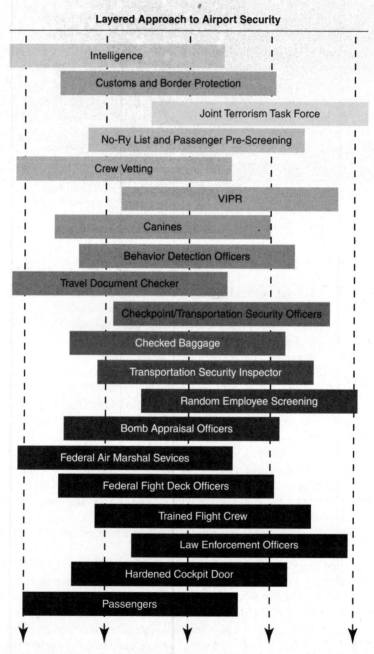

Layered Approach to Airport Security

- Intelligence
- Customs and Border Protection
- Joint Terrorism Task Force
- No-Ry List and Passenger Pre-Screening
- Crew Vetting
- VIPR
- Canines
- Behavior Detection Officers
- Travel Document Checker
- Checkpoint/Transportation Security Officers
- Checked Baggage
- Transportation Security Inspector
- Random Employee Screening
- Bomb Appraisal Officers
- Federal Air Marshal Sevices
- Federal Fight Deck Officers
- Trained Flight Crew
- Law Enforcement Officers
- Hardened Cockpit Door
- Passengers

FIGURE 9.1   Layers of Security: Airports (Transportation Security Administration)

Note: VIPR—Visual Intermodal Protection Response. To learn more about the individual layers of security, see Transportation Security Administration at *http://www.tsa.gov/approach/layered_strategy.shtm*

Al Qaeda's approach to the jihad is centered on deception and imagination. Al Qaeda's strategy seeks to wear down its enemies, attacking them when they are least prepared. An integral part of al Qaeda's strategy is the use of threats in an effort to exploit our fears and anxiety, forcing us to divert a large part of our resources to security. So far security systems in the United States have worked and al Qaeda is on the run.

In the long term, the establishment of such security options would restrict easy access to aircraft and airports by determined skyjackers. Unquestionably, the proposed options would increase the risk for skyjackers and decrease the possibility of carrying out a successful skyjacking. Certainly passenger morale and sense of security would improve with the presence of sky marshals, television monitors, and bomb detection devices. The proposed layered-security options can help solve the problem of skyjacking, but they are not without some drawbacks. Airport security managers must also consider possible disadvantages that on the surface may not be as readily apparent.

The proposed security options are expensive, inconvenient to passengers, time-consuming to implement, and may infringe upon individual rights in a free and open society. The development of sophisticated detectors requires high-cost research. The presence of sky marshals may endanger the lives of passengers since an armed confrontation with skyjackers is more likely. For example, most airports have resisted any increased security measures because passengers dislike being searched or having their behavior monitored by television cameras. Increased security measures also result in displacement so that terrorists shift from high-security targets to less likely ones. The clandestine nature of terrorist groups poses problems for security personnel. In order to deal successfully with the potential threat of terrorism, security authorities need information about terrorist groups and their strategies. The planning of preventive security measures requires solid information-gathering techniques.[10]

Relevant information must also be provided to the general public. It is a well-documented psychological observation that individuals who are threatened react more confidently to the threat if their awareness is heightened by practical information. Subsequently, the U.S. government has provided a color-coded terrorist threat alert system (see Table 9.1). The then Secretary of Homeland Security Tom Ridge established the threat advisory chart six months after the 9/11 attacks. The national threat level has not changed from yellow (elevated) since January 2004. The threat level for the aviation industry has been set at orange or "high" since the 2006 arrests of several terrorist suspects charged with planning to blow up commercial aircraft flying from Great Britain to the United States.

President Obama referred to the color-coded alert system as "the politics of fear." He has appointed former governor of Arizona Janet Napolitano as the new "czar" of Homeland Security. In March 2009, Secretary Napolitano launched a review of the color-coded system.

The type of information that could be most useful in desensitizing the general public about terrorism falls into three broad categories. First, the historical background of specific terrorist organizations can reduce the mystery of clandestine operations and political objectives of a campaign of terrorism. However, the dissemination of such information may provide terrorist groups with much needed publicity. The information must then emphasize the indiscriminate nature of the extranormal violence of the terrorist act and must not reflect the propaganda designed to generate sympathy for so-called freedom fighters.

Second, information about counterterrorist strategies can reassure the general public that active steps are being taken to reduce the threat of future terrorist actions. Third, forecasts about the capacity, frequency, and intensity of future terrorist operations may reduce the individual fear and general feelings of dread in democratic countries under siege by terrorism. Without such information, the public may envision an escalation of terrorism more threatening than what has actually occurred. In sum, the mass media must provide reliable, factual, and accurate information about

TABLE 9.1 Terrorism Alert Levels	
The five levels of terrorism alerts outlined by the Office of Homeland Security	

Red	Yellow
Severe risk of terrorist attacks	**Significant risk of terrorist attacks**
• Assign emergency response personnel and pre-position specially trained teams. • Monitor, redirect, or constrain transportation systems. • Close public and government facilities. • Increase or redirect personnel to address critical emergency needs.	• Increase surveillance of critical locations. • Coordinate emergency plans with nearby jurisdictions. • Assess further refinement of protective measures within the context of the current threat information. • Implement, as appropriate, contingency and emergency response plans.

Orange	Blue
	Guarded condition; general risk of terrorist attacks
High risk of terrorist attacks	• Check communications with designated emergency response or command locations. • Review and update emergency response procedures. • Provide the public with necessary information.
• Coordinate necessary security efforts with federal, state, and local law enforcement agencies or National Guard or other appropriate armed forces.	

	Green
• Take additional precautions at public events and possibly consider alternative venues or cancellations. • Prepare to work at an alternate site or with a dispersed workforce. • Restrict access to threatened facilities to essential personnel only.	**Low risk of terrorist attacks** • Refine and exercise planned protective measures. • Ensure emergency personnel receive training. • Assess facilities for vulnerabilities and take measures to reduce them.

Source: USA Patriot Act.

terrorism and the political objectives of terrorist groups. Factual information is also required in the gathering of accurate intelligence data on the nature of terrorist groups and potential terrorist targets.

INTELLIGENCE FUNCTION

The need for adequate intelligence is of vital importance. Intelligence information is the first line of defense against political terrorism. The organizational structures, methods of operation, and political objectives of terrorist groups must be fully understood by police and government authorities. This is a difficult undertaking since terrorist groups strive for secrecy in order to ensure the advantage of the element of surprise. Terrorist tactics depend on the use of surprise to achieve tactical objectives. Wardlaw suggests that by utilizing surprise terrorists achieve the following goals:

1. Force police and military personnel into unplanned actions.
2. Create violent situations that police and security planners are unprepared to deal with.
3. Capitalize on the use of unexpected tactics.
4. Disperse security personnel by diversionary tactics.
5. Create the illusion of the relative strength of the terrorist group.[11]

FIGURE 9.2 Former Homeland Security Director Tom Ridge describes the color-coded alert threat system with the Homeland Security Advisory Council. (AP/Wide World Photos)

Obviously the element of surprise puts police and security forces at a great disadvantage, thus the need for pertinent intelligence information. But surprise is not the only disadvantage.

Terrorist groups are typically small, and their clandestine operations are organized in such a manner as to limit the flow of information even within the terrorist organization itself. Contemporary terrorist groups such as those inspired by al Qaeda prefer the cellular model of organization with three to five members in each cell. The cellular organization places its greatest emphasis on the secrecy and security of group communication. Therefore, before any counterterrorist measure can be undertaken, overt or covert, police and government planners must have in their possession solid documentation of terrorist objectives. So when U.S. State Department officials, for example, argue about a military strike against terrorist training camps, how do they locate these terrorists?

Historically, a covert operator, whether a government agent or an informant, has proven to be the most valuable source in obtaining intelligence information on terrorist groups. However, the use of undercover operatives is extremely dangerous. The fanaticism and intensity of terrorist groups today make covert penetration of terrorist groups especially difficult. Most terrorist groups have international ties to some extent and therefore are suspicious of new group members. An alternative to the undercover operative is the cultivation of an informant who is an active member of the terrorist group. Several democratic countries, including the United Kingdom, have used this strategy successfully.

In the early 1980s, police in Northern Ireland broke through the organizational structure of the PIRA. Under intense questioning and the promise of immunity from prosecution, several PIRA men agreed to inform. Acting on information supplied by informers, the Royal Ulster Constabulary (RUC) was able to make a number of arrests and uncover several weapons caches.[12] The use of informants continues to be an important tactic in attempts by British intelligence, the British army, and the RUC to curtail the terrorist campaign of various IRA-affiliated terrorist groups. Wilson reminds us that having productive informants is essential and indispensable in virtually all criminal terrorist cases.[13] If, however, the use of undercover agents or the development of informants proves to be too dangerous and difficult, other sources of intelligence gathering may be pursued.

A variety of intelligence information useful to police and government officials can be found in an analysis of the political, military, economic, and scientific and technical operations of proclaimed terrorist groups.

Political intelligence includes intelligence about the terrorist group's support for a specific political ideology or philosophy. A variety of issues might be relevant: the group's relations with Iraq, Afghanistan, North Korea, Sudan, Iran, Syria, Libya, or Cuba; policies and attitudes relating to the Israeli–Arab conflict; support for other terrorist or revolutionary groups; and the perception of the United States, particularly related to the presence of U.S. military bases on foreign soil.

Military intelligence is required for several situations. For example, what types of weapons do terrorist groups prefer and who supplies those weapons? In addition, the size and capability of terrorist forces as well as the location of training bases and readiness to carry out acts of violence must be continually monitored. George Tenet, former director of the CIA, stated that the free world is engaged in a new form of low-intensity warfare carried out by highly trained and dedicated terrorists under the military control of various nations that sponsor surrogate warfare.[14] This low-intensity conflict is directed by an enemy that is difficult to locate and even more difficult to defend against; thus, there is a need for relevant military intelligence information.

Economic intelligence involves the evaluation of evidence concerning financial resources. How do terrorists get their money and how do they spend it? Adams insists that no serious study on how terrorists obtain funding existed until he published *The Financing of Terror*.[15] In this excellent volume, Adams describes several strategies terrorists use to fatten their war chests. These strategies include the sale of illegal narcotics, armed robbery, kidnapping for ransom, control of illegal activities, donations from individual contributors, charitable front organizations, lotteries and raffles, and gifts from states that sponsor terrorism.

On September 24, 2001, President Bush issued an executive order freezing all U.S. assets of terrorists, terrorist organizations, and their sponsors and associates and banned all financial dealings with terrorist organizations. The prohibited transactions include making donations and contributions to or for the benefit of terrorists. The list of terrorist organizations, individual sponsors of terrorism, and charitable front organizations for terrorist groups continues to expand. As of this writing, over 200 terrorist organizations, individuals, and charitable organizations have had their assets frozen in the United States and around the world by cooperating governments. To date, over $300 million in terrorist assets have been frozen. This is money that would have been used to finance terrorist operations, purchase weapons and explosives, and conduct research on weapons of mass destruction.

Scientific and technical intelligence includes monitoring the development and availability of new technologies to terrorist groups. The capability of acquiring chemical, biological, or nuclear weapons should receive intelligence priority. The unknown factor revolves around the question: What are the possibilities that a terrorist group can somehow obtain weapons of mass destruction? According to the U.S. Office of Nuclear Material Safety and Safeguards, hundreds of pounds of weapons-grade uranium and plutonium have disappeared and are unaccounted for.[16] After the fall of the Soviet Union, it was widely believed that weapons of mass destruction, chemical, biological, and nuclear, had fallen into the hands of state sponsors of terrorism or terrorist groups. George Tenet told Congress "documents recovered from al Qaeda facilities in Afghanistan show that bin Laden was pursuing a sophisticated biological and chemical weapons research program."[17] In sum, the collection of terrorist intelligence information is costly, and a plethora of intelligence organizations disseminate intelligence information to various police and military authorities.

In the United States, intelligence information is collected via aircraft, ships, reconnaissance satellites, radar, clandestine operations, and covert intelligence stations. In general terms, the cost of collecting *all* kinds of intelligence information exceeds $20 billion per year in the United States. There are sixteen known intelligence agencies in the United States collecting information concerning terrorist activities. However, some intelligence organizations are well known, such as the Central Intelligence Agency (CIA), the National Security Agency (NSA), the State Department Bureau of Intelligence and Research (INR), the National Reconnaissance Office (NRO), and the Defense Intelligence Agency (DIA). However, other intelligence agencies, services, and offices exist that only marginally collect and disseminate intelligence on terrorism. For example, the International Association of Chiefs of Police provides update reports on terrorism in *Clandestine Tactics and Series*.[18]

In order to consolidate and enhance the analysis of terrorist intelligence gathering, President Bush in 2002 announced plans to create a new **Terrorist Threat Integration Center (TTIC)**. The TTIC will bring together the FBI's Counterterrorism Division, the CIA's Counterterrorism Center, and the Division of Homeland Security (DHS). The TTIC is designed to help minimize any problems that may result from collecting terrorist intelligence overseas and inside the United States. A new data management system has been implemented to ensure that terrorism-related information is shared by all appropriate intelligence agencies. In addition, the Information Analysis and Infrastructure Protection (IA/IP) unit allows the DHS to take specific action to protect the critical infrastructure of the United States.

Regardless of the source of data used, the process includes the collection, collation, analysis, and dissemination of data gathered on terrorism incidents and terrorist organizations. Table 9.2

TABLE 9.2   Intelligence Information Cycle

STEP 1 **Collecting Information/Intelligence**

Use established lines of communication
- Open sources (libraries, newspapers, periodicals)
- Criminal information sources (ICID, FBI, LEIN, CLETS, local/state/federal law enforcement agencies)
- Intelligence (military, federal, CIA, NSA, NRO, foreign intelligence services)
- Clandestine agents

STEP 2 **Analysis of Collected Information/Intelligence**

Determine if information meets requirements of three Rs:
- Relevant
- Reliable
- Rational

STEP 3 **Dissemination/Disposition**
- Determine classification (consider classified and unclassified sources)
- Get information to individuals who are decision makers
- Store information for easy retrieval
- Destroy information after use
- Develop new needs (forward requirements to the collector)
- Forecast trends and developments
- Evaluate problems
- Conduct threat analysis

describes the intelligence information cycle. The first step in the process is to collect information, data, and intelligence. The next step is the analysis of the information. Some information may be difficult to analyze since terrorist groups often conceal their true objectives by engaging in media campaigns of disinformation. The analyst must decide the validity and reliability of each piece of information. Then that information must be compared with existing information to determine new trends and to specifically identify individuals and terrorist or criminal organizations. The final step is to disseminate relevant information to police and military personnel by the most expedient and secure means available. Only by carefully analyzing terrorist information can command authorities conduct a relevant threat analysis.

A threat analysis is a comprehensive review of all available intelligence information in order to evaluate security measures in terms of potential terrorist targets and vulnerabilities. The elements of a complete threat analysis are included in the following proposition:

Threat analysis = terrorist information/intelligence + threat + vulnerabilities

The failure to review continuously the organization's overall threat assessment could seriously restrict police and military antiterrorism measures and the ability to conduct counterterrorist operations. If security measures prove inadequate and potential targets easy for terrorist groups to penetrate, and if intelligence indicates a dangerous threat to the safety and security of the state, then police and security managers must consider the use of elite military or police forces.

COUNTERTERRORIST OPERATIONS: RETALIATION AND PREEMPTION

Lethal acts of political terrorism continue to escalate in both numbers and ferocity despite improved physical security around potential terrorist targets, a public somewhat better informed about terrorism, and the collection of relevant intelligence information. Terrorist groups now appear to be more inclined to conduct large-scale, indiscriminate attacks against completely innocent victims. The trend in the twenty-first century is to attack public places such as airport terminals, subway systems, trains, residential housing areas, and public gatherings. Such attacks are calculated to kill as many innocent people as possible. This lethality of terrorist assaults has led democratic nations to consider the use of retaliation and preemptive military strikes against terrorist bases, training facilities, and countries that sponsor terrorism.

Since 1981, U.S. government officials have declared that the United States would employ force to preempt or retaliate for terrorist attacks. The purpose of such retaliation is to punish terrorists or criminals who have committed terrorist assaults and retreated to the safety of bases beyond the reach of conventional police or military forces. The guiding example of this type of retaliation is the Israeli commando raids on suspected Palestinian terrorist strongholds.

Israel was the first nation to articulate a deliberate and official policy of retaliation against terrorism. However, there certainly is a great deal of moral ambiguity about **preemptive strikes**. Many innocent bystanders have become victims of Israeli preemption. At times retaliatory strikes seem as terroristic as suicide bombings or random car bombings. Since 1951 the Israeli Defense Forces have conducted large reprisal raids and preemptive strikes against Palestinian guerrilla bases and hostile Arab countries. In practice, Israel frequently goes beyond the principle of "an eye for an eye," seeking to inflict maximum casualties on Palestinian extremists and hostile Arab countries. Such was the case in October 1953 at the Palestinian village of Qibya, where Israeli forces killed forty-two men, women, and children in retaliation for the terrorist murder of an Israeli woman and two children.[19] On June 7, 1981, Israel destroyed the Iraqi nuclear facility at Osirak in a preemptive bombing raid. Israel claimed Iraq was close to attaining a nuclear military option that they would unleash against the state of Israel. In an earlier preemptive campaign, Israeli agents assassinated German scientists who were working on Egypt's military long-range rocket program. The campaign was known as operation Damocles and resulted in the deaths of at least five German scientists between 1961 and 1963.[20] Israel has conducted hundreds of retaliatory raids and preemptive strikes against "hostile" Palestinian targets. The practice was sanctioned by the Israeli people and was especially popular among the nationalistic elements of the Israeli population. This has not been the case in the United States.

Although public support in the United States for retaliatory strikes against terrorist groups and sponsoring nations is strong in the wake of a major terrorist episode, that support quickly vanishes once the terrorist incident ends. Many government officials and citizens of the United States are uncertain about the use of military force to cope with terrorism. There is no doubt that the democratic principles embraced by the United States create ambiguities about the moral aspects of using military force, particularly bombing raids. One school of thought argues that retaliation only invites terrorists to escalate their strategy of indiscriminate violence. Another school of thought believes that retaliation is necessary to demonstrate American resolve not to be passive victims of indiscriminate acts of terrorist violence. During the course of intense debate and heated rhetoric on this issue, President Reagan signed, on April 3, 1984, the National Security Decision Directive 138, which permits the United States to use retaliatory military force legally against terrorists who attack U.S. citizens, interests, or allies.[21] U.S. targets of retaliation have been identified as individual terrorists, terrorist training camps, or any country that sponsors, aids, or abets terrorist organizations.

The United States is now committed to a policy of retaliation, which was not always the case. In fact, former Vice President George Bush and Secretary of Defense Caspar Weinberger resisted the concept of retaliation and preemptive strikes against terrorist facilities. One writer summarized the opinion of many observers who felt that because of a lack of information it is doubtful that the United States will ever carry out a successful retaliatory military strike against terrorist bases.[22] President Reagan acknowledged this fact, stating that the lack of precise information regarding terrorists keeps the United States from retaliating against known terrorist strongholds.[23]

But on April 4, 1986, the United States finally struck back at terrorist training operations. U.S. intelligence services allegedly intercepted several messages between Muammar Gaddafi of **Libya** and his agents in West Berlin.[24] According to the U.S. State Department, the intercepted messages provided the first clear and detailed evidence of Libyan participation in a terrorist attack. Libyan terrorists had bombed a Berlin nightclub frequented by U.S. servicemen. One U.S. soldier was killed and several were seriously injured. The evidence of Libyan complicity in terrorist attacks directed against U.S. citizens was viewed as irrefutable by the Reagan administration. Amid controversy and internal dissension, President Reagan made plans for a retaliatory air strike against suspected Libyan terrorist training bases.

The planned "surgical" air strike, code-named Operation El Dorado Canyon, began on Monday, April 14, 1986. Twenty-four F-111s from the 48th Tactical Fighter Wing along with various support aircraft left southern England and headed toward the Mediterranean and Libya. Five hours later, after a 2,800-mile flight, the aircraft, now reduced to thirteen fighters, began their attack on Tripoli, Libya. The targets consisted of two military airfields, a military barracks, a training center for elite naval personnel, and Gaddafi's headquarters. While all the targets were hit, several nontargets came under attack as well. The fears expressed by critics of the retaliatory strike were all too accurate. The primary fear concerned the impossibility of reliably distinguishing between military targets and civilian areas. Several civilian houses were hit as well as the French and Swiss embassies, a community park, and a children's playground. Six men, three women, and two children were killed, including Gaddafi's 15-month-old adopted daughter. Sixty civilians were injured, including two of Gaddafi's other children. Later it was reported that forty people were killed. The Libyans used the casualties to great political advantage. The world's press focused on the injuries to the innocent victims, visiting hospitals and photographing dead children. These pictures were spread throughout the world, depicting the United States as a military superpower that badly overreacted.[25]

All aircraft, except one F-111 that had been hit by anti-aircraft fire and crashed, returned safely to their bases.[26] The mission, viewed in strictly military terms, was deemed a success. But the political fallout that resulted from the raid was far greater than the military success. The United States' NATO allies in Europe condemned the raid. Politicians and citizens in Britain, France, Spain, and Italy overwhelmingly opposed the raid. In contrast, Americans hailed the raid, and support for President Reagan's tough new stand against terrorism was high.

More practically, the immediate aftermath of the raid seemed to confirm earlier observations that retaliation equals greater retaliation and escalation. Two British and one American hostage being held for several months in Lebanon were executed. The British ambassador's residence in Beirut was attacked; also in Beirut a British journalist was hanged and another was taken hostage. A U.S. employee was shot in Khartoum, and an attempt to bomb London's Heathrow Airport was uncovered by British security police. Attacks were made on U.S. embassies in Mexico, Indonesia, and Tokyo, and U.S. military bases in West Germany, Spain, and Japan. Certainly this violence was in reprisal for the U.S. raid on Libya. Given the high cost of the U.S. preempted air strike on Libya, did the benefits make it worthwhile?

On the one hand, Adams concludes that the United States made a serious political, military, and moral mistake by bombing Libya.[27] He concluded that the result of the bombing raid created new complications within the NATO alliance and an escalation of terrorism against NATO targets. The distinction between state-sponsored terrorism and reprisals by democratic nations then became difficult to evaluate. On the other hand, former Secretary of State George Shultz argued that terrorists are murderers and lawbreakers, and the United States should take forceful action against them.[28] Shultz claimed there was no moral question. The United States merely responded to acts of indiscriminate murder by considering both the use and effectiveness of military force as a weapon against future attacks. The argument maintained that failure to strike back forcefully encourages more attacks against Americans. A policy of retaliation would make it clear to international terrorist groups that Americans traveling abroad are not soft targets and that the United States has an obligation to its citizens to punish murderers beyond the reach of the U.S. legal system.

There is little doubt that Libya was an easy target. Repeating such attacks to counter an expected rise in anti-American terrorism in the future would be extremely difficult. The United States is not Israel. The Israelis are determined to destroy the PLO/PA, Hamas, and Hizballah and refuse to yield to hostage takers, skyjackers, or bombers. But Israel is engaged in an undeclared war with several Arab states and various Palestinian terrorist groups and, as such, has no moral ambiguity over the use of retaliation or preemptive air strikes. Like Israel, Livingstone and Arnold believe that the United States and other Western democracies are involved in a state of war with nations that sponsor international terrorism.[29] Only by acknowledging the magnitude of the terrorist problem can the United States take active steps to combat it.

Undoubtedly, in the current global "war on terrorism" (GWOT), the United States and allied forces have been successful. The U.S. response to terrorist threats since 9/11 has been to move from a traditional law enforcement investigative approach toward preventive intervention. The U.S. has moved from a defensive position to one of preemptive war. The Taliban regime in Afghanistan has been on the run. Al Qaeda training bases in Afghanistan have been destroyed, and many key figures of al Qaeda have been killed or captured. The preemptive U.S. attack on Iraq resulted in the ouster and capture of Iraq's brutal dictator Saddam Hussein. The attacks on the Taliban in Afghanistan and Iraq all began with retaliatory preemptive air strikes, followed by ground assault troops. When there is no other effective response to counter an immediate terrorist threat, preemptive military strikes can be justified. The United States and its NATO allies are only now beginning to realize that a state of low-intensity warfare exists with nations that support terrorist activities. In his first term as Israeli prime minister, Netanyahu unequivocally stated that the United States and other Western democracies were clearly justified in waging defensive as well as offensive war against nations such as Afghanistan, Sudan, Libya, Iraq, Syria, and Iran, which sponsor international terrorism.[30] The current rhetoric proposed by the U.S. State Department supports not only retaliatory air raids but also the organization of a covert counterterrorist squad that would infiltrate and make preemptive military strikes against terrorist training facilities.

COVERT MILITARY OPERATIONS: PROACTIVE MEASURES

The objectives of commando-type assaults would be to inflict casualties on terrorists and destroy their base of operation. The plan would use a clandestine military force to track down and penetrate terrorist groups in an effort to defeat the terrorist threat. This clandestine, or Special Operations Force (SOF), is not new to U.S. military adherents of guerrilla-style warfare. However, military traditionalists who prefer to plan for an all-out, conventional-style war oppose the formation and use of small guerrilla-type commando forces. High-ranking military staff planners opposed to special operations are concerned that an emphasis on clandestine tactics will reproduce Central Intelligence Agency involvement in mini-military projects. Military planners fear that the misuse of such SOFs by the CIA will create long-term problems for the United States by contributing to the escalation of terrorism and low-intensity warfare.[31]

CIA covert actions have been directed at all major areas of conflict in the world—Africa, the Middle East, Eastern Europe, Asia, and Latin America. Covert actions by the CIA include a wide range of activities: (1) political advice, (2) subsidies to individuals, (3) financial support to political "democratic" groups, (4) disinformation and propaganda campaigns, (5) private training of insurgent forces, (6) paramilitary operations designed to overthrow a government, and (7) assassinations.[32] Probably the best known of the CIA covert actions are the ones directed at Cuba. Not only did the CIA attempt to assassinate Castro several times, but it also planned the Bay of Pigs invasion, trained guerrilla forces in the swamps of Florida for that invasion, conducted sabotage and economic warfare, and was involved in a variety of propaganda and disinformation activities.[33] But the covert action that has generated the greatest adverse publicity was the one directed at the Sandinista government in Nicaragua. The Nicaraguan CIA paramilitary operation clearly highlights the issues involved in covert activities.

The issues of adopting a policy of **covert operations** in the United States are both ethical and practical. Under what conditions are covert actions morally justified? Does the history of U.S. covert operations suggest that such actions have a long-term benefit for U.S. national interests in the complicated world of foreign policy in efforts to defeat international terrorism?

Several U.S. presidents have sanctioned military covert operations. President Kennedy authorized a program of sabotage against Cuba. President Ford argued that covert military operations were acceptable international strategies. President George W. Bush stated that "every country" has the right to use covert actions when it believes its national interests are threatened.[34]

The implication of such presidential remarks is the acceptability of covert military operations when there is a direct, immediate threat to the national security of democratic nations. There is no doubt that the U.S. government feels physically threatened by a variety of international terrorist groups, especially al Qaeda, the jihadist movement, and the countries that support them. The benefits of adopting covert military operations as a planned governmental policy are several:

1. The directness of the military assault would cause the terrorists to lose face and prestige.
2. Covert operations would be less objectionable than air strikes and would likely lessen world criticism by eliminating "collateral damage."
3. Actions could be accomplished with military forces already trained and in position to act.
4. Military objectives would be selective and attacks on specific terrorist targets would lessen operational casualties.
5. The costs would be much lower than air strikes.
6. Democracies are not morally, ethically, or legally bound to deal in a civilized fashion with those who seek to destroy the democratic way of life.

On the other side of the issue, it is difficult to justify a policy of covert military operations to attack terrorists or their sponsors. Such a policy has several pitfalls:

1. The operations unit would be in danger of capture.
2. A failed mission would be embarrassing to the United States and discredit a policy of planned retaliation.
3. If the commando unit is withdrawn before completion of the mission, policymakers run the risk of escalation of the problem.
4. Intelligence information in covert operations often is inadequate and inaccurate.
5. The cooperation of friendly forces and nations is essential for success; however, most nations would not support such covert U.S. actions for fear of retaliation by terrorists or their sponsors.
6. Small wars have a tendency to escalate into larger wars.
7. The history of U.S. covert operations does not support the view that such operations serve the long-term interests of the United States.

The issue of covert military operations has been debated for decades. But until the policymakers face up to the realities of terrorism and low-intensity conflict, the United States will remain a highly visible and too often helpless target. Traditionally, the role of the U.S. military in counterterrorist operations has been one of "reaction" rather than "proaction."

COUNTERTERRORIST OPERATIONS: REACTIVE MEASURES

In the recent past, the deployment of military forces for internal security duties in democratic nations has produced much controversy. The increase of random political terrorism has caused the governments of Britain, Canada, Germany, Australia, France, and Italy to call out the troops to provide internal protection and to assist the police in searching for terrorist hideouts. In 1970, the Canadian government invoked the War Measures Act, enabling government troops to conduct a search of residential areas of Montreal in an attempt to apprehend terrorist hostage takers of the

Front Liberation du Quebec (FLQ), who had abducted James Cross, the British trade commissioner. The War Measures Act gave the Canadian government forces broad legal powers of detention for questioning and abrogated individual rights related to search and seizure. The act remained in force for approximately six months. Since 1969, British security forces have seen duty in Northern Ireland attempting to defeat the terrorist activities of the PIRA and various reactionary Protestant paramilitary groups. In Germany, Spain, and Italy, government troops have been called into action to provide security for airports, to guard transport routes, to protect government officials, and to search the countryside for terrorist bases and safe houses. In October 2002, elite Russian troops were used to rescue hostages being held by Chechan terrorists in a Moscow theater. All these incidents have caused heated arguments about the role of governmental armed forces in support of civil authorities responding to terrorist attacks. In sum, what are the specific roles of the armed forces and the police in internal security problems in a democracy?

Nearly all writers on terrorism are concerned with the need to maintain a balance between security measures used to protect against terrorism and individual rights of liberty and freedom. Dershowitz argues that as far as possible the local police should provide for the internal security of citizens and that the distinctive roles of police and military security forces need to be clearly defined.[35] Heavily armed detachments of military troops responding to control local internal matters, whether for homeland security or public order, may only serve to incite the citizenry against the government.

Using the military for homeland security raises many important legal questions. There are several laws that prohibit the use of the military in domestic civil situations. The most widely known is the **Posse Comitatus Act** of 1878. Historically, the United States has been reluctant to use military armed forces for internal security. In general, the Posse Comitatus Act prohibits the use of federal military forces' participation in frontline law enforcement activities, such as arrest, search, seizure, surveillance, or pursuit of suspected or convicted felons, except where authorized by the U.S. Constitution or the U.S. Congress. Hammond believes that the Posse Comitatus Act should be modified to further tighten legal restrictions on military law enforcement.[36] However, the U.S. military has been used to support several homeland security missions. For example, in October 2002, military reconnaissance aircraft were used in an attempt to locate the Washington, DC–area sniper.

On October 1, 2008, the Bush administration announced that the 1st Brigade Combat Team (BCT) of the 3rd Infantry Division will be an on-call federal response team used to respond to natural or human-made disasters, including terrorist attacks. This action marks the first time an active U.S. Army combat brigade has been given a specific civilian mission. By 2011, the U.S. military will have 20,000 troops in place to respond to domestic disasters. The formalized role of U.S. troops and the Bush administration's interpretation of the Posse Comitatus Act are the direct result of how ill prepared state and local police agencies were during Hurricane Katrina in 2005. The Bush administration advised Congress that the BCT only be used would in an advisory and support role as opposed to conventional law enforcement.[37]

Nonetheless, widespread confusion exists about Posse Comitatus and other statutes, such as the Insurrection Act, and the use of the military in domestic law enforcement situations. The *National Strategy for Homeland Security* states that laws governing the use of the military should be consolidated and that the federal government should publish a document that clearly delineates these laws.[38]

Acts defined as terrorism are crimes already proscribed by state and local statutes. Certain terrorist acts also violate federal criminal statutes. These include hijacking, kidnapping, hostage holding, bombing, and assassination. The lead agency for the management of terrorist incidents is the FBI. The initial tactical response and the resolution of incidents defined as terrorism are also the responsibility of the FBI. However, in the event that a prolonged terrorist attack erupts and exceeds the capacity of local civil police agencies or the FBI to control and resolve the incident, then the president has the option to use specially trained and equipped military forces to restore order and preserve life. For example, this presidential option was used during the urban riots of the 1960s when President Johnson stationed federal troops throughout the United States.

Civil authorities often call upon the U.S. military to assist in dealing with natural disasters such as fires, floods, or hurricanes, as well as civil unrest such as urban riots and drug trafficking. Large-scale incidents can create a significant demand for the use of military units. In fact, after the attacks on the World Trade Center and the Pentagon on 9/11, authorities discovered that a fourth hijacked plane was heading for the nation's capital. The U.S. Air Force scrambled several fighter aircraft to intercept and shoot down the hijacked jet, but the heroic efforts of some of the passengers to regain control of the aircraft caused it to crash in a field, killing all on board. Thus, certain actions by terrorists may raise the level of military involvement. The military may have to take the lead in responding to situations that take on the features of an "invasion."

President Bush has recognized the challenge ahead to protect the United States in the *National Strategy for Homeland Security*. The *National Strategy* has outlined three broad roles for the military to perform in the event of a domestic terrorist attack, including (1) carrying out homeland defense missions with support from other agencies, (2) responding to emergencies to provide support that civil agencies do not have, and (3) supporting lead federal agencies for "limited scope" missions such as national security for special events. Furthermore, the *National Strategy* also foresees specific details in combating terrorist operations:

> Military support to civil authorities pursuant to a terrorist threat or attack may take the form of providing technical support and assistance to law enforcement, assisting in the restoration of law and order; loaning specialized equipment; and assisting consequence management.[39]

SPECIAL OPERATIONS

Besides the protection of the homeland, the United States also has **special operations** forces ready to respond anywhere in the world to protect U.S. interests. Special operations forces include specially trained military units and some police units that specialize in unconventional operations. Although fairly large units can be deployed, small teams of operatives most often carry out special operations. For example, a large special operations force was deployed to Afghanistan in 2001, where they destroyed al Qaeda training facilities and forward bases. Special operations forces are trained for long-range reconnaissance, hostage rescues, punitive raids, surveillance, liaisons with allied counterterrorist teams, and abductions. One such abduction involved the apprehension of **Mir Aimal Kansi**.[40]

On January 25, 1993, an unknown assassin armed with an AK-47 assault rifle opened fire on employees of the Central Intelligence Agency who were sitting in their cars waiting to enter the main gate of the CIA's headquarters in Langley, Virginia. Two people were killed and three were seriously wounded. Mir Aimal Kansi, a Pakistani who lived in the United States since 1991, was the shooter. After the incident Kansi fled the United States for sanctuary in Afghanistan and Pakistan where he found refuge among family members and al Qaeda supporters.

The United States posted a $2 million reward for Kansi's capture and distributed wanted posters throughout the Middle East, Pakistan, and Afghanistan. After almost five years, the search for Kansi ended when an unidentified informant contacted U.S. authorities in Pakistan, revealing the location of Kansi. He was apprehended and arrested in June 1997 by an FBI special operations team with the assistance of the Pakistani government. Kansi was returned to the United States to stand trial for first-degree murder in a Virginia state court. At his trial, the prosecution argued that Kansi was motivated by revenge for the U.S. bombing of Iraq during the Gulf War. Kansi was convicted of murder on November 10, 1997, and was executed by lethal injection on November 14, 2002. The value of special operations and counterterrorist operations has been proven many times. The following illustrates the mission of special operations forces in the United States.

The secretive military unit known as **Delta Force** operates covertly in small teams outside of the United States. The mission of Delta Force includes hostage rescues, reconnaissance, and probably abductions. The Green Berets, or Special Forces Group, operate in units called A-teams. A-teams comprise military specialists whose skills include languages, intelligence gathering, medicine, and explosive and demolitions expertise. The primary mission of the A-teams is to provide military training to local or friendly insurgents, thus maximizing their operational strength. Another special operations group is the Navy Seals. The mission of the U.S. Navy Sea Air Land Forces (SEALs) is to conduct seaborne and harbor operations, although SEALs have also been used for land operations. However, when a large highly trained combat unit must be deployed, the United States sends the Army's 75th Ranger Regiment into action. In 2001, the 75th Ranger Regiment was deployed to Afghanistan to locate and destroy al Qaeda training bases. The Marines also have their own elite force called Recon units. These Recon units have basically the same mission as the A-team and SEALs. The dedication of a small number of specialized "rapid reaction" forces will enhance U.S. efforts to track down and bring terrorists to justice.

UNITED KINGDOM AND ISRAEL

Allies of the United States also have highly competent special operations forces that are worthy of a few words. The **Special Air Service (SAS)** is a secretive unit attached to the British Army that has been used repeatedly in counterterrorism operations. It is organized at a regimental level but operates in very small teams of four to five operatives. The SAS is similar to the U.S. Delta Force. It often trains with other antiterrorist units in the world, including the Delta Force. The SAS has been deployed to assignments in Northern Ireland and elsewhere throughout the world. It also responds to domestic terrorist incidents, such as rescuing hostages, defusing improvised explosives, and protecting governmental leaders. For example, in May 1980 the SAS rescued several hostages from the Iranian Embassy in London, killing the hostage takers.

The **Special Boat Service (SBS)** is another clandestine military unit under the command of the British Royal Navy. The SBS specializes in operations against seaborne targets and along the harbors and coastlines. For example, during the Gulf War in 1991 the SBS made raids on the Kuwaiti coast to draw Iraqi troops away from the frontal land assault by U.S. troops. The liberation of the British Embassy in Kuwait was the SBS's most successful operation. The SBS is equivalent to the U.S. Navy SEALs.

Yet another British counterterrorism team is the Royal Marine Commandos. The Royal Marines are a rapid-reaction force that can be deployed in large numbers or smaller clandestine units. Royal Marines joined the U.S.-led coalition against the Taliban and al Qaeda in Afghanistan. The unit of Royal Marines in Afghanistan specializes in high-mountain and extreme cold weather warfare. The Royal Marine Commandos are similar to the U.S. Marines Recon Units in size, training, and counterterrorist mission.

In Israel, the **Sayeret Matkal (SM)** or General Staff Reconnaissance was formed in 1957 to carry out top-secret intelligence-gathering missions against hostile Arab states and Palestinian guerrilla bands. The SM operates in small clandestine units where it has engaged in counterterrorism operations, often being quite ruthless, against a variety of Palestinian terrorist groups. An SM unit killed several top PLO leaders in reprisal for the Munich Olympic massacre of Israeli athletes. The SM's best-known operation occurred in 1976 with the rescue of 106 Israeli hostages at Entebbe Airport in Uganda. The Sayeret Matkal has been deployed in small units to penetrate deep into territory hostile to Israel, such as southern Lebanon. The primary target of the SM in southern Lebanon has been Hizballah.

The use of the military in a counterterrorist role, however, is not without its critics. Schoch writes that counterterrorism is basically a police function at which regular military units have generally shown themselves to be inept. Schoch identifies several problems. First, the deployment of large numbers of uniformed troops implies a serious terrorist threat exists that could be used to the propaganda advantage of terrorist groups. Second, the presence of military troops may incite violence rather than prevent it. Third, the commitment of troops indicates that less violent methods, such as negotiation, have failed, and terrorism cannot be controlled no matter how much force the government has at its disposal. Fourth, armed troops are more likely to be used for political reasons unacceptable in a democracy, where the roles of police and military are significantly different. Finally, counterterrorist operations should be limited to specific strike actions where there is no other option, and not expanded to include order maintenance or security responsibilities. In the case of skyjackings, every effort should be made to peacefully negotiate the release of hostages rather than attempt an ill-planned rescue mission.[41]

The containment of terrorism, as far as police are concerned, should be a police function handled by police agencies. Each police agency should have a specialized unit prepared to deal with explosives, hostage negotiations, and firearms. Only in extreme situations that the police are unable to handle should armed military troops be called out. In the absence of widespread social unrest, there is little justification for the use of large numbers of military troops or specialized counterterrorist units to respond to incidents of terrorism. The military should be assigned as a counterterrorist reaction force and again only in the most extreme circumstances. Presently in the United States and other democratic nations, with the exception of Israel perhaps, no situations exist that the police cannot cope with, although admittedly that could change. In the event that it does change and acts of terrorism present widespread threats to social order, then the use of elite military counterterrorist units may be needed. As long as democratic nations can avoid the use of military forces, they should do so. Attempts to control terrorism will always focus on the police response and the legal and treaty obligations rather than action-oriented military responses. The excellent research study of Jones and Libicki argues that terrorist groups usually end for two reasons. They decide to give up the use of violence and join the political process or police authorities kill or arrest key members of the terrorist group. The use of military force is effective only on terrorist groups that evolve into an insurgency; for example, al Qaeda in Iraq.[42]

NATIONAL GUARD

At the national level, the United States has organized several units that have counterterrorist responsibilities. The need for homeland security concerns has focused attention on the domestic role of the National Guard. The Guard is well prepared to provide assistance to civilian law enforcement agencies in an emergency situation involving acts of indiscriminate terrorism. The National Guard's potential contribution is an important dimension in responding to the threat of terrorism.

FIGURE 9.3   An armed National Guardsman on duty at the Jacksonville, Florida, International Airport alertly watches as passengers pass through a metal detector. (Oscar Sosa/AP/Wide World Photos)

The National Guard serves not only the citizens of the state but the president as well. Technically, the president has the authority to declare a state of emergency and take over all National Guard units in the United States, even if the governors of the states object to such a federal takeover. In the event of a disastrous terrorist incident equal to 9/11, the demand for National Guard support begins with a governor's call-up of guard personnel and moves through a call to federal service. In other words, the president can federalize Guard units to move between states or out of the United States as part of a national response to terrorism. The National Guard's experience in responding to the September 2001 terrorist attacks illustrates the challenge associated with its dual state–federal role. The magnitude of 9/11 compelled an immediate national response: The president wanted a coordinated national effort in response to the attacks on the World Trade Center and the Pentagon. Improving airport and border security measures were immediately required to prevent future terrorist attacks. The Guard continues to provide airport security and assist with border security.

The events of 9/11 and the anthrax attacks in the following weeks illustrate the challenge local, state, and federal governments face in responding effectively to pending terrorist threats. The problem the United States faces is to determine the most appropriate way to employ police personnel and National Guard units to protect citizens of the United States and to respond in a decisive manner to the terrorist threat. The pervasiveness of the terrorist threat, the increased probability of a terrorist attack, and the need to prepare for an effective response to terrorism are now well understood by government policymakers. Between 9/11 and January 2008, Osama bin Laden appeared in thirty videotapes or audiotapes threatening to destroy the United States. Ayman al Zawahiri has been even more prolific, starring in twice as many video and audio productions, delivering vague threats of future attacks against the United States. The possibility of a major terrorist attack on the U.S. homeland that would overwhelm even the best-prepared cities and states warrants consideration of deploying the National Guard. The deployment of National Guard units offers a great advantage to the nation in the long-term nature of the war on terrorism.

HRT AND NEST

Also at the national level, the United States has organized several law enforcement units that have counterterrorist capabilities. The most well known of these law enforcement units is the FBI's **hostagerescue team (HRT)**. The mission of the HRT is to be prepared to deploy to any location within four hours of notification by the director of the FBI. In 1982, the HRT was created as a special counterterrorist unit to offer a tactical operation for any extraordinary hostage crisis occurring within the United States. As part of the FBI's Critical Incident Response Group (CIRG), the HRT is composed of ninety-one special agents who are trained in hostage-rescue techniques and high-risk arrest situations. In its brief history, the HRT has been deployed over 200 times to negotiate and rescue hostages held by terrorists and violent criminals.

Not as well known is the Department of Energy's **Nuclear Emergency Search Team (NEST)**. In 1975, an extortionist threatened to blow up the city of Boston with an improvised nuclear device if he was not paid $200,000. To prove he was not bluffing, the extortionist sent a diagram of the nuclear weapon along with the ransom note to the Boston police. The accuracy of the diagrammed nuclear device caused police and Boston city officials to give in to the extortionist's demand and pay the $200,000 ransom. However, the unknown extortionist never picked up the ransom payment, leaving police officials wondering if the threat was just a hoax. Regardless, the alarm bells were sounded.

The Boston incident caused the federal government to establish NEST. NEST is responsible for disarming nuclear devices. It is comprised of more than 750 volunteer scientists, engineers, and technicians from the U.S. national scientific laboratories, such as Los Alamos, Scandia, and Lawrence Livermore. When deployed, NEST works closely with the U.S. Army's 2nd Ordinance Group, which specializes in disarming nuclear devices. Since 1975 NEST has evaluated over 110 nuclear threats and mobilized to respond to thirty credible threats. Even so, there has not been a successful attack on an operating nuclear reactor, a deliberate release of radioactive material, or a detonation by terrorists of a nuclear device.[43]

CHEMICAL AND BIOLOGICAL TERRORISM

The threat of terrorist attacks using chemical, biological, or radiological weapons with potentially catastrophic consequences is also of major concern to the *National Strategy for Homeland Security*. Al Qaeda's quest for chemical, biological, radiological, and nuclear (CBRN) weapons continues to this day. Jenkins reports that Osama bin Laden has met with Russian organized crime figures, Pakistani scientists, and Islamic jihadists in an effort to obtain CBRN.[44] There is no hard evidence that al Qaeda had any success in acquiring CBRN. Nonetheless, the Environmental Protection Agency is evaluating the upgrading of air monitoring stations to allow for the detection of certain chemical and biological substances, specifically sarin gas, smallpox, and anthrax. The ability to quickly recognize and report chemical and biological attacks will minimize casualties and allow responders to first effectively treat the injured. However, medical countermeasures cannot address all possible biological agents. For example, the federal government has explored the possibility of vaccinating the entire population of the United States against smallpox. President Bush organized the National Biodefense Analysis and Counterterrorism Center to conduct risk assessments of the great variety of potential biological weapons. In addition, the Department of Homeland Security will oversee the Select Agent Program to regulate the shipment of certain hazardous biological organisms and toxins. The Select Agent Program has the responsibility of "policing" over 300 scientific laboratories that handle highly dangerous pathogens that could be used for a bioterrorism attack. Protecting a diverse population of all ages and health conditions requires a coordinated national effort to interdict a chemical or biological terrorist attack.[45]

LEGAL FRAMEWORK: APPREHENSION, PROSECUTION, AND PUNISHMENT

The international community has considered several treaties or **conventions** specifically to fight the growing threat of terrorism. The central problem confronting the international community is agreeing on a common definition of terrorism. Since most treaties or conventions are formalized legal proceedings, all participants must accept a common definition of terms. Consider the definition of terrorism proposed by former U.N. secretary general Kofi Annan: "any action constitutes terrorism if it is intended to cause death or serious bodily harm to civilians or non-combatants, with the purpose of intimidating a population or compelling a Government or an international organization to do or abstain from doing any act."[46] Annan's definition of terrorism was unacceptable to the U.N. Security Council. The issue of what constitutes an act of terrorism is the most perplexing, unresolved problem in arguments about terrorism. Undoubtedly, the dissent and confusion surrounding an agreement on terrorism for the purpose of international conventions has probably contributed to the escalation and lethality of terrorism.

The precedent for establishing antiterrorist cooperation is the 1937 Convention for the Prevention and Punishment of Terrorism. This convention was initiated after the assassination of King Alexander I of Yugoslavia and French Foreign Minister Louis Barthou in Marseilles in 1934. The assassins represented an obscure group of Croatian freedom fighters, or terrorists, depending on how terrorism is defined. The 1937 convention defined terrorism as "criminal acts directed against a state and intended or calculated to create a state of terror in the minds of particular persons, or a group of persons, or the general public." The 1937 convention considered two provisions relating to terrorism: (1) that attacks on heads of state or internationally protected persons are a criminal act regardless of motivation and (2) that the destruction of public property or the willful endangering of citizens of one country by another be proscribed under international law. The most controversial issue of the convention was the extradition of offenders. Most countries refused to extradite offenders for political crimes. Because of these problems—lack of a precise definition, how to handle the extradition of offenders, and the impending signs of world war—the 1937 convention was never ratified, thus making it impotent and unenforceable. Since 1963 and the escalation of international terrorism, the United Nations has adopted sixteen multilateral antiterrorist treaties or conventions relating to the suppression of terrorism.[47]

The focus of these conventions is to establish a formalized structure for international cooperation among nations to prevent and suppress international terrorism.[48] The 1973 Convention on the Prevention and Punishment of Crimes Against Internationally Protected Persons requires the cooperation by all signatories to prevent attacks on diplomats, to coordinate administrative measures against such assaults, and to exchange information on terrorist groups and individual offenders. In the event that a diplomat is attacked and the offender flees the country where the attack occurred, the signatories are obliged to make every effort to identify the offender and assist in determining his or her whereabouts. Additionally, if the offender successfully flees the country where the attack occurred and takes refuge in another country and is apprehended, then the offender must either be extradited or prosecuted for the crime committed.[49]

In 2005, the U.N. General Assembly adopted an international convention relating to the threat of nuclear terrorism. The convention criminalizes the possession, use, or threat of use of radiological devices by non-state offenders. Beyond criminalizing acts of nuclear terrorism, the convention requires governments to prosecute nuclear terrorists in domestic court or extradite them to their country of origin.[50]

The most controversial issue of U.N. conventions and treaties is the **extradition** of offenders. Strictly speaking, the extradition of offenders is not required in them. Rather, they contain language that strongly induces nations to extradite the accused offender, and if extradition fails, the accused must be prosecuted in the country where apprehension took place. In a more practical sense, the U.N. conventions also obligate the signatories to apprehend and detain suspected terrorists. However, there is no general agreement that absolutely obliges the requested country to return the accused to the requesting country to stand trial for the crimes. Usually individual countries will have agreed-upon extradition treaties for the return of fleeing suspected terrorists.

U.N. treaties and conventions can often prove hypercritical, embarrassing, and contradictory. For example, at about the same time the United States was demanding the extradition of two Iranian hijackers who murdered two American civilians, a U.S. federal judge invoked the "political exception" rule and refused to return to the United Kingdom a PIRA member who escaped while on trial for murdering a British soldier from ambush. The British requested that the PIRA terrorist be extradited to serve his prison sentence for the murder. The PIRA escapee who had taken refuge in the United States resisted extradition on the grounds that his crimes were political, citing a treaty between the United States and Britain that forbids extradition for crimes of a "political character." The political exception rule has been used by several IRA guerrillas, allowing the United States to become a safe haven for Irish political terrorists. However, on July 17, 1986, the United States and the United Kingdom ratified a new treaty that would prohibit criminals, particularly IRA terrorists/revolutionaries, from taking refuge in either country. On October 21, 1986, the United States finally extradited a PIRA assassin to the United Kingdom to stand trial for the murder of a London police officer.[51] Then on November 21, 2008, a new extradition treaty was ratified between the United States and United Kingdom that streamlines the earlier treaty, making it easier to extradite fleeing terrorists or international criminals.[52]

In this way, Western democracies retain their discretion to grant political asylum to offenders when they consider the offense to be of a political nature. According to framers of the conventions, the entire extradition process is ambiguous, time-consuming, and cumbersome.[53]

To overcome some of the problems of international conventions, three earlier conventions with a regional scope have attempted to fight the spread of international terrorism and still have application in contemporary society. These include:[54]

1. The Convention to Prevent and Punish Acts of Terrorism Taking the Form of Crimes against Persons and Related Extortion That Are of International Significance, Organization of American States (OAS) Convention, Washington, DC, February 2, 1971.
2. The European Convention on the Suppression of Terrorism, European Convention, United Kingdom, October 25, 1978.
3. The Agreement on the Application of the European Convention for the Suppression of Terrorism, Dublin Agreement, 1980.

The basic focus of these three conventions is somewhat different in their approach to combat the threat of terrorism.

The OAS convention, for example, is limited to the protection of diplomatic personnel. The convention is also ambiguous with reference to establishing workable extradition treaties. In fact, a country is not obligated to extradite the alleged offender; and it may also refuse to prosecute the alleged offender without violating the provisions of the convention.

The European convention deals directly with the most frustrating international problem in combating terrorism—the "political offense exception" rule. Extradition treaties commonly provide an exception for political offenses. Unfortunately, the convention fails to define what constitutes a political offense. The approach of the convention is to list a series of crimes that are to be excluded from the political offense exception rule. The convention failed to agree on the distinction between political crime and common crime. Equally, the convention failed to provide a definition of terrorism acceptable to all participants.

The Dublin Accords attempted to strengthen the provisions of extradition outlined by the European convention. First, the conditions of extradition would apply to all signatories without reservations, even if one state has enacted a political offense exception. Second, any dissent made to the European convention would not apply in extradition proceedings. Nine European nations participated in the Dublin Accords and have yet to ratify the proceedings. Again, a disagreement over the definition of terrorism and political crime has prevented the extradition of terrorists.

Both international and regional conventions have taken only a limited approach toward reducing the incidence of political terrorism, and cover only specific manifestations of international terrorism. Accordingly, when a terrorist commits an act of terrorism in one country and flees to another, he or she can be prosecuted only if the country where he or she is apprehended agrees to return him or her to the country where the offense was committed. In today's world, return is highly unlikely, since terrorism to some is heroism to others. In the absence of strong international provisions against terrorism, some democratic countries have enacted tough antiterrorist legislation and invoked emergency powers.

EMERGENCY POWERS

Unfortunately, the emergency powers that democracies must enact to defeat terrorism are the same powers that totalitarian states use to subjugate entire populations. In Germany terrorist groups have forced the federal government to enact antiterrorist emergency legislation that is the most repressive in a liberal democracy.[55] Even the names given to these emergency powers connote a need for extreme action to cope with outbreaks of terrorism. In Spain, a "State of Exception" exists; in Northern Ireland, "Special Powers" have been enacted; in India, certain areas are declared "Terrorist Affected"; and in the United States, "Homeland Security" has resulted in the enactment of the Patriot Act.[56] Typically, in an emergency situation democratic governments will enact the following broad categories of draconian legislation to defeat terrorist threats to internal security:

1. All citizens are required to carry identity cards that include a photograph, fingerprints, and signature. Identity cards, for example, were required in Italy and Spain during the most recent outbreaks of terrorism. In Germany and Northern Ireland, police can establish roadblocks to make identity checks.
2. Firearms, ammunition, and explosives are controlled. The tactic is to make the legal acquisition of weapons as difficult as possible.
3. Special courts are established to try suspected terrorists for heinous political crimes. In India special courts try offenses that impinge on the security and territorial integrity of the country. India has also imposed the death penalty for terrorist acts. France and Northern Ireland have abolished jury trials involving charges of terrorism.
4. Other harsh penalties were enacted in hopes of deterring future acts of terrorism. Italy now imposes a mandatory life sentence for the killing of a police officer. In Northern Ireland,

suspects can be interned indefinitely for possession of firearms or explosives. In Germany, anyone who disseminates "terrorist" literature can be imprisoned for three years.

5. Security forces in several countries are now permitted to arrest and question people without charge, to search houses and vehicles without warrants, to intern suspects, and to impose curfews. The situation in Northern Ireland during the "troubles" between 1965 and 2006 is an example of this type of infringement of rights.

6. Substantive rights such as free speech and the right of assembly are curtailed; censorship and the banning of organizations are frequently imposed. In Northern Ireland, the assembly of three or more people is a violation of Special Powers.

The obvious question concerns the effectiveness of emergency legislation. Does the enactment of emergency provisions to fight terrorism have a greater impact than international or regional treaties? Hewitt states that the results are mixed, but most often emergency legislation has no discernible impact on terrorism.[57] Wardlaw argues that democracies should not arbitrarily disregard all emergency legislation as ineffective.[58] Extreme circumstances may exist in which security forces need extensive powers to stop, search, question, or detain people suspected of terrorist involvement. The proper evaluation of terrorist legislation, emergency powers, and international treaties is an important consideration for U.S. lawmakers. The U.S. Congress only recently began to vigorously pass legislation to improve the apprehension, prosecution, and punishment of terrorists and the control of terrorism.

In 1984, the U.S. Congress passed several antiterrorist bills. This legislation made it a federal offense to commit an act of violence against any passenger onboard civilian or government aircraft. Hijackers can now be prosecuted for the destruction of foreign aircraft outside the United States if they take refuge in the United States. Crimes against high-ranking federal government officials can now be prosecuted under special legislation. The new "Murder for Hire" legislation makes it possible to prosecute persons who travel interstate or use foreign transportation for the purpose of murder or assassination. Congress has posted reward money under the direction of the FBI for information leading to the arrest and conviction of international terrorists. Laws concerning traffic in arms have been expanded to make it illegal to train any foreign national in the use of firearms, munitions, and explosives. The death penalty has been approved in hostage-taking situations where hostages are deliberately murdered. Anyone who kills, assaults, or kidnaps a U.S. citizen outside the United States can be prosecuted if returned to the United States. The most difficult legislation has involved the debate over extradition proceedings. The United States continues to negotiate with several countries to revise the extradition process and the political offense exception rule.[59]

In 1996, the U.S. Congress passed the **Antiterrorism and Effective Death Penalty (ATEDP) Act**. The passage of the ATEDP Act was largely the reaction to the Oklahoma City bombing in 1995 and the bombing of the World Trade Center in 1993. The major provisions of the ATEDP Act:

1. Established a special court that could use secret evidence to deport noncitizens accused of association with terrorist groups.

2. Gave the Executive Branch the power to criminalize fundraising conducted by organizations labeled as terrorists.

3. Established the designation of Foreign Terrorist Organizations.

4. Repealed the Edwards Amendment, which prohibited the FBI from opening criminal investigations based on First Amendment activities. In other words, the FBI can now monitor First Amendment activities, such as marches, meetings, rallies, conferences, and demonstrations, as

well as write down license plate numbers, even when there is no reason to believe that evidence of a crime is being planned or has been committed.

5. Barred aliens from entry into the United States based on their association with terrorist groups or known terrorists.

6. Expanded the use of pretrial detention and loosened rules governing federal wiretap laws.

Critics of the ATEDP Act opposed the legislation, claiming that it was unnecessary and dangerously unconstitutional.

Despite the increased terrorist attacks on Americans overseas prior to 9/11, citizens in the continental United States had been virtually free from terrorist attacks. Therefore, critics maintained that in the United States the rule of constitutional law should prevail. There is no need for "emergency powers" or the diluting of individual and civil rights. However, this situation changed dramatically after the attacks of September 11, 2001.

POST-9/11 LEGAL MEASURES

In the weeks following September 11, 2001, the Bush administration proposed legislation titled Uniting and Strengthening America by Providing Appropriate Tools Required to Intercept and Obstruct Terrorists Act, popularly known as the **USA Patriot Act**.

Chief Justice Rehnquist wrote that the "government's authority to engage in conduct that infringes on civil liberty is greatest in time of declared war."[60] The war on terrorism began on October 8, 2001. The Patriot Act is a 342-page document that sped through the U.S. Congress six weeks after 9/11. The Act was instrumental in defining how the president should respond to terrorism and conduct the war on terrorism. The U.S. Congress held no hearings, provided no committee reports, and did not debate the controversial aspects of the Act, especially the new standards for the abridgement of civil liberties. The lone dissenter to the Patriot Act was Senator Russell Feingold of Wisconsin, who stated, "Preserving our freedom is one of the main reasons that we are now engaged in this war on terrorism. We will lose that war without firing a shot if we sacrifice the liberties of the American people."[61]

Historically, the U.S. Congress has enacted legislation during periods of war that tip the balance between security and liberty in favor of tighter security. For example, in 1798 the U.S. Congress passed into law the infamous Alien and **Sedition Acts**. President John Adams referred to the Alien and Sedition Acts as war measures. In 1798, there was rampant fear and anxiety of the enemy within. French emigrés in America were beginning to "take over" public institutions in New York and Philadelphia. At the time, the United States was involved in an "undeclared" war against France. In addition to the French, there were dangerous Irish refugees from the Irish Rebellion of 1798 who harbored an underlying distrust of the United States and President Adams. Even though President Adams supported the Alien Act, he was not in favor of massive deportations of French and Irish emigrés.[62]

Of greater consequence was the Sedition Act, which made any false, scandalous, and malicious writing against the government, Congress, or president, or any attempt to excite against them or to stir up sedition crimes punishable by fines and imprisonment. Clearly, the Sedition Act was a violation of the First Amendment guaranteeing free speech. Proponents in Congress, like President Adams, insisted it was a necessary war measure. The Sedition Act was strictly enforced and dozens of people were imprisoned between 1798 and 1802.[63]

During World War I, over 2,000 people were prosecuted for "sedition" after speaking out against the war effort. In 1940, the U.S. Congress enacted the Aliens Registration Act, or the

Smith Act, which forcibly interned 110,000 people of Japanese descent. The internment of the Japanese, of whom two-thirds were U.S. citizens, was carried out in the "national interest" following the Japanese surprise attack on U.S. naval forces at Pearl Harbor.[64]

On April 27, 1861, President Lincoln suspended **habeas corpus**. Also known as *The Great Writ*, the writ of habeas corpus is an important legal instrument for the safeguarding of individual freedom against arbitrary action by government officials. President Lincoln was convinced that the only way to suppress the Southern insurrection that eventually evolved into the Civil War was to suspend the writ of habeas corpus.[65]

Once again, the writ of habeas corpus is being tested in the U.S. court system. Since the beginning of the war on terrorism in Afghanistan in 2001, 775 enemy combatants of the Taliban and al Qaeda were incarcerated at the U.S. detention center at Guantanamo Bay, Cuba. Subsequently, over 500 were released without charge. As of May 2008, approximately 270 enemy combatants remained at Guantanamo. In June 2008, the U.S. Supreme Court recognized the habeas corpus rights of the Guantanamo detainees. Basically the Supreme Court ruled either charge the Guantanamo detainees with a crime or release them. On October 7, 2008, the United States began releasing some of the Guantanamo prisoners.[66] After the election of President Barack Obama, his first act as President was to close down the Guantanamo detention center. However, other detainees such as Khalid Sheikh Mohammed, who confessed to planning the 9/11 attacks, and Ramzi Binalshibh were charged by the U.S. government for the September 11 atrocities.[67]

In sum, during periods of war the U.S. government has reacted in a predictable way. Fearful people worry incessantly about being attacked and subverted from within. Fear often causes government officials to overreact. Fearful populations look to tightening security and reducing individual freedom to protect the homeland. Thus, the events in 1798, the Civil War, World Wars I and II, and currently the war on terrorism have resulted in legal reforms that would chip away at our individual liberties. So it is with the USA Patriot Act.

The Patriot Act has ten titles outlining new powers for the U.S. government's war on terrorism. Title I enhances domestic security, creates funding for counterterrorist operations, expands electronic intelligence gathering beyond the ATEDP Act, increases technical support for the FBI, defines presidential authority in response to terrorism, and prohibits discrimination against Arabs and Muslim Americans.

Some of the most controversial features of the Patriot Act appear in Title II. The purpose of Title II is to reshape the U.S. government's ability to collect electronic evidence. Police officials can now monitor a variety of communications media. Title II of the Patriot Act now allows the police to request a wiretap search warrant from the court to engage in electronic surveillance to investigate any foreign intelligence information for terrorist, chemical weapons, or computer crime investigations. Before the Patriot Act, police had to identify a specific alleged foreign intelligence activity to obtain a wiretap warrant. The Patriot Act also allows law enforcement officers the use of "roving wiretap warrants" against unspecified persons across all jurisdictions. Title II provides police with a blank warrant that can be used along with the roving wiretaps. Police in the jurisdiction under police surveillance can then use the blank warrant. Hence, prior restrictions on police warrant requests, such as identifying the suspect and location for the wiretap warrant, have been replaced by Title II enhancements in the case of foreign intelligence investigations or counterterrorism activities.[68]

Before enactment of the Patriot Act, police search warrants were required for announcement and notification. One exception to the announcement provision was the "no knock" rule, where search warrants could be authorized by federal courts when alerting the suspect would put the police officers' lives in danger or cause the suspect to destroy evidence. Today, the Patriot Act authorizes "sneak and peek" warrants, whereby police officers can conduct surreptitious searches or wiretaps without announcing their presence at the time of the search. Unannounced searches allow police the opportunity to prevent destruction of evidence, risk of suspect flight, threat to the safety of investigating police officers, and interference with investigative strategies. The "sneak and peek" aspect of the Patriot Act brings about a significant change in search warrant procedures outlined by the Fourth Amendment.[69]

Federal law enforcement agencies can now share noncriminal information with each other. Private corporations are required to share personnel records and data with law enforcement officials during criminal investigations. The FBI can seize materials, public or private, when it believes national security is in jeopardy.

Other sections of the Patriot Act impact the war on terrorism in a variety of ways. Title III empowers the FBI to interact with banking regulators and provides arrest powers for federal law enforcement outside the borders of the United States for financing terrorist activities and money laundering. Financial institutions are now required to inform federal authorities of "potentially unlawful activity" of current or former bank customers or employees. Title IV increases border patrols, the monitoring of foreign nationals living in the United States, and mandates the detention of "suspected" terrorists. Title VII supports the sharing of investigative information by federal law enforcement agencies, especially the reorganization of the Regional Information Sharing System (RISS). Title VIII strengthens the criminal laws against terrorism, providing for a definition of domestic terrorism and expanding biological weapons statutes. In addition, educational institutions are required to disclose all educational records to police, once directed by a court order, during a terrorism investigation.

Since the 9/11 attacks, the U.S. government has enacted over 400 counterterrorist resolutions, twelve executive orders, and ten presidential orders. Even so, the USA Patriot Act has become the cornerstone of U.S. federal statutes that have expanded the legal requirements in the war on terrorism. On March 9, 2006, Congress renewed the provisions of the Patriot Act. The USA Patriot Act has retained its original authority and is being used successfully in foreign intelligence and counterterrorism investigations (Table 9.3).

Proponents of the Patriot Act are convinced it will enhance federal law enforcement's ability to effectively respond to terrorism. Supporters also maintain that the threat of terrorism will be greatly reduced by strengthening law enforcement agencies by expanding the ability of gathering intelligence on terrorist groups, by the **seizure of terrorists' assets**, and by authorizing secret searches of e-mail. Opponents of the Patriot Act argue it is incompatible with core civil and individual rights. They are especially concerned about the federal government's increased power to monitor the activities of average American citizens. Civil libertarians also are concerned about other attacks on civil liberties, such as requiring a national ID card, infiltrating domestic groups by undercover police officers, authorizing military tribunals, restrictions of freedom of speech, racial profiling, nonlethal torture of terrorist suspects, and rendition.

Rendition, or *irregular rendition*, is a term that describes the extrajudicial transfer of a terrorist suspect from one country to another. Rendition is a secretive practice that bypasses judicial and administrative due process. The major criticism of rendition is that it often involves transporting terrorist suspects to countries where torture is routinely used during interrogation. The CIA was granted authority to use rendition in a presidential directive signed by President

TABLE 9.3	Summary of USA Patriot Act
Title I	Improving Domestic Security • Counterterrorism fund • Presidential authority
Title II	Enhanced Surveillance Procedures • Intercept communications relating to terrorism • Sneak and peek search warrants • Amends Foreign Intelligence Surveillance Act (FISA)
Title III	Money Laundering Abatement and Antiterrorism Financing Act • International monetary cooperation • Counterfeiting domestic or foreign currency
Title IV	Border Security • Mandatory detention of suspected terrorist • Foreign student monitoring • Visa security
Title V	Removing Obstacles to Investigation of Terrorism • Authority to pay rewards • Disclosure of educational records
Title VI	Providing for Victims and Victims' Families of Terrorism • Payment of heroic public safety officers • Crime victims compensation
Title VII	Increased Information Sharing for Critical Infrastructure Protection
Title VIII	Strengthening Criminal Laws Against Terrorism • Definition of domestic terrorism • Material support for terrorism • No statute of limitations for terrorist offenses
Title IX	Improved Intelligence • Terrorist asset tracking • Expansion of Foreign Intelligence Surveillance Act • Defer disclosure of intelligence information to Congress
Title X	Miscellaneous • Define electronic surveillance • Critical infrastructure protection

Source: 107th Congress, *http://epic.org/privacy/terrorism/*

Clinton in 1995.[70] Since the 9/11 attacks, the United States has operated an extensive rendition program. Supporters of the U.S. rendition program maintain that culturally informed native language interrogators are better prepared in gaining information from terrorist suspects.[71] Accordingly, the goal of the U.S./CIA rendition program is to protect Americans from another 9/11-type terrorist attack.

As you recall, one of the goals of terrorism is to panic citizens into surrendering their civil liberties for more security. Dershowitz writes that many citizens prefer security to liberty in times of the widespread fear associated with indiscriminate acts of terrorism and at the first sign of danger are willing to give up their civil rights for safety. Dershowitz got it exactly right when he concluded, "We must maintain our preference for liberty even in the face of the most pressing claims of security."[72]

The post-9/11 era has brought numerous changes in the relationship between terrorism threats, the safety of U.S. citizens, and expanding police powers. The war on terrorism has produced a myriad of legal, social, psychological, and political effects on the U.S. government's effort to balance security and liberty. Any effective approach to responding to terrorism within the rule of law must be multifaceted. More important, the response to terrorism must remain consistent with the core principles of legality and morality. The war on terrorism is a new phenomenon, not adequately addressed by current legal precedents. Thus, the need for new laws, such as the Patriot Act, addresses the concerns of keeping society safe and tracking down terrorists. To remain credible and effective, law must change with experience so that society can be protected from unpredictable acts of terrorism. The challenge for lawmakers is to strike the right balance between individual liberty and security, which is certainly a difficult challenge since citizens demand both safety and freedom.

Conclusions

So what do we have to do to fight and defeat the spread of terrorism? The first line of defense against terrorism is to tighten security measures. The protection of people and places is quickly evolving from the total reliance on poorly trained, undereducated, and underpaid security guards to the development of high-technology intrusion systems. The media's concentration on terrorism has provided the general population with current information, even though media coverage of terrorist incidents often sensationalizes the violence. The effective management of the many diverse components and assets of the intelligence community is crucial in order to acquire the most pertinent, relevant information on terroristic activities.

The second line of defense in response to widespread terrorism is the use of elite military forces for retaliation, preemption, or prevention. The willingness to use the armed forces in such actions as air strikes or covert operations is indispensable to defeat international terrorism. Otherwise, the deterrent capability of liberal democracies would be nonexistent. Commando-style raids against known terrorist installations are considered by the United States and other democracies to be a credible alternative in the fight against terrorism. However, it must be remembered that military force should be used only as a last resort.

Nations typically respond to terrorism by strengthening existing laws and enacting emergency legislation. Often this emergency legislation deprives the population of various individual and civil liberties. Detention without trial, warrantless searches and seizures, establishment of special courts, and other extreme legal measures should be used with great caution. However, emergency powers may be justified to illustrate the government's determination to defeat terrorism. The enactment of such legislation provides a proscribed legal framework for security forces, police or military, to respond to the potential threat of terrorism. Finally, the improvement of extradition treaties would enhance the prospects of bringing international terrorists to justice. The U.S. Congress needs to reform the extradition laws of the United States to make them more effective to combat the spread of international terrorism.

As of this writing, there certainly appears to be a great deal of confusion and hypocrisy on the appropriate U.S. response to terrorism. The response to terrorism must be unambiguous and most of all consistent if the United States and its allies hope to defeat terrorism in the twenty-first century.

Key Terms

Antiterrorism and Effective
  Death Penalty (ATEDP) Act
conventions
covert operation
Delta Force
extradition
Front Liberation du Quebec
  (FLQ)
habeas corpus
HostageRescue Team (HRT)

Libya
Mir Aimal Kansi
Nuclear Emergency Search
  Team (NEST)
Office of Homeland Security
Posse Comitatus Act
preemptive strike
rendition
Sayeret Matkal (SM)
Sedition Act

seizure of terrorists' assets
skyjacking
Special Air Service (SAS)
Special Boat Service (SBS)
special operations
Terrorist Threat Integration
  Center (TTIC)
USA Patriot Act

Discussion Questions

1. Describe the intelligence information function.
2. Do you believe the United States should pursue a policy of retaliation or preemption? Why or why not?
3. What major measures can the international community take to prevent terrorism?
4. How can the United States and its allies "win" the war on terrorism?
5. Do you think the United States should follow Israel's example in fighting terrorism? Explain fully.
6. What is the most insidious consequence of responding to the potential spread of terrorism? Discuss your response.
7. Respond to the following statements:
   a. Most politically motivated murders of U.S. citizens in recent years have come as a result of international terrorism.
   b. Violent actions conducted by surrogates are preferable to direct U.S. attacks on terrorists.
   c. Terrorism is low-intensity warfare in which innocent civilians are targets.
8. Identify and explain at least three international conventions organized to suppress terrorism. Develop your own international treaty.
9. Evaluate the provisions of the Patriot Act.
10. Discuss the impact of emergency powers on defeating terrorism.
11. Debate the pros and cons of the United States rendition program.
12. Discuss Title II of the Patriot Act, for example, do you think Title II is a violation of Fourth Amendment rights?

Web Sites

Gilmore Commission, Advisory Panel to Assess Domestic Response Capabilities for Terrorism Involving Weapons of Mass Destruction
http://www.rand.org/nsard/terrorpanel/

Central Intelligence Agency: War on Terrorism. DCI Counterterrorism Center
http://www.cia.gov/terrorism/ctc.html

National Guard Association of the United States
http://www.ngaus.org/

The White House, President Barack H. Obama
http://www.whitehouse.gov/

U. S. Department of Homeland Security
http://www.dhs.gov/dhspublic/index.jsp

Endnotes

1. Secretary of Defense, *Annual Report to Congress, Fiscal Year 1986* (February 4, 1985), p. 23.

2. Office of Homeland Security, *National Strategy for Homeland Security* (Washington, DC: U.S. Government Printing Office, July 2002).

3. Federal Aviation Administration, *Semiannual Report to Congress on the Effectiveness of the Civil Aviation Security Program* (Washington, DC: Federal Aviation Administration, April, 1985), p. 8.

4. Ibid.

5. Greg Schneider, "Terror Risk Cited for Cargo Carried on Passenger Jets," *Washington Post* (June 10, 2002), p. A1; Bruce Hoffman, "Aviation Security and Terrorism: An Analysis of the Potential Threat to Air Cargo Integrators," in *Aviation Terrorism and Security*, ed. Brian M. Jenkins (New York: Routledge, 1999), pp. 54–69.

6. Anatoly Burshtein, *Introduction to thermodynamics and Kinetic Theory of Matter* (New York: John Wiley and Sons, 1995); See also Kathleen W. Sweet, *Transportation and Cargo Security: Threats and Solutions* (New York: Prentice Hall, 2005).

7. Transportation Security Administration, *Innovation and Technology* (December 12, 2008), *http://www.tsa.gov.*

8. U.S. Department of Homeland Security, *Prevention and Protection* (December 14, 2008), *http://www.dhs.gov/xprevprot/.*

9. Transportation Security Administration, *Layers of Security: Strengthening Security Through a Layered Approach* (April 4, 2006), *http://www.tsa.gov.*

10. For example, see Paul Wilkinson and Brian Jenkins, eds., *Aviation Terrorism and Security* (New York: Frank Cass Publications, 2000).

11. Grant Wardlaw, *Political Terrorism: Theory, Tactics, and Countermeasures* (Cambridge, MA: Cambridge University Press, 1982), pp. 131–34; See also Michael Ronczkowski, *Terrorism and Organized Hate Crime: Intelligence Gathering, Analysis and Investigations* (Boca Raton, FL: CRC Press, 2003).

12. "Provos versus the Crown: A Review of Contemporary Terrorist and Antiterrorist Operations in Northern Ireland," *Clandestine Tactics and Technology*, Update Report 8, no. 7 (1983), p. 2.

13. James Q. Wilson, *The Investigators: Managing F.B.I. and Narcotics Agents* (New York: Basic Books, 1978), p. 61.

14. George J. Tenet, *Johns Hopkins University Diploma Ceremony* (May 25, 2000), *http://www.cia.gov/.*

15. James Adams, *The Financing of Terror: Behind the PLO, IRA, Red Brigades, and M19 Stand the Paymasters* (New York: Simon and Schuster, 1986).

16. Ovid Demaris, *Brothers in Blood: The International Terrorist Network* (New York: Charles Scribner's Sons, 1977), p. 392.

17. George J. Tenet, *Worldwide Threat—Converging Dangers in a Post-9/11 World* (February 6, 2002), http://www.cia.gov/.

18. For example, see Jeffrey T. Richelson, *A Century of Spies: Intelligence in the Twentieth Century* (New York: Oxford University Press, 1997).

19. Fred J. Khouri, *The Arab-Israeli Dilemma* (Syracuse, NY: Syracuse University Press, 1985), pp. 187–98; John Quigley, *The Case for Palestine: An International Law Perspective* (Durham, NC: Duke University Press, 2005), pp. 154–56.

20. Stewart Steven, *The Spymasters of Israel* (New York: Macmillan, 1980), pp. 145–71; Dan Raviv and Yossi Melman, *Every Spy a Prince: The Complete History of Israel's Intelligence Community* (New York: Houghton-Mifflin, 1990), pp. 122–25.

21. *Public Report of the Vice President's Task Force on Combating Terrorism* (Washington, DC: U.S. Government Printing Office, February, 1986), p. 15.

22. James B. Motley, "Target America: The Undeclared War," in *Fighting Back: Winning the War against Terrorism,* eds. Neil C. Livingstone and Terrell E. Arnold (Lexington, MA: Lexington Books, 1986), p. 73.

23. *New York Times* (January 27, 1985), p. 12.

24. *Sacramento Bee* (April 15, 1986), sec. A, p. 8.

25. *New York Times* (April 15, 1986), p. 1; *Time* (April 21, 1986), pp. 17–29; *Newsweek* (April 21, 1986), pp. 21–26; Dick Vandawalle, ed., *Qadhafi's Libya,*

1969–1994 (New York: Palgrave Macmillan, 1995), pp. 62–65.

26. *Sacramento Bee* (April 16, 1986), p. 1.

27. Adams, *Financing of Terror*, pp. 31–32.

28. George P. Shultz, "The U.S. Must Retaliate Against Terrorist States," in *Terrorism: Opposing Viewpoints*, eds. David L. Bender and Bruno Leone (St. Paul, MN: Greenhaven Press, 1986), pp. 197–203; See also R. A. Davidson, *Reagan vs. Qaddafi: Response to International Terrorism* (Bangor, ME: Booklocker.com, Inc., 2003).

29. Neil C. Livingstone and Terrell E. Arnold, "The Rise of State–Sponsored Terrorism," in *Fighting Back: Winning the War Against Terrorism*, eds. Neil C. Livingstone and Terrell E. Arnold (Lexington, MA: Lexington Books, 1986), pp. 11–23.

30. Benjamin Netanyahu, *Fighting Terrorism: How Democracies Can Defeat Domestic and International Terrorists* (New York: Farrar, Straus and Giroux, 2001), pp. 129–46.

31. Tim Weiner, *Legacy of Ashes: The History of the CIA* (New York: Anchor Books, 2008), pp. 363–65.

32. Victor Marchetti and John Marks, *The CIA and the Cult of Intelligence* (New York: Knopf, 1983), p. 334; See also Ishmael Jones, *The Human Factor: Inside the CIA's Dysfunctional Intelligence Culture* (New York: Encounter Books, 2008).

33. Warren Hinckle and William Turner, *The Fish Is Red: The Story of the Secret War Against Castro* (New York: Harper and Row, 1981), p. 106; John Ranelagh, *The Agency: The Rise and Decline of the CIA* (New York: Simon and Schuster, 1986), pp. 349–82.

34. President's Foreign Intelligence Advisory Board, *Presidency in Action* (May 13, 2003), *http://www.americanpresident.org*.

35. Alan M. Dershowitz, *Why Terrorism Works: Understanding the Threat, Responding to the Challenge* (New Haven, CT: Yale University Press, 2002) pp. 165–221.

36. Matthew Carlton Hammond, "The Posse Comitatus Act: A Principle in Need of Renewal," *Washington University Law Quarterly*, 75 (Summer 1997), *http://www.law.wustl.edu/WULQ/issues.html*.

37. For example, see Gina Cavallaro, "Brigade Homeland Tours Start October 1," *Army Times* (September 30, 2008), *http://www.armytimes.*

com; John R. Brinkerhoff, "The Posse Comitatus Act and Homeland Security," *Journal of Homeland Security* (February 2002), *http://www.homelandsecurity.org/journal;* Spenser S. Hsu and Ann Scott Tyson, "Pentagon to Detail Troops to Bolster Domestic Security," *Washington Post* (December 1, 2008), *http://www.washingtonpost.com*.

38. Office of Homeland Security, *National Strategy for Homeland Security* (Washington, DC: July, 2002), pp. 47–51.

39. Ibid., p. 44.

40. Jessica Stern, *Terrorism in the Name of God: Why Religious Militants Kill* (New York: Harper Perennial, 2004), pp. 172–81.

41. Bruce P. Schoch, "Four Rules for a Successful Rescue," *Army*, 16 (February 1981), pp. 22–26.

42. Seth G. Jones and Martin C. Libicki, *How Terrorist Groups End: Lessons for Countering al Qaeda* (Santa Monica, CA: Rand Corporation, 2008), p. 9.

43. Lynne L. Snowden, "How Likely Are Terrorists to Use a Nuclear Strategy," *American Behavioral Scientists*, 46 (February 2003), pp. 699–714.

44. Brian Michael Jenkins, *Will Terrorists go Nuclear* (Amherst, NY: Prometheus Books, 2008), p. 87.

45. Dana A. Shea, *The National Biodefense Analysis and Counterterrorism Center: Issues for Congress*, Congressional Research Service (Washington, DC: US Government Printing Office, February 15, 2007), pp. 1–15.

46. *United Nations Action to Counterterrorism* (September 19, 2006), *http://www.un.org/terrorism/*.

47. For example, see Douglas C. Lovelace, *Terrorism Documents of International and Local Control* (New York: Oxford University Press, 2008).

48. United Nations' Office on Drugs and Crime, *Conventions Against Terrorism* (May 16, 2003), *http://www.unodc.org/unodc/terrorism_conventions.html*.

49. Ibid.

50. Clair Applegarth, "U.N. Adopts Nuclear Terrorism Convention; Treaty Seven Years in the Making," *Arms Control Association* (May 2005), *http://www.armscontrol.org*.

51. *Sacramento Bee* (July 18, 1986), sec. A, p. 1; *Sacramento Bee* (October 21, 1981), sec. A, p. 8.

52. United Kingdom, *Documents and Texts for American Government; United States—United*

Kingdom Extradition Treaty (November 21, 2008), *http://www.usembassy.org.uk/gb080.html.*

53. John F. Murphy, *Punishing International Terrorists. The Legal Framework for Policy Initiatives* (Totowa, NJ: Rowman and Allanheld, 1985), pp. 9–11.

54. Ibid., pp. 11–16.

55. For example, see M. Radvanyi, *Antiterrorist Legislation in the Federal Republic of Germany* (Washington, DC: Law Library, Library of Congress, 1979); Herman Blei, "Terrorism, Domestic and International: The West German Experience," *Report of the Task Force on Disorders and Terrorism* (Washington, DC: U.S. Government Printing Office, 1976), pp. 497–506; Karlheinz Gemmer, "Problems, Means, and Methods of Police Action in the Federal Republic of Germany," in *Hostage Taking*, eds. Ronald D. Crelinsten and Denis Szabo (Lexington, MA: DC Heath, 1979), pp. 119–26.

56. For example, see James X. Dempsey and David Cole, *Terrorism and the Constitution: Sacrificing Civil Liberties in the Name of National Security* (Los Angeles, CA: First Amendment Foundation, 1999); Government Institutes Research Group, *Homeland Security Statutes: 2003 Edition* (Rockville, MD: Government Institutes Publication, 2003).

57. Christopher Hewitt, *The Effectiveness of Anti-Terrorist Policies* (New York: University Press of America, 1994), pp. 61–67; See also, Stewart A. Baker, *Patriot Debates: Experts Debate the USA Patriot Act* (Chicago, IL: American Bar Association, 2005).

58. Wardlaw, *Political Terrorism*, 1982, p. 130.

59. *Vice President's Task Force*, 1985, pp. 15–16; Dempsey and Cole, *Terrorism and the Constitution.*

60. Stephen J. Schuhofer, *The Enemy Within: Intelligence Gathering, Law Enforcement, and Civil Liberties in the Wake of September 11* (New York: Century Foundation Press, 2002), p. 7.

61. "U.S. Senate Role Call Votes 107th Congress—1st Session" (October 25, 2001), *http://www.senate.gov.*

62. David McCullough, *John Adams* (New York: A Touchstone Book, 2001), pp. 504–07

63. Ibid., p. 506.

64. John F. Christgau, *Enemies: World War II Alien Internment* (Bloomington, IN: Authorhouse, 2001), pp. 144–62.

65. For example, see George Clarke Sellery, *Lincoln's Suspension of Habeas Corpus as Viewed by Congress* (Whitefish, MT Kessinger Publishing, 2007); Mark E. Neeley, *The Fate of Liberty: Abraham Lincoln and Civil Liberties* (New York: Oxford University Press, 1972).

66. Radio Free Asia, *Guantanamo Uyghurs Release Blocked* (October 7, 2008), *http://www.rfa.org.*

67. Margot Williams, *Khalid Shaikh Mohammed* (December 8, 2008), http://www.nyties.com.

68. Amitai Etzioni, *How Patriotic is the Patriot Act?: Freedom Versus Security in the Age of Terrorism* (New York: Routledge, 2004), pp. 443–65.

69. For example, see M. Katherine Darmer, et al., eds., *Civil Liberties vs. National Security in a Post 9/11 World* (New York: Prometheus Books, 2004); Paul A. Ibbetson, *Living Under the Patriot Act: Educating a Society* (Bloomington, IN: Authorhouse, 2007).

70. Presidential Decision Directive 39, *The White House, Washington* (June 21, 1995). *http://www.fas.org/irp/offdocs/pdd39.htm.*

71. David Ignatius, "Rendition Realities," *The Washington Post* (March 9, 1995), p. 21.

72. Dershowitz, *Why Terrorism Works* (2002), pp. 190–93.

CHAPTER 10

Future of Terrorism

CHAPTER OBJECTIVES
The study of this chapter will enable you to:

- Reexamine the Palestine question
- Explore the growth of Islamic fundamentalism
- Discuss the theory of state-sponsored terrorism
- Describe low-intensity warfare
- Discuss the future prospect of "super terrorism"
- Evaluate the influence of terrorism on the quality of life in the United States
- Estimate the future of terrorism and political violence

INTRODUCTION

After nearly forty years of political and criminal terrorism, there can be few who have not been exposed to the atrocities and fanaticism of commandos, freedom fighters, and guerrillas throughout the world. The ritualized massacre of hundreds of innocent civilians is all too well known. The drama of terrorism has been brought into sharp media focus as a result of indiscriminate bombings, such as those in Madrid, Bali, and London; suicide bombings, which are so numerous that today several are recorded each week; and the monthly hostage-taking incidents. The media have made certain that millions are now familiar with the dreams of Palestinians and obscure Islamic religious jihadi fundamentalists, with the fantasies of pan-Islamic groups, and with the alphabets of murder—PFLP, PIRA, FALN, and Hamas. Lebanon, Syria, Iraq, Israel, and Iran are now found in daily media headlines of terrorism instead of travel brochures depicting the exotic Middle East. Terrorist attacks are planned for the prime-time viewer, and after each attack there is a plea for vengeance or at least for instituting tighter security measures. The repetition of terrorist attacks, especially suicide bombings, has become so ritualized that now each terrorist drama is a rerun. The script never seems to change. The deaths of innocent victims of terrorism are brought to us close up and made very personal by the media.

Capturing the attention of an audience may be easy, but terrorist groups need to heighten the drama in order to sustain that interest. This requires changing demands, locations, performers, and types of terrorist incidents. The most ingeniously contrived terrorist action can, if repeated too often, cause the intended audience to become bored and disinterested in the grievances of the terrorist group. To be effective, then, terrorists cannot attack the same target or continually use the same strategy.

Both sides, government and terrorists, like to be able to predict within reason the outcome of a terrorist incident. A government's interest in predictability is to reduce the element of surprise that gives terrorists a great advantage, but terrorists are equally interested in predictability. Terrorists want to attract media attention and create interest in their cause without damaging their image as freedom fighters or inviting massive government retaliation such as the Israeli retaliation against Hizballah, Hamas, and al Aqsa, or the U.S. retaliation against al Qaeda in Afghanistan. The inevitable outcome of a terrorist incident in no way detracts from government involvement; if anything, predicting the outcome of a terrorist incident heightens anticipation and involvement for both terrorists, government, and police officials.

The prediction of future directions in terrorism and the threat that acts of indiscriminate violence will pose for democratic societies is an obvious consideration for government planners. The attempt to forecast future terrorist actions is an exercise ladened with danger and uncertainty, for the ability to accurately predict future events may be a form of crystal ball gazing that produces an unrealistic picture of increased terrorism.[1] There is little agreement among scholars whether terrorism will continue to escalate or decline. Jenkins rightly predicted that by the end of the twentieth century a new generation of terrorists would have taken the field, compelled to escalate their terrorism so as to maintain public attention or to react to restrictive governmental power.[2] Apter argued that terrorism will gradually decline in the twentieth century as terrorist groups recognize the futility of indiscriminate campaigns of violence that only serve to alienate the general society.[3] The Proteus Trends Series predicts that terrorism will escalate worldwide once "freedom fighters" return to their native countries from the Iraqi insurgency.[4] Still others conclude that the prospect of nuclear, chemical, or biological terrorism poses the greatest threat to the stability of the world.[5] Bearing in mind these conflicting observations, can we accurately predict the future directions of terrorism in the twenty-first century?

In this chapter, we focus on the factors presented in earlier chapters that are currently thought to contribute to the escalation of world terrorism. In the first section, the continuation of the Israeli–Palestinian problem is explored. The second section contains a review of Islamic fundamentalist terrorism in the context of the September 11 attacks. The third section attempts to evaluate the concept of terrorism as a form of low-intensity warfare and the role of state-sponsored terrorism. The prospect of superterrorism is detailed in the fourth section. How accurate are earlier warnings that terrorists will inevitably use weapons of mass destruction? Finally, the influence that terrorism has on the quality of life in a democracy is examined.

ISRAEL VERSUS PALESTINIAN RESISTANCE MOVEMENT

The Palestinian Resistance Movement is no closer today to recovering Palestine than it was in 1948 when Israel was granted the right by the United Nations to proclaim its statehood. The Palestinians and the Israelis are implacable enemies, and they will remain so for considerable time to come. Netanyahu maintains that the spark of contemporary international terrorism was ignited by Palestinian attacks against soft Israeli targets.[6] Eventually, Palestinian terrorism directed against Israeli targets expanded to include attacks against moderate Arab nations, moderate Palestinians, and the United States. Israel and the Palestinians have been engaged in an undeclared "shadow" war since the mid-1960s. In June 1982, that war was broadened when Israeli Defense Forces launched a blitzkrieg-style assault across the Lebanese border to finally destroy the infrastructure of Palestinian unity—the PLO. In the process the Israelis captured several documents that revealed the central role played by the PLO in contributing to the escalation of worldwide terrorism. In 1982, the PLO had apparently created a mini-terrorist state in Lebanon, where training centers and launching areas of international terrorism had been established.[7] However, the Israeli raid developed into a full-scale war lasting for three years. The major objective of the Lebanon war—the destruction of the PLO—was never accomplished. In fact, it is doubtful whether the Israeli blitzkrieg strategy had any effect at all on the PLO. Adams reported that the assets of the PLO in 1985 exceeded an impressive $6 billion.[8] With that kind of money, it did not take the PLO long to rebuild. Thus, the armed struggle to liberate all of pre-1948 Palestine continues.

Today Israeli citizens face several enemies determined to destroy the state of Israel. In Lebanon, Hizballah continues to harass the northern border of Israel with Katyusha rockets. In Gaza, Hamas has fired thousands of **Qassam rockets** and mortars indiscriminately into southern Israel towns and villages. On the West Bank, Fatah, al Aqsa, PFLP, and Islamic Jihad search for opportunities to send the next suicide bomber into Israel to kill and maim innocent noncombatants. Then, there is the unmistakable intention of Iran to develop deliverable weapons of mass destruction that are capable of reaching Israeli cities. Iran's leaders have threatened to "wipe Israel off the map." The greatest danger Israel faces in the near future is from Iran's nuclear weapons. Iran also provides the major financial and weapons support to Hamas and Hizballah, while Syrian tanks sit on the Golan Heights waiting for an opportunity to attack Israel. In addition, the hatred of Israel has basically healed the millennium-long schism between Shias and Sunnis.

Through the years several peace plans for a reduction of hostilities between the Palestinians and Israelis have been proposed—the Reagan Plan, the Soviet Plan, the Fez Plan, the Saudi Plan, the Oslo Accords, and, most recently, the "Road Map." The best-known variant of all plans advocating the territorial compromise is the so-called **Allon Plan**.[9] All plans support the concept of "territory for peace." The major conclusion of the plans is that the creation on the West Bank and Gaza of an independent Palestinian state that meets certain minimal requirements would do much to bring peace not only to Israel but also to the entire Middle East. However, almost all Israelis regard the creation of a Palestinian state as an immediate threat to their security and a long-term threat to the existence of the State of Israel. Israel pulled out of Lebanon in 2002 and from Gaza in 2005, yet Gaza and Lebanon now serve as launching pads for attacks on Israeli civilians. Territorial withdrawals only bring continued violence.

Critics of territory for peace believe that Palestinian terrorist groups, that is, Hamas, Fatah, PFLP, and Islamic Jihad, would use the territory as a base for the destabilization of both Israel and Lebanon.[10] They point to the Hamas' charter, which is clearly incompatible with the existence of the Israeli state. Still others write that Israeli fears are unwarranted and that a Palestinian state could peacefully and easily coexist if the Israelis would withdraw to their pre-June 1967 borders.[11] Even if the Israelis and the Palestinians were able to come to terms over the West Bank and Gaza, extremists within the Palestinian community would certainly attack the Palestinian "traitors." In January 2006, Hamas was elected to govern the Gaza Strip and other Palestinian territories. Subsequently, Israel pulled out of Gaza and physically removed Israeli settlers. Hamas, now in control of Gaza, defeated the Palestinian Authority in a bitter internecine war and assumed de facto control over the entire Gaza Strip. The leadership of Hamas then instructed its military wing to launch Qassam rockets at civilian targets in southern Israel. Between April 2008 and December 27, 2008, over 8,000 rockets and mortars were launched from Gaza by Hamas against Israeli cities in southern Israel. Once again Israel was under attack by a terrorist group (Hamas) that vowed to destroy the Jewish state. On December 27, 2008, Israel struck back and began an eight-day air assault on Hamas rocket-launching sites as well as attacks on other Hamas locations. Israel is determined to destroy the infrastructure of Hamas.[12]

Attractive as the territory for peace sounds, it does not appear to be a feasible option for Gaza or the West Bank. Israel will remain in control of the West Bank for a long time to come. As Conor Cruise O'Brien writes, "The idea of Israel withdrawing to its pre-June 1967 territory and living there behind secure and recognized frontiers, in peace with all its neighbors, is an agreeable international pipedream. The reality is that Israel will stay in the West Bank where its presence will continue to be challenged from within and without."[13] The presence of Israel on the West Bank is likely to be continuously challenged by the Palestinian Authority. As noted earlier, in September 2000, for example, there were several days of uncontrolled rioting on the West Bank after Israeli occupation of the al Aqsa Mosque. Several Palestinians were subsequently killed as the rioting escalated throughout the West Bank, Gaza, and Israel proper. In one sense, the West Bank has become another Northern Ireland and Jerusalem another Belfast.

Additionally, as the years of Israeli occupation of the West Bank continue, the controversy over the establishment of Jewish settlements will also continue. The Palestinian Arabs, of course, strongly oppose any Jewish settlements in the "occupied territories." The Palestinians are supported by the international community, where it is widely believed that Jewish settlements on the West Bank are illegal and violate international law and the Geneva Convention. Israeli opinion supports the position that the West Bank is part of the sovereign state of Israel, and further, if Jews want to settle on the West Bank, they have the legal right to do so. There is fairly widespread agreement within Israel on the intrinsic right of Jews to settle in "**Judea and Samaria**," the land of the ancient Hebrews. Some of the settlements are little more than paramilitary outposts, whereas others are substantial agricultural or residential ventures, often with mystical Jewish historical connotations. A Palestinian state would surely prevent further Jewish settlement and might possibly mean the relocation of those Jewish settlements already established on the West Bank.

However, several Jewish religious fundamentalist groups vowed never again to be driven out of Judea and Samaria. For example, the issues of religion and land are inseparable to the Kahane Chai, Kach, and the **Gush Emunim** (Block of the Faithful). Members of the Gush Emunim strongly believe that both the Jewish nation and the Jewish land are sacred, since they were both chosen by God. The Gush maintain they are fulfilling a religious prophecy and reviving the Jewish spirit of pioneers by settling on the West Bank, that is, Judea and Samaria. The ultimate objective of the Gush, Kahane Chai, and Kach is to drive all Arabs out of the West Bank and re-establish a secular Jewish nation. The relentless growth of Jewish religious communities on the West Bank dooms any prospect of the formation of a viable Palestinian state. Today the Gush refer to themselves as the "Ne'emanei Eretz Yisrael," or those who are faithful to the land of Israel.[14]

The combination of religious fervor and the question of Israeli security make the establishment of a Palestinian state in the West Bank and Gaza a highly unlikely proposition at this time. Furthermore, Heller observes that the physical characteristics of the West Bank complicate the task of defending Israel's vital core area in which over 60 percent of its population and 80 percent of its industry are concentrated.[15] The geographic features of the West Bank, then, make it a formidable defensive asset for Israel and a definite threat if occupied by hostile Palestinian forces. On the Gaza Strip, the Israelis have constructed a security barricade that surrounds Gaza. Israel reports that since the construction of the security fence, not a single suicide bomber has carried out an attack in Israel.

In sum, after nearly 2,000 years, the Jews had finally regained Jerusalem, Judea, and Samaria; and to expect the Jews to hand over Jerusalem (the ancient city of David), the home of the ancient Hebrews, is to ask the impossible. Realistically the Israelis will continue to dominate the West Bank, and the 3.5 million Palestinians living under Israeli occupation will undoubtedly continue to resist. Most Palestinians living on the West Bank are loyal to the Palestinian Authority although Hamas has been growing stronger. One can only conclude that this loyalty will continue, and terrorism and resistance supported by various PLO-affiliated groups will continue to escalate. The debate over the illusory and highly publicized pursuit of territory for peace is likely to continue. The critical question of how to make the sharing of territory less dangerous and less uncomfortable for Israelis and Palestinians will continue to dominate international politics. Palestine is still the issue. Most likely the Israelis will not yield, and the Palestinians will continue their struggle to recover Palestine. Terrorism, then, can be expected to escalate as desperate Palestinian extremist groups such as Hamas, Islamic Jihad, and al Aqsa fight for self-determination. In spite of the Palestinian–Israeli conflict and widespread acknowledgment of the justification of Palestinian political violence, a new strain of terrorism has spread throughout the Middle East. The results have been more deadly than any trend in international terrorism since the Palestinian–Arab–Israeli conflict began in 1948.

ISLAMIC EXTREMISM

After the 1979 Iranian revolution, the Middle East erupted into a spasm of political violence and terrorism that continues to this day. The early targets were not U.S. citizens or Europeans but Middle Easterners. The terrorist incidents were dramatic attention-getting events designed to provide maximum publicity to yet unknown Islamic religious fundamentalist groups. The assassination of Egyptian President Anwar Sadat, the attempted assassination of the president of Iraq, the 1981 plot to overthrow the government of Bahrain and install an Islamic republic, the plot to overthrow the Kuwaiti government in 1982, the 1987 seizure of the Grand Mosque in Mecca, and the Islamic uprisings in Saudi Arabia, Lebanon, Egypt, and Syria have all generated extensive news coverage. But other less publicized terrorist incidents have passed and been forgotten. Skyjackings of Arab jetliners, kidnappings of Arab government officials, assassinations of Arab civilians, and attacks on Arab businesses and cultural centers have become commonplace in the Middle East.

Amorphous groups with exotic-sounding names such as **Islamic Amal**, Islamic Jihad, Hamas, and Hizballah began to attract media attention in the early 1980s. The groups responsible for this new surge in Middle East terrorism are primarily Shi'ite Muslims. Islamic Amal of Lebanon, for example, attracted worldwide attention after involvement in several well-staged skyjackings. One Amal skyjacker has become a legend in the Shia community of the Middle East for successfully hijacking an astonishing six aircraft. In the 1980s, the largest Shia movement in Lebanon was Amal. Amal is the Arabic word for "hope," as well as an acronym for the "Lebanese Resistance Battalions." Wright reports that by 1982 Amal split into two factions, and a more extremist faction called Hizballah, or "Party of God," emerged.[16]

Hizballah derives its name from a verse in the Koran that promises eternal life for those who join the Party of God and spread the message of Islam. With the support of Iran, Hizballah has grown among the disaffected Shi'ite minority, especially in Lebanon. Proclaiming world

Islamic revolution and martyrdom, Hizballah followers represent a variety of Muslim fundamentalist beliefs. Attempts to understand the religious crusade of Hizballah led to predictions that a revengeful Islamic world is preparing for a *jihad*, or holy war, against Christianity, Judaism, capitalism, and godless communism. The extremist Islamic world allegedly mobilized for such a jihad against the Israel presence in Lebanon in the early 1980s. Eventually Israel withdrew its military forces from Lebanon. Jihad, or holy war, promotes the concept of conscious martyrdom or purification through death, which is apparently the core belief of the radical Shi'ite sects of Hizballah and Islamic Jihad.[17]

Only when the United States and other Westerners came under attack was the concept of jihad taken more seriously. In 1982, suicide car bombers attacked the U.S. Embassy, the U.S. Marine Command Center, and the French, British, and Italian multinational peacekeeping force in Lebanon. Suicide car bombers also blew up the French and U.S. embassies in Kuwait, and several theatrical skyjackings were staged between 1983 and 1986. At one point, Iranian officials were quoted as saying that 1,000 suicide bombers were prepared to strike targets in the United States. By the end of 1983, the Reagan administration labeled the attacks on Western targets as "state-sponsored terrorism." The United States charged that Iran was providing the financial and technical support for terrorist acts directed against the United States. Eventually the Shi'ite Islamic sect became synonymous with the term *terrorism* in the United States. The Shi'ites had replaced extremist Palestinian groups as the most determined and feared international terrorist groups. The growth of Shi'ite extremism is complex, but undoubtedly the Lebanese civil war contributed to the escalation of Shi'ite terrorism.

As the cycle of international terrorism shifts from one group to another, terrorist attacks become more devastating. Under Osama bin Laden, **al Qaeda** has emerged as the leading patron of international terrorism. Osama bin Laden's support for terrorism was more damaging than anything experienced by the PLO, Hamas, or Hizballah. Unlike most terrorist organizations that have definite objectives—the recovery of Palestine or the destruction of Israel—al Qaeda–sponsored terrorist groups divided the entire world into two distinct categories: enemies of Muslims and enemies of Islam. However, the two categories are not mutually exclusive. Since the bombing of the World Trade Center in 1993, U.S. citizens have become a prime target of al Qaeda–sponsored terrorists. Al Qaeda terrorism culminated with the mass murder of 3,000 Americans on September 11, 2001. Its surrogates also attacked U.S. interests in Europe, North Africa, Asia, and the Middle East.[18]

The Islamic terrorists of al Qaeda are convinced that they have been unfairly treated by the Arab countries of the Middle East and manipulated by the West. Osama bin Laden has taken Islamic discontent and molded it into a combination of religious fervor and national pride. Bin Laden apparently views his destiny as one of destroying the heretics of Islam and diminishing the seductive influence of the "Great Satan," the United States. Since September 11, 2001, al Qaeda–sponsored terrorists have carried out dozens of devastating terrorist attacks. The majority of these attacks were directed against innocent civilians around the globe.[19] The indiscriminate bombing of the London subway, the Madrid commuter train bombing, and the Bali nightclub bombing are just a few examples.

The growth of al Qaeda–sponsored extremism is particularly alarming to Western nations because Islamic religious fanatics are willing to sacrifice their lives for religious beliefs. Previously, all terrorists had carried out their terrorist attacks with well-devised plans of escape. Such logical planning does not apply to most acts of suicide terrorism. In many cases, in fact, the opposite seems true. Some Muslim martyrs choose death and gladly welcome the opportunity to enter paradise in exchange for the killing of Western nonbelievers and the eradication of Islamic heretics. For example, during a British trial of eight Islamic terrorists who planned to blow up seven planes flying from London to the United States, it came to light that the terrorists' wives and children were to accompany them in order not to arouse suspicion as they went through airport security. It is unclear whether the terrorist bombers intended to inform their wives and children that they were about to become martyrs for the jihad.[20] How should Western democracies fight against an enemy whose leaders preach a preference of death over life? There seems to be little disagreement that Osama bin Laden and al Qaeda have planned for some time to export its "terrorism" to other parts of the Islamic world, especially Middle Eastern and Islamic countries.

Western society, particularly the United States, is ill prepared to combat the twenty-first century strategy of al Qaeda–sponsored terrorism, which draws heavily on its eleventh century religious philosophy. Religious zealotry and suicidal fanaticism are virtually unknown to the United States. Al Qaeda, under the guidance of Osama bin Laden, may now have a chance to influence the Islamic world by their dedication to fanatical religious principles. Al Qaeda–sponsored terrorism plays an important role in the formation of international terrorist groups and will undoubtedly continue for some years to come.

The attacks on the World Trade Center and the Pentagon represent a dramatic increase in the lethality of terrorist attacks. The trend in the lethality of terrorist attacks is directly correlated to changes in terrorist groups' motivations. A new generation of terrorists has emerged supporting extremist religious beliefs that vow to create a pan-Islamic empire. Recent terrorist attacks have also created economic chaos. For instance, Osama bin Laden and al Qaeda supporters were reportedly elated by the economic losses caused by the September 11 attacks. In an October 2001 videotape message, bin Laden was exhilarated by the economic devastation caused by the attack on the World Trade Center. Even if the objective of the al Qaeda September 11 attacks were not economically disruptive, the attacks raised an awareness of how fragile the world economy can be to indiscriminate acts of terrorism. In fact, bin Laden warned the world that "the youths of God are preparing for you things that will fill your hearts with terror and target your economic lifeline until you stop your oppression and aggression."[21]

As U.S. intelligence services, law enforcement, and the military continue to disrupt al Qaeda and its affiliated groups to carry out future mass casualty attacks in the United States, al Qaeda may attempt attacks on softer, smaller-scale targets. In the future, smaller-scale attacks could take the form of suicide bombings, assassination of public officials, car or truck bombings of symbolic targets, or low-level biological or chemical attacks. In fact, the spiritual leader of Hizballah encouraged Muslims to carry out global suicide attacks against the United States.[22] **Abu Zubaydah**, chief of operations for al Qaeda, currently in U.S. custody, warned that al Qaeda terrorists were planning attacks on nongovernmental buildings where large numbers of Americans gather, such as airports or sporting venues.[23]

Historically, contemporary terrorist groups have been more imitative than innovative. For instance, al Qaeda's attack on the U.S.S. Cole emulated the tactics of the Japanese kamikaze suicide pilots who successfully targeted U.S. naval vessels in the Pacific during World War II. However, the September 11 attacks illustrate al Qaeda's ability and planning skills to exercise the tactics of deception and innovation. Furthermore, Gunaratna reports that al Qaeda operatives are seriously evaluating the possibility of deploying chemical, biological, radiological, and nuclear devices against targets in the "West."[24] Italian police uncovered a plot by an al Qaeda terrorist cell to use **cyanide gas** in an attack on the U.S. embassy in Rome in March 2002. The significance of the planned cyanide gas attack demonstrates the innovative nature of the al Qaeda cell that included known members of the Algerian Armed Islamic Group (GIA) and the Salafist

Group for Call and Combat (GSPC). The plan was to release the cyanide gas in the underground utility tunnels that surrounded the American Embassy. Along with the cyanide compounds, the police also recovered a quantity of gunpowder that the conspirators planned to use to disperse the cyanide gas through the utility tunnels.[25]

In early May 2003, Pakistani police uncovered a plot by al Qaeda to crash an explosives-laden aircraft into the American Consulate in Karachi, Pakistan. The plot was in its late stages when Pakistani police arrested several al Qaeda figures who had over 300 pounds of explosives and a cache of weapons in their possession.[26] Even though the cyanide gas attack and the 9/11-style attack were foiled by superior police investigative work, dedicated members of al Qaeda carried out a devastating multiple suicide bombing in Riyadh, Saudi Arabia, on May 12, 2003.

Typical of previous attacks by al Qaeda, three suicide bomb vehicles carrying three suicide bombers each struck almost simultaneously at three gated compounds housing Americans and Westerners in Riyadh. Over forty people were killed, including several Americans and the nine suicide bombers. Over 200 people were seriously injured. The attacks were well planned and successfully carried out despite a U.S. State Department warning of an imminent terrorist attack against U.S. interests in Saudi Arabia. In all three attacks, the suicide bombers killed the security guards at the compounds, opened the gates, and drove a vehicle packed with high explosives deep inside the compounds before igniting the explosive material. The Riyadh attacks illustrate that al Qaeda is still capable of carrying out coordinated attacks, even in tightly secured gated compounds.[27]

Hoffman observes another disturbing trend in Islamic terrorism, described as the evolution of "loose networks" of al Qaeda–directed terrorists.[28] It has indirect influence over a much larger group of people that range from local supporters or "walk-ins" to like-minded guerrillas, terrorists, revolutionaries, and insurgents. Therefore, group affiliations are not always clear, making it difficult for the United States to determine responsibility for future attacks. In the aforementioned suicide bombing in Riyadh, no one claimed credit for the attack. The Riyadh attack was followed by another multiple suicide bombing attack in Casablanca that killed thirty-four people.[29] In fact, there are a number of loose networks of Islamic terrorist groups forming on the basis of their common hatred of the United States and the West.

In one respect, Islamic terror networks support Osama bin Laden's "America first" policy of driving Americans from Islamic countries, deposing pro-Western governments from the Islamic "umma," and the creation of a pan-Islamic society. The best example of how Islamic terrorist groups rally around the ideology of bin Laden can be found in Central Asia. In September 2002, several Islamic extremist groups joined forces in an effort to create a single Islamic entity. The Islamic Movement of Uzbekistan (IMU), separatists from Kyrgyzstan, Chechnya, Tajekistan, and the East Turkestan Islamic Movement (ETIM) joined forces to create a single Islamic terrorist entity. The anti-Western agenda of al Qaeda to sell its propaganda of worldwide jihad and the restoration of the Islamic Caliphate is gaining momentum in the Islamic community.[30] As can be seen from a now declassified National Intelligence Estimate, the U.S. intelligence community concluded that al Qaeda and affiliated groups were more powerful in 2007 than they had been before the "war on terror" began. The National Intelligence Estimate cites two reasons for the future danger posed by al Qaeda: continued U.S. support for Israel and a new generation of jihadis inspired by the Iraqi insurgency.[31]

Al Qaeda also relies heavily on technology, such as the Internet, video- and audiotapes, to spread their hatred, promote internal communications, and intimidate their enemies; that is, the West. In the future, Internet-based crime may serve as a funding source for al Qaeda. The availability of public records and other information over the Internet should provide new opportunities for al Qaeda to select potential targets. Al Qaeda has always been quite proficient at external communications and enhancing its worldwide image. Al Qaeda has used both videotapes and audiotapes to warn potential targets of impending attacks and to relay messages directly to its followers. The use of audio- and videotapes serves two purposes for al Qaeda and Osama bin Laden: (1) The tapes convey the message that the organizational structure of al Qaeda is still functioning and (2) the organization is still capable of carrying out successful terrorist missions.[32] Al Qaeda and affiliated groups not only use audio- and videotapes to spread propaganda but have created several Web sites to spread messages of hate and violence.[33]

Finally, the threat from individual Islamic extremists, or "little al Qaedas," appears to be increasing. Individuals acting of their own volition, who sympathize with the aims of al Qaeda or the Palestinian cause, pose a significant threat. There is little doubt that lone terrorists are diffi-cult to detect, particularly the terrorist who may have loose ties to a terrorist organization. Marc Sageman refers to the lone terrorist or unaffiliated terrorist group as leaderless jihad.

The concept of **leaderless resistance** (jihad) was first introduced by Louis Beam to continue the right-wing militia's struggle against the U.S. government. Beam was a member of the Aryan Nations and an avowed white supremacist who preached that Jewish conspirators (the ZOG) controlled the U.S. government. Abu Musab al Suri, a prominent al Qaeda planner, outlined a similar analysis of leaderless resistance or the "lone wolf" extremist.[34]

Al Suri's theory calls for a strategy of fighting a more powerful enemy using self-organizing clandestine networks. The strategy is to convince likeminded people to organize independent groups that will continue the struggle without contacts with other groups or leaders. The groups operate independently and are protected from detection when members of another group are apprehended and interrogated by police. Several examples of terrorist plots and bombings illus-trate the concept of leaderless jihad: the Madrid training bombings of March 2004; the Asparagus 18 case in Belgium of March 2004;[35] the Taba, Egypt, bombings of October 2004; the Sharm el-Sheikh bombings in July 2005; the London subway bombings in July 2005; the Melbourne and Sydney bombing plots in November 2005;[36] the bomb plot to blow up Sears Tower in Chicago in June 2006;[37] and the plot to bomb London and Glasgow in June 2007.[38]

Not one of these terrorist plots or terrorist bombings had any significant link to al Qaeda or Osama bin Laden. Likewise, when offenders were apprehended, police discovered that the primary motive behind the bombing plot was the Iraq insurgency and U.S. support of Israel.

The most important asset related to al Qaeda in the United States is certainly the recruit-ment of individuals who are U.S. citizens. American citizens who tacitly support al Qaeda or the objectives of other terrorist groups present a dangerous threat to American society.

Another growing danger is an attack against U.S. commercial aircraft using Stinger-type shoulder-fired anti-aircraft missiles. The world is saturated with Stinger-type missiles, including ones made in the United States, Russia, China, and North Korea. On November 28, 2002, two anti-aircraft missiles barely missed an Israeli plane taking off from Mombasa, Kenya. A missile strike on a jet flying over the United States would undoubtedly bring commercial aviation to a standstill. In fact, even an attempt or credible threat could bring commercial air traffic to a halt. The potential threat from Stinger-type missiles is no longer hypothetical.

LOW-INTENSITY WARFARE

Several commentators maintain that al Qaeda positively supports a variety of terrorist groups, partic-ularly in the Middle East and Southeast Asia where the focus of terrorist attacks is directed toward destabilizing local governments.[39] Conventional warfare is out of the question for al Qaeda since the

United States and its allies are militarily too strong. The military and economic capacity of the United States has led al Qaeda to support international terrorism, insurgency, guerrilla wars, and wars of national liberation as a substitute for traditional warfare. Gunaratna adds that al Qaeda–sponsored international terrorism should not be misunderstood since al Qaeda support of terrorist groups is essentially to attain its political, religious, and military objectives.[40] Those objectives are to destabilize the United States and the West, spread al Qaeda's influence throughout the world, and assist pro–al Qaeda "liberation" movements to gain power. More pragmatic objectives involve the use of terrorism to eliminate pro-government forces in various countries, to provoke Western democracies to overreact, and to disrupt the military establishment and the criminal justice system. A variety of unconventional conflicts and episodes of indiscriminate terrorism are currently a permanent feature of the international community. Whether al Qaeda is directly responsible for all these conflicts is still debatable. Falk argues that it is absurd to place the blame for the increase of worldwide, unconventional conflicts on al Qaeda.[41] There is, however, considerable disagreement regarding the definition and nature of unconventional conflicts and al Qaeda support for such conflicts.

The term *low-intensity conflict* is widely used to describe various forms of unconventional wars. The U.S. Army defines low-intensity conflicts as "conflicts ranging from terrorism, revolution, counterrevolution to limited small war operations conducted by a political group to achieve a major political goal that can include the overthrow of the existing system and replacing it with a new leadership and political-social order."[42] Other writers give little credence to the notion of unconventional conflicts and divide all violent political conflicts, including international terrorism, into low- and high-intensity areas.[43] In the end unconventional conflicts include a broad range of extranormal types of political violence. The most common and damaging to the survival of democracies is terrorism/counterterrorism and revolution/counterrevolution. Terrorism is a strategic and tactical concept fundamental to the success of a well-planned guerrilla war, insurgency, or revolution. Marighella reminds us that "terrorism is an arm the revolutionary can never relinquish."[44]

Sarkesian presents a unique model for categorizing unconventional conflicts. He argues that to respond effectively to acts of political violence and terrorism, a more comprehensive understanding of unconventional conflicts is necessary. He identifies five types of world conflict. At one end of his conflict spectrum are conflicts unlikely to escalate into total warfare, that is, terrorism; at the other end is the ultimate conflict—nuclear holocaust.[45] (See Table 10.1.)

In sum, as yet the concept of low-intensity conflict and al Qaeda involvement is ill defined. However, al Qaeda officially supports the use of terrorism as a tactic to destabilize the West and proclaims its involvement in unconventional world conflicts. Currently forty-six countries are engaged in some type of unconventional warfare, ranging from the indiscriminate terrorism of Peru's communist-inspired Sendero Luminoso (Shining Path) to the several guerrilla wars being waged in Africa to the conventional land wars, such as the Iraq–U.S. war, or the Russian–Chechnya war.[46] Moreover, Janke identifies 568 terrorist guerrilla organizations that have been active throughout the world between 1945 and 1994 and have posed a dangerous threat to the overthrow of established governments.[47] The motivation of terrorist guerrilla activity is indeed complex, covering such concepts as colonialism, ethnic separation, religious fundamentalism, and ideological convictions. To say that al Qaeda has organized and planned the terrorist operations of the many world conflicts and financially and ideologically supported terrorist guerrilla groups that exist in the world seems somewhat farfetched. However, documentary evidence is available that indicates that once unconventional conflicts begin or Islamic terrorist groups emerge, al Qaeda surely will attempt to exploit the situation.[48]

In fact, al Qaeda does support various terrorist groups, national liberation movements, religious fanatics, and revolutionaries. This support generally involves training, technical

TABLE 10.1 The Conflict Spectrum

Terrorism	Counter Terrorism	Low-Intensity Conflict	Conventional Warfare	Nuclear, Biological, or Chemical Warfare
Indiscriminate acts of political violence Attacks on "soft" targets (civilian or military) PFLP, Hamas, ETA al Qaeda, criminal acts	Special tactics (Delta Force, SAS, GSG-9, private militias, vigilante groups)	Revolution/Counterrevolution (Wars of national liberation, civil war, ethnic and religious turmoil)	Major land wars (Iraq and United States; Chechnya and Russia; Afghanistan and United States)	First strike options? (Total destruction)

The History Guy: The War List, February (2009), *http://www.historyguy.com*

Source: Adapted from Sam C. Sarkesian, *America's Forgotten Wars: The Counterrevolutionary Past and Lessons for the Future* (Westport, CT: Greenwood Press, 1984), pp. 229–48.

assistance, and, at times, direct participation. As you recall, al Qaeda operatives have participated in terrorist attacks against a variety of symbolic targets. Al Qaeda has been organized into a highly specialized and trained force capable of conducting low-intensity warfare and as a major disruptive terrorist force.[49]

Hoffman predicts that the future course of unconventional conflicts will involve an escalation in international terrorism, guerrilla war, and limited conventional war.[50] In some respects, the future course of low-intensity conflicts is reflected in the Sri Lankan civil war. Political violence in Sri Lanka encompasses four levels of Sarkesian's conflict spectrum. It involves indiscriminate suicide terrorist bombings, private militias, regular military forces, guerrillas, revolutionaries, and counterinsurgency forces, some of which are assisted by foreign states, by other terrorist groups, or political religious fanatics. But the most dangerous future escalation of international terrorism is the growing fear that terrorists, guerrillas, revolutionaries, or insurgents will use weapons of mass destruction.

SUPERTERRORISM

Among all forms of terrorist activity, there is little doubt that terrorist acquisition of weapons of mass destruction is the most threatening to the security of the world, specifically nuclear, biological, or chemical weapons. Symbolic terrorist attacks such as hostage taking, bombing, murder, and assassination, carried out for a variety of political motivations, have killed thousands of innocent people. However, no mass casualties have as yet resulted from a single terrorist attack using weapons of mass destruction. Terrorist groups prefer automatic weapons and suicide bombs and seldom use more sophisticated weapons, although Palestinian terrorists have attacked Israeli El-Al jetliners with rocket-propelled grenades and surface-to-air missiles. Livingstone reports that it is not uncommon to find rocket-propelled grenade antitank missile launchers or Soviet-built SA-7 anti-aircraft guided missiles in the arsenals of at least a dozen international terrorist groups.[51] But according to Stern, high-tech weapons are least preferred by terrorist groups since tactical success has been achieved by using more conventional weapons.[52] Nonetheless, the vulnerabilities of a high-tech attack are so obvious and so threatening that real security measures are needed even if the threat remains theoretical. The greatest threat comes from the possibility of some type of nuclear terrorism.

In the years since India's single nuclear test in 1974, the spread of nuclear weapons has slowly gone underground. The declared nuclear weapon states of the United States, Russia, United Kingdom, France, and China announced their membership in the nuclear club by openly testing nuclear weapons. Thereafter, they publicly acknowledged the progress of nuclear weapons research as it advanced to hydrogen bombs, neutron bombs, strategic defense initiative (SDI), long-range missiles, and other high-tech weapons systems.

In contrast, the emerging nuclear weapon states of India, Israel, Iran, Pakistan, and North Korea have concealed their programs of nuclear weapons testing, although India and Pakistan acknowledged testing nuclear weapons in the 1980s with the objective of creating a nuclear military option in the event of war with a hostile nation. Nonetheless, emerging nuclear states often deny any interest in the development of a nuclear military option. Fortunately, not all emerging nuclear states have the capacity to test or construct nuclear weapons. The testing of nuclear weapons can be achieved through computer simulations, and reliable nuclear weapons can be developed without a test explosion. Clearly a few nuclear weapons could have a devastating impact on regional global conflicts. Moreover the clandestine development of nuclear weapons technology heightens the underground proliferation of unrestricted nuclear weapons programs. This global trend toward the secret development of nuclear weapons is a matter of grave concern for the planet.

Israel, for example, is believed to have acquired nuclear weapons in the late 1960s. However, in the absence of a known test, the certainty of Israeli possession of nuclear weapons is unknown. In addition, Israel has never proclaimed publicly that it now has a nuclear military option. Today the possible size of the Israeli nuclear military arsenal and the capacity of delivering nuclear warheads to a projected target are a mystery, although evidence suggests both are growing.[53] The Israeli government has maintained a well-planned, ambiguous position about its ownership of nuclear weapons, neither confirming nor denying their existence.[54] There is no doubt Israel has used this ambiguity as a veiled threat against hostile Arab nations. Of all parts of the globe where nuclear proliferation could occur, none is more volatile than the Middle East. Israeli nuclear development has provided a justification for several Middle Eastern nations to seek nuclear weapons. The race is on. Muslims believe that if Christians, Jews, godless communists, and Hindus have nuclear weapons, then so should the Muslims. The list of nations includes the key opponents of Israel: Jordan, Syria, Egypt, and Iran. As long as the status and self-determination of the Palestinians and Arab hostility toward Israel exist, there may be little that can be done to stop the escalation of nuclear proliferation in the Middle East.

The increase in the number of nations experimenting with nuclear weapons also increases the number of nations in the world handling weapons-grade, enriched uranium and plutonium. Emerging nuclear powers may also have fewer security measures to protect such weapons-grade fuel. Obviously, if such weapons-grade material were obtained by a fanatical terrorist group such as al Qaeda, it could pose a significant threat to the entire world.

The spread of nuclear weapons to terrorist groups requires that terrorists possess at least two essential elements. First, the knowledge of how to construct a nuclear weapon is an obvious requirement. However, this is no longer a serious obstacle. Cameron points out that unclassified material is readily available to provide enough technical information for terrorists to manufacture a crude nuclear device that has a known probability of detonation.[55] Furthermore, states that sponsor terrorism have access to trained physicists who can probably figure out how to build a workable nuclear weapon. The technology could then be shared with terrorist groups. Logic suggests that sooner or later terrorist bombs will be nuclear.

Second, sufficient quantities of weapons-grade material are necessary to manufacture a nuclear weapon. Experts are in general agreement that terrorists would require not only design information but also fissionable material, high explosives, a high-tech laboratory, extremely tight security, years of dedicated effort, advanced education in physics, and millions of dollars.[56] With this in mind, the possibility of terrorists building a workable, fissionable nuclear device seems remote. Jenkins agrees that constructing a nuclear terror device is beyond the capabilities of terrorist groups.[57] Nevertheless, Willrich and Taylor early on argued that the acquisition of nuclear material and the construction of a nuclear device are not beyond the capacities of a few terrorist groups with governmental sponsorship.[58] Hughes estimates, for example, that nuclear terrorists would require no more than 4 kilograms of plutonium or 11 kilograms of highly enriched uranium (HEU) to construct a crude fission bomb that upon detonation would produce an explosion equal to 100 tons of TNT or any high-velocity explosive and would be small enough to transport in a compact automobile.[59] In the Norton and Greenberg text, several scenarios are presented where **dirty bombs** or radiological devices are used that include radioactive isotopes such as cobalt, iodine, and **cesium**, which are commercial products that are more vulnerable to theft than plutonium or enriched uranium.[60]

In November 1995, Chechen terrorists planted a device in Ismailovsky Park in Moscow. The device has been described as a lead container with radioactive cesium-137 surrounded by dynamite—a so-called dirty bomb. One expert states that hundreds would have died soon after exposure to the radioactive cesium-137. However, the Chechen terrorists made no attempt to detonate the "dirty bomb." Instead, the Chechens called a local television station describing the type of bomb and its location. The Chechen terrorists then heightened the fear and panic in Moscow by claiming additional radiological devices had been planted at other Moscow locations. Russian police found the device at Ismailovsky Park and disarmed it without incident. No other devices were located. This is most likely the only confirmed incident of a terrorist group possessing a "dirty bomb."[61]

Awareness of the danger of terrorists acquiring a nuclear weapon has been growing for some time. Warnings in the United States and abroad have continually been issued that thefts from nuclear plants could provide the fissionable material to construct a terrorist nuclear device. In an effort to reduce the availability of weapons-grade materials, the United States and Russia have cooperated more than on any other issue since the fall of the Soviet Union. The two nuclear countries have a clear interest in keeping the nuclear weapons club as small as possible, both for security reasons and political power. Nuclear proliferation not only implies that terrorists could easily penetrate lax security systems, but it also entails a geometrical increase in the number of pairs of nations that could engage in a nuclear confrontation. To date, al Qaeda has made a determined effort to acquire a tactical nuclear weapon. In fact, Jenkins notes that al Qaeda is the only terrorist group that actually has a nuclear policy.[62]

Even so, by November 2001 al Qaeda's leadership was on the run, leaving behind in Afghanistan hundreds of documents, including manuals regarding potential target selection, records of meetings, and schematics regarding dirty bombs and nuclear, chemical, and biological weapons. The documents confirm al Qaeda's ambition to acquire weapons of mass destruction but provide no conclusive evidence that al Qaeda was successful in its pursuit of weapons of mass destruction. It would be extremely difficult to pursue a nuclear program while al Qaeda's bases in Afghanistan were being destroyed and its key operational planners were being killed or captured. The difficulties in acquiring trained scientists and nuclear material have not deterred al Qaeda from creating the impression that it has weapons of mass destruction and is just waiting for the opportunity to use them.

By contrast, a real threat exists that terrorists might capture an intact nuclear weapon. The possession of such a nuclear weapon could undoubtedly create an international crisis, even if the terrorists could not overcome the technical security systems required to fire or launch the weapon. The United States now has commando teams equipped with "backpack nuclear weapons."[63] If such small, easily concealable nuclear weapons were to fall into the hands of terrorists, they could be used to hold the U.S. hostage for a considerable time.

Numerous scenarios of nuclear terrorism have been proposed by scholars as well as authors of popular literature. Some obvious possibilities that appear technically possible and politically convincing include a group of religious fanatics with suicidal tendencies who adhere to a belief that preaches heavenly rewards; antinuclear activists attacking nuclear facilities as an act of symbolic violence; organized criminal gangs attempting to extort large sums of money from affluent nations; emerging Third World nations seeking to influence international policy; revolutionaries, insurgents, or terrorists engaged in a low-intensity conflict with a strategic desire to escalate that conflict; or a band of highly trained terrorists who could take over a nuclear facility near a major city and destroy it, resulting in the deaths of millions of people.[64]

The scenarios should be taken seriously. Researchers at Stanford's Institute for International Studies have compiled a database of lost, stolen, and misplaced nuclear material, depicting the world "saturated" in weapons-grade uranium and plutonium that is unaccounted for. For example, over the past ten years at least 40 kilograms (88 pounds) of weapons-grade uranium and plutonium had been stolen from nuclear facilities in the former Soviet Union. Subsequently, most of the weapons-grade material has been recovered. However, at least 2 kilos (4.4 lbs.) of HEU is still missing. Other thefts have included nuclear fuel rods, as well as radiation equipment from scientific labs. The Institute paints a bleak picture of nuclear thefts and concludes the ultimate destination of the stolen nuclear material remains a mystery.[65]

The seizure or theft of nuclear weapons in the United States and from NATO military installations has also been the object of many scenarios. One scenario explores the takeover of a Minuteman missile site by a dedicated team of terrorists, thus providing the terrorists with the means to launch a nuclear strike.[66] Jenkins hypothesizes that a dedicated team of three to five terrorists armed with automatic weapons and explosives could easily carry out a surprise attack on a nuclear power plant or a nuclear military facility.[67] On November 7, 2007, four intruders attacked the nuclear research facility at **Pelindaba**, South Africa. The Pelindaba site is South Africa's main nuclear facility, where nuclear bombs were developed, tested, and stored. South Africa disarmed its nuclear arsenal in the late 1990s. However, the stockpile of nuclear fuel, in the form of HEU, was stored at the Pelindaba site. Four armed intruders were able to penetrate two layers of security before they escaped, being driven off by security personnel. No doubt the object of the attack was the HEU, which is a difficult substance to process. It takes only a few pounds of HEU to make a crude nuclear device. Over 1,000 pounds of HEU, worth millions of dollars on the black market, is stored at Pelindaba. The Pelindaba incident illustrates the importance of protecting nuclear facilities.[68]

Countering any future nuclear terrorist threat requires teamwork by federal, state, and local law enforcement agencies. The FBI maintains federal jurisdictional responsibility for the investigation of nuclear extortion threats or any incident involving radioactive materials or the attempted construction of nuclear explosives. The Department of Energy is also responsible for the security and management of nuclear materials. Search personnel with high-tech detection equipment, known as the Nuclear Emergency Search Team (NEST), are trained to respond when incidents include improvised nuclear weapons, "dirty bombs," lost or stolen radioactive material, or improvised radiation devices. NEST can be mobilized and transported to a nuclear crisis scene anywhere in the United States in two hours. The role of NEST is to assist the FBI and local law enforcement in a search for suspected nuclear explosives material. Because of the seriousness of the nuclear terrorist threat, criminal justice students and law enforcement personnel should be familiar with at least a few of the technical terms associated with nuclear weapons technology. The following terms are described:[69]

> *Enriched uranium*—uranium that contains a U-235 concentration, which is the only naturally occurring fissile isotope.
>
> *Plutonium-239*—a fissile isotope created by the use of U-238. Excellent material for construction of nuclear weapons those are human-made and radioactive.
>
> *Special Nuclear Material (SNM)*—fissionable material in the form of uranium-enriched isotopes consisting of Uranium-233 and Uranium-235 or Plutonium-239.
>
> *Radioactive Dispersal Device*—any nuclear device containing radioactive material designed to spread contamination.
>
> *Weapons-Grade Plutonium*—plutonium that contains approximately 7 percent of Plutonium-240 used in the design of nuclear weapons.

The U.S. Energy Department reports that the United States now has two nuclear facilities to manufacture enriched uranium for eventual use in U.S. nuclear strategic weapons.[70] As production and supply centers increase, serious security and control problems also increase the possibility of the theft of weapons-grade material. For the first time in the evaluation of nuclear weapons technology, any nation with an advanced industrial base, a corps of nuclear scientists and technicians, and a modern military establishment familiar with weapons-delivery systems can build a formidable nuclear strike force. This obviously creates additional opportunities for terrorists to "go nuclear." The greater fear is that emerging nuclear weapons states such as North Korea or Iran, who have been identified by the United States as state sponsors of terrorism, would sell or give nuclear weapons to terrorist groups. Cranston points out the real threat to the security of the world lies not with the acquisition of nuclear weapons by some fanatical terrorist group but by the formation of a nuclear terrorist state such as Iran.[71] The United States first accused Iran of pursuing an active nuclear weapons program on May 7, 2003. The U.S. government reports that Iran's nuclear weapons program is so advanced it no longer requires foreign assistance to construct a nuclear bomb. Iran refuses to submit to UN inspection of its nuclear facilities.

Jenkins states that assuming Iran eventually acquires a nuclear military option and is willing to risk nuclear retaliation, why would it give or sell nuclear weapons to a radical terrorist group?[72] Mearsheimer and Walt agree that the danger of a "nuclear handoff" to terrorists from Iran is a remote possibility since Iran could not be sure the transfer would be undetected by Israel or the United States.[73] Thus, Iran runs the risk of retaliation from the United States or Israel. Former President Jimmy Carter also supports the position that Iran would not be willing to risk retaliation from the United States or Israel if it provided nuclear weapons to terrorist groups like Hizballah or Hamas.[74] Jenkins, Mearsheimer and Walt, and President Carter may be underestimating the danger posed by a nuclear Iran. For example, Iranian leaders have repeatedly threatened to "wipe Israel off the map." The president of Iran Mahmoud Ahmadinejad firmly believes that nuclear war with Israel will bring about the arrival of the Twelfth Imam.[75] Even Iranian moderate leaders proclaimed that an Iranian nuclear attack on Israel would kill 5 million Jews; and if Israel retaliated with its own nuclear bomb, Iran might lose 15 million people, a small price to pay from among the world's billion Muslims.[76] This seemingly irrational rhetoric by Iran's leaders pushes the world closer to a nuclear holocaust.

Even though Iran, with nuclear weapons, presents a dangerous threat to the world, Pakistan may present an even greater threat since they already have a moderate nuclear arsenal. Pakistan always appears to be on the edge of sectarian and religious upheaval, with Shia and Sunni Muslim and Hindus constantly attacking each other. Pakistani government officials also sympathize and/or support Islamic extremists like the Taliban and al Qaeda. The instability in Pakistan has created fears that Pakistan's nuclear weapons are no longer secure. The concern is that other states or terrorist groups could obtain material or expertise related to nuclear weapons from Pakistan.

Beginning in 1970, Pakistan organized a clandestine network led by Abdul Qadeer Khan to procure information on the development of nuclear weapons. By the mid-1990s, Pakistan had successfully developed a nuclear military option. The Abdul Qadeer Khan network subsequently supplied nuclear technology to North Korea, Libya, and Iran.[77] Al Qaeda has also sought assistant from the Khan network. George Tenet, former Director of the CIA, reported that al Qaeda had sent "emissaries to establish contact" with **A.Q. Khan**.[78] Furthermore, al Qaeda allegedly established contact with other Pakistani scientists, who indicated that the material needed to construct a nuclear weapon would be difficult to obtain.

Insofar as the United States knows, A.Q. Khan did not sell nuclear technology to any terrorist organization. By 2004, the A.Q. Khan clandestine network of nuclear weapons technology proliferation was dismantled and A.Q. Khan confessed to his involvement in the network and was arrested. The Pakistani government claims it has taken efforts to prevent further nuclear proliferation. After spending five years in confinement, A.Q. Khan was released by the Pakistani government on February 7, 2009. A.Q. Khan is a hero in Pakistan for developing the country's nuclear weapons program—the Islamic bomb. Pakistani government officials believe that development of nuclear weapons has saved Pakistan from a nuclear attack by archrival India.

Nevertheless, nuclear weapons represent only one dimension of the threat of so-called superterrorism. Other weapons of mass destruction include the introduction of biological and chemical agents into the target population by terrorist groups. The use of chemical or biological weapons, like nuclear weapons, can produce several million casualties in a single episode, causing widespread public fear and disruption of normal governmental operations. Unlike nuclear weapons, no insurmountable technological problems exist. Chemical and biological agents are easy to obtain, the methods of delivery are manageable, and they can be dispersed over a wide area. Thus, the resort to chemical or biological weapons can be accomplished with the minimum of risk by terrorists.

Several chemical terrorist incidents have been recorded. For example, in 1975 West German police received several threats from the Red Army Faction that mustard gas stolen from the military would be used against the German people unless all "political prisoners" were released and granted amnesty.[79] In another incident Middle East terrorists mailed a Jewish target a parcel bomb that was designed to detonate a vial of nerve gas when the parcel was opened.[80] European police discovered a clandestine laboratory in Paris producing *clostridium botulinum*, which secretes botulinal toxin (BTX), considered to be the most lethal toxin known.[81] Hersh maintains that BTX is so lethal that it would require only 8 ounces dispersed by vapor or aerosol to kill every living creature on earth.[82]

There exist a substantial number of highly toxic chemical agents available to terrorists or criminals. The use of such toxic chemicals is widely discussed in the available literature. Books, monographs, and professional papers are easily obtainable at most university libraries. The information needed to synthesize toxic chemical agents from raw materials is, therefore, available, and determined terrorist groups could easily brew up a chemical weapon capable of killing thousands of people. Four methods of dissemination of chemical weapons appear possible: (1) contamination of beverages and food products, (2) spreading lethal vapor concentrations in an enclosed location, (3) dispersal of aerosols in an enclosed location, and (4) widespread dispersal of vapors or aerosols in open locations.[83]

Chemical agents are man-made supertoxic chemicals that can be dispersed as a liquid, gas, vapor, or aerosol. Basic categories of chemical agents include nerve agents such as VX or **sarin** that disrupt the central nervous system, causing convulsions and death by respiratory paralysis. A single drop of VX on the skin is sufficient to kill a person. A second category of chemical agents is blood agents such as hydrogen cyanide or cyanogens chloride that complicate cellular respiration. A third category is blister agents such as phosgene, mustard gas, and lewisite that cause severe burns to the skin and lungs. Chemical agents vary greatly in toxicity and durability. For example, sarin disperses rapidly, whereas VX nerve agent or sulfur mustard gas can remain toxic for several weeks.[84]

Chemical agents were first used on a massive scale during World War I in Europe. During World War II the Allies and Axis countries produced large quantities of chemical weapons. However, fearing retaliation, chemical weapons were not used in Europe; but Japan used significant amounts of chemical agents against China. Since the end of World War II chemical agents have been used in several low-intensity conflicts such as the Yemen Civil War between 1963 and 1967, the Iraq–Iran War between 1980 and 1988, and the conflict between South Africa and Mozambique in 1992. On March 17, 1988, Iraqi military forces spread sarin, VX, and sabun over the Kurdish village of Halabja in northern Iraq, killing an estimated 5,000 people. Unconfirmed allegations of chemical agents include use by Bosnian Serbs against Muslims in 1995 and by the former Soviet Union in the early part of the Afghanistan war in 1981.[85]

Besides the use of chemical weapons during warfare, an attack on a commercial or industrial chemical plant can cause devastating results. In 1984, for example, an incident that happened at a Union Carbide plant in **Bhopal, India**, caused the death of thousands of people. A disgruntled employee precipitated an explosion in a storage tank by adding water to highly volatile chemicals. The explosion released noxious fumes that killed nearly 4,000 people and disabled another 11,000 people. The Bhopal incident illustrates how dangerous a single angry worker can be. This incident eventually resulted in the passing of laws requiring chemical companies to report industrial risks in Europe, Asia, and the United States.[86]

The first terrorist group to use the chemical weapon was not Aum Shinrikyo but the LTTE of Sri Lanka. In June 1990, the LTTE used **chlorine gas** in an attack on a Sri Lankan military base camp at Kiran in Sri Lanka's Batticaloa district. Several large drums of chlorine gas were positioned around the base camp's perimeter. When the wind currents were judged to be just right, the LTTE terrorists released the gas, which then drifted into the Sri Lankan military camp. It is not known how many Sri Lankan soldiers the chlorine gas affected. However, we do know that the Sri Lankan armed forces were unable to defend themselves against such a chemical assault. Furthermore, the LTTE reportedly broadcast over its radio net the fact that the military base was under a poison gas attack. The strategy of the LTTE was to create panic and fear in the ranks of the Sri Lankan military throughout the island. Apparently, this incident was the only time the LTTE used a chemical agent.[87]

The first acknowledged indiscriminate terrorist attack using a chemical agent against innocent noncombatants occurred on March 20, 1995, when Aum Shinrikyo released eleven packages of sarin nerve gas on five Tokyo subway lines. Ultimately twelve people died and 5,000 others became ill from the deadly gas. The attack marked a turning point in the strategy of terrorism. The Aum attack has become the defining incident for all academic discussions about the use of chemical, biological, radiological, or nuclear weapons. In fact, Aum experimented with a wide variety of chemical agents, including sarin, tabun, soman, VX, and hydrogen cyanide, phosgene, and mustard gas. Kaplan states that Aum selected sarin because it was apparently the safest and most convenient to manufacture.[88] Aum also attempted to develop and deliver biological agents against a variety of "soft" targets. After the subway attack by Aum, Japanese police discovered a large quantity of biological weapons. Aum only turned to chemical agents after unsuccessfully attempting to use biological weapons.

Mengel asserts that even though the threat of chemical or nuclear terrorism can be devastating, the greatest casualty-producing potential appears to be the threat of biological agents available to terrorists. The most lethal of these biological agents are **anthrax**, smallpox, and botulism. Terrorists could easily disperse anthrax by a truck-mounted spray. Once the anthrax was inhaled, it would take about two minutes for infection to set in. Not all victims would die, but sufficient casualties would produce chaos and confusion. In a more confined space, such as domed athletic stadiums, lethal doses of anthrax could be spread by aerosols. Furthermore, Mengel estimates that in a domed stadium one fluid ounce of anthrax would infect 70,000 people in less than one hour.[89]

Experts believe that the probability of a major biological terrorist attack by a foreign government or a terrorist group against the United States seems remote.[90] In contrast, smaller acts of biocriminality are the more likely biological terrorist attack. In the last twenty years, there have been only two significant cases of bioweapon use in the United States. The first case involved a religious cult group located in Oregon, known as the **Rajneeshees**.[91] The Rajneeshees intentionally and indiscriminately contaminated ten salad bars with a strain of **salmonella** that is a common cause of food poisoning. The salad bars were located in ten restaurants in the Dalles region of Oregon. The motive for the Rajneeshee attack was an attempt to influence local elections by sickening voters who might vote against their candidates. Although no one died from the salmonella, 751 people were diagnosed with the illness, and twenty people were hospitalized. The police did not recognize the intentional aspect of the outbreak of the salmonella poisoning for over a year. Members of the Rajneeshee cult revealed the details of the salmonella attack only after they were arrested on other criminal charges.

The second case occurred in October 2001 following the 9/11 attacks when a series of anthrax-laced letters were mailed to several political and media targets. Letters containing powdered anthrax were delivered to Senator Tom Daschle, Senator Patrick Leahy, and NBC news anchor Tom Brokaw. This was the first case of intentional anthrax infection in the United States. Although the letters never reached the intended targets, five people who came in contact with the letters died, and seventeen people contracted the disease. Five people died from inhalation of anthrax and eleven contracted cutaneous anthrax. Despite the low number of casualties, the anthrax attacks caused considerable alarm. Congressional sessions were canceled, the U.S. Senate and the U.S. Supreme Court were evacuated, and people were afraid to open their mail. Initially the sophisticated nature of the anthrax attacks indicated that only a state-run anthrax weapons program could have produced the material. However, the FBI could find no connection between a nation state, for example, Russia, Iran, or Iraq, and the anthrax letters. Investigators then turned their attention to an individual or a group that may have access to the lethal powdered anthrax. The expertise required to carry out such an attack opened new frontiers for the use of biological weapons.[92]

Eventually, the FBI determined that the anthrax originated at Fort Detrick, Maryland, and was part of an experiment by the United States to weaponize anthrax. Subsequently, the FBI developed a list of suspects from the employees at Fort Detrick. After pursuing several suspects, the FBI began to build a case against **Bruce Ivins**. However, before the FBI could present their case before a grand jury, Bruce Ivins died of an apparent suicide on July 29, 2008. Ivins was a microbiologist who worked at the U.S. Army Medical Research Institute of Infectious Diseases at Fort Detrick, Maryland, for twenty-eight years. Based on the evidence collected by the FBI over a two-year period, the FBI concluded that "Dr. Ivins was the sole person responsible for the 2001 anthrax attacks." The motive behind the anthrax attacks by Ivins is unclear.

Presently, only nation states are capable of carrying out large-scale biological attacks, and they are reluctant to do so since they run the risk of retaliation. While some terrorist groups

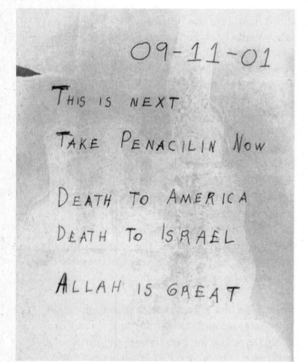

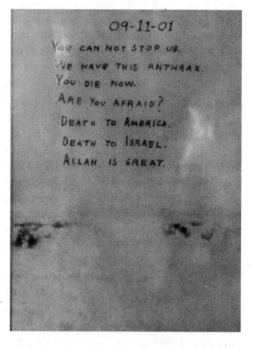

FIGURE 10.1 Letters containing anthrax included the above messages. Five people were killed after exposure to the powdered anthrax contained in the letters. (Top and bottom right: Photos by FBI/Getty Images, Inc.; Bottom left: AP/Wide World Photos)

like al Qaeda would like to attempt a large-scale biological attack, the possibility seems remote without the help of a state sponsor of terrorism, such as Iran. Limited attacks using biological agents as common as salmonella or as rare as anthrax are highly probable. One reason that terrorist groups avoid the use of biological agents is that other strategies, such as suicide bombings, serve the dual purpose of attention-getting and causing mass casualties.

Although the threat of superterrorism covers a broad spectrum of probable events and the nuclear, chemical, and biological weapons club continues to grow, how realistic is the threat? Mengel and Jenkins argue that the probability of terrorist groups successfully combining the proper skills, material resources, and motivations necessary to carry out an act of superterrorism is extremely low.[93] Nonetheless, it must be recognized that in the event of a successful act of superterrorism, the results could be catastrophic, causing death, injury, and destruction beyond the magnitude of any past terrorist attack. The concept of superterrorism represents an unknown but realistic future terrorist threat that merits the attention of law enforcement officials at all levels of government. Regardless of the type of terrorism, whether conventional or super, the results could be devastating to the future of democracy in the United States. What influence would a sustained terrorist climate have on the quality of life in the United States?

Table 10.2 illustrates the menu of the most likely biological and chemical agents used by terrorist groups that could inflict massive casualties in the United States. The viruses, bacteria, toxins, and gases show the many possibilities of chemical and biological weapons available to terrorist groups, psychotics, or individual criminals.

TABLE 10.2   Biological and Chemical Agents

Biological			Chemical		
Agent	*Lethality*	*Contagiousness*	*Agent*	*Persistence*[a]	*Rate of Action*
Anthrax			Nerve		
Inhalation	95–100%	None	Sarin	Low	Very Fast
Cutaneous	5–20%	High	Tabun	Low	Very Fast
Gastrointestinal	100%	None	Soman	Moderate	Very Fast
Plague	100%	High	VX	Very High	Fast
Ebola	50–90%	High	Blood		
Dengue Fever	Rarely	Moderate	Hydrogen Cyanide	Low	Rapid
Botulism	60–90%	None	Cyanogen Chloride	Low	Rapid
Smallpox	30–70%	High	Blister		
Salmonella	Rarely	None	Phosgene	Low	Immediate
			Mustard	High	Delayed
			Lewisite	High	Rapid

[a]Rate at which the agent degrades in the environment.

Source: Adapted from Richard A. Falenrath et al., *America's Achilles Heel: Nuclear, Biological, Chemical Terrorism and Covert Action* (Cambridge, MA: MIT Press, 1998); Jessica Stern, *The Ultimate Terrorists* (Cambridge, MA: Harvard University Press, 1999), pp. 164–67.

INFLUENCE OF TERRORISM ON DEMOCRACY

The use of indiscriminate and random acts of terrorism has the potential to influence future U.S. society in the following ways. First, tighter security measures will continue to predominate strategies to defeat terrorism. The sight of armed military units stationed outside the White House reflects the heightened concern about terrorism in the United States that has also contributed to the growth of the domestic security industry. Private corporations now spend approximately $50 billion yearly to strengthen security systems against possible terrorist assaults. The U.S. State Department currently spends 15 percent of its budget on security, and Michael Chertoff in 2008 asked Congress for an additional $50 billion over the next five years to strengthen homeland security. Surveillance security systems, their maintenance, and the specialized personnel required to operate them are all very expensive. Additionally, kidnap and ransom insurance has become a growth industry in several European countries and the United States. Private corporations are now taking out insurance policies to help cover possible ransom payments for high-risk employees. In sum, the increased security costs for both government and private corporations could be reflected in higher taxes and higher costs for consumer items. Most experts believe this trend will continue well into the twenty-first century. The escalation of the potential threat of terrorism has created a new industry that could involve a combination of security systems that dramatically increases consumer prices.[94]

Second, a prolonged campaign of terrorism in the United States would undoubtedly result in changes in the legal system beyond the current Patriot Act. Legal concepts of habeas corpus, intent, individual rights, and precedent reflect the character of the legal system in the United States. Given a sustained terrorist campaign of indiscriminate bombing and assassination, would the U.S. legal system strictly adhere to the principles of constitutional law and the protection of individual rights? Thus far, there has been no need to invoke total emergency powers in the United States to defeat a campaign of random terrorism. However, there have been a number of incidents in the United States where normal legal procedures were suspended to prevent widespread disorder.

For example, in May 1971 in Washington, DC, the police reacted in an unusual way to quell a massive anti-Vietnam War demonstration. Fearing uncontrollable rioting, the police began arresting anyone they found in the streets. The dragnet sweeps resulted in 13,400 arrests in a four-day period—a record that still stands. Few arrestees were ever charged with any crime; in fact, most were peacefully demonstrating and a good number were totally uninvolved. But order was preserved, violence was kept to a minimum, and the chief of police was congratulated for taking such decisive action. Two years later a federal judge declared the arrests unconstitutional and awarded monetary damages to those individuals who were illegally arrested. This example could well prove to be a model for future responses to random terrorism in the United States. Unquestionably, a campaign of prolonged terrorism in the United States would result in the federal government assuming direct police powers; and the temporary suspension of civil liberties would be deemed necessary to maintain order and locate offenders.[95]

Third, a campaign of terrorism certainly can affect the general mental health of a community living in a terrorist "war zone." General feelings of dread and fear result from prolonged exposure to bombings, arson, assassination, and hostage taking. Fanon observed that continued exposure to acts of extranormal violence creates mental disorders that he referred to as "reactionary psychoses."[96] Inner feelings of fear take on an apocalyptic sense in which eventually everyone will be consumed by the "fires" of violence and terrorism. The effect on children is especially acute. Children exhibit a noise phobia so intense that an unexpected sound often triggers a panic reaction, and their often chronic, sadistic behavior can manifest itself in the torture of small animals or other children.[97] In the terrorist war zones of Lebanon, Belfast, Israel (West Bank and Gaza), Afghanistan, Iraq, or Colombia, children often display nervous depression, motor instability, chronic apathy, and loss of appetite.[98] The symptoms are not unlike those associated with battered children.

The effect of a terrorist campaign on U.S. citizens could be even more profound. It is well documented that Americans already suffer from a wide variety of mental illnesses, including severe forms of neurosis and paranoid schizophrenia. The impact of an indiscriminate terrorist campaign could conceivably be more devastating on the mental health of Americans than, say, citizens of Baghdad or Kabul, where intercommunal violence has become almost a way of life and part of traditional culture. Just how Americans would respond to indiscriminate terrorist attacks is difficult to evaluate. The very randomness of terrorism makes it more fearful. Suicide attacks, for example, give the impression of an unstoppable enemy, contributing to even greater fear. Jenkins concludes that many Americans live on the brink of doom, underscored by end-time visions, 9/11 nightmares, weapons of mass destruction, worldwide economic collapse, and apprehensions of a nuclear terrorist attack.[99] But one thing seems certain. General feelings of fear, hopelessness, and dread would surely intensify.

Fourth, the growth of paramilitary groups to counter the actions of an indiscriminate terrorist campaign would intensify the violence. In the United States, there are several well-known "paramilitary" organizations that could be quickly mobilized into reactionary vigilantes. These include right-wing groups such as the American Nazi Party, the KKK, the Order, the Jewish Defense League, and/or such left-wing groups as the Earth Liberation Front or the New Black Panther Party. In addition, there are armed groups that support no political ideology but have a penchant for terror and violence. A variety of prison gangs, like the Aryan Brotherhood, Mexican Mafia, and Black Guerrilla Family, or a host of juvenile gangs and motorcycle clubs, which are made up of elements of criminal society looking for opportunities to exploit, could easily be mobilized into vigilantes.

An indiscriminate terrorist campaign could mobilize groups like these and possibly produce anarchic situations of the kind that exist in Afghanistan and Iraq. For example, as terrorism escalates, a "warlord" mentality could emerge where communities and urban neighborhoods would "contract" paramilitary groups, for example, juvenile gangs, to protect lives and property. In its final stages, such as in Afghanistan, foreign intervention would be required to restore some semblance of order, although social deterioration such as this in the United States does seem somewhat remote.

Finally, demographic changes would occur as potential victims of terroristic violence flee areas where random terrorism is prevalent. As people flee, real estate values decline along with the tax base of the community. Eventually, businesses and industry will move to safer locations since increased terrorism prohibits people from daily shopping or attending their jobs. The result is chronic, high unemployment and economic chaos. Conditions like these exist in several parts of the world, most notably in Gaza, the West Bank, Iraq, and Afghanistan, where political terrorism has a stranglehold on communities. There is no reason to believe that a terrorist climate in the United States could not produce similar conditions.

In sum, the future influence of terrorism on the quality of life in the United States could have the most profound effects in the following areas: (1) increased security costs,

(2) changes in the legal system reflecting a loss of civil liberties, (3) increased mental health problems associated with the fear of terrorism, (4) growth of paramilitary groups that would heighten the level of violence, and (5) demographic changes reflected in patterns of settlement and commerce.[100]

Conclusions

If the future appears dismal, what measures are likely to be the most appropriate to defeat terrorism? The liberal view is that objective causes of terrorism should be overcome. Therefore, the focus could be on the establishment of a Palestinian homeland or the settlement of the justified claims of a variety of ethnic, religious, and racial issues. For example, Catholics in Northern Ireland, Shi'ite Muslims in Iraq and Lebanon, and blacks in South Africa all strongly believe that they have been unjustly treated by the established governmental system. Obviously, justice for all people should be pursued with vigor if terrorism is to be defeated. However, the reality is that the concept of justice for all will probably never be achieved and certainly not quickly enough to raise the hope of "disadvantaged" groups.

The most difficult problem in attacking terrorism is still agreeing on a definition of terrorism. The Obama administration has yet to define terrorism, scholars have yet to define terrorism, and the mass media, which exploits terroristic violence, has yet to adequately define terrorism. For example, nonaligned nations representing seventy countries recently condemned the repeated U.S. aggressions and provocations against Iraq, Iran, Syria, Sudan, Serbia, and Afghanistan as acts of state-sponsored terrorism. Pillar et al. states that there is no universally accepted definition of terrorism.[101] This lack of a precise definition makes it virtually impossible for established governments to pursue policies that would remove many of the conditions or grievances, real or imagined, that motivate terrorists.

The future of international terrorism is bound to escalate as forms of low-intensity conflict increase. Terrorism, as a strategy of low-intensity warfare, is a serious threat to open democratic societies and one that will be exacerbated in the future. Failure to respond firmly to the threat would be to give up a way of life based on individual and civil liberties. Democracy must not overestimate the threat nor overreact, but keep the violence associated with terrorism in perspective. In the end, acts of terrorism, that is, suicide bombing, assassination or murder, hostage taking, and other criminal acts, are law enforcement problems. Therefore, the law enforcement community and more specifically the criminal justice system must be prepared to defeat the newest form of criminal behavior—terrorism. It is hoped that the considerations outlined in this text will contribute toward an understanding of the causes, strategies, and responses to terrorism.

Key Terms

A.Q. Khan	cesium	Leaderless Resistance
Abu Zubaydah	chlorine gas	Pelindaba
Allon Plan	cyanide gas	Qassam Rockets
al Qaeda	dirty bomb	Rajneeshee
anthrax	Gush Emunim	Salmonella
Bhopal, India	Islamic Amal	sarin
Bruce Ivins	Judea and Samaria	

Discussion Questions

1. Describe the concept of "territory for peace." How would you solve the Israeli–Palestinian problem?
2. Who are the Kahane Chai? Why are Judea and Samaria so important to Jewish fundamentalists?
3. Discuss the anthrax attacks of October 2001. Do you think the FBI "got their man"?
4. What is low-intensity conflict? Cite examples.
5. Discuss Sarkesian's conflict spectrum.
6. What should the United States do to counter al Qaeda support for world terrorism? Does the United States support terrorism, as many nations claim?
7. What is the likelihood that terrorists will use weapons of mass destruction? Be specific.
8. Who is the greatest threat to the U.S.—nuclear nations such as Pakistan or Russia or Islamic terrorist groups such as al Qaeda?
9. What changes would most likely occur in the United States if a sustained campaign of terrorism were initiated?
10. What can the law enforcement community do to meet the future threat of terrorism in the United States?
11. Do you think terrorism is a law enforcement problem or a military problem? Explain fully.
12. Compare and contrast the terrorist attacks by the Aum Shinrikyo, the Rajneeshee religious cult, and Bruce Ivins.

Web Sites

J. David Singer, University of Michigan, Correlates of War (COW) Project, May 26, 2003
http://www.umich.edu/~cowproj

U.S. Department of Homeland Security, FEMA
http://www.fema.gov

Terrorism Reporter, Chemical Weapons
http://www.terrorismreporter.com

Center for Strategic and International Studies (CSIS)
http://www.csis.org

Centers for Disease Control and Prevention
http://www.cdc.gov/

FBI, "Amerithrax,"
http://www.fbigov/anthrax/amerithraxlinks.htm

Nuclear Terrorism
http://www.nci.org/nci-nt.htm

Endnotes

1. David Carlton. "The Future of Political Substate Violence," in *Terrorism: Theory and Practice*, eds. Yonah Alexander, David Carlton, and Paul Wilkinson (Boulder, CO: Westview Press, 1979), pp. 201–04.
2. Brian Jenkins, "The Future Course of International Terrorism," *TVI Report*, 6 (Fall 1985), pp. S3–7.
3. David E. Apter, "Notes on the Underground: Left Violence and the National State," *Daedalus*, 108 (Fall 1979), pp. 155–72.
4. Marvin J. Cetron and Owen Davies, "55 Trends Now Shaping the Future of Terrorism," *The Proteus Trends Series*, 1, no. 2 (February 2008), p. ix.
5. For example, see Richard Barnet, "Nuclear Terrorism: Can It Be Stopped," *Current*, 211 (March/April 1979), pp. 30–40; David M. Krieger, "What Happens If . . . ? Terrorists, Revolutionaries, and Nuclear Weapons," *Annals*, 430 (March 1977), pp. 44–57; Jessica Stern, *The Ultimate Terrorists* (Cambridge, MA: Harvard University Press, 1999); Albert Mauroni, *America's Struggle with Chemical-Biological Warfare* (Westport, CT: Praeger, 2000); Gavin Cameron, *Nuclear Terrorism: A Threat Assessment for the 21st Century* (New York: Palgrave MacMillan, 1999); Brian Michael Jenkins, *Will Terrorists Go Nuclear?* (Amherst, NY: Prometheus Books, 2008).

6. Benjamin Netanyahu, ed., *Terrorism: How the West Can Win* (New York: Farrar, Straus & Giroux, 1986), p. 11.

7. Ibid., pp. 11–13.

8. James Adams, *The Financing of Terror* (New York: Simon & Schuster, 1986), pp. 83–131.

9. Mark A. Heller, *A Palestinian State: The Implications for Israel* (Cambridge, MA: Harvard University Press, 1983), p. 35.

10. For example, see Doron Goldenberg, *State of Seige: Report from a Middle-Eastern War Zone* (New York: Gefen Books, 2003).

11. For example, see Noam Chomsky, *The Fateful Triangle: The United States, Israel and the Palestinians* (Boston, MA: South End Press, 1999); Edward W. Said, *The Question of Palestine* (New York: Knopf Publishing, 1992); Richard Falk, *The Great Terror War* (New York: Olive Branch Press, 2002).

12. Alan Dershowitz, *The Case Against Israel's Enemies: Exposing Jimmy Carter and Others Who Stand in the Way of Peace* (Hoboken, NJ: John Wiley and Sons, Inc. 2008), p. 151.

13. Conor Cruise O'Brien, *The Siege: The Saga of Israel and Zionism* (New York: Simon & Schuster, 1986), p. 650.

14. David Newman, *Jewish Settlement in the West Bank: The Role of Gush Emunim* (Durham, NC: University of Durham Centre for Middle Eastern and Islamic Studies, 1982), pp. 27–30; See also Ian S. Lustick, *For the Land and the Lord: Jewish Fundamentalism in Israel* (New York: Council on Foreign Relations, 1988); Amnon Rubinstein, *Zionist Dream Revisited: From Herzl to Gush Emunium and Back* (New York: Knopf, 1990); Avraham Berg, *The Holocaust Is Over: We Must Rise From Its Ashes* (New York: Palgrave Macmillan, 2008), pp. 48, 180–83.

15. Heller, *A Palestinian State*, pp. 12–14.

16. Robin Wright, *Sacred Rage: The Wrath of Militant Islam* (New York: Simon & Schuster, 1986), p. 82.

17. For example, see Amal Saad Ghorayeb, *Hizbullah: Politics and Religion* (London: Pluto Press, 2002); Hala Jaber, *Hezbollah* (New York: Columbia University Press, 1997).

18. Rohan Gunaratna, *Inside al Qaeda: Global Network of Terror* (New York: Columbia University Press, 2002), pp. 54–74.

19. Ibid., pp. 47–58.

20. For example, see "Plotters Made Martyrdom Video," *BBC News* (April 4, 2008), p. 1.

21. "Bin Laden Tape: 'Youths of God' plan more attacks," *Associated Press* (October 7, 2002), *http://www.ap.org/*.

22. Paul Martin, "Hezbollah Calls for Global Attacks," *Washington Times* (October 29, 2002), p. A3.

23. Gunaratna, *Inside al Qaeda*, pp. 228–29.

24. Ibid., pp. 36–38.

25. Courtney C. Walsh, "Italian Police Explore al Qaeda Links in Cyanide Plot," *Christian Science Monitor* (March 7, 2002), *http://www.csmonitor.com/*.

26. CBS News, *U.S. Stops 9/11 Style Attack in Pakistan* (May 2, 2003), *http://www.cbsnews.com/*.

27. Glenn Kessler, "Death Toll Could Top 100 in Triple Blast," *Sacramento Bee* (May 14, 2003), p. A1.

28. Bruce Hoffman, "Lessons of 9/11," *Testimony before House and Senate Select Committee on Intelligence* (October 8, 2002), *http://www.rand.org*.

29. "Terrorist Blasts Hit Morocco," *Sacramento Bee* (May 17, 2003), p. A1.

30. Gunaratna, *Inside al Qaeda*, pp. 167–74.

31. Tom A. Peter, "National Intelligence Estimate: al Qaeda Stronger and a Threat to U.S. Homeland," *Christian Science Monitor* (July 19, 2007), *http://www.csmonitor.com*.

32. For example, see Ben Venzke and Aimee Ibrahim, *The al Qaeda Threat: An Analytical Guide to al Qaeda's Tactics and Targets* (Alexandria, VA: Tempest Publishing, 2003); Henry J. Hyde, *Al Qaeda and the Global Reach of Terrorism* (Collingdale, PA: Diane Publishing Company, 2003); Bruce Riedel, *The Search for al Qaeda: Its Leadership, Ideology and Future* (Washington, DC: Brookings Institution Press, 2008).

33. For example, see *http://www.mojahedoon.net*; *http://www.hezbollah.org*; *http://www.almus-limoon.com*; *http://www.kavkaz.org.uk*; *http://www.jihadonline.net*.

34. Brynjar Lia, *Architect of Global Jihad: The Life of al Qaeda Strategist Abu Mus'ab al Suri* (New York: Columbia University Press, 2008).

35. Elaine Sciolino and Helene Fouquet, "Belgium is Trying to Unravel the Threads of a Terror Web," *New York Times* (October 10, 2005), *http://www.nytimes.com*.

36. Greg Ansley, "Supergrass Tipped Off Spies," *The New Zealand Herald* (November 2005), p. 18 Islamic extremists planned suicide bombing attacks across Australia, *http://www.nzherald.com.nz.*

37. *Seven Charged over Chicago Plot* (June 23, 2006), *http://www.news.bbc.co.uk.*

38. Henry Chu, "Doctor Found Guilty in London-Glasgow Bomb Plot," *Los Angeles Times* (December 17, 2008), *http://www.latimes.com.*

39. For example, see Jane Corbin, *Al Qaeda: In Search of the Terror Network That Shook the World* (New York: Thunder Mouth Press/National Books, 2002); Paul L. Williams, *Al Qaeda: Brotherhood of Terror* (Parsippany, NJ: Alpha, 2002); Paul K. Davis and Brian Michael Jenkins, *Deterrence and Influence in Counterterrorism: A Component in the War on al Qaeda* (Santa Monica, CA: Rand, 2002); Philip Margulies, *Al Qaeda: Osama bin Laden's Army of Terrorists* (New York: Rosen Publishing Group, 2003); Hyde, *Al Qaeda and the Global Reach of Terrorism.*

40. Gunaratna, *Inside al Qaeda*, pp. 60–74.

41. Falk, *The Great Terror War*, pp. 6–19.

42. Army FM 100–30, *Low Intensity Conflict* (Washington, DC: Department of the Army, 1981), p. 24.

43. *Executive Risk Assessment* (Alexandria, VA: Risks International, 1986).

44. Carlos Marighella, *The Terrorist Classic: Manual of the Urban Guerrilla* (Chapel Hill, NC: Documentary, 1985), p. 84.

45. Sam C. Sarkesian, *America's Forgotten Wars: The Counterrevolutionary Past and Lessons for the Future* (Westport, CT: Greenwood Press, 1984), pp. 229–48.

46. The History Guy, *The War List* (February 2009), *http://www.historyguy.com.*

47. Peter Janke, *Ethnic and Religious Conflicts* (Hanover, NH: Dartmouth University Press, 1994).

48. Gunaratna, *Inside al Qaeda*, pp. 167–220.

49. Ibid.

50. Bruce Hoffman, "Rethinking Terrorism and Counterterrorism since 9/11," *Studies in Conflict and Terrorism*, 25 (September–October 2002), pp. 303–16.

51. Neil C. Livingstone, "The Impact of Technological Innovation," in *Hydra of Carnage*, eds. Uri Ra'anan et al. (Lexington, MA: Lexington Books, 1986), p. 139.

52. Stern, *The Ultimate Terrorists.*

53. Thomas C. Schelling, "Who Will Have the Bomb?" in *Studies in Nuclear Terrorism*, eds. Augustus R. Norton and Martin H. Greenberg (Boston, MA: G. K. Hall, 1979), pp. 42–43; Seymour M. Hersh, *The Samson Option: Israel's Nuclear Arsenal and American Foreign Policy* (New York: Random House, 1991); Shlomo Aronson and Oded Brosh, *The Politics and Strategy of Nuclear Weapons in the Middle East* (Albany, NY: State University of New York Press, 1992).

54. Leonard S. Spector, *The Nuclear Nations* (New York: Vintage Books, 1985), pp. 129–49; Avner Cohen, *Israel and the Bomb* (New York: Columbia University Press, 1998), pp. 8–34.

55. Gavin Cameron, "Nuclear Terrorism Reconsidered," *Current History*, 99 (April 2000), pp. 154–58.

56. For example, see Neil C. Livingstone and Joseph D. Douglass, Jr., *CBW: The Poor Man's Atomic Bomb* (Cambridge, MA: Institute for Foreign Policy Analysis, 1984); Stanley P. Berard, "Nuclear Terrorism: More Myth Than Reality," *Air University Review*, 36 (July–August 1985), pp. 30–36; Karl-Heinz Kamp, "An Overrated Nightmare: There Are a Lot of Dangers Out There, But Terrorists Wielding Nuclear Bombs Probably Isn't One of Them," *Bulletin of the Atomic Scientists*, 52 (July–August 1996), pp. 30–35.

57. Jenkins, *Will Terrorists Go Nuclear?* p. 131.

58. Mason Willrich and Theodore B. Taylor, "Nuclear Theft: Risks and Safeguards," in *Studies in Nuclear Terrorism*, eds. Augustus R. Norton and Martin H. Greenberg (Boston, MA: G. K. Hall, 1979), pp. 59–84.

59. David Hughes, "When Terrorists Go Nuclear: The Ingredients and Information Have Never Been More Available," *Popular Mechanics*, 173 (January 1996), pp. 56–60.

60. R. W. Mengel, "Terrorism and New Technologies of Destruction: An Overview of the Potential Risk," in *Studies in Nuclear Terrorism*, eds. Augustus R. Norton and Martin H. Greenberg (Boston, MA: G. K. Hall, 1979), pp. 189–245.

61. Anatol Lieven, *Chechnya: Tombstone of Russian Power* (New Haven, CT: Yale University Press, 1998), p. 137.

62. Jenkins, *Will Terrorists Go Nuclear*, p. 91.

63. *Time* (June 3, 1985), p. 52.

64. Some examples of scholarly scenarios: Louis Rene Beres, "Terrorism and the Nuclear Threat in the Middle East," *Current History*, 70 (January 1976), pp. 27–29; Augustus R. Norton, *Understanding the Nuclear Terrorist Threat* (Gaithersburg, MD: IACP, 1979); Robert H. Kupperman, "Fighting Terrorism: A National Security View," *Georgetown Center for Strategic International Studies* (Public Broadcasting Stations, September 17, 1986); Friedrich Steinhausler, "What It Takes to Become a Nuclear Terrorist," *American Behavioral Scientist*, 46 (February 2003), pp. 782–96. The popular literature has produced hundreds of nuclear scenarios: Larry Collins and Dominque La Pierre, *The Fifth Horseman* (New York: Simon & Schuster, 1981); Karl Lorimar, *Special Bulletin* (movie) (Irvine, CA: Lorimar Home Video, 1986); Christopher Matthews, *The Butcher* (New York: Stein and Day, 1986); *Final Option* (movie) (MGM/UA, 1984); Alistair MacLean, *Goodbye California* (New York: Doubleday, 1978); Jenkins, *Will Terrorists Go Nuclear*, pp. 323–53.

65. Stanford University, *Institute for International Studies: Center for International Security and Cooperation* (2008), *http://www.cisac.stanford.edu/*; Graham Allison, *Nuclear Terrorism: The Ultimate Preventable Catastrophe* (New York: Times, 2004), pp. 17–61.

66. Bruce G. Blair and Gary D. Brewer, "The Terrorist Threat to World Nuclear Programs," *Journal of Conflict Resolution*, 21 (September 1977), pp. 386–89.

67. Brian Jenkins, *Terrorism and the Nuclear Safeguards Issue* (Santa Monica, CA: Rand Corporation, March 1976), pp. 2–7.

68. Scott Pelley, "Nuke Facility Raid An Inside Job?" *CBS News* (November 23, 2008), 60 Minutes Presentation, *http://www.cbsnews.com/*.

69. Norton and Greenberg, *Studies in Nuclear Terrorism*, pp. 443–46; See also, Jeremy Bernstein, *Nuclear Weapons: What You Need to Know* (New York: Cambridge University Press, 2007).

70. *San Francisco Chronicle* (December 21, 1986), p. AA4.

71. Alan Cranston, "The Nuclear Terrorist State," *Terrorism: How the West Can Win*, ed. Netanyahu, pp. 177–81.

72. Jenkins, *Will Terrorists Go Nuclear?* pp. 143–44.

73. John Mearsheimer and Stephen M. Walt, *The Israeli Lobby and U.S. Foreign Policy* (New York: Farrar, Straus and Giroux, 2007), pp. 5–7.

74. Jimmy Carter, *Palestine: Peace Not Apartheid* (New York: Simon and Schuster, 2007), pp. 13–18.

75. Charles Krauthammer, "In Iran, Arming for Armageddon," *Jewish World Review* (December 16, 2005), *http://www.jewishworldreview.com/cols/krauthammer.*

76. Alan Dershowitz, *Preemption: A Knife that Cuts Both Ways* (New York: W.W. Norton & Co., 2006), p. 175.

77. Paul Kerr and May Beth Nikitin, "Pakistan's Nuclear Weapons: Proliferation and Security Issues," *Congressional Research Service* (June 20, 2008), p. 10.

78. George Tenet and Bill Harlow, *At the Center of the Storm: My Years at the CIA* (New York: Harper Collins, 2007), p. 261.

79. *Washington Post* (May 13, 1975), p. 22.

80. Ibid.

81. Livingstone, *Hydra of Carnage*, pp. 142–43.

82. Seymour N. Hersh, *Chemical and Biological Warfare* (Garden City, NY: Doubleday, 1969), p. 83.

83. For example, see Richard A. Falkenrath, Robert D. Newman, and Bradley A. Thayer, *America's Achilles' Heel: Nuclear, Biological, and Chemical Terrorism and Covert Attack* (Cambridge, MA: MIT Press, 1998); Walter Laqueur, *The New Terrorism: Fanaticism and the Arms of Mass Destruction* (New York: Oxford University Press, 1999), pp. 59–61.

84. Jonathan B. Tucker, ed., *Toxic Terror: Assessing Terrorist Use of Chemical and Biological Weapons* (Cambridge, MA: MIT Press, 2000), pp. 3–5; Andre Richardt and Marc-Michael Blum, *Decontamination of Warfare Agents* (New Jersey: Wiley VCH, 2008), pp. 55–65.

85. Michael L. Moodie, "The Chemical Weapons Threat," in *Terrorism and Counterterrorism: Understanding the New Security Environment*, eds. Russell D. Howard and Reid L. Sawyer (Guilford, CT: McGraw Hill/Dushkin, 2002), pp. 184–203.

86. For example, see Ashok S. Kolelkar, *Investigation of Large-Magnitude Incidents: Bhopal as a Case Study* (May 1988), *http://www.bhopal.com/infoarch.htm*; Dominique La Pierre and Javier Moro, *Five Past Midnight in Bhopal* (New York: Warner books, 2002); Themistocles

D'Silva, *The Black Box of Bhopal: A Closer Look at the World's Deadliest Industrial Accident* (Victoria, Canada: Trafford Publishing, 2006).

87. Bruce Hoffman, *Terrorism and Weapons of Mass Destruction: An Analysis of Trends and Motivations* (Santa Monica, CA: Rand Corporation, 1999), document #P-8039-1; Hoffman, *Inside Terrorism* (New York: Columbia University Press, 2006), pp. 268, 361–62,

88. David E. Kaplan, "Aum Shinrikyo (1995)," in *Toxic Terror: Assessing Terrorist Use of Chemical and Biological Weapons*, ed. Jonathan B. Tucker (Cambridge, MA: MIT Press, 2001), pp. 207–26.

89. Mengel, "Terrorism and New Technologies of Destruction," pp. 195–96; See also Leonard A. Cole, *The Anthrax Letters: A Medical Detective Story* (Washington, DC: John Henry Press, 2003).

90. Hoffman, *Inside Terrorism*, p. 196; Stern, *Ultimate Terrorists*, pp. 49–68; Tucker, *Toxic Terror*, pp. 1–14.

91. W. Seth Carus, "The Rajneeshees (1984)," in *Toxic Terror*, ed. J. Tucker (Cambridge, MA: MIT Press, 2001), pp. 115–37; Judith Mkiller, Stephen Engleberg, and William Broad, *Germs: Biological Weapons and America's Secret War* (New York: Simon and Schuster, 2001), pp. 15–33.

92. For example, see Senator Bill Frist, MD, *When Every Moment Counts* (New York: Rowman and Littlefield Publishers, Inc., 2002); Cole, *The Anthrax Letters*, p. viii–x.

93. Mengel, "Terrorism and New Technologies of Destruction," pp. 244–46; Jenkins, *Will Terrorists Go Nuclear?* pp. 183–215.

94. For example, see Jonathan R. White, *Defending the Homeland: Domestic Intelligence, Law Enforcement, and Security* (Belmont, CA: Thomson Wadsworth, 2004); *The National Strategy for the Physical Protection of Critical Infrastructures and Key Assets* (Washington, DC: U.S. Government Printing Office, February 2003); Ibp USA, *U.S. National Homeland Security Strategy Handbook* (Washington, DC: International Business Publications, USA, 2009).

95. Don Hazen, "What a Difference a Generation Makes," Alternet.org (April 21, 2000), *http://www.alternet.org.*

96. Frantz Fanon, *The Wretched of the Earth* (New York: Grove Press, 1968), p. 251.

97. San Francisco Chronicle, *This World section* (November 11, 1994), pp. 7–8.

98. For example, see Johnathan Kozol, *Children of the Revolution: A Yankee Teacher in Cuban Schools* (New York: Delacorte, 1978); Howard Tolley, *Children and War: Political Socialization to International Conflict* (New York: Teachers College Press, 1973); Roger Rosenblatt, *Children of War* (Garden City, NY: Anchor/Doubleday, 1983).

99. Jenkins, *Will Terrorists Go Nuclear?* p. 213.

100. H. C. Greisman, "Terrorism and the Closure of Society: A Social Impact Projection," *Technological Forecasting and Social Change*, 14 (1979), pp. 135–46.

101. Paul R. Pillar, *Terrorism and U.S. Foreign Policy* (Washington, DC: Brookings Institution Press, 2001), pp. 12–18; Sageman, *Leaderless Jihad: Terror Networks in the Twenty-First Century*, pp. 15–16; Jerrold M. Post, *The Mind of the Terrorist: The Psychology of Terrorism From the IRA to al Qaeda* (New York: Palgrave Macmillan, 2007), p. 3.

GLOSSARY

17 November a terrorist group formed in 1973 in Athens, Greece, in honor of thirty-four university students who were killed by police during a student demonstration.

Abimael Guzman founder of the Sendero Luminoso or Shining Path terrorist group in Peru.

Abu Abbas leader of the Palestine Liberation Front (PLF).

Abu Musab al Zarqawi founder of al Qaeda in Iraq. Killed by U.S. forces in Baghdad on June 7, 2006.

Abu Sayyaf the "bearer of the sword" is an Islamic insurgency movement on the island of Basilan in the Philippines. Abu Sayyaf has links to al Qaeda.

Abu Zubaydah chief of operations for al Qaeda; currently in U.S. custody.

al Aqsa Martyrs Brigades a Palestinian nationalistic group affiliated with the PLO noted for its use of suicide bombings against Israeli civilian targets.

Allon Plan probably the best-known peace plan for the Middle East, advocating a territorial compromise between Israel and the PLO.

al Qaeda an international terrorist network founded by Osama bin Laden, responsible for the September 11, 2001, attacks against the United States.

al Qaeda in Iraq (AQI) Abu Musab al Zarqawi faction of al Qaeda that carried out actions of violence in Iraq.

al Zawahiri founder of Egyptian Islamic Jihad and co-founder of al Qaeda. He is also a qualified surgeon.

Amal Arabic for "hope"; a Lebanese Shi'ite terrorist group active in the 1970s.

Anarchism a political ideology that opposes governmental controls of human activity.

ANO the Abu Nidal Organization is a Palestinian terrorist group.

Anthrax a lethal biological agent used to kill five people in the United States in October and November of 2001.

Antiterrorism Act sets forth a formal list of foreign terrorist organizations; enacted in 1996. This was the first comprehensive American antiterrorism legislation.

A.Q. Khan Father of Pakistan's nuclear weapons development and the Islamic bomb.

Asahara the founder and leader of the religious cult Aum Shinrikyo.

Assassins a division of the Shi'ite Islami Muslim sect. The term *assassin* is derived from the Arabic *hashashin* or "hashish eaters."

ATEDP Act the Anti-Terrorism and Effective Death Penalty Act passed by the U.S. Congress in 1996. This was the first comprehensive U.S. antiterrorism legislation.

Atrocity a brutal and barbaric attack on innocent noncombatants.

Balfour Declaration a statement of British policy from Foreign Secretary Arthur J. Balfour on November 2, 1917, that promised to create a Jewish state in Palestine.

Bali bombing the first recorded suicide bombing in Indonesia that occurred on October 12, 2002, killing over 190 people.

Basque nationalist terrorist group formed in 1969 seeking to establish an independent Basque nation in the regions of northern Spain and southwestern France.

Beirut the capital of Lebanon where the first recorded suicide bombing occurred in the Middle East at the American Embassy on April 18, 1983.

Bhopal a city in India where a chemical storage tank of a Union Carbide plant exploded, killing 4,000 people.

Black Panthers an African American organization founded in Oakland, California, in 1966.

Black powder a low-velocity explosive used to make clandestine bombs.

Black September a Palestinian terrorist group founded in 1970 that carried out the terrorist hostage-taking event at the Munich Olympics in 1972.

Black Tigers suicide units of the Tamil Tigers (LTTE) comprising both men and women "willing" to carry out suicide bombing attacks.

Black Widow female Chechen suicide bombers.

Blast relates to the amount of energy released during an explosion.

Bojinka Plot, or the "Big Bang." Involved plan to blow up eleven commercial jets while in flight, to assassinate Pope John Paul and President Clinton, and to blow up the CIA Headquarters in Langley, Virginia.

Bruce Ivins Responsible for the anthrax attacks in the United States in 2001.

C-4 a high-velocity military explosive.

Car bombs a vehicle bomb introduced by PIRA that has become a favorite bombing technique of terrorists worldwide.

Carlos Marighella author of *The Mini-Manual of Urban Guerrilla Warfare.*

Censorship the concept of curtailing a free press.

Cesium a chemical element used by Chechen terrorists in a dirty bomb.

Chechnya located in the North Caucasus Mountains, is a federal subject of Russia fighting for independence from Russia.

Chlorine gas a chemical agent that destroys the cells in the respiratory system; cited as the first use of a chemical weapon by a terrorist group.

Cluster refers to an increase in suicide activity after widespread news reporting of suicide incidents, for example, suicide bombings.

Contagion effect the theory that anytime someone does something new or novel and are successful others will attempt to emulate that success. The copycat syndrome.

Conventions international treaties agreed upon to fight the growing threat of terrorism.

Covert operation counterterrorist measures that seek to disrupt, resolve, or destroy terrorist operations and planning, for example, Delta Force.

Cyanide gas a rapidly acting chemical agent that prevents the cells of the body from getting oxygen. Cyanide is most potent in enclosed spaces.

D.B. Cooper the first to successfully hijack a commercial jet liner.

Delta Force a specially trained American counterterrorist unit that operates in small covert teams.

Desert One the code name used for the rendezvous point used in an attempt to rescue American hostages in Iran in April 1980.

Dev Sol Revolutionary Way; originally formed in 1978 for the purpose of attacking Turkish national security interests and military targets.

Dirty bomb a conventional explosive combined with radioactive isotopes in order to spread nuclear material over a wide area.

Disinformation the deliberate spread of false, misleading, or incomplete information.

Dynamite a high-velocity explosive invented by Alfred Nobel in 1867.

Emile Durkheim a noted sociologist who studied suicidal behavior.

Entebbe an airport in Uganda where Israeli commandos rescued over 100 hostages who had been taken hostage by the PFLP.

Extradition international agreements to return criminal fugitives to law enforcement agencies of cooperating countries.

FALN a Puerto Rican nationalist/terrorist group active in the United States in the 1970s and 1980s. Historically, the most active terrorist group in the United States.

FARC Fuerzas Armadas Revolucionarias de Colombia was formed in 1964 as a military wing of the Colombian Communist Party, a marxist-motivated terrorist group determined to overthrow the Colombia government.

Fatah the largest group within the PLO founded by Yassir Arafat in 1957. The term means victory, conquest, or freedom.

fatwah an Islamic religious decree.

Fear the focus, purpose, and direction of terrorism is the creation of fear and panic.

Fentanyl an opiate-based narcotic a hundred times more powerful than morphine.

Fertilizer ammonium nitrate bombs used by a variety of terrorist groups.

FLQ the Front for the Liberation of Quebec was active in Canada in the late 1960s and early 1970s and took credit for a series of bombing incidents and hostage takings.

Fragmentation one of the primary effects produced during an explosion.

George Habash founder of the PFLP (Popular Front for the Liberation of Palestine).

GIA the Armed Islamic Group; the most active terrorist group in Algeria.

Good Guys an electronics store located in Sacramento, CA, where forty-one people were taken hostage, three were killed, and eleven were wounded on April 4, 1991.

Guilt transfer a propaganda technique.

Gush Emunim "The Block of the Faithful"; a Jewish religious group that strongly believes that the Jewish nation and the Jewish land are both sacred since they were both chosen by God.

Habeas corpus   the Great Writ, a judicial mandate ordering that an inmate be brought to the court so it can determine whether or not a person is imprisoned lawfully.

Hamas   the Islamic Resistance Movement well known for its suicide attacks against Israel civilians. The goal of Hamas is to destroy Israel, the PLO, and the Peace Talks.

Hanafi   a Muslim sect that took over 300 hostages at three different locations in Washington, DC, in 1977.

Hizballah   the Party of God, an Islamic Movement that supports an Islamic revolution in the Middle East; responsible for the bombing of the U.S. marine barracks on September 23, 1983.

Hostage reaction   psychological states that a hostage goes through during captivity.

HRT/NEST   the Hostage Rescue Team/Nuclear Emergency Search Team. The HRT is organized under the authority of the FBI, while NEST is controlled by the U.S. Department of Energy.

Hunger strike   a classic political tactic to obtain widespread media attention.

Imad Mughniyah   Hizballah leader responsible for numerous acts of terrorism against U.S. targets. Assassinated on February 12, 2008, in Syria.

INLA   the Irish National Liberation Army was formed in 1974 after a split in the ranks of the PIRA and the IRA.

Interdiction   to prevent suicide bombings before they are carried out.

Irgun/Stern Gang   Zionist terrorist organizations responsible for the terror attack on the Palestinian village of Dir Yassin in 1948.

Islamic Amal   Arabic for "hope"; a Lebanese Shi'ite terrorist group active in the 1970s.

Jammu/Kashmir   Territory in Northern India where ethno-national and Islamic extremist movements are waging a terrorist war against Indian occupation of Kashmir.

JDL   the Jewish Defense league founded by Rabbi Meir Kahane.

Jemmah Islamiyah   an Indonesian terrorist group responsible for the Bali bombing in October 2002.

Judea and Samaria   the land of the ancient Hebrews whereby the religious Jews maintain they have an intrinsic right to settle.

Kamikaze   literally, "divine wind" in Japanese. During World War II kamikaze suicide pilots flew bomb-laden planes into U.S. naval vessels in the Pacific.

Kashmiri   a native inhabitant of Kashmir.

Khobar Towers   on October 25, 1996, Islamic terrorists detonated a truck bomb at Khobar Towers in Dhahran, Saudia Arabia, killing nineteen U.S. Air Force personnel and injuring 500 others.

Ku Klux Klan   a white supremacist organization founded in Pulaski, Tennessee, in 1866. The KKK is the oldest continuous terrorist organization in the United States.

Leaderless Resistance   is the concept of the "lone wolf" or the single terrorist who operates without the sanction of a host terrorist group.

Letter bombs   a bombing technique first introduced by Russian terrorists in the 1880s.

Libya   a Middle East nation that was attacked by the United States after a terrorist incident that killed an American soldier.

London Syndrome   refers to a situation in which a hostage continuously argues or threatens the hostage takers and the hostage is killed by the hostage takers.

LTTE   the Liberation Tigers of Tamil Eelam, a Tamil separatist/terrorist group of Sri Lanka.

Marine compound   on October 23, 1983, the Marine Compound in Beirut, Lebanon, was destroyed by a suicide bomber that killed 241 marines.

Martyrs   people who die for their religious faith or for some other greater cause. A term often used to describe suicide bombers.

Meir Kahane   founder of the JDL and the Kach party in Israel, who was assassinated by an extremist Muslim in 1990 in New York City.

MEK   the national liberation movement of Iran that seeks to overthrow the Iranian government.

Mir Aimal Kansi   a Pakistani gunman who killed two and wounded three CIA employees on January 25, 1993. Kansi was eventually captured and executed by lethal injection on November 14, 2002.

Morality   the conformity to ideals of virtuous human conduct.

Mujahedin   Islamic extremists who wage war in defense of Islam. Literally translated as Holy Warriors.

Munich Olympics   on September 5, 1972, Israeli athletes were taken hostage by members of the Black September Organization. Eleven Israeli athletes were killed by the hostage takers.

Narodnaya Volya the People's Will, a nineteenth-century Russian terrorist group.

National Alliance a white supremacist group that follows the teachings of William Pierce.

Negotiator professionally trained hostage mediator.

NPA the New People's Army; a Filipino-Marxist guerrilla group formed in 1969 that specializes in urban terrorism.

Ocalan the founder of the Kurdish Workers' Party (PKK).

Occupied Territories a Palestinian reference to the West Bank and Gaza.

Office of Homeland Security U.S. federal agency created to secure the U.S. homeland from terrorist attacks.

Omagh on August 15, 1998, the town center of Omagh was destroyed by a powerful car bomb killing thirty people, the deadliest bombing in the thirty-year history of the "Irish troubles." The RIRA took credit for the bombing.

Operation Cast Lead Israeli incursion into Gaza Strip during Israeli–Hamas war of 2008–2009.

Oslo Peace Process granted Palestinians control of Gaza and a limited area of the West Bank. The Oslo Peace Process was an attempt to gradually partition Palestine into an Arab and Jewish state.

Palestinian Authority is an autonomous Palestinian government established after the Oslo Peace Accords in 1993.

Pan Am 103 an airliner that exploded over Lockerbie, Scotland, on December 21, 1988. Two hundred seventy people were killed, and Libya took credit for the bombing.

Patriot Act following the September 11, 2001, attacks, the Bush administration proposed legislation titled "Providing Appropriate Tools Required to Intercept and Obstruct Terrorism Act," popularly known as the Patriot Act. The Act gives law enforcement far-reaching police powers to detain immigrants, expand wire tapping, to use the military to patrol U.S. borders, and to conduct warrantless searches.

Pelindaba South African nuclear weapons site.

PETN a high-velocity explosive in linear form.

PFLP the Popular Front for the Liberation of Palestine founded by George Habash in 1967. The first terrorist group to introduce sky jacking to attract media attention.

Phalangist a right-wing Lebanese Christian militia responsible for the massacre at Sabra and Shitila.

Phineas Priesthood a white supremacist movement that follows the religious principles of the Christian Identity Movement. The name is taken from a verse in the Bible, Numbers 25:6.

PIRA the Provisional Irish Republican Army known for its use of car bombs. The goal of PIRA is to unite Ireland and drive the British out of Northen Ireland.

PKK the Kurdistan Workers Party. The PKK is a nationalist/separatist group seeking to establish an independent Islamic Kurdistan in Turkey.

Political objective the motivation for acts of indiscriminate terrorism.

Posse Comitatus Act enacted in 1878, the act prohibits the use of U.S. military forces in domestic civil situations, such as riot control.

Preemptive strike counterterrorist actions that proactively search for terrorist organizations prior to any terrorist episode.

Qassam Rocket simple steel rocket filled with explosives. Made by Hamas. Named after Izzad-Din al Qassam Brigades, military wing of Hamas.

Rajneeshee followers of a religious cult leader who poisoned ten salad bars in Oregon with salmonella bacteria.

RATF the Revolutionary Armed Task Force; a left-wing terrorist group active in the United States in the 1980s.

Red Brigades an Italian terrorist group most active in the 1970s and 1980s.

Rendition the apprehension and extrajudicial transfer of a person from one country to another.

Salafist a branch of Islam that adheres to rigid and utopian principles of life. Salaism is followed by the GSPC of Algeria.

Salmonella a bacteria that is a common cause of food poisoning. The Rajneeshees intentionally contaminated ten salad bars with a strain of salmonella in the Dalles region of Oregon in September 1984.

Sarin gas a potent nerve agent; the Aum Shinrikyo cult released sarin gas into the Tokyo subway system in March 1995, killing twelve people.

SAS the Special Air Service is a secretive counterterrorism military unit attached to the British Army.

Sayeret Matkal an elite Israeli counterterrorist reconnaissance unit.

SBS the Special Boat Service is another British counterterrorist unit attached to the British Royal Navy.

Sedition Act Signed into law by President John Adams in 1798 to stop seditious acts from weakening the United States by alien citizens of enemy powers.

Seizure of terrorists' assets the seizure of the financial assets and records of known terrorists and drug dealers.

Self-immolation a rare form of suicide by fire and almost always associated with political protests.

Shoah the catastrophe or a term used to describe the Holocaust.

Sicarii Jewish rebels who opposed Roman rule in 66 A.D. Considered by historians to be the first terrorist group.

Sikh an adherent of a monotheistic religion of India founded about 1500 A.D.

Skyjacking the hijacking of commercial jet aircraft.

SLA the Symbionese Liberation Army; active in the United States in the early 1970s. The SLA took Patty Hearst hostage in 1974.

Special Operations elite military units deployed to interdict terrorist operations.

S.S. *Mayaguez* on May 12, 1975, a Cambodian gunboat seized the *Mayaguez* off the coast of Cambodia; thirty-nine Americans were taken hostage.

Stockholm Syndrome a psychological aberration in which hostages begin to identify and sympathize with their captors.

Suicidology the study of the theory, causes, and motives of suicidal behavior.

Taliban "Students of Islamic Knowledge Movement." An Afghanistan ruling faction allied with al Qaeda.

Tanzim in Arabic meaning organization; associated with Yassir Arafat's Fatah movement.

Terrorism the premeditated, deliberate, systematic murder, mayhem, and threatening of the innocent to create fear and intimidation in order to gain a political or tactical advantage, usually to influence an audience.

Time and trust generally considered the most important factors in a hostage-taking episode.

Timothy McVeigh responsible for the ammonium nitrate and fuel oil (ANFO) bomb that destroyed the Alfred P. Murrah Federal Building in Oklahoma City on April 19, 1995, killing 168 people. McVeigh was executed in June 2001.

TTIC the Terrorist Threat Integration Center is a newly organized U.S. government agency to coordinate the intelligence-gathering capabilities of the FBI, CIA, and the Division of Homeland Security.

Tupac Amaru a Marxist terrorist movement in Peru most active in the 1980s and the early 1990s.

Tupamaros a Marxist terrorist movement active in Uruguay in the 1960s and 1970s. One of the first groups to exploit terrorism and media attention.

Turner Diaries a novel written by William Pierce, founder of the National Alliance, under the pseudonym Andrew MacDonald. Considered by white supremacist to be the "bible" of right-wing activity in the United States.

Typology a way of categorizing hostage takers; the classification of terrorist groups based on types.

Uighurs the largest Turkish-speaking ethnic minority in Xinjiang province in China. The Uighurs support a moderate form of Sufi Islam.

Unabomber the name given to Ted Kaczynski, a serial bomber who carried out attacks with mail bombs, killing three people. Kaczynski was sentenced to four life sentences.

Uzbekistan part of the former Soviet Union created in 1998.

WCOTC the World Church of the Creator founded by Ben Klassen in 1973. A white supremacist organization that believes in a coming racial holy war.

William Pierce the founder of the National Alliance and author of the *Turner Diaries* and *The Hunter.*

WUO/BLA the Weather Underground Organization and the Black Liberation Army. Left-wing terrorist groups active in the United States between 1968 and 1984.

Xinjiang Islamic-dominated province of northwestern China.

Yom Kippur War on October 6, 1973, the Syrian and Egyptian armies simultaneously attacked Israel. Yom Kippur is the Day of Atonement in the Jewish religion.

Zakarias Moussaoui a suspect in the September 11, 2001 terrorist attacks; considered by the FBI to be the "20th hijacker."

Zionism the revival of Jewish national life, culture, language, and religion in the Holy Land.

APPENDIX: MAPS

ISRAEL

Israel
- ✪ National Capital
- Haifa • City
- —— International Boundary
- —— District Boundary
- *Haifa* District Name

50 km

0 ——— 50 Miles

LEBANON

SYRIA

GOLAN HEIGHTS (Israeli occupied)

• Nahariyya
• Akko
• Haifa
Haifa
• Tiberias
• Nazareth

• Hadera
• Netanya
• Herzliyya
• Nablus
• Tel-Aviv Yafo
Tel Aviv **WEST BANK**
Ramla •
• Ashdod
Jerusalem ✪
• Ashqelon • Bethlehem

Mediterranean Sea

GAZA STRIP • Gaza
• Hebron
• Rafah

• Beersheba *Dead Sea*

• Dimona
Oron •

JORDAN

• Mizpe Ramon

EGYPT

• Yotvata

Elat
Gulf of Aqaba

* Israel occupied with current status subject to the Israeli-Palestinian Interim Agreement - permanent status to be determined through further negotiations

EUROPE

Serbia and Montenegro have asserted the formation of a joint independent state, but this entity has not been formally recognized as a state by the United States.

F.Y.R.O.M. - The Former Yugoslav Republic of Macedonia

Scale 1: 19,500,000

Lambert Conformal Conic Projection, standard parallels 40°N and 56°N

SOUTH AMERICA

MIDDLE AND FAR EAST

INDIA

CHINA

INDEX

Note: The notations *f*, n and *t* indicate figures, note numbers and tables cited in the text.

Abu Abbas, 114, 135 n3
Abu Nidal Organization (ANO), 80, 109*t*, 113, 135 n1
Abu Sayyaf Group (ASG), 109*t*, 116–117
Abu Zubaydah, 258
Achille Lauro, 114, 135–136 n3, 149, 169 n33
Afghanistan, 108, 112, 121*t*–122*t*, 208–209, 221, 226, 234–235, 253, 262*t*, 273–274
Aircraft bombs, 188–191
al Aqsa Martyrs Brigade, 13, 93–94, 109*t*, 113, 201
   qassam rocket launching, 93
Alert levels, 224*t*
al-Fatah. *See* Fatah
al-Gama'a al-Islamiyya (IG), 110*t*
Algerian groups, 114, 119–120
Allon Plan, 254
al Qaeda, 3–7, 13–14, 29, 63–65, 94–98, 211–212, 260–262, 264, 267, 271
   against civilian population, 102
   attacks of, 98*t*–99*t*, 100–101, 208–209
   beheading of U.S. citizen Nick Berg, 102
   dirty bombs and virus bombs, 103
   foreign fighters of, 102
   iraq insurgency, 101
   vs JI, 119
   links to, 114–117, 119–120, 126–127, 130–132, 221–225
   mindless terrorism, 102
   penetration of airline security, 221–222
   reasons for success of, 99–100, 257–260
   suicide bombers, 204, 208–209
   theft of nuclear weapons, 265
   vehicle bombing, 183–184
   website announcement, 63, 102
   Zarqawi's reign of terror, 102
AQIM (al Qaeda in Islamic Maghreb)
   attack strategy, 120
   goals of, 120
   merging of GSPC, 109, 120
al Saiqa, 84–85, 85*t*
al Suri Abu Musab, 260, 276 n34
   fighting strategy, 260
American Nazi Party, 40, 273
Anarchism, 29–33
Anderson Terry, 164*f*

Animal right advocates, 41–42, 42*f*, 43*t*
Annual Threat Assessment of the Director of National Intelligence, 102
Anthrax, 121, 196, 269–270, 270*f*, 271*t*
Antiabortionists, 41
Antiterrorism Act, 31, 242, 246*t*
Arab Liberation Front (ALF), 41–43, 79, 85*t*
Arab nationalism, 74–77
Arab Nationalist Movement (ANM), 78
Arafat, Yasir, 77–80, 85*t*, 86*t*, 87*t*, 88, 113, 116
Argentina, 66–67
Armed Islamic Group (GIA), 109*t*, 119–120, 161, 258–259
Armed Resistance Unit (ARU), 37
Armenian Revolutionary Army, 57
Army of God, 41
Aryan Republican Army, 38
Asahara, Shoko, 120–121, 121*f*
Asbat al-Ansar, 109*t*, 114
Asia. *See* Central Asia; Southeast Asian groups
Assassins, 23–26, 31, 125, 239
Assets seizure, 245
Atrocities, 14–15
Aum Shinrikyo, 109*t*, 120–121, 137 n9, 216 n16, 268, 279 n87
Ayn-al-Hilwah, 114
Ayyash, Yihya, 87*t*, 89

Baader-Meinhoff, 56–57, 199, 215 n12
Bakunin, Mikhail, 27, 30, 46 n35, 185
Balfour Declaration, 74, 86*t*
Bali bombing, 118*f*, 118–119, 136 n7
Basque Fatherland and Liberty, 122–123
Begin, Menachem, 3*f*, 23
   The Revolt, 24, 44 n5, 75
Beirut, 81–82, 102, 110*t*, 114, 147, 164, 177, 178*f*, 184, 195, 200–201
Bhopal, India, 268
Bin Laden, Osama (Usama), 5*f*, 24, 43*t*, 53–54, 63–64, 96–98, 101*t*, 114, 117, 119, 129, 132, 208–210, 237, 238, 257–260
Biological and chemical terrorism, 203–204, 226, 238–239, 267, 271*t*
Black Liberation Army (BLA), 15, 35–37
   arresting of members, 36
   police killing of, 36
   San Francisco 8, 36
Black Panthers, 59
   anti-vietnam war demonstration, 60*f*

Black powder, 172–174, 176, 178*f*, 179–180, 187
Black September, 50, 57–58, 86*t*, 149, 150*f*
Black Tigers, 205–206
Black widows, 209
Blast pressure, 171, 176–179, 177*f*, 186
Bojinka plot, 117
Bombing and terrorism, 171–191. *See also* Suicide bombers/suicide bombing
   aboard aircraft, 188–191
   effects of explosion of, 176–181
   historical perspective, 172–176
   letter, 185–188
   Marine compound U.S., 178*f*
   Murrah building, 175*f*
   vehicle, 181–185
Bombs, types of, 181*t*, 181–191
Bray, Michael, 41
   Time to Kill, 47 n72
Bush, George Sr., 33, 229
Bush, George W., 42, 87*t*, 101, 102, 182, 204, 220, 226, 227, 232, 233–234, 238, 243

C-4 (Composition 4), 173, 176, 180, 181*t*, 187, 190
Canada, 2, 24, 50, 51, 90, 189, 232
Car bombs, 181–182, 184, 189, 201
Censorship, 65–67
   arguments for and against, 67*t*–68*t*
Central Asia, 129–132
Chase, William, 154
Chechen groups, 112*t*, 131–132, 162–163, 191, 198*t*, 209, 264
Chemical and biological terrorism, 14, 65, 96, 120–121, 174, 203–204, 212, 226, 238–239, 244, 253, 258, 262*t*, 264, 267–268, 271*t*
China, 24, 112*t*, 128, 130–131, 200, 260, 263, 268
Chlorine gas, 268
Christian Identity churches, 38, 41
Christian Identity Movement (CIM), 40*t*
Clinton, William, 33, 43*t*, 117, 146, 246
Clusters (suicide), 83, 211
Columbia, 23, 31, 112*t*, 189, 190
Communist Party of the Phillipines (CPP), 110*t*, 117–118
Conflict spectrum, 261, 262*t*
Contagion effect, 49–53
Conventions, international, 239–241

Cooper, D. B., 11, 50–51, 143, 144, 168 n15
Copycat syndrome, 49–53
Counterterrorist measures, 219–247
  alert levels of terrorism, 224*t*
  color-coded alert threat system, 225*f*
  covert military operations, 231–232
  intelligence function, 224–228
  layers of security in airports, 222*f*
  legal framework, 239–241
  metal detector, 237*f*
  reactive measures, 232–239
  retaliation and preemption, 228–231
  security, 220–224
Covenant, the Sword and the Arm of the Lord (CSA), 38
Covert operations, 231–232
Croatian groups, 48–49, 166, 239
Cuba, 6, 50–51, 122, 130, 162, 226, 231–232, 244
Cyanide gas, 258–259

Delta Force, 155–156, 235, 262*t*
Democracy and terrorism, 272–274
Desert One, 155
Deterrence, 212, 247
Dev Sol, 125
Deir Yassin attack, 75–76
Dirty bombs, 103, 264, 265
Disinformation, 4, 63, 228, 231
Document on Terror, 29, 45 n30
Durkheim, Emile, 203
Dynamite, 173–174, 176, 177, 178*f*, 179–181, 264

East Turkistan Islamic Movement (ETIM), 112*t*, 130–131, 134*f*, 259
Ecoterrorists, 42–43
Egypt, 51, 78–79, 86*t*, 91, 97, 98*t*, 99*t*, 110*t*, 111*t*, 114, 149, 151, 187, 198*t*, 204, 209, 256, 260, 263
Egyptian Islamic Jihad, 92, 99*t*, 100, 209–210
Elbridge Cleaver, 36
Emergency powers, 241–243
Entebbe Airport rescue, 86*t*, 160–164, 236
ETA (Euskadi Ta Askatasuna), 122–123, 262*t*
European groups, 122–126
Explosives, 171–192
  secondary forces, 177*f*
  types, 181*t*
Extradition, 239–242, 247

FARC, 126–127
  Colombian lawyers death, 126
  conflict with Colombian government, 126–127
Fatah, 77–80, 84, 85*t*, 86*t*, 87*t*, 88, 90–93, 113, 116, 254
  power struggle, 91
  rule of West Bank, 91

Fatwahs, 97–98
FBI, 31, 33, 36–40, 42, 43*t*, 49, 61, 96, 119, 145, 177, 184, 187, 221, 227, 234–235, 238, 242, 244, 245, 265, 269–270
Fenian Brotherhood, 24
Fertilizer bombs, 173, 181*t*
Fighters for Free Croatia (CFF), 48
Films and terrorism, 52, 63, 160
Foreign Terrorist Organizations (FTOs), 6, 63, 94, 102, 108–133
  State Department list, 109*t*–112*t*
  threat severity, 134*f*
Fragmentation of bombs, 176–179
France, 11, 29–30, 49, 50, 109*t*, 112*t*, 113, 119, 120, 122, 142, 161, 184, 230, 232, 241, 243, 263
Front for the Liberation of Quebec (FLQ), 2, 233
Fuerzas Armadas de Liberation Nacional (FALN), 32–33, 183, 252
Future of terrorism, 252–274
  conflict spectrum, 262*t*

Gama'a el-Islamiya, 209
Germany, 49–50, 77, 101, 130, 142, 149, 150, 199, 232, 233, 241, 242
Giotopoulos, Alexandros, 124
Goldstein, Baruch, 35, 87*t*, 89, 148
Good Guys, 52, 156–160
Government terrorism. *See* State terrorism
Greece, 29, 112*t*, 124–125, 183
Guevara, Ernesto (Che), 29, 61
Guilt transfer, 4, 18 n6
Gush Emunim, 255
Guzman, Abimael, 128

Habash, Dr. George, 78, 85, 86, 115*f*, 116
Hamas, 3, 4, 24, 65, 76, 80, 84, 85*f*, 87*t*, 88–93, 94, 101, 103, 116, 183, 198*t*, 200–203, 206, 210, 230, 252–257, 262*t*, 266
  bus bombing, 90*f*
  power struggle, 91
  rule of Gaza, 91
  victory of, 91
  vs Israeli Defence Forces, 89*f*
Hanafi, 61–62, 151
Harakut ul-Mujaheddin (HUM), 99*t*, 129, 110*t*, 129–130
Hearst, Patty and Randolph, 60–61, 146, 147
Hizballah, 4, 24, 64–65, 71 n39, 76, 81–88, 92, 93, 101, 110, 113, 144, 183, 184, 198*t*, 201, 203, 204, 205, 206, 207, 210, 216 n32, 230, 236, 253, 254, 256–258, 266
Homeland Security, 220, 221, 223, 224, 225, 227, 233–234, 236, 238, 241, 249 n8, 272
Hoskins, Richard, 39–40
Vigilantes of Christendom, 39

Hostage taking, 67*t*, 68, 74, 141–167
  American hostages, 152*f*, 156*f*
  data, 141
  early history of, 142–143
  good guys planning, 159*f*
  guidelines for hostage events, 149–152
  normal and pathological response, 166*f*
  reactions to, 166*t*
  rescue efforts, 153–164
  surviving situations, 164–166
  in Tehran, 155–156, 156*f*
  typology of, 143–145, 145*t*
HRT (hostage-rescue team), 161, 163, 238
hunger strikes, 55–56, 199
Hunter (Pierce), 39, 52
Hussein, Saddam, 115, 132, 133, 203–204, 231

Imad Mughniyah
  car bomb killing, 82
India, 24, 99*t*, 110*t*, 111*t*, 129, 184, 189, 198*t*, 205–207, 241, 263, 267, 268
Intelligence, 100, 102, 131, 154–155, 161–162, 222*t*, 224–228
  information cycle, 227*t*
Internet
  adverse publicity, 64
  al Qaeda's psychological waefare, 63–64
  fund soliciting, 64
  usage by 9/11 hijackers, 65
  terrorist exploitation of, 63
Intifada, 84, 86, 87*t*, 88, 90, 93–94, 97, 115, 116, 205
Irish Republican Army, 15, 23, 52, 110*t*, 112*t*, 122, 123–124, 183, 199. *See also* PIRA (Provisional Wing of the Irish Republican Army)
Iran, 6, 51, 81, 82, 83, 84, 85, 87*t*, 90, 91, 92, 103, 110*t*, 111*t*, 116, 119–120, 126, 132–133, 145, 147*t*, 152*f*, 174, 184, 226, 231, 252, 254, 256, 257, 263, 266–269, 271
Iraq, 3, 7, 23, 30, 51, 63, 64, 87*t*, 97, 101, 102, 109*t*, 111*t*, 113–115, 120, 125–126, 131–133, 171–172, 174, 181, 183–184, 195, 197, 198*t*, 203–205, 211, 213, 226, 229, 231, 235, 236, 252, 256, 260, 261, 262*t*, 268, 269, 273
  evolution of al Qaeda, 101*t*
Ireland. *See* Northern Ireland
Irgun Zvai Leumi-al-Israel (IZL), 3*f*, 23, 74–75
Irish National Liberation Army (INLA), 55, 56, 199
Islamic Amal, 256
Islamic extremism, 256–260
Islamic International Brigade (IIB), 112*t*, 131

Islamic Jihad, 3, 24, 80, 84, 87*t*, 88–94, 99*t*, 100, 110*t*, 111*t*, 144, 198*t*, 201, 209–210, 254, 256, 257. *See also* Palestine Islamic Jihad (PIJ)
Islamic Movement of Uzbekistan (IMU), 108–109, 110t, 130, 134*f*, 259
Israel, 3*f*, 6, 22, 23, 34–35, 49, 57, 58, 64, 65, 73–74, 76–84, 86*t*, 87*t*, 88–94, 97–98, 100, 103, 110*t*, 113*t*, 114, 115–116, 121–122, 144, 150, 184, 195, 197, 198*t*, 201, 202, 211, 213, 228–230, 235–236, 253–256, 257, 259, 260, 263, 266, 273
  boundaries of, 75*t*
  defence force *vs* hamas, 89, 91
  major wars, 76
  suicide bombing of PFLP, 116
  suicide bombing of PIJ, 92
Italy, 29, 51, 58–59, 114, 142, 166, 230, 232–233, 241
Izz al-din al-Qassam, 90

Jaish-e-Muhammad (JEM), 99, 110*t*, 129, 134*f*
Jammu/Kashmir, 129
Jemaah Islamiah/Jemaah Islamiyya (JI), 110, 118–119, 173
Jerusalem, 22, 75, 88, 90*f*, 91, 92, 93, 103, 122, 201, 255–256
Jewish Defense League (JDL), 35, 121, 137 n10, 273
Jibril, Ahmad, 114
Jihad, 88–93, 100, 101*t*, 110*t*, 116, 119, 120, 129–132, 144, 176, 198*t*, 201, 205, 207, 209–210, 223, 254, 256–260
Judea, 22, 255–256

Kach, 34–35, 109*t*, 111*t*, 121–122, 255
Kaczynski, Theodore, 185, 186*f*
Kahane, Rabbi Meir, 34, 121–122, 137 n10
  JDL founder, 34*f*
Kahane Chai, 109, 111*t*, 121–122, 134*f*, 255. *See also* Kach
kamikaze, 17, 181, 196–197, 198*t*, 202, 208, 215 n2, 3, 4, 258
  headband wearing, 197*f*
Kansi, Mir Aimal, 234–235
Kashmir/Jammu. *See* Jammu/Kashmir
Khaalis, Hamaas Abdul, 61–62
Khobar Towers, 98*t*, 184
King David Hotel bombing, 75
Klassen, Ben, 39
Klinghoffer, Leon, 149
Ku Klux Klan (KKK), 25–27, 45 n14–15 n17
  empire knight, 26
  hot-button issues, 26
  Houston ralley, 25*f*
Kurdistan Workers' Party (PKK), 111, 125–127, 207–208

Lashkar e-Jhangvi (LIJ), 129
Lashkar-e Tayyiba (LT), 109, 111*t*
Lebanon, 66, 76, 80–84, 86*t*, 87*t*, 93, 103, 110*t*, 111*t*, 113, 114, 122, 147, 164, 184, 198*t*, 200–201, 205, 207, 230, 236, 252, 254, 256, 257, 274
Letter bombs, 185–188
  recognition of, 188*f*
Liberation Tigers of Tamil Eelam (LTTE), 111*t*, 113, 205–206
Libya, 6, 85*t*, 87*t*, 103, 111*t*, 116, 122, 174, 189, 226, 229–231, 267
List of foreign terrorist organization, 109*t*–112*t*
London Syndrome, 148–149
Low-intensity warfare, 226, 231, 253, 260–262

Macdonald Andrew. *See* Pierce William
McKevitt, Michael, 123–124
McVeigh, Timothy, 38, 174*f*
Major, John, 183
Marighella, Carlos, 29, 172, 261
Mini-Manual of Urban Guerrilla Warfare, 29, 36, 66
Marine Compound Beirut (1983), 177–179, 178*f*, 184
Martyrs, 202–203, 206, 207, 208, 209, 210, 257–258
Marxism, 40*t*, 124–126
Masada, 22–23
May 19 Communist Organization (CO), 35–37
Media and terrorism, 48–69
  propagandist uses, 62*t*
Mexico, 23, 142, 230
Mini-Manual of Urban Guerrilla Warfare (Marighella), 29, 36, 66
Moro National Liberation Front, 116–117, 210
Moussaoui, Zakarias, 96
Mughniyah, Imad, 82, 87*t*, 105 n30
Mujahedin-e-Khalq Organization (MEK or MKO), 111*t*, 132–133
Mujahedin, 96, 100, 101, 117
Munich Olympics (1972), 52–53, 149–151
Murrah Building (Oklahoma City), 174*f*, 175*f*

Nail bombs, 10, 10*t*, 92–93, 176, 178*f*
Narodnaya Volya (People's Will), 27–29
National Alliance, 38, 39
National Counterterrorism Center (NCTC), 171
National Guard, 32–33, 98*t*, 224, 236–237
National Liberation Army (ELN), 55, 111*t*, 126–127, 133, 134*f*, 138 n17–18, 142, 199
National Strategy for Homeland Security, 220, 233–234, 238, 249 n2, 250 n38

Nechayev, Sergei, 28–29
  Revolutionary Catechism, 28–29
Negotiation
  cultural dimensions of, 156–164
  guidelines, 149–152
  time and trust, 145–148
Neo-Nazis, 26, 38, 40*t*
NEST (Nuclear Emergency Search Team), 238, 265–266
Netanyahu, Benjamin, 87*t*, 231, 254
New People's Army (NPA), 110*t*, 117–118
  Bali bombing suspect, 118*f*
  terrorist attacks, 118
News coverage and terrorism, 17, 52–53, 56, 69, 211, 256
Nguyen brothers, 157, 159–160
Nicaragua, 122, 231
Nidal, Abu, 80, 84, 85, 87*t*, 113, 135 n1
Northern Ireland, 2, 4, 6, 11, 15, 22, 24, 53–56, 66, 110*t*, 112t, 122–123, 142, 182–183, 188–189, 190, 199, 225, 233, 235, 241–242, 255
North Korea, 4, 6, 154, 226, 260, 263, 266, 267
17 November, 112*t*, 124–125, 137–138 n13
Nuclear weapons and materials, 76, 96, 203, 226, 254, 263–268

Ocalan, Abdullah, 126, 208
Occupied territories, 79, 80, 86, 87*t*, 93, 213, 255
Office of Homeland Security, 220, 249 n2, 250 n38
Official terrorism. *See* State terrorism
Omagh, 123–124, 137 n12
Order, 38, 40
Oslo Peace Process, 88

Palestine, 22–23, 69, 113, 201, 202–203, 211
  vs al Qaeda, 73–103
  vs Israel, 253–254, 256, 257
Palestine Islamic Jihad (PIJ), 85, 92–94, 111*t*, 201, 202, 203
Palestine Liberation Army (PLA), 85
Palestine Liberation Front (PLF), 79, 85, 111*t*, 114–115
Palestine Liberation Organization (PLO), 58, 73, 77–91, 113, 116, 147, 230, 236, 254, 256, 257
  affiliated groups, 84, 85*t*, 256
  Arafat's UN General Assembly addressing, 79*f*
  holocaust survivors, 77*f*
  significant events, 86*t*–87*t*
Palestine National Front (PNF), 85
Palestine question, 73–103
Palestinian Authority (PA), 82, 88, 90, 116, 255–256

Palestinian Resistance Movement, 50, 97, 253–256
Pan Am Flight, 189
PATRIOT Act. *See* USA PATRIOT Act
People's Revolutionary Army (FARC), 126–127
Peru, 112, 128–129, 133, 139 n20, 161–162
PETN, 173, 174, 180, 181
Phalangist militia, 81
Philippines, 109*t*–110*t*, 116–118, 133, 198*t*, 210
Phineas priesthood, 39–40
Pierce, William, 38, 39*f*
    Hunter, 39
    Turner Diaries, 38–39
PIRA (Provisional Wing of the Irish Republican Army), 4, 15, 23, 54–57, 112*t*, 122
    decommissioning, 56
    fighting communist party, arresting, 59
    funeral procession, 55*f*
    vs justice department, 59
    New black panther party
PKK (Kurdistan Workers' Party), 111*t*, 125–126, 198, 207–208
Plastic explosives, 182, 190
Popular Democratic Front for the Liberation of Palestine (PDFLP), 78, 84, 85*t*, 86*t*
Popular Front for the Liberation of Palestine-General Command (PFLP-GC), 49–50, 78, 79, 84, –85, 111*t*, 114, 116, 136 n5
    killing of Jihad Jibril, 116
    Soviet SA-7 missiles, 116
Popular Front for the Liberation of Palestine (PFLP), 32, 49–50, 66, 78, 84–86, 111*t*, 114–116, 134*f*, 198*t*, 201–203, 252, 254, 262*t*
    founder of, 115*f*
Posse Comitatus Act, 233, 250 n36, n37
Preemptive strikes, 228–229
Product tampering, 51–52
Propaganda, 4, 15, 27, 29, 30, 33, 35, 53–59, 61–63, 67*t*, 90, 155, 165, 210, 223, 231, 236, 259, 260
Provos. *See* PIRA (Provisional Wing of the Irish Republican Army)
Puerto Rican separatists, 31–33

Rajneeshees, 269
Real Irish Republican Army (RIRA), 112*t*, 123–124
Red Brigades (Italian), 32, 58–59, 249 n15
Reid, Richard, 190–191
Religious cults, 120–121
Republic of New Africa (RNA), 35–36, 37
Rescue of hostages, 153–166
Ressam, Ahmed, 119

Retaliation, 3, 22, 23, 27, 62, 76, 78–79, 116, 129, 142, 181, 189, 198*t*, 208, 210, 228–232, 253, 266, 268, 269–270
Revolt, The (Begin), 23, 44 n5, 75, 88, 104, 136 n6
Revolutionary Armed Forces of Columbia (FARC), 112*t*, 122, 126–127, 133, 134*f*, 138 n17, 142
Revolutionary Armed Task Force (RATF), 35
Revolutionary Catechism (Nechayev), 28–29
Revolutionary Nuclei (RN), 112*t*, 124–125, 138 n14
Revolutionary Organization 17 November, 112*t*, 124–125
Revolutionary People's Liberation Party/Front (RPLP/F or DHKP), 112*t*, 125, 138 n15
Revolutionary People's Struggle (ELA), 112*t*, 124–125
Ridge, Tom, 223, 225*f*
Riyadus-Salikin Reconnaissance, 112*t*, 131
Rocket launching
    AQSA, 93
    PIJ, 93
Russia, 2, 27, 29, 30, 76, 109*t*, 112*t*, 130, 141, 162–163, 198*t*, 209, 260, 262*t*, 263, 264, 269

Sabotage Battalion of Chechen Martyrs (RS), 112*t*, 131
Salafism, 114, 120
Salafist Group for Call and Combat (GSPC), 109, 112*t*, 114, 119–120, 259
Salmonella, 269, 271
Samaria, 255–256
Sands, Bobby, 55, 55*f*
Sarin gas, 109*t*, 120–121, 238
Saudi Arabia, 97, 98*t*, 100, 184, 204, 256, 259
Sayeret Matkal (SM), 236
Schultz, George P., 230
Secondary fires of bombs, 176, 177*f*, 179
Secret societies, 23–25
Self-immolation, 199–200
Sendero Luminoso (SL), 13, 112*t*, 128–129, 261
September 11, 2001
    burning of World Trade Center, 95*f*
    impact of Antiterrorism and Effective Death Penalty (ATEDP) Act, 242–243
    as Islamic extremism, 257–258
    post leagal measures, 243–247
    Obama's action, 244
    prevention of suicide bombing, 213
    role of Office of Homeland security, 220

skyjacking and suicide bombing, 94
suicidal hijackers, 96
website announcement, 63
Setton, Dan, 202
Sharon, Ariel, 88, 97
Sherif, Bassani Abu, 50
Sheriff's Posse Comitatus (SPC), 38, 233, 250 n36, n37
Shi'ite extremism, 23, 81, 83, 101–102, 201, 205, 256–257, 274
Shinrikyo, Aum, 109*t*, 120–121, 121*f*, 137 n9, 216 n16, 268, 279 n88
Shoah (the Catastrophe), 77
Shock front, 177, 179
Sicarii and Zealots, 22–23
Sikh separatists, 206
Single issue terrorism, 9, 12, 13*f*, 41–43, 46 n70
skyjacking, 56–59
    by al Qaeda, 94
    Arabians, 256
    as communication strategy, 58
    during 1968–1970, 86*t*
    during 1983–1986, 257
    by Hum (Kashmiri group), 99*t*
    media attention, 49–51
    negotiation, 236
    by PFLP, 115
    security measures, 220–221, 223
Southeast Asian groups, 110*t*, 116–119, 199, 260–261
Spain, 14, 30, 69, 109*t*, 122–123, 142, 144, 183, 230, 233, 241
Special Air Services (SAS), 148–149
Special Boat Service (SBS), 235
Special Operations, 163, 231, 234–235
Special Purpose Islamic Regiment (SPIR), 112*t*, 131
Sri Lanka, 66, 111t, 144, 173, 184, 198t, 205–206, 211, 262, 268
S.S. *Mayaguez*, 154–155, 169 n45
State terrorism, 5–7, 12, 17, 29
Stern Gang, 74–76
Stockholm Syndrome, 142, 145–148, 165
Students for a Democratic Society (SDS), 37
Suicide bombers/suicide bombing
    of al Qaeda, 208–209
    analytical arguments, 3
    of 9/11 attacks, 98
    of Buddhist monk, 200*f*
    of Chechen, 209
    definition, 199–200
    during 2005, 98*t*
    events, 198*t*
    female, 93, 191
    as freedom fighters, 52
    of Hamas, 89–91
    insurgency of Iraq, 203–205
    of Iran in U.S., 257
    of Kashmir, 206–207
    of Kurdish, 207–208

of LTTE, 205–206
Middle East, 200–203
media intervention, 211
of Palestine, 115
and security, 212–213
other terrorist groups, 209–210
religious motivation, 56
of Sikhs, 206
vehicle attack method, 184, 259
Suicide clusters, 211
Suicidology, 199, 211, 215 n1,
218 n68
Superterrorism, 253, 262–271
Symbionese Liberation Army (SLA),
60–61, 66, 146
symbol, 61*f*

Taliban, 96, 103, 111*t*, 129–132,
208–209, 231, 235, 244, 267
Tamil Tigers. *See* Liberation Tigers of
Tamil Eelam (LTTE)
Tanzim, 85, 93
Tenet, George, 226, 267
Terrorism
and bombing, 171–191
and censorship, 65–68
characteristics, 10*t*
chemical and biological,
238–239, 271*t*
definition, 8–9
definitional problems, 2–4
influence on democracy, 272–274
and internet, 63–65
morality of, 4–7
purpose of, 15–16
religious roots, 22–31
role of mass media, 48–63
superterrorism, 262–271
in U.S, 31–43
violence typology, 13*f*, 15*t*
Terrorist Threat Integration Center
(TTIC), 227

Thatcher, Margaret, 54–55, 69
Time to Kill (Bray), 41
TNT (trinitrotoluene), 173, 176–177,
180, 181*t*, 182, 184, 190, 201, 264
Tran, Cuong, 157, 160
Truman, Harry, 31
Tupac Amaru, 161–162, 170 n58
Tupamaros, 1, 66
Turkish groups, 4, 57, 112*t*, 124–126,
130, 198*t*, 207–208
Turner Diaries (Pierce), 38–39, 192 n5
Typologies of terrorism, 9–14
table, 15*t*

Uganda, 69, 160–161, 236
Uighurs, 130–131
Unabomber, 185–186, 186*f*
United Freedom Front (UFF), 37, 54
United Kingdom, 2, 56, 69, 114, 187,
225, 235–236, 240, 263
United Self-Defense Forces of
Columbia (AUC), 112*t*, 127–128
United States
al Qaeda attacks, 96–103, 208–209,
257–262
anthrax, 269
Asbat al-Ansar, 114
comparison of left and right wing
terrorist groups, 40*t*
counter terrorism measures, 221–235
future of terrorism in, 43*t*, 271–274
Hamas in, 90–93
high-tech weapons, 263–269
hijackings and skyjackings, 50–52
ideological left, 35–38
ideological right, 38–41
Iraqi insurgency, 203–205
law enforcement, 238–247
media exploitation, terrorist groups,
59–62
quality of life, 271, 273–274
rescue of hostages, 153–156

role of rejectionist PLO, 80–81
single issue terrorist, 41–43
suicide bombers, 195–199
superterrorism, 262–271
terrorism in, 31–35
widely used bombs, 180–191
Uruguay, 1, 66–67
USA PATRIOT Act
antiterrorism legislation, 31
Homeland Security, 241
law enforcement, 2, 220
post 9/11 leagal measures, 243–247
summary of, 246*t*
U.S.S. *Cole*, 24, 98*t*, 99*t*, 100, 109*t*,
195, 196, 208, 258
U.S.S. *Pueblo*, 154
Uzbekistan, 108–109, 110*t*, 130, 259

Vehicle bombs, 181–185
Velocity and explosives, 179–181
Vigilantes of Christendom (Hoskins),
39–40

Weapons of mass destruction, 14, 98,
120–121, 137 n9, 196, 204, 212,
226, 253, 254, 262, 264, 267, 273
Weather Underground Organization
(WUO), 36
Website listings, 18, 44, 70, 104, 135,
167, 192, 215, 248, 275
Werther Effect", 211
Wholesale (government) terror, 7
World Church of the Creator (WCOTC),
39, 46

Xinjiang province of China, 130

Yom Kippur War (1973), 76, 78–80,
86*t*, 104 n11
Yousef, Ramzi, 117

Zionism, 35, 74, 276 n13